A SYSTEM OF RIGHTS

A SYSTEM OF RIGHTS

Rex Martin

CLARENDON PRESS · OXFORD
1993

Oxford University Press, Walton Street, Oxford OX2 6DP
Oxford New York Toronto
Delhi Bombay Calcutta Madras Karachi
Kuala Lumpur Singapore Hong Kong Tokyo
Nairobi Dar es Salaam Cape Town
Melbourne Auckland Madrid
and associated companies in
Berlin Ibadan

Oxford is a trade mark of Oxford University Press

Published in the United States
by Oxford University Press Inc., New York

British Library Cataloguing in Publication Data
Data available

Library of Congress Cataloging in Publication Data
Martin, Rex.
A system of rights / Rex Martin.
Includes bibliographical references and index.
1. Political rights. 2. Natural law. I. Title.
K258.M37 1992 340'.112—dc20 92-17833
ISBN 0-19-827374-6

Typeset by BP Integraphics Ltd, Bath, Avon
Printed in Great Britain
on acid-free paper by
Bookcraft (Bath) Ltd, Midsomer Norton, Avon

Acknowledgments

I AM conscious of many debts—of collaboration, of influence, and more generally of support and encouragement and constructive criticism—which I am very happy to acknowledge here.

Much of the writing of the first five chapters of this book was completed during tenure of a sabbatical-leave grant from the University of Kansas and a Rockefeller Foundation Humanities Fellowship in 1983-4. I was also fortunate to enjoy, during spring 1984, a period of uninterrupted writing at the Institute for Advanced Study at Princeton, New Jersey, where I was a visiting research fellow in the School of Historical Studies.

Of the remainder of the book, all but the last two chapters was completed during 1986-7 when I had a research fellowship from the Hall Center for the Humanities at the University of Kansas. The College of Liberal Arts and my own department made the necessary arrangements and the Center (and ultimately the National Endowment for the Humanities and the Hall Family Foundation) provided the additional funds that made this particular research leave possible.

The final draft of the book was completed during my sabbatical leave from the University of Kansas in 1990-1. I was pleased, for a part of that period, during Whitsunday term in spring 1991, to be a visiting research fellow at the Centre for Philosophy and Public Affairs in the Department of Moral Philosophy at the University of St. Andrews. Here the final chapter was concluded. The funding for the particular fellowship I had there was provided by the Royal Bank of Scotland.

Let me say, then, simply that progress over these years (from 1983 on) has been slow but—in my eyes, at least—certain. Various stages of completion were marked at the points already mentioned and at others by aid generously given. And I have been aided as well by research grants from my university. I am deeply grateful for this assistance.

My work on the book has also been aided greatly by the support of friends and colleagues. I am especially indebted, for comments and criticism and general conversation about rights, to Richard De George, Gerry Mac-Callum, Donna Martin, Jim Nickel, Carl Wellman, and Georg Henrik von Wright. I want to thank Pam LeRow (who did the bulk of the typing) and Cindi Hodges, Jean Lowe, Sandy Lafferty, Beth Ridenour, and Sandee Kennedy; and also Susan Daniel (who provided bibliographic and other research assistance during 1984–7). George Trey and Michael Hinz and Ted Vaggalis provided valuable editorial and other research help during the subsequent years, for which I am very grateful. The assistance of all these good persons is acknowledged with heartfelt appreciation.

Acknowledgment is also made to various publishers for my use of portions of (or quotations from) my own writings. References to these published writings, in the endnotes, will be in shortened form; full details can be found in part 2 of the Bibliography.

Contents

Introduction   I

1. On the Logic of Justifying Political Authority   5
2. The Concept of Rights   24
3. Rights as Valid Claims   51
4. Human Rights   73
5. Civil Rights   98
6. Democratic Institutions   127
7. Democracy and Rights   152
8. Allegiance and the Place of Civil Disobedience   185
9. Justifying Coercion: The Problem of Punishment   218
10. Modes of Punishment   251
11. The Right of Inmates to Work   280
12. A System of Rights   303
13. Critical Justification   323

Notes to Chapters   340
Appendix: Addendum to Chapter 7   413
Select Bibliography   417
Index   433

Introduction

THIS is a philosophical book on rights: their nature, justification, and systematic connection with other political concepts. In it, I attempt to develop a general account of the most important kinds of rights—that is, human rights and constitutional rights—and then to show how such rights connect up with other political notions and practices (democratic institutions, obligation to obey law, punishment) to form a coherent system, a system of rights.

Let me begin with a very brief history of my interest in this topic and then offer a short sketch, a prospectus, of the argument of the book.

Initially, my interest focused on the conceptions of authority and obligation found in contemporary Western political society, and this led to a consideration of the ideas of rights and of consent developed by the so-called contract theorists. Surprisingly, the great classics of Western political thought, such as those of Hobbes and Locke, while identifying certain things as natural rights, failed to make clear just what a *right* is. And some of the most prestigious contemporary thinkers, such as John Rawls and Robert Nozick, though using the language of rights, have not penetrated to the question of the nature of rights or the character of their justification. Such omissions seem especially noteworthy when one considers that many of our most engaging problems and the very language of our political discourse center on rights. I concluded, then, that any systematic study of the concepts of politics pertinent to our own political culture—as found in Europe, in the Americas, in Australia and New Zealand, and perhaps elsewhere—would have to begin with rights, for reasons both theoretical and practical.

Regarding rights, I have attempted to develop the following overall line of argument. (1) Contrary to the view that a right is a claim, a valid claim, or an entitlement, I advance the notion that a right is an established way of acting. (2) I argue that for there to be rights (for ways of acting to be established) norms must be formulated and given value and, where they conflict, they must be harmonized. (3) My conclusion, then, is that specific agencies are required to formulate, maintain, and harmonize rights. (4) And, of course, one needs (in order to fill in behind this conclusion) to extend this analysis of rights to cover not only liberties of action (for example, the freedom to travel) but also avoidance of injury (such as the injuries of bodily harm) and even the receipt of services (including such things as public schooling, retirement benefits, and medical care).

In the present book I attempt to elaborate this analysis of rights into a systematic political theory. An introduction to the character of this book and an overview of its main themes is provided in the first chapter, on authority. Here three elements are identified—a government's rightful title to issue rules, a reasonable expectation of compliance with them, and the propriety of using coercive force to back them up—and I argue that they need to be linked together in order for one to speak of political authority as justified. In the first chapter I argue, further, that the connection of these elements requires us to move to a background theory, which is itself an internally coherent system of political institutions and conceptions. And I suggest that a system of rights could afford us such a coherent background theory.

This introduction is followed by four chapters on rights which develop the line of argument indicated earlier; these chapters concern the concept of rights (Chapter 2), rights as valid claims (Chapter 3), human or natural rights (Chapter 4), and civil rights, that is, ways of acting (or of being treated) secured by law for *all* members of a given political society (Chapter 5). The main point I try to establish in these chapters is that rights (in particular, those rights which are universal within a given polity, including human rights) are institutional practices which require an institutional setting.

Having argued that government enters the picture in such a setting as a coordinated set of agencies to formulate, promote, and harmonize rights, I will want to propose that a democratic government would inherently tend to be rights-producing. This is not an obvious or easy point to make when one considers the history of democratic political philosophy, in particular if one considers democracy to be primarily a decision-making procedure in accordance with a principle of majority rule.

In any event my central claim is that the setting required by civil rights can be provided by democratic majority rule government. Democracy, in its turn, needs a justification and this can be provided by giving priority to preferences that include, as a proper subset, universal political (or civil) rights.

Thus, in the next two chapters of the book (Chapters 6 and 7) I attempt to elaborate the idea of democratic institutions and to show that that which justifies a democratic principle in decision making would also prescribe and undergird a tendency to be productive of rights. Two key notions (civil rights—of individual persons—and democratic government) are mutually supportive and form the central undergirding of the internal justification of the system in question.

From this particular foundation certain secondary lines of support run: to the character of compliance with law in a rights-producing state and, then, to the general features of an eligible justification for using coercion to enforce rights of individuals. In tracing these lines we are, in effect, concerned with two of the classic problems of political philosophy: the presumed obligation of the citizen to obey the law and the alleged justifiability of a government's backing up its laws with coercive sanctions. The chapter devoted to political obligation (or allegiance, as I prefer to call it) consists of materials concerned not only with political obligation, as traditionally conceived, but also with civil disobedience (Chapter 8). And to the question of punishment I have devoted three distinct chapters: one (Chapter 9) deals with the basic issue of justifiability; the next (Chapter 10) takes up the respective place of penalty, of compensation, and of treatment and rehabilitation as (justified) coercive responses triggered by an adjudged violation of law in a political system of rights; and the third (Chapter 11) focuses on the aspect of rehabilitation in particular, while taking up the rather specialized issue of work in prisons. With this account of coercion we will have all but completed our sketch of a system of rights (a form typical of many contemporary political societies, though found imperfectly in any one of them).

The main idea I try to advance in these four chapters is that the other elements in a justified scheme of political authority (that is, obligation to obey the laws and the use of coercive sanctions) can be incorporated as necessary features of the background theory. Thus, an internally coherent system of rights has resulted.

In the last two chapters of the book I return to the issue of the justification of authority raised in the introductory chapter. Here (in Chapter 12 especially) I want to bring home the original argument, from the first chapter, that the notion of political authority is internally justified in a given political system if the main elements in that notion—that is, the title to issue rules, a reasonable presumption of compliance, and the government's rightful monopoly in the use of coercive force—are actually ingredient in the theoretic structure of that system. For it is the coherence of the background theory, in which each of the authority elements can be shown to have a necessary place, that justifies political authority in any given political system. In the case at hand, a system of rights, these elements have been shown to be present; thus, that system has a justified authority.

Then, after the question of the internal justification of political authority has been canvassed within these confines, the book turns, in its concluding chapter (Chapter 13), to address the difficult subject of the possibility and character of an ultimate critical vindication for such a system. Here I want to suggest something about the proper tasks of political theory.

Political philosophy is an old subject, with a long history. And one would be foolish to claim any considerable novelty in one's treatment of its traditional themes.

Even so, I would say that some features of my work are distinctive. Two features, in particular, are worth noting. First, there is the program of explicating the notion of rights (including human rights) as established patterns of acting or of being treated and hence as institutional in character. This program of explication (which occupies Chapters 2 through 5) is, I believe, a fairly novel one (and, I have been assured by many of my friends, wrong-headed). Then, second, there is the program of providing an internal justification of political authority. Here rights are substantively connected (in Chapters 6 through 12) with other political institutions and conceptions (with majority rule democracy, etc.). Thus, my analysis forms in the end a systematic approach to one 'style' of government in particular. So far as I know such an approach has not been taken by other philosophers.

I believe, further, that rethinking some of the main topics in political theory, particularly allegiance and punishment, in the light of a theory of rights is much overdue. Whether my book performs this task successfully I am not in a good position to judge, but it is something that can only be done in the systematic, comprehensive way I have here attempted.

I

On the Logic of Justifying Political Authority

THE justification of political authority is one of the central problems of philosophy. It is the topic of this chapter and, in a way, of the entire book.

The notion of political authority and the logic of its justification are intimately tied in with the concept of the state. This connection is helpful, for 'state' is widely used as a descriptive term and, indeed, has been given a degree of technical precision by political scientists. We are aware, of course, that the technical sense captures only the idea of a *de facto* state; nonetheless, it should be possible to construct a *de jure* conception on this foundation.

I. THE STATE AS A POLITICALLY ORGANIZED SOCIETY

We should briefly note, however, an ambiguity in the term 'state' in that it can refer either to a politically organized society or to an agency for making laws, and so on, in a society. There is no philosophical advantage in deciding which of these is the proper reference. For, whether one takes 'state' to refer primarily to a politically organized society or primarily to such an agency, the problem remains: What is involved in calling something a state? It is easy enough to avoid ambiguity, though, either by explicitly identifying which sense of 'state' one intends ("the state as ... ") or by using two distinct terms: 'polity' (to refer to a politically organized society) and 'political agency' (to refer to an agency for making laws, and so on).

I.I. *States and Government*

A society is said to be politically organized if it contains a determinate agency (or correlated set of agencies) to formulate, apply, and maintain rules (and principles) for all the people in that society; if these rules are generally adhered to (that is, usually and by most people); and if the agency itself has a monopoly in principle on the use of physical force for coercion, at least in the sense that it can forbid, more or less successfully, the use of such force on the part of the citizens.

As I have already indicated with the term *de facto*, this preliminary characterization of a state is intended principally as an empirical one; it is meant to cover instances at different times in history and it is supposed to be in rough accord with ordinary usage, again from various cultural and historical periods. It is successful to the extent that it allows us to say that Plato and Aquinas, Locke and Marx were all talking about the state (about a politically organized society), even though we are aware that they probably had widely different things in mind when they used the words we translate as 'state.' Our account should aim only at capturing important common elements, while allowing for significant variation and nuance. Moreover, it should enable us to accommodate the differences that exist between, say, a modern territorial state with sovereign power, a medieval kingdom, a Greek *polis*, and a seminomadic tribe.[1] And it should allow us to differentiate between a polity (a society that is politically organized) and a society that is not politically organized, or a mere association (like a university or a club), or a church.

As I suggested above, the usual way in which we would distinguish a politically organized society from a voluntary group or from a church is by stressing the notion that one of the agencies in that society has a monopoly in the use of physical force. The agency in question could, of course, simply proscribe altogether the use of force to all those who live in the society—or perhaps it would allow for (but regulate) some use of force by those who are subject to its rulings. In either case, though, it would have a monopoly *in principle* of the use of force. But if we put the point in precisely this way we would fail to distinguish a politically organized society from a comprehensive church of the medieval sort (or, for that matter, from a utopian community). The crucial difference we are looking for is that the political agency characteristically *uses* force itself, or threatens to, as a way of backing up its rules and commands. Thus, when Thoreau was released after his one night in jail he tells us he "joined a huckleberry party"; in half an hour they had gotten to the huckleberry field "on one of our highest hills, two miles off" and, he adds significantly, "then the State was nowhere to be seen." In short, states are different from such things as huckleberry-picking parties and the difference largely comes down to a matter of courts and jails (and things even more severe than these).

Governments do not simply forbid physical force to others; they normally use it themselves. And it is only when a politically organized society is organized by government and uses its coercive devices that we would call the society a state. We could imagine, however, a politically organized society which had failed to take this final step: its agencies did not, typically could not, use physical force. Such a society would not be a state as we understand it; rather it would be an organized society that had no government (and hence was anarchist in that respect).

We could simply say, then, that there is an intrinsic connection between being a government and using or threatening physical force. And if we wanted to say that a government has rightful or legitimate authority we would have to show that it could justifiably back up its laws with force and employ this force against lawbreakers. Here, then, the justification of political authority would be the justification for a government's forbidding, or being in a position to forbid, the use of coercive force to its subjects while maintaining coercion and the threat of coercion on its own behalf. And the logic of justifying political authority would amount to the logic of justifying the possession by a government of precisely this sort of coercive power.

1.2. *A Map for Authority*

We are now able to mark a distinction between *de facto* and *de jure* political authority. We can do so by setting alongside our earlier empirical definition a definition in normative form. And this normative form can be achieved simply by adding a word to the empirical definition, thereby amending it to read that the political agency itself has "a *rightful* monopoly . . . of the use of physical force for purposes of coercion." Or, if one prefers, it could be said here simply that the agency is "*rightfully* able to forbid the use of force to its subjects while exercising such use (or the threat of such use) itself."

But, surely, this wording suggests also that the political agency is somehow entitled to issue rules (or definitively to interpret guiding principles) in the first place. It would be unreasonable to say that a government has a title to back up decrees with threats and even the use of force without also saying that it—or someone—has some sort of rightful license to issue these decrees. More to the point, it would be self-contradictory to say that a government has a rightful capacity to prohibit *all* or almost all use of force to its subjects while denying that it had a rightful title to issue any rules whatsoever. At least someone—some agency—would have to have such a title. For a capacity to prohibit by right requires and would involve a title to issue at least prohibitive rules.

So, two things are really involved here: the license to issue certain rules and a title to enforce them coercively. Accordingly, the introduction into our definition of the notion of a *rightful* monopoly in the use of physical force also requires the introduction of the notion of a determinate agency having a *rightful* license to formulate and issue commands and rules (or definitively to interpret guiding principles).

It would follow on this analysis that the authority of a government resides mainly in the notion that, quite properly, it can and does formulate laws (or settle on guiding principles) that enable it rightfully to prohibit force to its subjects or to use it to enforce its own rules. Government, so conceived, then, involves closely coordinated agencies of two main sorts (agencies to issue rules or to interpret guiding principles and agencies to enforce these laws or principles coercively).

But we have not yet provided a ground for these rules to be obeyed. One could say that this is provided for by the coercive element in our analysis.

People would obey, or we could reasonably expect them to, because they are forced to. But it is not clear that we can add a normative component to this idea of obeying, for it is not clear that the reasonable expectation of general compliance is here a rightful one. People might obey because they feared to do otherwise, but that they *ought* to obey in any case raises a wholly different issue.

We can connect the title to enforce rules with the title to issue them and the capacity to prohibit subjects from using force with the license to issue rules. But we have not as yet brought in an *obligation* to obey the rules. We have failed to make our empirical definition wholly normative, for we cannot connect the normative capacity of the government in its monopoly (in principle) of the use of force with any normative expectation of general compliance.

I think a similar defect would plague us were we simply to start with a rightful expectation or presumption of compliance. We could, perhaps, move from there to an original title to issue rules or definitive interpretations; but it is not clear that we could take a further required step. For even if one started with the contention that these commands ought generally to be obeyed, it would not necessarily follow that such commands should be coercively enforced in the absence of compliance.

The notion of the state has three main elements: the issuing of rules, the expectation of general compliance, and the possession by government of a monopoly (in principle) of the use of coercive force. And, if my claim is sound that the notion of political authority should be mapped onto that of the state, it would follow that the notion of political authority has these same three parts. Where that notion is made normative, as it would be in the idea of a justified political authority, these same three elements will still be present.

Thus, to say that a government has authority or that a politically organized society has a legitimate government would require that such a society exhibit all three of these elements. And I have suggested that these three elements (in their normative form) are to be thought of as connected.

The notion of a justified political authority is a systematic one, and the logic of its justification involves establishing systematic connections between these three elements (in their normative form). What we would need to show, then, is that a rightful license to issue rules does connect with a rightful presumption of compliance and that such a connection does confer an eligible title to back up these rules coercively.

2. A STANDARD APPROACH TO JUSTIFYING POLITICAL AUTHORITY

Now, it might be contended that I have been alleging a problem in relating two notions—the rightful license to issue rules and the obligation to obey them—but that no such problem exists. The two notions are already connected, in virtue of their meaning, and the problem vanishes simply in seeing this. It is a persuasive reply and has considerable vogue among contemporary political philosophers; hence it might be worth examining at some length. Even so, it will not allow us to dispense with the problem I have raised, for there remains the question of a connection between the rule-issuing license and the citizen's obligation to obey, on the one hand, and the coercive enforcement of these rules, on the other. But I want to turn to that matter only after I have first dealt with the linkage between rule-issuing and obligation.

Many contemporary political philosophers see a close connection between the rule-issuing authority of government and the obligation of the citizen. It is, for them, an analytic connection. To say that a government has such authority means, or entails, that every citizen has an obligation to obey its particular laws. Thus D. D. Raphael says, "The authority of the State implies that those who exercise it have the right (of action) to issue orders and the right (of recipience) to have those orders obeyed, and that, corresponding to the second right, the citizens have a duty or obligation to obey the orders."[2] A conventional political philosopher like Raphael is not alone in thinking this; many defenders of the anarchist point of view hold the connection to exist, as an analytic one, as well. For example, we find Robert Paul Wolff saying that legitimate authority is "a matter of the *right* to command, and of the correlative obligation *to obey the person who issues the command*."[3] Even philosophers who are not defenders of the anarchist or of the statist viewpoint and who would claim to restrict themselves to conceptual analysis endorse the notion of a connection of entailment between rule-issuing authority and obligation. Here Thomas McPherson says, "Now, to hold that some person or some body has authority is to hold that he or it ought to be obeyed. This, again, is part of what we mean by 'authority' ...."[4]

Accordingly, on the basis of this belief that a connection of entailment holds here, the statist undertakes to defend political authority by affirming political obligation, as one of its implications, and the anarchist undertakes to deny political authority by denying political obligation. For what each position means by 'authority' is "that which requires obligation"; they occupy a common ground. As Wolff put it, "The normative concept of the state as the human community which possesses rightful authority [that is, as a rule-issuing authority which correlates with the citizen's obligation to obey] thus defines the subject matter of political philosophy proper."[5] Here both parties to the dispute are able to agree that rule-issuing authority logically requires the citizen's strict obligation to obey the rules issued.[6]

For them, then, the logic of justifying political authority can be reduced to the single crucial consideration that a government has authority to issue rules only if its citizens have a strict obligation to obey those rules. The anarchist and the statist differ here only in that one denies and the other affirms such an obligation.

This dispute between the anarchist and statist comes down to the issue whether the citizen is bound to obey all laws just insofar as they are laws. The essence of what is at issue between them is the notion that citizens have a special obligation towards laws as such, as distinct from an obligation to do a certain thing whether it is prescribed by law or not. The nature of this obligation is that one is to do what one is told to do simply because it is mandated by law. The obligation is a strict one; it attaches to all laws and can be overridden, if at all, only in exceptional cases.

I think the Socrates of Plato's *Crito* held something very like this view, and held it in a particularly strong and uncompromising version.[7] Kant, too, was a political obligationist. Unlike Socrates, who espoused a doctrine of unmitigated obligation, Kant held that the obligation to obey the law could be overridden only if what the law commanded was immoral.[8] The position of most political obligationists is more akin to Kant than to Socrates in that they regard political obligation as strict but allowing of mitigation.

Hobbes, who is often thought to hold the doctrine of an absolute obligation to obey, actually allowed that a matter of life or death could exempt the citizen, even the citizen under criminal penalty, from the obligation to obey.[9] And Locke, who sounds like an uncompromising absolutist when he lays down his doctrine of civil obligation on the basis of his theory of consent, limits the obligation significantly in his subsequent discussion of the so-called right of revolution.[10] But the examples do suggest that the obligationist view has been a fairly common one in the history of political philosophy and that the dispute between the philosophical anarchist and the statist is deeply embedded there.

Now, if we are not merely going to assume the fact of authority, political obligation must be grounded in something other than such an assumption. And where obligation has become the focal issue, as it is in the perspective under discussion, it would be question begging simply to posit rule-issuing authority.

From the perspective of the traditional approach, then, we must go outside the political system, outside the idea of the state, to find the ground of political obligation. We must look for an obligation-conferring trait external to the body politic and bring that to bear on the issue of the citizen's standing before the law.

For example, one could allege that a person has a standing of obligation toward the law if it is divinely commanded that people obey laws, that is, obey laws simply insofar as they are laws. Or, again, the person who was bound to obedience by an oath or some sort of promise would have an external ground of obligation to obey all particular laws.

Perhaps the best example, though, is the well-known theory—usually associated with Hobbes and Locke in particular—in which a contract is said both to authorize a government to make laws and to bind subjects to strict obedience. It may be that the theories of Hobbes and Locke are not so simple as this, however.

For Locke argues that, at a certain point (that is, upon reaching adulthood and then by staying on, more or less voluntarily, in the face of an unexercised right of emigration), people become members or parts of a particular body politic. The main function of any such body is to create a constitution or form of government and, presumably, there is a consensus (what Locke calls a majority) among the citizens as to where—that is, in what institutions—the main powers of government (legislative, executive, etc.) have been lodged. Indeed, Locke says, if there were not this consensus the body politic would come apart, would simply disintegrate, and could only be held together by obvious and clearly improper force. Now, from these two facts—that one is a member of a body politic and that there is a constitutional government for it—it follows for Locke, as a matter of logical entailment, that each citizen (each member of a political society so organized) is strictly bound to obey the laws duly issued by such a constitutional government. Or it follows logically from these two facts plus one other—if laws were not obeyed people would in effect have returned to the unwanted state of nature—that each member has the strict obligation in question. One has, in short, not consented (contracted, promised) in so many words to obey the laws; rather, one has consented to be a member of a body politic and from that fact, plus one or two others, it follows as a matter of logical entailment that the citizen has a strict duty to obey laws duly issued. One is thus obliged *as if* one had in fact expressly consented to obey.[11]

The doctrine of consent in Hobbes is, perhaps, simpler. He dispenses with such ideas as the body politic (as something conceptually prior to government) and legitimate or constitutional rulership and argues that all subjects consent in one and the same fundamental respect. Persons "stand aside" from their own exercise of natural rights; and thus each one individually consents (or, in effect, promises) permanently but conditionally to waive that exercise in deference to the exercise of those selfsame rights by the governmental person(s), the sovereign—the condition here being the noninvasion of the subject's unmistakably vital interests by the sovereign. Hence, the subject consents to be under the sovereign's will and is obliged to comply with it in all or almost all cases.[12]

It could be said, then, that both Hobbes and Locke do ground political obligation in consent (albeit not straightforwardly, as the usual interpretation would have it). And Rousseau, in contrast to either theorist, does seem to put the obligation to obey right into the contract, as one of its terms, so to speak.[13] So Hume, who is, of course, no partisan of the original contract theory, interprets the theory as asserting that citizens have an obligation to obey because they have, in effect, signed on or promised to do so.[14] This would be, perhaps, closer to the mark as an account (and ultimately a criticism) of Rousseau than it is of Hobbes or Locke but, clearly, in all these cases, the theorists do ground obligation on some specific act of undertaking on the part of the citizen-member of the body politic.

In sum, the standard approach when filled out (as it was by the political obligationists just examined) yields a definite theory of authority and its justification. In the next section I want to look more closely at the central notion in this theory (as it has taken shape from the hand of the obligationists) and to criticize that idea. Then I want to deepen our understanding of the model, more generally, by sketching its logic, its characteristic pattern of reasoning. This pattern is a form of what might be called externalism. But it is not the only form, or the best one, as we will see in time.

3. A CLASSICAL MODEL FOR THE JUSTIFICATION OF POLITICAL AUTHORITY

The crucial point in this theory or model is that the citizen's obligation to law is derived from the citizen's being a party to a contract—or from being treated like such a party. The social contract governs the relevant obligation just as any contract would in establishing the duties that attend it, whatever its nature or whoever the contracting parties. Political obligation is here a species of contractual or consensual obligation. And where it is indeed the presumed fact of a contractual relationship that grounds the citizen's obligation to law, then clearly, such obligation is conceived as externally grounded. (Or, alternatively, the grounding feature could be some undertaking like contracting, sufficiently like it to count in the present consideration. Note, thus, the parallel case in which Socrates regards himself as having made an agreement with the laws to obey them so long as they remain in force.) It is evident that in many theories the relationship of citizens to the government is construed as a case of some nonpolitical undertaking, like promising, agreeing, consenting, or signing a contract, which is obligation-creating in character.

I would argue that such an external ground of political obligation never creates an obligation to obey laws as such (that is, just because they are laws). When God commands us to obey all laws, we obey them because God says so. Our obligation is to what God commands and not principally to the laws at all. Nothing about law itself or about the system of political concepts, without the superaddition of the will of God, makes obeying laws obligatory. Similarly, when utility commands us to obey all laws, we obey them because it is useful to the end of the greatest happiness of the greatest number. Our obligation is, logically, to the principle of utility; our obligation to subordinate rules holds only insofar as they accord with it. Again, nothing about law, except under the superordinate principle of utility, makes obedience obligatory. And the same could be said for contracts and promises or for the categorical imperative as a ground of political obligation.

Perhaps I can make this crucial point clearer with an example. Suppose I have promised my neighbors to feed and otherwise care for their cat while they are away on a two-week vacation. Indeed, since they are both rather finicky, I have made that promise to them quite explicitly (and they in turn have given me a key to their house, some supplies, and a lot of instructions). The task I have undertaken is somewhat onerous since (among other things) the cat becomes ill during their time away. But I carry out my duties, nonetheless, consoling myself with the thought that I have done all these unwanted things *because* I have promised.

We can also call it the doing of a neighborly duty, if we want; for this locates the duty, tells what it is about. But it is in fact a promise-based duty. Someone might still say: you had the duty as a (good) neighbor regardless of the promise. But I do not know that this is so. For we have not yet worked out exactly what neighborliness demands, what precisely it requires; we do not have a conception of such a duty in hand. And if in the end what I basically say is "I promised" and that promise carries all or much of the normative weight for how I should conduct myself in the project at hand, then we will not have gotten to the duties of neighborliness at all. Even if we had them in mind (which we do not), they are doing little work; at most they are a reason for making the promise or for carrying it out (when things occur that are more than we bargained for). But these reasons do not govern or ground the agent's action in the relevant case.

By the same token, we might call the duty to obey law—as based on a promise, agreement, act of consent, or contract—a political duty. For this locates the duty, tells what it is about. But it does not tell the *ground* of that duty. If it is a duty based entirely or principally on a promise (even on a promise that is reasonably made), it is not as such a political duty. (Recall here the point just made about neighborly duty.) It would be a political duty, a duty based on the demands or requirements of the political institutions among which one lives, only if those requirements were laid out and understood as such a basis. But this has not been done. And, clearly, insofar as one sticks to the notion of a promise-based duty, then those requirements are not being laid out or understood as a ground for duty. Indeed, if one sticks resolutely enough to that one base (the promise), there is a sense in which the other possible base is simply dispensed with or even excluded altogether.

What counts as its ground is what mostly shapes a given duty; the ground is whatever has preponderant weight within the overall balance of reasons, within the set of relevant normative considerations. By sticking resolutely to the promise, one thereby rests the case for a duty to obey laws on something nonpolitical, on something whose normative force derives from and is settled in another context (a context external to the political). Here then we can distinguish between a promise-based duty and one that is politically grounded.

The traditional approach to the justification of political authority (as grounded primarily or entirely on a promise or contract or undertaking of some sort, in the way the obligationists would have it) is essentially nonpolitical. For the duty to obey law is like the duty I had toward my neighbors and their cat; it is grounded on a promise (and not on an analysis of what our relations, as neighbors among neighbors, might require). I do not mean here that the question never comes up as to how fellow citizens relate to one another or to their shared political institutions (or that these matters are never cited as reasons). I mean, rather, that what grounds the citizens' duty (however else that duty might be described or rationalized) rests preponderantly on certain undertakings, or professed undertakings, which conventionally have normative force and have it nonpolitically.

The ground here is located in such undertakings as promising and so on. The controlling metaphors are used with some effect, and are intended here to have that effect.

All these external ground analyses (so long as they are taken as basic) effectively rule out the notion of a special obligation to laws as laws. They do not allow us to take as focal the consideration of what institutions generate the laws or the consideration of what these laws reflect in their normal operation or of what political ends they serve; such external ground analyses do not allow us to make central the matter of how fellow citizens relate to one another or to their shared political institutions (or how an individual citizen should relate, given the demands of those institutions, shaped as they are). Whatever the ground of the duty is, it is not configured to the requirements of the political domain, nor to the laws *as laws*, but to something else. And this, I think, is the crucial consideration.

3.1. *Externalism as Simple and Direct*

The external ground analyses follow a distinctive logical pattern. (1) A tight connection is assumed between political authority, in the rule-issuing sense, and political obligation. The first is said to logically imply the second. (2) This stick, though, can be picked up from either end. In the perspective we have been examining, the issue of justifying political authority is focused on the question whether citizens have a strict obligation to obey laws just insofar as they are valid laws. (3) Since obligation is made the eligible issue here, the justification of strict political obligation has become central and the question of the justification of political authority is thought to turn on it. (4) But since obligation is now logically prior to any other political concept, the task of justifying it requires that we go outside the whole system of political concepts and institutions. (5) Hence the justification, whether it can be accomplished or not, must be attempted by reference to some external, nonpolitical standard.[15]

The very procedure of justification here creates, though, a deep conceptual problem. As we have seen, the ground for an obligation to obey law on this view (whether it be a strict obligation or not) lies in some politically external standard. But to repair to this standard, as the logic of this externalist justificatory argument requires, is to treat these obligations as nonpolitically derived. Hence, all external grounds (as they are conceived in this argument) exclude political obligation, that is, special obligations to obey laws *qua* laws, in principle. It follows, then, that we may have obligations to the law but these can never be special ones; thus, none of the obligations we may have can be obligations to the laws *per se*. We are left with only one conclusion: that we can have no *political* obligations at all, hence no strict political obligations.

The perception of this fact has been seized upon by the philosophical anarchist. But the anarchist's claim that where we have external justifying grounds we have no special obligation to law—no political obligations as such—is merely a redescription of the contention that our standing before the law is governed by external grounds of obligation. Nonetheless, the anarchist's strictures are telling against traditional justifications of political authority which rely on tethering that authority to the citizens' contract-based (or agreement-based) obligation—indeed, strict obligation—to obey the laws issued. For these accounts, as we find them, for example, among the political obligationists, are subject to the conceptual pressures generated within any such scheme of external justification. And since the traditional accounts share that scheme with the anarchist, they can never free themselves from the toils of the anarchist's argument.

One might be tempted to solve this problem by a simple expedient: simply reverse the priorities involved—by picking up the other end of the stick and putting rule-issuing authority ahead of political obligation. Indeed, this style of analysis represents another common pattern in the history of political philosophy.

3.2. *A Plausible Move: Some Examples*

Consider, for instance, the case of St. Paul. The famous thirteenth chapter of his letter to the church at Rome, verses 1–7, addresses the matter of politics; it begins, "Let every person be subject to the governing authorities. For there is no authority except from God, and those that exist have been instituted by God" (Romans 13:1). One is first of all subject to God, the supreme rule-issuing authority. If there are other rule-issuing authorities, they are there because they have been established by God; accordingly, one is subject to them also. But the highest level of authority—that of God—always takes precedence over the lower. It follows that we ought to "obey God rather than men" (Acts 5:29) in cases of conflict. The martyrdom of Peter and Paul at the hands of the Roman state indicates the clear perception each had of the order of priority of authorities, of the subordination of the authority of the state (and its laws) to that of the divine will.

It should be obvious, however, that the move to make political authority in the rule-issuing sense conceptually prior to political obligation cannot solve the problem I have identified. For, where the ground on which political authority is to be justified is itself politically ulterior (as it is in the case of resorting to God as the source of all authority or of using the analogy of parental authority over young children), nothing political grounds the justification. We are still locked into the same pattern of external justification.

Nor does any particular problem lie in the requirement that the citizens' obligation to obey the law be a strict one. Even if that requirement were to be relaxed, as it is in theories of civil disobedience, the obligation may still be externally grounded, and to that extent it would not be an obligation toward the laws simply as laws.

A precise example of the moves I am discussing—that is, making rule-issuing authority the prior concept rather than obligation, while dropping the notion of a strict obligation to obey the laws—is offered by Jeffrey Reiman's argument. The question is whether he offers a significant alternative to the externalist program for justifying political authority.

I think not. Reiman's arguments remain externally grounded in that they simply identify justified political authority with morally justified (political) authority.[16] Or, to be precise, they identify justified political authority with the achievement, or the tendency to achieve, morally good results. Indeed, in Reiman's account the political system itself (e.g., the kind of constitutional democracy which he seems to prefer) is not the principal locus of moral evaluation but, rather, the laws that are produced; and these are simply judged by their effects. That such laws, when followed, give rise to morally worthy results (as determined by some superordinate ethical standard, here a utilitarian one) is all that ultimately counts. Any political system, in producing such laws and hence results, would be equally justified. So Reiman reduces political authority in the rule-issuing sense to the effects of the rules issued. Political authority, insofar as it can be established, is focused in these rules; their assessment, in Reiman's view, is straightforwardly derivative from high-order moral norms.[17] And the problem I have cited remains.

Whatever the ground for justifying political authority is here (whether we are talking about Paul's injunctions to the Romans or Reiman's arguments), it is not a ground within, not an integral feature of, any theoretic system of political concepts and institutions. Authority attaches not to the law-making role or the system of concepts in which it is embedded but to the external ground. The political system and that which confers authority on it are, necessarily, separated conceptually.

This is all that philosophical anarchists would need to reintroduce their arguments. This capacity of anarchism, however, represents not so much the peculiar vulnerability of political authority to critique as it does the exploitation by the anarchist of inherent defects in the externalist program for justifying political authority (that is, in the defects of what I have been calling simple and direct externalism). But locating these defects is another matter.

3.3. *Main Defects of Simple Externalism*

As I have already indicated, I don't think the defect lies in making political obligation the prior concept over rule-issuing authority rather than the other way around. The same problem clearly exists under either option.

For in both cases we first establish directly (on *external* grounds) the justification of a *single* focal element, be it (1) rule-issuing authority, or (2) an obligation for citizens to obey the laws issued. And then we reason from there, using (for simplicity) the idea of a mutual entailment between rule-issuing authority and obligation. In case (1), we say that citizens thus must have an obligation of obedience—some have said a *strict* obligation—or, in case (2), we say that, since they do have a standing obligation to obey laws, government then must have a title to issue such rules in the first place.

These two prior element approaches have constituted, I would say, the traditional and standard answers to the ancient question of whether citizens are bound in conscience to obey the laws of the land. But these standard answers are deeply problematic: for each is committed to the externalist program.

The logic of that program (as set out earlier in Section 3.1) requires that we take *one* element in the idea of political authority— say, the license to issue rules or the reasonable expectation of compliance—and lift it clean out of the realm of the political to bring it *directly* under some external normative standard, such as the divine will or an ultimate ethical principle (like that of utility). Hence, the classical externalist program (the program of simple and direct externalism, as found in the traditional political obligationists or in the Pauline idea of the "governing authorities") commits us to a piecemeal treatment of the constituent elements of the notion of political authority. More important, by removing elements of that notion from the particular theoretic system in which they are located we sunder the connections that any such element has within that system to the other conceptual elements ingredient there.

Where external justification (so conceived) remains our focus, it forestalls any serious effort to exhibit the systematic connections that might arise from within the set of theoretic political conceptions and institutions. Instead, we are encouraged to single out some element from within the set and to moralize it, or baptize it. But what is taken out of the system, no longer having its internal connections and its place there, is no longer characteristically political.

For example, the obligation to obey the law is not treated in the accounts we have examined as a political obligation. On the contrary, it is treated (so far as its justifying grounds are concerned) exclusively as a *moral* one, or as a divinely commanded one; and it takes its place, if it has one, in a list of moral rules, on a par with the obligation to keep promises.[18]

The defect of the program of classical externalism (of simple and direct externalism) as regards obligation, then, is that it effectively short-circuits the effort to exhibit the internal or systemic connections that might yield a distinctive notion of *political* obligation. For, if we take up that program (treating its one project as focal, and regarding that one focus as determinative and conclusive), we have adopted a perspective from which it is systematically impossible to determine whether the peculiar *political* standing of a citizen before the law can be morally approved. For it is never determined, and never could be, that, for example, some specific requirement on action is inherent in the citizen's standing before the law in a system determined by a given set of political concepts and institutions.

Similarly, the question whether some authoritative rule-issuing agency is actually required by such a set, and hence is a necessary feature of any state so organized, cannot be answered in the classical externalist program. Indeed, that question does not even arise there.

A solution to the problem posed, though, is perhaps suggested by these very considerations. The logic of classical externalism (as set out in Section 3.1), relying on a supposed analytic or conceptual connection between any two of the main elements in the idea of political authority, requires that we select *one* of these elements—be it the title to issue rules or the reasonable presumption of compliance or the government's rightful monopoly in the use of coercive forcing—and ground that one element *directly* in some external normative source. Thus, we get the classical externalist model for justifying political authority. But we might, instead, consider working the elements up together. Or, to be precise, we might try to work up a theoretic system of political concepts in which these three elements would be seen to be in place there once the system is fully described and hence could be said to be required for that system to be instantiated.

The simple and direct approach, as we have it in classical externalism, does not encourage or even allow for the project of making such substantive internal connections. In contrast to this approach, we now have the germ of an alternative scheme: of a program for an *internal* justification of political authority.

4. INTERNAL JUSTIFICATION

As I see it, whether or not political authority is an intrinsic feature in a theoretic system of political concepts and institutions actually depends on what that system is. Hence, to see if a particular theoretic system really can support the category of political authority we would need to give body to the notions that actually make up that system.

In concluding the argument of this chapter I want to sketch out some preliminary features of just one example of an internal justification of political authority. To do this I will identify, but only very schematically, certain main details of a particular political system. I will try to show, in a very general way, how political authority could be justified internally in that system. I will not, of course, attempt a full-scale justification at this point.

4.1. *A Preliminary Illustration*

Let us imagine a theoretic schema for a political system which would include at a minimum such notions as constitutional rights and democratic procedures. I think it arguable, whatever one might think about so-called natural or human rights, that constitutional or civil rights require stating. They must be issued by some body. Moreover, they must be applied, at least in the sense of being given some determinate content, and then lived up to. And, where rights conflict, they must be harmonized. When we have rights, issued and applied and coordinated, we have a *system* of rights rules. And we could not have such a system without agencies to do those things. These agencies, in turn, would have to exhibit some degree of coordination themselves. Here, then, government as a coordinated set of agencies would enter the picture as instrumental to the production of rights.

But how could agencies of government issue rules which constituted, or at least helped define, civil rights of individual persons? What basis could we have for believing that the rules and practices generated by governmental action were really rights rules, really rights practices? This is a hard question, but it might be answered that this is where democracy comes in. Having democratic procedures available does not assure that the rules issued will establish or maintain rights. But one can at least presume—a refutable presumption in the individual instance—that they would. Why?

Governmental agencies in a democratic society not only represent a majority—or plurality—of citizens but also must appeal to these pluralities for their foundation and must constantly strive to create them anew. Accordingly, when we have rules produced in conformity to democratic procedural norms—in conformity with the consent of the subjects, as it is sometimes put—we can have some assurance that many people (by hypothesis, at least a majority) have affirmed, or would affirm, such rules. And this would include, if democratic procedures stay in character (as determined by what could justify majority rule, a point I will amplify later), rules which assign and help maintain benefits for all persons, individually, in the society—rules which identify and establish ways of acting, or of being acted toward, that every person arguably would want for himself or herself.

So we see, in sum, that civil rights rules do require an agency or set of agencies to issue and apply them. And we have reason to postulate that agencies based on democratic procedures would presumptively be able to issue just such rules. Though I will not argue the point here, there does seem to be an affinity between the idea of civil rights and that of democratic procedures. They are somehow connected and, accordingly, the idea of a system of rights—at least that of the one we are interested in—would have both these as features of it.

Now it might be alleged that good citizenship in a rights-producing polity, one where presumptive civil rights rules were issued in accordance with democratic procedures on a democratic electoral basis, involves some sort of standing commitment to abide by the laws that define and maintain these rights. Here the conduct appropriate to the citizens in such a system would involve compliance generally and on principle with civil rights laws in particular. Whether the idea of a system of rights requires compliance with *all* its laws or whether it involves *strict* compliance even with all civil rights laws are clearly matters for dispute. But I doubt that there is any real dispute that the standing of the citizens toward the law in this particular system is a special one, a standing that attaches to the laws—that is, to the laws that formulate and help maintain civil rights—and hence attaches to the polity as such.

In this brief sketch, then, I have indicated how two of the elements in the traditional notion of political authority—the title to issue rules and a reasonable expectation of compliance with these rules—might be regarded as implicit in a particular theoretic system of political conceptions and institutions—in the illustration used, a system of rights. Even so, it should not be a foregone conclusion that a political agency which has a justified title to issue rules and to expect compliance thereby has the title to punish, that is, a license to attach sanctions clauses to its laws and to carry these out against lawbreakers. The matter is more complex than that.

Again, I do not want at this point to express any but a very preliminary judgment. I would merely suggest that punishment as a political–legal practice is itself located in a particular political system and that it is to be justified by reference to its system-located aim or function. Here, to justify punishment is to display its rationale, to show its place, and the necessity for it there, within a particular system of political institutions and principles. Accordingly, the practice of punishment would be justified, to one degree or other, in the particular political system we have been concerned with, a system of rights, if (1) it would help maintain the condition of noninterference with determinate rights, and (2) it was necessary either because no alternative way would do the job at all or because no alternative way could do the job as effectively.

In a quite natural way, then, the third and final authority element—the government's use of physical force for purposes of coercion—has been brought into the picture. Thus, we see how it might be possible to extend an analysis of a system of rights to include an internally justified practice of punishment in it.

In sum, I have tried to show that the notion of political authority has three main elements: rule-issuing, general compliance, coercive enforcement. And theories of justifying such authority approach this grouping of elements in radically different ways.

The classical externalist approach reduces the issue of justification by focusing on a single one of the elements, on, for example, a strict obligation to obey laws *qua* valid laws. The implications of this reductionist move are striking, as I have tried to show; for just insofar as the obligation to conform to laws, say, is not thought to be grounded in or derived from elements in the notion of authority—or for that matter from other political concepts at all (such as from the notions and institutions of democracy)—the justifying grounds for that obligation must be sought *outside* the body of political concepts altogether. Hence we must, in accordance with the classical model, turn to some external obligation-conferring trait: be it biological or sociological, theological or moral. This externalist approach makes it systematically impossible to justify *political* obligation—and thence political authority—as itself politically grounded. Or at least I have so argued (recall here the parallel case of neighborly obligation).

The alternative approach, which I have so far developed only in outline, attempts to work up a theoretic system of political concepts in which all three of the elements composing the notion of authority can be shown to be ingredient. Here the justification of political authority involves establishing systematic connections between the three main elements (in normative form) in the notion of authority.

The intuitive point of internal justification, which is what I have called this second or alternative approach, is that the connection is mediated through a background theory. (For I doubt one could ever do so on the basis simply of analytic connections, of mere relations of logical entailment between the elements.) Thus, it would be the coherence of the idea of a system of rights, in which subsequently each of the authority elements can be shown to have a necessary place, that justifies political authority. Not in general but within a system of rights. For it is within such a system that the authority elements have been successfully linked together.

4.2. *A Plan of Attack*

It seems, accordingly, that if my sketch of this second approach can be filled in, these conclusions sustained, and the connections they involve amplified, we will have a clearer idea of what is involved in the internal justification of political authority respecting at least one political system. Hence, the chapters that follow discuss rights; democratic procedures and institutions;

the obligation (or allegiance, as I prefer to call it) of citizens in a rights-producing state and the question whether civil disobedience might be allowable there; the case that could be made for justifying punishment in such a setting; and, finally, the variety of punitive responses that might properly be triggered by the violation of law in a political system of that specific sort.

Though these many topics are canvassed, the underlying motif will remain the justification of political authority. For it is the object of this book to determine whether the principles of a system of rights do constitute a coherent set and, in particular, whether they can ground, through this coherence, the presence of the elements of political authority in states properly said to be rights-producing.

I realize that if a different system had been chosen for illustration, a different analysis and perhaps different conclusions would have been required. Even so, I think the basic logical points involved here would be invariant for all such systems.

4.3. *Externalism Revisited*

There is, in particular, an interesting connection between what I have been calling an internal justification of political authority and a possible externalist scheme for such justification. The externalist scheme I have in mind would, of course, be structured quite differently from the way it was in the classical model. In its revised version the externalist scheme requires simply that, in the end, we bring political authority under some politically ulterior standard. But for this to be done properly, or so I have argued, any acceptable externalist scheme would have to presuppose—hence require—the very internal justificatory procedure I have been describing. For without first establishing that political authority is both a political and an internally justified authority, any externalist program would seem to have little point.[19]

However, once the internal justification is completed, the externalist (in the revised account I am suggesting) is in a position to ask an important question. The externalist can ask whether a given theoretic system of political conceptions and institutions, in which the elements of authority have been established as embedded, can be morally approved, that is, approved in accordance with the standards of a critical theory of moral justification. This is the same as asking whether political authority can be morally justified.

The externalist program for justifying political authority is, as revised, one step removed from where, in its earlier version, it was normally thought to operate. Rather than deal with the question of justifying on moral grounds the elements of authority, seriatim and head on (as in the classical model), it is peculiarly suited to raise the question whether an authority that is politically justified can be *morally* justified. For, if there is such a thing as an independent critical moral justification of political authority, it is probably at the level of justifying an entire political system (or at the level of justifying salient features of an entire system) and, hence, can be a justification of political authority only after the accomplishment of a prior internal justification.

In short, then, classical externalism, having regard to each of the elements of political authority in turn (to *either* rule issuing *or* compliance *or* coercion), was simple and direct. In its revised form, however, it is complex and indirect: indirect because it presupposes a prior internal justification; complex because what it must justify is not a simple thing (not a single authority element, on its own) but a complicated one (an integrated theoretic system of political institutions and conceptions which, as a set, supports all the authority elements together). On the revised account, then, which I am recommending, internal justification and external justification are *conceived as complementary* in character.

It follows too, from the two-step pattern of justification I am here discussing, that certain changes in the strategies of philosophical anarchism will be entailed. For on the analysis I have developed, the characteristic device of the philosophical anarchist, to remove the elements of political authority simply on external grounds, would be a category mistake, since the notion of political authority is an intrinsic one, belonging always to a particular theoretic system of political concepts. Accordingly, it is not open to the philosophical anarchist, if the elements of authority can be coherently integrated within a given theoretic system, to say that legitimate political authority is an incoherent or contradictory notion and, for that reason, is impossible.

In the very last part of the book I will return to the issue of critical moral justification raised in the present chapter. To move toward this end, either to justify political authority morally or to deny it in the manner of the philosophical anarchist, one must start by attempting to establish or justify the elements of authority with respect to the notions that constitute a particular theoretic system of political concepts. To this extent, then, the program for an internal justification of political authority is logically inescapable. And to begin the program I have outlined for the present book we will turn, in the next chapter, to the concept of rights.[20]

2

The Concept of Rights

THE philosophy of rights has been a perennial subject of discussion not only because it is embedded in the intellectual tradition and political practices of many countries but also because it exhibits deep divisions of opinion on fundamental matters. Even a cursory survey of the literature on rights since, say, the time of the Second World War would turn up a number of perplexing questions to which widely divergent answers have been given: What are rights? Are rights morally fundamental? Are there any natural rights? Do human rights exist? Are all the things listed in the UN's Universal Declaration (of 1948) truly rights? What are moral rights? Legal rights? Are basic moral rights compatible with utilitarianism? How are rights to be justified? What is the value of rights? Can infants have rights, can fetuses have them, or future generations, or animals? And so on.

The existence of deep philosophical disagreement need not be an occasion for alarm or despair; it could, instead, point the way to a fruitful method of proceeding. Thus, a theory of the character and value of rights might be expected at the very minimum to identify certain crucial issues—where philosophers are divided—and then to sketch out the main grounds of the positions taken. What we would be looking for is the crux, the hinge on which the issue turns, so that it might be resolved one way or the other.

A theory arises on a body of problems; it has a context and ultimately reflects a limited aim. Theories of rights should be regarded, then, as partial explications or characterizations rooted in an attempt to resolve some particular crucial issue or other. It is tempting, but misleading, to regard the ensuing theories as concerned with the nature of rights; it is much more likely that an attractive and suitable characterization is but a successful way to avoid certain errors which unfortunately keep cropping up in the field of rights theory. Such characterizations make it possible to think about concrete and accredited rights carefully with the result that we may be able to take them seriously.

In the present chapter I want to move toward consideration of just one crucial issue on which philosophers have been sharply divided. It bears on the question "What are rights?"

I. SOME MAIN FEATURES OF RIGHTS

To fix our thinking at the very outset on a specific matter, let us imagine the following scene. A group of people live in an out of the way place, a forest perhaps. In that place is a pond and the people there are used to going to the pond to fish. There are several well-worn paths by which they can go to the pond, depending on which part of the forest they are coming from. One day a fence is put across one of the paths and the people are told that the path is closed. One of them responds that this cannot be. They are going to the pond to fish and it is their right to do so and they have taken this path and it is their right to do so; the fence maker should remove the fence or, at the very least, the people should be able to climb over it and continue to the pond.

I presume the scenario is recognizable: the talk of rights seems natural and appropriate. There is, of course, much about the setting that we do not know and that would require filling in. We do not know, for example, what the political status of the people is: whether they are subjects of the same political jurisdiction or, for that matter, whether they are subjects of any political jurisdiction. For all we know these people might be bucolic inhabitants of a benign state of nature, of the sort imagined by Locke (at least in its very earliest stages) or by Rousseau. Nor do we know anything about the status of property among these people: whether they have private property or which persons, if any, can be said to have particular property interests. We do not even know what kind of right the fisher-to-be was asserting: whether it was a customary right or a legal one or a moral right of some sort. None of this is clear.

Yet the claim that there was a right here did not seem unintelligible and the suggestion that the fence maker should therefore give way seemed appropriate enough. Why should things be clear even to this extent, when so much else was indeterminate? I suppose, then, that we can tell something about the character of rights from this relatively uncluttered story and that, whatever this character is, it is independent of the many things we do not know from the story. What we might gather here, in particular, is the character rights would have regardless of whether they were customary or legal or moral in nature.

One conclusion we could draw from the story, once we assume that the way of acting in question is indeed a right, is that rights are fairly determinate things. The disputation seems to require such determinateness; for it matters, crucially, whether going to the pond *on this particular path* is a right. If simple access to the pond had been all that mattered, where other paths were available, the dispute would have reduced to issues merely of custom or convenience. I do not, of course, want to suggest that people never dispute about more abstract matters (the right to travel, for example). It's just that if we could not reach something fairly determinate from the abstract assertion of the right, then the assertion of a right here is irresolute; it would not tell people what they could or could not do and they would soon lose interest. So we can say that there is an appropriate determinateness to such disputes and that one of the points to an argument about rights is to settle on what that is: to decide what, specifically, the right is *to* in the context of the dispute.

A second conclusion we could draw is that whatever the right is to—considered determinately—it must be to something distributable, something that could (practicably speaking) be given to or provided for or engaged in by those who are relevantly said to be the rightholder(s). For any given right must define a class such that every member is assigned the thing in question. Thus, in the story, the people (presumably all those who live in the forest) are said to be the rightholders and all have the right of going to the pond on any of several paths, this one included. Going along on this particular path was something the relevant persons physically could do; in that way, clearly, it was distributable. But the sense in which we are interested is whether the capacity so to walk is itself parceled out to each of them in the defining rule, as it was presumably in the right we are discussing. When a distributable physical capacity is thus distributed to all the relevant individuals, the resulting arrangement is said to be "individuated." Following Dworkin (whose term it is) we can say, then, that all rights are individuated: they are rights to something which can be distributed to all the rightholders (be they natural individuals or collective bodies or what have you) and they assign the same capacity to each of them to enter into that distribution in the appropriate way.[1] That thing can be said, in some relevant way, to be *due* to the rightholder, and due in the same way to each of the rightholders.

Yet another conclusion we could draw, coming close on the heels of the one just sketched, is that rights are—or involve—accredited ways of acting. This is, of course, the conclusion I most want to draw; it is, indeed, the hypothesis from which my argument in this chapter starts. And the question I will address is the character, in its main dimensions, of that accrediting.

We can readily imagine from the story that initially, before it is challenged, the way of acting is relatively unself-conscious—unreflective and routine. Here the right and the practice are virtually indistinguishable. Now, when a way of acting has been challenged or infringed, the practice in question may well be referred to by its proponent, explicitly, as a right. More important, the features in the practice that make for a right will be brought out or, at least, there will be an attempt to do so.

How, then, does the person whose action has been challenged make good a rights claim? Certainly that person could do so, for example, by drawing forth an acknowledgment that the action was indeed his or her practice, and the practice of others, if that was the case. More significantly, the claimant could elicit confirmation that this practice had been an accepted one, not merely by those who engaged in it but also by others whose judgment seemed relevant. The practice in question (going to the pond on this particular path) was accredited, then, by an appropriate social ratification—in the case at hand, it might be, by an unreflective and unspoken social acceptance. And, presumably, any practice can be said to be a right insofar as the way of acting involved is backed up—that is, endorsed and accredited—by some form of social recognition.

We say *social* here, for it is unlikely that a right could ever arise except in a social setting: it would be odd, and probably pointless (practically speaking), to talk of the rights of a wholly and permanently isolated individual. But my point is not simply about the setting of rights; I want, rather, to suggest that this factor of social recognition or ratification is actually a constituent of rights—that is, of our characterization of something as a right. Of course, the precise description of the social recognition involved would probably vary somewhat, even within the same society, depending on whether the right in question was said to be customary or legal or moral in nature.[2]

Now, the situation on the path is one that could actually happen. If it had happened, we would want the disputation about it to be similarly realistic. Thus, one of the considerations that would surely be evoked by practitioners of the challenged way of acting is a specification of the interest(s) at stake in the way of acting. And the way of acting and the interest would be connected by an explanatory account which would render the action plausible as a means to a certain end, that is, to the interest(s) being served. In short, the way of acting would be endorsed or accredited on the ground of common acknowledgment, and the reasonableness of that in turn would be underwritten by the soundness of the explanatory account which could be provided for the way of acting, by exhibiting it as the means to or as a part of accomplishing some interest or perceived benefit or other good (or desirable) thing.

Sometimes there may prove to be difficulties in the way of our saying that the social acceptance has been, or still is, a reasonable thing. Thus, if the person who wanted to stop the practice said there were no longer any fish in the pond, then the practice of going to the pond to fish would appear to be unreasonable. And if the practice was unreasonable, the social ratification of the practice, on the grounds given, would also be unreasonable. There would be a basis then to revoke the common acceptance or, if the acceptance had been of an unconscious sort, to let it wither.

Indeed, reflection on the reasonableness of social acceptance could follow any of several channels, as marked out by the theory of practical inference.[3] Hence, consideration would be relevant not only of the claim that the practice was a means to a certain end, or a part of accomplishing it, but also that the practice was, among available alternatives, a preferable one. Thus, on this point in particular the fence maker might say that there are other ways to get to the pond and this path should not be taken because it cannot be used without fouling the water supply or trampling the berry patches of some of the people.

Such contentions would, no doubt, multiply our difficulty in determining whether a right existed or whether it should be exercised. But it is important to see that the line of connection between an accredited way of acting and the notion of explanatory reasonableness is not a direct one. Rather, when one says that a way of acting is accredited that contention is supported in a quite particular way, by the fact of social ratification (in some appropriate form). It is this factor, then, which is focal. Here reasonableness would tend to support the ratification and unreasonableness, we presume, to erode it. Thus, explanatory reasonableness affects accredited ways of acting by operating on what accredits or supports them, by affecting social acceptance. I doubt, then, that the right would be extinguished short of revoking the crucial factor of social recognition, in whatever form it was appropriate to give it.[4]

In any event, my concern here is not with cases in which rights might be doubtful but with those in which they are not in serious dispute. For we are trying to conceive what rights are. To do this we must try to envision the successful cases.

And I am particularly concerned, for now at least, to avoid cases where rights conflict (where the fence maker had, for example, asserted a competing right). For, in order to contemplate this interesting possibility, we would first have to assume that the way of acting being infringed was indeed a right and thus we would necessarily presuppose a simpler case in which that way of acting was a right whether or not the thing infringing it was also said to be one. In a preliminary account it is best to keep things simple and to avoid deflecting attention from the central understanding, which would be presupposed by *both* the competing rights, of what a right is and of what its vindication amounts to.

Thus, we can usefully imagine that sometimes the elements I have identified would concur; here a way of acting would be socially acknowledged and the acknowledgment certified as reasonable, that is, reasonable so far as the practical inferences involved are themselves sound. In such a case there would be good ground for saying that a well-founded or proper right existed: that the practice was socially accepted, hence a right, and that the acceptance was reasonable.

Here one would have a basis for giving directions to the fence maker or to others: the infringer can justifiably be asked to desist. And if the infringer does not, then, arguably, steps could be taken to remove the interfering measure or to prevent it. And this capacity to issue such directives and, perhaps, to take other steps, would add a further degree of establishment, or fastness or security, to any way of acting in question. It is often said that rights are guarantees to the individual that a certain pattern of activity is accredited and will be maintained socially, and we can readily see how such a notion of guarantee could arise from this point.

We must recognize, of course, that the account of rights so far given is very abstract, very general, and the features we have identified would undergo revision and acquire peculiar emphases depending on which kind of right we were said to be concerned with—legal, moral, or what have you. In particular, the account would be amplified by appeal to the standards and content of political or moral or religious discourse, as determined by philosophy or, what is more likely, by the practices of such reasoning in a given time and place. But I believe these various specialized modes of justification (each emphasizing its own preferred kinds of reasons—I mean here *material* reasons, such as the common good or the scriptures as interpreted by Calvin—and its own style of supporting argumentation) would all build on the standard I have used, that of explanatory reasonableness as attached to social acceptance. These forms of conventional justification would not set that standard aside. This standard, then, seems to me not so much minimal as indispensable.

Thus, I would want to suggest that the central intuitions in my account would be preserved intact throughout the elaboration of a theory of rights. A right is *to* something which is both determinate and distributable. An identical or, at least, a similar capacity respecting that thing, as specified in the right, is assigned to every person who can relevantly be said to be a rightholder; in this regard, all rights are individuated. A right so understood is an accredited or established way of acting. The ground of this establishment, what accredits the way of acting and what principally qualifies it as a right, is something variously described as social recognition or acknowledgment or common acceptance (in a form appropriate to the kind of right involved, and with whatever reasons and argumentation that might be deemed necessary there). This acceptance would be supported as reasonable in the minimal sense given by the notion of explanatory reasonableness. And directives could be issued to others, to those who are not rightholders, and further initiatives taken on the basis of—or as part of—any such successful claim to rights status.

In the present chapter I want to discuss two of these features in particular: the idea that rights can be understood as accredited ways of acting and the idea that rights always involve some sort of normative direction of the behavior of others (the so-called second parties). I will begin with the latter contention, for it represents one of the views commonly held nowadays as to the character of rights.

2. RIGHTS AND NORMATIVE DIRECTION

This view is often put by saying that rights correlate with duties—meaning that a right always implies or has attached some closely related duty of others. But there are, I think, serious difficulties in the way of holding a thesis of correlation in precisely this form.[5]

The most interesting arguments against correlations of this sort derive from Wesley Hohfeld's classification of rights; on his view a legal right could be constituted by any one of four elements: by a claim, but also by a liberty, by a power, or by an immunity. Let me be more specific here. Hohfeld identified four basic types of rights, each type having a unique second-party correlative. For a legal *claim right* the correlative element is a legal duty of some second party. Analogously, the legal *liberty* to do X—which consists in the absence of any duty on the agent's part to refrain from X—is matched with other people's lack of a claim that X not be done by the agent. A legal *power* to do X consists in a person's legal competence to perform an act which will create, or at least bring to bear, certain legal consequences for a second party—and the situation of the second party constitutes the party's liability (or susceptibility) to that particular power. Finally, a person's *immunity* from X is necessarily correlated with a lack of power on the part of others to do X, and thus the correlative of an immunity is a disability or what Hohfeld calls a no-power.[6]

Now, an example developed in terms of Hohfeld's classificatory analysis might help to indicate the difficulty in the way of the thesis that rights always correlate with duties. Take the constitutional right of Americans to free speech. This right does not create an area of free choice by imposing obligations on others; instead it does so by imposing a normative disability or lack of authority on Congress. The First Amendment "deprives Congress of the authority . . . to enact laws requiring or prohibiting speech of certain kinds." An attempt by Congress to legislate in this area could presumably be challenged successfully in court and declared null and void. Thus, although the right to freedom of speech has a conceptual correlative, "it is not an obligation; it is a legislative disability . . . ."[7]

The point here is this. We are not saying that Congress has a constitutional duty not to pass such laws and, hence, that it *should* not; rather, we are saying that Congress is constitutionally unable to legislate in this area and, hence, that it *cannot*. By analogy, we might say that a person cannot legally contract two marriages over one and the same stretch of time; for one of the marriages, the second, is necessarily invalid. This says something quite different from the injunction that one should not have two same-time marriages, for this suggests merely that such a course would be legally wrong (and not that it would be—or would also be—in some sense legally impossible). Hence, duty and disability are distinct notions in law and some legal rights imply legal disabilities, not legal duties. Of course, one might believe that prudent people should not (or have a duty not to) do what is legally impossible or inadmissible or invalid, but this is a clearly a derivative sense of 'should' (or 'duty') and depends entirely on a prior and independent notion of legal disability, which is here basic.

Suppose that we, under the influence of these examples, decide to deny that every right is attached to a duty of some sort. We would immediately be challenged, no doubt, to imagine someone asserting the existence of a right while allowing (at the same time) that no one is under any duty regarding the acts covered by the right. In such a case, the challenger continues, "the alleged right has turned out to be a right that has no meaning. ... The alleged right does not protect [the holder]; it does not even give him a ground for complaint. There is nothing for him to gain in invoking it before, during or after any attempts at interference."[8]

But we can imagine such a right being useful if we imagine it to be correlated with a disability on the part of other persons. Thus, when a person purports to do what that person or anyone else lacks the legal authority to do (e.g., legislate away freedom of speech, or deprive someone of citizenship on grounds of race or religion) there is a ground for complaint—at least if this harms one's interests—and there may indeed be something to gain in invoking such a right, namely that the invalidity of the action will be officially declared and the act deprived of practical effect. More generally, the most important means of institutionalizing some rights may be to create second-party disabilities (or, sometimes, to create what Hohfeld called liabilities) rather than duties. This will often be the solution in cases where a legal duty cannot be expected to be particularly effective (where, for example, it would prove difficult to enforce the duty against individual police officers and prosecutors or even against a branch of government).

Of course, it may continue to be said that Congress has a duty not to make laws "abridging . . . the freedom of speech"; but this particular duty cannot be fully stated (as I indicated above) without bringing in the notion of a disability, or "no-power" as Hohfeld called it, nor is it enforceable along the lines of most duties but requires instead the "sanction" of nullity. There is considerable bite, then, to the contention that a normative disability or lack of authority rather than a duty may sometimes be the main correlative of a given right.

It seems, therefore, that arguments based on the existence of rights of the sort we have been discussing—immunity rights—are telling against the view that every right is necessarily connected to a closely related second-party duty. But we can still accept the important point that a right which doesn't guide anyone's behavior is no right at all; but to do this we should add that this guidance need not involve a duty—a disability or liability will do as well in some contexts.

The truth, which the rights-correlate-with-duties thesis skews, is that any genuine right must involve some normative direction of the behavior of persons other than the holder—for example, direction of the sort given by the Hohfeld elements mentioned earlier (duty, disability, liability). And it is this truth about normative direction, crucial to the concept of rights, which I want to endorse here and which I tried to suggest in my earlier discussion of directives. The idea that all rights attach to certain directives for the conduct of others is weaker than the claim that they are necessarily linked to specific duties, but it is, I believe, a sounder and more defensible notion.

There is, however, a serious problem in holding even this weaker thesis, that all rights involve normative direction of persons other than the rightholder. For it seems to run up against the authority of Hobbes, one of the founders and still a presiding genius of rights theory.

3. A PROBLEM: HOBBES AND HOHFELD ON LIBERTY

In his account of natural rights Hobbes appeared to argue roughly as follows. A natural right is a liberty; such a right specifies a way of acting that is rational for anyone in the state of nature and, on reflection, we determine that it would be rational for persons in such a state to do anything to preserve their own life and substance. Hobbes's account here is specifically intended to endorse as rational, hence as a natural right, each person's following a policy of first-strike violence. But the conduct of other people was in no way normatively directed by these liberty rights. True, they had what Hohfeld would call a no-right (or no-claim) against any exercise of a natural right, but this amounts simply to saying that others could call on no duty of the rightholder *not* to do the thing he or she was doing. But beyond this there was no positive normative direction that could restrain their conduct, not even given by such other duties as might exist in a state of nature. In this respect their responsive conduct towards another's exercise of a liberty right was completely ungoverned normatively: just as the rightholder could (normatively) do anything that the holder was physically able to do so all other individuals could in anticipation or in response do literally anything, presumably in virtue of *their* natural right. Hence, we could say for Hobbes that no person—no second party—is given any normative direction as to how that person is supposed to act in virtue of the natural liberty rights possessed by others. And we conclude, then, that for Hobbes at least, a right *qua* right involves, can involve, no normative direction of the behavior of others. For if he had *conceived* rights differently, as always involving second-party obligations or directions of some sort, he would simply have been unable to talk in the way that he did of rights in a state of nature.

Now, Hobbes stands at the very beginning of the tradition of talking about rights with which we are concerned in this chapter. He wrote at a time when the concept of rights was actually being molded. And we might do well to ask how we got from there to here.

I want to suggest, briefly, that there were problems within Hobbes's own theory which would force even his talk of rights onto lines we are familiar with; that is, force it toward the view that rights characteristically involve normative direction for the behavior of second parties.

I think it is generally accepted that Hobbes endorsed a theory of rights *in civil society* in which rights (here the rights of the sovereign) are paired with duties of others (the obligation of the subjects to conform). Here then, quite simply, the conduct of subjects was normatively directed in relation to the sovereign's rights. And, where rights of individual subjects to act were decreed by the sovereign's will, others were prohibited from interfering.

The problem is that Hobbes now appears to be using 'rights' equivocally. In his theory of civil society, the crucial case of rights (those of the sovereign) seems to carry second-party obligations in its train; but in his theory of the state of nature, the very opposite is so. Hence, we cannot say, for the former theory, that rights *imply* second-party obligations whereas, for the latter, they do not. We cannot say this, that is, if we mean to suggest something about the definition or the concept of rights.

It's not merely that the term 'rights' is being used equivocally. For, more important, these two uses would be incompatible insofar as we took either to represent correctly the notion of a right. Hence, if we started with the state-of-nature definition of a right then we could not get to the civil society account, as Hobbes had seemingly attempted to do, for these are logically incompatible.

One could attempt to preserve the basic consistency of Hobbes's account by contending that the duties of subjects are not *implied* by the sovereign's right but are merely superadded to it in civil society (for reasons of prudence, as given in Hobbes's theory). Even so, when we consider that for Hobbes the sovereign's right has the character it does have in civil society only because the subjects have a duty (to conform) attached to that right, then it becomes imperative for him to say that the sovereign's right is always paired with such obligations. Thus, Hobbes could never contend about rights that normative directives were not attached, that is, imply that there are no corresponding duties or even that such duties were *necessarily* omitted, if he was to have the theory of the right of the sovereign in civil society which he had espoused.

Hence, rights could not be *conceptually* identified with mere natural powers, as Hobbes had initially done, or with (Hohfeldian) liberties. For that would in effect entail a sheer absence of significant obligations on the part of others. And this would make Hobbes's account of the rights of the sovereign (in civil society) simply impossible, simply incoherent. On pain of equivocating or, even worse, of falling into logical contradiction, then, Hobbes must leave off such conceptual identifications as that of mere natural powers or mere liberties with rights.

On the likely supposition that Hobbes would want to retain his talk of rights as mere liberties in a state of nature, his only recourse, then, would be to leave the *concept* of rights neutral on the point of implying or not implying second-party obligations. Whatever Hobbes is to *mean* by "a right," then, it must not include or entail that such obligations are *not* attached. He would have to rely on a reduced conception of rights (where the attachment or not of the normative direction of second parties is left wholly indeterminate, such direction being neither implied nor not implied).

Whether this reduced conception would hold much interest is, of course, a matter for concern. Moreover, there is some question whether even this minimalist view is consistent with some of Hobbes's key arguments. One of his main claims, as we noted in Chapter 1, was that each person as subject, in order to move out of the state of nature and into the civil relationship, was required to waive, conditionally but permanently, that person's own exercise of natural rights. But it does appear that, for Hobbes, this waiving does imply at least one *duty*: that the subjects not exercise their rights, that they no longer act as if they even had such rights (except under certain very restrictive conditions). That is, for Hobbes, the waiving of a right, or of its exercise, by *A* logically implies such a duty of *A*. And this implication is not consistent with the minimalist thesis that neither normative direction nor its absence is ever *implied* by any proper right.

Be that as it may, this watered-down minimalist version is much less threatening to the account I have been developing than the Hobbesian theory of rights in a state of nature at first glance appeared to be. And there remains, beyond this, the serious problem that in Hobbes's account rights so understood (as in the minimalist account) would, without any restrictive duties on the part of others, give rise to constant conflict and ultimately, under conditions like those of the state of nature, to chaos. Further, rights so understood can be effective (as opposed to defective or even to chaotic) only with the superaddition of normative direction on the part of others. These are, of course, both points that he saw clearly.[9]

We can, thus, begin to sense why the development of rights theory has tended to go against Hobbes (even against the suggested minimalist account) and to side with Locke. For Locke did see normative direction attached to all rights, even rights in a state of nature. Thus, on the Lockian view, rights as rights (and hence as natural rights or human rights or constitutional rights or civil rights, what have you) always correlate with some significant normative direction of the conduct of others (the so-called second parties); and in the absence of such directives one could not speak of rights.[10]

Following along the line I have traced from Hobbes to Locke, a consensus has since developed that rights have a normative character and, among other things, have the normative force of implying (or, if not that, of always being correlated with) significant normative directions for conduct incumbent on second parties. Now, it is important to see that the issue we have been considering is in no way special to just Hobbes's thinking about rights; rather, it applies to the whole category of Hohfeldian liberty rights (with respect to which Hobbes's account of natural rights is but an example). Accordingly, my proposal is that we use this consensus, insofar as its credentials have progressively passed muster and will continue to do so, to justify reshaping the entire Hohfeldian category, so similar in essential respects to the Hobbesian idea of a natural right of liberty, to bring it into conformity with what has now become the traditional view.

We should note at the very beginning that Hohfeld, unlike Hobbes, actually subscribes to the basic thesis of the consensus, at least formally; for he does appear to believe that every proper right logically entails some normative direction for the conduct of second parties (but varying, of course, from case to case, depending on what *kind* of right we are concerned with). Thus, a liberty right implies a 'no-right' of others. And a no-right is the total absence of a claim on the duties of others. Thus, the second party, in the case of a liberty right, can claim no duty of the rightholder *not* to do that action respecting which the holder is said to have a liberty.

One of Hohfeld's classic illustrations of a liberty so conceived is the right of someone to eat a salad. Here the others at the table can call on no duty of the rightholder not to eat it. Presumably, they would be unjustified, then, in simply restraining the eligible eater from proceeding in due course to eat the salad, or in otherwise making that eating physically impossible. But, interestingly, Hohfeld specifically denies this. His point here is a rather technical one. He wants to emphasize that the *one* thing specified as certain that these others cannot do is point to a duty, on the rightholder's part, to forbear eating. Indeed, in Hohfeld's actual example, this is the only normative direction that relevantly pertains to *their* conduct. So we are free to imagine a number of scenarios: thus, the others might feel perfectly free to put their forks into the rightholder's salad and help themselves to portions of it as the holder nibbles along; or (in the scenario Hohfeld actually cites) one of them might feel free to grab the bowl away from the rightholder.

If this is a paradigm example of a liberty right, such a right is indeed an odd one. Why so? Not because *no* normative direction is involved but because no *significant* normative direction is involved. If, perhaps, the relevant duty had embraced at least two explicit features in particular—the Hohfeldian no-right (or no-claim) *and* a duty of second parties not to interfere directly with a proper exercise of the liberty (and maybe to restrain themselves in other ways as well)—that would be all right. But the Hohfeldian correlate to a liberty right does not require this (and Hohfeld goes out of his way graphically to point that fact out); rather, only the first of the these directives on conduct is actually entailed in Hohfeld's view.

It would follow from the analysis I have been developing, then, that those liberties (in Hohfeld's sense) that provide *insignificant* normative direction to the conduct of others (in being correlated with mere no-rights, for example) and that do not rest in any significant way on standing duties (which, though independent of the liberty in question, do afford its exercise a considerable degree of protection) would be bracketed off from the class of rights. They would simply be licenses or *mere* liberties or 'privileges,' as Hohfeld called them, but they would not properly be called rights.[11]

This conclusion follows, in short, as I have already indicated, from the thesis that every right has the normative force of implying (or, if not that, of always being correlated with) significant normative directions for conduct incumbent on second parties. And I have taken this thesis to be at the core of the consensual or traditional understanding of rights that has emerged from the disputation between Hobbes and Locke.

But is it enough to cite this consensus, this tradition: are our reasons for including such normative direction within the concept of rights merely historical ones? Is there no other foundation for the assertion that rights always involve normative direction? These are questions that must be answered. For we are concerned here not merely with what the traditional understanding of rights is, and some of the reasons for its acceptance historically, but also with whether that understanding is a coherent one, specifically on the point at issue. And to see this we need an analysis of how the *other* elements implicated in the notion of rights link up with the one factor, that of the normative direction afforded the conduct of second parties.

4. PRACTICAL INFERENCE AND THE NORMATIVE DIRECTION OF CONDUCT

A plausible account of the connection here can, I think, be generated by emphasizing the idea of action found in the notion that rights are endorsed or accredited ways of acting. Let me sketch it briefly. In my analysis the main ground of this endorsement—that which did the accrediting—was some sort of appropriate social ratification of the way of acting in question. This could take the form, if the right were a legal one, of official recognition, if it were a conventional or a customary one, of common acceptance, and so on. In any event persons in that society understand that the accomplishment of that way of acting has, in that society, a kind of endorsement. We suppose them as well to see the point of such ratification: by identifying an interest—a perceived benefit or good—of the rightholder(s) appropriately said to be provided in or through that way of acting.

One could say, then, on the basis of such ratification and the support given by its presumed reasonableness, that in this society the way of acting specified (e.g., going to the pond on this particular path) is one that is allowed or encouraged or sometimes even required; in sum, its accomplishment is supposed and accepted. The crucial point here is that the endorsed way of acting is set in a network of other actions such that it, toward them, serves as a sort of end-in-view, as an object that is to be thought of as brought about or accomplished. Suppose we take a rightholder's successfully walking on this particular path as properly exemplifying such an end (as something that is allowed or encouraged or required in that society).

Now, if we adopt the perspective of practical inference here, the actions of other people toward that end—and toward that particular action—are not to thwart its realization, that is, not to do so insofar as they affect the end or the action at all. Thus, the proper conduct of others, normally, would be to forbear preventing or interfering with the action of the rightholder. But whether others act to interfere or not, there is normative direction given to their conduct in the case at hand: they are not supposed to interfere; it is improper to do so.

The crucial fragment of reasoning would go something like this. We first suppose that the doing of *A* by an agent is socially endorsed. Here the accomplishing of *A*—as an end-state or goal, as something that is to be brought about—is socially approved. More specifically, we could say, for example, that the accomplishment of *A* is allowed. Now,

IF   (1) the accomplishment of *A* is allowed, and
      (2) an agent (*X*) sets himself or herself to do *A* (not a particular action, but any action that has the character indicated), and
      (3) another agent's (*Y*'s) doing *B* can be judged by *Y* to interfere with or prevent the performance of *A* or its accomplishment; here doing *B*—not a particular action, but any action that has the character indicated—is believed to be sufficient, or likely to be so, for *A* not to be accomplished and hence is believed to be inconsistent with the accomplishment of *A*, and thus
      (4) the not-doing of *B* becomes a means to or part of the accomplishment of *A*, which accomplishment is allowed (as in 1) unless, we could add, there are adequate countervailing reasons for doing *B* or for not allowing the accomplishment of *A*, and
      (5) the other agent (*Y*), though that agent might have reasons (such as personal dislike for *X*, or expectation of inconvenience), does not have countervailing reasons that would be judged adequate in the context in question (as in 4), and
      (6) *Y* is personally and situationally able to avoid doing *B*,
THEN   the action specified and expected, where *Y* acts in accordance with these conditions, is that *Y* forbears doing *B*.[12]

The conclusion here, I should add, is indifferent to the question whether one takes an external point of view (toward the endorsement) or an internal one.[13] Suppose, for the moment, a person who does not approve the relevant endorsement, and in that sense has an external viewpoint (as might someone from another society, for instance). This could well affect such a person's conduct, negatively, towards the action of the rightholder in question; but it should not affect that person's understanding that if the accomplishment of the way of acting was in fact endorsed then the conduct of others regarding it, given that endorsement, can be rated as proper or improper within the perspective of that endorsement. All that my account requires here is that people understand what such an expectation amounts to, that they be able to follow, perhaps even generate, the arguments that display such expectations, as that which is specified by the endorsement. Thus, if a way of acting is established as a norm within a domain (or perspective), then there is normative direction provided, given that establishment, for the conduct of others.

Or to be precise, an exercise of practical inference can tell us which action(s) would be performed by the relevant second party, if that person acted in accordance with the endorsement. And this understanding of what conduct is specified, given the satisfaction of the conditions in the "if ..." part of the formula, together with the statement of aim expressed (if only implicitly) in the endorsement tell us how that individual (as second party) *should* act, in some generic sense of 'should'. Suppose the statement of aim (or maxim) expressed is: "The accomplishing of A is to be allowed." If that maxim were a moral one, for example, a maxim of positive (or conventional) morality, then we are saying the second party *morally* should do X (e.g., morally should forbear doing B insofar as it interferes with or prevents A). If the maxim or rule, as expressed in the endorsement, is of a legal nature, then we are saying that the second party *legally* should do X: that that person is legally required not to do B, that he or she is legally prohibited from doing B. And so on with custom and other kinds of norms or rules. In this way, then, the conduct of others is normatively directed in each such case. And I have tried to capture this idea, in a general way, with the generic sense of 'should.'[14]

It should be clear, I hasten to add, that the normative direction exists here solely within the convention established for each particular right. But nothing is implied as to how that right stands in comparison with other normative considerations. Quite conceivably, the normative direction given by that right could be overridden, on a particular occasion or even altogether, by another normative consideration. Thus, for one example, the normative direction given in a right that was justified by standards of positive morality might be overridden altogether by a principle of critical morality (such as the Rawlsian first principle, as it was conceived in his *Theory of Justice*, 1971). Or, for another example, the normative direction given in a constitutional right might be set aside on a particular occasion by reference to a normative consideration of a completely different sort (a nonrights consideration of national security, for instance). And, of course, if one believes that rights can conflict, say, legal right A with legal right B, then one must believe that the normative direction afforded by any particular right is not determinative, even within the class of rights of the same kind (a point I will return to in Chapter 5). Thus, the sense in which second parties are directed by rights, in my analysis, is not to be understood as normatively *conclusive*. We must sometimes go to the final analysis, that famous place where "all things are considered" (and in a cool hour, one would hope).

We are now in position, I think, to see as well that this normative direction is not something logically entailed. We can do so in two steps. First, let us take the important features that I have identified in my account of rights as established ways of acting. Thus we would say: (1) that a right is *to* something which is both determinate and distributable, (2) that the right is individuated, (3) that the ground of this individuation—the establishment in the defining rule of a capacity on the part of each rightholder to the benefit in question—is social ratification, (4) that this ratification is or could be supported as explanatorily reasonable, by resort to standard means–end reasoning. Now, I want to suggest that if we take *all* these features—and call the conjunction or collective set of them (*a*)—then we could not get by mere logical entailment from (*a*) that (*b*) the conduct of others is normatively directed.

One could, of course, urge that we don't have a proper right unless we combine (*a*) and (*b*), for this is what we *mean* by 'a right.' And I do not dispute this; so, now, we do have a logical entailment: (*a*) & (*b*) → (*b*). But it is a trivial one. Thus, I would argue that if the presumed entailment here is supported merely by the putative *meaning* of 'a right,' then where we *separate* (*a*) and (*b*), as I have done, (*a*) does *not* logically entail (*b*).

Since (*a*) does not by itself entail (*b*), the question naturally arises as to how they are to be linked. This brings us to the second step. My analysis was meant to suggest that this connection is mediated by practical inference—by the capacity of people to reason practically, or, if you will, by the practice of such reasoning. Now, there seems to me only one way in which the connection so understood could be a matter of logical entailment. It could be only if the practical reasoning involved could be set out in a schema—call it (*s*)—and, further, only if that schema itself expressed a logical entailment. For we could then get that (*a*) & (*s*) logically entail (*b*):(*a*) & (*s*) → (*b*).

Thus, the question whether the connection I have discussed is, more precisely, one of logical entailment would depend on carefully developed views as to the logical character of a schema for practical inference (for example, a schema like the "if . . . then . . ." formula I introduced above). I do not think we could usefully pursue the matter beyond this point in the present study. So I will say no more than to record my belief that the analysis would ultimately not support a thesis as strong as logical entailment.[15] But it could still be said that the connection, though not one of logical entailment, is in some sense a conceptual connection—or, as I would prefer to say, a connection of practical inference.[16]

With this point, about a schema of practical inference as the connecting device, my account of the general characterization of a right is substantially complete. And the coherence of that conception has been made out, at least as regards the connection of the element of normative direction with the other main factors. We have seen that this element is not an adventitious feature, a mere historical happenstance, within the concept of rights; rather, it belongs there—insofar as rights are accredited ways of acting, having these other main features—in virtue of the character of practical reasoning.

5. WAYS OF ACTING AND WAYS OF BEING TREATED

I want to turn next to a further consideration, one that on reflection forces an expansion in my account. Up to now I have spoken of a right as if it specified, invariably, something that the rightholder as agent does or can do. True, many of the things typically captured in talk of rights would be so characterized—for example, the free exercise of religion, the liberty to travel, the right to vote or to own personal property. For each of them identifies a right to a specific way of acting, on the part of an agent, which way is secured or made fast—to a degree—for that agent by the relevant normative direction of the conduct of others. Thus, any one of these rights (as a right to a way of acting) could be given the now standard construal of a liberty or a freedom developed by MacCallum: here someone (as an agent) is able to do A (for example, to make his or her own judgments in matters of religious or moral or scientific or philosophical belief) free from proscribed interferences with A (such as would be afforded by a state establishment of religion). These proscribed interferences give us, in effect, a clearer idea of the normative direction of the conduct of others insofar as that conduct is responsive to the endorsed way of acting, the liberty in question.[17]

But not all rights identify ways of acting in precisely this sense. For not all of them identify things that agents (rightholders) do or can do.[18] The right to life, for example, is construed by some theorists as the right not to be killed. And this says something about what *others* do or can do. Thus, if person 1 has a right to life then person 2 is to do something: person 2 is to forbear killing person 1 and even, perhaps, to prevent that person's being killed by person 3. And none of this is something the rightholder does or can do.

The crucial point I am making does not rest on a single example; others are at hand. The right not to be tortured, for instance, is fulfilled perhaps exclusively by what others do or can do. In short the way of acting is theirs, not the rightholder's. They forbear, they prevent, they set up alternatives. And someone has an effective right not to be tortured when these things are so. Indeed, one has this right even when one does and can do nothing.

A person has the right not to be tortured even when unconscious. It might be countered that a person has, even when asleep, the right to travel. That is so. But the way of acting is the rightholder's; it is, or essentially involves, something the rightholder does or can do. Or that others, acting on the rightholder's behalf, do or can do. Not so with the right not to be tortured.

The two rights we are discussing are classical in character; the right to life and the right not to be tortured clearly were contemplated by the

philosophers and manifesto writers of an earlier time. And the rights themselves are enshrined in the great American documents of the eighteenth
century: the right to life in the Declaration of Independence and the right
not to be tortured in the Eighth Amendment (as part of the Bill of Rights)
of the U.S. Constitution.

Thus, if we intended, when we talk of rights, that the specified way of
acting is to be the rightholder's way of acting, we run afoul of the fact that
some important rights are not captured by such an analysis. For they do
not specify the rightholder's way of acting but, principally, the ways of
acting of others toward the rightholder. Let us accept, then, that we must
be able to classify rights as including both liberties of conduct *and* so-
called freedoms from injury (that is, avoidance by others of causing such
injuries to rightholders). And, since the latter are not ways of acting available to rightholders—something they do or can do—we would need to
amend my formula to say that rights are established ways of acting *or*
established ways of being acted toward, ways of being treated.

Now that I have made this accommodation, to include avoidances of
injury among rights, it is much easier to address the problem posed by
so-called social and economic rights: the right to a minimum wage, to an
education, to disability or retirement benefits, to medical care and ser
vices, and so on. It is often said that the notion of rights as liberties
represents the classical or earlier view of rights, characteristic of the seventeenth and eighteenth centuries; and that an enlarged view of rights, to
include the positive services of others, is a later graft onto this earlier stock
and represents the agitation for social reform in this century and the one
previous. But this view, as we have seen, is too simple; the foundation of
these social and economic rights already exists to an important degree in
the classical rights to a certain kind of treatment by others (not to be killed,
not to be tortured, etc.). For the economic and social rights have in
common with rights to avoidance of injury a significant feature: all these
rights concern, crucially, ways of being treated. Essentially then, they
involve at their core, not ways of acting on the part of the rightholder, but
ways of acting on the part of others towards the rightholder.[19]

But the social and economic rights are not simply or even mainly rights
to the forbearance and preventive actions of others; rather, they are principally rights to services on the part of others. Thus, one has an effective
right to education when, on a basis available to all, schools are built,
teachers are trained and certified, a general curriculum established, and an
environment thus created for learning to read, write, do sums, and so on.
The right to education, like the other social and economic rights, is not
restricted to mere avoidances of injury. Indeed, the prevailing pattern for
such rights is that a benefit is first provided generally and then the society
follows through to assure its availability by (among other things) preventing people from denying it to eligible individuals. Here the preventive

action *presupposes* the provision of the service and cannot be understood as independent of it.[20]

Thus, we are able to distinguish this case from one where individuals act mainly to prevent someone from harming another person—while providing nothing but this prevention, or while providing principally only such prevention. And we need, accordingly, to identify a third major class of things one has a right *to*: not merely to liberties in the proper sense (as liberties of conduct or ways of acting for the rightholder) and to avoidances of injury but also to the provision of services (where this, like avoidance of injury, crucially involves ways of acting by others toward the rightholder).

These three classes are wide enough to cover the things typically regarded as rights. To accommodate these classes, then, we need only affirm our *amended* characterization of rights to say that rights are established ways of acting or of being acted toward, of being treated. For what is established in some cases is action by the rightholder but in others it is action toward the rightholder.

Before we leave this point as settled, however, I think it would be useful to consider a possible rejoinder to the argument in favor of amendment which I have just conducted. Someone could say that all rights really are things the rightholder, as an agent, does or can do; that is, under suitable and careful analysis, they are. Accordingly, my gesture towards pluralism (by including as rights things other than liberties of conduct) and my amended characterization are misplaced and unnecessary in a theory of rights.

For example, the rejoinder continues, the right not to be killed can be suspended or can be waived by the rightholder. This act of suspending, this act of waiving, would allow suicide or voluntary euthanasia—things not allowed in the present account of the right to life as a right not to be killed. More important, the counterargument would continue: if the individual is allowed, under a suitable construal of the right in question, to kill himself or herself or allowed to be killed in a benevolent act of euthanasia, then we must assume it was because of some act of the rightholder (at the minimum a signal of consent) that this was so.

Now, the line of argument goes on, the fact that we do regard some acts of others as wrong reflects our belief that the rightholder has not acted so as to allow that conduct. And if we can treat forbearings as actions (as in fact I did in my earlier analysis), then we can treat such forbearances here as acts of the rightholder. Thus, the right not to be killed can be understood, quite plausibly, as something the rightholder does or can do as an agent. There is, then, an essential liberty of conduct involved even in a right to noninjury, and without this element of liberty the so-called right would not be a proper one.

It would, of course, be possible to extend the objector's line of analysis to cover cases under the heading of services. Thus, one has a right to a pension or to a disability payment (both of them services provided by another), but the rightholder must trigger this payment by a positive act of his or her own. Here we must distinguish having a right to a service from simply receiving it, however justified that receipt might be. Effective or proper rights to services are always acts of the rightholder in the first instance, for without some such signal (a signed voucher form, for example) no service can be provided as a right of the recipient.

I am not inclined to give much credit to the line of objection we are here considering. It rests on doubtful premises. The objection comes down to the view that all rights to be counted as rights involve an element of (voluntary) action on the part of the rightholder. The payoff—the benefit provided in the right—may come more from others in some cases; but in all such cases the initiation of the right's exercise, hence the payoff's being provided, is the prerogative of the rightholder. But this account would yield some strange results.

A person might drink enough wine to become dead drunk; it does not follow that such a person, incapable of invoking or exercising any of the rights he or she might have, could be tortured or killed. It might be said that we cannot count mere lapsing into stupefaction as the waiving of a right; here, then, we should presume that the right has not been waived and is still in effect. But, equally, we could not say with any show of plausibility that the rightholder, while indulging in drink to the point of insensibility, had *forborne* waiving the right. In such a case the right's not being revoked (waived or suspended or forfeited) is itself *not* an action, nor the result of an action, that the rightholder has performed. Rather, we presume the right in question to be in effect without regard to an action of the rightholder. And that is the crucial point.

The point can be illustrated graphically. Many people regard infants as having a right not to be killed or as having a right not to be tortured. The effectiveness of the right here cannot be regarded as involving something the rightholder has done or can do. Nor could the absence of revocation, in such cases, be itself regarded as an action of some sort, e.g., as a forbearance. Infants are not agents. Thus, there is no possible way for the rights of infants to involve an element of (voluntary) action on their part.

We realize, of course, that infants could have representatives who act in their behalf and, presumably, in their interest. A parent, perhaps, or a hospital board. And these people *can* do things (demand services, revoke protections, etc.). But this fact is of no moment if we believe, as many do, that a newborn infant would have a certain range of rights regardless of whether it was so represented. And that rightholder—that unrepresented newborn—has done nothing, can do nothing. If this is so, then agency is simply irrelevant here, even for the rights of those infants that do have representatives.[21]

But my argument in no way depends on whether newborn infants have rights. For we think agency irrelevant in a large number of cases. We think it irrelevant in cases of victims in need of emergency medical treatment or old people in visible need of various services. The claim that service rights have to be invoked by the rightholder or that noninjury rights have to be regarded as not revoked, where the latter involves some sort of action the rightholder has performed (even if only silently or inwardly), is open to many damaging counterexamples.

More important, the claim fails to capture the presumption on the basis of which people are normally said to be the recipient of the intended noninjury or of the intended benefit in the case of many rights. As I said, we presume the rights in question—such as the right not to be killed or the right not to be tortured—to be in effect without regard to an action of the rightholder. Such an action, an appropriate normative gesture by the rightholder, might defeat the presumption. But it does not *ground* the presumption. Nor is any action of the rightholder thought to initiate the right (or the holder's having it).

I do not want to argue this presumption for all rights. But since it holds for some, unearthing it is sufficient to rebut the general claim that all rights to be counted as rights must involve an element of (voluntary) action on the part of the rightholder.

The claim also has the defect of implying, inasmuch as all rights depend on voluntary action, that *any* right could be revoked or made ineffective by the rightholder. Thus, on the view I am criticizing any right to a service, on behalf of a given rightholder, could be made inoperable simply by that person's not claiming the service, or by that person's revoking an earlier claim; similarly, any right to a noninjury could be made inoperable by holders' waiving that right and, hence, removing the restraint on the conduct of others toward them. But it is not clear to me that the right not to be tortured, for example, could be waived for a specific purpose or revoked altogether, even by the rightholder. (As Jacopo Timerman was thought to have been willing to do, when he said that he wanted to appear on television and to be tortured there so as to educate viewers about torture and especially to inform them about torture in his native Argentina at that time.) I say this, not to deny the good intentions or even the heroism of such a person, but to deny that others could ever be warranted in crossing the line of restraint against torture that the right establishes. In this sense, the right cannot be waived or revoked, even voluntarily.[22]

So there are significant barriers in the way of accepting any analysis that reduces all rights, or even a component of all rights, to things that the rightholder does or can do.[23] Accordingly, we should have no compunction about expanding the concept of rights to include both ways of acting on the rightholder's part *and* ways of acting toward the holder on the part of others. And we have a strong reason to make such an expansion in order to encompass the whole range of things normally regarded as rights, as captured, albeit rather loosely, under three main (and sometimes overlapping) headings: ways of acting (in particular, liberties of conduct), avoidances of injury at the hands of others, provision of services by them.

6. THREE MAIN HEADINGS FOR RIGHTS

In any of these cases, the central content of a right is specified by what might be called an action-universal or generic description of a way of acting.[24] The generic description (the way of acting at issue or the way of being acted toward) does not give us the whole of the right but it does give us its main content. For it is this core content that is said to be socially recognized, and the various protective measures, when adopted, are attached to this central content as a way of securing or making it fast, for the benefit of the rightholder. Persons who have the right have the right *to* whatever it is that this core specifies.[25]

In the account I have given, the central content of some rights will be a liberty of conduct of some sort (e.g., going to the pond on a particular path). But at the core of other rights will be a noninjury of some sort or, alternatively, the provision of a service. And corresponding to each main heading or class of rights (as determined by these cores) there is an appropriate or characteristic normative response enjoined for the conduct of others. But the essential character of this normative direction of the conduct of second parties shifts from main case to main case.

In a liberty of conduct the doing at the core of the right is the rightholder's responsibility and second parties are normatively directed to allow that conduct, to forbear interfering with it, and perhaps even to prevent such interference or remove it when it occurred, and so on. And if the doing at the core of the right were not simply allowed but specifically encouraged, then the normative direction afforded the conduct of second parties would be reworded, in an appropriate way, to reflect this point. Thus, they would not merely forbear interference; rather, they would actively facilitate the liberty—the rightholder's way of acting—in question.

In the other main cases, though, the doing at the core of the right is an action of second parties. In an avoidance of injury the doing, or more precisely the not-doing, is the responsibility of second parties. And the incumbent normative direction on their conduct is to prohibit a certain line of conduct (and not to give it liberty). Here the active agents (who are persons other than the rightholder) are mainly to forbear doing something but they may also be directed to act, positively, to prevent its being done, to dismantle attempts to do it, to provide acceptable alternatives to the proscribed conduct, and so on. In a provision of service, finally, the stress is on the doing of something beneficial for or to the rightholder. And the incumbent normative direction of the conduct of second parties—the agents of the service—is principally to require that doing. But they, of course, may also be directed to forbear interfering with the provision of service, to prevent others from doing so, to remove such impediments as might arise, and so on.

Thus, with the shift to accommodate ways of being treated as included within rights, a corresponding shift occurs in the fundamental character of the normative direction of the conduct of others. For just as allowing or encouraging a piece of conduct is what they are normatively directed to do in the case of a liberty, so prohibiting the doing of an injury or requiring of them a service is the incumbent directive in the other two cases.

The Hohfeld elements, if I may call them that, could enter the account at precisely this point. They come, as we may recall, in pairs (claim/duty, power/liability, immunity/disability, and so on). One member of the pair lodges with the rightholder, or with persons acting on the rightholder's behalf, and the other member lodges with the second party. The Hohfeld elements, then, connect the rightholder with the second party in certain quite definite ways. Accordingly, they could come within the broad framework already sketched (as to what specific way of acting, or of being treated, the right is *to* and what the characteristic form of normative direction is). Here their job would be to help particularize and give finer detail to the standing of rightholder and second party, in relation to one another, under a given right.

It is important to be clear that the function the Hohfeld elements would or could perform here is entirely subsidiary to points already established in the present chapter. Thus, they do not justify the idea of normative direction, nor have any role in that justification; they do not play any part in establishing the fundamental claim that every right affords some significant direction to the conduct of second parties and, hence, that every right is two-place, always involving two parties; finally, these elements have figured in no way in the distinction of rights into three main kinds (with a type of normative direction being identified, as fundamental and appropriate, for each of these kinds). Instead, I would argue, any use of the Hohfeld elements actually presupposes these very things. In my account, then, the use of the elements would merely build on foundations already laid, in particular, by practical inference.

Thus, the use of the various Hohfeld elements would presuppose the basic analysis of a right (as to whether it is a right to a liberty, or an avoidance of injury, or a service of some sort). For it is the basic analysis which identifies a pattern (e.g., liberty to do by someone/noninterference by others) that serves as a point of orientation. And the understanding of the right, as exhibited in this pattern of analysis, would guide the deployment of Hohfeld elements (in the form of specific powers/liabilities, etc.) in any given case. In short, the main thing the Hohfeld elements would do here is help make more determinate the normative direction afforded the conduct of second parties in the case of any right, once the main lines of understanding have been fixed through the sort of analysis I have been developing. Nonetheless, they would have a useful part to play in making determinate rights even more determinate.[26]

Now, the basic analysis (regarding whether a right is to a liberty, a noninjury, or a service) may fail, for some rights, at least, to capture significant features. For rights are often complex; and the preliminary account, though it is essential, indeed fundamental, does not always touch all the details, or even all the important ones.

For example, the right to vote involves a number of features (and in discussing this we can, perhaps, see more clearly the way in which the Hohfeld elements can make normative direction, in the case of any given right, more determinate). Thus, one is eligible to vote if that person is properly enrolled or has met residency requirements (Hohfeldian claim element); that individual can vote for whom he or she pleases (Hohfeldian liberty element); the vote is to be counted and to have the requisite effect, along with other votes (Hohfeldian power element); voting is something that adheres to citizenship and is, in the normal case, not removable from the individual citizen (Hohfeldian immunity element). And here—in characterizing the right to vote as a liberty to do, coupled with noninterference by others—it might be alleged that we have not brought out that the act of voting creates a liability on the part of others (vote registrars, incumbent officials) to count the vote and give it effect.[27]

Such omissions are to be expected in a preliminary account. I would readily concede that this Hohfeldian power element is important to the right to vote and should not be omitted in any full characterization of it. Accordingly, we should not take the description of the right to vote as a liberty of conduct (i.e., as a rightholder's liberty to do coupled with noninterference by others) as somehow licensing or suggesting the omission of this Hohfeld element or any of the others. More to the point, there is no implication to *any* of the Hohfeld elements—to their presence or to their absence—in the case of a right when so described.

I would also suggest that the characterization of this particular right in terms of agency—a characterization which is fundamental to my characterization of it as a liberty—might bring out the right's essential features more handily. Thus, we could describe the right to vote as one in which we are concerned principally with what the rightholder does or can do. That would serve not only to identify the right as to its basic type, and thereby distinguish it from rights to noninjury or to a service, but also to incorporate the rightholder's power into the basic analysis in a perspicuous way. For the rightholder's power to have the vote counted and to give it effect is something the holder can do: it is a part of what the holder does or can do as a voter (or that an agent of the holder does or can do as the agent of a voter). Hence, the analysis I have given of this kind of right—cast now in terms of agency—seems adequate to capture this important feature for subsequent elaboration, in particular as regards the normative direction it affords, in its main dimensions, for the conduct of others.

By the same token we ought to be able to count the official capacities and competencies of civil authorities as rights in the same way. For they are legal powers of an office—things designated officials do or can do—and, hence, could be rights of a quite recognizable sort in the analysis I have given. But little is lost, I would add, if we simply were to call these things competencies rather than rights.[28]

Which Hohfeld elements are present and which are important ones, in the case of any given right, are matters of significant detail, but we do not look to and determine this in the basic analysis. Rather, the function of the basic analysis (where we determine whether a given right is, say, a liberty of conduct) is to justify the use of any or all of the Hohfeld elements as devices useful to a certain end, as given in the basic analysis: to the end of giving appropriate normative direction to others in order to secure to the rightholder the central content of the way of acting involved or, alternatively, of the way of being treated.

The basic analysis moves on a different track. And, though rights can take elements of any one of the four Hohfeldian kinds as part of characterizing their important features (in particular, of making more determinate the character of the normative direction involved), and though some rights may contain all four of these elements, each right has in common with other rights that they are secured ways of acting or secured ways of being treated. It is this unity, the coming together under this conception, that gathers rights into a well-defined family—not the presence of some particular Hohfeld element, or all of them for that matter, in the characterization of a particular right.

Rights to ways of acting (on the part of the rightholder) I have called rights to liberties of conduct (or, more generally, agency rights). Some rights on the part of rightholders to ways of being treated (by others) I have called rights to the avoidance of injury and other such rights, rights to a service or its provision. There may be individual rights that come under more than one of these headings. I do not claim that these categories are mutually exclusive, only that they are exhaustive with respect to those things that are normally called rights. For everything so called will ultimately lodge under one such heading, as its principal heading. Hence, where our goal is to lay out a general profile of the main *contents* of rights, the basic analysis of rights (as liberties, noninjuries, provisions of benefit) seems serviceable enough.

In arguing this, it should be noted again, I have introduced a crucial amendment into our original account, the amendment that ways of being treated are counted as rights. But beyond this crucial amendment, introduced to recognize the complexity of the central content of rights under the three main headings, the general characterization offered in this chapter remains intact. For rights to noninjury and rights to services follow the pattern of analysis already established for rights to liberty of conduct.

As before, the noninjury or the service will function as a sort of end in view, as an object that is to be brought about or accomplished. And (1) the accomplishment of the way of being treated in question is something determinate (not being killed, for example, or having schooling provided) and something distributable. (2) It can be individuated: the capacity specified (as a way of being treated) can be parceled out to all the rightholders. (3) The end in view (not being injured in some proscribed way, having a service provided or available) is appropriately ratified, socially. (4) The achievement of such an end can be supported by reference to an interest or perceived benefit or a good of the rightholder—supported, that is, as itself a plausible or appropriate means to, or part of obtaining, the benefit in question. And (5) the accomplishment of any such end does provide a basis for the normative direction of the conduct of second parties.

Even here, though, the connection between (1)–(4) and (5), the normative direction of others, is not one of logical entailment. For the relevant conduct of others would have to be necessary or sufficient to the end in view. It would have to be practicable. And thus we would require—as before, in the case of a liberty of action—a chain of practical reasoning to complete the linkage here.[29]

But once we identify the right of person 1 by reference to a way of being treated (as we do in [1]–[4] above) then it simply follows, given a sound practical inference argument, that (5) the conduct of person 2, as second party, is normatively directed. For the proper line of conduct, given these factors, is then spelled out.

Now, when this particular linkage has been completed we have license to add (5) to the characterization of a right. I would not want to say that we had a right until this element was added (for I have endorsed the view that all rights do involve the normative direction of the conduct of other persons). One might claim, indeed, and quite reasonably, that the way of acting (or, conversely, the way of being treated) had not been secured or made fast until this was done.

And when it is added then, of course, we do have a logical implication: it follows from a right so characterized, as including (5), that (5) is so. But that is not the issue; the issue is how (5) got there in the first place. Thus, the entailment here presupposes the practical inference connection and it has no independent weight in the initial establishment of (5), the normative direction of the conduct of others, among the elements of a right. For it plays no role at all in the crucial determination that where (1)–(4) are so, then (5) follows—when it follows—as a matter of practical inference.

It may well be true, I would add, that the normative directions (to others) could be derived more readily on a foundation of practical inferences here than in the earlier case of liberties of conduct. But this is another matter and is of no real moment to the main argument.

Accordingly, we can regard ways of being treated as rights in the same sense as rights to liberties. For in all these cases the central content of a right is some generic way of acting (sometimes on the rightholder's part, at other times on that of the second party). And all these rights, to ways of acting and to ways of being treated, come under the same formula and they are all susceptible of the same analysis. In particular, measures to make fast the way of acting or of being treated, to secure it in appropriate ways (at least through the issuing of relevant normative directions), would have been taken on the basis of a number of considerations (including some sort of social recognition). It is, accordingly, these factors (including the factor of social recognition) that principally qualify a practice as a right in all these cases.[30]

7. A PROBLEMATIC FEATURE IN THIS ACCOUNT

I realize that the overall account here is a rough one; it serves, though, to block out the main dimensions. But much more would have to be filled in for any particular right. I have in this chapter attempted to provide only the main features of rights—in particular, the main features of the sort of rights we encounter under such headings as constitutional or civil rights, fundamental or basic rights, human or natural rights. These are features that are among those that would be emphasized as belonging to rights—to *all* rights—in what might be called a general description. Thus, the account is intended to hold true of rights regardless of whether they are customary rights or social arrangement rights or moral rights or legal ones. And to provide such an account one must ignore those distinctions which tend, in precisely the ways indicated, to differentiate rights.

I am also aware that I may have done justice to some of these general features but not, perhaps, to others. Thus, the feature of social recognition has received very little attention and yet it is, I am sure, one of the most controversial parts of my analysis. In the two chapters that follow I will address this feature directly and try to provide more of a defense than I have so far that social recognition is indeed a generic feature of rights. In these chapters I hope as well to elaborate my account of rights as accredited ways of acting (or ways of being treated) by reference to the two main categories of rights that have historically dominated discussion, that is legal rights and human (or natural) rights.

3

Rights as Valid Claims

Do rights, in order to be rights, require social recognition? In considering this question one school of thought has tended to emphasize that individuals simply have rights willy-nilly or at least they can have them independently of organized society, of social institutions, and hence of social recognition and maintenance in any form. The classical natural rights theorists apparently held some such view and this would likely be Robert Nozick's view also.[1] Many contemporary advocates of human rights would probably regard this characterization as an essential feature of the conception of rights they hold. And, though it is not so apparent, I would suggest that Ronald Dworkin adheres to this conception, at least as regards certain basic moral rights endorsed in his theory, such as the right of all persons to an equality of concern and respect.[2] Even Mill, in his discussion of rights as valid claims, could be taken as subscribing to the view that people have some basic moral rights independently of their station in life, independently of whether those rights have been recognized by government or in the society's ethical code or by other individuals.[3]

I. THE ISSUE

I think the rather common characterization that rights are essentially claims can be taken as a way of emphasizing that rights hold irrespective of whether they have been acknowledged, either in the society or, more specifically, by that person against whom the claim is made. This characterization stresses that claims have the normative force of rights whether or not there are existing social institutions that recognize, promote, and maintain these claims.

Against the view that rights are essentially claims are ranged a number of philosophers, some of them well known and influential. Bentham comes most readily to mind, and his polemic on this very point against natural rights as "nonsense" still adds relish to philosophical discussions.[4] T. H. Green, in his insistence that rights require social recognition and that without it they are something less than rights, would be another.[5] And, oddly enough, Lenin would be a third.[6]

One might be permitted the thought that any philosophical theory which commended itself to three such unlikely co-adherents as Jeremy Bentham, T. H. Green, and V. I. Lenin would be sound and acceptable, almost automatically, to any right-minded person. But this would be too easy a resolution of a philosophical problem.

Instead, we might want to consider what would motivate a person to identify rights with valid claims in the first place. The backdrop here, I think, is the common view that to have a right is to have a justification for acting in a certain way, or a justification for being treated in a certain way.[7] To put this point somewhat differently, most people regard rights as, in some sense, justified (though not all of them have advanced explicit theories of justification, or clearly identified the justificatory strand in their characterization of rights).

For many theorists the notion that rights are justified has meant that rights can be shown to follow from or square up with some standard which is itself taken to be a source of justification. Thus, a federal judge might measure a right affirmed in a state statute against the U.S. Constitution to determine whether the affirming statute was justified. Or a utilitarian might measure a practice (otherwise capable of being a right) against the standard of the "greatest happiness of the greatest number" to determine whether it was justified and hence a right. And so on. In all such cases an item that requires justification is referred to some standard that could provide the justification but is not itself in need of that same justification.

But not all theorists view the matter in precisely this way. Rather, they regard rights—or, at least, some important rights—as themselves ultimate standards of justification. These rights are simply fundamental within the universe of discourse, be it legal or moral, that we are concerned with. For some specific rights, then, it is not so much that they are justified as it is that they are themselves the very standards of justification. Dworkin, for example, seems to regard the right to equality of concern and respect as being of this sort.

So, in order not to beg important questions, we should say about particular rights that they are justified or, alternatively, that they are ultimate standards of justification. In either case, though, where one had a right that person would have a justification for acting in a certain way or for being treated in a certain way (and duties could justifiably be imposed on second parties toward that end).

Now, suppose we were able to say for a particular right-to-be that it had all the rights-making features I identified in the previous chapter: it was relatively determinate, was individuated, had social recognition, afforded normative direction to the conduct of others, etc. And it could be said, in having all these features, to be fully justified. Let us say for simplicity here that it was fully justified *morally*. Then it would be a right, specifically, a moral right.

Suppose next that it had all the rights-making features but one. It lacked social recognition. It ought to have social recognition, no doubt about that. For its being socially recognized *would* be justified—we can say without cavil—whether that recognition had actually occurred or not.

The question is why the lack of such recognition should deprive it of rights status. For, if we modeled the rights-making features on what was justified, the thing was already a right even before it was recognized, even before it became a practice. And when it was recognized it would be recognized *as a right* (as something that was fully justified) and would not simply *become* a right in being recognized.

There appears no clear reason to accept my version of this situation, as developed in the previous chapter (where it is the fact of social recognition that is the essential rights-making feature), over the alternative version (where it is the *justification* for such a state of affairs, should it occur, that is the rights-making feature). At least there appears no clear reason in the way we ordinarily talk about rights, for each version can be found in the way we ordinarily talk. Thus, although my account up to now has depended heavily on facts about rights as found in ordinary parlance and in the history of rights, it cannot depend on these facts to carry it through this pass; for here the relevant record supports both accounts. Yet both cannot be sound.

So, we must leave the ordinary considerations and try another path: that of philosophical argument. But there seems great difficulty for my account on this route. For I have already acknowledged the point about the importance of justification and this would appear to give an edge to the alternative account at the very outset. In any event we reach the crux.

Are rights sometimes norms specifying a practice that should be socially recognized and hence socially supported—or are "intermediate conclusions" lying between such norms and such practices, as Raz sometimes has it[8]—or, alternatively, are rights always actual practices based on social recognition and social support which can be, independently, adjudged to be justified? In order to answer this question we will need to consider not merely the crucial matter of what social recognition is but also the more basic issue of whether rights are existing practices, with normative direction and perhaps other protective measures already in place, or whether they are principally the norms (or intermediate conclusions) specifying the justifiability of such practices.

This is the fundamental question that my account of rights (as developed in the previous chapter) must face. For the rights as claims view, the view that rights are justifying norms or "intermediate conclusions" from them, is the main alternative to the account of rights I have developed. To opt for this alternative is to reject a fundamental part of my account. It is to this question of alternative accounts that we must now turn.

2. VALID CLAIMS

I will do so by considering what has probably become the most influential of the current analytical theories of rights: a theory in which a core characterization of rights is identified (as claim or valid claim) and in which the nature of a right is said to be the same for both *human* rights and *legal* rights. The difference between kinds of rights is accounted for, then, within a single generic theory of rights (of rights treated as claims).

The theory of rights as valid claims best articulates the view that is the alternative to my own account, on the crucial point at issue, whether social recognition and maintenance are essential to rights properly understood. It avoids entangling details and centers resolutely on the very features in the characterization of rights that serve fundamentally to differentiate such a characterization from my own (as set out in Chapter 2). Thus, I find engaging with it unavoidable.

In order to provide needed focus I will examine critically and in some detail the most extensively elaborated and the most philosophically subtle of the various versions of the theory of rights as valid claims: the one provided in the writings of Joel Feinberg.[9] For it seems to me to that this particular version does an especially good job of gathering in the threads of the rather large group of theories which, though they differ in much else, agree in the view that rights—irrespective of social recognition and maintenance—are essentially justifications of ways of acting or of being treated, justifications sufficient to hold second parties to the having of duties relevant to those ways. Indeed, it not only gathers in these particular threads but highlights them. Thus, it concentrates and exhibits the essence of a fundamentally different perspective that one can take on rights from the one I have been developing.

Our main project in this chapter, then, is to get clear on valid claims. And my emphasis throughout will be the contention that legal rights in particular, as one of the main kinds of rights, are valid claims.

Feinberg thinks that much can be learned about the nature and value of claims by attending to the activity of claiming. This emphasis on performative claiming has led some writers (for example, David Lyons) to locate Feinberg among those who see rights as an important social currency, as a way of demanding one's due.[10] But the basic notion for Feinberg is, not making a claim, but *having* one: to have a claim is to be in a position to *make* a claim.

Claiming is the main function of rights in Feinberg's view; self-respect is, no doubt, one thing that results from so acting and in this way can be said to justify the practice of making claims. It would be a serious confusion, though, to think that this result justifies one's *having* a claim, for the validity of the claim was antecedently established, presumably on other grounds.

What Feinberg does emphasize, when talking about validating force here, is the role of legal and moral principles. Thus, "To have a right is to have a claim *to* something and *against* someone, the recognition of which is called for by legal rules or, in the case of moral rights, by the principles of an enlightened conscience."

To be a right, then, a claim must be conclusively established by the appropriate governing principles.[11] Feinberg tries to explain what else is involved in such validation by distinguishing between claims-to and claims-against.[12]

Claims-to can go through several stages. A mere claim (as distinct from a demand) is a worthwhile claim to something: it merits a hearing, deserves consideration. When such a claim is accepted as sound, is said to fit in with the rules and to deserve satisfaction, it becomes a potentially valid claim (that is, a valid claim-to, if or when a certain level of satisfaction is practicable). Where such a threshold of satisfaction has actually been achieved, the claim becomes a valid claim-to. It has then become the ground of other people's duties. Even so, a valid claim-to never entails or implies specific duties of others.[13]

Hence a valid claim-to is only part of the justification for a claim-against; the latter claim requires, as well, the existence of duties of assignable individuals. It would be pointless to speak of claims-against in the absence of specific duties, for such a claim is always on a duty (or on some sort of normative direction of the conduct of others). Equally, though less obviously, it would be pointless to speak of a *claim* against a duty simply in virtue of the existence of that duty or of that normative direction. For one might be the designated or qualified recipient of a duty done and in that way its assigned or proper beneficiary, but the beneficiary could be said to have a *claim* on the performance of the duty only where that individual had some status (vis-à-vis the duty) other than that merely of designated recipient.[14]

To put this matter somewhat differently, a claim-to is a necessary condition of a claim-against. If the claim-to did not exist, then we would not describe our standing with respect to the duties or obligations of others as a *claim*: for, though a qualified recipient of what the duty brings when done, we might have no claim on its being done. But where we have both claims-to and the duty of others, we can intelligibly speak of claims against (or on) such duties. In short, when we can latch onto (or generate, as the case may be) the requisite duties or other normative direction, the status of claimant in claims-against is marked precisely by those criteria which belong to our earlier analysis of a valid claim-to.

As we have noted, a claim-to can never entail a claim-against: because it can never *entail* the specific duties of assignable (other) people to which such claims-against are necessarily attached. It can, however, provide a justifiable basis for a claim-against on the grounds of an existing duty or other normative direction—or a justifiable basis for generating such a duty or other normative direction. Claims-against, then, are validated (as claims) insofar as they can be grounded on valid claims-to.[15]

Valid claims are those in which practicable, rule-endorsed claims-to hook onto specific duties, duties which can then justifiably be called upon to satisfy or help satisfy such claims-to. In a valid claim, that to which claim is made is due the individual and the dutiful actions of others are, when justifiably invoked, *owed* to providing that satisfaction. A proper valid claim is the conjoining of a valid claim-to with a valid claim-on or -against.

And there are, correspondingly, a variety of ways in which a claim can fail of full validity: A claim to something can lack evident rule-authorized title; it can fall short of covering the full class of persons intended or be otherwise impracticable. Claims-against are equally susceptible to defect, in lacking the specific duties (or other normative direction) or the assignable people which such claims require in order to be valid. In this account, then, rights as valid claims have satisfied two distinct dimensions: they are valid claims to something and, as claims on the specific duties of assignable people, they are valid claims against someone.[16]

The idea that rights are valid claims allows Feinberg to treat a moral right and a legal right as parallel in character: both are rights in the same sense. What differentiates them is the kind of norm from which they derive validity. Moral norms figure in the case of moral rights. For it is by reference to moral rules and principles that claims to something are adjudged to be morally valid; and moral duties are involved in moral claims-against. Correspondingly, for legal rights, legal rules and principles determine the validity of claims-to; and legally created duties are invoked in legal claims-against.

Human rights are a special class of moral rights, differing from other moral rights, largely, on the point of universality. They attach to all persons and do so simply because of the moral rules themselves without consideration of any undertakings, express or implicit, or of special relationships to others in which such persons might stand.[17] Some human rights may be full-fledged moral rights; others—the ones Feinberg calls "manifesto" rights—lay claims to things which are not fully practicable at present; hence these claims are at best only emerging or proto-rights.[18]

Thus, one has a moral or human right when one has a valid claim to something—as determined by moral principles—which underwrites, when practicable, that individual's claims on the moral duties of others (for example, to provide or not impede, as the case may be, that to which a legitimate claim exists). Hence Feinberg analyzes human rights as morally valid claims (insofar as such claims are universal): the right is fully present, as a right, in the validity of the claim.

The question we want to consider especially closely at this point is whether legal rights owe their status as rights solely to an element of valid claim. For, if a legal right has the sense of legally valid claim, it would follow that the analysis of it should parallel that of human rights as morally valid claims (allowing only for a difference between moral contexts and legal contexts). And such a parallelism does seem well established in Feinberg's texts.[19]

Indeed, it is precisely this parallelism that allowed Feinberg to extrapolate from the two distinct cases, of legal right and of moral right, a generic characterization of rights. Thus, "To have a right is to have a claim ... whose recognition as valid is called for by some set of governing rules or moral principles."[20]

Now it is relatively unproblematic to catch the drift of the statement that the governing *moral* rules "call for" recognition of a claim as valid. But the meaning is by no means obvious when it is alleged that the relevant rules "call for" the official recognition of a claim (as valid) in the case of a *legal* right.

Specifically, what could it mean to say that a legal claim right is "a claim against the state [for] recognition and enforcement"?[21] If it is not already recognized by the state how could it be called a *legal* claim right?

A similar problem arises in the brief characterization, above, of a legal right as being parallel to a moral one. For, if the governing rules are *legal* ones, what could be meant by "calling for" *official* recognition? Indeed, it would appear that if the governing rules are legal ones that already counts as official recognition.

It would, then, be distinctly odd if the valid claims definition of rights implicitly disavowed that governmental recognition or promotion is (necessarily) involved in a *legal* right. For, clearly, a right could never be a legal right, not even a nominal one, unless that right figured in the "governing rules" and hence was recognized and formulated there.

Let us grant, then, that a legal right could exist only if it was somewhere specified in the law (in a constitutional provision, in a statute, in an administrative decree, in a judge-made common law, or in a binding decision by a high court) and grant, as well, that attendant duties or other sorts of normative direction would themselves likewise be specified there (or, when generated, would likewise be specified there). How then could it make sense to claim recognition *by government* of a right that was, in the way just indicated, already legally recognized?

It would make sense to claim it *on an occasion.* We could make claims against governmental officials for recognition if, on a given occasion, we wanted to avail ourselves of what was already specified in law as, say, a liberty (together with attendant duties that attached to other people).

The basis of any such claim, however, is that the thing sought—the liberty, the forbearance of others—is already encoded. Hence, what one is claiming is that an existing legal right be extended on that occasion, presumably appropriately, to the claimant. Government is being asked (1) to recognize (reaffirm or acknowledge) that a valid claim-to does exist in law and (2) on the occasion in question, to recognize (affirm) that it does attach to the claimant. The claimant, in seeking recognition of this sort, wants to invoke attendant legal duties; the claimant wants to be able, in the particular set of circumstances envisioned, to enter into what is officially recognized as a legal right. Here it would make sense to make a claim, directed to the government, for recognition—as in (1) and (2) above—of a (pre-existing) legal right. But what would underwrite or validate the making of such a claim is simply the existing right (in law and practice) together with the appropriateness of the circumstances for the claimant's entry into that right on that particular occasion.

My analysis suggests that a legal right is not principally a claim at all, at least it is not purely a claim, not even a valid one, but is, rather, something recognized by government. For it is this factor of official recognition that provides a ground for making claims—that is, legally valid ones—on a given occasion.

3. PROMOTION AND MAINTENANCE

I think this same analysis could be extended to cover the case of claims on government for the promotion and maintenance of that which is being claimed as well. For I want to argue that the point, touched on above, about a legal claim right constituting a claim on government for promotion and maintenance of that right—including therein its enforcement—should be taken as presupposing that the right in question already has the status of being so treated legally.

This reading is supported by the discussion that follows, below, on conflict of legal rights.[22] When legal rights come into conflict, the result is that one such right is enforced at the expense of the other. That is, one right is infringed by the legally allowed exercise of another.[23]

How should one construe such conflict? Does it mean, as some have suggested, that the first right ceases (perhaps for a time only) to be a right at all? If so, then this right (indeed any right not regarded as absolute or as incapable of being infringed under law) is merely a prima facie right. Such a right holds as a right only presumptively, only provisionally, until a conflict of rights brings into play the mechanisms of legal annulment whereby one right is canceled, if only temporarily, in the interests of the other right(s).[24]

But this is not an answer that Feinberg, for one, can accept. On his view rights are not properly regarded as "something that one has only at specific moments, only to lose, regain, and lose again as circumstances shift."[25] For "Rights are themselves *property*, things we own, and from which we may not even temporarily be dispossessed. Perhaps in some circumstances rights may be rightfully infringed, but that is quite different from their being taken away and then returned."

His solution is to say that the government's recognition of the validity of the rightholder's claim can be distinguished (even in those cases where that right is infringed) from its maintenance—the government's promotion and protection—of this claim. Hence, the crucial element of recognition could be retained in the face of a government's not enforcing the duty, say, of noninterference on the part of others, or retained even in the face of a government's not following through on its other prescribed duties to provide the services or the legal protection (e.g., in the courts) which are normally required of it in the case of a given right.[26]

In short, the state, in the person of one of its courts or of one of its administrators, can both affirm that the way of acting vouchsafed to the rightholder does obtain generally (and hence is a right) and deny its being entered into on that particular occasion. Here the state's recognition of the right in question is held to be intact while the protection of that right is sacrificed to some degree in the interest of the exercise of another, and, on that occasion, conflicting right. Indeed, we can even imagine on the basis provided not merely that the element of enforcement or protection is suspended but that an actual exercise of the right (especially where it consists in a liberty of action) is denied or coercively suppressed on the occasion in question.

It is important to note here that the right in question (the one that is being abridged) does not consist *solely* in the ongoing statute and in the attendant legal practices of recognizing—affirming or acknowledging—this right and spelling out the normative directions (regarding other people's forbearance, and so on) which are normally attached to it. Any such right also consists in practices of governmental promotion and protection (in case assignable persons don't do their specified duties). It is the addition of this second feature— promotion and maintenance—that allows us to describe the conflict of rights as a situation in which some of the practices which characterize a particular right are retained (that is, the practices of recognition) even though others (that is, those characteristic of promotion and maintenance, for example, the enforcement of the duties of others to hold off) are suspended.

Thus, unless one holds the view that actual conflicts of rights are wholly eliminable (an issue I will discuss further in Chapter 5), there remains a point to the discussion of how such conflict could be resolved in a particular case. Thus, one would try to establish an account or model of what the resolution of a conflict of rights amounts to. Indeed, one might do so even though one believed (as does Feinberg) that any such conflict was climinable in principle. For there is virtue in recognizing that what is so in principle may not be so in fact.

Now, the point about distinguishing recognition (and hence possession) from enforcement, as a way of solving the problem of conflict of rights, actually presupposes the notion of *practices* of recognition and of maintenance and makes sense, as a solution, only if we assume that nonprotection, though it may happen on occasion (and sometimes may even constitute an unlicensed infringement), is not a general rule. Hence, where the nonprotection happens only on occasion and in accordance with the relevant procedures and standards, we would have a full-fledged existing right—but not, of course, an absolute right.[27]

I have emphasized here that this suspension of the mechanisms of promotion and maintenance—in the case of a given right—must be *on a particular occasion*. Suppose, though, that the suspension was general, that promotion of a particular given right was never forthcoming. Imagine here that there was no element of service or protection afforded it as a general practice at all, no attempt made to harmonize the right in question with other rights within a system of rights, no enforcement of the forbearance of others (if that is what is being required of them) even where a valid claim on that forbearance could be discerned as founded in law. In that case we would very likely call the right a merely nominal one, especially if no one, or hardly anyone, honored or respected it. The discussion about how a conflict of rights is properly to be handled has substance, then, simply because the practices of promotion and protection and enforcement are conceived as suspended on occasion only. For if they are always suspended (as is the case with nominal rights) there would be no special point in mentioning nonenforcement, say, as a way of dealing with the conflict of rights.

It follows that just as recognition in law must deepen the notion of valid claim in order to have a *legal* right so the notion of governmental promotion and maintenance must supplement that of legally recognized valid claim in order to have anything more than a merely nominal legal right. For promotion and maintenance—in the broad way I have described it—is not merely a characteristic of legal rights; it is ingredient in the very notion of such a right, excepting those that are merely nominal. Thus, for any particular legal right, there would have to be certain practices of promotion, protection, enforcement, etc. on the part of government and at least forbearance by (other) private persons. Or if the right were to a service, to positive provision of a benefit by second parties.

4. RIGHTS AS ESTABLISHED PRACTICES

We see, then, with a bit of dialectical pressure applied to the notion of rights as valid claims, the plausibility of the alternative view that rights, certainly legal ones, are established ways of acting or of being acted toward. They are not *merely* that which would justify the establishment of such ways (and of the attendant duties of second parties). Thus, a legal right, on the account I have been offering (as set forth initially in Chapter 2), would be a way of acting or of being treated secured for an individual within a complex public practice, one where governmental agencies played an essential role. And here we would want to include the ongoing statute and its provisions (or its analogue in administrative law or in constitutional law or in common law adjudication) together with the normatively directed appropriate conduct on the part of other people respecting a specified liberty of action or freedom from injury or provision of welfare and together, finally, with the practices of providing, protecting, enforcing and so on which fell to government to do, as mandated (usually) in the rights rule itself.[28]

The idea that legal rights—or, more broadly, institutional rights—are involved in practices can, of course, be amplified in a number of ways. We might do so by noting that the primary dutyholder (or, better, the addressee) in the case of such rights will vary from right to right. Thus, some rights will have as their principal addressee another person or a private corporation (e.g., the right of an insurance beneficiary will be addressed primarily to the insuring company). Such rights will count as legal rights, then, to the extent that government can be called in to enforce these second-party duties or otherwise protect the rightholder. Other rights will have government or some agency of government as its main addressee (e.g., the constitutional right of peaceable assembly is addressed primarily to Congress and, secondarily, to law enforcement agencies). Still others are addressed to the community at large (e.g., the right to life or to property specified in the Fifth and Fourteenth Amendments is usually thought to be addressed to all private individuals and groups and to government at both the federal and state levels).

Again, the kind of Hohfeld element(s) emphasized will differ from right to right. Thus, a creditor's right to repayment will probably focus on the associated claim against a debtor for repayment. The constitutional right to freedom of speech will properly emphasize the disability laid on Congress that it cannot validly pass laws abridging that freedom. (And the disabling of such laws will by and large be carried out by the courts, through their power of declaring invalid acts of Congress or of the state legislatures.) The legal right to sue, to make a contract or a valid will, or to marry will stress a certain legal power that one has. And the legal right to dress, or not dress, as one pleases in one's own living room or to paint one's barn purple, if that's what the individual wants, will identify a liberty of action that one has under this, that, or another legal category—be it privacy or property or what have you.

Some liberty rights may be specifically identified by name, and even spelled out, in a constitutional or legal document (as was the liberty to travel, which was mentioned in the U.S. Articles of Confederation, though not in the Constitution).[29] But most of them, like the ones mentioned in the paragraph above or like the right to scratch one's left ear (and Hohfeld's right to eat a salad, from Chapter 2), are not.[30] Accordingly, their status as legal rights would require a somewhat more complicated analysis in order to bring them into line with the account I have been giving.

4.1. *Problems: Unspecified Liberties, Competition*

One notable feature of these unspecified liberties is that they consist in the mere absence of any legal duty to do or not do that particular thing (e.g., paint one's barn purple), on the part of the agent, coupled with the absence of a legal claim on the part of others that it not be done by the agent (which would imply, of course, that they had no duty to prevent it). Since such liberties exist in all areas where there is such an absence of legal inhibition they are apt to be rather numerous. More important, there may be in most of these cases no duties which specifically protect the particular liberty in question. Even so, there might still be standing duties that prohibit such things as trespass and violence against persons or property and that effectively restrain the neighbors, who detest the barn's color, from stopping the owner or from repainting it. These unspecialized standing duties—which tell people things they cannot do—constitute a sort of 'perimeter' upon which any number of these liberties could rest for legal support and protection.

In sum, many determinate liberty rights have the rights character of being, at least on their face, mere liberties. For both the liberty to do that thing and the normative direction of others respecting the liberty are wholly unspecified in law, or largely so. Since the law makes no explicit recognition of the liberty in question (or oftentimes even of the main headings under which it could conveniently be lodged) and affords no protections *per se*, offering instead only a perimeter of unspecialized duties, we can call such rights in that context, the context of law, *weak* liberty rights.

Thus liberty rights—certainly the weak ones—may not be formulated in legal rules at all; rather they are more like authoritative conclusions drawn on a particular occasion. But they count as legal rights because they can be seen and officially accredited as special cases of very general legal categories—like property—or, more crucially, because significant normative direction of the conduct of other persons toward the liberty in question is provided by a standing perimeter of legal duties, which are themselves standardly enforceable by governmental action. In these ways liberty rights can be regarded as involved in rather general practices of the sort I have specified and hence as conforming to the account of legal or institutional rights I have been developing.[31]

It could be alleged, however, that competition rights, a special case of liberty rights, prove peculiarly recalcitrant to the analysis I have given. Though such rights occur in many places, a specific example might help fix attention. In a baseball game, a runner is at third base with no outs; a sharp ground ball is hit between second and short. The runner has a right to run and she heads for home. But the catcher, guarding home base, has no duty to allow the runner to score. Indeed, he has a right to try to stop her.

Thus, the catcher can, if he has the ball (or, perhaps, even if he is awaiting the throw), stand athwart the base path and block the runner. But it is an illusion to think that there is, in these cases, no normative direction afforded the competitors in their responses to the other side. For the catcher cannot stand there at his pleasure, without the ball or without awaiting the throw on the instant. Why not? Because the rules of baseball do not allow these things.

Although the catcher has no duty specifically correlated with the baserunner's liberty right to run home and has himself a right to prevent the runner from scoring, the catcher's conduct towards the baserunner is, nonetheless, normatively directed by the rules of baseball. A number of duties, institutional duties, are built into the playing of the game and these duties govern this case insofar as it comes under the relevant rules. No competition right, in baseball or in any other game, is wholly free of such constraints.

By the same token, the catcher cannot pull out a gun and shoot the baserunner. For this would violate not only the rules of the game but also the laws of the land. I realize that not every reader will be familiar with my example. Accordingly, it might be helpful simply to state my main point directly here. It is an error to think that in cases of competition we have a small-scale state of nature. In general, then, competitors should not be imagined as standing toward one another, on the model of gladiators, bereft of obligations that correlate, if only loosely, with each other's right to 'win, score, or advance.'

There is, in sum, no such thing as an uninhibited competition right, a liberty (nonetheless called a right) toward which there is no significant normative direction afforded second parties. Even in relatively unstructured cases of competition, some constraints would apply. Thus, they would apply to two persons both rushing to pick up an unclaimed five-dollar bill or to people fishing who are angling for the same trout or to business competitors in a contest to obtain a contract or to put a new state of the art personal computer on the market. For no one of them could shoot the other. Here, then, the laws provide normative direction to the conduct of these competitors also, for all are citizens or subjects of the laws. A perimeter of legal duties, standing duties designed to provide security to persons, surrounds the playing of games and other, less-structured forms of competition just as it surrounds a whole host of situations in life, circumscribing all liberties in the process.

The case really is no different, then, with the liberties or rights of competition. Such liberties exist in the presence of explicit authorization or, alternatively, in the absence of specific legal or institutional inhibitions. They have the status of liberty *rights*, however, largely because they come under recognized conventional or institutional rules and because, in virtue of these rules, significant normative direction constrains the conduct of the competitors as regards the liberties of their opponents. And the less significant the normative direction is, the less inclined we are to call such liberties rights, as distinct from *mere* liberties (or simply privileges).

I do not, of course, want to say that competition rights are, flatly, legal rights. For their implication in the network of laws and so on is at best a peripheral one. Under their proper names, so to speak, they are never or only rarely mentioned in law or in judicial proceedings. But they are legal rights—or, better, they can come to be involved in legally valid claims and hence count as legal rights—simply insofar as relevant normative direction is provided by a perimeter of standing legal duties, duties made effective by the action of government. Competition rights can be seen to conform, then, in the same way as all other liberties do, to the general analysis of rights that I have set forth in this chapter and in the previous one.[32]

4.2. *A Conclusion about Legal Rights*

We have taken a set of rights, all of them presumed to be legal rights to one degree or another, through a series of amplifications—involving differences in the primary addressee, differences in the Hohfeld element emphasized, or the complications posed by competition and other liberty rights. In all cases, though, the rights we have examined, insofar as they plausibly can be regarded as legal rights (or as legally valid claims), have in common that practices of governmental recognition (or at least authoritative inclusion) and protection are involved. The notions of recognition in law and of government promotion and maintenance of claimed ways of acting or of being treated mark out, then, an important structural feature in all these rights practices. And they constitute a crucial feature in all cases where we regard the right in question as a legal right—or, if you will, regard a claim as being a legally valid one. My analysis, accordingly, has served to specify governmental recognition and maintenance in particular as among the particularly important practices that go to make up a legal right.

5. BEYOND POSITIVISM: LEVELS OF LEGALLY VALID CLAIMS

Now that we have in hand the idea of a legal right as a practice with certain essential features (of recognition and maintenance), let me add a brief aside. I begin with a confession: I find the account I have just given to be altogether too positivistic and, beyond that, too cut and dried. I do not think the account needs to be rejected, for it is fundamentally sound; but it does need to be qualified. I think it can be, without losing what is essential to it. I will introduce the necessary qualification by elaborating the notion of stages or levels at which claims can be legally valid (in more or less Feinberg's sense).

5.1. *First Level: A Day in Court*

In a brief discussion, Feinberg distinguishes between having a legal right (as equivalent in sense, roughly, to having merely a *valid claim*) from having an *effective* or *recognized* legal right.[33] He does so by considering the case where a judge applies "rules to particular claims and counterclaims" on a particular occasion. Now it is clear, in such a case, that claims which are valid under the governing rules might nonetheless not be judicially recognized as valid—might, incorrectly, not be seen as properly holding and as subject to exercise and protection in the particular set of circumstances on that particular occasion. And, of course, the very opposite is possible: a claim that is not valid might still be judicially recognized as valid. So, if we allow for the possibility that rules could be "authoritatively misinterpreted or misapplied," then we could have the sort of situation Feinberg has envisioned. A person there would have a right (that is, a legally valid claim) even though it is *not* recognized by the authorities that day and, hence, is not subject to protection and enforcement by them.

However, the very point that the judge has misinterpreted or misapplied the rules, on which Feinberg's example depends, suggests the priority of the "governing rules" and of the practices of promotion and protection which attach thereto. Feinberg's example, accordingly, provides no ground for making an intrinsic separation of valid claims, on the one side, from rights practices (recognition in law, governmental promotion and maintenance, including enforcement), on the other.

Indeed Feinberg's analysis must actually presuppose these practices of recognition and of protection at the statute level. Thus, his account presupposes the having of rights in a sense of 'right' that is not captured by the notion of a valid claim. It would, then, be a logical solecism to identify the right with the claim, which happens to be a valid one, while suggesting the excludability or dispensability of practices of recognition and enforcement in law. But Feinberg has in effect done precisely this.

A right can reside in a so-called valid claim (which underwrites the making of claims on particular occasions) only because it is there, essentially, in what gives validity to the claim in the first place: that is, the laws and relevant rights practices in which that claim is embedded. The contention that a person has a legal right, though it is not authoritatively recognized, is here derivative from, and depends on, the further point that a statute (or a rights rule of some sort) does exist and that the practices of protection and enforcement which normally attached to it would, but for judicial error, have let that person enter into the particular secured way of acting, or of being treated, for which he or she was petitioning. In the case Feinberg was considering, then, we identify the right with the valid claim only because such an error was made.

It is this fact and not the nature of rights that is crucial to the identification Feinberg effects. For the judge's error alone has prevented a valid claim from being *judicially* recognized (affirmed as holding for the claimant) in the case at hand. It is the error that has kept what legally should be an effective right from exercise—and from protection and enforcement—on that particular occasion. Accordingly, it would not be permissible to say that what was being claimed, presumably validly, could lack authoritative recognition altogether; for what gave validity (that is, *legal* validity) to such a claim would be some statute to which claims of that sort could appeal.

We could, building on this point, imagine a hierarchy of higher levels at which valid claims could be lodged: the level of statute and that of constitutional provision or norm. Thus, at the next level up (statute), one could be said to have a legally valid claim even though it had not been accredited in any given statute.

5.2. *Second Level: A Statute*

Here there is, by hypothesis, no authoritative recognition at the statute level of the right in question. Nonetheless, the way in which any such claim would be determined to be valid is by reference to some higher order of law, say, some constitutional provision or standard interpretation, under which claims of that sort were already given official legal standing.

The question is, would it be permissible to say, as Feinberg and Raz apparently want to do, that one had the right simply in virtue of a valid claim (one that *should* be recognized) whether or not that claim had been authoritatively recognized in fact? Suppose that a court, at this second level and after a due consideration of the various constitutional materials, had ruled that a person did not have the legal right alleged. The withholding of authoritative recognition would appear to be important. For it might not be permissible to say that something, even though well founded in law, was a right where the court had quite explicitly denied authoritative recognition to that thing.

Suppose now, at this second level, we had not a court but a legislative body considering the issue. A committee of that body or an advocate for some interested group might say of a certain candidate for legislative enactment that what was being proposed—for example, that a person could not properly be denied lodging in an inn on the basis of race or religion—is well founded in the relevant constitutional and other legal materials. This might be urged, then, as a reason for authoritatively recognizing this particular freedom from injury in a statute as a right. If the legislature then went on to assert by statute such a right, as was done in the U.S. Civil Rights Act of 1964, then clearly it was that authoritative recognition which made the thing in question definitively a legal right. On the contrary, the explicit rejection of the legislative proposal, the denial of authoritative recognition, would mean that it was not to be regarded as a right. By parity of reasoning, then, we should say that a court's denial would have the same effect. It would appear, then, that being well founded in law, and in that sense a valid claim, is not sufficient to make of something a right in the face of an explicit denial of authoritative recognition.

One could say that the legislative body or the court was wrong. But it is not clear that such a contention gains any purchase. If another court or another legislative body affords authoritative recognition on a later day that action might vindicate the contention that the earlier action was wrong; it was, however, the fact of the subsequent authoritative recognition that made the crucial difference, converting the supposed valid claim to the status of a right. Imagine, though, that no later court or congress did so act. Then we still have the reason we earlier had—that its authoritative recognition had been explicitly denied—for saying that the thing claimed is not a right. Definitive denial appears decisively to block a valid claim from counting as a right; whereas authoritative recognition—together with practices of promotion and maintenance—seems sufficient to make of something, say, a liberty of some sort, an effective legal right.

What, though, are we to make of the mere *absence* of explicit authoritative recognition, or authoritative denial? Could a valid claim be a right in such a circumstance? To answer this question let us move to a third and even higher level.

5.3. *Third Level: The Constitution, its Provisions and Norms*

Here one might be said to have a legally valid claim even though it had not, in precisely those terms, been granted in existing constitutional law. There is, by hypothesis, no explicit, literal authoritative recognition of what is being claimed. Even so, the way in which such a claim would be determined, and defended, would be by constructive interpretation of precedents or by appeal to constitutional principles which could be shown to have controlled previous decisions. In so doing one could show that the thing claimed was well founded in law, even though that had not been said before in so many words.

Thus a distinguished constitutional lawyer might argue before a court, as did Thurgood Marshall, that the maintenance of a dual public school system, segregated by race, was inherently unequal and could not be allowed to stand in view of the principle that each citizen is to have equal protection under the laws (a principle stated in the Fourteenth Amendment but not spelled out there *vis-à-vis* segregated public education). If Marshall's argument is correct, it would provide a good reason for urging, on anybody's part, that this particular freedom from injury be explicitly and authoritatively recognized as a right, as it would be if racially segregated public schooling were declared unconstitutional. But it was the action of the Supreme Court in *Brown* v. *Board of Education* (1954) that transformed this claim, presumably a valid one, into a right.[34]

If the matter had not been before a court but merely in the public forum, then it might have been permissible to call the valid claim, merely in being well founded, a right. At least people do colloquially talk about rights in this way, and I do not want to insist they should quit. Accordingly, I would not say, were we to presume the mere absence of explicit authoritative recognition or denial prior to 1954, that someone was wrong to contend that a right existed in those circumstances before the court acted. For they might be saying, elliptically, that the basis for the right is there but not as yet the right itself. In any event the determination of the truth of any such contention is a highly speculative matter, however it might be interpreted. More important, if the claim really was valid in the sense of *legally* valid, the determination that it was would have to rely, as did Marshall's argument, on constructive interpretation of precedents and on appeal to constitutional principles (and these, of course, are ways of pointing to a kind of prior authoritative recognition and of legal effectiveness of that which is being claimed). Without such things as these—constructive interpretation and so on—whatever validity the claim might be thought to have (that of moral validity or historical necessity or the sanction of religion), it would not have *legal* validity.

The conventional usage is unlike Marshall's arguments in one respect: the colloquial claim, presumably a valid one, was not put before a court and could be said to exist merely in the public forum. But such a claim is significantly like Marshall's arguments in other ways: it is in effect a legal claim which lacks *explicit* authoritative recognition; this is what, crucially, the claim awaits and what, if achieved, would mark the transition from a speculative and shadowy but presumably valid claim to an accredited legal right. In any event we can attach no great weight to the conventional usage I have here allowed, for it will not permit us to dispense with the authoritative recognition of a right altogether.

Of course, someone might say that a court could just go to the relevant legal materials and construct a right *de novo*. This would allow us to dispense completely with any notion of a prior authoritative recognition in law of the right itself. The court simply appeals directly to a legal rule or principle, or interprets a right as derivative from some rule-applying practice in law, in order to show that a claim is valid and hence a right. Even so this would not remove the need for authoritative recognition for which I've been arguing; it's just that now the recognition comes at the point where the court in question makes *its* declaration. If that court failed to put its stamp on the claim, then there is no right, no *legal* right. The court might be wrong in so acting, but unless *some* court validated the claim, there would be no right in law. Resort to this *de novo* approach would, nonetheless, interestingly, make the situation with courts very like the usual one with a legislative body. Such a body need not appeal to a prior rights rule in doing its business, and we can presume that there is no such rule to draw on in a given case, but unless some rights rule is passed there is simply no legal right here at all.[35]

Often courts, and especially the U.S. Supreme Court, operate at these higher levels—at the levels where a claim could not be decided simply by reference to explicit, literal authoritative statements in a statute or to such statements in a constitutional provision or in a standard interpretation. But at whichever of the levels we are, the claim will have fastened—if it is a legally valid claim—on practices of recognition and enforcement in law and it is to them that it appeals. It is dependent on those practices of governmental recognition and maintenance which determine its validity in the first place. Thus, even in the absence of explicit official statements one way or the other, there is a kind of implicit authoritative recognition which is relied on when valid claims are treated as rights. But explicit definitive statements have here an overriding weight. Thus a definitive authoritative recognition is sufficient to make of something a legal right; just as its definitive and relevant denial would be sufficient for us to deny of a claim, otherwise a valid one, that it constituted a right.[36]

I have also emphasized throughout my argument that a right, unless it is merely a nominal one, must be promoted and protected. Accordingly, if the rights of which we have been speaking are all of them effective legal rights, then this requires that they be not only authoritatively recognized—though obviously such enunciations can often count for a great deal—but also maintained in practice. In this regard it is significant that the U.S. Supreme Court followed its initial declaration of unconstitutionality, in the 1954 Brown case, with subsequent decisions that had the effect of dismantling a system of state-supported separate education in which segregation was intentionally achieved by explicit reference to race.[37] Only in this way could there be a real right, an effective right as distinct from a merely nominal one, of persons to be free from this particular injury.

A legal right is an established way of acting or of being acted toward, distinctively legal insofar as governmental action is required, or essentially involved, in the formulation, enforcement, and harmonization of rights such as these. If this is so, then the identification of legal rights with (valid) claims or with what would justify such claims, where that suggests leaving aside altogether recognition or enforcement in law as necessary features, is simply incoherent.

5.4. *Postscript: Justified Duties*

Raz tends to identify rights (including legal rights) with norms or reasons, particularly interests, or with "intermediate conclusions" from them that are sufficient to justify holding some people to duties relevant to the fulfillment of those interests.[38] This analysis, a variant of the valid claims theory, would fail for the same reasons valid claims failed. Where the interest-relevant duty is justified as a *legal* duty, it must be either that (1) there are grounds in existing law (whether explicit or not) that would support such a duty, whatever might be said of the interest *per se*, or (2) that the interest itself is supported by grounds in existing law and the case can be made (again by reference to grounds in existing law) that such a relevant duty should be promoted and maintained by law.[39]

Of course the legal duty in question need not be in place. Such duties might be generated, assuming satisfaction of (1) or (2), by the action of courts or legislatures. And, where (1) and (2) were satisfied, it might be permissible at *that* point to say a legal right exists (as Americans might have said in 1954, after *Brown*, about a right to desegregated schooling). But if, after that point, the duty was never in fact generated—or it was neither complied with nor maintained—it would, of course, be necessary to say that the right in question was merely nominal and not an active right. And, clearly, if some such duty could not be generated at all—could never be generated—within a given legal system, then the ground of the interest-justified duty would simply fail to be a legal right, period. For the failure of the legal duty to jell, in those circumstances, would be fatal to the rights ground, disqualifying it entirely as the ground of either a potential duty, one that could be generated, or an actual duty in that legal system.

In the end, the same sorts of things might be said about grounds of justified duties as legal rights that was earlier said about valid claims as legal rights. Thus, at each of three levels, there would be a clear sense in which these things can be legal rights even in the absence of explicit authoritative recognition and maintenance. There is always room for interpretation and for non-deductive, interpretative arguments. Legal rights are not and never have been matters solely of black letter law; there is much that is indeterminate about them. And there is always the public forum, where interpretation and assertion are freer and less constrained than in courts of law or legislative chambers (but are, perhaps for that very reason, not legally definitive).

None of this, however, gives a ground for saying that one can have a legal right simply in virtue of a sound practical argument to the effect that there is a clearly identified important interest, or an "intermediate conclusion" from an interest, sufficient to justify a duty. That is, none of it provides a basis for saying a sound argument is sufficient whether or not that argument is supportable by reference to relevant ways of acting or of being treated and to other things already authoritatively recognized and maintained in law. For it is true, just as it was earlier, that a definitive authoritative recognition is sufficient to make of something a legal right, whether or not the duty in question can ultimately be justified by an important interest (or "aspect" of one's "well-being"); and, more important, it remains true too that a definitive and relevant authoritative denial of that duty (or of the interest that grounds it) would be sufficient for us to deny of a duty so justified and of its ground that it constituted a right in law. Or, if not sufficient, it certainly gives us a strong reason for drawing some such interpretive conclusion.[40]

6. LEGAL RIGHTS AND HUMAN RIGHTS

The fatal flaw in the theory of rights as grounds of justified duties, as in the theory of rights as valid claims, is the suggestion that practices of recognition and enforcement in law are dispensable in the case of legal rights. Neither theory is up to the task assigned it. If a valid claim is conceived strictly as a *claim* (rather than as a recognized claim or a claim granted or an effective one), or if the reason or ground and the duty it justifies are conceived simply as a valid argument (or simply as a morally grounded valid argument), then this claim or this argument excludes the very things—the practices of recognition and maintenance—that would serve to make it a legal right; but if these things are left in the picture, as somehow essential to a legal right, then we find it impossible to identify any such right simply with a valid claim or simply with a valid argument.

I have contended in this chapter, accordingly, that the characteristic and fundamental sense in which a legal right is a right is not captured by the notion of a valid claim or its variant and that, indeed, another sense is basic to and presupposed by such claims. The notions of authoritative recognition (if sometimes only in effect) and governmental promotion and maintenance (usually on a wide variety of occasions) are, I've tried to show, themselves internal to the notion of a legal right, that is, where we are concerned with something other than a merely nominal right. It is such factors as these that crucially constitute a way of acting (say, a liberty of some sort) as a legal right, or, correspondingly, a way of being treated (say, a freedom from injury of some sort) as such a right.

These conclusions bear, in an important way, on the general theory of rights. Presumably, both Feinberg and Raz wanted here to isolate a significant feature common to rights of all sorts. The point, then, of identifying rights with valid claims or practical arguments was to fix upon just such a feature. But if my analysis is correct the notion of a valid claim or its variant does not and cannot give us that in virtue of which a legal right is to be counted as a right.

I have argued, accordingly, that we cannot define rights by reference to claims or justifying interests; such a definition would fail, if it were offered, because the notion of a claim (even a valid claim) or a duty-grounding reason is singularly unrevealing of what is involved in the concept of a right. It will not do, then, to offer the notion of valid claim, or its variant, even in an "informal elucidation" (Feinberg's phrase) of the idea of a right; for it is not apt to elucidate.[41]

The idea of a valid claim or a valid practical argument simply does not give us a useful characterization, let alone the nature of a right. For if we consider just one kind, the legal right, that which characterizes it *as a right* is not describable, in any significant way, as a valid claim.

It might be said in response that the institutional features I have identified—recognition, promotion and maintenance, harmonization (where there is a conflict of rights)—are characteristic features of a legal system and hence, derivatively so, of legal rights; but it does not follow that these are characteristic features of rights *per se*. Now, it is true that I have not shown there are analogues to these institutional features in the case of moral rights. But I have shown that one cannot bridge directly from legal rights to valid claims or to valid arguments without leaving out features, perhaps the most important features, of legal rights. Accordingly, we cannot contend that it is especially revelatory to treat (valid) claims as the genus to which legal rights stand as a species. It is precisely the identification of rights with claims for these purposes that I have tried to oppose in the present chapter. And the contention that valid claims provide the essential element in a generic theory of rights is appreciably weakened thereby.

The theory of rights as valid claims or its variant represents, so far as legal rights are concerned, a deep philosophical mislocation. For the main configuration of legal rights lies outside its boundaries.

The question remains, though, whether rights of some other sort, specifically human rights, can conveniently be construed within the framework provided by the theory of rights as valid claims. But this is another story, better told on another day; I will take it up in the next chapter.

4

Human Rights

THE development of measures for the international promotion of human rights since the Second World War has brought the concept of human rights into use around the world. The Universal Declaration of Human Rights of the United Nations (1948) gave fairly definite content to the category of human rights; and the European Convention on Human Rights (1954), the two United Nations Covenants (1966, entered into force 1976), and the Helsinki Agreement (1975)[1] have made human rights part of international relations and to some extent of international law.

Nonetheless, one of the most difficult subjects in philosophy is, and continues to be, the status of human rights and the bearing of such rights on domestic and international codes of law. No point has given more trouble here than the apparently different sense in which the term 'right' is used in *human* right and in *legal* right. It is not a matter of great surprise to learn, then, that since the time of the UN's Universal Declaration philosophers have been at work on this problem. And this very problem surfaced in effect at the conclusion of the previous chapter.

For the analysis that rights are valid claims, which was explored in that chapter, did seem on the face of it especially congenial to the traditional or usual idea of human rights. But if my argument from the previous chapter is to be credited, then the account of valid claims won't do as providing a generic notion of rights, one that includes legal as well as human rights. Thus, if the valid claims analysis is upheld for human rights, that would force a special sense of 'rights' on human rights. This seems undesirable in itself and some would question, even, whether these were rights at all. But if the alternative view is upheld—that human rights are themselves practices of some sort (ways of acting or being treated), practices that specifically include such things as social recognition and maintenance of these ways— then we can regain a unified conception of rights. And the acceptability of this conception is strengthened by the fact that it comports well with legal rights, indeed on those very points where legal rights are distinctive and peculiarly interesting. The only problem is that the practices conception may provide an inferior or even an unacceptable account of human rights, as normally understood.

We have arrived here at a point of tension in the philosophy of human rights and at a significant problem with the argument of my book. In the present chapter, then, I will develop further the dialectic between the two main options, the practices view and the conception of rights as valid claims, in an attempt to resolve this tension.

I. HUMAN RIGHTS AS MORAL RIGHTS

Let us begin with a point that does not seem in serious dispute, for one finds general agreement among philosophers that human rights are moral rights. But the implications of this characterization are not wholly clear. Feinberg says that "the term 'moral rights' can be applied to all rights that are held to exist prior to, or independently of, any legal or institutional rules"; that is, they are rights which are "independent of *any* institutional rules, legal or nonlegal."[2] And Maurice Cranston contrasts moral rights with positive rights; the former, unlike the latter, are not necessarily enforceable and their existence cannot be established by appeal to some authority.[3]

The word 'moral' seems to be doing much of the same work in this context that the word 'natural' used to do.[4] Describing rights as natural implied that they were not conventional or artificial in the sense that legal rights are, and the same is implied here by describing human rights as moral rights. The latter description—"moral rights"—has the advantage over the earlier one—"natural rights"—of not committing one to the view that human rights norms are somehow built into human nature or the universe.[5]

I do not want to beg important questions. But it does seem that nowadays philosophers and others use the language of human rights and natural rights more or less interchangeably. And these notions do have much in common—for example, the ground marked out by the sense of 'moral' we are here considering. So in what follows, where no significant distinction will be drawn between human rights and natural rights, I will emphasize points that overlap the two notions and that constitute common ground between them.

Describing human rights as moral rights also implies that the norms which constitute human rights are moral norms, and thus human rights can exist only if substantive moral norms in some sense exist (or, at least, can be objectively described and argued for). Now, it is possible for moral, and hence human, rights to exist even if moral norms are conventional or are relative to culture. But if human rights are to serve their role as international standards of political criticism then such a conventional morality would have to include some norms that are accepted worldwide. More important, if such norms are to have weight and bearing for future human beings in societies not yet existing (and this much would seem to be involved if we are to call these norms *universal* in any significant sense), then these norms cannot be merely conventional. (For there can be, existing now, no moral conventions of the future—conventions of the people living *then*.)

Thus, in classifying human rights as moral rights one may wish to distinguish between actual and critical moralities. A utilitarian like Mill might allow that there is little agreement worldwide or over time in actual moralities about basic rights but nevertheless claim that human rights exist in the most defensible critical morality, namely utilitarianism. Or a critical moralist like Rawls might want to make a similar claim respecting a preferred set of principles in the Kantian mode. What seems especially crucial to human rights, then, is the belief that there are objectively correct, or objectively reasonable, critical moral principles.[6]

In calling a principle objectively reasonable I mean to suggest that, once it was understood, the principle would be regarded as reasonable by persons at different times or in different cultures. And such principles, again cross-culturally, would be thought to have connection—as rationales, for example—with a fairly wide range of differing conventional moralities. There are probably several moral principles that could be regarded as objectively reasonable in this way. But in any event a controlling belief in the theory of human rights is that there are such principles.

A slight qualification to the view that human rights are moral rights is now perhaps in order. For it should be noted that human rights can be and have been institutionalized in national and international legal systems. It is obvious that a constitutional bill of rights can institutionalize human rights, and a fundamental purpose of human rights manifestos has been to promote such institutionalization. Moreover, human rights have also been institutionalized at the international level, to a limited degree. So when people say that human rights are moral rights (that is, are noninstitutional in character), they do not mean that anything institutional would fail to be a human right. They mean, rather, that human rights norms are, or derive from, sound substantive critical moral principles and that these principles hold (and, arguably, that the human rights themselves exist) without being encoded; that is, the principles hold (or the rights exist) prior to being encoded in national or international laws. But when such rights are encoded they do not cease to be human rights, for they retain their essential character. They are incorporated as rights, as preexisting moral rights, and their being such rights does not depend on any constitutional or legal embodiment.

Our project is to examine this apparently plausible contention, that human rights are moral rights, with some care. And it is the special province of the view that rights are valid claims to provide a distinctive interpretation of it. So we begin with that.

2. HUMAN RIGHTS AS MORALLY VALID CLAIMS

As we saw in the previous chapter, rights as valid claims have two distinct dimensions: they are justifiable claims *to* something and, as claims on the specific duties of assignable people, they are claims *against* someone. A right in the full or proper sense is both these things; it is a merger of the two dimensions. Thus whatever is to be counted as human right, in the proper sense, must hold in both these dimensions.

When it is said that a human right is a valid claim one means at a minimum that the thing claimed is endorsed by moral considerations or, as Feinberg sometimes puts it, by the "principles of an enlightened conscience."[7] It is for this reason especially that human rights are regarded as a class of moral rights. But any such claim to a service (or a freedom from injury or a liberty) must hold good on other important counts in order to qualify as valid: the thing claimed must be morally endorsed for each and every person; and that thing must be practicable and, hence, able to serve as a justifiable basis for calling on duties (of other people) in the fulfilling of that which is claimed. Only such claims-to as are fully valid in the way just described can properly figure in a human right. And, if we turn to the other main dimension of what can be called valid claims, that of claims-*against*, it is clear such claims require that there be specific duties which fall on determinate or assignable individuals. Lacking these, claims-against could not take hold and would thereby be defective. The filling in of the requisite background here (with established duties) may involve creating new duties, or it may involve simply hooking on to existing ones. In both cases, though, a fully valid moral claim, hence a human right, will combine a valid claim *to* something with a valid claim on or *against* someone.[8]

The important thing to note here is that in this account a moral claim can be valid even though it has not been "answered," so to speak, by governmental or by individual action; for the validity of the claim is in no way rendered infirm here by the fact that the called for responses have not been forthcoming. A morally valid claim can be purely a claim, for it is possible to conceive of any such claim as one which holds in the absence of practices of acknowledgment and promotion, and yet is fully valid as a claim.

Thus in assessing the thesis that human rights are valid claims we must test it by considering valid claims as claims, whether responded to or not. For the proposed thesis stands or falls on the point that morally valid claims, just in virtue of being morally valid, are rights and that human rights owe their status as rights solely to the element of valid claim. Hence the thesis analyzes human rights as morally valid claims (which are, as well, universal): such rights can be conceived of, without loss, as justified or valid claims and nothing more.

A valid claim can exist solely in the domain of critical moral argument, but that which satisfies the claim cannot. It cannot because what satisfies the claim is the maintenance of a course of action and such maintenance is not confined to the realm of argument. Simply because human rights (as valid claims) have the capacity to be theoretical entities in the moral domain, which are then responded to in a somewhat different mode (for example, in the law), a certain instability has crept into our conception of them.

More generally, we should note that a peculiarly elusive feature of human rights, in their role as moral norms, is that the procedure for deciding whether something is a human right is not wholly settled. We find that the vocabulary of human rights may actually be used at any of several steps: that of moral entitlement (where only the claim-to element is settled), that of fully validated moral claim, and that of satisfied claim (where the appropriate measures required to support or to fulfill the claim have been given effective embodiment as well). The presence of these stages has introduced a degree of ambiguity into assertions that a human right exists. We should, if possible, attempt to fix the notion of human rights more firmly through analysis.[9]

Let us concentrate for now on the account given in the theory of valid claims (as initially set forth in the previous chapter). Here a human right, as equivalent to a valid moral claim, comprises two elements (a morally justified claim-to and a morally justified claim-against) under a condition of practicability (which applies to all moral rights) and a condition of universality (which applies to human rights in particular). But could it be limited to these factors? The question is whether a moral right, including therein any human right, could be limited to being simply a claim (as defined by those two elements under the conditions named)—as that and nothing more—and still count as a moral right. Could such a right exist, in short, without any sort of social recognition or promotion whatsoever?

2.1. *First Problem: Recognition*

In order to answer this question we need to put a certain amount of logical pressure on the notion of a valid claim. For a moral justification could exist (as a valid argument, as a logically sound relationship between critical moral principles and the so-called morally justified claim, perhaps via some "intermediate conclusion") without people even knowing it. For example, they might lack knowledge of the relevant first principles, or what have you. In such a case persons could not acknowledge and approve the claim-to. These claims-to (so understood) would not, in the required sense, be morally justified or approved claims to something or other.

It is questionable, then, that persons could be said to have a duty to respect that claim in such a case. For, whatever duties they might have, there could be no valid claims against their duties, that is, no claims-against which were grounded, in the case we are considering, by morally valid claims-to. I doubt even that one would affirm the existence of a relevant duty in this circumstance, since having such a duty, presumably, would involve being able self-consciously to argue in a certain way. But this would not be possible, by hypothesis, in the circumstances envisioned (where a sound argument to a valid claim existed in principle, but no one there knew of that argument).

It seems that a person's being normatively directed—being held to be under some sort of duty or obligation—necessarily involves that person's being aware of that direction, aware of it as normative and aware of it as applicable to them. Or, if that is not so, they are positioned so that, through discussion and reflection, they could become aware in those respects. Thus, if the appropriate awareness does not exist in the case of given individuals, then there would at least have to be a real possibility for persons in a particular society, including those on whom the duties fell, to acknowledge such duties by the lights they had (by reference to moral and other standards actively ingredient in that society).

In the simplest case, it would have to be plausibly believed that actually incumbent duties could in fact be derived or endorsed in virtue of standards of critical morality. For obligations or duties that cannot be acknowledged in a given society, or that cannot be shown to follow, discursively, from accredited principles of conduct which are at least reflectively available to persons in that society, cannot be regarded as proper duties which could normatively bind conduct in that society.[10]

This last point strikes me as crucial; there is a need to connect the justifying argument, no matter how sound it might be, with the real moral beliefs and practices of people. For one cannot have an obligation (or a duty) of which one literally cannot be aware. An actual person's conduct cannot be determined by duty (or obligation) if it is not possible for that person, even upon reflection or through discussion with fellow moral agents, to be aware of that duty as a duty. By the same token, if one cannot even be aware of a particular reason for doing one's duty, or cannot credit it as a good reason, then one cannot be said to have a duty to act for that reason. That particular reason can make no claim on that person's duty.

Where the high-order beliefs people have (their scientific beliefs, their religious beliefs, their overall moral beliefs, and so on) effectively block acknowledgment of something as a duty, or as a claim on the doing of their duty, then we have precisely the unawareness of which I am speaking.[11] Thus, if a duty is removed or a supposed moral reason for performing one's duty is removed, in a given time or place, through such unawareness then the valid claim dissolves; it becomes something effectively unavailable.

I dare say the Aztec priest's heart would be as hard and strong toward our arguments against the ritual sacrifice of human beings as his knife was toward its victim, or as was the block on which it was done. For the duty not to do this, or a good moral reason for acting otherwise (as a claim on the duties the priest did have), was simply unavailable to people in that society.[12] Let us suppose this is so.

It would follow, accordingly, that even where a valid argument exists and exists in the awareness of some people—as, for example, now in contrast to times past—there might still be no moral right, no valid moral claim as regards people in the past in that case. In order for there to be a valid claim, in the full or proper sense, there must be relevant duties in place, or makable for them, and there must be a relevant reason, for them, to do that duty (that is, there must be a valid claim to something which grounds that duty, a claim-to of which the dutyholder must be aware, or at least capable reflectively of becoming aware). But in the case I have described, in the previous two paragraphs, there could be no fully validated moral claim, one that included such a duty or such a reason, in any society where the appropriate awareness was simply lacking and where it was blocked by important beliefs they did have and thus could not be generated there through reflection and discussion.

Let me fill in behind this line of argument a bit. I am not arguing here that people have only the duties they believe themselves to have. For, in the account I have been giving, they can properly be held to be under a *moral* duty which they do not now believe themselves to be under if the argument for that duty can be constructed from the overall social set of moral beliefs they do have (subject, of course, to the constraint that this particular construction is not blocked by *other* important beliefs they have, for example, by their scientific or religious beliefs). My point, then, is that people can have only the duties that they are reflectively able to have.

Of course, if we require that critical moral principles be brought to bear, as the theory of human rights as morally valid claims does require, we would need to add yet a further dimension to our account. We would need to add that the duties (either in place or generatable) that people reflectively are able to be under can themselves be reflectively seen to follow from such critical moral principles. And, in turn, these principles would have to be ones that people are reflectively able to accept as reasonable, given their overall set of moral beliefs and the other important beliefs they have. My point remains, though, even with this addition, that people can have only the duties they are reflectively able to have—or, more to the point, that they cannot have duties they are reflectively unable to have.

Why so? Two linked considerations seem pertinent. I would rely, first, on the consideration that moral beliefs, whether mine or someone else's, should themselves exhibit intellectual coherence and should be coherent as well with other important, high-order beliefs. A certain duty, then, is reflectively available when it can, and reflectively unavailable when it cannot, arise in the context of and cohere with the overall set of moral beliefs and other important beliefs people have. It follows that people cannot, when their beliefs are true to the standards of intellectual coherence, have duties that are reflectively unavailable to them in the way just described. Nor can we—where we adhere to these same standards of coherence—reasonably expect them to.

One might reply that this matters little. If someone holds beliefs that cannot be made to cohere with critical moral principles (or with scientific norms or with true religion), so much the worse for that person. We should be concerned only with the best set of beliefs (which will be, presumably, a coherent one). Such a set would include, of course, all critical moral principles and, let us assume, the theory of human rights as morally valid claims as well. Thus, that theory, based as it is on critical moral principles, lays down a standard for us all and, clearly, we and others should be held to that standard. Accordingly, people can be *held* to be under—can be *held* to have—those genuine duties that follow from critical moral principles, as elaborated in the notion of morally valid claims, even when those duties are in fact reflectively unavailable to such people.

But can anyone really hold the position implicated in this response? This brings me to the second main consideration: that reflective availability is a necessary condition for a detail of morality (be it a duty or a principle or a reason) to count, in the relevant sense, as properly *moral*. At this point, note, we leave off talk simply of what intellectual coherence demands and, instead, ask about the demands of morality in particular.

In order to do this, let us keep in view here only one case, the case of moral duties. It seems to be accepted, by Kantians and utilitarians alike, that people cannot be said to be performing a duty *as a moral duty*, that is, in the way proper to such a duty, unless they act with the consciousness that it is their duty—or could come to that consciousness after discussion and reflection.[13]

This foundational idea can be broken down into a series of steps: (3) people can't be acting dutifully (as distinct from merely acting according to moral duty) unless (2) they perceive or can come to perceive that they are required to act that way by a moral principle or a moral reason which (1) they accept, or can accept. We have, in effect, a chain of reasoning here (though I have numbered it backwards).

Now let us reverse the order, this time starting with (1). In doing so, we can come to see more precisely that reflective *unavailability* (in the sense already spelled out) does figure in morality in the way I earlier said it did. Thus, where one satisfies the standards of intellectual coherence, (1) one cannot accept principles or reasons which are reflectively unavailable; accordingly, (2) people cannot perceive or come to perceive that they are required to act in a certain way (the way spelled out by a proposed genuine duty) by a moral principle or a moral reason which they cannot accept, as in (1); it follows that (3) people can't act dutifully (in the moral sense of dutifully), even when they act in the way required by the duty, where (2) is so. Next, we take one further step. It follows from (3) that (4) when people act in a way forbidden by a supposed genuine duty (but where [2] is so), or when people do not act in a way that is required by such a duty (but, again, where [2] is so), they do not act contrary to their moral duty. For, in the case envisioned, they do not and *cannot* have that particular duty, if they have it at all, as a *moral* duty.

Here we have mapped, or tried to map, some of what is specifically presupposed by moral oughts and moral ought-nots. In doing so we have shown that *reflective* availability or unavailability does figure in *morality*. In short the sense of 'cannot' here (as used at the end of the previous paragraph) is complex: it combines two considerations. One bears on reflective unavailability (as grounded in a notion of intellectual coherence and the reasonable expectations it generates); the other bears on how substantive moral theories construe the notion of 'a moral duty' (and, hence, is in effect a conceptual claim about the term 'moral' in moral duties in particular).

And we have, in (4), reached a conclusion that directly opposes the idea that people can be properly *held* to be under—can be morally *held* to have—those presumed genuine duties that follow from critical moral principles, even when those duties are in fact reflectively unavailable to them. Now let us apply this conclusion, and the chain of reasoning that led to it, directly to the theory of human rights as morally valid claims.[14]

The most plausible interpretation of the idea of valid moral claims—certainly the most interesting interpretation—is one that treats such a claim as a sound justifying argument, an argument from critical moral principles to a conclusion respecting rights and duties. It is an argument which, though possibly known to some, is not necessarily available to those on whom the duty fell, since it is specifically allowed that the claim need not have been responded to or the duty recognized in any way whatsoever. But in view of the account developed so far in this chapter I'm not sure that such an idea is workable. For, since it allows exclusion of the very conditions that make duties or claims on duties meaningful (as matters of effective normative direction) for those who have the duty and since the duty actually vanishes as a moral duty in the absence of those conditions, there simply could be no *morally* valid claim which altogether excluded the appropriate awareness. In short, the notion of a morally valid claim, understood as so excluding, is incoherent, and it could not be used to analyze moral rights—nor, as a special case, human rights.

A parallel argument could be developed to show that if a certain claim to (e.g., to a specific liberty) was similarly unavailable in a given society, or could not be understood in that society as following from principles of critical morality, then it could give rise to no valid claim-to there. Nor could it be a ground for calling on the duties of others.

Rights involve significant normative direction of the conduct of others, and that would be missing in these cases. Thus, there might be a valid moral claim in the crucial sense we are examining; that is, there might be a sound argument from objective moral principle(s) to a valid conclusion which holds, insofar as practicable, for each and every human being against as-signable or determinate persons. But where that valid moral claim (equal to a sound moral argument of the sort just described) effectively failed to con-nect with such direction as was available in a society, then it would not be a right, or constitute an element in a right, in that society. So there is, we must conclude, an unexpungeable element of social recognition built into the idea of rights (as valid claims)—at least in the sense that the existing moral beliefs and practices of a society are, on reflection, compatible with or ultimately amenable to the strictures of critical morality. For social recognition, an actual and appropriate awareness on the part of people in a society, is a necessary condition of a morally valid claim's being (or becoming) a moral right.

So I doubt the defender of the valid claims analysis would want to say, in the end, that the moral right existed simply in the fact of moral justification (at the point where the mere abstract argument could be constructed in principle), even when no one (or no one alive in a certain generation, say) knew of this argument or was able to state it as a moral argument.

Thus, the existence of a morally valid claim in the sense we are interested in would probably require, at a minimum, that there was a well-founded principle of *critical* morality (such as the utilitarian principle of general welfare or the Kantian one of respect for free and equal persons) which was, if not explicitly present, at least reflectively available to those who might formulate the claim. And there would have to be as well a good argument, one that could be stated by them, which connected the moral principle with the claim-to. Otherwise such a claim could not be said to be endorsed by moral principles. There would have to be, similarly, a good argument (preferably an explicit one) connecting the moral principle (or the derived claim) to duties of assignable people: duties that either already existed or could be constructed for those persons.

2.2. Second Problem: Promotion and Maintenance

Let us take this one step further, from recognition to maintenance. Here we will complete our canvass of the issue of what counts as an exemplification of a moral right and, in particular, of a natural or human right so conceived.

Let us imagine the case of innocent travel. Suppose we were able to formulate matters fairly precisely here: we could distinguish travel from emigration; we could exclude some obvious cases of unlawful travel; we were able to add a reasonably good exceptions clause (allowing for restrictions for reasons of public health or to avoid the dangers of a war zone—or of a bridge out). Not only this; we could show also a decisive moral endorsement of travel so conceived: at least up to the point that no morally good reasons could be advanced to prevent travel, as we have been conceiving it; whereas morally good reasons could be put forward that a practice of innocent travel, of the sort specified, should be maintained.[15]

Citizens the world over might declare for it. Pronunciamentos are issued, editorials written, sermons preached. Panels of thinkers mull it over and see the moral force of such declarations. The liberty to travel is espoused in essays and from platforms. A book entitled *The Liberty to Travel* wins acclaim and then awards. It is not really an original book (since it mainly derives from Mill and his wife, Harriet Taylor, though the book often draws on Kantian arguments as well), but its author appears on television and her ideas are widely disseminated, unusually so for philosophical ones. The idea of a liberty to travel enters the reflective consciousness of humankind as something morally endorsed and well grounded. The claim is valid: the liberty in question has an impeccable moral title, is widely practicable, the relevant duties are in place, etc.

It would seem then that there is a human right to travel. But the guard at the border or the ticket agent at the airport counter says no.

Now, clearly, what the balky official was doing did not satisfy the claim. But that wouldn't detract from the integrity of the claim; it would still be a valid one. Even if everyone acted as these officials did, the claim would still stand; there would be no defect in the claim, as a claim, on that account. (Though we would begin to suspect that the widespread assent to the claim was merely rhetorical.[16])

But the matter stands differently with a right: the right to travel would be vitiated *as a right* if it were not protected or promoted at all. In such a case the right would be a merely nominal one, a right that existed in name only but not in fact. A merely nominal right—at least the paradigm case of one—is in principle never enforceable; enforcement simply does not belong to its nature. Its permanent recognition could be assured (the liberty put in writing, enshrined in a declaration or bill of rights, honored by lip service) but its perpetual nonenforcement would be equally assured. Such rights do not, as some have suggested, constitute a special class of full-fledged rights.[17] Rather, they constitute a limiting case; they are rights only on paper.

To be sure, nominal rights are rights. The point is, though, that we regard the total absence of promotion and maintenance as making a right infirm, as rendering it defective. Nominal rights are rights *in one sense only* (that of recognition) but they fail to function as rights. A merely nominal right gives no effective normative direction to the conduct of other persons; such persons act as if the right did not exist even on paper. No one of them takes the nominal existence of the right as a reason for doing, or not doing, as the right directs. The right here has in actual practice no justificatory or directive force. Where social recognition effectively counts for so little the rightholder is without any effective security respecting that which has been recognized and formulated as a moral right. Such a right—when merely nominal—has failed in a crucial respect. It represents at best a marginal and precarious example of a right. It is a degenerate case.

Perhaps the force of this point can be brought out more clearly by a distinction. I have in mind the different directions that promotion and maintenance can take. Sometimes we start, more or less, with an appropriate recognition and move from there to compliance, a compliance which grows greater and more widespread with time. This would be analogous, then, to the situation with the U.S. Supreme Court's decision of 1954 (which authoritatively affirmed that racially segregated schools were unconstitutional) or to the situation with the U.S. Civil Rights Act of 1964 (which declared illegal the refusal of hotel or restaurant services to people when it was done solely or basically on grounds of race or color). Thus, the right is not merely nominal in such cases; what happens, instead, is that the appropriate social recognition constitutes a basis, a reason of sorts, for the subsequent widespread promotion and maintenance of the recognized way of acting or of being treated. This is one direction in which a right can move; here the right, never merely nominal, becomes a full and proper right as the factor of social recognition progressively secures compliance and measures to enforce compliance.

But we could also envision the case in which things move in the opposite direction. Compliance withers and fades away; measures to ensure compliance atrophy and finally cease to have effect at all. What results now is a merely nominal right; such a right is, properly speaking, a right only on paper and nowhere else. It is this kind of right, a *merely* nominal right, that I had in mind when I said that such a right would be a degenerate one.

Let us assume that the rights under discussion here are not merely nominal; then, for any particular moral right, there would have to be certain appropriate practices of promotion, protection, enforcement, etc. on the part of society, including at least forbearance by (other) private persons. For we do regard total noncompliance and total nonenforcement—when there is a seated disposition in that direction—as effectively invalidating the right, as rendering it defective as a right.[18]

2.3. *Third Problem: The Parallelism of Human Rights and Legal Rights*

Let us briefly double back here to an earlier argument. It was recognition, of some appropriate sort, that allowed us to describe the right in question as even a nominal one. Were a morally valid claim to lose that too—the recognition itself—we would have to say that it had ceased to be a right altogether. And if we supposed that it never had been recognized at all, we would have to say simply that it never was a right. We do not, then, regard a right simply as a morally valid claim; rather it is more like the combination of a claim with what it takes to satisfy the claim.

The defender of the view I am criticizing might have here a ready reply. The defender could say that what my argument licensed was merely the conclusion that there is not, or never has been, a legal right in such cases of nonrecognition. But the matter is different with a human right.

This would be a damaging rejoinder for the defender to make; it supposes that legal rights differ significantly from human rights on the point at issue: the existence of appropriate mechanisms of recognition and promotion.

Thus, whatever a legal right as valid claim might be, it does appear to include those very things which are (in this rejoinder) specifically excluded from moral rights as valid claims. This suggests, in turn, that 'claim' does not have the same sense in the one case that it has in the other. The defender might, indeed, be forced to make this concession. But to do so explicitly would have serious effect. For such a rejoinder would diminish appreciably the attraction of one of the contentions put forward originally on behalf of the theory of rights as valid claims, where it was alleged that this theory gave us a univocal sense of 'rights,' one moreover that was capable of capturing both legal and human rights under a single generic heading.

More important, the rejoinder is beside the point. For it was not said in the discussion of the example cited (the liberty to travel) that this right was to be regarded as a legal one; the suggestion, rather, was that it was a moral or human right. And the argument there was perfectly general, covering without distinction moral as well as legal rights.

To sharpen the argument, however, let us direct it specifically to moral rights. (1) Moral rights which are more than merely nominal are appropriately promoted, as maintained ways of acting etc., and appropriately enforced. Correspondingly, nonpromotion or nonenforcement renders such a right infirm *as a right*. For a moral right would be a merely nominal right if it were not maintained or promoted at all. (2) Take away that thing which gives the nominal (moral) right the little status it has, that qualifies it as a right, though only a nominal one, and you have no right left. (3) And were the thing in question never even recognized as a morally accredited way of acting (or of being treated) it would have failed to be a right at all.

This argument suggests that the concept of a human right as moral right includes within it practices of recognition and promotion of some appropriate sort: these things are internal to the concept in that they are necessarily considered in determining whether any such right has been instantiated. And since a morally valid claim would fail to instantiate a human right at precisely the point where that claim is just a claim, it follows, contrary to the analysis we have been examining, that a human right is not simply a morally valid claim.

A morally valid claim, when effectively recognized and maintained, is a claim *plus* something else (the "something else" being precisely what is lacking in the claim considered simply as a claim). A morally valid claim is not defective in the absence of these things, but a right is. A human right is defective, not as a morally valid claim but as a right, in the absence of appropriate practices of recognition and maintenance. The absolute difference between morally valid claims and human rights, then, is that rights do, and claims do not, include such practices within their concept.

Of course, it is not implausible to say that a morally valid claim could appropriately secure a way of acting simply by qualities the claim has, by elements in it: by the fact of accreditation in accordance with sound moral principles or the fact of widescale practicability, or what have you. I grant this, but these elements would do no securing if they weren't recognized (or if they didn't help to maintain the way of acting or of being treated in question). The point is that if we focus just on the claim, and on the elements that make for its validity, then we leave out features that would qualify such a claim as a right.

It is possible, though, to restate the thesis that human rights are morally valid claims so as to make it effective against this particular line of attack. If a proper claim with some sort of appropriate recognition etc. can be a right, then there could be rights which are peculiarly moral in character. Some rights are secured by law, some by social convention or arrangement, some by moral recognition and the practices of maintenance appropriate to moral life (education, the development of character, reproof, encouragement, putting oneself imaginatively in the place of others, etc.). Here the notion of what is to count as morally valid is thickened so as to include those very points (acceptance into conventional morality or explicit recognition in moral argument, promotion and maintenance) which had earlier been urged against the valid claims thesis. Still, a distinction would remain between ways of acting (or of being treated) secured by moral considerations alone and those that involved recognition in law and maintenance by governmental action as well. So the crucial sense in which human rights are morally valid claims is that they are ways of acting (and being treated) that are established by normative measures but not necessarily by legal ones.

Clearly, this restatement amounts to a rejection of the thesis from which we started (in that human rights are no longer being regarded merely as valid claims, merely as sound justifying arguments, whether responded to or not). We cannot, therefore, regard it as an acceptable restatement of that thesis; for the hallmark of the approach there was that recognition and maintenance (under which heading we also would put enforcement) were specifically excluded from any part in the characterization of 'a right' in the full or proper sense. It was precisely this exclusion that made talk of valid claims distinctive and gave the thesis philosophic bite. Even so, the position as restated does seem to capture what is intended by many of those who characterize human rights as morally valid claims. And this seems justification enough to consider it.

I do not think, however, that the thesis even when restated is adequate. My reason can best be brought out by considering an important feature which it shares with the argument I have been advancing. In both cases it is accepted that appropriate practices of recognition and maintenance are intrinsic to human rights. These points, then, are not at issue; they mark common ground between my argument and that of the theory of valid claims.

What is at issue, though, is to determine what is *appropriate* for a human right. This becomes, then, the exact point at issue.

The great human rights manifestos were intended to impose restraints upon governments. Individuals were involved as beneficiaries of these restraints but, for the most part, were not the parties to whom the manifestos were addressed.

Thus, I would want to argue that, insofar as human rights claims are addressed to governments in particular, we have to regard practices of governmental recognition and promotion as being the appropriate form that such recognition and maintenance must take. To that degree, governmental practices are included within the notion of human rights. They are (or have become) a part of the concept in question. On this view, the right is not just the claim, to which there were added the called-for protective devices; instead, the right is the valid claim as recognized in law and maintained by governmental action.

A human rights claim which lacks such recognition is still a claim, and may even be a morally valid one; but it cannot qualify as a human right. And the issue of whether something is a human right, or whether such rights exist or whether people have them, cannot be decided without consideration of the whole range of relevant practices, which include recognition in law and governmental maintenance of the claimed ways of acting or of being treated. Such practices are ingredient in the very notion of what it is for something to be a human right, or so my argument is meant to show. Thus, I would want to argue that there is a deep parallelism—or, better, a convergence at a deep level—between legal rights and human rights.

3. THE ROLE OF GOVERNMENT IN HUMAN RIGHTS

Many people are not prepared to accept this. They will balk at the contention that human rights require governmental practices of recognition and maintenance. But this point about government was not inserted capriciously or casually into the human rights picture. It is there as a result of an argument.

Specifically, I argued that the notion of a right (hence a human right) contains the element of appropriate practices of recognition and maintenance within it. And I argued that since human rights claims are conventionally addressed to governments, governmental practices of recognition and promotion are necessarily included within the range of relevant practices.[19] It follows, then, that this kind of practice is specifically to be considered as one of those appropriate to human rights.

I see no way of effectively deflecting this argument short of denying that human rights are addressed to governments in particular. Thus, Cranston does not mention governments at all in his characterization of human rights. On his view human rights are rights of all individuals *against all individuals*: "To say that all men have a right to life is to impose on all men the duty of respecting human life."[20] A similar position is taken by Raphael, who distinguishes two senses of 'universal moral right.' He says, "In the stronger sense it means a right of all men against all men; in the weaker sense it means simply a right of all men, but not necessarily against all men." The latter rights involve the responsibilities of states and are viewed as "rights of the citizen." Universal moral rights in the stronger sense are viewed as genuine "rights of man"—although Raphael thinks it appropriate to include rights of the citizen in international declarations of rights.[21]

Cranston's view ignores history. It also has the implausible consequence that the right to a fair trial, which he gives as an example of a human right, is a right which one has against all people individually rather than against governments in particular, especially one's own.[22]

The example is by no means atypical; others are ready to hand. The right to travel (UN Universal Declaration, article 13) certainly contemplates the absence of restraints imposed by governments; indeed insofar as the issue is the liberty to travel, as distinct from the wherewithal to do so, it is primarily government that is addressed. And the right to freedom from the injury of torture is peculiarly held against governments; this is clear from the context—court proceedings and, in particular, punishment—in which the right is set (article 5).[23] The same pattern holds with rights to the provision of a service. The duty of providing social security is explicitly enjoined on governments (articles 22, 25), and the duty to provide for elementary education, which "shall be compulsory" (article 26), is clearly addressed, in this crucial detail at least, to states in particular.[24]

It seems, then, that government's being an intended addressee of human rights claims is too deeply embedded to be erased. Whether we look at details of specific rights, as we have just done, or at the theory of human rights (including its actual history),[25] we find that government is in fact an addressee, often the principal addressee. So a consideration of the relevant governmental practices is never a dispensable or even a negligible matter as regards the human rights status of these moral claims.

It seems, of course, obviously true that some human rights claims are "double-barreled" (the term is Feinberg's); thus the right to life (as a freedom from injury) is addressed both to the world at large as a demand that individuals respect life and to the state as a demand for its respect—in the form of legal security and enforcement for protection of life.[26] It would be a serious mistake, then, for my account to leave the individual out completely as an addressee of some human rights. For everyone can agree that individual persons, as distinct from organized governments, will sometimes—perhaps often—have such a role.

Among the double-barreled human rights, the right to freedom from the injury of torture is probably properly placed. In the UN's International Covenant on Civil and Political Rights (in article 7) the only point added to the original language of the Universal Declaration (1948), respecting the right not to be tortured, is that "no one shall be subjected without his free consent to medical or scientific experimentation." Even here, though, where the norm is addressed to individual persons (as well as to governments), there is a claim against governments to see that this particular way of acting, on the part of the individual persons toward others, is effectively recognized and maintained. Thus, the right to life or the right to be free from torture is, insofar as it is claimed against individual persons, ultimately also a claim against government for backup promotion and maintenance. My point, then, is that governmental practices (of recognition and maintenance) are *necessarily* involved even in such cases.

It may be, I would add, that for some universal moral rights the role of government is incidental or even nonexistent. These rights hold strictly between persons. The moral right to be told the truth (or at least not lied to), the moral right to gratitude for benefits provided, and, perhaps, the moral right to have promises kept are examples. Such rights differ from, say, the right not to be killed—even when we're talking about the latter right as held against individuals—in being rights maintained exclusively, or almost exclusively, by conscience. They are moral rights merely and in no way claims against the government. Interestingly, though, it is often in these very cases that, while we are willing to call such rights moral rights, we would tend to withhold the name of human (or natural) right.[27]

There is a sound basis for saying, then, that human rights norms (i.e., morally valid claims) are addressed to governments in particular, often to governments primarily. And natural or human rights can be distinguished from other universal moral rights in this very circumstance.

It is not clear, however, that from the point just made about addressees it follows that governmental practices are intrinsically relevant let alone that they are properly regarded as included within the *concept* of human rights. Thus Bernard Mayo, though he stresses that human rights are principally claimed of governments and not of persons in general, alleges this is so for historical rather than conceptual reasons.[28] I cannot follow him on this point. It may be that our conception of human rights might have been different from what it is. In any event, it is admittedly a conception that came into being at a certain time (somewhere between Ockham and Hobbes) and has had a definite history (natural rights theory, the eighteenth-century declarations, nineteenth-century criticisms, human rights theory and practice today). It is even arguable that what Hobbes intended by his talk of natural rights (and presumably meant by 'a right') is quite different from what we mean and intend today with roughly the same language—a point already touched on in Chapter 2. But none of this justifies saying that governments and public law are subject to rights claims for merely historical reasons, for reasons extraneous to the notion of human rights.

How is the matter to be decided? We could begin by recalling that human rights often and, perhaps, typically are not claims made on people in

general—not directly, anyway. There is, we also should note, an important asymmetry here between the claims-to part and the claims-against
part of a complete (or full) valid moral claim. The rights we have in mind
when we speak of human rights are, on their claim-to side, universal and
unconditional.[29] A valid moral claim holds good for everyone, or at least
for everyone who is alive at a given time—for the ground of the claim is
simply a title to something or other given to every person, merely in virtue
of their being persons, in accordance with critical moral principles. Critical
moral principles are the ground of universality in the case of human rights.
By occupying the perspective they afford, one is able to stand outside the
perspective of any given conventional morality. Thus, on their claim-to
side human rights are like natural rights in the traditional sense.[30]

Yet it does not follow automatically here that the claim-against element
will be similarly universal. For example, all human beings are, or were at
one time, children and all have (or had) the appropriate claims to care and
concern: to nourishment, upbringing, and so on. But these claims on the
part of each child are principally addressed, not to anyone and everyone,
but to that child's parents or guardians in particular. Rights so restricted
are called special (rather than general) rights. I want to suggest that something like this functions in the case of human or natural rights; they too are
special rights.[31] The claim-to element is unrestricted: it holds of every
person. But the claim-against element is typically restricted: not all persons, but only some (usually and in particular, agencies of government)
are addressed as having the primary responsibility in question.[32]

There is an important reason, which needs bringing out, for precisely
this restriction. It is assumed in talk of specifically human or natural rights
that human beings live in organized (or relatively organized) societies. The
goods that are identified in claims-to are here conceived as goods obtained
and enjoyed in such a social setting. That is, such goods are conceived as
provided peculiarly or especially through life in a society. They are not, in
short, thought to be attained principally, if at all, on a mere individual-
person-to-all-others basis. Here then, where the social context is emphasized, claims against others are for the most part addressed not to
individuals as such but, rather, to individuals insofar as they exercise the
powers of some assigned agency in that particular social setting. Such
claims-against hold not against everyone individually but against an
organized society; and it is of the institutions—or agencies—of that
society that satisfaction is expected.

In cases of this sort, individual persons play only a derivative and sometimes incidental role. And since individuals *per se* are not addressed here in
claims-against, it follows that the class of all persons—the class of all
individuals considered simply as individuals—is not the intended
addressee either. Hence there is a definite sense in which the universality of
human rights is not defined by the (universal) class of all persons, and that

sense obtains when we have regard to the class of those addressed in such claims.

Moreover, though the claim-to element properly understood holds for all persons, the group of claimants (in which any human person could possibly be included) is actually—for any given society—not humanity *per se* but, rather, those who live in that society or who are significantly involved with it. Even if some other person actually did the claiming, it would be done mainly on their behalf; for they are the specific group to whom is due that which was claimed of the society in question. These important points, though little noted, set a powerful constraint on the sense in which human rights can be regarded as universal.

The role and character of government in human rights claims follows from these facts. Admittedly, it is not so much governments as it is organized societies that are selected out by claims-against. The point, though, is that such societies are correctly regarded as *politically* organized; and it is governments that typically play, and have played, a major role in such organization. Thus government enters the human rights picture as the organizer, and as one of the major agencies, of the kind of organized society against which a human rights claim is characteristically lodged.

Even if an organized society happened to be big enough and complex enough and overarching enough to be so addressed, but did not have over it a government in the conventional sense (lacking certain coercive mechanisms or, perhaps, a territory of operation), it would still in some sense be a politically organized society. And there would still be significant analogues to government as we understand it. Thus the addressing of claims would not be markedly different from the way I've been describing it even in an anarchist society (so long, that is, as it is—relatively speaking—an organized society and not a disorganized one).

What I have argued, then, is that those institutions and agencies which are central to organized society are necessarily relevant to the status of human rights claims in all societies. In any given society it is these institutions that count. And it is their job—their moral duty, if you will—to arrange things there so as to incorporate the substance of these claims-to for the benefit of their respective inhabitants.

The relevant facts here—that all human societies are local and particular, and not coextensive with our biological species, that all or almost all such societies are organized by and with governments, that human rights norms (i.e., morally valid claims) are primarily addressed to governments in particular—are all facts of history. They are certainly not logical truths. It would be singularly misleading, however, to say these facts bear on the notion of human rights only historically but not conceptually. Rather, since these facts identify pervasive and long-standing conditions, our concept actually embodies them; the facts have been built into it. Just as these root facts could be different, so could our concept of human rights; but it is the concept it is because these facts are assumed in its formation. They are constitutive elements, disclosed by philosophical analysis, of our notion of what a human right is.

If my analysis is correct or even plausible, we have a reason for the central place occupied by government in our concept of human rights. Given this reason, we find it natural that recognition and maintenance by governmental action—the satisfaction principally sought in human or natural rights claims—should be relativized to particular societies. For these claims, insofar as we have regard to their primary addressee, are satisfied by political devices (say, laws) having an appropriately universal scope within a particular society. Such a law would exist when, for example, a freedom to travel on the part of every citizen (or preferably, every person) was recognized in the law of that society and scrupulously enforced. We can call any such operative and universal political right (that is, universal within a given society) a constitutional right or a basic right or, as I would prefer, a general political or civil right.[33]

4. HUMAN RIGHTS AND CIVIL RIGHTS

Civil rights fit the picture here simply because there is a significant restriction on universality inherent in the concept of a human right. Civil rights reflect the fact that human rights typically are special rights and are claimed on moral grounds which hold good for all persons, simply in virtue of their being persons, against particular politically organized societies—specifically, against governments. And the question whether a particular valid and universal moral claim has been appropriately responded to in law is answered by considering the class of active civil rights. Such rights, when molded and subsequently shaped under the influence of these claims, are the kind of right involved. Their existence is a necessary element in a morally valid claim's being (or becoming) a human right.

I want to avoid a possible confusion here. In my account human rights and morally valid claims are not the same notion. Therefore, it would be incorrect to contend that since governments are the principal addressee in human rights *claims* in my account they are, therefore, the second parties on whom a duty or other normative direction is imposed in the case of any human *right*.

Now let me put the point positively. Human rights *claims* (as morally valid claims) are addressed to governments: that they are to recognize and promote a variety of claims-to in appropriate ways. Such claims are responded to, properly, when governments create active civil rights laws having that end. Human rights *laws*, then, are civil rights laws with a certain kind of moral backing. It is these civil rights laws that impose duties or other normative directions on second parties; they do so variously, sometimes directly on agencies of government, sometimes directly on private persons.[34]

We recognize, of course, that there may be some constitutional or civil rights which do not have the sort of direct backing, in a valid and universal moral claim as determined from the perspective of objective moral principle(s), that we have been discussing. These would not, then, be human rights.

A human right is never simply a civil right, for it should be clear that what constitutes something a civil right and what constitutes it a human right are not the same. Thus the mere existence of a civil right is not sufficient to make of it a human right.

Look at this another way. A morally justified claim to a way of acting or of being treated, even when built into law, doesn't become just a legal right and nothing more; for it continues to carry with it the idea of *moral* validity (and not merely that of legal validity). There is always a standard external to distinctively political standards (that is, such political standards as constitutionality, due enactment, the tradition of judicial interpretation, or current political consciousness) on which the validity of human rights, in its moral aspect, is founded.

Hence there will always be a difference in the way one determines civil rights (*qua* legal rights) from the way human rights are determined. Civil rights as legal rights are determined by reference to the laws themselves or to principles already embodied in law. (A U.S. citizen's right to be free of "cruel and unusual punishments" is itself determined, for example, by taking the Eighth Amendment as touchstone.) But the determination of a human right to freedom from torture requires that accredited standards of critical morality explicitly be brought to bear. Here even the basic constitutional source is counted a human right only if its moral, as distinct from its legal, title can be made out.

A legal right is an established way of acting, or of being treated, the establishment of which is peculiarly legal in character: recognition in law and maintenance by governmental action. A human right goes one level beyond this. It is a civil right, hence a legal or political right, established by moral reasoning; it is a way of acting or of being treated for each and all that ought, morally speaking, to be secured by law. And this security, not given by law, is not exhausted by it either.

Natural or human rights are confined to those constitutional or universal political rights that have the appropriate moral support.[35] But if a particular civil right is missing in a given country, then, lacking this necessary ingredient, the would-be human right fails to take shape or it dissolves, for that country or for that time and place, and we are at best left with a moral claim (presumably valid) that something should be a civil right.

Or to be precise: something (that otherwise would be a human right) would be, in a society in which the relevant civil right was lacking, *merely* a morally valid claim there (in the suitably broadened sense, of course). It would be a valid claim that holds, insofar as is practicable, for each and every human being in that society, against the government there (and in many cases against private persons also). The claim would hold in virtue of being a proper conclusion to a sound argument from objective and accredited moral principle(s). It would be, then, a universal and valid moral claim (as assumed in the wider account mentioned above). And the principal import of the claim—where that claim was reflectively available in the society in question and where it could be seen already to have some purchase in the moral beliefs and conduct there—would be that the thing identified in the claim-to element (be it a liberty or a freedom from injury or a service of some sort) should be established as a universal legal or civil right in that society.

Any such claim would have significant uses insofar as it was or could be acknowledged by people in the society. (And most likely it would be where the conventional morality of that society was such that the claim could be affirmed when that conventional morality was reflected on.) For the claim would provide a realistic and reasonable basis for criticizing the conduct of government, or of people generally in that society. Thus, the government could be criticized—that is, the society in question could be criticized—for failing to take even the first step, that of authoritative recognition in law. Or it could be criticized for failing adequately to promote and maintain a course of action, or way of being treated, that it had incorporated in law as something to be promoted and maintained.

These would be criticisms characteristic of traditional natural or human rights advocacy. And they would be powerful criticisms to the extent that the moral claim—suitably individuated, universal, practicable, and so on—really was a proper conclusion to a sound argument from objective principles and really could be made to connect up with the normative directions on conduct provided people in that society by their existing morality or by their system of law.[36]

Indeed, the point of all such criticism is that the mechanisms of a civil right—the mechanisms of authoritative recognition in law and promotion and maintenance by governmental action of a particular way of acting, or of being treated—would be fully justified (morally) in a specific case in *any* society in which these circumstances (of social recognition, and so on) were fulfilled. For a justified moral claim (to a particular liberty of action or avoidance of injury or service of some sort) counts under those conditions as a conclusive argument that there should be a correspondent and active civil right in a given society. It does this because the argument holds, in the circumstances specified, for each and every human person against any organized society with which that person is significantly involved, in particular as a member. And this is what human rights, on their moral side, are all about.[37]

Thus, for instance, we might reasonably assume that there are sound arguments of critical morality against slavery (arguments which could connect up, on reflection, with elements in the conventional morality of the day). Suppose we had in mind the conventional morality of the slaveholding South in the United States in the late eighteenth or early nineteenth century. Here we would consider such elements as the intellectual or moral opposition to slavery exhibited by many who were themselves slaveholders (as in Jefferson's initial draft of the U.S. Declaration of Independence) or the fact that persons were required by statute *not* to teach slaves to read (statutes that inadvertently testified to capacities that slaves held in common with those who would be their masters). Obviously, the matter here is very complex. The point is that, with such considerations in hand, one could plausibly say that slaves at that very time had a morally valid claim to personal liberty despite what the United States Constitution said or implied (or despite what intellectual defenders of slavery, such as Aristotle, might have said).

More important, there was a morally valid claim against American society that this particular freedom from injury should be embodied as a constitutional or civil right (specifically as a right not to be enslaved) for every human being in that society. The intended result of authoritatively acknowledging such a claim in that society is that slavery would cease to exist there—as it did in fact, first as a legal institution and then as an acceptable idea in the minds of people. (Compare this with the *Brown* decision of the U.S. Supreme Court in 1954.) But until slavery did cease to exist there, the right established by that acknowledgment would lie somewhere between a merely nominal one and a full and effective civil right. We should expect, though, that the personal freedom from injury in question would become in time a proper or full-fledged right—that is, an active constitutional or civil right in that particular society (as in fact the history of the matter has borne out).

The moral soundness of this criticism of slavery does not require that there be some right superordinate to conventional morality or to existing systems of law. Indeed, legally sanctioned slavery may violate no one's rights in those cases where the relevant way of being treated has not been incorporated as a civil right, especially where its incorporation is effectively blocked by the beliefs people have (as in the earlier example of the Aztec practice of ritual human sacrifice). The crucial point remains that legally sanctioned slavery may, nonetheless, always be immoral (from the perspective of a critical theory, insofar as that theory has been apprehended in morality).

Any moral argument strong enough to support a specific valid claim (of the sort involved in human rights) is strong enough to support in *any* society (where the conditions of recognition and so on, already identified, are met) the claim that there should be, *morally* should be, a particular civil right there. Indeed, there will not be an instance where the moral argument holds in the former case but not in the latter. The two things stand or fall together. And if the moral argument is too weak or otherwise inadequate to support a particular valid claim of the sort found in human rights norms, then it won't support the requirement for a specific civil right, under those conditions, in a given society either.

One frequent criticism of the account of human rights I have been developing is that it makes the human rights people can have wholly dependent on what government chooses to provide. We are now in position, I think, to assess this criticism.

As regards morally valid claims, the criticism is quite wide of the mark, for two reasons. First, I have argued that people can have the duties they are reflectively able to have; thus, where discussion and reflection have successfully brought the matter home, agents of government (like all other persons) can be held to be under the duty, the moral duty, to satisfy certain claims-to. We note, second, that much of the argumentation on this head would take place in the public forum. And I have allowed (in the previous chapter) that rights-by-argument can properly be called rights in the public forum (so long as it is understood that what this means here is that such morally valid claims are in effect socially recognized, in the conventional morality of that society, and should now be given legal validity and maintained, as accredited ways of acting or being treated, by action of government). It follows, then, that where such a case can be made out for a given morally valid claim, that claim can count in this way—in the public forum within a given society—as an existing human right. Finally, it is not at all an arbitrary matter, once we have reached this point, that something should be a civil right; nor is it an arbitrary matter, among the civil rights people have, which ones are human rights.[38]

It does not appear, then, that the theory of human rights I have advanced is in any way inferior to the valid claims thesis on the side they have in common, the moral side. And where they do differ, as to whether operative civil rights are required as a necessary feature of a valid moral claim's being (or becoming) a human right, I have provided independent and, I think, compelling arguments against the view that such operative civil rights are not required. Thus, of the two options, only the practices view seems able to provide an adequate account of human rights.

One peculiar strength of the practices view has yet to be noted. By providing for two main elements in the account of a human right, the advocate of that view is able to distinguish between something's being morally justified (as, for example, a way of being treated such as nonenslavement is said to be justified) from its being justified *as a human right*. The importance of this distinction is brought out in a question one often hears asked: What is added to the point that something is morally justified by calling it a right? The practices account provides a ready answer. Social recognition and maintenance—in the case at hand, *governmental* recognition and maintenance—make the difference.

5. THE DUALITY OF HUMAN RIGHTS

Whether or not something is a human right raises a somewhat different set of questions from whether its elements conform to those of a morally valid claim. Natural or human rights are not simply demands of morality, not even of distributive justice. Rather, as I've argued in this chapter, the crucial issue is whether appropriate practices of social recognition and promotion are in place for that kind of right. Without such recognition and maintenance, whatever was said to be justified on moral grounds would not be a proper human right.

Social recognition, in particular, serves to constitute a justified claim a right and serves in so doing to preserve the integrity and distinctiveness of human rights within the domains of both morality and civility. For without social recognition and maintenance whatever was said to be justified, on moral or other grounds, would not be a proper right. But, equally, a proper civil right which lacked the appropriate moral backing would not be a human right.

The analysis I have been developing suggests, then, that our ordinary idea of human rights is a hybrid. It consists of two principal elements: one of them moral and the other legal. A human right, properly speaking, is never one of these to the exclusion of the other.

There is an irreducible duality to human rights. On the one side they are morally validated claims to some benefit or other. And the theory of valid claims has proven particularly serviceable, I think, in bringing out this dimension. Each claim is an endorsement of a way of acting or of being treated: as morally worthwhile, as practicable, as supportable by duties (existing or generatable). Each is, in effect, a set of good moral reasons why such a way open to each and every person ought to be recognized, of reasons—reflectively available reasons—why it ought to be allowed or maintained and ought, indeed, to be protected and promoted. Such a moral claim can be wholly sufficient as a claim and fully valid without entailing that it is recognized or maintained by those against whom the claim is made; this feature preserves the integrity of the moral element in the case of any human right.

On the other side such rights require recognition in law and promotion by government of the claimed way of acting, or of being treated. The addition of these features, which serves to constitute the claim a right, also serves to maintain the integrity of the political–legal element.

The notion of a human right cannot be confined within the framework of the theory we set out to examine. It is not possible to *identify* human rights with morally valid claims alone.[39] For neither the legal nor the moral side is dispensable in a human right.

On its legal side a human right would have the form of a civil right. If there are any human rights at all, it follows that there are civil rights in at least some countries.

5

Civil Rights

THE basic argument of the last chapter was that human rights necessarily have an institutional (or practices) side and that, on this side, they would have in a given society the form of active constitutional or civil rights. We recognize, of course, that in such a society, even where the moral dimension of human rights has made some significant connection with the conventions of belief and conduct in that society, there may be some constitutional or civil rights which do not have the sort of direct backing we were discussing there—that is, backing in an individuated and practicable and universal moral claim which serves as the proper conclusion to a sound argument from objective moral principle(s). These would not, then, be called human or natural rights. Human rights are confined, we are supposing in the present argument, to those constitutional or civil rights that have the appropriate moral support.

I. UNIVERSAL POLITICAL RIGHTS

Nonetheless, what human rights as civil rights and these other civil rights have in common is that they are all universal political rights within that society. They are ways of acting, or ways of being treated, that are specifically recognized and affirmed in law for each and all the citizens there (or, ideally, for all individual persons there) and that are promoted or maintained by the actions of those on whom express, relevant normative directions for conduct have been laid (including at some point, necessarily and always, the actions of government agents).

Not all political rights will be universal rights in the sense just described. Indeed, rights are often specific to given classes. For example, sumptuary rights in an aristocratic society, or the right to vote of whites only or of males only at an earlier time in our own society, or today the right to freedom of worship for Muslims only (in some Islamic societies) or of freedom of political expression (in some states) only for supporters of the existing government or present constitutional arrangements—and never for the critics of those things, not even the loyal ones. In some societies the tendency is for rights to be class rights.

Thus, the leading idea in a traditional class society is that there are, as a matter of permanent fact, different classes or castes and that rights (if the term is used at all) are apportioned wholly or largely by class. Where rights are so apportioned they are not civil rights, not universal political rights in the sense already described. Indeed, there may be no rights which are universal in that society.

And in an ideological or monopolizing society there may be classes that do not now conform to the governing ideal; members of such a class are not accorded the same rights as those who do conform. Hence, these rights, as apportioned only to those in the conforming class, are not civil rights, not universal political rights of every individual. Of course, the governing intention here is to eliminate all such opposition, to see an end to all opposing classes—so that in time all persons will conform to the governing ideal. Then the rights of the conforming will be the rights of each and all. But the point remains that if, by hypothesis, some opposing class did exist, a class that did not or could not conform to the monopolizing religion or the monopolizing political ideal (even though the person or persons in that nonconforming class posed no threat at all to the predominance of this ideal or its continued existence), its members would not have freedom of religious expression, in the first instance, or of political expression, in the second. Thus, the existence of such a class, whether actual or hypothetical, in such a society indicates that the rights there (if there are any) are rights of certain classes only and not of each and every individual simply as citizen or simply as subject of law.

Even in societies that do have or aspire to have universal political rights, we will find some rights that are not civil rights, not rights of each and all as rights of the citizen or of the subject of law there. Some legal rights in such a society will be restricted positional rights (for example, the rights of the U.S. President to veto acts of the Congress or to command the armed forces). These will not be rights of each and all so long as it is understood to be the case—and it is the case—that only one or a few can have these positional rights at any given time; and over time (over a lifetime, say) only one or a few have actually had them. Such restricted positional rights could not be civil rights.

Nor, indeed, could the weak liberty rights we described in Chapter 3 be civil rights. For their character was that the liberty in question (for example, to scratch one's left ear) was not specified in law nor specifically recognized in law. Such ways of acting were not, as such, afforded promotion and maintenance by government action. No one's conduct toward them was normatively directed at all, except in the weak sense that no one could say that the agent had any legal duty *not* to do the thing in question. The only relevant restraint on anyone's conduct was provided by certain standing but nonspecific duties ('perimeter' duties). Weak liberty rights as weak necessarily lack the very things that would constitute them *civil* rights. They are neither specifically recognized in law nor expressly promoted and maintained either by government action or by the actions of fellow citizens (backed up by government action). If such things as these were ever ways of acting everybody engaged in (each of us scratched his or her own left ear without interference from anybody, ever), they would be only accidentally universal. They would be universal rights only by happenstance; there would be no social commitment to them as rights, no effort expended on their behalf to the end of establishing and maintaining them.

Civil rights are rights of each and all by design, by express intention. They represent a social commitment.

Ways of acting, when civil rights, are expressly recognized in law as something that is to be allowed or encouraged or required of everyone (every citizen, every subject of law) in a given society; interference with any such way of acting is expressly forbidden. And governmental resources, as a matter of conscious public policy, are put at the service of promoting and maintaining such ways of acting. Ways of being treated, when civil rights, are expressly recognized in law as an injury that is not to be done to any person (if the right is to an avoidance of injury in a given society) or as a benefit that should be provided or made available to each and all (if the right is to a service of some sort in a given society). And the injurious conduct of others is expressly prohibited, in the first case, or their service-providing conduct expressly mandated, in the second. And governmental resources, as a matter of public policy, are put at the service of promoting and maintaining such ways of treating each and all the citizens, or each and all of those subject to the laws in a given society.

What all morally based civil rights and all other civil rights have in common, then, is that they are universal political rights of the sort just described. In this chapter I want to consider all civil rights simply as civil rights, having the properties that belong to them in that one respect; I want to leave aside the other properties they might have (for example, the property of being morally based in the way appropriate to a human right as civil right). This chapter is concerned, then, with the character of civil rights considered solely as civil rights.

Some civil rights are important because they have the requisite moral pedigree. And the social commitment to them, presumably, reflects this consideration to one degree or another. But social commitment could be there even in cases where that moral pedigree was lacking or was negligible.

Consider, for example, a society that was committed to the idea of schooling and, in particular, to the idea that every citizen should have the benefit of a college education. And resources were deployed, in great amounts, to this end. In the same way that young people today can be said to have a right to an education, people in that society could be said to have a right to a college education. This was the nature of the civil right to an education in that particular country.

Many societies in the past—good ones, too—had no commitment, or little, to schooling, to education in that sense.[1] Ours does. Most societies today do. But a commitment to a college education for everyone goes considerably beyond what any society today is willing to provide, or to declare a civil right. We could presume any society that did would attach importance to such a service, and making it a civil right would indicate a commitment to that project—a commitment that would serve, then, as a token of the importance attached to the project. (And the importance attached is equally an emblem of the commitment.)

The reasons for this commitment may not be primarily moral. They may reflect more readily the technological level of the society's industrial and service economy, or the fact that people there live longer (or move about frequently) and need resources of the sort college education can provide, or the fact that the society is nontraditional and innovative and requires a highly adaptable citizenry who are able to do a 'quick study' and still keep their bearings. Or it just may reflect the fact that education, including higher education, is one of the ways in which people are 'processed' in that society, made ready there, efficiently and effectively, for adulthood and the workaday world.

Consider next a society that made not just medical care available to all citizens, as a civil right to a service provided, but also high-level dental care. Or beyond that all sorts of other expensive medical procedures (face lifts, hair transplants). The goals of people in doing this were not merely hygienic but largely cosmetic. They put a premium on certain appearances (as most societies do, though few would make it a matter of social commitment). Such cosmetic medical and dental treatment could be a universal political right to a certain kind of treatment (in the case at hand, a provision of service) available to each and all the citizens, promoted and maintained by government action, and at considerable cost. I doubt, though, many people would regard this civil right as a human right; it lacks the appropriate moral backing. Nonetheless, it is important in that society; it represents an express commitment to providing a service for each and all.[2]

All civil rights represent social commitment. Some for reasons of moral pedigree, at least that in part; some for other reasons (and not necessarily bad ones either).

Without putting too fine a point on it, we can say that a society that had civil rights would probably afford such rights a fairly high standing, as measured by the resources committed and by the competitive weight of such rights in relation to other normative considerations. And the whole set of civil rights would reflect a major social commitment.

Let us note one further step. A people might make the whole set of such rights the principal political object in their society, thereby giving priority to civil rights over other possible competing values (over, for example, the common good understood collectively rather than distributively, over the advantage and interests of a certain class, over holiness, and so on). Here we could say that civil rights were politically fundamental in that society and, in a sense, constituted part of its body politic or "basic structure" (in Rawls's term).[3] In such a case I think it would be proper to use the terms 'civil rights' and 'constitutional rights' interchangeably.

But the set of civil rights need not be given priority. In the present account, to this point at least, no such priority has been argued for. In this chapter, rather, we are concerned simply with civil rights, without regard to whether they are constitutional rights or not.

2. JUSTIFICATION OF CIVIL RIGHTS

All civil rights are important rights and all reflect a high level of social commitment. But not all can be justified as representing individuated, practicable, and universal moral claims which serve as proper conclusions to sound arguments from objective principle(s) of critical morality. Nonetheless, all are susceptible of being justified in a distinctive way—in accordance with one and the same pattern—and we turn to that pattern now.

The governing supposition (initially laid down in Chapter 2) is that all rights are, in some way, beneficial to the rightholder. Thus, all civil rights (all universal political rights), in being true to this notion, could be represented heuristically as identifying ways of acting, or ways of being acted toward, which would upon reflection be claimed by all persons for themselves individually; for these claimed ways of acting or of being treated are, arguably, part of the 'good' of each person or instrumental to it. A particular line of conduct (or of treatment) might be established, then, on the foundation that it was in the interest of each and all the members. Each one could plausibly claim it for oneself and acknowledge it for all others on that basis.

We must, though, take some care with this notion of a 'good' of each. The goods in question are not necessarily the goods of self-interest—things that give the agent advantage over others or that enlarge the self, by increasing a person's self-regarding expected utility. For we can, reasonably enough, speak of a set of parents sacrificing so that their child can have a better life than they have had, and we can understand the remark that somebody was selflessly committed to a certain enterprise (to an archaeological dig, say). These are, nonetheless, goods *for* those people. I have in mind, then, a notion of goods that would include such examples when I speak of something as part of the 'good' of each, or a means to it. Often such goods are things individual people share with others (in families, in voluntary associations, and so on).

Given such a notion of goods, individuals could reasonably conclude that certain specified, available liberties and noninjuries and services ought to be civil rights—ought to be formally acknowledged and specially maintained—because they are part of the 'good' *for* each, or a means to it, because they are, in this way, significant universal interests of all citizens (all subjects of law). Thus, a given civil right (an established way of acting or of being treated) can be regarded as so grounded, and hence justified as a civil right, if it is capable of being exhibited in some such form of mutual acknowledgment, if it can plausibly be said to be, and could be perceived to be upon reflection, in the interest of each and all—as constituting a part of their good or a reliable means to it.

I would not want, however, to leave the factor of time and experience out of the picture. Sometimes rights rules do not meet with widespread favor and their initial effect may be somewhat divisive socially. But if they really are rules specifying *justified* rights, time and experience will tell in their favor and the degree of social approval and the identification of one's own interest and of the interest of others in such rules will grow extensively over the years. This has certainly been true of the American experience in such matters as the abolition of slavery and the ending of racial segregation in many of its aspects.[4]

There may have been a time when white Southerners did not think, for example, that a policy of public accommodation without regard to race (in inns and restaurants) was in their interest. But they might come to see that it was in everybody's interest—theirs included—to have such a policy as part of the law and practice of the land. Such things do not happen overnight; they take public discussion, reflection (where, for example, the whites might imagine themselves as a racial minority in a somewhat hostile place), and experience. Thus, even here, the element of mutual perceived benefit with respect to a particular way of acting or of being treated (where that way belongs to the good of each and all, or is instrumental to it) constitutes the significant justifying feature of universal political or civil rights.

One might say, in sum, that an appropriate social recognition identifies a feature of all rights. Social recognition, then, belongs to the *definition* of rights, to the concept of rights (or so I have argued in Chapters 3 and 4). But even where an appropriate social recognition exists in law, there can be no such thing as a fully *justified* universal political right without the element of mutual perceived benefit. For that element belongs to the dimension of *justifying* something as a right. Or at least it belongs to the justifying of perhaps the most important kind of right, the universal political right.

The fact that all civil rights are important, the point with which this discussion began, is supervenient on the very justifying norm I have identified. Now, mutual perceived benefit is not *per se* a moral notion. To be that it would have to be brought into line with overt moral norms— those of conventional morality or, to stay with the case at hand, the principles of a critical morality. And this would involve taking another step, a distinct step beyond the perception of mutual benefit. If this is so, then such benefit can correctly be affirmed (and used as justification) even though the right in question has not been, or cannot be, justified in the way appropriate to a human right. (This was the point of the example about the right to higher education, and especially the one about cosmetic dental care.)

It may not even be possible convincingly to ground all civil rights by reference to sound arguments from objective critical moral principle(s). Indeed, the conventions of a particular society—given beliefs that it has or its current state of intellectual development—might be effectively blocked from any significant contact with or penetration by the standards of critical morality (insofar as these are known to us). Nonetheless, justified civil rights could exist there, on the ground given.

All civil rights have in common, then, that they can be justified by the standard of mutual perceived benefit. For it is always feasible and reasonable to bring this standard to bear on any universal political right, regardless of what other standards (in particular, moral ones) might also have bearing in a given case.

And the normative force that appropriate social recognition carries— where the way of acting (or of being treated) is appropriately recognized and maintained for all within a given society and where its recognition and maintenance there is reasonable (as plausibly serving certain identifiable ends)—dovetails nicely with the good of each and all that is aspired to and affirmed, after a manner of speaking, in every justified universal right. Thus, the standard of mutual perceived benefit sets an appropriate and uniform justifying pattern for all civil rights.

3. THE SAME WAY OF ACTING OR OF BEING TREATED

I do, however, want to caution against a possible misreading of this standard (and, by extension, of civil rights). I have claimed there must be an interest on the part of each and everyone in a society that a certain way of acting (or of being treated) be officially acknowledged and maintained. We need a clearer idea of the sense in which these interests must be the same for all.

Take a specific liberty of conduct, like the civil right to free speech, for example. One might defend such a liberty and its exercise as instrumental only (say to scientific controversy and truth, or to social harmony). Or one might defend it as having intrinsic value, as part and parcel of authentic good character, for example, or of rational participation in political life by free and equal citizens.[5] Such diversity must be accommodated and allowed for; the interest in question (here freedom of speech) may be a means to some and an end in itself, or part of such an end, to others. What is identical, though, is that all perceive (or could be reasonably expected to perceive upon reflection) that the way of acting in question is an interest they individually have. Putting it crudely, we would say here that it is the *same* way of acting (as identified in the notion of liberty of speech, including its exercise) that is perceived as an identical interest of each.[6]

We do not, of course, think or suggest that this liberty will be exercised in precisely the same way by each individual (by G. E. M. Anscombe, for example, when compared with Erica Jong) or that, when exercised, it will have the same value (in terms of personal satisfaction or vocational utility or political clout) for each.[7] Rather, what is identical is that each perceives, correctly we presume, that it is in that individual's benefit (as a means or as an end) to have such a way of acting available to enter into. And for each person it is the selfsame way of acting that is here referred to.

I do not claim that having such a way of acting available (as something allowed, let us say), or entering into it, will maximize an individual's interests or maximize them when that and *other* liberties (and noninjuries and services) are guaranteed as available. Nor that the individual can maximize personal interests by prudently achieving the full measure that can be gotten from the exercise of each and all of his or her civil rights. Maximization of an individual's interests is no part of the picture I am sketching. Rather, we are talking merely of an interest that is identical for each citizen or subject (in the way already indicated). We are speaking only of an interest that is, when identical, mutual (though probably not, for that very reason, maximal for many people, if for anyone).

Interpreting the justifying idea of mutual perceived benefit as one that involves an identical interest (that is, the same way of acting or the same way of being treated, for each and all), we can further distinguish civil rights from class rights in an important respect.

It could be said, for instance, that the ideal state in Plato's *Republic* embodies at least one rights-like norm: that each person (as subject or citizen) should exercise the competency for which that person is best fitted, subject to the proviso that all others do the same. Now, supposing that the exercise of this competency is a way of acting that each could engage in, one could say that it was in the interest of each so to act and, in an ideal state or 'perfect city,' would be perceived that way. Hence, such a way of acting would be, when socially recognized and maintained, a civil right and that right could be justified as a right by reference to the standard of mutual perceived benefit.

But this analysis will not do. For the interest that each of Plato's citizens has, insofar as it is an interest in a specific way of acting, is not an identical interest, not an interest in one and the same way of acting.

Let me fill in behind this point a bit. For any universe of discourse there is an appropriate specificity to action descriptions. With civil rights it is given initially in the description under which the way of acting (or of being treated) is socially recognized and maintained. Ultimately, though, these action descriptions must be conveyed with a specificity and determinateness that could guide and inform the agents themselves (that is, the first and second parties of the various rights involved).

Some lines of conduct for these agents will, under the relevant descriptions, prove to be single-track. Here there will be, roughly, some single thing (e.g., voting in a given society) that one can do or must do in order to carry out the action specified. The point is that this single way of acting (or of being acted toward), as described in the rule, must be one that *all* citizens can enter into in order for it to count as a civil right.

In other cases, of course, there is no single line of conduct specified. Instead, there are a variety of things, disparate ways of acting (of being treated), that come under one and the same descriptive heading in the rights rule. Here the lines of conduct, under this heading, can be said to be multi-track. Nonetheless, if it is a civil right that we are concerned with, these multiple ways of acting (of being treated), or at a minimum some of them, must be identical for all the citizens, for all the subjects of law.[8] We can at least begin with this claim.

Consider here the case of the right to privacy in U.S. constitutional law. For it is multitrack in character. According to my analysis, if that right is a civil right, then there will be some ways of acting that it identifies, or that can be specified as coming under it, which are identical for each and all. The famous right of a woman to have an abortion at her discretion, at least in the first trimester, would probably not (under *that* particular description) be a way of acting that is, or could be, the same for each and all of the citizens.[9] But *some* ways of acting would have to be, if the right to privacy was in fact a civil right. And presumably some would be (for example, intimate conduct—of certain sorts—in one's own home or other acceptable place or having autonomy in areas—such as the birth and rearing of children—that fundamentally touched one's own essential sense of self, that trenched on one's innermost well-being and the way one's life was to be conducted).

Now, Plato's theory, quite explicitly, emphasizes the variety, the disparateness, of the lines of conduct that come under his norm (the norm that each should do what each is best fitted for). There simply is no single thing involved in carrying out that norm. Rather, the lines of conduct, under the descriptive heading given in this norm, are multitrack.

Thus, we should analyze the presumed right here in parallel fashion to the privacy example. According to that analysis, then, if Plato's norm is correctly understood as conveying a proper civil right, there will be *some* determinate ways of acting (of being treated) under it that are the same for all the citizens.

But on inspection we find nothing of the sort. For the rulers, theorizing and setting policy is the way of acting proper to their station; that's what they do. For the auxiliaries it is carrying out that policy; for the ordinary citizens it is unthinkingly accepting and conforming to that policy, as executed by the auxiliaries. (Though the ordinary citizens do many others things as well—some farm, others are artisans, yet others engage in trade—and all may have family life and other temperate comforts as well.) Thus, all the citizens may be said to have an identical interest (that each is to exercise the competence for which each is best fitted), but all may not be said here to have an identical interest in one and the same way of acting (or of being treated).

Indeed, the *only* way we could get a uniform action description, one that applies to each and all of the citizens, is to subsume their relevant ways of acting or of being treated (otherwise various) under some general redescription (for example, under the very one given in Plato's norm). The problem with the alleged Platonic civil right (that is, the way of acting where each does what each is best fitted to do), then, is that it identifies no uniform determinate way of acting except by means of the merely verbal subsumption I've just described. All of its determinate descriptions of actions, excepting this one, refer to actions under the description they would have as class-specific actions; and none of these would be actions, under those descriptions, which could be identical for citizens in all walks of life. There simply is no across-the-board uniformity of action (except for citizens of kindergarten age) in the republic.[10]

Thus, there is no significant universal political right in Plato's theory. And there is no mutually perceived benefit, or practically none, of the sort my account has been at pains to describe.

Of course, we could shift at this point to some other notion of a common good, the good of the *polis*, say (but one that was not distributively the same for each and every member). Though this might defend or even justify Plato's ideal, it would take us even further away from the main case I had in mind with civil rights.

Here it is the *same* way of acting (or of being acted toward) that one has an interest in when one has the right to that way. The identity of interest focuses in civil rights on specific ways of acting (or of being treated) for each and all of the citizens, and those ways are perceived to lead to benefits or to be benefits, or parts of them. And here mutual perceived benefit is an appropriate standard for justifying, as rights, the universal political rights to such identical ways of acting or of being treated in a given political society.

It follows from this account of civil rights and of mutual perceived benefit as their justifying norm that civil rights are equal rights for each citizen, for each subject of law. They are equal in two respects. First, all citizens have them. All citizens (with but a few well-accredited exceptions: children, perhaps prisoners, possibly convicted felons) have toward them the same status, that is, the status of full holder of civil rights. Second, and more important, these rights are equal in content for each citizen. The rule that formulates the way of acting (or of being treated) identifies the *same* way for each and all of the citizens.

Thus, the content of the right to privacy would be equal for all the citizens. It would be equal not only when it specified a way of acting (or of being treated) that was universal for all under that right—as, for example, the right to engage in intimacies, of certain sorts, within the privacy of some acceptable place (e.g., one's own home) or to choose certain forms of medical care for oneself—but also when it specified a way of acting (or of being treated) under that right for some only—as, for example, the right of women to a discretionary abortion. For this is an equal right, of all women as citizens or subjects of the laws, under those higher-order descriptions of actions that pertain to the right of privacy.

Equality in the content of rights rules, an identity in the ways of acting (or of being treated) that are formulated and maintained as being for each and all, is built into the notion of justified civil rights, that is, when they are justified by the standard of mutual perceived benefit. For the idea here is that the same way of acting (or of being treated) is perceived as a benefit, or as a means to some benefit, by each of the citizens. Thus, insofar as we regard this standard as the significant justifying norm for universal political rights, it follows that each right in the set of such rights should be equal in content.

We can, at least, presume that equality so understood, as equality in content when set forth in the operative rules, is the settled tendency or normal pattern for civil rights, given that justifying ground. And the equality presumed for civil rights, when such rights are justified in accordance with the standard of mutual perceived benefit, can be sacrificed only on an exceptive and interim basis, to be regained within a lifetime, and only for a reason that would satisfy the perspective of equal citizenship—that it be for the sake of a more extensive or a more secure set of equal civil rights for all persons in the society in question.

The root idea—and main rationale—here is that a temporary inequality as specified in the content of a given rights rule or as determined by administrative or judicial action, can be tolerated (under certain conditions) but that lifelong inequality cannot. For any permanent and unequal restriction on civil rights would run afoul of mutual perceived benefit. It would go against the idea that served to justify civil rights in the first place, the idea that such rights concern universal interests in identical ways of acting (or of being treated), in which those ways can be perceived as benefits themselves, or parts of them, or as reliably leading to such benefits for each person. Hence, any lifelong inequality could not be justified in the account I have given—so long, that is, as we occupy the perspective in question, the perspective of civil rights.

Thus, the inequality allowed for here should not affect the lot in life of the representative citizen (or any class of representative citizens). For the inequality is to be rectified within the life span of the citizens, or at least that is the reasonable intention behind the deviation, with the result that all are better off with respect to equal civil rights. No one, no one class, is to be sacrificed in this regard.

The general principle that emerges, then, is that civil rights, as justified by the standard of mutual perceived benefit, must be equal for all. Within the perspective identified, they can be restricted—whether on a temporary and exceptive basis or on a standing and regular basis, that is, permanently—only in a way compatible with mutual perceived benefit. This is true whether a given right is restricted by another right or by a wholly different sort of normative consideration. And rights so restricted, especially when restricted permanently, must remain and will remain (if only in prospect) equal ones.[11]

We speak of rights here (in the plural), for we have been presuming throughout that people will normally have *several* civil rights. More important, we think of these rights as standardly restricted by other rights (or by other normative considerations). The leading ideas in my analysis (identical ways of acting or of being treated, mutual perceived benefit, equality in the content of rights rules) are all consistent with the supposition that individual rights will ultimately have to fold into some overall pattern, thus taking their place within a *set* of civil rights.

4. THE PROBLEM OF THE CONFLICT OF RIGHTS

But the very fact of multiplicity, and with it the very possibility of a justifying consensus regarding civil rights, requires that such rights not conflict. For if these rights conflict—such that, for example, a person's exercising right A will normatively direct another person to do something which that person is normatively directed *not* to do by right B—and if such conflicts are unresolvable in any principled way, then a fundamental incoherence has been introduced into rights. If civil rights cannot constitute a harmonious and workable set, then the notion of a justifying consensus (as to benefits) will constantly be under siege.

If a deep conflict of rights is possible, if civil rights cannot in fact be gathered into a stable system made up of compatible elements, then the solution proposed in the present chapter, regarding mutual perceived benefit as the justifying ground of civil rights, will have to be disowned or significantly rethought. The analysis of the present chapter requires that we be concerned with the status of civil rights *as a set*. We must, accordingly, attempt to deal with the problem posed by conflict between equal civil rights.

I do not mean to suggest, in saying this, that conflict of rights is inevitable (for that is the very point that needs resolving). Rather, I want simply to note that such conflicts are very common. Thus, we find frequent conflicts between, say, the right to a free press and the right to a fair trial (a recurring issue, as evidenced by the De Lorean tapes and the CNN–Noriega phone taps) or between either of these rights and the right to privacy. And because specific rights do tend to conflict or conflict at points, we are prepared to say, in a more general way, that rights can conflict. Usually the conflict is not wholesale but, instead, is limited to an incompatibility between an instance of exercising or enjoying right *A*, by one person, and an instance of exercising or enjoying right *B*, by another.

But conflict, even of this limited sort, is avoidable. It is avoidable (at least in part) through careful drafting, and redrafting, of the content of potentially competing rights. Here steps must be taken in the direction of "definitional balancing," that is, toward delimiting the content of each civil right in relation to that of the others. Let me be more specific now.

Every right has conditions of possession, a scope, and weight. The conditions of possession specify who has the right and how, indicate when it is said to be suspended or forfeited, and so on. The scope of a right specifies what the right is to (be it a liberty of conduct or an avoidance of injury at the hands of others or the provision of a service of some sort) and includes any limitations that are built into or decided upon for this right. The weight of a right is a determination, sometimes explicit and sometimes not, sometimes quite exact and sometimes rather imprecise, of how it stands with respect to other normative considerations and whether it would give way to them, or they to it, in cases of conflict. The question that we want to address is how these notions (of possession, scope, and weight) could be used to reduce or eliminate entirely the conflict of rights, in particular, conflict within the class of civil rights.[12]

One gambit would be to say that when right *A* and right *B* appear to conflict, we will eliminate the potential for conflict by saying that one of the rights is not possessed at the time, or not possessed at all, by the person who wants to exercise or enjoy it. This expedient is sometimes resorted to as part of justifying punishment for lawbreakers. Thus, we might believe that strong measures are required as a response to a violation of person *C*'s right by person *D*; we might also believe that these measures are likely to infringe *D*'s rights (though they ought not to do so insofar as these rights of *D* are equally stringent with those of *C*). The potential conflict here between the vindication of the rights of *C* and the rights of *D* is short-circuited by saying that *D*, in violating *C*'s rights, had forfeited *D*'s own rights—or at least had forfeited those rights which would be invaded by the punitive countermeasures. But the expedient of denying possession, I would suggest, is not available as a *general* solution to the problem of conflict between civil rights—a point I will return to in Chapter 11.[13]

Thus, to eliminate conflict between civil rights, we must look elsewhere than to restrictions on possession. The likeliest solution would come, then, in limitations on scope or in the fine tuning of weight. We can see this most clearly by examining one right in particular, taking as our specimen the civil right to freedom of political speech and of the press.

4.1. *Sample Procedures for Avoiding Conflict*

For convenience we can visualize a civil right as a sort of 'space'; marked off by a rectangle, say. The content of that space is given by the liberty (or the avoidance of injury or the provision of a service, as the case may be) named in the civil right. Thus, we can initially envision liberty of speech and press as simply covering all that is spoken and all that is printed. This is its operating space; we reach the basic liberty through successive partitionings of that space. What we would be left with after all the partitioning was completed is the central core of the right. This would be the indisputably protected or guaranteed part of the civil right in question.

The first boundary drawing, the one that defines the original space, is the distinction of speech from action. Thus, a distinction is made between advocacy and incitement. Crying "Fire!" in a crowded theater, to adapt Justice Holmes's famous example, is not speech but action—direct incitement to direct action. And again, so-called fighting words, as direct incitements, are not considered to be speech. We can consider this particular partitioning to have been made, then, in all our subsequent discussions.

Of course, persons in the policy process could introduce further partitionings, this time *within* the domain of speech and press. Thus, obscene speech or libelous speech might be partitioned off. Although these things count as speech, such speech is not within the protected area of the liberty of speech and press. It is not part of the basic liberty—the civil right—in question.[14]

There is another kind of constraint on the protected area which is not reached through partitionings. We should note it briefly. Speech often occurs—political speech, in particular—in a parliamentary setting or in some other relatively orderly give-and-take situation. Rules of procedure (such as General H. M. Robert's *Rules of Order*) are thus required in order to allow everyone to be heard and to assure that interested persons do not fail to speak, or fail to speak effectively, through misunderstanding of the process.[15] Often these rules of procedure are spontaneously arrived at, on the spot, as representing a consensus about what is fair. I would suppose, even, that rules for sporadic heckling and harassing of speakers by members of the audience could be codified in some such rules of fair procedure. Also, courts and administrators often undertake to regulate permissible speech, not in content, but in regard to its time, place, or manner (e.g., through permits to hold a large rally at a certain time and place and under conditions that ensure sanitary facilities, crowd safety, etc.).

These belong—in particular, the rules of orderly procedure—to what might be called (in Rawls's term) the "self-limiting" character of a basic liberty. Thus, we can distinguish (as Rawls does) between the *regulation* of a liberty (which has to do with acceptable limitations within its protected area) and its *restriction* (i.e., by partitioning). Restriction simply removes an activity from the protected area altogether; the thing that is partitioned off no longer lies within the scope of the right in question (as, for example, libelous speech is said to fall outside the protected area of the right of free speech). Regulation, however, does not remove an activity from the protected area of a right; rather, its function is to restrict or qualify a permitted action (as, for example, parliamentary speech is qualified in being subject to procedural rules). Partitioning *defines* the protected area by leaving some activities out; whereas regulation *modifies* those activities that remain within. Thus, regulation is part of the correct understanding of the activities (including both ways of acting and of being treated) that come within the area protected by a right; hence, regulation is part of the proper characterization of the activities within the central core of any given civil right.[16]

The point remains that without restriction, without partitioning, the civil right in question (as defined by this central core) will conflict with other accredited civil rights. For simplicity, I will begin by limiting our account here to conflicts between rights and will stipulate further that we shall be concerned in such cases only with conflicts that could arise between one civil right to a liberty (or to a noninjury) and another. Thus, for example, we must engage in further partitioning to mark the limits at which the civil right of speech and press is allowed to impinge on the civil right to a fair trial. There will, of course, be areas of overlap where the two rights can normally coexist; but there will have to be some ultimate lines drawn—for there must be some restrictions, at the margin, on what is to count as within and what is to count as outside the area protected. And a similar partitioning would probably occur between the civil right of free speech and press and, say, a right to privacy.

Not all of the restrictions introduced after this point, however, will concern the conflict between rights, because it is possible for a given right to conflict with other kinds of normative values. Thus, for example, the liberty of speech and of the press could conceivably conflict in time of war with a society's interest in national security. It might be argued in this regard that a justifiable restriction on speech and press could occur in a "constitutional crisis of the requisite kind," which means that "free political institutions cannot effectively operate or take the required measures to protect themselves" and that, without some such measures, those institutions cannot survive.[17]

Now, national security and public order are corporate or aggregate goods; they are, as values, extraneous to rights. But it should also be evident that national survival and public order are here only proximate and instrumental values. The more direct consideration, within a system of rights, is whether the failure of national survival or of an existing public order would virtually annihilate civil rights or lead to a severe restriction of them. Clearly, the failure of some governmental systems to survive could threaten the continuation of civil rights in the society in which that government existed, but in other cases (e.g., Nazi Germany or most contemporary Third-World dictatorships), where there were no such rights in the first place and no real prospect of ever having them, the failure of *that* governmental system would not. So the point is that civil rights (in the crisis here contemplated) are being restricted for the sake of other civil rights— indeed, for the very survival of a particular set of civil rights. And some (but not all) restrictions, of an interim nature in time of emergency, could be justified on the principles for restriction set forth earlier in this chapter (in Section 2) and thereby made compatible with the justifying ground for all civil rights, mutual perceived benefit.

Thus, a restriction on grounds extraneous to rights—such as a security-based restriction on freedom of speech, even one that applied equally to all in time of war, or a program of universal conscription for wartime service— would nonetheless have to meet certain constraints, within the perspective afforded by rights. (1) The restriction is not encoded into the rule that defines the right except as an emergency and interim feature; for otherwise it would cease to be a deviation from the rule and the rule itself would become, presumably unjustifiably, simply a more restrictive general rule. Rather, the restriction—even when legislatively enacted—is regarded as an exception, as a justifiable *ad hoc* constriction, to a rule which otherwise does not include that restriction in the scope of the right or in its defining content and would not tolerate it there as a permanent feature. (2) The restriction is short-term, for otherwise it would count as a lifelong restriction on some (all those citizens alive in a certain period) in the interest of others (other citizens alive at some future date). Even if the restriction was willingly undertaken, it could not justifiably be required, as reasonable, within the perspective afforded by the universal interests of the representative citizen, as grounded in mutual perceived benefit. (3) The restriction would have to be justifiable from that same standpoint. It must, even when done equally, serve to improve or, if need be, to preserve the system of equal civil rights.

The general principle (I repeat) is that a civil right, as part of a system of equal rights, can be restricted on a standing and regular basis—that is, permanently—only in a way compatible with mutual perceived benefit. Thus, any civil right, when so restricted, must remain an *equal* right. This general principle together with the constraints, as specified above, afford a unified account of the allowable restrictions on equal civil rights (including those that operate on a principle extraneous to rights). For the constraints govern the apparent exceptions to the general principle: covering both those interim and exceptive restrictions that restrict equally and those restrictions that deviate from equality. In effect, then, the general principle and the constraints spell out the preferred meaning of the idea that civil rights, when justified on the ground of mutual perceived benefit, are equal rights within a set of equal rights.[18]

Now it is, perhaps, unlikely that a "constitutional crisis of the requisite kind" will ever occur; it is certainly unlikely that one would occur frequently or in a predictable fashion. So we need not partition liberty of speech against that unlikely event. More important, we may not be inclined to limit the exercise of the national security interest in advance. It is very hard to draw such lines, especially in the abstract, and we realize that sometimes the interest of national security will involve great efforts and many sacrifices (including voluntary and self-imposed restrictions on speech and press). We might prefer, then, to let the right and the interest coexist, albeit uneasily. (Just as we prefer a similar coexistence between the civil rights to free speech and to a fair trial.)

We do not try, then, to limit conflict through redrafting of scope. That would often prove unnecessary and would probably prove to be too restrictive, of the interest or of the right or both. For, after all, there is nothing out of bounds about the speech in question except for its conflict with the national security interest. It is only because of such conflict, with another value or another right, that the speech might fail of protection *on a given occasion*. Thus, we do not treat it like libel, as being intrinsically outside the area of protection.

What we do instead is to allow for an area of overlap, an area for concern, in which national security interests and liberty of speech could conflict in a significant way, and then specify a test (rather like the "clear and present danger" test) that would determine when liberty of speech was to give way to the interest of national security. The test would be stronger than the one invoked by the U.S. Supreme Court, for it would link the "clear and present danger" test specifically to the imminent and unavoidable danger of a "constitutional crisis of the requisite kind".[19] Thus, we resolve the problem of conflict here by specifying the *weight* of the liberty of speech against that of national security (in itself an aggregate or collective good): the weights are such that liberty of speech is normally given precedence as a consideration, in cases of conflict, except when that one very stringent test is satisfied.

Indeed, we can generalize from the present case. We can say that whenever there is an area of overlap, and hence of possible conflict between two rights or between a right and another value, then the respective weights should be specified—at the points where significant and otherwise intractable conflict could arise—by reference to appropriate tests.

We have here a rough sketch of the civil liberty of speech and of the press as a civil right. We have identified (1) the area in which speech and press are protected (i.e., the central core of that right, as determined by successive partitionings) and, within that area, (2) the zones of competitive overlap between that right and other normative considerations. The area of basic protection—(1)—gives us the scope of the basic liberty; that space, as modified by 'self-limiting' regulations and by the notion of competitive weight (which operates in [2]), gives us an almost graphic representation of the proper understanding of significant features of the basic liberty in question.

At the beginning of the present discussion we said that we were concerned specifically with liberty of *political* speech and press. Accordingly, in order to reach this exact liberty of conduct, under this rather precise description, we need not consider commercial speech (e.g., nonpolitical advertising). This can be bracketed off, not because it is somehow ineligible for protection but because it is not *political* speech. Thus, we can presume the presence of this particular functional partitioning from this point on. We have now reached, by a rather elaborate process, the main scope and the central core of the civil right of *political* speech and press.[20]

Repeated applications of this same procedure—introducing limitations on scope through partitionings, identifying the main internal regulations, and establishing competitive weights in the zones of overlap—would allow us to achieve a similarly deep understanding of other civil rights to liberty of conduct. There is, moreover, nothing in principle that would prevent the employment of this same procedure to work up the profile of those civil rights that come under the heading of civil rights to an avoidance of injury at the hands of others or of civil rights to the provision of various services by others.

More important, such repeated applications of the procedure would be, precisely, the way in which to reduce or even to eliminate conflict between civil rights. Thus, the possibility of a harmonious set of such rights is strongly supported by the analysis, here, of the scope and weight of a right.

4.2. *A Harmonious Set of Rights*

In their work of establishing and balancing civil rights, both parliamentary bodies and the courts (and to some extent constitutional delegates) are concerned to restrict the main scope and to devise internal modifications for particular rights so as to prevent conflict between those rights and, so far as possible, to preserve intact the central core of each (as that idea, of central core, is understood, by reference to the liberty or noninjury or service involved in each case and to the main kind of normative directive thereby invoked). We would expect these political agencies, then, to have due regard for each of the civil rights individually. But the work of these bodies, as I've described it, also results, in effect, in a set of rights. Thus, we would want the bodies to be guided not merely by a concern for particular rights but also by the ideal of harmonization, more specifically, by consideration of what would make for a coherent overall arrangement of the basic liberties and noninjuries and services.

The main thing is that we understand this rather loose ideal of harmonization or compatibility as ranging over all the civil rights. They are all to be molded under it. For all civil rights, insofar as they are justified on the pattern I suggested earlier, are justified by reference to one and the same standard, that of mutual perceived benefit. This standard is the enframing one for all civil rights and, hence, can serve as the ground of their coherence in a set.

Now, in meeting this standard for being a *justified* civil right, all civil rights stand on the same footing. They are all equal and no one of them, on the ground given, has priority over the others. Thus, there can be no such thing, within the domain of justified civil rights simply *qua* civil rights, as the priority of one civil right to another. It is necessary, then, to adjust them one to another without regard to any notion of inherent priority. The coherence sought is the coherence of equal civil rights toward one another in a single, harmonious set of rights.

Of course, we could introduce certain standards of priority internal to the class of civil rights. We could, for example, revert to the earlier distinction between those civil rights that were morally based (in a way appropriate to human rights) and those that were not, with priority presumably going to the former, as somehow more basic. Or we could rely on other standards to determine basicness: we could revert to standards of justice, as with Rawls, or of personhood, as with Nozick, or of constitutionality, as with Dworkin and with American jurisprudence generally, or of conventional moral or religious judgment, or what have you.

The point is, even if we admitted some such standard of basicness, though we would be able to distinguish nonbasic from basic civil rights, we would not, within the subclass of basic civil rights, be able to distinguish one of them from another. Thus, the point about nonpriority already made would be duplicated now within the class of *basic* civil rights. For all basic civil rights would meet not only the standard of mutual perceived benefit—we can presume this—but also the standard (whatever it is) for basicness. Thus, all basic civil rights would be equal and no one of them, on the grounds given, would have inherent priority over the others.

There is no conceptual advantage, then, in moving from civil rights *per se* (all of which, if justified, are justified by the standard of mutual perceived benefit) to some subclass of *basic* civil rights. For there is no way to avoid the issue of the mutual adjustment of civil rights to one another under conditions of nonpriority (for at least *some* civil rights). That possibility must be explored in any event. So we can stay with civil rights—that is, civil rights pure and simple—as our favored case for the time being.

Here delegates and legislators and judges, in doing their work of formulation (through partitionings and limitations of scope and through the assignment of weight at points of overlap), cannot assign a greater weight, say, to a civil right to a liberty than to a civil right to an avoidance of injury (where these overlap and hence potentially conflict) on the ground that the former is a right to a liberty. Such a move is ruled out by the coherence ideal, understood in the way that I have specified it. The priority of any civil right over another is simply not a relevant concern under the supposition we have made.

This, of course, should not inhibit legislators and judges from drawing boundary lines between civil rights. They draw them all the time between one civil right (to a specific liberty) and another in situations in which no notion of priority could be said to operate. Hence, there is no problem, in principle, in their drawing boundary lines, again without resort to notions of priority, between civil rights to a liberty, on the one hand, and civil rights to a noninjury or to a provision of service, on the other—or between rights of the two latter sorts.

Nor does the coherence ideal rule out, under conditions of nonpriority, all assignments of competitive weight to civil rights. For properly designed assignments can satisfy that ideal.

Thus, it might be reasonable for a parliamentary body to assign more weight to a policy that is attached to one civil right (e.g., a policy of not allowing discrimination to burden the free choice of occupation and employment) as opposed to another policy that is attached to a different civil right (e.g., a policy of allowing *all* sports events, as attached to the right of free association, even where one or both teams were constituted on invidious racial grounds). It would be reasonable, that is, if the former policy were judged, after due consideration and careful argument, to be closer to the central core of the one right than the latter is to the core of its right, or if the former policy were judged to be more tightly associated with its core, in historical or popular experience, than the latter is with its core.

These are difficult judgments to make. Nevertheless, one could say that a policy is close to the central core of a right if, when that policy is discontinued or disallowed, other policies under that same right are weakened. Or again, it is close if there was thought to be a significant gap in the area protected by the right when the policy was absent.

All such judgments require that we have a proper understanding of the rights involved. Thus, if the *political* character of the right of free personal association were emphasized, as it would be with freedom of speech or of peaceable assembly, we would probably conclude that a policy of allowing sports events is less closely associated with that right, properly understood, than the policy of not burdening the marketplace with racial discrimination is with the right to free choice of occupation and employment.

It follows, by the same token, that it would be reasonable for a judge or an administrator to give greater weight to the exercise of one civil right (by person *A*) than to the exercise of a different civil right (by person *B*), if the former was close to the central core of the right or was done regularly (by everyone) and if the latter was remote from its core or done infrequently (by anyone).

These are merely sample considerations. My concern is principally to exhibit the kind of reasoning that goes into the determination of the weight of policies under respective civil rights and to show that such a determination can be compatible with the idea of universal interests (as grounded in mutual perceived benefit) under conditions of nonpriority. Thus, such assignments of weight can satisfy the ideal of systematic coherence set forth earlier.

The political agencies ought, in principle at least, to be able—through judicious partitioning and limitation of scope, internal modifications within scopes, and assignment of competitive weight in zones of overlap—to adjust civil rights one to another. Where these rights have been satisfactorily balanced definitionally, they cannot conflict with one another. Or in the rare but foreseeable case in which one right and another might conflict, the drafting bodies could add a determinate weight to policies under each, such that the possibility of real conflict would be wholly forestalled. Within its assigned scope and given its determinate weight, a well-defined right simply governs all applicable situations that arise in the domain of rights.

If the relation between a well-defined right (e.g., the right to free political speech) and other normative considerations (e.g., the interest in national security) is set up in the same way, then that right would govern literally all applicable situations. Thus, there would be no true conflict (conflict outside of the rights-defining rules) even here.

What the analysis suggests, in short, is that the boundaries of rights *could* be drawn so as to prevent any conflict between rights or between rights and other sorts of normative considerations. We should avoid exaggerating, however, the degree to which this can actually be done, especially *in advance* of situations in which conflict could occur. Accordingly, there will probably always be a need for courts and administrators to balance and weigh competing rights on the spot, even within the situation that we have been examining.

I would be willing to concede, however—if only for the sake of argument—that rights could have a sufficiently well-drawn scope. I would also concede, though more reluctantly, that rights could be assigned a tolerably determinate comparative weight by the drafting body. I am willing to concede these points because it is at least *theoretically* possible (as I said) that scopes and weights could be competently drafted into the rules defining rights, by constitutional delegates or by legislators and judges in their work. Let us suppose, then, that this drafting has been done expertly—to the point where conflict between rights (and between rights and other values) could be eliminated.

Thus, on the supposition of expert drafting, all conflicts between different determinate rights and between a determinate right and another sort of determinate normative consideration (for example, the national security interest) are eliminable in principle. Accordingly, naïve examples of conflict between two rights (say, property and life in time of famine) or between two different specifications of the same right (as when, for example, the moving of a house obstructs a highway) are easily set aside by means of this supposition.[21]

4.3. *Internal Conflict*

Even so, a problem with conflict of rights remains. It is unlikely that, even with a well-defined scope and a clear central or core content and carefully calibrated assignments of weight, a right could be so formulated that conflicting claims within that selfsame right could never arise.[22] I would suppose, for instance, that conflicting claims could arise under the right to freedom of conscience (a civil right, we can assume, in the society under study).

Consider the case of two persons, married to each other, who belong to quite different religions: the husband is of the Mormon faith; the wife, of the Jewish. Each feels a special religious obligation—that is, it is a significant internal feature of the religion that each faithfully adheres to—to include their son (aged about 11) in the religious beliefs and practices appropriate to that parent's respective religion. Each parent is devout and dedicated to the religion in question; neither wishes to coerce the other parent or the son; but neither is willing to let the matter ride—to leave it to the son to decide, for example, after he has come of age—and neither thinks that a nuisance, or anything offensive, is created by the practice of the other's religion (nor could anyone reasonably allege so). Clearly, if these people stick to their convictions and exercise their religions freely, there will be a conflict between them: for each in exercising the right of freedom of religion will run athwart the allowed exercise of the other's selfsame right.

This conflict is between instances of one and the same right and would, although it is technically a conflict within a single right, be described as a conflict of rights. Even if one were to set this description aside, as being somehow peculiar, the fact remains that such a conflict would challenge the coherence of a system of rights.

For the important point is that we are here dealing with the core, or essential liberty, of the free exercise of religion. The right has been carefully defined, and the exercises under consideration are uncontroversially within its scope, well away from the boundary (and well away from any zone of overlap).

Now, it might appear that the son has a right not to be indoctrinated—that is, a right to freedom of conscience on his own part. Suppose that he does. The fact remains that this right could conflict with the right of the parents at some point. It might even be that at some point continued activity by the parents would be regarded as coercive of the son and as impermissible under the right to free exercise of religion. In the present example, however, I have supposed that such points have not yet been reached.

Of course, we could vary the example somewhat. We could, for instance, focus the right of conscience of the parents, not on religion, but on the education of their children in moral matters or in general philosophic orientation. If such educational matters are not undertaken by somebody, the growing child will lack significant values and traits of character—perhaps permanently. And, although the indoctrination of young people may burden their development as rational and autonomous beings, people believe that *some* indoctrination is necessary to that development, as well as to other ends. Even if the moral education of a young person consists principally in exposing that individual to selected paradigms of conduct and to the behavior of role models, with little or no explicit verbal instruction, that person is nonetheless being instructed or, if you will, indoctrinated. The issue is simply the acceptable limits (up to a certain age, at least).

Thus, assuming that we were within acceptable limits, we could pose the issue as one of freedom of conscience, insofar as that concerns moral or philosophic education. Nonetheless, we would still have a conflict of rights here; it's just that the conflict would now involve, not the free exercise of religion by the parents, but instead their right of conscience to educate their own children in matters moral or philosophic.

But clearly, if the parents had been of a single faith, their religious instruction of their son would be regarded (in our own society, for instance) as an acceptable exercise of liberty of conscience and in no way an affront to any rights of the son. It follows, then, that each parent in trying to instruct the son in the respective faith and practice of that parent was acting acceptably within the norms of that same liberty. My point, accordingly, is that the exercise of the right of conscience would, within limits thought to be acceptable, include religious instruction of the sort described in our example.

I would not claim, by the way, that every society will have a religious dimension (and, hence, that religion will inevitably be included in the notion of liberty of conscience). Nor would I claim that it is necessarily true that a religion would always have the character here described: that of being exclusive and requiring the indoctrination of minors and their incorporation into the religion of the parent(s). But if a society has a notion of religion of this sort, then the right to liberty of conscience, as incorporated into the set of civil rights of that society, would cover religion so understood.

The inclusion of religious freedom within liberty of conscience in such a society would probably be done with the understanding that religious attachment (like ethical commitment or advocacy of social policy) is one of the ways in which people develop and display strong attitudes about good and bad, right and wrong, and, further, that such attachment will often prove harsh and controversial and divisive. Nonetheless, where there are competing religious alternatives available (or ethical convictions or social policies to be advocated), the free exercise of conscience can be achieved only where the free exercise of these competing alternatives is allowed. Religious conviction and even indoctrination of the young (as one feature of that conviction) are consistent—in particular, under conditions of religious diversity and advocacy—with the interest of persons in liberty of conscience.

In a society like our own, with its peculiar history and present character (of religious pluralism), the civil right to liberty of conscience would have to include, within its central core, the free exercise of religion. It would have to include it, and exercises of the sort contemplated (within acceptable limits, that is), even when the competing creeds were sectarian and exclusive. Thus, the specific kind of religious activity identified in our example (incorporation and indoctrination of their children within the religion of the parents) is within the scope of the right to free exercise of religion, itself a specification of the right of conscience.

Hence, conflict of the sort that I have described could arise. And insofar as we restrict the matter to the right of each parent to free exercise of religion, the conflict here is between two equally eligible and equally central instances of the same right. Although the envisioned conflict would not be easily resolvable, it is possible that strategies could be devised that both maintained the full exercise of the right and avoided the specific conflict. There is no built-in guarantee of such a resolution, however. The parents might even feel the need to go to some impartial third party to help mediate their dispute. In the unhappy event that the matter did pass into the hands of a court—perhaps when one of the parents had yielded to the urgings of relatives or of coreligionists—then the court, in choosing between them (and such choice might prove unavoidable), would override the one exercise of the right in the interest of the other. So long as conflict *within* rights is possible, a problem remains, then, for the theory I have been developing.[23]

The crux of the problem is that the conflicting exercises which we are contemplating are equally eligible instances of the same right and that, by hypothesis, the profile of this right has been competently determined in accordance with the ideal of compatibility with mutual or universal interests. Hence, it would not be useful to employ that perspective in deciding between them. Nor would it be useful to revert to the grounds for determining scope and weight in making such a decision, for these are already incorporated in the scope and weight actually—and expertly— assigned to that right. The ideal of compatibility with universal interests, interests that are shared identically by each and all as the ground of rights, fails to give us guidance in resolving the conflict between exercises of the same right, exercises that come equally under the core or central content of the right, under the very same clause, so to speak.

Conflict of rights becomes an intractable problem only when there is no way to resolve the conflict in principle—that is, by reference to the principles that were used to settle the matters of possession, scope, and weight, and so on, in the first place. Here resort to any such relevant principle (to resolve conflict within a right) would be evidence that the scope and weight of that right had not been expertly and competently formulated, contrary to the governing hypothesis (set out at the end of Section 4.2).

My account has emphasized one such relevant principle in particular, that of mutual perceived benefit, as a principle of justification, and compatibility with it, as a principle of systematic coherence. I have, of course, left it open that other principles might be employed as well, supplementary to this one. For example, all *basic* civil rights would require both the principle of mutual perceived benefit and some other compatible principle, the principle for basicness (whatever it was), to achieve coherence. And further complications are possible. But however many principles there are, we have an intractable conflict of rights when the choice between exercises of a given right cannot be made by reference to the relevant principles for formulation and justification.[24]

A court, of course, need not be doing formulation (or justification) work here. It might decide, rather, merely to select one exercise of the right over the other and to give it judicial protection. That, and nothing more. And in so doing, it might draw on technical procedural points or on rules of precedent and other relevant traditions and existing rules of law that are appropriate to the bench the judge occupies, things that did not touch the essential matter, as determined by the principle of universal interests.

Thus, where we have an intractable conflict of rights, where the choice between exercises of a given right cannot be made by reference to the principles for formulation or justification, then choice can only be made—and must be made, by judges and administrators—on technical grounds. Here the court would resolve a particular conflict of rights but would do so in such a way as to acknowledge the possibility of conflict of rights, then and in the future.

I conclude, then, that conflict of the sort that I have described is probably inevitable, even where stringent measures have been taken (under carefully specified conditions) to prevent conflict of rights. Accordingly, any theory of rights must recognize the possibility of such conflict and take it into account. We cannot assume that principles which are appropriate to the formulation and competitive weighting of rights, etc., even when the principles are expertly applied, can be used to resolve all disputes concerning conflict of rights. The dispute I have characterized is peculiarly immune to the sorts of considerations one brings to bear in such matters: that is, in the determination of the core content, the precise scope, and the weight of various rights. In regard to such matters, the coherence criterion we would have constitutional delegates and legislators and judges rely on—that of compatibility with mutual perceived benefit—was effectively out of commission at the point where conflict arose *within* a given right. Thus, any theory which asserts or implies that individual rights can never conflict or never conflict internally in given exercises, simply by virtue of being well-defined rights, justified in the appropriate way, must founder on this point.[25]

The failure of the claim that well-drafted rights can never conflict does not, however, jeopardize the central features of my account of civil rights. The point on which the claim foundered—namely, that *internal* conflict within given well-drafted rights is still possible—does not touch the more basic contention that conflict between different rights can be avoided, or at least appreciably reduced, through judicious drafting of the scope of potentially conflicting rights. Such drafting allows identification of the central core and protected area of each right, and it includes assignment of determinate weights to govern the conflict of rights, in cases of overlap between adjoining rights, and to govern the conflict between rights and other normative considerations. Thus, this important idea in my account of the coherence of a set of civil rights remains substantially intact. And, although we cannot say that every eligible exercise of a well-drafted right will give relevant normative direction to others within a system of rights (for this is precisely what the possibility of internal conflict would preclude), we can say that with agencies of harmonization available (such as courts) the relevant directives can be determined and can be given.

In brief, my argument has been that conflict between rights (and between rights and other normative considerations) is avoidable in principle. It is, that is, except where conflict arises within a well-drafted right (between two different exercises), for such conflict is intractable. Here the only recourse is to resolve the matter procedurally, technically, institutionally.

I do not want to suggest that all conflicts are resolvable in practice, however. For rights are often not well drafted and technical solutions are not always available. Accordingly, I think some conflict of rights is inevitable. And some may prove to be deep, divisive, resistant to solution.

My argument is designed to show only how conflicts could be avoided (or reduced), by showing that conflict of rights is resolvable in principle within a system of civil rights. And resolvable in ways compatible with the ideal of mutual perceived benefit. Even a resolution of the sort I contemplated as a last resort (a technical resolution of a conflict between two eligible exercises of the same right), while sufficient to give normative direction to the parties in the case, does not run athwart their universal interests. For the interest in the free exercise of religion that each has (and that all other citizens have) was unchanged on all the essential points—of possession, scope, and weight—by the technical basis of the decision. What governed, ultimately, was simply the judge's need to give determinate normative direction in the case at hand. Since the decision was made by reference to existing institutional patterns of behavior, patterns appropriate to judges or administrators in a given political system, it was not an unjustified infringement in that system of the right in question and was compatible, presumably, with the perspective of the universal interests of the representative citizen.

The losing party did, of course, forgo some benefit and this loss could be the occasion for some remedial moves by courts or by administrators. But no issue of principle was surrendered by the losing party; the rights of all are still as they were.

5. AN INSTITUTIONAL SETTING FOR RIGHTS

In order to have these features—of systematic coherence and the capacity to give determinate normative direction—civil rights must be made incumbent within an institutional setting. They must come to have well-defined scopes, with identified core contents and assigned weights. Care must be taken to reduce and, as much as possible, to eliminate conflict of rights.[26] They thus become in intention, in prospect, a coherent set of rights.

The ideal of harmonization of rights—the creation of a coherent set of civil rights—is served not only by the work of scope drafting and weighting but also by the low-level work of judges and administrators who, relying on established institutional processes and on standards and rules that are internal to these processes, resolve conflicts *within* given civil rights. The sort of work that is done in the latter case is different from what is done by the drafters and assigners of weight (be they delegates or legislators or judges), and it cannot be done solely on the principle that primarily governs all expert determinations of scope and weight, that is, the principle of universal interests—as determined from the perspective of the representative citizen, the perspective of mutual perceived benefit.

The work at the lower level—the level of judges and administrators— supplements the work at the basic drafting and weighting level. Thus, the use of facts (and their assessment) and the development of institutional processes that are appropriate to each level work together to help create and preserve a reasonably coherent family of civil rights.[27] And the closure of the set of civil rights is thus completed.

To my mind, the single most important point that emerges in the analysis set out in this chapter is the indispensable role of political agencies and of institutional processes in the development of rights. Such agencies, acting in concert, are required in order to formulate civil rights, to promote and maintain them (as is necessary, if they are to be more than merely nominal rights), and to harmonize them through judicious drafting.

Here we reach again, but by a different route, the conclusion of the previous chapter. Human rights (natural rights in *that* sense), like all other civil rights, require institutional harmonization just as they require institutional formulation and maintenance.

But what, one might be tempted to ask, about natural rights in the old sense, in the sense they had in the debates of the seventeenth and eighteenth centuries? Have natural rights as traditionally conceived been shunted aside? The main problem with them, as I see it, is that traditional natural rights cannot form a coherent set and, hence, are conspicuously open to the very problem that the argument begun in Section 4 was designed to resolve.

Whatever such natural rights are, they are noninstitutional in character. Hence, in one famous formulation, they are the rights we would have in a nonsocial state of nature, where individuals are conceived as isolated and wholly independent.

But I have argued that the scope of rights must be authoritatively set (to preserve their central content) and that without such setting and adjustment of scope, rights will conflict—conflict internally and with one another and with other (nonrights) considerations. Since such conflict can only be resolved or prevented by the action of agencies that can formulate and harmonize rights (through scope adjustment, competitive weightings, and so on), rights that lacked such agencies would necessarily conflict and the set of them could not be coherent. Natural rights, resolutely non-institutional in character, as they are, lack such agencies in principle. Hence, natural rights (as traditionally understood) cannot provide a plausible alternative, or even a useful addition, to the account I have given.

Perhaps, the most likely way to save natural rights theory from this crucial disability is to relocate its main thrust somewhat. Thus, we could redescribe such rights as moral norms (reached by sound inferences from the objective principles of a critical morality). Such norms, which are allowed for in my own account (in the discussion of human rights in Chapter 4), provide reasons or grounds for saying that certain ways of acting or of being treated *ought* to be civil rights, ought to be formulated in law and maintained for all people in a given body politic.

Such norms, when they are authoritatively acknowledged (as they were in the Declaration of Independence, as the rights to "life, liberty, and the pursuit of happiness") are rather like the relatively unspecified rights (for example, the right to privacy) discussed earlier in this chapter. But, like such unspecified rights, these norms or proto-rights in order to be active civil rights require, as we have seen, specification of content (so as to identify some *identical* ways of acting or of being treated for all) and they require as well scope setting and scope adjustment, competitive weighting, institutional devices for the on-site resolution of conflicts, and so on. For, otherwise, such norms will conflict with one another and collapse into an incoherent set. And, equally, they require promotion and maintenance; for, otherwise, they will be mere nominal rights and not active, functioning civil rights.

Accordingly, natural rights (conceived merely as norms of critical morality that can underwrite some civil rights—presumably compatibly with the appropriate justifying ground of mutual perceived benefit) do have a place in my account. But we cannot think adequately about such natural rights (where they are correctly thought to be true rights, as distinct from mere norms) by dispensing with the institutional features—content specification, scope adjustment, competitive weighting, promotion and maintenance—I have emphasized throughout. It is these features that are necessary to make such norms into civil rights and into a compatible set of such rights; in these very facts, we have the decisive rationale that would disqualify natural rights, understood in the old eighteenth-century way, from being themselves a compossible set of true rights.[28]

In the case of each justified civil right, then, a central or *core content* would have to be specified. This core content would have to be *individuated* (parceled out equally to all individuals within a certain class) in some *determinate* amount or to some determinate degree, under publicly recognized *rules*. And devices would have to be put in place for *assuring* this distribution as a *benefit* to each and every member of that class (here the class of all citizens in a given political society).[29]

Such assurance is to be understood as involving not simply the maintenance by government action of the relevant ways of acting (or of being treated) for each individual but also the use of the offices of government to harmonize rights in a principled way. And, where conflict that is virtually unmanageable, or even merely difficult to resolve, does arise (between rights or within a given right) we should expect the use of existing institutional devices and patterns of behavior—at the judicial or administrative level—to resolve these conflicts in a way compatible with the justifying ground of all civil rights, through the preservation within the content of a given rights rule of the principle of mutual perceived benefit.[30]

Now that the possibility of coherence of a given family of civil rights as a set has been affirmed, in part through the workings of the institutional processes of a political society, and the problem of conflict of rights resolved, at least at the level of rules, we are in a position to turn to an issue raised in Chapter 1. For we are now ready to take up the question of what particular institutional processes, if any, are apt in the production of civil rights—that is, in their formulation especially and also in their maintenance and harmonization.

6

Democratic Institutions

IN the previous chapter I argued that the set of universal political or civil rights in a given society is important because it includes all human rights in that society and, more generally, because the set includes many, perhaps most, of the high-level commitments in that society for the well-being of individual persons as individuals. Now, we cannot assume that civil rights will be a feature of every society. So the question naturally arises: What would it take for there to be active universal political rights in a given society?

Clearly, it would take a coordinated set of agencies to formulate, maintain, and harmonize rights. Thus, it would take a government of a fairly specific sort. But what sort? of what form? We are asking, then, whether there are any kinds of governmental agencies that could reasonably be expected to formulate and promote civil rights, that could be expected as part of their *characteristic* operation to produce and maintain such rights.

It would not be implausible to suggest in this regard that democratic institutions are somehow conducive to rights, for many people see a connection here. But the exact relationship, though often thought to be positive, is peculiarly elusive and has remained quite unclear. In what follows I want first to spell out more fully in the present chapter what might be meant by democratic institutions in such a claim and then to show in the next, as precisely as I can, what the crucial relationship is between these institutions and having civil rights.

More specifically, in the present chapter I want to begin by characterizing democratic institutions. Here democratic institutions are identified under three main headings: (1) universal franchise, on a one person, one vote principle, (2) competitive voting, (3) majority rule (understood, in the focal case, as decision making by a majority of first-place votes). Then, I will consider what might justify democratic government (in particular, majority rule) so understood. There is, however, as we will note, a deep ambiguity in the proposed justifying ground insofar as majority rule is concerned, for a variety of disparate kinds of outcome are all supported there. Some plausible move to dispel this ambiguity is required. Accordingly, a decision apparatus is constructed (by reference to the *other* features of democratic institutions) so as to remove this ambiguity (or order these kinds of outcome) and, hence, complete the justification. The leading idea here, which entirely animates this chapter and the next, is that that which *justifies* majority rule—indeed, justifies the whole set of democratic institutions—is what makes democratic government peculiarly conducive to the production of civil rights. Or, to put the leading idea more precisely: coordinated agencies which follow a program of *justified* democratic procedures can be expected, when staying in character, to tend to the formulation and maintenance of civil rights.

1. A CHARACTERIZATION OF THE THREE DEMOCRATIC INSTITUTIONS

The three institutional headings identified in the previous paragraph—for simplicity I will call them the three institutions—do not define practices that would be found in all societies that call themselves democratic today. This is partly because democracy is an essentially contested concept, and there is rivalry about how democracy is properly to be understood.[1] So I hesitate to describe these particular institutions, without qualification, as democratic ones. It may be that they are institutions only of one form, one preferred interpretation of democracy. And even where we restrict ourselves to just the one historic form, as found today principally in Western parliamentary democracies, we learn that these institutions have come to be emphasized, as primary institutions, only in comparatively recent times.

We can see this last point readily by looking at eighteenth-century parliamentary democracy in the United States in contrast to its presentday version. Two main differences would be immediately noted: in the extent of the franchise and in the degree to which the staffing of the offices of government (here restricted to those involved in lawmaking) is to be decided by contested elections. Let me say a word about the first of these.

1.1. *First Institution: Universal Franchise*

Voting in colonial and in early constitutional America was highly restricted. All women were excluded, as were slaves and, of course, children and resident aliens. In short, the situation was not significantly different from what it had been in Athenian democracy during the fourth and fifth centuries B.C. Moreover, where some property qualification was in operation (as it was in most places in the United States), the restriction was quite possibly even greater than it had been in classical Athens.

In contrast, the voting privilege (or franchise) in the United States today is virtually universal. Women now have the vote (a phenomenon largely of this century); there are now no slaves and property qualification has disappeared. For practical purposes, the franchise is coextensive with the class of adult citizens.

Children (that is, all young people below the age of 18) and resident aliens are, admittedly, still excluded. But young people are not excluded once they reach a certain age; then they are included along with everyone else. And resident aliens can have the vote if they decide to become citizens (an option open to most, indeed most all, of them).

For our purposes, we can say that the franchise is universal when all those normally subject to the laws in a given country are able to vote; and where they are not, the exclusion is not invidious and not permanent, for it is not set on grounds of unalterable traits—that is, traits unalterable over time—with respect to any given person subject to the laws. The idea of universal franchise, understood in this way (as 100 percent of those subject to the laws, at least in principle and over time), defines one important institution in contemporary parliamentary democracies.

The idea of one person, one vote is to be understood within this context, for it serves here merely to qualify the notion of universal franchise. It means that each participating citizen has the same vote—one and only one vote—in any given voting round (e.g., a general election) on any given topic (e.g., a particular contested election between two candidates or a yes/no vote on a single proposition, such as a specific amendment to the state constitution). Thus, on this principle any voter (chosen at random) in any given voting district will have a vote-casting capacity identical to that of any other voter in any given voting round etc. for which each is eligible.

The principle of one person, one vote is to be contrasted with plural voting: that is, with the situation as described above except that some voters do have more votes than others—three votes, for example, as compared with someone else's one. Some actual voting situations have come close to plural voting in effect. For instance, Britain ended—but only in 1948—a system of voting (available to graduates of Oxford and Cambridge) which allowed each of them two votes for parliamentary representatives: one as residents of a constituency and one as members of a university corporation that elected its own representative.

Plural voting, though it has been advocated by influential people such as John Stuart Mill, never really caught on.[2] Instead, the notion of one person, one vote has taken hold in all parliamentary democracies today. One can say, loosely, then, that in such a democracy everyone has the voting privilege and they have it equally (no one of them having more votes to cast than anyone else).

There are, of course, other ways to interpret the one person, one vote principle.[3] But I will continue to emphasize this interpretation, in particular, in the account as it proceeds, for it identifies the central case.

In any event, what distinguishes contemporary parliamentary democracy from other forms prevalent today is not the institution of universal franchise, but rather that of contested voting. Indeed, universal franchise is important in our account largely as a backdrop to this institution.

1.2. *Second Institution: Contested Voting*

Contested or competitive voting, on a basis of a universal franchise, is a rather complex idea. For our purposes, three features can be identified as central: (1) there is fairly frequent periodic voting, (2) competition occurs between alternatives in the vote, (3) the alternative selected is the one with the most votes.

Different models can satisfy the idea of contested voting. Let us consider first a simple "direct" model (for example, voting in a club or in a department of a university). Here the voters, acting mainly for themselves and not as agents for someone else, meet on a fairly regular basis to decide issues by ballot. The ballot is itself shaped by preliminary discussion and sometimes by preliminary voting. At each stage people can speak for or against the alternative proposals that are to be voted on. And when the vote is held the alternative with the most votes is the one selected, either to go on to some further stage of voting or to be the final choice.

We might allow the preliminary voting to proceed on a somewhat different principle. For example, in my department a vote is taken on candidates nominated for an annual lectureship. Usually the list is long and names are systematically eliminated by dropping the name with the fewest votes in each round. It occurs, though, that in the final round the alternative selected is the one with the most votes. What is crucial in competitive voting is that this be so. The final choice must go to the alternative with the most votes.

Voting on this model is called competitive or contested for several reasons. Alternatives are on the ballot (and we presume them to be genuine alternatives in the sense that they are different and only one can be chosen). Relevant alternatives can be added to the ballot on the initiative of members. The merits and demerits of the different alternatives are debated and various points of view heard (or at least there is opportunity for them to be heard).[4] And, finally, the alternative with the most first-place votes is selected and the others are defeated. Or, if some sort of weighted vote is involved (taking account of first-, second-, third-place votes, etc.), then the one with the highest weighted total is selected and the others are defeated.

This means that the winning proposal is put into effect or kept in effect (for now at least) and the losing ones are not. The qualification ("for now at least") is added because the decision now made could always, in principle, be overturned or significantly modified at some later point on the same basis, that of contested voting. For it should be clear that the resort to contested voting, as a way to make decisions, is not a one-time thing but recurs instead on a regular basis.

We have now canvassed, if only briefly, the central features of competitive voting. The notion of contested voting is to be understood as defined by *all* of these features. Let us take one further step. When many decisions, including important ones, are made by the procedure of contested voting (as defined), we can say that this particular procedure has been institutionalized. In our account we are interested only in institutionalized contested voting.

So far we have a model, a simple one (that of direct voting on issues or proposals), for institutionalized competitive voting. It is not, however, the model that best fits the case we actually began with, the case of contemporary parliamentary democracy. For one of the distinguishing features of this particular form of democracy is that most of the decisions made by voters, as participants in a universal franchise, are not decisions on issues or proposals *per se* but, rather, decisions on representatives, who then do the bulk of the job of voting and thereby deciding on issues. Even when the voters do decide directly on issues (such as a school closing or a state constitutional amendment or some issue of public policy, e.g., a state lottery or a municipal nuclear-free zone) it is often the case that the issue has already been framed and to that extent determined through debates and votes by those representatives.

In any event, it is correct to say that the voters in a parliamentary democracy exercise their franchise largely by electing or not electing persons as representatives. Thus, in order to accommodate the fact of "indirect" or representative democracy—a fact characteristic of contemporary parliamentary democracies—we need to qualify our simple model.

We could do so by identifying a model with two distinct stages, in the order indicated: (1) the electoral stage, in which voters, on a basis of universal franchise, engage in institutionalized competitive voting in order to select their lawmaking representatives, (2) the lawmaking stage, in which the duly elected representatives, themselves acting on a basis of universal franchise within a representative body, engage in institutionalized contested voting in order to organize their business and to decide policy proposals, public laws, and so on. Insofar as each stage reproduces the leading features of institutionalized contested voting, in a way appropriate to that stage, the elaboration of the simple model to cover the special case of lawmaking by elected representatives does not seem arbitrary.

Of course, we realize that some changes might be made, or thought desirable, once we had this expanded model in view. For example, the electoral stage (if it involved competing parties) might be organized to reflect, in the body of elected representatives, the proportion of votes each party had in the election that chose that body. Thus, the principle that the alternative with the most votes wins (and the others lose) would be modified to say that the alternative with the most first-place votes ends up with the most representatives, and so on, down to the alternative with the least number of votes (which loses out altogether or, if not that, has the least number of representatives). Or proportionality could be allowed to range not over the first place votes but over weighted-vote totals (where preference orderings had been expressed as well). Or some method of selecting individual representatives in individual electoral districts might be chosen, on the principle that the most votes win in any given district. And here some care would have to be taken to see to it that the individual districts were more or less equal in size (so long, that is, as the districts were being conceived of as *electoral* districts and not as something else, as ethnic blocs, for example, or as geographic entities or as "sovereign" states).

But the leading idea in all the cases mentioned is that the lawmaking stage—once the representative body was constituted by election—would duplicate the main features of the simple model (for contested voting) in its decisions about policy and public law. There might, even so, still be important differences between representative lawmaking and direct lawmaking by voters. For example, in a direct democracy voters might stay more involved or become better informed. And their characters might be improved by such active participation (or at least Aristotle and Mill thought so).

In any event, the inclusion of a model for indirect democracy is intended to accommodate the fact that such a model is prevalent in parliamentary democracies today. My aim here is simply to show what would count as competitive or contested voting in such a setting and to show why people in these democracies are inclined, by and large, to regard parliamentary government, when it conforms to the two-stage model I have outlined, as democratic.

1.3. *Third Institution: Majority Rule*

Or, at least, they are so inclined when the institution of majority rule is incorporated into the two-stage model. For it is one of the signal features of contemporary parliamentary democracy to require that the winning alternative in the *lawmaking* stage is to be decided, not merely by the most votes, but by a majority vote—by over 50 percent of the first-place votes of those voting.

I realize, of course, that other patterns of majority—or plurality—voting are possible (for example, using preference scales rather than first-place votes, with first-place votes used to break ties), but I have chosen this one, to fix attention, because it is the one particularly emphasized by advocates of parliamentary democracy. And it does define, to some extent, one of the main strands in the actual pattern prevalent today in parliamentary democratic states.

The important thing to note here is that majority rule, like universal franchise, is intended to qualify the notion of contested voting. Specifically, it identifies and makes more precise the idea of a winning vote. It says that—in a sequence of votes—the final vote, the winning vote, the vote that is put into effect (for now) is to be a majority vote.

And if we followed through on our earlier two-stage analysis of contested voting, we could insert into the electoral stage as well the requirement that the winning vote is to be a majority vote. Thus, we would have majority rule in that two-stage model when (1) the voters select their lawmaking representatives under the requirement that each representative selected is to have a majority of the first-place votes cast in the particular contest in which he or she was involved and, then, when (2) the elected representatives, a working majority of whom have the support of a majority of the *total* election vote cast, subsequently organize their business by majority vote and decide on the final form of laws and public policies, again, by majority vote (by over 50 percent of first-place votes in every case). Thus, the idea of a majority electoral base for any given elected representative translates (by the qualification introduced in [2]) to the representative body as a whole.[5]

Now, quite obviously, it is not the case that important decisions regarding law or policy are always going to be decided within the context of the two-stage sequence just identified. For unelected courts (e.g., the U.S. Supreme Court) and unelected administrators (e.g., the U.S. Federal Reserve Board) often do make important decisions. In order to talk of majority rule in such a situation, we would have to say that most important decisions of law and policy are made in accordance with the model of the two-stage sequence, by majority vote, and that other decisions (by courts and administrators) are subject to these majority decisions.

The notion of 'subject to' here is quite vague. It could mean that the decision of a court could be overturned by a majority decision (e.g., a modified version of a law struck down by a court is subsequently passed, this time with success) or that an administrative agency or a court acts within the confines of a law itself passed by majority vote—or could be so constrained if such a law were passed.

One thing does seem clear, though. The decisions of courts and administrative agencies could not be subject to the majority votes of elected representatives unless there was an appropriate publicity about these decisions. The legislators would have to know, or be able readily to know, what these administrative or judicial decisions were and know—in at least a general way—what was being done by court or administrative officials in order to carry out these decisions. By the same token, if we took seriously the extension of majority rule to include (as it does in the two-stage model) a majority electoral base, then the notion of appropriate publicity would itself have to be extended in that direction. Voters too would need to be in a position to learn about and discuss administrative or judicial decisions and to know or feasibly come to know, in reasonably timely fashion and at least in general outline, what policies and actions had been taken pursuant to such decisions.

Of course, it would be difficult, in advance of all contingencies, to spell out and especially to institutionalize the notion of appropriate publicity; but we often are in a position to know that the notion has not been well served in an individual case. More important, we are always able (given the two-stage model for majority rule) to insist on the importance of the principle of appropriate publicity. I will return to this point again, later in this chapter and in Chapter 9.

In the account I am suggesting, then, we have an ideal model of majority rule—or rule consistent with the principle of majority rule—when (1) the final stage of many important decisions is decided by more than half of the first place votes cast, (2) where those votes are cast by elected representatives who have engaged in institutionalized contested voting at the lawmaking stage and who themselves have been selected, in such a way that the working majority of the representative body reflects a base of majority electoral support, by (3) universal franchise electors who have themselves engaged in institutionalized contested majority decision voting in a prior electoral stage, and when (4) decisions about law and policy not reached as in (1) through (3), for example, by courts and administrators, are subject to those that are.

1.4. *Problems with Majority Rule*

There are many problems with the account of majority rule I have offered, even after we set aside its vague, almost impressionistic character. Let me mention two problems in particular.

First, I have specified that better than half of the first-place votes actually cast is sufficient to count as a majority decision. Why not say over 50 percent of *all eligible votes*?

Take a legislative body with 100 members (e.g., the U.S. Senate). If we specified a vote of better than half of all eligible voters, then every winning vote in this body would require at least 51 votes. But often fewer than 100 votes are cast in a given contest. (Senators are frequently away or they abstain from voting.) It does not seem reasonable to count these nonvotes as, in effect, votes *against*. Rather, the option chosen has been to subtract the nonvotes from the voting pool and to require a decision only by a majority of the votes actually cast. So long as no significant inhibition on voting is imposed on those who take the nonvote route, there seems to be no issue of principle involved. For a vote of more than half of the first-place votes of all those eligible to vote was always a viable possibility.

By the same token, a winning vote of less than half of those eligible to vote can be tolerated at the electoral stage if no significant inhibition on voting was imposed on those who chose or took the nonvote option. For, again, a vote of over 50 percent (of first-place votes) by all those eligible to vote was always a viable possibility; and the decision, then, to go with better than half of the votes actually cast poses no problem of principle.

This is an important consideration when, as is consistently the case in many Western parliamentary democracies, large numbers of eligible voters do not vote in any given election; for here the winning vote, in any electoral contest, is never or only rarely going to be better than 50 percent of those eligible to vote. Accordingly, we will simply specify from now on that any vote—at the electoral or at the lawmaking stage—will be acceptable, under the stipulation of no significant inhibition, if it constitutes over 50 percent of the first-place votes actually cast.

This brings us to the second and more serious problem. For the real problem comes, not in choosing to go with a vote of better than 50 percent of those actually cast, but in making a decision with a mere plurality vote—that is, a vote of less than 50 percent of the votes actually cast. Yet this, in fact, is what the Western parliamentary democracies routinely do at the *electoral* stage. Thus, to take a typical case, candidate *A* might have 48 percent of the vote cast and *B*, the nearest rival, 44 percent. On the principle of contested voting followed in most parliamentary democracies, candidate *A* would be selected—though on a principle of majority rule *A* ought not be.

The thing I just described is not exceptional but is, rather, typical. And, multiplied many times over, it can lead to a mere plurality base, at the electoral stage, for the working majority in representative bodies. Let me be more concrete now.

All contemporary parliamentary democracies operate with political parties. Three main patterns have emerged: disciplined parties in a two-party framework (e.g., Great Britain), loose parties in a two-party framework (e.g., the U.S.), and a multiparty system (e.g., Italy).[6] The problem is that, in each of these cases, events have transpired to make majority rule at the electoral level difficult to achieve. Thus, the party that comes to power through electoral victory in a two-party framework, a frame designed to secure majority rule, is often too loosely organized to function as an instrument of majority will. And, more important, there often is no discernible majority will (since Presidents in the U.S. can be elected, and the majority party in Congress too, with only a plurality of the total vote in an election). Or the party that comes to power may be a disciplined party (as in Great Britain) but quirks of the electoral system and the gradual weakening of the two-party framework has led in these cases as well to mere plurality government, not government that reflects majority support at the electoral level. It may well be that *disciplined* parties (or, to take another case, ideologically oriented ones) in a situation of universal franchise and contested voting at the electoral stage, especially in a class-divided society like Great Britain, naturally tend to a multiparty framework. And multiparty systems are notorious for the fact that no one party has, or even realistically could have, a majority electoral base. The tendency in multiparty systems, then, is to form a coalition government. But the coalition itself does not have—since it is typically formed after the election and was not voted on *as a coalition*—majority electoral support. And, more important, it is possible for coalitions to be formed, as governing coalitions for purposes of making law and policy, even though the parties involved had only a plurality of the total election vote and not a majority.

One might be tempted, given these facts, to see plurality rule in elections as an acceptable alternative to electoral majority rule (as most parliamentary systems do in practice). And it might well be acceptable, practically speaking, if the winning vote was high enough (say, over 40 percent) or runoffs were allowed or parliamentary or presidential elections were held fairly frequently.

Thus, one might be tempted to revise the earlier account of majority rule so that it now reads (1) plurality rule at the electoral stage, (2) majority rule at the lawmaking stage. But such an amendment would run directly counter to the reigning ideology (as distinct from the practice) of all contemporary parliamentary democracies—for that ideology embeds majority rule, specifically, at the electoral level and regards representative lawmaking as peculiarly justifiable for this very reason, that it rests on a foundation of majority electoral support.

This, then, is the crux: the ideal of majority rule, to which all these democracies subscribe, is belied by their consistent inability to put this ideal into play. What we have here is a serious gap between ideology and practice.

Whether this is a cause for concern—and, if so, what should be done about it—is something we cannot yet say, however. For we have not yet determined that majority rule is an ideal that matters, that it is a reasonable or desirable procedure to follow.

Clearly, if it is, then practice would need to be reformed at a number of points—through equalizing electoral district sizes, through changes in ballots and in the way tellers assess returns, through use of runoff elections between, say, the top two vote getters, through submitting coalition governments to electoral ratification, what have you. Even then it may be, since the set of constitutional institutions in any society is very complex, that no perfect coordination of democratic institutions with the other institutions is feasible. So we should aspire, at a minimum, to incorporate improved democratic institutions into the constitution in such a way that majority rule (as *originally* defined, as functioning at both the electoral and lawmaking stages) is more likely, rather than less likely, to occur in a given parliamentary democracy. But we need not, as I have already noted, turn to this question of institutional design until we have resolved the prior question of the intrinsic desirability of democratic institutions.

In this chapter I am discussing one issue only: what might make contested majority rule voting on a basis of universal franchise desirable. I will not be, except incidentally, engaged with questions of institutional design.

I will assume for now, however, that the instinct expressed in democratic ideology is sound—the instinct that majority rule at the electoral level is, arguably, an essential institution among those that go to make up the form of government we call parliamentary democracy. On this conception, then, the set of democratic institutions would define one important aspect, perhaps the most important aspect, of the political constitution in such a society. Here (1) voters, on a basis of universal franchise, (2) engage in institutionalized contested majority decision voting to elect representatives, who (3) subsequently engage in institutionalized contested voting, in a way wholly consistent with the principle of majority rule, to organize their business and to decide on important matters of law and public policy. We would, of course, add the proviso that decisions not reached as in (1)–(3) would be subject to those that are.

This schema, designed to identify the main democratic institutions in a so-called indirect or representative democracy, would have to be modified to be applicable to direct democracy. Here we would simply say that (1') people, on the basis of universal suffrage, (2') engage in institutionalized contested voting in order to decide, but only by majority vote, on important matters of law and public policy, with the proviso that (3') decisions not reached as in (1') and (2') would be subject to those that are.[7]

Thus, if electronic direct democracy ever replaced representative democracy—thereby allowing people (by using home computers or telephone buttons) to vote directly on laws and policies—this is the form it would take.[8] But in either case—that of direct democracy or that of representative democracy—the same institutions would be present in a recognizable and appropriate form: universal franchise (on a principle of one person, one vote), contested voting, and majority rule.

2. THE DESIRABILITY OF DEMOCRACY: A PLAUSIBLE ACCOUNT

Now the problem we have set is to determine why these institutions, in particular, the institution of majority rule, would be thought reasonable or desirable ones for a society to have in its political constitution. Or to pose the issue slightly differently, we could ask, Why might these constitutional institutions commend themselves to people who were already committed, or fated, to living together in a single society in which there would be, inevitably, some rules binding on all? Our concern in such a setting is the rationale for making decisions, under conditions of universal franchise, by contested voting on a principle of majority rule—regardless of whether these decisions are made in accordance with a simple direct democracy model or with a two-stage representative democracy model.

One thing seems clear here: a decision procedure based on majority rule is not designed to secure the interest or the advantage or the maximum benefit of some one particular person, known to us by proper name, or some relatively small groups of such persons. For it is surely too much to expect that, as a matter of course, majority rule voting would routinely support or advance the prospects of that one person or that one group in particular.

More generally, a policy endorsed by majority decision, though it might offer some advantage to any one person *A* or to persons in any relatively small group *A*, would probably be less in the interests of *A* than policies directly tailored to *A*'s preferences or than policies which might be developed if that person or group were acting on its own, in relative isolation or with a relatively free hand. For we expect majority voting to identify and advance interests that are widely, rather than narrowly, shared in the voting population, and to advance these more general interests even where, for any person or group *A* (taken at random), there was some other policy that was more in *A*'s interests.

Majority rule is a mechanism, not of individual, but of *social* choice. It is a mechanism designed to secure general interests, the interests of many people, not the preferred interests of a given individual or of a relatively small group. The question is, Why should a group of people install this decision procedure, rather than some other, for choices involving matters of social or general interest?

2.1. *The Basic Rationale for Democracy*

Rule by a majority of first-place votes is thought desirable, presumably, because it is a relatively stable way of coordinating interests of people in the overall group. In short, the main rationale for contested voting, on a principle of majority rule combined with universal franchise, is that this is a reasonably reliable way of identifying policies or laws that serve interests common to the voters or to a large number of them and, then, of implementing such policies.[9]

The argument in support of this rationale sets out from the claim (presumably intuitively sound) that each voter is, more likely than not, able to judge that a policy or law is in his or her *own* perceived interest. Now, we have no reason for thinking that, when some policy also happens to be in the perceived interests of others, voters would be any less able so to judge. Accordingly, we can extend the claim to cover these cases explicitly. Indeed, that claim might seem even more acceptable when it was focused specifically on shared or coordinated interests, especially those perceived interests that are widespread among the voters.

For here there is no need—or considerably less—for the individual voter to estimate and discount the contrary interests of others. And there is no need, or considerably less need, to calculate over a heterogeneous and potentially divergent set of interests and to engineer complicated majority coalitions from among them (and to continue to effect the tradeoffs required to keep such coalitions together). Here, instead, the discussion of issues would tend to focus on the various widespread interests being served and on the connection of policy with them, and this connection would be brought home to each voter—with the result that the voters would be better informed about the connection in their own case and the identifiable interest being served. Further, we might be inclined to think that the judgment of any given voter is more perspicuous or more reliable when it is able to discern some single policy that served an interest common to all, or one shared at least by a great many.

Thus, we might emphasize common or widely shared interests as a favored case. Here the focal claim would be that any given voter and hence each voter is, better than half the time, reflectively able to judge correctly that a policy or law is in the voter's own interest (as the voter perceives that interest), in particular when the interest is common to all the voters or is shared by indeterminately many of them or can be coordinated with such common or shared interests.

Putting the claim this way seems closer to the main rationale for majority rule as initially set out. And the claim does accurately reflect the democratic ethos, which reposes great faith in the judgment of individual voters in precisely such cases. Whether this faith is misplaced has been a matter for much discussion, for the claim is certainly not *empirically* true of literally everyone in the actual political world. But we need not enter into that discussion here, except to note that the claim in this form—and taken for the most part—is not inherently implausible, especially where the standard of appropriate publicity has been met and voters are reasonably well educated and attentive.

Now that we have these preliminaries in hand let us turn to the main consideration. I will lay it out as a single argument, with two parallel formulations. In the first formulation we assume a probability, for each voter, that the voter is correct more than half the time about whether or not policies or laws are in the voter's own interest (as the voter perceives that interest). For simplicity of presentation we will assume as well that each voter has an *equal* ability to make such a judgment. It follows, then (for it can be shown to follow), that there is an even *greater probability* that the majority of voters will be correct about whether or not policies or laws are in *their* interests—that is, in the interests of a whole group of them, presumably at least a majority.

Certainly, some of the things in the interest of any such majority of voters will be things common to all the voters or widely shared by them. In accordance with the central claim, then, we will focus on precisely such common or shared interests. We take up this particular standpoint—that of the central claim—because it is probably the most plausible way to state the contention at issue. But we should be clear about the point being made here: it is not that the probability value of the social decision is higher in the case of common interests than in the case of a mere majority interest, say; it is, rather, that the claim which emphasizes them (that is, the so-called central claim) is more likely to be true than any parallel claim which speaks simply of majority interests, without further qualification.

This should be obvious for the reason already given, at the beginning of the previous paragraph, that things in the majority interest are often things common to all voters or widely shared by them. It is also obvious because all mere majority interests are actually *included* within the central claim, as but one of several available special cases that it is intended to cover. Thus, as more likely to be true, the central claim is a more acceptable claim; so we reformulate our argument in accordance with it. And this reformulated argument becomes, then, the basic argument.

In this revised formulation, we conduct roughly the same argument, this time starting out from what I have called the central claim. Here we focus, when we make the assumption that the voter is able to judge correctly more than half the time respecting policies or laws that are in the voter's perceived interest, on those interests common to the voters or shared by them or by indeterminately many of them. And we utilize the same simplifying assumption we made in the initial formulation, of an equal probability in each voter's case. It follows, then, that a contested majority vote, on a universal franchise basis, would exhibit an even greater probability than any given voter on his or her own of being correct about policies or laws in the voter's perceived interest, whether that interest is an interest common to all the voters or an interest shared by indeterminately many of them (presumably a majority) or an interest that can be coordinated with such common or shared interests.

Thus, we reach the rationale that majority rule is a reliable and stable social decision procedure to follow when we want to identify, in order to implement, policies or laws that are likely to serve just such widely shared interests, the interests of a lot of people. Namely, interests that are common to all voters, etc.[10]

The point with which I began this chapter—that there is a positive connection between the creation of civil rights laws, on the one hand, and the use of democratic procedures, on the other—is seemingly supported by this analysis. (More, of course, would need to be said, though, to make this particular contention perspicuous and to bring it to conclusion.)

Before we proceed, though, two things about this rationale should be noted. First, it draws on the *direct* democracy model in justifying rule by a majority of first-place votes. And, second, it justifies such rule on *epistemic* grounds. Let us consider these points in turn, briefly.

2.2. *The Compatibility of the Two Models*

Even though the direct democracy model was used in the basic argument, it is not clear that laws and policies would be better under direct rather than indirect lawmaking (each on the same principle, that of rule by a majority of first-place votes) or even that such laws and policies would necessarily be more representative of the public will, or the preferences, of voters. For we can readily conceive a *majority* of elected representatives, in accordance with the central claim, as exhibiting an even greater probability than any given representative on his or her own of being correct about policies or laws in their and the voter's perceived interest, especially when that interest is an interest common to all (voters and representatives) or an interest shared by indeterminately many of them (presumably a majority) or an interest that can coordinated with such common or shared interests. Here, in this indirect democracy version of the argument, the voters are conceived principally as exercising a check on representatives, removing some through electoral defeat and helping others to form legislative majorities through election and reelection.

The same considerations are seemingly at play in elections as were present in voting on policies (at least as regards those considerations that were captured in the direct democracy argument). For it is not implausible to say (especially where the assumptions of appropriate publicity, an educated populace, reasonably attentive voters, and so on, hold good) that individual voters do in fact correlate their interests with policies, as one factor in their decisions about whom to vote for, and do in fact make a rough-and-ready calculation about which candidate is more likely to act or vote in favor of preferred policies, should the occasion arise. Thus, a rough parity between laws and policies approved by a majority of representatives and those approved by a majority of the voters, the benchmark goal, is a viable outcome—indeed, a not unlikely outcome under institutions well designed for achieving that particular goal (and assuming appropriate publicity, etc.).

It is essential to make this very last point, for otherwise any preference for representative government rests simply on practical grounds or reasons of economy. The point is, representative government can be preferred on such grounds over so-called direct democracy, within the confines set by a theory of democratic institutions, only where the benchmark goal is a viable outcome, or can be made so through refinements in institutional design.

Of course, there is one special interest legislators have that may be incompatible with the interests of voters. I mean the desire of legislators (and administrators and judges) to stay in office, to gain special perquisites, and to get big pensions at the public's expense. Many legislators will, in effect, conspire to give advantage to incumbency and to preserve themselves in their positions. The voters need to offset this special interest in incumbency, as best they can, by setting limits on campaign financing (or even by replacing private with public financing), by requiring fair exposure of the main parties and positions and candidates in the media, by setting limits to tenure in office, and so on. The basic incompatibility between legislators' and voters' interests here cannot be wholly resolved; it can only be controlled (to a degree). Institutional design is needed to accomplish this. Though the incompatibility is serious and chronic, it need not disrupt, in any fundamental way, the benchmark goal just described.

2.3. *The Epistemic Understanding of the Basic Rationale*

We turn next to the point that, in the basic argument, majority rule was justified on epistemic grounds. For, as we saw, the main move was from a presumed correctness in judgment on policies, of at least better than half, by *individual* voters to a demonstrated greater likelihood of correct policy judgment by them *collectively*, when they use a contested-voting procedure based on majority decision and on universal franchise. And correctness here means that voters—including here voters in an election or representatives in a policy vote—can perceive when a policy is in their own interest and, presumably, when it is in the interest of others as well. For we do not assume that the voter is any less likely to perceive which policies or laws are in the voter's interest when the voter has an interest in common with, or shared with, many other voters.

This epistemic understanding of the justification of majority rule is in line with the classical rationales offered by Aristotle and Marsilius and Rousseau.[11] And it is quite different from saying that majority rule is justified because it gives more people, rather than fewer, what they want or desire.[12] Or from saying, as did Locke, that the body politic can stay intact only if it moves that way "whither the greater force carries it, which is the *consent of the majority.*"[13]

It is important to be clear also on the argument that supports this particular epistemic rationale or justification for majority rule. The argument is probabilistic in form. The argument, put starkly, is that a probability of correctness, for each individual voter, of greater than half (and for simplicity we assume an equal probability for each voter) would yield a majority rule social decision having an even greater probability of correctness (as to which policies were in the perceived interests of an indeterminately large number of these voters). And it could be shown, further, that the probability value of the social decision will increase with an increase in any (or in two or in all) of three factors: (1) the absolute size of the difference between the number of majority voters and the number of minority voters, (2) the probability of correctness of each individual voter, (3) the size of the majority vote, expressed as a percentage of all votes.

Take just (1) and (3). To illustrate, Brian Barry says:

[I]f we have a voting body of a thousand, each member of which is right on average fifty-one percent of the time, what is the probability in any particular instance that a fifty-one per cent majority has the right answer? The answer, rather surprisingly perhaps, is: better than two to one (69%). Moreover, if the required majority is kept at fifty-one per cent and the number of voters raised to ten thousand, or if the number of voters stays at one thousand and the required majority is raised to sixty per cent, the probability that the majority (5,100 to 4,900 in the first case or 600 to 400 in the second) has the right answer rises virtually to unity (99.97%).[14]

One final point of clarification is in order. The supporting probabilistic analysis here is best understood—properly understood—as *ordinal* in character. Thus, we should say merely that where the probability of correctness of each individual voter is presumed greater than half—i.e., $p(c)$ > 1/2 (and, for simplicity, we assume that the value $p(c)$ is the same for each voter)—then a majority vote yields a social decision $p(s)$ with an even greater probability of correctness, i.e., $p(s) > p(c)$. And, moreover, the probability value $p(s)$ increases here, $p(c)$ remaining constant, with an increase in either (or both) of the factors identified in the illustration just quoted. The important point here is that we need not plug in precise amounts to give a cardinal value for $p(s)$, such as 69 percent or 99.97 percent, or for $p(c)$, such as 51 percent (the percentages given in the illustration above).

A formula, such as the one relied on in the illustration, that included precise evaluations of probability would, of course, support the ordinal claim; thus it can provide evidence for the truth of any such claim. But the ordinal claim does not reduce to any such precise formula nor does it require one. All that is needed to make the crucial probability analysis work is the idea that one probability value can be estimated as greater than another—e.g., that $p(s) > p(c)$—and that one such value can be estimated as greater at one time than it is at another—e.g., that $p(s)$ at $t_n > p(s)$ at t_{n-1}.

The main value of using the ordinal approach is that it captures the important relations but without commitment to precise probability values. For often we have only passable ordinal estimates, that this probability (say, p_1) is greater than that one (say, p_2), but are quite unable to say how much greater it is (as, typically, we are unable to say exactly what the probability of voter correctness is over against the probability of voter error in a given case). Thus, the use of an ordinal analysis is to be preferred to Barry's (and Rawls's) cardinal analysis for the crucial probability values.[15]

In sum, I have distinguished an ordinal from a cardinal form of probabilistic analysis and have indicated that the ordinal analysis is sufficient to support an epistemic rationale or justification for a contested-voting decision procedure that incorporates universal franchise and majority rule. The rationale is that, assuming an equal and better than even chance of correctly judging by each individual voter what policies are in that individual's interest, we can say that a majority decision[16] by such voters would be a reliable and stable social decision procedure to follow when a social group wants to enact policies or laws that are likely to serve the interests of its individual members taken overall, in particular when those interests are common to all the members or are shared by indeterminately many of them (at least a majority), or can be coordinated with such common or shared interests.

We do not, in conducting the argument in ordinal form, desert the fundamental standard of perceived interests; for we still start with the point that each voter is reflectively able to determine, more likely than not, when policies are in that voter's interest (especially when that interest is common to all the voters, etc.) and we still end with the rationale that rule by a majority, as specified (with universal franchise, etc.), is even more likely to enact laws or policies that tend to serve widespread interests—perceived interests—of members of that majority, taken overall.

The rationale here does not involve saying that some *independent* standard (such as the public good or the voter's true interest) emerges in the majority vote. Rather, the same standard operates throughout (that of perceived interests, for each voter, in relation to policies); what changes is simply that majority rule, as specified, provides a higher probability of correctness in such cases—regarding common perceived interests, interests of indeterminately many, and so on—than the presumptive probability of correct judgment by each voter taken one by one. It is this higher probability of correctness, then, that lies at the heart of the rationale for majority rule developed in the present chapter.

3. A DEEP AMBIGUITY IN THIS RATIONALE

There is, however, a significant ambiguity in this rationale, for it covers a range of different possibilities. First, there is an ambiguity in the notion of common interests, interests shared in some common object by *all* the members. Does this 'all' here mean (1) in the interests, or in the overlapping interests, of *each* and all or does it mean (2) in the interests of all—that is, of the corporate *group* of which each is a member—though not necessarily in the interest of each?[17] Then, second, there is a need to distinguish these common interests—as found in (1) and (2)—from (3) interests shared by indeterminately many of the members (presumably a majority) though not by all, interests that may indeed be harmful to the interests of some (presumably a minority). Finally, these interests—as in (3)—can be distinguished into (3a) those interests that are compatible and can be coordinated with the common or shared interests—in (1) and (2)—and (3b) those that are not compatible and cannot be coordinated.[18] So, when we talk of a rationale for a majority rule, it is not evident whether we are relying on (1) or (2) or (3a)—or even (3b)—or on some combination of them. And there may be other ambiguities as well.

Clearly, then, if the rationale is to be meaningful we need some principled way to resolve the ambiguities we have noted. Or, at the minimum, we need some device for ordering these options as features of the rationale for majority rule.

3.1. *Dispelling the Ambiguity: Preliminary Remarks*

I would suggest that one way, perhaps the best way, to remove these ambiguities—or to order them—would be to generate a procedure for assessing the main options from within the notion itself of contested voting on a basis of universal franchise and majority rule. Let me, briefly, indicate the merit of this suggestion.

We might decide to choose between the options by some random device—for instance, throwing dice. Then if, e.g., (3*b*) won the toss, we could say that simply settles it. This is what we are now going to intend with the rationale, and where the interests identified in (2), say, conflict with those identified in (3*b*) in a given vote, we should choose those in (3*b*). Or we could decide to choose among the options by using some property of the voters—for example, the ability to win relay footraces (assigning to each option a relay team representative of the voting population). One could always say about such devices (first) that, insofar as we were trying to refine the rationale for majority rule more precisely, these devices seemed wholly irrelevant or (second) that they simply would not afford a good reason for choosing among options at all—at least not as a general rule. Both ripostes seem wholly appropriate.

One could, responding in the light of these ripostes, say that we should decide among the options by using an acknowledged good reason for choices. Thus, we might turn to utilitarian calculation and presumably choose (2) or possibly (3*a*). Or we could let the Pope decide and probably get (2). Or we might introduce Kantian considerations, about respect for each person as an equal and never treating anyone as a mere means, and decide to choose (1) over (2). And so on.

But we could always say about these devices that they are good ones *if* one is a utilitarian or a Catholic or a Kantian in the first place (or, if the account were extended further, a Marxist, a Hobbesian, a rational choice theorist, what have you). In addition, and more important, it is not clear that any one of these devices is necessarily *the* device one should use in trying to decide about a rationale for majority rule in particular. For none of them has anything to do with majority rule *per se*. And it seems—if we are trying to determine something about what is best intended in the rationale for majority rule—we should find reasons for refining that rationale which are themselves somehow intrinsic or connected to majority rule.

Such a stance would be especially appealing to someone who had already accepted the basic probabilistic argument for the rationale and who wanted now merely to choose between the eligible options as a way of suitably clarifying that rationale. Such a person could regard the issue as one of determining more precisely the purpose or point of majority rule, once the probabilistic argument had set the main options in place. Now it should be clear that such persons cannot rely, in order to solve *this* problem, on the probabilistic reasoning that was originally employed. (For that reasoning incorporates the very ambiguities we are here being called upon to resolve—indeed, they were introduced at the very beginning, in the intuitive claim from which the main argument set out.) So, such persons might think it reasonable as well as most likely to lead to resolution, in determining the principal object to be achieved in a practice, to go to features of the practice itself. In doing so they would try to establish the best *internal* rationale for majority rule.

Rationales of this sort are never conclusive, as we know, all things considered. But they are often a good place to start. And if we then go on to approve or reject internally rationalized majority rule by reference to other standards, we do have some confidence that the things we are here accepting or rejecting are pertinent to the rationale for majority rule in particular.

Thus, we reach again my proposal that the best way to resolve the issue, at least as a first step, is to see if there is something about the practice of contested voting conjoined with universal franchise and majority rule that would allow us to choose among the options or to order them. There is nothing circular about such a procedure, for the main options—as features of the basic rationale—have already been argued for and decided upon on other grounds, and these grounds are not being gone over again.

3.2. *Dispelling the Ambiguity: The Construction of a Decision Apparatus*

Our project, then, is to use the resources of the practice we recounted earlier in this chapter, use them to help us choose between options in the rationale for that practice (a rationale itself independently established). If this revision to our earlier account of democratic institutions is successful (so that the preferred option, or the ordering of options, can be explicitly mentioned in the rationale), we will have a resolution of the ambiguity that has so troubled us. And by building this resolution into the overall account, we will also have the most convincing rationale for majority rule that could be offered from within the perspective of majority rule.

In the earlier account of democratic institutions, two main models were developed: a simple direct model and a two-stage indirect or representative model. Some contrast between direct and indirect democracy is probably in order, but I do not think (as I have already indicated) that the difference is sufficiently great to draw forth any significant difference in principle. For the point, in any case, is that each can be justified in the same way. This is something we will come to see more clearly as we go along.

From these two models we could plausibly construct a single model which abstracts the features that they have in common. For in each model voters, leaving it undetermined whether they are electors or policy makers, engage in a regular and continuing way in institutionalized contested voting on a basis of universal franchise and of majority rule. And the decisions so reached are regularly put into effect; such decisions are the dominant decisions in the example we are focusing on.

My proposal, then, amounts to this: that we take the arena or forum identified by such a composite or abstract model as the framework for assessing and deciding about the main options in the rationale for majority rule. The justifying rationale that emerged, in accordance with this proposal, would consist of the original rationale as modified through the ranking of options, where some or all of them had been determined to be permissible.

Here the choice and ranking of the main options has become, in effect, a feature of the justification of democracy. And the most plausible such justification is the one in which that choice and ranking is done within the forum—the framework and assumptions—of the contemporary idea of democracy itself. I will not attempt to construct this forum in every detail. I will, however, simply call attention to some of its more important features.

Now, the choice in question (the ranking) has to be done by *someone*. For reason, though it may be impersonal, is never disembodied. It requires voice and location. But who are these someones going to be? Who should they be?

They are representative citizens, people who will live under and with the democratic institutions and whose deep instincts have been informed by them. For just as we have specified the composite or abstract model so we can specify (if that is the word) the representative citizen. These are people who have traits that typify main features of that model and who will conduct their reasoning about the options (choosing some as preferred and ranking them) within the confines of those typical traits.

These participants (the assessors) in the arena formed by the composite or abstract model—for short we can call it simply the abstract model—would necessarily have a certain reflexive understanding of themselves. They know, or could come to know, that they are persons and fellow citizens. They know that all the members of the particular political society involved—given the stipulation of universal franchise—could be participants and are to be counted as assessors respecting the determination to be made. (I mean all the citizens except as noted at the very beginning of the chapter—excepting, then, for example, children.) The participants know as well that, in the deliberation about the permissibility and the ranking of the main options, the assessors have an equal status (an equality reflecting the stipulation of one person, one vote and the stipulation of interchangeability).[19] And they know that all the assessors are reasonable beings— that is, reasonable within normal limits. For, according to the stipulation of institutionalized contested voting and of the interchangeability of voters, each participant (each assessor) is presumed able to contribute to the discussion, able to follow it, and able to reach a reasonable decision (as already specified, in the discussion of probabilities) about the main options.

We should note that no radical constraint on the knowledge of the assessors is imposed. Thus, we presume them to know that they have interests and to know, at least in a general way, what their interests are. We can also presume them to know that others have interests as well, some common, some compatible, some incompatible with their own. But, although each is able (more likely than not) to make a reasonable estimate of whether a particular choice (in particular, a given policy) is in his or her own interest, no one is able to predict exactly what decision(s) would be reached by majority vote on a given occasion. Indeed, this is often very unclear. Moreover, matters grow progressively dim where we to put the vote and its ingredients further and further into the future.

The knowledge elements here identified precisely overlap those I identified earlier (in the basic argument) as elements each voter could be presumed to have. In the basic argument, individual voters were deciding, with a better than even probability of correctness, about particular policies, which had definite connections to determinate interests they had; and they were in usable possession (or could be, assuming appropriate publicity, etc.) of relevant local facts and the immediate historical backdrop attendant to the vote on particular occasions. The same could be said for the assessors, as I have just characterized them.

I did not add earlier (as I have now) that the *voters* might be less clear about the connection of their interests to policies in distant and hypothetical circumstances, where local facts could only be guessed at (or were far different than from those at present), where the policies themselves often took some getting used to (for they represented things the voters were unfamiliar with and, accordingly, did not readily understand), and where the historical background, leading from the present to a remote future, was simply missing. Nor did I add that the voters would have an even harder time predicting outcomes of votes in the distant future than do voters respecting outcomes of present votes (where, even so, the probability is presumably not high—perhaps below one-half).

I did not add these things at the earlier point; nonetheless, they are so. If they were added, as they could be (to complete the record), then the voters as earlier characterized (in the basic argument) and the assessors as now characterized would be *identically* described.

I did not add these things earlier (about preferences in distant votes or about the voter's ability to predict voting outcomes, either now or in the future) because they did not seem relevant to the situation described in the basic argument. For the concern there was with an individual majority rule decision on a given occasion about a particular policy (where there was, presumably, a set of determinate options and of first-place preferences and a fairly definite localized and historical setting in which these arose).

But these things do seem relevant to the situation we are here contemplating. For we are now concerned with majority rule as an ongoing practice—concerned, that is, with the *institution* of majority rule itself and with whether it should be restricted on some principle or, alternatively, designed to be wholly unrestricted. (And, for our purposes, majority rule will be regarded as unrestricted if *all* the main options are allowed and no ordering is imposed on them.)

As noted, we do not assume here that the participants (the assessors) will always have a clear idea of the details of their preference scales in advance of the on-site voting contests in which the elements in the scale and the preference order itself become determinate (for the situation we are now contemplating goes beyond the highly localized assumptions of the earlier basic argument). More important here, we now add explicitly that these assessors are unable to foresee the long-term history of contested voting, and thereby are unable to tell what the outcomes will be and, for the most part, how these outcomes will relate to their individual interests. That is, they cannot foresee these outcomes or attendant effects on interests when no ordering constraint has been imposed on majority voting.

But each person involved in this assessment of options within the forum constructed—and this person could be any one of us—is able to imagine what effect a long-term regime of unrestricted majority rule might have on his or her interests in particular, or on the interests of others. And to free each from dogmatic or unthinking slumber, we ask everyone to imagine that they do not know at what point they enter into the continuing sequence of such votes. Thus, each must carefully assess what tendencies a practice of *unrestricted* majority rule might have. Each might reasonably conclude here that such a practice is likely at some point to be inimical to the interests of any given person—certainly to some of that person's interests, perhaps to a great many. And each is able to communicate this assessment to fellow assessors and to expect a considered response. For all know that, unless things change, they must live their lives under the decisions made by a regime of contested voting on a principle of unrestricted majority rule.[20]

The knowledge conditions I have identified in this case are ones I take to be peculiarly characteristic of a continuing but unrestricted scheme of contested voting under democratic institutions. Thus, the abstract model, so like Rawls's model of the "original position" in other respects, is singularly unlike it in the very limited "veil of ignorance" here imposed.[21]

And, of course, the object of the two models is quite different as well. Rawls's original position constitutes an arena for deciding about the principles of distributing certain "social primary goods" through the basic structure of a society, principles chosen from a short list of principles of political justice. My abstract model constitutes an arena for deciding, in a society governed by democratic institutions, about the proper characterization of the rationale for majority rule—through choosing from among options that were ambiguously present in the original rationale for such rule.[22]

Specifically, the object of assessment in the abstract model is to decide about the permissibility and ranking of these options, to determine which options to embed within the rationale for majority rule and in what order.

The main options (and here I simplify a bit) are that the rationale for majority rule is to be understood as affording priority to choices, and ultimately to policies, which are (1) in the interest of each and all, (2) in the interest of the corporate group of which all are members, though not necessarily in the interest of each, (3) in the interests of indeterminately many (presumably a majority) even though harmful to the interests of some (presumably a minority). What has to be decided in the abstract model is which of these options should be preferred. (And if none should be preferred, though all these options are retained, that too is a decision. It is a decision in favor of *unrestricted* majority rule.)

Now, since the options are the ones described in (1)–(3), we need posit no special motivational assumptions about the participants. For any of the three options, absent the claim about priority, is consistent with what any participant could probably tell by introspection about oneself or others—or at least what anybody could tell from the past history of democratic voting itself. I mean each could learn that the participants are fairly self-interested (outside the immediate circle of family, friends, co-workers, and so forth), that the participants prefer to advance their interests rather than not to (especially when there is little or no cost in doing so), that they are willing to live with cooperative arrangements (where all benefit, though not necessarily equally) over Hobbesian state of nature arrangements, and so on.

It would, in fact, be desirable to let the idea of participant self-interest remain sufficiently indistinct so that it directly attaches to no one of these options as preferred. For if it did so attach, then we do not have an arena for decision but, instead, a decision—one that has been built, perhaps arbitrarily, into the motivational assumption. Thus, that assumption should be realistic (for the model) but weak in that by itself it does not determine one of the options as the preferred one.

Indeed, no single feature—not even *all* the features—of the arena should decide the preferred option, as though by logical entailment; rather, it is the admissible arguments which could go on within the forum that should be determinative. Here the participants try to see if some arguments afford considerations that, on balance, decide the issue.[23]

4. THE ASSESSMENT PROCEDURE

Individual persons here are trying to determine what would be a reasonable ranking of the options and, if that could be decided, whether all are permissible as ranked. They make this determination about what is reasonable by assessing which option it is likely the participants would prefer, that is, prefer after reflection on admissible arguments within the constraints afforded by the abstract model, where all are identically situated.

Let me elaborate a bit on the decision procedure outlined here. Each assessor, within the framework described, makes a subjective estimate of which institutional option it is most likely that an individual assessor would come to prefer in light of an estimate of what most others would come to prefer. It is an assessment made in the shadow of the uneasy uncertainty each feels about the success or even survival of the individual's own interests in the face of, or with the backdrop of, a long-term regime of unrestricted majority rule. This estimate, then, comes within the general province of decision theory insofar as it concerns subjective judgments as to preferred outcomes under conditions of uncertainty.[24]

The estimate is, I have emphasized, based at least in part on arguments (though they are arguments yet to be heard). These arguments articulate the principal reasons that could be offered for selecting one option over the other two. When one finds any such argument convincing, it is (in the arena designed) convincing to all, or almost all. Thus, on the presumption that the argument for one option is likely on balance to be convincing, that argument regiments the estimates of the individual assessors into a concurrence of estimates—each estimate reflecting an individual's subjective judgment as to which institutional option it is most likely that that assessor and most others (indeed, almost all) would prefer.

It is the *concurrence* of individual subjective estimates that we are looking for, then; for such concurrence decides the matter. It is the function of the arguments developed in the abstract arena to make for concurrence.

It is wholly reasonable, I think, to refer the assessment, as we do here, to individuals rather than to the collective group. For only individuals can assess. We know of no intelligence—no human intelligence or intelligence comparable to human intelligence—in a group. Thus, the consensus of individuals in a reasonable assessment can be our only standard.[25]

And if we polled people to see if such a consensus existed, we might have a basis for saying that such a consensus did exist, but that poll would be in no way itself a vote. Indeed, we could never reach the required consensus through voting. For no vote, even a majority of first choices or, beyond that, unanimity, could be considered satisfactory until we had first determined the order of considerations within the rationale for majority rule. And this is the very thing we are here called upon to decide.

So we go then to the relevant arguments. I will take these up in the next chapter.[26]

7

Democracy and Rights

I SUGGESTED in the previous chapter that the main priority concern is whether interests in ways of acting or of being treated that benefit everyone have priority over corporate goods or collective goals (such as efficiency or national security or the wealth of a nation and the growth of its GNP) which are in the interest of the body politic of which all are members, though not necessarily in the interest of each individual member. This is an especially significant question to pose because there are, in fact, a good many aggregative considerations which come under the heading of such corporate or collective goods, with respect to which the issue of the priority of individuated interests could be raised. Several are worth singling out for special mention. Besides the ones already named (market efficiency, national security in time of war, overall wealth, and GNP growth) there are such aggregate goods as (1) the self-determination of a nation or a people—a goal much favored in Third World rhetoric, (2) national defense—a value much favored in the rhetoric of the other two worlds during the Cold War period, and (3) things such as roads, parks, urban transportation, measures to prevent ecological deterioration, public safety or order, in particular police protection.[1]

So, the question whether individuated interests have priority over corporate aggregative schemes can be posed over against a large number of eligible candidates. But I do not want to be sidetracked into considering a single one of these specific confrontations, just on its own. In the present account, rather, I want to treat in its most general terms the problem posed and to ask why one kind of scheme—specific individuated interests which are in fact coordinated as a set—might be preferred or given precedence over aggregative schemes of the sort we have identified, that is, over those that are in the interest of the corporate group of which all are members, though not necessarily in the interest of each individual member.

Since, as we saw in Chapter 5, civil rights are public policies in the interest of each and all—policies that establish and maintain identical ways of acting or of being treated that benefit everyone or lead to such benefit—and since civil rights have been harmonized by public agencies to form a coherent package (or, at least, we can assume that a significant effort in this direction has been made), they constitute a proper subset of the sort of individuated interests we are here concerned with. In order to focus discussion, then, we can confine our attention to civil rights in particular.

I. THE PRIORITY OF CIVIL RIGHTS

The main reasons, I think, for according priority to such rights, individually and as a coordinated set, can be found in the following set of considerations. Specific civil rights so harmonized have distributive features which corporate aggregative schemes—or many of them—lack. First of all, not all such aggregative schemes can be individuated, that is, set up to allow for the parceling out of the good in question to individual persons. For instance, there is no clear sense in which GNP or market efficiency could be individuated. We might describe those schemes which in principle lack individuation as *essentially* aggregative schemes; they can be taken as providing only aggregative goods, goods that can (under the characterization they have) be enjoyed only collectively. Any individual effect they have is indirect, incidental.

But other of the aggregative schemes can result in or have direct effect for various individuals. This can be granted even though they have these effects on no certain or definite basis. Thus, a policy of national security in time of war, though it might serve the good of the whole (of which all are members) and might have good effects on the interests of many or even most of its individual members, would surely have bad effects on the interests of some of them (those killed or maimed in the war). Or, to take another well-known example, the achievement of the greatest happiness for the group overall, will have effects—for some good, for some ill—for a whole variety of individuals. But for either of these cases it is never clear in advance, from the relevant principle itself, what the effect would be for any given individual or, for that matter, that there would even be an effect for every individual (and here I have in mind principally just the greatest happiness case). Nonetheless, what is distinctive about the aggregative schemes in this second grouping is that each could, while staying in character, have effects for all or most individuals. For it is part of their intention, unlike the case with the nonindividuated schemes, to have direct, nonincidental distributive effects.

What differentiates a scheme of civil rights even from these latter aggregative schemes, insofar as these schemes can be said intentionally to have distributive results, is that civil rights will have, at least in intention, distributive results for *all* individuals. These results will be of a determinate sort, in a definite amount or at a definite level; and these distributive effects on each individual will be, so to speak, predetermined and on strict principle. It will be the same thing (the maintenance of the same specific way of acting, or the same specific way of being treated) for each and everyone. These ways of acting or being treated, each of them representing (by hypothesis) a mutually perceived benefit, are understood by each individual—or could be so understood, upon reflection—to be for the good of that individual and for all others. So understood, civil rights identify

important interests and the coordinated set of them identifies a major social
commitment—one that is of great importance to the members, each and
every one.

Three points, then, seem particularly relevant here: that civil rights are
individuated (or inherently distributive) in character, that they are
determinate in their distribution, and that they are *important*, in belonging to
the good for each or serving as a reliable means to it. With these three points
in mind as background, were the assessors (the participants) described in
Chapter 6 to consider a coordinated scheme of civil rights in competition
with corporate aggregative schemes, we have reason to believe (given the
three points) that they would prefer it, within the context provided by the
abstract model, over any corporate aggregative scheme.

For a coordinated set of civil rights commends itself to the participants
not only because such rights distribute certain liberties and noninjuries and
services on a principle (of universality and equality) that would be appreci-
ated by these assessors (these participants) in the abstract model but also
because such rights have predictable and desirable distributive effects in
accordance with that principle—effects which could be reliably delivered by
the operations of democratic institutions (and could even be guaranteed
there, *if* civil rights were given priority over corporate values).

What we need to do now is to see whether this brief sketch of the relevant
assessors' reasoning will hold up, as leading to the conclusion that civil
rights, in a coordinated scheme, should be given a certain priority. To do
this we need to add further considerations and thus embed the crucial
stretch of reasoning in a fuller argument. More specifically, what we need to
construct is an argument which deploys the reasons identified—that civil
rights are individuated, determinate, important—in coordination with
main points developed in Chapter 5 (in particular, the justification of equal
civil rights by the standard of mutual perceived benefit and the construction
and harmonization of rights by public agencies) and in Chapter 6 (the
constraints of the abstract model and, in particular, the focus on the long-
run effects of unrestricted majority rule under conditions of uncertainty).

The full argument here, some parts of which are already familiar to us
from Chapter 5, would go roughly along the following lines. It would begin
with the recognition that civil rights—certain publicly established and
maintained ways of acting and of being treated—are important to the individual and the set of them important to the social group. No individual,
thus no participant/no assessor, should be willing upon reflection and due
consideration to tolerate, or to risk, either the entire loss of such ways of
acting, or of being treated, or the unequal specification and distribution of
them.

It might be retorted that sometimes risk taking is reasonable, even in
matters of importance. But in all these cases of reasonable risk taking the
relation of policies to interests can be calculated (using realistic probability

values); the order of individual preferences can then be made determinate, and the outcomes of votes and elections can be predicted within reasonable limits (at least as well as pollsters can do with elections, or legislators can do with votes, that are but a couple of days in the future). None of these conditions hold, for the distant future, in the abstract model. That is, none of them hold in the forum within which the deliberations of the assessors (the participants) occur. Thus, the risk to civil rights here contemplated (by subjecting them to the vagaries of a long term of unrestricted majority rule under these conditions of uncertainty) is unreasonable. No one, not even persons disposed to risk taking, wants to be unreasonable.

The participants or assessors can be presumed to accept the claim (developed in Chapter 5) that ways of acting and of being treated when recognized and maintained are appropriately justified, as rights, by the standard of mutual perceived benefit. Here certain identical beneficial ways of acting and of being treated are to be specified and maintained for everyone. And the participants or assessors are inclined, in the forum created by the abstract model, to disallow risky alternatives. A scheme that allowed such risks, where the risk could be avoided, should be regarded as inferior. It follows, then, that no such scheme (for example, no one of the corporate goods identified earlier) should be allowed to control or override the distribution of civil rights.

Under the knowledge conditions characteristic of the long-run operation of democratic institutions, as set forth in the abstract model (in Chapter 6), the participants or assessors there should prefer equal civil rights and their assurance over any of the corporate aggregative schemes, which are either nondistributive in principle or distributive on an uncertain principle and which, even though uncertain, do presume—at least in effect—to govern the distribution of these mutually beneficial ways of acting and of being treated. Accordingly, the participants (the assessors) should accord a settled priority to civil rights, as a matter of reasoned principle, over corporate goods in cases where considerations of these two sorts conflict, or might conflict.

It would follow also that the participants or assessors, again from the perspective of the abstract model, should give to an egalitarian scheme of civil rights a decided priority (or preferential standing) over corporate aggregative schemes that settled arrangements and made policies respecting *other* social matters (such as a tax policy or an appropriation for roads, bridges, harbors, schools, and so on) so long, that is, as these schemes affected, or likely could affect, civil rights.

In sum, the priority of civil rights holds over aggregative considerations insofar as these considerations concern policies for civil rights directly or concern such rights in relation to other social policy matters. Thus, any corporate aggregative scheme would have to be wholly compatible with civil rights (in the results such a scheme gives).

Civil rights, certain specific ways of acting and of being treated, would be given a standing exemption, individually and as a set, from the discounts that might be imposed on equal civil rights by corporate aggregative concerns. These concerns would yield to civil rights, not rights to them, because the determinate and distributive results of having such a scheme of coordinated rights could then be counted on—and affirmed—by each and all.

The line of argument I have been describing captures what might be called the public reasoning (the discourse) of the participants (the assessors) with one another, when they consider what everyone or most everyone would conclude—hence, anyone *should* be expected to conclude—from arguments carried on within the confines of the abstract model. Would the *private* reasoning (the reasoning in the heart of each) be any different? I think not.

I.I. *Private Reasoning Here*

For each individual in the abstract scheme would privately reason as follows. Each sees the value of the specified and maintained way of acting (or of being treated) for himself or for herself. Each sees as well that the way in question is a good for others also. Each has reason to believe that these two perceptions are mutually shared, by themselves and all the others. Each concludes, then, that if they are to have this good secured for themselves they must acknowledge it and see to its security for all, for themselves and all the others.

If each sees as well that a whole set of such goods is involved, and that trouble must be taken to coordinate them as a coherent set, then each individual sees that—in buying into first one of these goods and then another and finally the whole coordinated set—each individual is buying into a very important arrangement that is for the good of each and all. And each presumably would be willing to enter into such an arrangement, for mutually perceived benefit, if others, for that same reason, are willing also. And presumably all are (given the motivational configuration that can reasonably be ascribed to each, as set forth in the previous chapter).

Let me make this last point a bit clearer. The argument I have just described, the one that goes on in the heart of each, does not depend on *denying* that persons are typically rational maximizers of expected individual utility. Nor, for that matter, does it depend on affirming that they are, either.

The point, rather, is that such maximizers can be brought to see that the 'equilibrium solution' which maximizes expected utility for *each* participant in an interaction, where each takes strategic account of what the other(s) could be rationally expected to do, could have less good results *for each* than would an 'optimal' cooperative solution designed to secure mutual benefit. An equilibrium game—played by absolute maximizers over a re-peated (but finite) series of moves—would end worse for each than a lengthy game in which the participants cooperated for mutual benefit, even though the average of benefits attained by each in the cooperative game is less than the benefit that could have been gotten, if sheer dumb luck (as distinct from tenacious game-theoretical reasoning by X in the face of tenacious game-theoretical reasoning by Y) had given X such a payoff on one or a few occasions in the absolute maximizers' game. The Prisoner's Dilemma, as it is called, is such a game, when played by absolute maximizers; so is an unrelieved Hobbesian state of nature.

A scheme of coordinated civil rights is a cooperative game, if we may call it that for now, in which all participate on terms of mutual benefit (though, as contrasted with possible alternatives, no one of them maximizes expected individual utility). There is no reason a maximizer would be unwilling to enter such a game, however, once it was seen on all sides that absolute maximizers' games are best avoided even by game-theoretical types. Thus, each maximizer would be willing to enter into such a scheme of civil rights for mutually perceived benefit, if other maximizers are, for that very same reason, willing also. And presumably all are (given the motivational con-figuration that can reasonably be ascribed to each, as set forth in the claim that each is a rational maximizer of expected individual utility).[2]

The end result, then, is simply that there is nothing in the maximizer's private reasoning (which is dominated by the conviction that *all* persons are rational maximizers and can be expected to follow game-theoretical reason-ing) that would preclude entering into a mutually beneficial cooperative arrangement of the sort represented by a scheme of coordinated civil rights. (Nothing that would preclude *making* 'the agreement,' as maximizers tend to call it.) Nor is there anything in their private reasoning that would go against the public reasoning (already described) that establishes the priority of civil rights, individually and as a coordinated set, over corporate aggregative goods.

For the rational maximizer, like everyone else in the abstract model, is concerned about the long-run operation of unrestrained majority rule. And here the rational maximizer, like everyone else, is unable to come up with realistic probabilities for outcomes in the distant future and is therefore unable to predict what the consequences of such rule would be for the maximizer's own interests. In these circumstances, putting a priority on some policies (those that determinately serve identical interests of each and all, where such interests are specifiable in advance) would seem as good an idea to the rational maximizer as it would to anyone else.

The characterization of the motivational structure of the participants (the assessors) in the abstract model neither requires that they be rational maximizers nor rules out their being so. Thus, we properly assume that some might be, though we are not required to assume that all or even any will be. In any event, we find that the peculiar motivational structure of rational maximizers does not change the picture, for the participants or assessors overall, as to what each would conclude. Here the conclusion in the heart of each is identical to the conclusion of public reasoning that, between a scheme of civil rights and a scheme of corporate goods, civil rights should have the priority.

As we noted in the previous chapter, any such priority is ultimately to be established by the preferences it would be likely to find, as a matter of consensus, among participants (assessors) who had a view of the overall character of democratic institutions, as expressed in what I called the abstract model. For their judgment about priority would have to be made under knowledge conditions typical of the long-run operation of these institutions, in particular, of the tendencies possible there when majority rule was unrestricted. We can presume the likely preference, should one emerge, to be reasonable under those conditions.

It is worth noting, then, that one and the same priority judgment has actually been reached here—whether the assessors (the participants) asked about what was good for them (and others as well) or asked about what others would likely opt for and, accordingly, what they should opt for (with the result that they should opt for x if others did so as well). This established preference, expressed in either way, is presumptively reasonable and is the basis for a subjective consensus among the individuals in the abstract model. As a matter of consensus, then, the participants (the assessors)—in their job of characterizing the rationale for majority rule—can be expected to give a priority to civil rights, as a proper subset of those policies that are in everybody's interest, over corporate interests.

There is, however, an important consideration which has not yet been made clear—and which, if brought out explicitly at this point, would help make more plausible the priority I have been arguing for. Thus, before we can claim to have reached the point of an established priority for rights, we need to round out more fully our interpretation of the preference that I have argued would emerge.

1.2. *An Interpretation of the Main Priority*

To that end let us suppose that individual civil rights are constructed and the set of such rights configured in accordance with the account given in Chapter 5. Here individual rights would be constructed through partitionings and limitation of scope, through internal modifications made within the content of a right once its scope was determined, and through the assignment of competitive weights.

Now, the important consideration for each civil right so constructed is that it specify a way of acting, or of being treated, that was in the interest of each and all. Thus, the *same* way is perceived by everyone as a benefit, or a part of one, or as reliably leading to benefits for everyone.

But it should be clear, as well, from the argument in Chapter 5, that the formulation of scope for any given right could take account of considerations that were not themselves rights. For example, the right to free speech could be partitioned by constitutional delegates or legislators or judges so that classified information, information which (in the interest of national security) should not be divulged, is permanently excluded as lying outside the scope of free political speech. Or the right of habeas corpus (the right not to be held in involuntary confinement unless charged or sentenced) might be suspended, as happened in the American Civil War, on an emergency basis when the "public safety" requires it "in cases of rebellion or invasion" (as the language of the U.S. Constitution has it). Or, to cite a more general example, a practice like punishment (not itself a right) might in effect restrict the scope of many rights through the establishment of punitive sanctions, any one of which could restrict the scope of some civil rights (as, for example, certain liberties are restricted by imprisonment).

The general principle used in Chapter 5 was that a civil right, as part of the scheme of coordinated equal rights, can be restricted only in such a way that what results is compatible with the central content of that right and is justifiable by the standard of mutual perceived benefit. Thus, any civil right when so restricted by a nonrights consideration must still be something—a way of acting or of being treated—that is in the interest of each and all. And the set of rights, as I argued there, is continually to be made coherent in a way consistent with these main concerns (with the central content of the various constituent rights and with the justifying principle of mutual perceived benefit).

In this context, the procedure of scope adjustment seems relatively unproblematic so long as these main concerns are still well served for the rights involved. Thus, when a nonright element (like national security, say) is acceptably incorporated *within* the scope of a given right, or of several such ways of acting or being treated, that incorporated element is necessarily compatible with the right(s) in question, given the way each such right has now been defined.

But built-in scope adjustments and competitive weightings, between rights and between rights and nonrights, cannot resolve all problems. It is important to see even here, then, that the priority I have argued for—the priority of policies in the interests of each and all and, hence, of civil rights as a set—is not absolute. For there are circumstances in which the priority of individual civil rights would not hold, even after careful scope adjustment and competitive weighting have been given their full due.

In Chapter 5, for instance, the idea of a "constitutional crisis of the requisite kind" (Rawls's phrase) was introduced. In such a crisis—where national survival could not be assured without restrictions—rights as a set and any right within the set could be restricted on an emergency or interim basis, and restricted either equally or unequally. But the correct understanding of such a crisis is not that a corporate aggregate good (here national security) now takes precedence over rights; rather, the restriction on rights is undertaken here in order that rights as a set can survive.

The two social interests, (1) having a set of civil rights and (2) national security, coincide at this point. Thus, it would be senseless to say that rights as a coordinated set have an absolute priority over corporate aggregative concerns, or that particular rights always prevail or always should prevail over corporate goods. There is, then, no all-out priority of rights over such aggregative values.

The notion of a constitutional crisis, as we saw in Chapter 5, is but a special case of a more general principle. That principle was that a given civil right, as part of a scheme of civil rights, can be restricted—on a temporary basis—for a reason that would satisfy the standard of mutual perceived benefit. That is, it can be restricted (usually by action of parliament or the courts) if and only if doing so would likely lead to a more extensive or a more secure set of equal civil rights in the society in question. Thus, any one of these rights, though each is important socially, might yield to restrictions in the interest of a common good or take on secondary status, relative to that good, even *before* we reached a constitutional crisis. But it could do so, given the argument for the priority of rights that was developed in the abstract model, only if doing so served to make the set of rights itself more extensive or more secure—or served, in the most extreme of cases, to assure the very survival of rights as a set. Thus, certain rights might be temporarily restricted, by a curfew or a roadblock, in the interests of making the set of rights more secure. Accordingly, the situations I have described (where particular rights are circumscribed on an interim basis in the interests of rights as a set) are situations consistent with the idea that corporate aggregate goods are never to *supersede* rights.

In short, the restrictions (the partitioning of scope on an interim basis) and the apparent reversal of weight orderings under a situation of constitutional crisis (or under less drastic situations) are consistent with the priority of rights so understood; that is, understood as requiring that corporate or collective goods are not to supersede rights, even in an emergency or other demanding but temporary situation, when rights are constructed in accordance with the principle of mutual perceived benefit and the central content of each has been preserved more or less intact and made coherent with other rights on principles compatible with such benefit. And it is this idea of priority that the analysis (using the resources of the abstract model) is properly said to establish.

Let me summarize this rather complex idea. The priority of civil rights, individually and as a set, is a priority over other normative considerations (specifically over corporate goods, such as economic efficiency or national security or the public safety) that are not rights. And this priority holds except where, in an emergency or other demanding but temporary situation, the interests of rights as a set and these corporate considerations actually coincide (and notions of priority are thereby out of place). Here civil rights can be outweighed by these nonrights if and only if such an outweighing is required on a temporary basis in order to make a given set of civil rights more extensive or more secure or, if need be, to preserve a scheme of civil rights in existence.

In short, in the normal case (that is, where the exception just mentioned does not hold) civil rights, individually and as a set, enjoy a priority over corporate aggregative goods. In *any* case (and not just the normal case), such goods never supersede civil rights.

This, of course, is in sharp contrast to an aggregative theory, which would allow an outweighing, all things considered, on the simple ground that it would increase the general well-being of the group as measured by one of these nonrights normative considerations (and where that increase might amount to nothing more than the increased well-being of *other* individuals). It is at this point that the guarantee provided by the priority of civil rights comes into play: for each individual is assured that the individual's civil rights will not be sacrificed simply to promote the general well-being so understood. This is a pledge that no aggregative theorist can make.

My approach to the outweighing of rights is geared to considerations that are internal to rights (as a set); the other approach is geared to aggregative considerations (to increasing the *total* net benefit of the corporate group as measured by one of these considerations or, alternatively, to increasing the *average* net benefit of members of the group). Not only are outweighings justified differently in these two approaches but also, it is likely, different ones would be allowed by them.

1.3. *A Further Ranking of the Priorities*

Now, let us see if we can extend this priority analysis to a yet another option, one in which we are concerned simply with policies that serve the interests of indeterminately many (presumably a majority), even where advancing these interests harmed the interests of some (presumably a minority). In order to distinguish this case from the one already canvassed, the case of corporate or collective goods, let us specify that the total number of people helped or harmed by such policies is considerably fewer than the total number of citizens and that the interest at stake is not a matter of corporate or collective good.

We might, then, call these newly identified interests *partial* aggregative interests (to distinguish them from the corporate aggregative interests discussed earlier). As examples of policies that served these partial aggregative interests we might have in mind such things as a policy on once-a-week closings that favored some (those who wanted Sundays off) but not others (those who wanted Saturdays off) or zoning (that is, land- and building-use) laws that helped some (residential occupiers) but hurt others (persons who had to give up business uses of their homes, for example, a microcomputer business service offered by a handicapped person) or a tax law that allowed interest deductions on home mortgages, even mortgages on *second* homes, but not interest deductions on car loans, consumer credit, etc., thus favoring some (home owners) and hurting or ignoring others (renters).

I think it could be shown that the participants (the assessors) in the abstract model, having regard to the long-run operation of democratic institutions and with a constraint on majority rule already established (one that gave priority to civil rights policies over corporate goods policies), would be likely to opt for the priority of civil rights over things in this particular set. For, presumably, what would justify preferring a mere majority interest—a partial aggregative interest—over a minority interest is that doing so would increase overall well-being or, at least, yield a greater number of satisfied than of dissatisfied people. But this rationale would form the very ground for preferring civil rights policies to such mere majority interest policies.

The reasoning would go as follows. If the set of civil rights has priority over aggregative well-being when all or almost all citizens are taken into account it would continue to have it when only some citizens, albeit a majority, were. And since the total or average amount of aggregative well-being (otherwise unspecified) did not outweigh the set of rights, or outweigh individual rights, in our earlier analysis of rights in relation to corporate goods (except where such outweighing, on an interim basis, made the set of rights more extensive or more secure or, in the extreme case, preserved the scheme of rights during a constitutional crisis), so the total or average amount of aggregative well-being identified by policies that served partial aggregative interests could not possibly outweigh the set of civil rights, or an individual right, in a situation where no issue of constitutional crisis or these other mitigating circumstances could even arise. And since the number of people satisfied (over against those dissatisfied) would always be greater when the interest involved was an interest of each and all, as measured against any partial aggregative interest under this third option, it follows that policies in the interests of each and all—hence, civil rights as a set— would always take precedence over these interests—that is, over any policy that served a mere majority interest while harming or not helping some minority interest.

The reasoning I have identified here becomes wholly persuasive once one recalls that it occurs within the confines of the abstract model among participants (assessors) who are concerned, not with deciding specific policies on determinate occasions, but solely with the question whether to restrict majority rule or leave it wholly unrestricted and who have already decided in that regard to give priority to one option (civil rights) over another (corporate aggregative interests). Thus, considerations that applied to this earlier priority choice would presumptively apply now to a choice between civil rights and yet a third option (that is, between civil rights and partial aggregative or mere majority interests).

In particular, under the knowledge conditions characteristic of the long-run operation of democratic institutions, as set forth in the abstract model (in Chapter 6), risk taking with civil rights, given their already established priority over corporate goods, simply would not be reasonable. The same three considerations that swayed the participants or assessors in their initial deliberation (as regards the preferred outcome in a competition of civil rights with corporate values) are still present. For it remains the case that (1) the relationship of policies to interests (in this case, partial aggregative interests) cannot be calculated for the distant future (using realistic prob-ability values); and that (2), absent such calculations of well-being, the order of individual preferences cannot be made determinate; and, finally, that (3) the outcomes of distant votes and elections cannot be predicted within reasonable limits, or even close to such limits. Thus, the risk to civil rights here contemplated (by again subjecting them to the vagaries of long-run unrestricted majority rule under these same conditions of uncertainty, and for an even less compelling purpose than in the initial case, where the pursuit of corporate goods was the end in view) is simply unacceptable.

I will not argue, but I think it could be shown in roughly the same way, that a corporate or collective interest would also have priority over third-option interests. Thus, we can say that a definite order of options would very likely be selected by the participants (the assessors) in the abstract model, where the long-term operation of democratic institutions was under con-sideration and where the knowledge conditions typical of that operation were appropriately invoked.

1.4. *The Order of Priorities: a Summary*

Applying this analysis now to the focal issue and very point of the abstract model (the rationale for majority rule), we would say that majority rule is justified because it is a reliable and stable social decision procedure to follow when a group of people living together on a more or less permanent basis wants to identify, so as to implement, policies or laws that are in the follow-ing order of priority: (1) in the interest of each and all and, where (1) is satisfied or, alternatively, not at issue, those that are (2) in the interests of the group of which each is a member (though not necessarily in the interests of each) and, where both (1) and (2) are satisfied or, alternatively, neither is at issue, those policies that are (3) in the interests of the majority though not in the interests of the minority.[3]

This analysis would also allow us to remove an ambiguity that figured in our earlier account of third-option interests. For sometimes the interests hurt under this option (always the interests of a minority) are not interests of each and all or interests of the corporate group. The priority ranking I have identified would include such a possibility. But if the interests hurt here are in fact interests that come under either (1) or (2), then this would not even be allowed—given the already established priority of the first and second options over the third. Thus, the only policies permissibly involved in option 3 are those policies that are compatible with policies under the first two options—that is, only those policies that concern (3a) interests the helping or hurting of which is compatible with serving interests under (1) or (2). Accordingly, packages of interests (where the interests, say, of group *A* and of group *B* are supported by a majority coalition of *A* and *B*) are allowable on this account, if they conform to (3a).

In summation, the ordering of permissible options in the rationale for majority rule, put in terms of the interests involved, is (1) over (2) and (1) or (2) over (3a). But some policies—policies that concern (3b) interests the helping or hurting of which is incompatible with serving interests under the first two options—would be ranked last and ruled impermissible by the participants (the assessors), under the constraints of the abstract model.

Using the same reasoning already deployed, I think a further priority could also be established: the priority of the first two options—(1) civil rights and (2) corporate goods—over some kinds of rights. I have in mind here rights that are not universal, rights that are not the rights of each and all, hence rights that are *not* civil rights. These are partial rights, rights that are rights of some only (analogous to the partial aggregative interests already discussed). Among such rights, for example, would be rights that attach to a particular role (like the tenure rights of college and university faculty) or rights that are grounded in some localized and partial undertaking (like the contractual rights of factory workers in industry *C* or in plant *D*).

If we designated the interests served by partial rights (which could, of course, include some legal rights) as (4), we could complete our priority rankings, schematically, when put in terms of interests, as follows: (1) civil rights interests over (2) corporate aggregative interests and (1) or (2) over (3a) partial aggregative interests and (4a) nonuniversal rights that are compatible, or compatible on most occasions, with (1) and (2). But no priority holds, however (or at least none has been established), between the interests in (3a) and those in (4a). Finally, noncompatible interests of either of two sorts, (3b) partial aggregative interests and (4b) nonuniversal rights, would be ruled out as impermissible.

The priority of civil rights holds, then, over other normative considerations, specifically over nonrights—corporate goods, such as economic efficiency or national security, and mere majority interests—and over rights that are not universal. And the priority over corporate normative considerations holds except where, on an interim basis (as given in an emergency or other demanding but temporary circumstance), the interests of rights as a set and these corporate considerations coincide. In short, in the normal case (that is, where the exception just mentioned does not hold) civil rights, individually and as a set, enjoy a priority over all the normative considerations or goods just named; in any event, such goods should never supersede civil rights.

This more extended priority schedule represents the conclusion it is likely the participants (the assessors) would come to in the end; it is, in effect, a settled consensus within the forum established by the abstract model, given the arguments that would go on there. Thus, this extended conclusion, this particular consensus, is to be built into the rationale for majority rule.

1.5. *The Completion of the Rationale for Majority Rule*

For, as I argued in Chapter 6, the choice and ranking of the main options becomes, in effect, a feature of the justification of majority rule, indeed, of democracy itself. And the most plausible such justification is the one in which that choice and ranking is done within the forum of the abstract model, within the framework and assumptions of the contemporary idea of democracy itself.

Thus, the rationale for majority rule (and, hence, of democratic institutions themselves) necessarily includes those restrictions on majority rule that could be established (if any could be) on the balance of reasons, by according a priority to some of the available options over others. The final justifying rationale for majority rule, then, would consist of the original rationale (concerning the aptness of democratic institutions for picking out interests common to indeterminately many—at least a majority—or even to all) as modified through the ranking of options.

Now, there are in fact other priority rankings that would be established as well (for example, the priority of corporate aggregative goods over mere majority interests). But the *main* ranking established is that policies in the interest of each and all—hence, civil rights individually and as a set— should have priority in the normal case over other norms, over norms that served the corporate or collective good or mere majority interests but were not themselves rights and over rights that were not universal.

It is necessarily the case that this main priority, established in the abstract model, would constrain majority rule. Otherwise, if majority rule remained unrestricted, this and the other priorities could not be observed, for policies could not follow them.

Accordingly, when the participants (the assessors) establish priorities, focusing as they do on those interests shared by the voters or by many of them or that can be coordinated to create a package of interests approvable by indeterminately many of them (presumably a majority), then such an establishment of priorities, within the confines of the abstract model, comes to the same thing as reaching the well-reasoned conclusion that majority rule should be restricted. It amounts to an acknowledgment, on grounds provided by the idea of democracy itself, that the operation of democratic institutions must be permanently constrained; these operations must, if they are to stay in character with their own justifying rationale, observe the established priorities.

At this point we have come to the end of a long argument, one that stretches back into Chapter 5 and that has occupied our attention through all of Chapter 6 and all the present chapter up to now. It is time, then, to determine how things stand overall and to take stock of important implications.

2. THE COORDINATION OF CIVIL RIGHTS AND DEMOCRACY

Perhaps the main conclusion in Chapter 5 was that active civil rights must be formulated (carefully constructed), maintained, and harmonized— harmonized, that is, if such rights are to form a coherent set and if internal conflict within given rights is to be avoided. Agencies are required, then, to formulate, maintain, and harmonize civil rights, and these agencies must be themselves well coordinated if the job of harmonization is to be accomplished.

But what agencies? In Chapter 6, it was suggested that democratic institutions—universal franchise (on a one person, one vote basis), contested voting, majority rule—constituted a coordinated set of institutions and that these institutions had a built-in tendency to be productive of civil rights (and to see to their maintenance and harmonization). This suggestion, then, was fleshed out in two stages. First, it was shown, in Chapter 6, that the operation of these institutions was especially prone to identifying and implementing laws and policies that serve perceived interests common to all (or almost all) of the citizens or that serve perceived interests or packages of interests suitable to indeterminately many (at least a majority) of them. And, second, it has been shown, in the present chapter, that democratic institutions, insofar as they stayed in character (as determined by what would justify them), would not only produce civil rights (as the argument in Chapter 6 had led us to expect) but would also accord a decided priority to such rights, to policies in the perceived interests of each and all, over policies that served the corporate good or that served a mere majority interest. Policies of these latter two sorts would never be allowed to supersede civil rights.

Thus, the main line of argument in these chapters has allowed us to reach one important conclusion. We have determined that what civil rights require for their completion—that, is, agencies to formulate, maintain, and harmonize rights—can be supplied by democratic institutions. For these institutions have (as the combined arguments of Chapters 6 and 7 show) a peculiar aptitude to produce and implement and harmonize civil rights when they operate in a way appropriate to that which most plausibly and convincingly justifies them in the first place.

The discussion of democratic institutions, though it did have this drift, was equally concerned with a problem of its own—the problem of justification. For democratic institutions, like all other institutions, require justification. The argument respecting justification proceeded here on a quite distinctive track from that of the rights discussion. At least, we can distinguish and even separate these tracks once the whole argument of the chapters has been laid before us.

On this distinctively democratic track, the democratic institutions themselves were first introduced and described (in Chapter 6) in such a way as to indicate that they, centering as they did on the practice of institutionalized contested voting, constituted a coherent set. Then, still in Chapter 6, the main line of their justification was set forth, focusing on the characteristic aptness of these institutions, in their operation, to produce laws or policies that serve perceived interests common to all of the citizens or to many of them. This particular justification probably marks common ground for all the defenders of democracy, but it was seen to be in the line of one important democratic tradition especially, the tradition of epistemic justification, if I may call it that, which runs from Aristotle through Rousseau to the present day. There was, however, an important ambiguity in this justification which required resolving.

Thus, in Chapter 6, an arena for resolution was created by abstracting a single composite model from features common to both direct and indirect democracy. This model, which I called the abstract model, was to provide a forum for arguments which, if any one could be established on the balance of reasons, would remove the ambiguity and thereby help constitute the most plausible or convincing justifying rationale for democratic institutions that could be afforded within the perspective of the idea of democracy itself. The arguments themselves were then developed in the first section of the present chapter.

Let me emphasize again that what is distinctive about this whole line of inquiry concerning the justification of democracy was that it was conducted on terms peculiar, not to rights, but to democracy. Indeed, it was *wholly* independent, insofar as the descriptive characterization of democratic institutions and the argument about aptness and the formulation of the abstract model were concerned, of the rights material that had gone before (in Chapters 2 through 5).

Now, I grant that the arguments developed in the present chapter, designed to resolve the ambiguity by establishing certain priorities, did refer in fact to civil rights and did say that they were determinate policies that specified identical ways of acting or being treated for everyone and did say that such ways were justified by the standard of mutual perceived benefit. But the governing argument here would have had the *same* content and the same force if civil rights had not been mentioned under their proper name at all.

To see this let us restate the argument, briefly. The restatement would frame the issue in terms of determinate specifiable interests of each and all the members and would then argue, just as I did earlier in this chapter, for the priority of such interests over corporate interests of the whole (of which each is a member), etc. Here the argument would show, to be precise, that that which justifies a majority rule principle in decision making would also serve to prescribe and undergird and give priority to the tendency to produce rules of precisely the sort identified: rules that specify and maintain certain identical policies which could, upon reflection, reasonably be seen to be for the perceived benefit of each and all.

Then, once this argument had gone through (with *no* mention made of civil rights and their peculiar pattern of justification), we could have turned to a second issue. What sorts of things exemplify interests of each and all justifiable by mutual perceived benefit? For these would be the *kinds* of things that had the priority just established. At this point, both civil rights and, presumably, individuated public goods (such as clean air or water and measures for public health) could have been introduced, as exemplifying such interests and as having thereby the already decided priority over corporate interests, etc. It should be clear, then, that in principle the argument about the justification of democracy could have been made *wholly* independently of the earlier characterization (in Chapter 5) of civil rights and their justification.

Using two distinct tracks of inquiry, as we have done (if my restatement of the argument for justifying democracy can be credited), allows us to reach two *independent* conclusions. Each conclusion is noteworthy on its own, but that they converge is even more striking. For converge they do.

Consider. We have seen, first, that civil rights require something (an agency or set of agencies to issue and apply and harmonize them) which democratic institutions, acting as a coordinated set, can supply. And we have seen, second, that democratic institutions require something (a principle of justification that itself makes sense from the perspective of democracy) which civil rights, as a proper subset of interests of each and all justifiable by mutual perceived benefit, can supply.

There does seem to be, then, a deep affinity between the idea of civil rights, individually and as a set, and the idea of democratic institutions. The main strands of the two arguments—one concerned with civil rights and their requirement of agencies to produce them, the other concerned with democratic institutions and their requirement of a plausible and convincing justification—turn out to be mutually supportive. The two strands are connected; accordingly, they can form a coherent system, with two elements, individual civil rights and democratic institutions.

The foundational justification of the elements in this system is, if anything, more unified than my account has yet made clear. For the two distinctive tracks of justification meet at a single point and merge there with one another.

The primary standard (in Chapter 5) for justifying civil rights, individually or as a set, was mutual perceived benefit. Thus, each way of acting or of being treated was identically the same way for everyone and that way was itself said to be a good for each (or a part of a perceived good) or to be a reliable means to such a good.

Then, in Chapters 6 and 7, the justifying rationale for majority rule (indeed, for democratic institutions as a set) was said to include the idea that such institutions tended to produce (among other things) and should give priority to policies specifying ways of acting or of being treated, identically the same way for everyone, that were themselves a perceived good for each (or part of it) or a reliable means to such a good. Thus, mutual perceived benefit—regarding ways of acting or of being treated, ways that are identically the same for everyone—underlies *both* civil rights and democratic institutions as the justifying rationale of each.[4]

This is a remarkable conclusion and it could only have been established, independently for these two concerns, where each was considered on its own, without presupposing the other. It is, I think, this unity of the justifying grounds together with the deep independence of each consideration from the other in reaching their respective justifications that allows us to form out of these factors one system with two distinct elements: (1) individual civil rights which have a standing priority, individually and as a set, over other normative values and (2) democratic institutions which tend to produce and maintain and harmonize policies of exactly the kind in question (universal political or civil rights) and which tend, when acting in accordance with that which justifies them, to accord priority to such rights over aggregative goods and over rights that are not universal.

For purposes of ready reference I think it would be useful if we had a specific name for a system of precisely the sort just described. I will call it a system of rights.

Let me add one further clarifying remark before I turn to the issue of main implications that I see in this system, as it has been developed to this point. It is important to interpret my claim about the relationship of democratic institutions to civil rights in the correct way.

3. A FINAL CLARIFICATION ON THE RELATIONS OF DEMOCRACY AND RIGHTS

I have not claimed that having democratic institutions is *necessary* to the production of rights. For, to cite one significant counterinstance to any such necessary relationship, the emergence of a form of civil rights (in the seventeenth and even eighteenth century) antedates in fact the full bloom of democratic institutions, as understood in the contemporary idea of democracy.

I call these early rights a 'form' of civil rights rather than simply civil rights because, though rights of all citizens, they are not universal within the body politic. Consider here the permanent exclusion, from the right to vote, of women (and of slaves in the U.S.) described in Chapter 6. Further, the famous rights of the U.S. Bill of Rights are universal in description, true enough, but they are rights of all persons (*excepting slaves*, of course) *only under federal law*; they are not legal rights, given the first of those italicized qualifications, of literally all persons. The important point here is that such rights as these *antedate* democracy.

Thus, insofar as we concern ourselves with some sort of historical relationship between democracy and civil rights, it is probably best to say simply that the two tend to go together. An insistence on civil rights (or even on a form of such rights) will often lead to democratization (as it did in the U.S. in the late nineteenth and in the twentieth centuries, when civil rights began to emerge in their full universality). We should not forget, though, that there were already independent tendencies in the direction of democracy, for example, in American colonial history and in the Lockian Declaration of Independence, as Tocqueville and Lincoln so ably pointed out. A reliance on well-conceived democratic institutions, by the same token, would tend to lead to the production of civil rights and to their priority over other normative considerations (as one might hope would happen in the 1990s and thereafter in the emerging post-Soviet bloc in Eastern Europe— though, again, one should not ignore the importance of existing independent trends in the direction of civil rights, piloted in this case by the UN's Universal Declaration of Human Rights and by the Helsinki Agreement of 1975 and by widespread criticism of the civil rights record in Eastern Europe in the era of Soviet domination).

This is the sort of tentative empirical or historical conclusion that my analysis would seem to allow for. In allowing even for this, we must remember that we are talking about tendencies and are abstracting a small number of institutions—civil rights as a set and the democratic institutions—from the constitutional and social context in which they occur in actual political societies. Any conclusion stronger than this tentative one, at least for now, is quite unwarranted.[5]

I have not claimed, then, that democratic institutions are the only way to produce rights or even that they are the best way. Rather, I have said merely that incorporating democratic institutions within a political society seems to be conducive to establishing rights for individual persons—not this person or that, but individuals across the board. I have claimed only that we can presume the operation of democratic institutions, taken on their own and over time, to have a decided tendency to be productive of determinate civil rights (and, as well, of policies for the corporate good and of policies, or packages of them, that further the interests of many) and, if that operation stays in character (by remaining true to its democratic charter), to accord a priority to such rights. On this account, accordingly, democratic institutions are conceived simply as providing a stable and reliable way to identify, in order to implement, civil rights and these other policies and as having, as determined by what could most plausibly *justify* majority rule from the perspective of democracy itself, a peculiar compatibility with civil rights in particular. For these other policies should not be allowed to supersede rights.

Given the intrinsic affinity set out here, we would expect democratic institutions to work at constructing rights, to give them shape by push and pull, but not to invade rights in a tyrannical way. Of course, this tendency to produce (among other things) civil rights and to protect them would not hold if the majority did whatever it wanted, whenever it wanted to. But if the majority stays within the confines already identified, as determined by what would justify democratic institutions, then it will take as its object the issuance of no rules incompatible with existing civil rights rules.

It is widely believed, though, that a dedicated majority—availing itself of the operations of democratic institutions—could win its way, over time, regardless. And civil rights, at least one or two of them, might fall. It is not clear, either, that a mere correct understanding of the relation of justified democracy to civil rights (even an understanding that was generally and expressly acknowledged) or the widespread having of good public habits by citizens (a sense of cooperation, civility of discourse, respect for others) will be sufficient to protect rights. For sound information is always a scarce resource, debate is often uninformed and the voters inattentive in any case, people do differ in good faith about the facts and about the tendencies of policies, special interests are unavoidable and have their weight, passions often run high, situations (sometimes amounting to emergencies) require immediate response. And education, in any event, is rarely up to snuff in matters of public philosophy.

The question of institutional set-up in a system of rights arises, then, inevitably. How can democratic institutions be kept on track in such a system, kept in line with their justifying rationale?

4. AN IMPLICATION FOR INSTITUTIONAL DESIGN

Attempting to answer this question, even in a sketchy way, takes us to the first important implication of my account of a system of rights, as it presently stands. We turn, then, to its implication for what might be called institutional design.

In a political society of the sort we have been discussing (that is, one describable as a system of rights), it would be correct to say that civil rights, individually and as a set, were politically fundamental in that society and, in that way, constituted part of its body politic or "basic structure" (in Rawls's sense).[6] In such a case, then, I think it would be proper to use the terms 'civil rights' and 'constitutional rights' more or less interchangeably.

Equally, the main democratic institutions—universal franchise, contested voting, majority rule—would also belong to the constitution or basic structure of that particular body politic. Thus, civil rights and democratic institutions, mutually coordinated in the ways I have indicated, would be among the institutional essentials of a system of rights. This much seems clear from what has gone before in the present chapter.

Now, I have argued that, in a system of rights, a *justified* majority rule would not infringe civil rights in a tyrannical way. This claim is compatible with—indeed, licenses—saying that an unrestricted majority rule (one that did not observe the constraints imposed in the very justification for majority rule) might violate rights and would need to be restrained. But such restraints, in a system of rights, would necessarily have to be compatible with justified majority rule itself—given that majority rule is an institutional essential there.

In order to gauge the character of the restraints that might be imposed here, we can take a brief page from American constitutional history. This will allow us a preliminary look at one sample of institutional design and an opportunity to consider what other institutional essentials there might be, besides the two already identified (that is, besides the set of civil rights and the three democratic institutions).

One of the important themes in the *Federalist Papers*, a series of essays published in support of ratifying the U.S. Constitution of 1787, is set out in paper no. 10 especially. Here it is argued that representative democracy, unlike direct democracy, would not readily succumb to the disease of majority faction (that is, to class-interested majority rule which is contrary to and invades the civil rights of some). But, though more compatible with such rights in point of practice, representative democracy has some tendencies to the same abuse and therefore needs additional controls.[7] At least, this is a reading that could plausibly be inferred here.

External checks, checks over and beyond those afforded by the representative principle, are required to keep majority rule from mischief. The authors of the *Federalist Papers* suggest several such checks: bicameralism, separation of powers, federalism (all found in no. 51), judicial review or the power of courts to declare laws unconstitutional and therefore void (found in no. 78). Later, in 1791, the American founders added a Bill of Rights to the U.S. Constitution. So we can include such a device on the list of external checks.[8]

Now, I am not inclined to differ so much from the institutional design afforded by the American constitution as from the historic rationale offered for it. That rationale, repeated by many subsequent writers down to the present time, is that majority rule is inherently inimical and threatening to civil rights in the long run and that specially listed constitutional rights and the other devices mentioned are needed as *external* checks (that is, anti-majoritarian checks) to majority rule.[9]

I find this rationale, despite its widespread currency, somewhat puzzling in view of the actual history of the U.S. Constitution. For, first, the Constitution itself was ratified by special conventions, voting on a majority rule basis, in the several states; second, every amendment has been passed, on a majority rule basis, by the Congress of the United States and, ratified, almost every one of them (again on a majority vote basis), by the legislatures of three quarters of the states. Thus, the rights in the Bill of Rights are themselves there in virtue of a sequence of majority votes.

Moreover, one could not adhere to the conventional rationale if one took account of the argument of the present book, in Chapters 6 and 7. For institutional design in a well-ordered system of rights proceeds, according to that account, from the principle of an essential *harmony* between democratic institutions (including justified majority rule) and civil rights. It proceeds, then, from that starting point to the creation of appropriate devices (e.g., majority rule lawmaking on a majority rule electoral basis) which generate, among other things, civil rights. And it proceeds from that same starting point to the creation of appropriate devices (e.g., a constitutional bill of rights or the practice of judicial review) which help preserve the essential harmony between justified majority rule and civil rights.

On the account I have been suggesting, then, these latter devices are to be regarded, not as antidemocratic or 'external' to majority rule, as they are in the conventional view, but, rather, as essentially democratic. The question is not whether they check majority rule (for, in a scheme of justified democratic institutions within a system of rights, democratic majority rule must be checked); the question, instead, is to determine the end served by such checking devices. If that end is to restrict majority rule so as to preserve civil rights—to accord them priority, in the normal case, over other considerations (such as the corporate good or mere majority interests)—then these devices cannot be antidemocratic. For they are helping carry out the proper purpose of democratic institutions, that is, their purpose as determined from within the perspective of democracy itself. And, necessarily, they would have to be justified in accordance with the *same* principle(s) by which majority rule is itself justified.

Of course, I leave it open whether existing institutional devices that check majority rule (devices such as judicial review) can in fact be justified on the grounds identified. The historical record would indicate that many of them have actually been justified that way, as protective of civil rights, or could plausibly lend themselves to such an interpretation—as, for example, the history of judicial review since the Fourteenth Amendment (1868) could probably do. (And Dworkin's name, especially, is linked with this particular view of the justification of judicial review.) And I leave it open whether other institutions, that is, other than the ones historically identified, could also play the role of democratically justified institutional checks on majority rule—play it as well as these more familiar ones have done or play it even better.

It is not, however, an open matter that *some* of the checking devices in place in the Constitution of 1787 (designed to control or replace majority rule at the electoral level) do run against the grain of democratic institutions and have, rightly, been rejected. I have in mind the election of U.S. Senators by the legislatures of their respective states rather than by the voters directly (rejected in the Seventeenth Amendment [1913]). And other checking devices would be rejected, if the occasion ever arose. For example, the electoral college method for choosing the President would, I believe, be jettisoned if the college ever again selected a President who had failed to gain even a plurality of the popular votes cast in the election.

In sum, the account I have developed (in Chapters 6 and 7) constitutes a very different—a radically different—way of looking at the relation of majority rule to individual rights than is afforded by the standard or conventional rationale, the rationale of an inherent conflict between majority rule and universal political or civil rights. My principal point here has simply been to suggest that another reading, alternative to the reading of these institutional checks offered by the conventional rationale, is available in the theory of justifying democratic institutions that has been offered here in these chapters; that, and to propose these particular institutional checks as examples of the sort of thing needed in order to keep democratic institutions on track.

Accordingly, if there are such institutional checks (as there would need to be) and if they are justifiable in accordance with the *same* principle by which majority rule is itself justified, then they too would be numbered among the institutional essentials in the typical constitution of a system of rights.[10] It follows that the main priority rule for civil rights would undergo an important modification in light of this analysis of the institutional essentials in a system of rights.

For civil rights—themselves institutional essentials in such a system—would not have priority over the *other* institutional essentials, where these essentials had the job either of producing civil rights (as do the democratic institutions) or of protecting them (as do such checking devices as judicial review). Here civil rights would have to be compatible with these other institutional essentials (just as these institutions would have to be compatible not only with civil rights but with each other as well).

Accordingly, if we were to speak of civil or constitutional rights in the way just indicated (as institutional essentials within the constitution of a well-wrought system of rights) we would mean that such rights, individually and as a set, (1) are compatible with the rights-producing and rights-protecting institutional essentials and (2) had a standing priority, at least within a certain domain (the public domain), over other normative considerations—over aggregative nonrights (such as the corporate good and mere majority interests) and over rights that were not universal.[11]

5. OTHER IMPLICATIONS

Now that I have addressed the first important implication of my analysis—the implication for institutional design, as just summarized in the revised version of the main priority rule—let me turn to certain other implications of the account of democratic institutions that I have offered in Chapters 6 and 7. Three strike me as worth mentioning, two of them relatively minor—or at least fairly obvious. Let me take these two up first.

5.1. *Two Minor Implications*

First, just as a majority in a well-ordered democracy cannot justifiably act against specific civil rights (as might happen in a racially or ethnically divided society) so it could not justifiably act against civil rights as a set, by ruling them out altogether (as might happen in a misguided society that tried to combine majority rule ideologically with fascism or with some familiar forms of socialism or of theocracy). The majority could not justifiably do so because, in accordance with what most plausibly justifies majority rule in the first place, any such course would simply be unjustifiable.

Nor, second, as in one of the so-called paradoxes of democracy, could a society decide by majority vote thence to end democratic majority rule forever.[12] Democratic majority rule requires continued, across-the-board contested decision making, on a regular basis, in accordance with majority rule and on the basis of universal franchise.[13] For it is a *set* of institutions that has been justified, when majority rule is justified. And majority rule could act against these other institutions, with which it is itself implicated in its justification, only in an unacceptable way.

These two implications, as I said, seem fairly straightforward. However, there is another implication, by no means obvious, that is both puzzling and important. And I will conclude my discussion of democratic institutions—and of their justification and of the place appropriate to them in a system of rights—by taking up this second important implication of my argument in the present and the previous chapters.

5.2. *The Tendencies of Democratic Law*

What I have in view can be sketched in lightly by considering one claim in particular. I have argued, at several points in these two chapters, that democratic institutions afford a stable and reliable way of developing policies that identify, in order to implement, civil rights and certain other policies. And the reason I have given for this claim is that we can presume the operation of democratic institutions, taken on their own and over time, to have a decided tendency to be productive of determinate civil rights (and, as well, of policies for the corporate good and of policies, or packages of them, that further the interests of indeterminately many—presumably a majority) and, where that operation stays in character (by remaining in line with its own justifying rationale), to accord a priority to such rights.

The problem, as I see it, is that this characteristic tendency to produce civil rights is only a tendency. Thus, in a society that incorporates democratic institutions nondefectively, a given majority vote—intended to identify a civil right (or to specify it further)—is a good way to proceed toward this end, but we cannot count on it to reach that end, always. This result is not surprising in view of the essentially probabilistic reasoning used to support the grounding rationale itself, that is, the epistemic rationale for democracy set forth initially in Chapter 6. At best, then, we can view any *given* vote (of the sort just described) as affording a presumption—a rebuttable presumption—that the way of acting or being treated, identified in a majority rule policy (where the intention is to implement that policy), is one that is in the perceived interest of each and all, at least over time and given experience and reflection.

Even so, we must realize, it is unlikely that *all* the rights established by majority vote are in fact justifiable by the standard just cited. The unlikelihood is, perhaps, not great; there are, moreover, ways to reduce it even further.

One of the stock (and even popular) justifications of democratic institutions is that they have a built-in tendency to correct their own mistakes. It is not meant that these mistakes are corrected through the checking institutions (like bicameralism and presidential veto or judicial review); rather, the contention is that contested voting on a principle of universal franchise and of majority rule *itself* has a tendency, over time, to correct its own mistakes.[14]

Thus, something adjudged a civil right of property at one time (like the right of owners to retrieve their property in slaves, as in the Fugitive Slave Law passed by the U.S. Congress in 1850) is determined at another to have been in error and thereby corrected (as it was in the Thirteenth Amendment [1865], the first of the three Civil War Amendments, passed by a majority of the two houses of Congress and by the ratifying action of legislative majorities in at least three quarters of the states).[15]

Still, the point remains that many *new* civil rights (say, the right in 1965 of travellers in the U.S. to stay in an inn without regard to such matters as their own race or color, a right established the previous year in the Civil Rights Act of 1964) have not been subject to these processes of self-correction. And it is these civil rights, the new ones, that are often the most controversial and divisive at any given time—and that are most called into question, as regards their justification.

One could reply that nothing is perfect and that democratic institutions, though they do have the problem just alleged (about new rights), are ones to stick with. For they do have a self-correcting tendency over time. In an imperfect world, where one nonetheless wants to take civil rights seriously, it is best to rely on democratic institutions now and in the long run; for their operation is likely, given this factor of self-correction, to *minimize* the likelihood that policies identified as civil rights are not in the perceived interest of each and all. Or, at least, they minimize it for long-established rights (like those in the body of the Constitution, for example, habeas corpus, or in the Bill of Rights or in the Civil War Amendments of 1865–1870, or the right to vote, found *both* in the body of the Constitution *and* in subsequent amendments).

This reply is wholly plausible. So we can incorporate and give it emphasis in our account of democratic institutions, thereby adding the factor of self-correction over time as yet another way that democratic institutions can stay on track, so as to produce and preserve civil rights.

6. SOME TROUBLING CONSIDERATIONS

But even when such incorporation has been duly noted, it is troubling to find that there are yet other considerations which continue to cast doubt on the pronounced tendency of democratic procedures to enact laws that embody civil rights justifiable by the standard of mutual perceived benefit. I want to turn now and address these troubling considerations directly.

6.1. *Cyclical Majorities*

Perhaps the most troubling consideration is provided by the notion of cyclical majorities. Suppose there are three policy options (or three candidates for office): A, B, and C. It is possible, then, that the voting population is divided as to its preferences, when expressed in a series of pairwise majority votes, in the following way: $A > B$, $B > C$, and $C > A$.

This pattern is often described as the "voting paradox," another paradox of majority rule, for it suggests that each of the options is preferred by a majority vote over at least one of the others but that there is, and can be, no majority of first-place votes for any of the options over all the others. Thus, a majoritarian method for determining policies (including civil rights policies) would seemingly fail in such a case.

The cyclical pattern is not really a paradox, however. Such a pattern is more than a mere logical possibility; it actually occurs, or can occur.[16]

The question we must ask then is, What effect would the possibility of cyclical majorities have on the analysis of majority rule developed so far in the argument of Chapters 6 and 7? That is, what effect would it have on the use of a majority of first-place votes as the decision procedure in cases of public policy?

A first answer would be, very little. For, in the account I have given, majority rule was conceived as operating in two distinct contexts, either as (1) a choice between two options or as (2) a choice between more than two. Here a majority of first-place votes would be decisive, and determinative of a given policy vote or election, if and only if, (1) between two options (say, A and B), there was a majority of first-place votes for one option (say, A) or, if and only if, (2) among more than two options (say, A, B, and C), there was a majority of such votes for one of them (say, [a] A over B and C jointly or, alternatively, [b] A over B and A over C separately).[17] On this rather particular understanding of majority rule, then, the problem of cyclical majorities would not even arise.

An aside. Pairwise voting, as in (2[b])is not the typical or prevailing pattern. Rather, the usual move in a parliamentary setting is to start with a policy that is deemed popular (and therefore likely to succeed) and, then, to discuss it, modify it through redrafting and, occasionally, through formal amendment, and, finally, to vote it up or down. Thus, policy decisions (of the sort we are concerned with here) are typically made at the legislative stage by an absolute majority vote, usually in a form that is more like (1) above, or like (2[a]).

Interesting variants are possible here. For example, some pieces of legislation are very complex and a bit heterogeneous; they are called 'omnibus' bills; in such cases it is possible that no part of the bill might command majority support, but the entire bill does. For another example, so-called log rolling allows voting tradeoffs and thereby achieves over time something of the same effect as the omnibus bill; thus, the first bill through the hopper, though it does not command majority support on its own, might garner enough additional support to pass—on condition that original supporters of the first bill also support a *second* bill which, though it too would not have commanded majority support on its own, does gain through the tradeoff enough additional support to pass. And so on. Again, policy decisions (of these sorts as well) are typically made at the legislative stage by an absolute majority vote.

But things do not always follow the path described, that of an absolute majority vote. Thus, cyclical majorities are possible. In the event that one did emerge (among, say, three options, A, B, and C), or we had the strong suspicion that it had (a suspicion that could be tested for by pairwise voting), we would simply say that here there was no majority decision. Or, better, we would say that the majority was indifferent as between these options.[18] And the body would pass on to other matters, where there was a majoritarian preference for one of the options. Or it would wait until a positive majority decision did emerge in this rather singular case. For the point is that in a majoritarian scheme, strictly conceived, positive decisions are taken only by a majority of first-place votes in accordance with the two patterns (called 1 and 2 above).

It is wholly appropriate, when discussing a theoretical system of political institutions and concepts (such as a system of rights), to use such strong or ideal-type notions as this one, of democratic majority rule, and to rely on typical or prevailing patterns. After all, if our project is to determine why decision making by a majority of first-place votes is thought peculiarly desirable, we should canvass that issue (as we have in Chapters 6 and 7) by looking at majority rule fairly strictly understood. The conclusion we have reached, following this procedure, is that majority rule (understood as positive decisions made by majorities) is desirable because it has a certain tendency.

This conclusion is not upset by the possibility of cyclical majorities. For where this possibility is realized, positive majority decision making, strictly understood, has not occurred. Indeed, the realization of either possibility, that is, either a cyclical majority or a positive majority decision (strictly understood), excludes the other. Accordingly, such cycles can never disable the tendency attributed to majority rule (so understood), for the two things are wholly independent of one another. Necessarily, then, the tendency operates only when cyclicity is not present. This would seem to settle matters rather conclusively, then, for the theoretical system of political institutions and concepts we have been discussing (namely, a system of rights).

The only real question remaining is whether such cycles might frequently be present. This issue, as I've indicated, does not arise at the level of ideal theory (which is concerned with other sorts of problems—normative or evaluative ones). It arises, rather, as a matter of fact in the real political world. For the problem here is that the occasions on which a positive majority decision obtains (and cyclicity is correspondingly absent) come nowhere near exhausting the occasions on which decisions are taken by voting, either electoral or legislative, in *actual* parliamentary democracies. The real issue, then, is that these democracies would encounter the problem of cyclical majorities—or would be likely to, were they to tally revealed preference orderings among the options by allowing pairwise voting (when there are more than two options).

Why so? Largely, because (as already described in Chapter 6) such democracies typically utilize the procedures of mere plurality rule at the electoral stage. The existing ethos in these polities is to allow mere plurality decisions at that stage (as the U.S. and Britain do) or, beyond that, to operate with a multiparty system and coalition governments (as Italy characteristically does—as indeed most of them do).

Moreover—because voting procedures, both electoral and legislative, are as they are in actual parliamentary democracies and because the phenomenon of low voter turnout is pervasive in many of them—the presence of cyclical majorities is usually effectively concealed. Accordingly, it is hard to say how often they do occur.

Not very often, I would suspect (at least where majority votes are taken rather than mere plurality ones).[19] Even so, we can suppose there was in fact a cyclical majority on some issue in one of these states, a cyclical majority that was there but was hidden from view by the electoral or voting procedures followed. And suppose as well that the vote in question did issue in an *apparent* positive majority decision and did involve an attempt to establish a particular way of acting as a civil right. What should we conclude about a putative right so established?

We should conclude, I suggest, that here universal franchise contested voting on such a defective foundation, as in this case, was not a *stable* way to identify (in order to implement) civil rights policies. Nor was it a *reliable* way to do so. We would not, in this kind of case, have even the presumptive basis, accorded majority rule in the strict sense, for saying that a legally enacted civil right specified a way of acting which was justifiable as being in the interest of each and all.

6.2. *Strategic Voting*

There is, besides cyclical majorities, yet another problem that can bedevil the theory of democratic voting and of majority rule. I have in mind here the problem of so-called strategic voting.

In strategic voting, an option once defeated (by a majority vote) is eliminated from further consideration. Thus, the order in which options are taken up could make a difference to the final outcome.

For example, if a pattern of cyclical majorities existed and one option could be eliminated by the first pairwise majority vote—say, B is eliminated (because $A > B$)—then C would necessarily win (because $C > A$), even though a majority preferred B over C. Clearly, given such a pattern, it would behoove partisans of C to eliminate B by strategic voting (by getting the eliminative pairwise vote between A and B placed first in the order of voting). Likewise partisans of A or of B would have their own strategic orderings in view.

Other patterns of strategic voting are possible than those given by cyclical majorities.[20] But in all cases strategic voting seems objectionable where the outcome of majority voting is determinable simply by the order in which the votes are taken. And we would conclude the same thing about any putative civil right so established that we had concluded earlier: that, in this kind of case, universal franchise contested majority rule voting on a principle of strategic voting was neither a *stable* nor a *reliable* way to identify, in order to implement, justifiable civil rights policies.

Cyclical majorities and, especially, strategic voting are not matters peripheral to the main line of argument in Chapters 6 and 7. They cut, or at least strategic voting can cut, into the fundamental epistemic justification for majority rule and into the role assigned majority rule of being especially conducive to the establishment of civil rights.

In addition, they help show clearly, along with the essentially probabilistic reasoning that supports the epistemic justification itself, that the real-world operation of parliamentary democratic institutions is an inherently imperfect way to realize that very thing which it is presumably a principal object of those institutions to achieve, the formulation and promotion of civil rights justifiable by the standard of mutual perceived benefit. They make the satisfaction of this goal one or two degrees less sure than it was at the beginning of the discussion, where we recognized that the operation of democratic institutions merely *tended* in a certain direction. For that tendency is now seen to be even less reliable—though not markedly so, I would add—than it was at the point we began.

Thus, even if we waved aside *any* weakening of the tendency noted, say, by ruling cyclical majorities out of bounds in an idealized account of the operation of democratic institutions, that would not avail in the end. For we would still have to face up to such weakening in situations where electoral and legislative voting actually counted for something. We would still have to deal with it in the real-world attempt of people, on a basis of electoral pluralities, to use democratic procedures to make laws, in particular, laws that identified and gave priority to civil rights policies.

7. MOVING TOWARD A PRUDENT RETRENCHMENT

In confronting this problem it would be foolhardy, though, to give up on real-world democratic procedures in the role assigned, that of producing and protecting rights. Or, to be precise, it would be foolhardy to give up here on the aptness of the institutional essentials (of the sort found in a system of rights) for establishing and maintaining justifiable civil rights.

For the historical record, such as it is, seems to show that civil rights and parliamentary democratic institutions do often go together. And the checking institutions, while themselves imperfect in their operation, do seem to stop some ill-conceived majority actions and do seem to afford long-term protection for some rights, once these rights have passed the double test of being proposed by legislative majorities and of surviving initial scrutiny by the checking devices.

Of course, some ways of acting or being treated that arguably would be in the interest of each and all might fail of legal enactment, and some that did secure legal enactment might not meet the standard of according benefits for everyone. But the self-correcting character of democratic procedures would work, over time and given experience, to reduce such likelihoods.

Thus, we might not ever be in a position to say that literally all civil rights policies are in the interest of each and all, but we do have adequate evidence for saying that many long-established civil rights, assuming here that a highly concurrent favorable social opinion exists in their case, are justifiable on the regulative standard of mutual perceived benefit.[21]

The prudent course, then, in the light of these considerations, is to qualify the claim that democratic institutions afford a reliable way of identifying, in order to implement, justifiable civil rights. Clearly, they are a way of doing so which it is *reasonable* to rely on at least in the case of long-established rights. (And if this so, then it is also reasonable, in a scheme of democratic institutions, to accord priority to such rights.)

Moreover, we can say, more generally, that democratic institutions (including the checking devices) do afford a reasonably reliable way—given time—to identify, in order to implement, justifiable civil rights. That they constitute an imperfect procedure, given the probabilistic undergirding of the epistemic justification and the uncertain footing afforded by cyclical majorities and strategic voting, is also clear and needs to be kept in mind.

But none of these grounds for imperfection are grounds for abandoning the democratic institutions in their assigned role, certainly not with regard to long-established rights. Even beyond such rights, the better project, rather, is to try to perfect parliamentary democratic institutions, to improve them by moving them in the direction of their own internal goal (as given in the model conception of a system of rights). That is, by moving these institutions toward the goal of achieving a rough parity between laws and policies approved by a majority of legislative representatives and those approved by a *majority* of voters; and within that, the goal of underwriting at least the matters of main priority, or a significant subset of them, with a strong social consensus.[22]

Now that a case has been made for the crucial tendency of democratic institutions even in the face of these troubling problems, it is easier to consider some of the less troubling matters often alleged against majority rule, in its role of producing civil rights. Two of these are worth mentioning briefly.

8. A FINAL REFLECTION ON DEMOCRATIC RULE: TWO CRITICISMS

Rousseau (and many others) have alleged that individual voters (especially in cases of the "will of all," the bad form of majority rule) often had their own personal interests in view, in voting, when they should have had only the public good or general well-being in view (as they do in "the general will," the good form of majority rule).[23] Thus, we cannot expect majority decisions to tend in the direction of general well-being when such wrong attitudes prevail or are very common.

But Rousseau's criticism is not well put, for he systematically failed to distinguish, within the general well-being or public good, between the good of each and all and the corporate good. If he had made the distinction, it would not have seemed plausible to say voters should disregard their own interests, where these interests were those of everybody individually. Moreover, given the extended priority rule adopted in the present chapter (in which priority was accorded the interest in civil rights and the interest in the corporate good over those mere majority interests compatible with them), it is not *per se* wrong for voters to consider their own personal interests, so long as these do not supersede everyone's interests in civil rights and the corporate good. Finally, the focus in the model conception of a system of rights has been, quite properly I think, not on the mind-set of individual voters, but on the *institutional* essentials (the democratic institutions, including the checking devices, and the priority of civil rights) in the context of which majority rule occurs. Or to make the same point differently, majority rule is more likely to stay on track with careful institutional design than it is by relying, primarily, on the goodwill of individual citizens and on public spiritedness (as Rousseau seemed to do).

Now we go to a second criticism of majority rule in its role as producer of civil rights. Some writers (Rawls is one) allege that the Black–Condorcet analysis requires, in order for majority decision to fill the role assigned, that the votes of the different voters be independent (that, in effect, the voters exhibit independently formed judgments and, accordingly, that they be uninfluenced by one another). Unless each person casts something like an independent vote, the objection continues, we cannot expect the majority sum of such votes to tend in the direction of the well-being of each and all. Unfortunately, the criticism then concludes, such independence sets a requirement impossible to be met.[24]

I do not find such an independence requirement in Black's account. And Condorcet says here simply, "We shall suppose that none of the voters influences the vote of others and that all express their opinion in good faith."[25] His remark could mean simply that others do not influence an individual voter illicitly or coercively, that is, in such a way as to undermine good-faith voting. The independence requirement baldly stated (as the noninfluence of one voter by others) is not, in my judgment, essential to the acceptability of the Black–Condorcet analysis.

It is not, in any event, an underlying assumption of the operation of democratic institutions in my account of a system of rights. Nor should it be; for, after all, one of the staples of the democratic tradition I have emphasized (the epistemic tradition stretching from Aristotle through Marsilius and Rousseau to the present) is that discussion and argumentation are a necessary part of the practice of contested voting.

The requirement Rawls takes exception to (as being unrealistic) would, as he notes himself, have the consequence of ruling out these very features. Clearly, something is amiss here. Rather than require the voter's wholly independent judgment (as though voters were "windowless monads") a sounder account would require, negatively, such things as the absence of force, fraud, intimidation, and bribery in the influence one voter can exercise upon another (which is what Condorcet could plausibly be taken to have meant) and require, positively, such things as an educated electorate and appropriate publicity. These things point to both a more plausible and a more realistic sense of voter independence.[26]

Thus, if these things are in fact required by my account, as they are, that account is not undermined by the alleged unrealism of its assumptions. The account is robust at that point (in the economists' sense of robustness). And we can look to institutional design, of the sort found in an actual parliamentary democracy, to build in or help build in such things.

Neither of these rather brief criticisms (the one bearing on voters having their own perceived good in view, when they should have only the common good in view, the other on an alleged requirement that voters exercise a wholly independent judgment) has material weight against the claim, developed in Chapters 6 and 7, that democratic institutions operating in a well-designed constitution are apt to produce, protect, and promote civil rights. But the earlier criticism (adducing cyclical majorities and, especially, strategic voting) does have some weight here. It must be considered. For it does show that this aptness, this tendency of democratic institutions, is an imperfect one at best and, indeed, that this tendency is less reliable than one would have concluded simply from noting the essentially probabilistic character of the tendency.

We have come now to the end of this long discussion of the relationship of democracy and civil rights. And we have examined two important implications of this relationship: (1) that institutional design restricting majority rule and of a quite definite character is necessary in a system of rights and (2) that the tendency of democratic institutions, so enframed, to produce civil rights is a reasonably reliable but imperfect one.

At this point we are ready to consider the further implications of this account of democratic institutions, within a system of rights, this time for the conduct of individual citizens there. In particular, we must consider whether we now have a reasonable basis for saying that citizens in such a system should comply with laws duly issued (or at least comply with those that are civil rights laws).

I shall turn to this issue in the next chapter.

8

Allegiance and the Place of Civil Disobedience

I HAVE argued, at several points, that for any given theoretic system of political institutions and concepts there is correlated to the rule-issuing authority in that system an appropriate allegiance on the part of citizens, some peculiar standing of the citizens toward the laws issued in that system. For the allegiance of a typical citizen, when acting in character in a given system of political institutions and principles, will vary from one system to the next. Thus, in Plato's State of the Guardians (*Republic*, books 3, 4, and 10) it is likely to be one thing, but in a system of rights quite another. I want to consider in the present chapter, then, the main lines of the case that can be made for saying that the citizens of the country do have a special standing (an allegiance) toward the laws in a system of rights and to determine more fully the character and ground of that allegiance.

I. THE ISSUE OF ALLEGIANCE

By 'political allegiance' I mean to include, among other things, consideration of what is often intended by the phrase "one's obligation to obey the laws." I have several reasons for preferring the term 'allegiance' over the more conventional 'political obligation'; let me begin by sketching them briefly.[1]

First, as we saw (in Chapter I), obligation tends to suggest a very strict tie between a citizen and the laws of the land; the suggestion is that the citizen is tightly bound to obey those laws. Allegiance, however, carries no such suggestion; rather, it connotes merely that the citizen has some special or characteristic standing with respect to the laws of the land (of that person's own country, in particular) but there is no suggestion of one's being tightly bound or tied to obedience—as though disobedience were categorically ruled out as impermissible. Second, political obligation is often construed (as it was by T. H. Green, who introduced the term) as one's *moral* obligation to obey the laws of the land.[2] But allegiance, on the contrary, carries no such freight, for it makes no suggestion that the matter of one's standing with respect to the laws is primarily a moral matter. Finally, many philosophers (e.g., Rawls, Hart) distinguish between obligation and duty.[3]

Having an obligation implies, for them, that one has voluntarily taken on that obligation through some sort of (morally approvable) transaction—a promise, for example, or an agreement. But duties, in contrast, imply no such voluntary transaction; thus, one might (as a child, or even when one becomes an adult) have duties to one's parents without any suggestion that these are based, or based primarily, on a voluntary transaction of some sort on the child's part. Allegiance, however, can accommodate either of these versions of being bound and, hence, is especially serviceable for this reason as well.

I do not want to be misleading here. When I talk about the typical or characteristic standing (the allegiance) of the citizen toward the law, in particular respecting whether the citizen owes compliance or not, I mean that person's institutional standing or expectation of compliance as determined within that system. Or, to put the point differently, the notion of allegiance is meant to capture an individual's proper standing, given the political practices and conventions of a society of a particular kind. Political obligation (if I may use that term) is one's institutional obligation within a particular political system.

I do not, however, deny that any such institutional standing can be subject to moral scrutiny (under some general critical principle of morality like that of the greatest happiness principle of the utilitarians, for example). My point, simply, is that the moral evaluation of this standing (and of any institutional duty of compliance) will include a moral evaluation of the character of the laws involved and, more important, of the system of political institutions and conceptions in which such laws occur and by reference to which they are initially justified. Thus, it is not law *per se* that is the object of moral evaluation but, rather, it is laws as typical of a given political system. One might say, then, that the locus of moral judgment is the whole system; here the citizen's institutional duty toward the laws (and ultimately the citizen's allegiance) stands or falls with the whole system of which it is a part.

Thus, the specific issue we are addressing is the character of the standing of the citizen in a system of rights toward the laws (and we assume that citizen to be a typical citizen in a system of rights). Here we are trying to determine, simply, what is the presumed proper way for such a citizen to act with regard to valid or duly enacted laws in such a system, in particular, the civil rights laws. And we go to the system itself to determine what is proper. Then, if we can make that determination respecting the citizen's allegiance (or standing toward the law, especially as regards conformity to law), we are free to go on to ask whether allegiance as defined in such a system could be morally endorsed by standards of critical morality.

The procedure here, in particular on this last point, is not the standard one in traditional political philosophy. Rawls, for example, contends that the citizen's duty to obey duly enacted laws in a well-ordered society is a special case of that citizen's natural duty (of justice) to support the institutions of a just society.[4] I would argue against Rawls that the institutional duty to obey rights-defining and rights-maintaining laws, presuming it can be established, would not presuppose the duty which Rawls takes as primary here, the duty to support *just* institutions. I say this because the former duty is established principally by reference to the notion of a system of rights and that idea has not itself been certified as morally correct or just.

Indeed, the independent establishment of a system-specific duty is actually crucial here, for unless we can show that support by the citizens is implicated in the features of the relevant institutions, we have no basis for saying that these institutions require anything of the citizens. Thus, if there were no settled expectation of citizen compliance with the laws in light of the institutions involved, then there simply could be no relevant expectation on their behavior at all, hence no expectation that would exist specifically when these institutions are just.

Rawls has conflated two distinct issues, that of our institutional duty as citizens in, say, a system of rights with that of our moral duty to support such a system *if it is just*. I have already argued (in Chapter 1) that a traditional external grounds analysis, of the sort Rawls gives us here, ultimately forces the conclusion that citizens have no normative requirements on their conduct to obey laws *qua* laws. Thus, if we could not develop a coherent account of the citizen's institutional duty toward the laws, then the very problem we began with, the problem of one's moral duty toward laws *qua* laws, would not even arise. In order to avoid such an unwelcome denouement and other philosophical difficulties as well, the proper procedure is first to take up the institutional duty of the citizen in a particular theoretic system (as to whether there is such a duty and what, specifically, it is) and only after that to turn to a moral assessment of that system. On the view I am developing the citizen's institutional duty can be morally approved only if the particular system can be, and that latter point can be determined only if we have first resolved, among other things, the question of a citizen's system-specific standing before the law.

2. ALLEGIANCE IN A SYSTEM OF RIGHTS

The first step toward determining the citizen's institutional duty in such a case is to make the idea of rights in such a system more specific. Briefly, I would suggest that we are principally concerned with civil rights, with legally established and protected ways of acting, or of being treated, that hold good for each and every member (and often for every person) in a particular society. Thus, our focus here (as elsewhere) is on universal political or legal rights within a given society—ways of acting or ways of being treated which are recognized in law and maintained by the actions of people in that society.

These rights identify ways of acting, or ways of being acted toward, which would (as I argued in Chapter 5) be claimed by all persons for themselves individually as well as for all others in the society; for these claimed ways of acting (or of being treated) are, presumptively, part of the 'good' or benefit of each person or are instrumental to it. Thus, the ground of any such arrangement is that identifying and sustaining these particular ways of acting (or of being treated) is, arguably, in the interest of everybody, of each and all the citizens. All could claim it for themselves individually and acknowledge it for everyone else on that basis. A way of acting (or of being treated) so secured, through some such form of mutual acknowledgement of interest or benefit, is *justified* as a civil right.

By *justified* I mean merely that it fulfills the idea relied on in the case of any civil right. For the presumption of mutual benefit has been cashed in here. The presumption holds good: what really is, legally speaking, a civil right actually is a way of acting (or of being treated) that is correctly understood to be in everybody's interest. Hence a justified civil right is simply a civil right that, in satisfying the criterion of mutual perceived benefit, meets the justifying standard for all civil rights.

It is often said that rights, certainly *justified* rights, correlate with duties— meaning thereby that a right always implies or has attached some closely related duty of others. The point here, put precisely (as I argued in Chapter 2), is that any genuine right must involve some significant normative direction of the behavior of persons other than the holder. And it is this truth, crucial to the concept of rights, which I want to emphasize.

Thus, for each right (for each established way of acting or of being treated on the part of a rightholder) there is some significant sort of normative direction given to the conduct of other persons. If the right is to a liberty of conduct (e.g., the liberty to travel), then the attached normative direction for those others is principally to forbear from interference with that conduct. If the right is to an avoidance of injury (e.g., the injury of being killed or tortured), then the attached normative directive for other persons is mainly that they are to avoid doing that injurious thing to the rightholder. And, finally, if the right is to the availability of some service (e.g., the availability of an education at public expense), then the normative directive incumbent on others is, chiefly, to provide that service (or, secondarily, not to interfere with its provision). But the main point in all these cases (as I argued in Chapter 2) is that there is *some* significant normative direction of the conduct of other persons in the case of every right—though it differs in important ways from one kind of right to another, depending on whether the right in question is to a specific liberty of conduct, or to a particular avoidance of injury, or to a service of some sort.

In a system of civil rights, the rights of individuals are maintained, at least in part, by the action of relevant second parties, for these are the persons on whom the *primary* directives for conduct have been imposed. Sometimes a given requirement is imposed on *all* the citizens as second parties (e.g., the prohibition against murder). And other times the requirement is imposed on some only (as, e.g., in the U.S. Civil Rights Act of 1964, where it might be on certain government officials—voting registrars—under one section of the act, hotel keepers and restaurateurs under another, school districts and other recipients of federal aid or, again, employers under yet a third, and so on).

But the point is, given the whole range of cases, that each citizen has toward the other citizens (all of whom are rightholders) the status of second party in the case of many determinate civil rights. And each rightholder can call on the government, or on other third parties, to help maintain these rights—to enforce these rights—when the second parties fail to act correctly, fail to act as directed. Hence, every individual citizen, in the argument so far, has some requirements imposed on his or her conduct—but variously—by civil rights.

Such requirements are imposed simply in virtue of the status these individuals have (as innkeeper or employer or, quite typically, as member and fellow citizen) in a system of rights. The normative directions given in civil rights come with the territory and, in a system of such rights, are imposed by the rule-making actions of government officials.

They are, thus, unlike standard voluntary obligations in a number of important respects. They do not necessarily involve undertakings or determinate transactions that serve to bring a citizen specifically under a given requirement; they are not characteristically owed to definite or named individuals (but, rather, to all citizens); they are not imposed *because* the individual has been the actual beneficiary of the selfsame way of acting toward which that individual's conduct is now being normatively directed in some appropriate way.[5]

I realize, of course, that people often assume vocations at particular points in life, and that they do so knowingly, often by taking certain steps (applying for the job, filling out forms, sitting at a certain desk and doing certain things). There is a transactional element involved here, and it would be quite proper to say that such a job has been taken on voluntarily. One normally becomes an innkeeper or a hotel clerk in the way just described. Even so, I would not want to retract my main claim.

For one thing, the public accommodations responsibility we are in effect citing (as a foremost example) is not a responsibility of innkeepers *per se*; it is, rather, a responsibility of innkeepers in a certain kind of society (and within a given system of determinate civil rights). For another, the responsibility in question conceivably might not antedate a person's taking up the job in question. For it is quite possible that the relevant requirement was imposed on given innkeepers subsequent to their taking that employment.

Nonetheless, such innkeepers would have that responsibility at the time of imposition; all innkeepers would, even though (by hypothesis) none of them had entered employment with that responsibility in place, as part of their job description.

The point is, in all the relevant cases, that the responsibility is one that now inheres in the status of innkeeper and it is not a necessary feature of having any such responsibility that it be the result of a transaction between the status holders and, say, the government. Accordingly, it need not be the result of any voluntary transaction by the individual innkeeper at all.

The same would be true for responsibilities that were assigned to all citizens—in their status as citizens. The requirement (enshrined in law) that citizens refrain from the injury of killing other people is not necessarily a result of any voluntary transaction between citizens or between citizens and lawmakers. The requirements come with the territory and, in a system of civil rights, are imposed by the rule-making actions of government officials.

For these reasons, then, I would prefer to describe the normative directions on conduct in such cases as more like duties than like obligations. Hence, I will sometimes refer to these normative directives as duties and to them, collectively, as the duty of the citizen.

For every right there are attached duties—that is, normative directives—which bear on and govern the conduct of individual citizens as second (or third) parties. In a system of civil rights, the relevant rights and duties are set forth in laws.

We are assuming, in short, that the main democratic institutions, as described in Chapters 6 and 7, are in place (universal franchise, competitive voting, majority rule, the checking devices) and that the civil rights laws have been duly enacted under these institutions. Accordingly, it is a reliable presumption (though a rebuttable one) that these laws do incorporate a mutual perceived benefit of each and all the citizens in the various ways of acting, or of being treated, that the law guarantees for all persons across the board. And it is a reliable presumption that these guarantees, in the form of the normative directives imposed on conduct, are defensible ones and effective to the end intended.

Rights carry normative directives for others and where rights are stated in laws (as they are in a system of civil rights), then the laws carry the relevant directives. It follows, then, that the typical member (or citizen) in such a society has definite duties to conform to these rights-defining and rights-maintaining laws. For, where rights are defined and maintained by law, to do one's duty under a given right simply is to comply with the law(s) in question. Thus, each citizen in a system of rights has a duty to conform to the relevant laws insofar as that citizen has a second-party duty to abide by the legally defined and maintained rights of others. In a system of civil rights, these duties come to the same thing. They are one and the same duty, described in different ways. Thus, subjects are expected—and reasonably expected—to obey civil rights laws.

Rights laws are binding on conduct not because laws are involved but because rights are. It is not, then, that each is to conform to the applicable rights norms because these are stated in laws, toward which, independently of that rights character, the citizens have a standing duty; it is, rather, the reverse. Citizens are required to obey rights laws—and correctly understand themselves to be under such a requirement—insofar as those laws properly state (as they presumptively do) relevant normative directions on conduct appropriate to the rights involved.

These duties to conform to rights laws define one aspect of the typical citizen's characteristic allegiance, the typical citizen's standing with respect to the laws, in a particular determinate system of rights. My argument here is meant to contrast to the conventional view that citizens have a binding duty to obey laws based on some sort of covenant, contract, express consent, promise, or agreement that they have undertaken.

In the argument I have been conducting, each citizen is, under the civil rights laws, a rightholder and has, toward all the other citizens, certain duties attendant on the rights specified in the governing laws. Thus, the relevant normative directives on conduct are those set by law and they oblige each and all citizens, variously, as second parties. It should be clear, moreover, that the rights each person supports by law-obedient conduct are rights which *that* person has. Thus, the reciprocity of a system of civil rights, as characterized in the earlier discussion about justification (in Chapter 5), provides the main rationale or justification for the citizens to do their duty by obeying rights laws.

3. CONSIDERATIONS OF CONVENTION

Let me fill in behind this last point a bit, by suggesting what I take to be a strong consideration—developed from the argument in Chapter 5 (as amplified in Chapter 7)—which would support saying that conformity with civil rights laws is a reasonable expectation on the conduct of the typical citizen.

In the account I have been giving civil rights practices are, at least in part, conventions. And conventions of behavior, as we know, can be beneficial to participants in two distinct ways. (1) They can be beneficial by introducing order and regularity in place of disorder, by achieving a resultant degree of efficiency and economy in patterns of behavior, by diminishing confusion and establishing expectations that can be relied on. (2) And they can be so by conferring on participants those specific benefits that are inherent or natural results of the determinate practice in question.

Driving one's car on the right (when in America) is an example of (1).

Indeed, type 1 or regularity benefits are the only ones that accrue to participants in that particular practice; for there is no inherent benefit of *this* practice that cannot be achieved by a similar but different rule of the road (such as driving on the left, when in Britain). Any cooperative practice (where benefits accrue from cooperation and are passed on to all participants in the practice) would be an example of (2). Civil rights practices (as the argument of Chapters 5 and 7 suggested) are of this sort also.

Now, the interesting thing is that conventions under (2) also generate the sorts of benefit characteristic of (1). Thus, the practice of civil rights, in a given determinate case, would generate not only beneficial regularities but also certain inherent benefits (whether actual or potential)—benefits that are brought about by or are part of various liberties of conduct, avoidances of injury, the receipt of services.

Even so, we cannot expect that literally every case of acting or of being treated in accordance with the conventions of a given civil rights rule will yield the expected benefit (that is, the inherent benefit identified above as [2]). Nor can we realistically expect people to comply every time they are supposed to or to comply always in the right way. Interestingly, though, when this sort of thing does happen (as it inevitably will), the practice does not collapse and the benefit evaporate. Rather, such practices, even when imperfect in the two ways indicated, continue to generate the two kinds of benefit (regularity benefits and inherent benefits), to do so for the most part and in a high enough degree to make those practices beneficial all around. Such a result, then, would continue to underwrite and make viable the preference each participant has already expressed (in Chapter 7) for according the first-place option to civil rights practices, over alternatives.

However, the account here (though it is consistent with the argument of the previous chapter) does create some problem for the argument of the present one. For an individual citizen could always reason as follows: though it is clear why compliance is a reasonable expectation (regarding the conduct of most people most of the time) it is not clear that I must *on this occasion* comply with the rights law and do my legal duty (that is, do what I am normatively directed to do as second party); for if I don't the practice won't be hurt substantially, and, in fact, a certain amount of noncompliance and of inept compliance (as well as of sometime failure of the benefit to occur) have already been factored in.

This chain of reflections is apparently sound (and could occur to any citizen). It might seem, then, that compliance—at least, *uniform* compliance—with civil rights laws by each citizen is not a reasonable requirement on conduct.

One might think this apparently sound chain of reasoning can be disposed of summarily. For, surely, some exceptions to uniform conformity will actually be written into any well-crafted set of rights rules. For example, the prohibition on conduct that is injurious to others (or even lethal on some occasions) would probably include an exception for cases of justifiable self-defense.

We can grant this, though, without touching the central issue. For the real problem is not with explicit exceptions of the sort just mentioned, but with discretionary *unspecified* exceptions. It was these, presumably, that were crucially at issue in the plausible chain of reasoning.

How might such exceptions be dealt with? We can do so by extending the plausible chain a bit further. Here each citizen considers the exceptions that the *other* citizens might want to make.

In their reflections on this point, I would suggest, it will become clear that people don't want others to make dubious exceptions or to make exceptions in the face of minor inconvenience or to make special exceptions in their own interest (that is, exceptions in the *other* person's interest). Equally important, people want to build up or to see built up an attitude of willing cooperation on the part of others, so that the benefits of the practice, even though it is an imperfect and somewhat porous one, will accrue generally and for the most part. So, if this is what one wants from others, then one must be willing to operate on these same terms oneself.

For—given that each citizen can engage in the same plausible chain of reasoning and that each can extend it to others, as we have just done, and that all know that each can do this and that each can know that this is known as well, and so on—the only reasonable thing each can conclude is that the same fairly strict expectation on conduct should apply to all the citizens, to every one of them. So the rule arises, and arises reasonably, that all expect each to comply uniformly, with a minimum of discretionary opportunities for noncompliance.

Uniform conformity here, then, is conformity to what the rights rules specify in the way of normative direction for second parties. Certain classes of exceptions are explicitly admitted and, beyond that, a few others allowed for, if they are wholly within the spirit of the rule, as that rule is generally understood. These latter exceptions are ones that might be called 'ruleworthy'; they are exceptions that, while not introduced explicitly into the rule, would be recognized and admitted as appropriate exceptions by all or most all of the citizens.

In sum, then, we have now supposed a scheme of civil rights laws that includes as well a rule (or reasonable expectation) of uniform compliance, understood in the way just indicated. Such a scheme is better to have than an alternative which included the same civil rights but a looser expectation of compliance (or no settled understanding on compliance at all), and it is presumably better than one which included an absolutely strict compliance clause and, hence, that allowed for no intelligent or reasonable discretion whatsoever. It is better, that is, on the point of securing the relevant regularity and inherent benefits. Thus, uniform compliance with civil rights laws, as understood here, is properly seen to be a reasonable expectation to place on the conduct of the typical citizen in a system of rights.[6]

4. PROBLEMATIC FEATURES OF ALLEGIANCE IN A SYSTEM OF RIGHTS

Now that I have completed the main argument, I would like to turn to some matters of clarification, of refinement. I will take them up in order of importance, beginning with the least important.

4.1. *Not the Whole Duty of Citizenship*

I have tried to show that the typical citizen in a system of rights has a characteristic duty, that is, an institutional duty internal to that system, to conform to the laws that define and maintain civil rights there. This is not, of course, the whole duty of such a citizen. For the allegiance of the typical citizen may embrace other significant duties as well. The citizen may, for example, have the duty to vote. The citizen may have the duty to understand the connection of civil rights laws with the principles of a system of rights. The citizen may even have the duty to argue, in a critical way, with fellow citizens and, perhaps, with unsympathetic hearers about this connection and these principles, as regards an individual law or an individual decision. And the citizen may have a duty to serve the country (insofar as it is modeled on a system of rights) and possibly even to fight in its defense.[7]

My argument has been concerned with one duty only—with but one detail of the citizens' allegiance—their duty to obey civil rights laws. Other duties (like voting or military service), if they can be established, will also be part of that allegiance and will probably come under principles other than or additional to those which are deployed to establish the duty of conformity to rights laws. They may even come to rest on grounds external to a system of rights. In any event, I have left discussion of them aside in the present chapter, as not bearing on the central or focal issue of conformity to law.

4.2. *But Some Laws Are Not Civil Rights Laws*

But there remains a matter for some perplexity. The duty I have been discussing is portrayed as one's duty—typically as second party, sometimes as third—to conform to civil rights laws. But not all laws in a system of rights are laws defining and maintaining rights. What about such laws? Do we have a duty to obey them? This brings us, then, to a second point of clarification and refinement in my account.

In order to canvass this issue, let us consider some sample kinds of laws of the intended sort. We will restrict ourselves to those laws that individual citizens could obey or disobey, conform to or not.

Take tax laws, for example. One does not regard the payment of a tax as a right that one has. So, if we regard tax laws from the perspective of payment, as designed to raise revenue in some gross amount (with the individual citizen contributing a share through tax payments), then we can say that such a law does not, at that point, at least, define a civil right of the citizen. Does the typical citizen in a system of rights have a duty to obey such a law? More precisely, the issue is whether the citizen has the sort of duty we have hitherto been considering, that is, a duty of allegiance internal to the system of civil rights to obey the tax law, given the way we have specified that law.

I would contend that the citizen does, on the following principle. The operation of a system of rights costs money. The money must be raised. Tax laws are a reasonable means of doing so. Other means are possible (state lotteries, a state liquor monopoly or other business ventures, such as off-track betting, and so on). But these may not be preferable. So, if the legislature decides to use a tax scheme, then the citizen, arguably, has a duty to conform.

Here that duty is not to obey a law that defines and maintains civil rights; rather, it is to support one of the conditions *necessary* to there being a system of operative civil rights laws. What is necessary is that money must be raised. The tax scheme is necessary only in view of the legislature's decision (which closed off the alternative options); nonetheless, it is now a necessary means to raise revenue, given that decision.

Thus, the citizen pays her property tax or the citizen pays his sales tax, knowing that a good bit of the overall revenue raised will support the public schools, thereby maintaining the civil right to public schools as an operative right in the political system in question. The duty to pay some taxes, to obey some tax laws, can be supported by the reasoning just exhibited. Hence, the duty to obey, as one feature of the allegiance of the typical citizen in a system of rights, can be extended to include laws other than those that directly define and maintain civil rights.

Consider now another example. In the United States until recently, federal law had the effect of requiring that highway speed limits be set at 55 miles per hour (maximum) in all states. There was, accordingly, such a highway speed limit set by law in every state. Then the federal law was modified to allow a somewhat higher speed limit (65 m.p.h.) on certain stretches of the Interstate Highway system and on a few other limited-access highways, as designated. And a fair number of states have set, by statute, differential speed limits that reflect these new standards. Does the citizen driving on a 'slow' road in Kansas, say, have a duty (of the sort we are interested in) to obey such a law?

Again, we could reasonably answer that there is, to all appearances, no right involved. The law in question does not seem to define or maintain a civil right. But this answer might prove hasty. True, when the federal standard was *originally* enacted in 1974, back in the salad days of OPEC and Jimmy Carter, its purpose was to conserve on fuel. It was noted as time passed, however, that a substantial reduction in highway deaths, accident costs, and personal injuries had also occurred. Thus, insurance companies became strong supporters of keeping these laws on the books, although there was and continued to be strong pressure, especially in the Western states, to set the limit higher.

Given these facts, the Kansas legislature could reason that the 55 m.p.h. speed limit was, on the one hand, safer on nondesignated rural highways than higher speed limits (say, 65 or 70 or 75) and, on the other, was the minimum reasonable highway speed limit on such roads. Both judgments seem sound enough; hence, one rationale for the 55 m.p.h. limit in such a case (given these considerations) is that it saves lives and is necessary to that end in that a lower limit simply would not be acceptable. The legislature has continued to impose this limit, on the roads in question, as one of many ways available to it to protect lives, to protect people from being killed by others. Hence, it would not be unreasonable to say that the law was in this respect *like* a law that expressly maintained a civil right and to say that the citizens should conform to it for that reason.[8]

The speed limit laws in question were a response to the same claim, the claim to an avoidance of injury at the hands of others, that laws against murder represented. Each sort of law was a way of specifying, and maintaining, that claim. Thus, we might be able to include some laws (like speed limit laws) that do not themselves expressly define and maintain rights as laws that the typical citizen has a duty to obey—insofar, that is, as such a citizen has a duty to obey civil rights laws. For here the speed limit law has been assimilated to the basic purpose of already existing and accredited specifications in law of the civil right to life.[9]

Perhaps one final example will prove useful: laws that require emission control devices (e.g., catalytic converters) on automobiles. The citizen can fail to conform to such laws by dismantling the devices (which can sometimes be expensive to maintain) or by using leaded gasoline (which costs less than unleaded). Does the citizen have a duty not to do these things, a duty to conform to the law? If so, is the duty anything like the one we have been examining, the duty to conform to civil rights laws?

One could plausibly answer, I think, that no civil right is involved here. (For we can always suppose that the legislature has not specified a right to clean air, at least as regards automobile emissions.) But one could say in response, nonetheless, that having clean air is a public good (in the economist's sense). As we saw in Chapter 7, public goods, where the market fails to provide them, are things that would have to be paid for publicly or at large (through increased auto costs and gasoline and repair costs) under some sort of cooperative or coercive mechanism, in this case a law requiring such things as operative emission control devices and, ultimately, even the phasing out of leaded gasoline. And we could rationalize (or justify) such a law by saying that it provides, as a corrective to a market failure, something that is in the perceived benefit of each and all.

Thus, even on the supposition that a right is not involved, we could, nonetheless, say that a form of justificatory reasoning appropriate to a system of rights is involved. And that form of reasoning would also support the citizen's duty to obey such a law. It would support that duty as effectively as the law would have, were it (contrary to the supposition) a law that defined and maintained civil rights.[10]

I do not, of course, contend that this form of reasoning is unique to a system of rights. I claim only that it is internal to such a system, for reasoning from mutual perceived benefit is the very line of reasoning that was used to justify civil rights laws in the main argument set out earlier. The form of reasoning here is internal in the following way. Once we specify something as a civil right, say, by enactment into law, we can justify its being so enacted by reference to the line of reasoning in question. And unless we could accomplish some such justification, there would be no ultimately sound basis for saying that normative direction for the conduct of others should attach to that right. Thus, the very thing that underlies the citizen's actually having a duty to obey civil rights laws, that is, the idea that normative directives for conduct are always involved in such rights, is itself implicated in an essential way with this line of reasoning from mutual perceived benefit. That line of reasoning, in its justificatory role, then, is internal to a system of rights.

Thus, in the analysis I have been developing there are probably many kinds of laws that come under the citizen's duty to obey civil rights laws. These would range from laws that expressly define or maintain rights, where all citizens are second parties under the law (e.g., laws against murder), or where only some are (e.g., innkeepers under the U.S. Civil Rights Act of 1964), to less obvious cases. Here would be included those laws that do not define or maintain a right but, rather, *apply* the purpose of such a right (defined elsewhere) to a special set of facts (e.g., the law requiring a 55 m.p.h. highway speed limit—or, as the case has proven to be, a 55 m.p.h. limit on some roads and 65 m.p.h. on others). Then there are yet other laws that are a necessary means to having a system of civil rights (e.g., some tax laws or laws which provide for police protection) or to the maintaining of a particular civil right (e.g., laws or ordinances that mandate the setting up of schools or the qualifications of teachers or other requirements for staffing, e.g., a school district's affirmative action or nondiscriminatory hiring plan). And, finally, there might be some laws that may not involve rights at all, but since they do involve the justifying reason behind civil rights laws—mutual perceived benefit—they could come within the orbit of our inquiry (e.g., laws requiring emission control devices on automobiles in order to make for cleaner air for everybody). For the duty to obey them binds the citizen in the same way *as if* they had been civil rights laws.

All the kinds of laws just mentioned constitute laws that, arguably, the typical citizen would have a duty to obey in a system of civil rights, a system where accredited ways of acting or of being treated are specified and maintained by law. For all these kinds of laws come, in one way or another, under the citizen's primary institutional duty to obey civil rights laws or, by extension, under the rationale of mutual perceived benefit (an idea which is part of the justificatory scheme appropriate to civil rights and, thus, internal to that degree to a system of rights and to the duty in question). Hence, conformity to such laws as these is part of the typical citizen's characteristic allegiance in a system of rights.

However, there are still many cases of laws that probably do not enter the picture I have sketched. For example, some laws are not requirements on conduct but instead are recipes for creating various kinds of legal facilities or instrumentalities. I have in mind such things as laws specifying the conditions for a valid marriage, a valid contract or will, standing to sue, conveyance of property, etc.[11] One must, of course, conform to these things in order to create the facility in question, but citizens are not required to make valid contracts, and so on. Hence, it is not clear that such laws are the kinds of thing one has in mind when we speak of a duty to obey laws. And even though some of these things may count as necessary means to having particular civil rights (e.g., the right to property), it is not clear that all would so count.

Again, the laws requiring persons to register for the draft (or with the Selective Service System) may not be laws that the citizen has a duty to obey in a system of rights. Arguments might be advanced, of course, that such laws serve the common good in a system of rights: that they are necessary to keep such systems in existence or to keep them from being seriously impaired. But, unless one had some reasonable assurance that wars would not be fought, or hostile countries not intimidated, except to preserve systems of rights, especially one's own system, from destruction (or from serious impairment), such arguments would not carry conviction. Indeed, in view of the adventurist and irresponsible war making that has characterized most of the wars on record (including those wars, up through the recent one in the Persian Gulf, waged by states that might claim to exemplify, albeit imperfectly, a system of rights), one could not reasonably claim that conscription laws or laws requiring registration were laws a citizen had a duty of allegiance to obey in a system of rights. If the citizen is to have any such duty it must be specified much more narrowly than this.

Finally, there are many laws that do not specify civil rights, and, in particular, do not identify and require conduct for the perceived benefit of each and all. They are simply duly enacted laws in which the advantage of some is served at the cost of the disadvantage of others. I have in mind here such laws as zoning laws (e.g., a land-use or building-use law that doesn't allow householders to take in tenants or doesn't allow them to create a nuisance through such matters as their care of their own yards and houses or through such matters as operating a business out of their homes or working on cars in their driveways). Or tax laws (where we are concerned with allowing tax deductions, credits, and so on). Or production control laws and laws that set rates. And there are laws concerned with the execution of public policy (e.g., the maintenance of the post office monopoly) or the efficiency of public operations (e.g., laws against the pilferage of post office writing pens) that do not seem to bear on rights in any direct way. I do not see that any of the laws mentioned here, then, would come under the duty to obey laws that we have been concerned with.

Thus, the only conclusion we can draw, in the end, is that many valid laws in a system of rights would come under the typical citizen's duty of allegiance to conform to civil rights laws, or could be brought under that duty in ways that I have indicated. But many other laws would not come under that duty and could not, reasonably, be brought under it.

I would not say that citizens, then, have no duties toward such laws. For they may well have. And if they do have the duties, then there would have to be other grounds to obey the law, available to a citizen in a system of rights, beyond the ones I have been at pains to delineate. My point is not to deny these additional duties; it is, rather, to suggest that the grounds of such duties would, most likely, not be internal to a system of civil rights.[12] Hence, they would not generate characteristic duties of citizens in a system of rights. They would not be a feature of the typical citizen's allegiance there. They are not, then, the sort of duty we are concerned with in this chapter.

Now, it is evident that theorists often seize upon these additional duties and their grounds—such grounds as agreement or express consent or gratitude for benefits received—and give them special emphasis. The reason for this we have already seen: these theorists treat the obligation to obey the law as primarily a *moral* one and thus the grounds that interest them are conceived as distinctively moral grounds. These theorists are interested in *general* grounds for obeying law—grounds operative in all or almost all societies, grounds that could cover all laws or, conceivably, all persons— and they disdain reasons which are local or distinctive only of a particular society (or specific kind of system). But their analysis, by its very nature, creates a deep problem; for they cannot show that duties so generated—by reference to these general, distinctively moral grounds—can ever be peculiar to a particular political system.

But is this really a problem? It will be if one wants to allege, as most theorists do, that citizens typically owe a duty to the laws of their own country *in particular*. It is clear that the theorist who occupies the perspective of classical externalism (the simple and direct externalism described in Chapter 1, Section 3) is systematically unable to solve this problem of particularity. For on the externalist view the grounds of so-called political duties are not even peculiar to a particular political system, let alone to the country involved.[13]

Some might take exception to this claim, for it is widely believed that one advantage of so-called contract theories is that they can handle not only the issue of obligation to obey laws but also the issue of particularity just raised. I am not disposed to think this, however. For, first, most citizens have never consented or contracted, in a way that can be regarded as plausible, to obey the laws of the country in which they reside. And, second, the notion of consent or contract is often used (as it was with Locke's notion of "tacit" consent) to justify an obligation, necessarily imposed in the relevant cases, that one has to obey the laws of countries that one was merely visiting or that one merely had business or property interests in. Thus, we could readily imagine the following scenario: a given citizen of country A has no 'contract' of obedience there (having never taken any sort of oath of allegiance, etc., respecting A) but does have one in country B, in which that individual is temporarily sojourning (a result of that individual's having explicitly promised, in an entry visa and over written signature, to obey all the laws of B while there).

Defenders of the contract view might say that I have missed an important point: lifelong members or citizens of a given country necessarily have a consensual or contractual basis for being obliged to obey the laws of that country in particular. I cannot see that this reply has force. It leaves obscure the crucial question of what the ground, in particular, the political ground, of obligation is. More important, it assumes that contract theory has provided a plausible account of such obligation, a point that has engendered and still engenders a vast amount of controversy.[14] Finally, the reply takes no account of my point that contract theory does not resolve the particularity issue (since it does not establish that one has a special relationship to the laws of one's own country, a relationship that one does not or could not have to the laws of other countries).

Can the theorist who occupies the perspective I have advocated do any better? This brings us to the third matter of clarification and refinement that I want to take up in the present chapter.

4.3. *The Problem of Particularity*

The problem of particularity, as I have posed it, has two distinct levels. First, there is the *systemic* level, the level of a particular theoretic system of political concepts and institutions (e.g., a system of rights). Then, second, there is the level of *particularity per se*, the level of the citizen's own individual country, a country which will fit under one or the other of these various theoretic systems as an (at best imperfect) exemplification of it.

There should be no problem in establishing a special obligation to the laws at the first of these levels. For I have argued that the typical citizen in a system of rights does have a peculiar or specific duty there, the duty to obey civil rights laws. This is not a duty to the laws *qua* laws; for there are, by hypothesis, some valid laws in that society that would not come under the duty in question. Thus, even for those laws that do, the duty is not owed merely to the laws as duly enacted ones but, rather, to them in some *narrower* aspect (in that respect which sets them apart from laws that do *not* come under the duty identified). The duty, in the simplest case, is a duty owed to the laws merely in virtue of their being valid civil rights laws, that is, in virtue of their having the characteristic form of law in the particular political system in question. This is the aspect we are looking for. Hence, we could allege that citizens have a special duty to some valid laws, simply as laws, within that given type of political society.[15]

But I think an individual would have this same system-specific duty toward the civil rights laws in *any* particular system of rights. Thus, if a citizen from country *A* (say, the USA) were to travel to country *B* (say, Great Britain), that American citizen would have the same kind of duty in either place—allowing here, for the sake of argument, that each country was sufficiently modeled on a system of rights to count as an exemplification, albeit an imperfect one, of such a system, or as an aspirant toward such exemplification. This citizen would, accordingly, have a duty to obey duly enacted civil rights laws in either place and would have such a duty, presumably, for the same reasons in either place: either because civil rights always impose normative directives on the conduct of people, applicably to our sample citizen in the case at hand, or because the things required by law here are in such a person's interest, as well as everybody else's, when each is involved in the goings-on within that particular society. Thus, we could expect the American visitor to Great Britain, on the grounds of the duty to obey civil rights laws, to comply with laws against murder, assault, theft, etc., to comply with laws that set speed limits on highways, that mandate emission control devices on cars, that require the payment of taxes, or that provide rules for setting up schools and for requirements on teachers and for standards of instruction, and so on.

The reasons given and the duty they support, are specific to a system of rights. They would not work in countries that exemplified other standards, say an Islamic state (like Iran) or a socialist country (like the former USSR, at least before the Gorbachev era) in which the dominant ideal was not civil rights but, rather, doing the will of God (Iran) or building communism (the pre-Gorbachev USSR). There would, of course, be laws against murder in such countries and probably highway speed limits as well. And I'm sure they should be obeyed. But a resident individual's characteristic reason for obeying such laws, and the specific duty under which they would be complied with, would be specific to these other standards.[16] Or it would be a moral reason, either conventional or general. In any event, the visitor's reason for complying with law in these cases would *not* arise out of any local duty to obey civil rights laws.

Nor should we expect that what was in the mutual perceived interest of persons in a Muslim society, especially one under a fundamentalist Islamic code, would necessarily be in the interests or for the benefit of a visitor (as specified, say, in the civil rights laws of that person's particular system of rights). But, of course, there might be some community of interest between visitors and inhabitants here, nonetheless (in laws against assault, for example).

Even so, if the visitor's duty to obey here actually came out of mutual perceived benefit it would not, in that case, count as anything like the duty to obey civil rights laws. For here mutual perceived benefit is not tethered to a system of civil rights but instead floats free, on its own. (Or it is in league with those standards specific to the society being visited.) There would thus be no coordination of matters of mutual benefit with existing rights: no attempt to put limitations on the scope of such matters so as to adjust them to adjoining rights, no harmonization of them with rights so as to create a coherent system of civil rights, no attempt to give weight to rights in competition with these other normative consideration, no commitment to the priority of rights—or, at least, basic rights—over other norms.

What I have said does not, however, in any way deny the power of mutual perceived benefit to ground duties to conform to law; it does, though, deny that in these cases the relevant duty, when so grounded, could be a duty to obey civil rights laws (or like one in the significant respects). Hence, arguing from mutual perceived benefit, even when sound, would not provide in such a case a reason characteristic of a system of rights nor would the duty so grounded, where there is one, have that character either.

So, we can leave aside such duties as might be found for respecting laws in countries like Iran or the one-time USSR (in its classical socialist phase). We still have remaining, then, certain reasons and a supported duty that are special to a system of rights (and special only to such a system) but not, apparently, to any *one* system of rights in particular. For these reasons appear to provide no claim on the individual citizen to the effect that citizens had a duty to obey the laws of their own country *in particular*. Thus, the second level of the problem—the level of particularity *per se*—is unresolved.

I don't know that I can deal with this problem in a wholly satisfactory way. It may be that particularity descends only so far; and to take it as far as we have may be enough, for we have already satisfied the terms of the analysis from which we set out initially. Nonetheless, we should attempt to account, so far as possible, for the apparently reasonable claim that citizens or life-long members have a special duty to one system of civil rights in particular, that is, to the one in their own countries.

I think we can make some headway toward doing so by attending to the justificatory ground appropriate to rights in any given system of civil rights—to the idea of mutual perceived benefit (but now confining it strictly to its role within a system of rights). The citizens or lifelong members of a given system of civil rights have pooled their efforts to achieve a limited but common set of values or norms for conduct in their society, as given in the civil rights laws that constitute or are among the main rules in this particular system of rights. Indeed, some features of that particular system may well be unique. And the citizens have accorded a sort of preference to the achievement of this precise set of rights. For they have put a priority on the achievement of these legally secured ways of acting or of being treated, ways that are in the interest of each and all. For there is (as I argued in Chapter 7) a priority of determinate universal rights—certainly of basic rights—in that society over certain other options.[17] It is a priority over (1) any common good that serves the social or corporate good but not the good of each individually (e.g., national defense) and over (2) majority decisions that serve the good of some individuals but not all (e.g., a particular tax code as regards allowable credits, deductions, exemptions, etc.).

Thus, a kind of reciprocity—a concern for the good of each and all—characterizes the conduct and ultimately the attitudes of typical citizens in a particular system of civil rights. And the texture of this reciprocity is spelled out not only in the specific list of civil rights that all enjoy but also in the normative directives imposed on the conduct of every person—but variously—by those rights.

Persons who are citizens or lifelong members of that particular society are rightholders there and have made their contribution to that society and to its system of rights, when they have acted in character as typical citizens, through their conduct in conforming to law. It is *their* system, for they have contributed to it in this way. Its flourishing is the work of their hands and of others like them. A system of rights so understood is always the work of its citizens or lifelong members; they are its primary beneficiaries but they are also its primary progenitors. Without them there would be no system of rights nor civil rights laws for the short-term visitor or the limited participant to enjoy or conform to.

Now, let us assume that an individual can be a citizen or a lifelong member of one and only one political society (at a time). Let us assume further that most people are in fact citizens or lifelong members of only one such society during their entire lifetimes. Both assumptions are reasonable enough and both fit the case of countries with which we started. For countries are territorially based, fairly large, relatively stable, long-lived, politically independent societies into which most of the inhabitants are born and where they spend their whole lives. And many others have joined, for reasons of their own, and have in effect cast their lots there. The important point for the vast majority of persons, then, is that each will count as a lifelong citizen or a contributing member of a single political society only.

If we stayed with the case at hand, that society would be a particular system of rights in a given country. And we will confine our attention to such a country.

It follows next that, since individual persons would have a system-specific duty toward civil rights laws, they would have that same duty toward such laws in the one country where they are now citizens or lifelong members. But they would have that duty in the context of a special status there. For this is the *only* political society, the only country, in which they currently have the status of citizen or lifelong member.

It is a mere contingent matter that people might be significantly involved, through travel, for example, with more than one particular system of civil rights. But it is not a contingent matter, for an actual individual person (indeed, for the vast majority of persons), that the citizen or lifelong member of a particular system of civil rights is significantly involved with one such system, that is, the one in that citizen's own country. It is this fact, the citizen's unique involvement with one system of civil rights in particular, and the fact of reciprocal contribution to that particular system through one's conduct, that constitute the peculiar standing each citizen or lifelong member has toward the civil rights laws of his or her own country.

I do not say that persons' individual duties of obedience will vary from country to country; rather, my point is that their allegiance—their standing before the laws—is different. And I have tried to mark out the points at which a citizen's relationship to that one particular system, the citizen's own country, is arguably different from any relationship to like systems in other countries. In the normal case the citizen's significant involvement in those other systems is a contingent matter and the reciprocity involved is, comparatively, minimal.

These differences are, no doubt, significant. But the psychological and practical differences involved are even more significant. I mean here the feelings and attitudes engendered by playing a role of the sort I've described within one's own system of rights and the habits and policies for action one builds up through reciprocal contributions over a long period of time. These matters are, perhaps, sufficient to *explain* the peculiar status or standing that we are here concerned with: that is, the citizens' special allegiance toward the civil rights laws in their own country in particular. It may well be that what I have called the typical citizen's special allegiance is more a psychological or a practical matter than a conceptual or theoretical one.[18]

My point, then, is simply that this special standing and the feelings and practical concerns that attend it are not unjustified. There is a rational foundation for the particularity, oft remarked on, of the citizens' allegiance to laws in their own country.

What function do these peculiar feelings and practical attitudes serve? Presumably, when they are apt, they help clarify and solidify a citizen's perception of the grounds of the justified institutional duty. And one's resolve to do one's duty and one's assiduousness in doing it can be strength-ened by such feelings and practical attitudes.

Of course, actual feelings and policies for action may not always run on this track, or have this result. For feelings can be wayward. Sometimes, indeed, when not apt in the way described, they can make a negative rather than a positive contribution, as measured by the standards of system-specific citizenship. In this event, thoughtful reflection and reasoned public discussion should be helpful toward the goal of reintegrating the texture of actual feeling and attendant practical attitudes with the justified duties appropriate to citizenship in a given political system.

Let me add, finally, that this analysis, just as it does not presuppose an existing bedrock of feeling (taken as an unchanging given), does not presup-pose a widespread social consensus (amounting to social homogeneity). Indeed, allegiance as I have been describing it is fully consistent with the idea of a permanently pluralistic society. If anything, it is more at home in such a setting. For the point is to construct a *shared* political focus, one which people of different race, ethnic background, religion, or gender can adhere to—both intellectually and in their feelings and practical attitudes as well. In any society (be it homogeneous or heterogeneous) such a focus is important, but in a pluralistic society it is essential. For the alternative here is simply Balkanization: a constant threat to the very existence of the body politic and a constant invitation to seek differential advantage by one party over others even at the expense of the common well-being—that is, of the good of each and all and of the corporate weal.[19]

My point, then, is simply that this shared focus would otherwise not be there in the absence of a political system of civil rights (or something like it). And the analysis I have sketched is intended to show only what is true for a typical citizen in a determinate system of rights and to show what charac-teristic line of behavior would be required or expected if that citizen stayed within the norms of the system in question.

In sum, we have been able here to generate the claim that in a system of civil rights the typical citizen has an institutional duty, a system-specific duty that holds good for every citizen, to obey—to conform to—laws that define or maintain civil rights. And the citizen has a special standing toward the laws in one system of civil rights in particular, that of the citizen's own country. For our rather limited purposes, then, this is the character of the typical citizen's political allegiance in a system of rights.[20]

4.4. *Democratic Process as an Imperfect Procedure*

Now, we know (from the argument in Chapter 7) that majority rule pro-cedures for making laws are inherently imperfect in that some laws, though duly made, may not satisfy the governing norms of the system. This is so for two reasons. First, the relationship between majority decision making and the existence of civil rights laws that can be presumed to be in the general interest is merely probabilistic. And, second, we cannot realistically expect the legislature always to stay within the governing norms (those that justify the democratic institutions in the first place), nor expect the checking devices always successfully to counteract the legislature when it so deviates. Thus, a constitutional government with truly democratic institutions and accredited procedures conceivably could enact a procedurally sound law or policy that—even though it purported to be a rights law—did not in fact identify and maintain for everyone a way of acting, or of being treated, that was for the benefit of each and all.[21]

In this chapter the citizen's institutional duty of conformity to law has been defined, properly, by reference to the notion of democratically enacted laws, specifically laws in the form of civil rights laws. Thus, that duty may cover some such laws that are, nonetheless, defective as rights laws. And since the citizens' duty attaches simply to laws of a certain sort (laws designed to support just institutions in Rawls's account, democratically enacted civil rights laws in mine), it would appear that the citizen has a duty of conformity even toward such defective laws. Thus, Rawls argues that members of a well-ordered society have a duty to obey unjust laws.[22] The parallel contention would be that citizens in a system of rights have a duty to conform to defective rights laws, or to such laws even when they are thought to be defective. But this is a paradoxical way to state the central claim.

Of course, the point might be, not that we are duty-bound to that particular law *qua* law, but rather that we are duty-bound to it in order to make the whole system work. But this seems a needlessly global view to take. For most of the laws we have examined in this chapter come under the institutional duty in question, not because they are individually necessary to the existence of the system of rights in general (or to any particular right in it), but because they have certain intrinsic features—I mean such features as being a rights law or *like* such a law or being justifiable by the same standard as a rights law, and so on. Thus, only a few 'unjust' laws, most of them tax laws, would even come close to being laws that the citizen, nonetheless, has an institutional duty to obey.

There may be other issues of workability here as well. For example, citizens might comply with an 'unjust' law in order to avoid offending the majority or the principle of majority rule. They might want to avoid large-scale social unrest or avoid giving encouragement to more dubious forms of lawbreaking. They might think noncompliance almost wholly ineffective, and so on. These are all prudential considerations, though certainly meritorious ones. But they do not touch the question whether citizens have a *duty* to comply with valid laws which are, arguably, unjust.

The crucial point seems to be, then, that citizens *do* have an institutional duty to obey all civil rights laws, on the presumption that these laws establish a mutual interest on the part of everyone in certain ways of acting and of being treated. And the duty attaches simply to such laws insofar as they are duly enacted by the democratic institutions because it has been presumed, on reasonable grounds, that when they are so enacted laws will likely have the desired character. Thus, the expected or presumptive response *is* conformity—uniform conformity—to duly enacted rights laws.

I would want to argue that this presumption or expectation is rebuttable. It can be defeated in a given case (though not in general). I do not want, accordingly, to argue that the citizen must *always* conform to the civil rights laws in a particular system of rights. For, as I indicated in Chapter 2 and, again, earlier in the present chapter, the positional or institutional duty of the citizen is not an 'all things considered' or absolute duty.[23] It can be overridden in the case of a given law, or overridden on a given occasion, for ruleworthy reasons, for reasons appropriate to the system of rights (and, I would add, for moral or religious reasons as well). My contention, in short, is that the political allegiance of a typical citizen in a system of civil rights includes or allows for the possibility that the citizen can be, perhaps will be, disobedient even of rights-defining and rights-maintaining laws in that society.

For as I have indicated, some laws may establish (as civil rights) ways of acting or ways of being treated that are not in fact in the interest of each and all. And the citizen might use such a contention to justify refusal to conform to such a law. Indeed, the idea of mutual perceived benefit built into both the notion of civil rights and the notion of justified democratic procedures might even license, conceivably, some cases of disobedience—where, for example, the citizen regarded an alleged rights law as positively inimical to the citizen's own interest and to the interest of many of those subject to it and, hence, as specifying a way of acting (or of being treated) that the citizen could not endorse.

Thus, a public official or a private citizen in the 1850s might refuse to deliver up an escaped slave in defiance of the Fugitive Slave Law (and the constitutional right of property that it presumably represented). Or the husband or lover of a woman might seriously interfere with her right to have, at her discretion, an abortion (a right which presumably existed on her behalf under the constitutional right of privacy as determined by a Supreme Court decision).[24] Or parents might withdraw their children from the schools, in a way not countenanced in law, in order to teach them at home.

The fact that the citizen in any of these cases could in effect appeal to rights principles against a contested right would, nonetheless, set limits to that citizen's disobedient conduct. So long as the citizen's conduct observes these limits and so long as the citizen appeals to rights as a prime justification for disobedience (or appeals to principles inherent in a system of rights) the citizen's allegiance to such a system remains intact.

This brings us, then, to the final matter of clarification and refinement that I want to take up in this chapter. It brings us to the issue of allowable disobedience, an issue often discussed under the heading of civil disobedience.

5. CIVIL DISOBEDIENCE

Some of the things that would be included, definitionally, under *civil disobedience* are relatively uncontroversial: that it involves a deliberate violation of public law (or policy or code), that it is done out of protest and is meant to serve some vital social or moral purpose. After these points, however, we come to a significant divergence in the way people talk about civil disobedience.

Some people will say that a knowing or deliberate violation of public law is *civil* only if it is peaceably done (nonviolent) and the violator more or less willingly takes the penalty for the violation. In America we are familiar with this *sense* of 'civil disobedience' from the practice and from the pen of Martin Luther King. This can be offered, then, as the crux of a general definition of the term in question: "civil disobedience is a public, nonviolent, submissive violation of law as a form of protest."[25]

But others will say that a knowing or deliberate violation of public law is *civil* only if it is done in such a way as to indicate recognition that the laws in question are duly enacted or authoritative. Thus, Rawls emphasizes that civil disobedience is within the "boundary of fidelity to law" and is, in his opinion, problematic principally because it is an act of disobedience by citizens who at the same time "recognize and accept the legitimacy of the constitution."[26] And Robert Paul Wolff attaches the notion of civil disobedience to that of the legitimacy of the state when he argues that the demise of the concept of legitimate political authority would completely undercut the very possibility of *civil* disobedience.[27]

Now, of course, these two senses of civil disobedience can get blended together in a variety of ways. The important thing to note, though, is that we have two distinct *basic* ways for conceiving of civil disobedience: the one way sees protesting and disobedient conduct as 'civil' insofar as it is nonviolent and submissive; the other sees that conduct as 'civil' insofar as it recognizes the authority of the lawmakers and the authoritativeness of the laws.

I want to suggest that the way one defines and, by extension, conceives civil disobedience has an important bearing on the way one would go about justifying it. For each of these basic ways of conceiving of civil disobedience marks out a distinctive way of relating relevant normative standards to the practice of civil disobedience.

I think it obvious that many kinds of judgments—including moral judgment, whether conventional or critical—can provide a *reason* for protesting actions or policies of government and for disobeying laws. But when would any such judgment provide a good reason for *civil* disobedience? Or, to ask the question another way, when would a conscientious action also be a case of justified civil disobedience? Let us deal with this question by taking the two basic senses in turn.

Let me add, parenthetically, that in what follows I will discuss civil disobedience by citizens (in the *plural*). My reason is that in our century civil disobedience has typically been a collective or mass phenomenon, done by people acting as a group or in a highly coordinated way. The classic cases in point here remain the mass confrontations against the British Raj in India led by Gandhi and the Montgomery Bus Boycott and the massive picketing and other agitations against the Birmingham (Alabama) police led by King.[28] Some would argue as well that such collective disobedience is more effective in achieving change and reform than is disobedience by individuals acting on their own. It has certainly proven more controversial. But I do not mean, of course, in emphasizing collective action, to exclude from consideration disobedience by individuals—not even by the Athanasian individual who stands alone against the world.

With this parenthesis concluded, we can return now to the main line of discussion. Here we suppose, first, the case of persons who individually feel constrained, even when they act in concert, to keep their disobedience to law *civil* in the sense of nonviolent and open to reprisals and other actions by the government. Now, why would they require these restraints? The answer might be that they have moral or, perhaps, religious reasons for eschewing violence and for performing their actions so as to be accessible and subject to penalty (as a sort of witnessing, perhaps, or piece of moral suasion). Here it may well be that the kind of reason that dictates their breaking the law in the first place is of the same sort as the reason which dictates that their violation be nonviolent and submissive. So, the question for them becomes: When do moral reasons (either critical or conventional) constitute good grounds both for breaking the law and for doing it in a nonviolent way and with a willingness to stand in court and even to accept penalty? The answer is that these reasons do so whenever civil disobedience, in the nonviolent sense, is *morally* justified.

In short, when the moral reasons for a certain line of conduct are consistent with or when they require civil disobedience, then we have the case where appeals to conscience can, or do, constitute *good* grounds for civil disobedience. For example, persons whose moral reasons for breaking the law included the belief that injury should not be done to other people would be constrained to the practice of civil disobedience in the nonviolent sense. On the other hand, if the agents' moral reasons for conscientious action did not themselves preclude violence, then the agents' conscientious actions (so long as they individually stayed in character as moral agents) would not be constrained by limits inherent in the notion of a justified civil disobedience: for those particular citizens there would be no justified *civil* disobedience and hence no such limits.

The point, in each of these cases, is that moral conscientiousness can constitute good grounds only when *civil* disobedience is *morally* justified: that is, when it is morally justified both to break the law and to break it in a nonviolent, submissive manner. Here, then, we have provided a kind of answer to the question. The answer is that morally conscientious actions can necessarily be limited only by conscience itself (that is, by moral rules themselves appropriately applied); nothing independent of conscience can properly serve as a limit under the first sense of civil disobedience (as, simply, nonviolent and submissive).

So, if an act is purely and truly conscientious—morally conscientious— then it cannot properly be limited here by mere civic standards. Surely, Thoreau thought this when he said, "The only obligation which I have a right to assume, is to do at any time what I think right."[29] And Howard Zinn when he said, "If the protest is morally justified (whether it breaks a law or not) it is morally justified to the very end, even past the point where a court has imposed a penalty." And again, "If a specific act of civil disobedience is a morally justifiable act of protest, then the jailing of those engaged in that act is immoral and should be opposed, contested to the very end. The protester need be no more willing to accept the rule of punishment than to accept the rule he broke."[30]

But there is another basic sense of civil disobedience, where *civil* has the sense of "recognizing authority." Can this notion of civil disobedience provide any sort of limitation on conscientious actions (even *morally* conscientious ones)?

To answer this question, we can again suppose the case of persons engaging in conscientious actions who individually feel constrained to keep their disobedience to law *civil*, even when they act in concert, but this time because they recognize the authority of the government to make laws and consider the relevant law to be duly enacted. Such persons would appear to have *political* reasons for feeling this constraint. I say this because their categories of thought, as described, are here political ones: the "authority of government" and "laws duly enacted." These persons conceive of civil disobedience politically.[31] So the question for them becomes, When do *political* reasons constitute good grounds for civil disobedience? The answer would be: When civil disobedience, in the authority-recognizing sense, is *politically* justifiable.

In short, when the political grounds that they have in such notions as "governmental authority" and "duly enacted law" are compatible with disobedience to law, under certain conditions, or when they actually license some sorts of disobedience to law, as a feature of the political system that they establish, then we have the case where authority-recognizing disobedience to law is possible. It is only here that the political grounds cited could constitute unequivocally *good* grounds for civil disobedience.

But we could well imagine a state in which the grounds of authority precluded *civil* disobedience, a state in which the acknowledged character of authority made it impossible both to accept that authority and to disobey its duly enacted laws. For instance, the character of authority in Plato's State of the Guardians (the state mentioned at the beginning of this chapter) is such that the decrees of the Rulers should not be disobeyed; indeed, we are explicitly told that the "virtue" of the ordinary citizen in such a state is simply to do what that citizen is told by the Wise Rulers.[32] Now, the citizen in that kind of state would have no concept of *justified* civil disobedience, where 'civil' has the sense of authority-recognizing and where the justification, if it had existed, would have to rest on the basic political ideal itself. Citizens while staying in character in that state could never, no matter what conscience told them to do, be civilly disobedient; for any time they broke the law, their so acting might be conscientious in some sense but it could never be civilly justified. Hence, for these citizens (*qua* citizens) the possibility of *civil* disobedience is never available.

Thus, when we talk about civil disobedience in the authority-recognizing sense, it is very important to have a particular kind of state in mind. For some kinds of state can 'take' civil disobedience and even incorporate it as a feature of their theoretic structure. But other kinds are logically incapable of doing this; the institutions, the theoretic structure of such states, won't allow it. When we talk about civil disobedience in the authority-recognizing sense the discussion must take place within a given or determinate theoretic system of political concepts and institutions, and the question whether civil disobedience is ever justified is decided by reference to the other elements within that same theoretic system. The ground of civil disobedience— whether it is to be allowed or not—and the ground of authority within a system are one and the same. Hence the kind of state, the exact nature of the theoretic system of political concepts and institutions for that particular state, becomes the crucial question.

And I have suggested that citizens who believed a particular government's authority to be founded on the task of specifying and maintaining civil rights would believe that sometimes disobeying a civil rights law is justifiable, or at least allowable, when that law was defective with respect to the standard for all civil rights laws—or possibly justifiable, or possibly allowable, when that law (though not itself defective) was effectively or symbolically connected with some law or policy that was defective by that standard. That is, disobedience would be justifiable here when it was a way of protesting an evident defect of this sort within a system of rights. Hence, even where we have a rights-producing state, individual citizens could disobey one of its civil rights laws, while at the same time recognizing the basic ground of authority; and that act of disobedience could be, by reference to that same basic ground, justifiable.[33]

More precisely, such an action would be justifiable *within* the political system only if it were done for an appropriate reason (for the sake of civil rights) and in a certain way (so as not to substantially threaten or damage the scheme of rights itself or the political institutions associated with it, in particular, the democratic institutions). This latter point needs amplification. For it leads us to consider and attempt to determine what conditions, if any, are required, over and beyond an appropriate reason, in order for an act of disobedience to be civil (in the authority-recognizing sense).

We can make such a determination by looking, again, at the theoretic system of politics in which the disobedience occurs. The conditions generated would be the conditions of a justified civil disobedience—that is, if there is such a thing—for given persons (each a typical citizen) in that particular state. We can view these conditions as a kind of bridge between those persons' recognition of the rule-issuing authority of government and its duly enacted laws, on the one hand, and their civil disobedience to the law, while *still* recognizing that authority, on the other. One might say, then, that the ability to construct such a set of conditions is to state what would count as justified civil disobedience in that particular system.

If we were to stay with our original example of a system of rights, then we could see more clearly how such conditions might be developed. For such a state the conditions would surely include the following two: (1) In disobeying the law, the citizens neither intend nor bring about, in a way that could reasonably be foreseen, a substantial violation of the civil rights of other citizens (including their right to property); for violation here would be incompatible with the basic goal of preserving the right to life and estate of those subject to that state's laws. (2) In disobeying the law, the citizens should be willing to undergo, if necessary, the appropriate legal or judicial scrutiny, as prescribed in law, for such lawbreaking; for otherwise they set themselves above the law and, by so doing, cannot be said to recognize its authority. There are, very likely, other conditions as well; I have specified these two in order to indicate the sort of thing I have in mind when I speak of conditions of a justified civil disobedience in a particular kind of state.[34]

Concern for the preservation of rights (which overlaps considerably with what was earlier described as nonviolence) and willingness to undergo legal scrutiny (including willingness to take the penalty for law violation, where punishment is an eligible option) are here conceived of as features, not of the *definition* of civil disobedience, but of its *justification*. This is one of the important differences between the moral sense of *civil*, in the definition of 'civil disobedience,' and the political sense, where *civil* has the force simply of authority recognizing.

It should be clear that civil disobedience in the authority-recognizing sense, where the justifying reason was appropriate to the system in question and where the relevant bridge conditions were observed, is precisely what I had in mind when I suggested earlier that typical citizens in a system of rights could, while staying in character, disobey some duly enacted civil rights laws. For here a ruleworthy exception to the convention of uniform compliance with civil rights laws can arguably be established. An act of disobedience on such a basis would not count as the breaking of allegiance to a system of rights if (whatever *other* reason the citizens might have— moral or what have you) their conduct was justifiable in the way I have described, that is, by reference to a system-specific reason and to the observance of the bridge conditions.

But my analysis is not limited to a single ideal type—to supposed typical citizens, each of whom stays in character as a good and proper citizen in what he or she does. Consider here a mixed case in which persons are living in a system of rights, for whom conscience (informed here principally by moral or religious considerations) might provide reasons for disobeying the law. Such reasons might even be described as good reasons; nonetheless, this act of disobeying the law would count as justified civil disobedience, in the *political* sense, only when the persons disobeying the law recognized the authority of the state and acted accordingly. In this event these agents, though acting in disobedience to law for reasons of conscience, would be acting in accordance with principles which underwrote the authority of the government, or at least they might be shown to have acted that way; and those agents, in disobeying, would in effect observe bridge conditions of the sort already indicated.

The important point is that the bridge conditions of civil disobedience (in the political sense)—such as not violating the rights of others and willingness to undergo legal scrutiny—would here impose certain limitations on these persons' performance of conscientious actions, that is, they would where they accepted *both* moral rules and political authority. Or, to put the matter somewhat differently, conscientious actions, even where they are properly regarded as morally approved actions, can be constrained by limitations inherent in a concept of civil disobedience only where that concept has a political as distinct from a moral sense. Thus, conscientious actions can be limited other than by conscience itself (that is, by moral rules and so on) only where an alternative standard is also accepted and that standard goes significantly beyond these moral rules into another domain, the political.

Where justified civil disobedience is itself a political idea, it can provide significant limitations to conscientious actions in which laws are disobeyed. Thus, the most important difference between the moral and the political sense of civilized disobedience comes at the point of the relationship between civil disobedience and conscientious actions.[35]

If my analysis is sound (and, as well, the mixed case I have described is a common one), there is an important intermediate case between that of strict obligation, on the one hand, and moralistic disobedience which is unrestrained politically, on the other; for we have the possibility both of recognizing authority in a government and of disobeying some of its laws. We have here the foundation for a theory of political allegiance significantly different from the obligationist one which prevailed in the past—and one that gives greater scope to the initiative of citizens in the fashioning of the laws. This idea, then, of politically justified civil disobedience is perhaps one of the most important contributions of contemporary thought to the stock of traditional civil philosophy.

Perhaps I can put my point more directly now, by reference to a system of rights in particular. In this system, obedience may not attach to all laws as a rule, allowing only for explicit or narrowly prescribed exceptions. Here there would be no rule mandating an absolute (or all but absolute) obedience to law and, hence, no exception to that rule. In a system of rights, *strict* political obligation, where obedience is either an unfailing rule (Socrates) or an unfailing one in a legitimate state (Locke) or an unfailing one except in a case of life or death (Hobbes), may not even exist. Rather, what might attach as a rule (or reasonable expectation) is simply *civilly* responsible and appropriate conduct—where ruleworthy exceptions in the form of civilly justifiable acts of disobedience are specifically allowed for.

This conclusion to my argument would suggest that something weaker than strict obligation is compatible with the notion of a rule-issuing authority in a system of rights from which we started. And in place of obligation we might put, or so I have argued, the notion simply of allegiance, understood in the way I have been describing it in the present section.[36]

6. AN ISSUE UNRESOLVED

One final point. My argument on this concluding issue, as to whether citizens in a system of rights have a duty of less than strict compliance with duly enacted civil rights laws, contains one element that goes beyond what has so far been established. For I have mentioned, several times, that one of the bridge conditions of civilly justifiable disobedience to law is the violator's willingness to undergo legal scrutiny and to otherwise be subject to the political processes attendant on and appropriate to lawbreaking. And clearly this may involve, probably will involve, the imposition of punishment on the lawbreaker.

In effect, then, my account supposes that in a system of rights sanctions clauses are justifiably attached to rights laws and may thereby be justifiably invoked when rights laws are violated (even invoked against those who have performed acts of justifiable civil disobedience). Here then I have written a check against funds not yet on deposit.

We must move, then, to remedy this deficiency by determining the justifiability of sanctions clauses and their application to law violators in a system of rights. Only after such a project is carried through successfully can we say that the topic of the present chapter, allegiance, has been given a full and satisfactory philosophical analysis.[37]

There is one other significant reason for turning to the justifiability of punishment at this point. It bears on one of the central arguments of the present chapter, the argument (in Sections 2 and 3) for uniform compliance with civil rights laws, allowing only for minimal exceptions.

Let me briefly recall, in order to focus on, an important point in that argument. In Section 3, I contended that a scheme of civil rights laws that includes as well a rule (or reasonable expectation) of uniform compliance, allowing only for certain explicit or other ruleworthy exceptions, is better than alternative civil rights law schemes. Since such a scheme is in each individual citizen's interest, the ingredient rule (or convention of uniform compliance), which is partly constitutive of that scheme, is in each citizen's interest. That is, on each particular occasion of (possible) compliance with civil rights laws, it is in each citizen's interest, when a second party, to comply with the normative direction involved. It does not, of course, follow that any given act of compliance is *more* in the interests of that citizen than noncompliance would be.

What, then, would keep the citizen from defecting on occasion from the reasonable expectation of uniform compliance? The simple and best answer is that each citizen is (as the argument in the earlier section made clear) a willing and convinced party to a scheme of civil rights laws which includes (among its several features) a mutual expectation of uniform compliance by all citizens with rights laws (allowing, as I just said, only for certain explicit or other ruleworthy exceptions). Such a scheme is better than alternative civil rights schemes and better, at least for rational maximizers, than anarchic state of nature alternatives too. Thus, a quite restrictive convention on the behavior of each has been clearly established. And every citizen can be presumed to know all these things.

Now we come to the important part. Not only are citizens willing and convinced parties; they are also (as the earlier argument in Section 4.3 made clear) typically habituated to such compliance, expecting it of themselves and of others as a matter of course, within the set of civil rights laws under which they all live. If we presume this arrangement to have longevity over time (an assumption appropriate to the favored case of a *country*), then typical citizens will have been brought up to have such an attitude or policy for practice (and have the feelings appropriate to it), and they will bring up their own children and encourage other citizens to have it.

Such habituation is to be expected (even among rational maximizers, were any to exist by hypothesis in a particular system of rights). For the parties to schemes of cooperation (including schemes of mutual perceived benefit) do not want and cannot afford grudging, suspicious, cost-counting compliance. So maximizers would have every reason to fit right in, to become habituated to compliance, once they had thought it over. Uniform compliance is, as I have emphasized, a reasonable mutual expectation in a system of civil rights.

But Hume's famous "sensible knave," a rational calculator and maximizer of expected personal utility, merely feigns or simulates an attitude of uniform compliance; for the knave (while operating under the protective cloak of feigned compliance) hopes at some decisive point to gain and to take an inadmissible advantage in an undetected act of noncompliance (without thereby suffering any attendant loss of the benefits of the relevant cooperative conventions). The knave would defect, or would be sorely tempted.

Hume's knave is something of a defector *ex machina*. For, if someone were habituated to compliance to a high degree (as the earlier argument suggested typical citizens would be), then compliance would not be feigned; it would be genuine. Real knaves (already formed) might resist habituation to a degree; but they could not resist it completely over the long haul, and they would come to be divided within themselves and to live with a kind of tension. They would be less inclined to defect than would a full-blown knave who had, say, dropped down from the sky—though they would be more inclined to be plagued by temptation (which, often enough, would lose the name of action).

More important, prospective knaves (when very little boys and girls) could hardly resist at all. For them, as adults, there would be even less tension. It seems, then, that real, fully fledged sensible knaves, drop-ins or otherwise, do not actually belong in this story—once we posit bodies politic (on the order of countries), and lifelong habituation is brought in, and the education of children.

It does not follow that noncompliance (or defection, as rational choice theorists call it) will never occur. But if it does, it will tend to occur on grounds other than full-blown sensible knavery. In the present account it could fairly readily occur on two distinct grounds: defective socialization and akrasia (classical weakness of will—including here as well, for convenience, straightforwardly irrational behavior).

Now, we cannot expect socialization to be effective in all cases, or perfectly so in any case; nor can we preclude actual instances of irrationality or other forms of weakness of will (for example, someone's better judgment being overcome by inappropriate appetites and so on—for, after all, feelings are, as we said earlier, sometimes wayward). So we must expect both defective socialization and akrasia to occur. Accordingly, reasonable countermeasures will be required.

In a political system, it is likely that sanction clauses in laws and the imposition of punishment on law violators will be among those measures considered. Thus, a new convention is contemplated, to remedy defects in the convention we have been discussing in the present chapter, the convention of uniform compliance with civil rights laws (or, rather, that convention, when viewed in the light of defective socialization and akrasia).[38]

Is the introduction of practices of punishment a required remedy or a good one for these defects? Is that introduction justifiable, in particular within a system of rights?

I turn to these issues in the next chapter. There I will observe, as my argument ultimately takes shape, the same limitation that has operated in the present chapter. For I will principally be concerned to establish whether punishment is justified in a system of rights, with respect to the civil rights laws there. But some of the laws in such a system do not support civil rights (i.e., some of them do not concern rights or have impact on rights at all and some legal rights are not civil rights) and the sort of justificatory scheme that I will discuss, again, is not intended to justify punishment in the case of such laws.

And now to the theory of punishment.

9

Justifying Coercion: The Problem of Punishment

THE issue of disobedience to law brings many problems in its wake. Chief among these is the appropriate social response, or range of responses, to lawbreaking. For every society is concerned to diminish lawbreaking or, more particularly, to prevent and control crime. Punishment is one possible option here, in a system of rights no less than in any other form of society.

Since punishment is in fact a widespread practice, existing in many kinds of societies and under many guises, we should characterize it so as to allow for the great diversity that has actually obtained there. Thus, our initial attempt at definition must be general, even minimal, touching on essential elements only. Even so, this characterization should be sufficient to fix attention on the main points and to allow a discussion of the justifiability of punishment to get under way.

This chapter is devoted exclusively to punishment under law; the locus of my topic is political–legal as opposed to parental, educational, natural, or divine punishment. Let me begin by identifying what I take to be the main elements of punishment when restricted to a political–legal institution or practice.

I. A CHARACTERIZATION OF LEGAL PUNISHMENT

First, there must be a rule of some sort, or a recognized practice or an acknowledged appropriate way of doing things, which can be broached. The rule need not be written down but, whatever it is, it must be fixed enough that deviations could be identified in advance, and firm enough that such deviations would be discouraged. The understanding here is that one is not supposed to break the rule. Violations would be judged, at least by most people in the society, as wrong or undesirable. Or possibly people there are simply afraid to break the rule.

Then, next, there must be an actual violation and, of course, an actual violator. Indeed, the violator here must be an adjudged violator. One of the peculiarities of punishment, and certainly one of the main reasons it is thought to require justification, is that punishment is carried out after the fact on someone who is no longer violating the law and who is, to all intents, confined or otherwise under the control of those who do the punishing. It is important, then, in any definitional account to bring out the difference between preventing a violation or stopping one in progress (which is what the police or ordinary citizens often do) and punishing a violator (which is what courts and jailers do, after the violation has already occurred). One rather economical way we have of bringing out this peculiar difference is to describe the persons properly liable to be punished not merely as violators but, more precisely, as *adjudged* violators.

Some systems of law might include others among those who are liable to punishment (members of the violator's immediate family, for example, or blood relatives) but there is, even here, an essential reference to an adjudged violator. For without that reference, without such a person and without procedures for identifying that individual (that is, for determining this person's guilt), there would be no way to pick out those who were to be punished in such a system. So, the emphasis on an adjudged violator is well motivated; it seems part of a proper understanding of punishment, even in a deviant system such as this. Accordingly, we will let it figure, as the standard case, in the definition I am developing. So we say that punishment, on this understanding, is applied to *adjudged* violators of a law, as a response to their violation of that law.

I do not want to appear to beg an important question; so let me say a brief word about my procedure here. The first object of a philosophical definition of punishment is merely to indicate what we are talking about; here we describe a widespread practice in a suitably general way by reference to some standard case(s). But we cannot expect such a definition to resolve all the important questions that could arise. For example, we could not use it to determine whether persons other than the adjudged violator *should* be subject to punishment. Rather, what would determine such an issue is that by which that practice of punishment is itself to be justified.

To rely on the definition alone in such an issue would be a philosophical mistake; for we could never, by reference to the mere definition, preclude consideration of the desirability of an alternative that was *like* standard punishment in every respect except that it was, sometimes or often, visited on those who were not themselves adjudged violators. Nor could we preclude consideration of justified exceptions to the standard practice (whatever we might choose to call them). But it would not be a mistake to rely on the composite claim (1) that the selection of elements which figure in the standard case definition of the practice of punishment gives a clear and common understanding of that practice and (2) that the practice as characterized in this definition is justified or can be and that the alternative practices (or the exceptions to the candidate practice) are not similarly justified. For what governs the question of who can properly be punished is not the bare definition of punishment but, rather, that defined practice *as justified* (in the way indicated).

Such a program of analysis requires, of course, that we shape the definition through the inclusion of standard case elements. The practice so defined also requires justification (a point I will be turning to shortly). Only by engaging in some such two-step procedure can we hope to keep a suitably general account of punishment in view and, at the same time, achieve a reasonably secure determination of the issue of who is properly subject to punishment.

Now, rules often carry on their face a clause which tells what is appropriate as a response to the rule's violation. (Or such information could be provided in a separate rule.) But such explicitness is not required. It is enough that there be an understanding—which could, of course, be communicated if the situation demanded—that *some* response would appropriately be forthcoming to violations and toward the violator. Thus, when I say that a violator is punished as a response to violation of law I do not mean to imply that it is expressly said somewhere that the rule's violation is to be punished, or that this is to be done in a precise way or to a particular degree. However, I will assume (as the simplest case) that the rules violated are explicit on these points—by themselves or along with other rules. And my account will proceed as though explicit, rule-given responses were the norm.

Even so, not every such response will count as punishment of the violator. Catching such a violator when that individual is suspected of crime or confining the suspect before trial will not count. Nor, if the suspect were to escape after conviction, would apprehending and forcing such a one to return to custody be counted as punishment either. These are all incidents on the way to lawful punishment, means to that end, but not parts of it. For what counts as punishing this individual is in some sense laid down by the rules in that there is *some* measure to be visited upon the adjudged violator, by some authorized person(s) as the proper or specific or mandated response to that person's violation.

So long as we are concerned with punishment, some rather general lines of response can be sketched here. We ought at least to be able to distinguish punitive responses from nonpunitive ones (from acts of reward or of mercy, for example).

In the main, the philosophical tradition has done this by characterizing punitive responses in a quite particular way: such responses are said to produce pain (on the part of the violator). This way of looking at punishment is very common: it is something that utilitarians such as Bentham and nonutilitarians such as Kant have in common.[1] Authoritative nonpartisan accounts, often take a similar approach to the characterization of punishment, defining it in reference to this element.[2] Even theories that take a curative approach to punishment, like the older theories of Plato and Aristotle, stress that punishment cures the soul of evil by being painful, in much the same way that a doctor cures sick bodies through painful procedures.[3] So, if we were to define punishment in accordance with this pervasive emphasis on the production of pain or suffering, we would say that the practice or institution of punishment involves the provision in law for painful measures to be applied, to those who are adjudged to be breakers of a law, as a specific response to that violation.

This emphasis on producing pain in the violator as the form of the punishment-specific response, as the very essence of the practice, is not universal among philosophers. Some have made coercion the principal feature of punishment. Such a view has been ably set forth by Hegel, for example, but it is by no means unique to him.[4] It is, nonetheless, decidedly the minority view.

The decision between these two lines of characterizing punishment is not easy to make. For one thing, the border between them often blurs: measures for coercion are themselves often painful. Indeed, if one holds with Mill that the desirable and the pleasant, or the undesirable and the painful, are names "for the same thing," then when one is coerced, one is presumably doing that which one doesn't desire; and, insofar as the undesirable and the unpleasant (or the painful) tend to mean the same thing, the coercive and the painful become blended conceptually, perhaps inextricably.[5] For another, even if we could separate the two conceptually, or at least distinguish things that were unpleasant merely because they were coerced from things otherwise unpleasant, reserving 'painful' for the latter class, the fact would remain that violators in being punished are often coerced to undergo that which is painful. They are *forced* to suffer. So I see no easy way to pull these two strands apart: coercion, on the one side, pain and suffering, on the other.

Perhaps the simplest expedient would be to incorporate *both* features into our preliminary definition; thus, we could speak of provision in law "for painful and/or coercive measures," to be applied to violators as a specific response to violations. Then we could leave the matter of choosing between these alternatives, if such choice can be made, to subsequent philosophical argument and attendant refining of the issues.

I would prefer, however, to simplify things at the very beginning by emphasizing coercion, treating it as the principal and definitive feature of the two. I do this for theoretical reasons that go beyond the narrower issue of punishment. In Chapter 1, I argued that the justification of coercion is one of the key ingredients in the philosophical justification of political authority. Or, as I put it there, the element of coercion is one of the features that would be included were one to succeed in justifying political authority within a particular political system. Now, punishment, it is agreed on all sides, is one of the main ways in which coercion enters and plays a role in any political system, excepting possibly those that are anarchist. So there is a good theoretical reason to emphasize coercion, at least preliminarily, in one's account of punishment, while leaving it open that an equally deep or even deeper characterization of punishment—as the production of pain—remains possible. (Here it would always and necessarily be pain and suffering that the adjudged violator is coerced to undergo.) And I have assumed throughout that if the coercion involved in the practice of punishment (where we not only provide for sanctions in law against violation but also sometimes actually carry them out) can be justified, then the coercion involved in having laws, in particular in having punitive laws (where the coercive measures are only threatened), can also be justified.

So, we reach by this path the starting point for my account of punishment; for we are now in a position to characterize the practice of punishment with which this chapter is concerned. Here, the institution or practice of punishment is understood to involve two things: first, it involves the provision in a law for coercive measures to be applied by an authorized person, to those who are adjudged to be violators of a particular law, as a specified response to that violation; second, it involves the actual carrying out of the provision, on the occasions when it is so applied, against an adjudged violator.[6] One is said to be punished—or punished properly—when such a provision does exist and when the coercive measures are carried out in accordance with that provision.

What one must principally justify, then, is having provisions for sanctions and having certain particular ones (with the understanding that these sanctions are sometimes carried out). If punishment cannot be justified at the level of such provisions—at the level of providing for legal sanctions—then there would not even be such a thing as a justifiable act of punishment on a given occasion.

2. JUSTIFICATION

Now that the concept of punishment has been suitably focused, we can turn to the issue of justifying punishment so conceived. The issue is whether there ought to be provisions in law for coercive measures to be applied as specified sanctions for the violation of laws. What would count as a justification?

2.1. *Standard Theories*

There are three standard normative theories of the justification of punishment: the reformatory, the retributivist, and the utilitarian-deterrent. These three normative theories have in common the belief that punishment has, or can be shown to have, a "General Justifying Aim."[7] Each of them is conceived to be a theory for specifying that aim (as, respectively, reformation of character, the righting of moral wrong, the deterrence of pain-producing actions as part of promoting general welfare). And in each case the practice of punishment, in one society or another, is to be brought directly under the preferred aim and inspected to see whether punishment there comports with that aim and hence whether or not that practice can be justified. Is it useful to voice any sort of dissatisfaction with this approach?

I want to raise a conceptual objection. In each case, a particular feature has been abstracted from a more general account of punishment (whether that feature be individual bad character, or moral wrong, or the production of pain by lawbreaking, with attendant lessening of general well-being) and given special emphasis. I do not say such emphases are out of place in an inquiry into the justifiability of punishment. But I do think each abstraction here involves displacing the very trait that centrally characterizes punishment in the account we have been considering. I mean the trait that punishment is being conceived as a political–legal institution.

Let me put my objection more positively now. Punishment under law is something that is dependent on the existence of governments and laws. It is a political institution which is essentially implicated, as a practice, with other political institutions.

Thus, the thing that triggers the carrying out of a punitive sanction is a violation of the law of the land (more precisely, an *adjudged* violation of that law). Such coercive measures have antecedently been provided for in duly enacted laws, as specified responses to such judgments. When any coercive measure is carried out, against an adjudged violator, it is done by governmental or other authorized agencies in accordance with law and with the previous decision of some public body.

We have not said, however, that violators necessarily have bad characters or that they have committed wrongs (as judged by utilitarian or other superordinate moral standards). Rather, we regard them as lawbreakers. The concern of punishment under law begins at this point, with crimes against the law of the land and with adjudged lawbreakers.

2.2. *An Alternative Account of Justification*

Punishment so conceived is located in a system of political institutions and principles. It is located in some *particular* political system. A justification of punishment that stayed with such a focus would itself be system-located; it would attempt to see how punishment fits in with the other main institutions, to see what job it is doing in relation to them.

This is the consideration I have foremost in mind. Here we would be concerned, then, not with punishment's "General Justifying Aim," but instead with its system-located justifying aim (or, better, function).

To justify punishment in such a case is to display its *rationale*. Punishment conceived as system-located can be justified by showing its role, its systematic relationships within a given kind of state. Such a justification of punishment is internal. An internal justification of punishment shows its place, and indeed, if possible, the necessity for it there, within a particular theoretic system of political institutions and principles. The ideal of internal justification is to see legal punishment as an integrated part of a theoretic system of politics.

Clearly, this question of rationale can arise in particular systems; indeed, I would argue that it will arise in *any* particular system. Thus, even as a political conception, punishment does require justification. It requires a political justification.

Now it may have, or come to be supplied with, some sort of critical moral justification as well; this I do not deny. I do not want to be taken as saying that, in the nature of the case, it is logically impossible to bring all cases (or practices) of legal punishment under the scrutiny of some comprehensive normative ethical theory. Indeed, I mean to leave that question open.

An ultimate justification, by reference to principles of critical morality, is certainly possible; here it would involve taking stock of the particular political system in which something conceived as punishment has its location and its system-specific justification. Thus, in the account I am offering, if there is such a thing as an independent moral justification of punishment, it is probably best played out at the level of considering—perhaps justifying— an entire theoretic system of political concepts and institutions, and it is then only indirectly a justification of legal punishment.

Thus, there are two ways of justifying legal punishment in the account I am giving: (1) directly, by locating something conceived as punishment within a particular political system and (2) indirectly, by considering the particular political system in which something conceived as punishment is located.

An attempt to escape this stricture—by bringing the practice of punishment in a given society directly and in relative isolation under high-order moral norms—would simply not grasp the point of legal punishment in its relation to political institutions and would fail to determine whether punishment was successful in fulfilling that point. Such a justification would be inappropriate insofar as punishment is indeed a political–legal institution. We would, in fact, have lost the distinctive sense of it as a political practice at all.

In following out a system-located analysis, where we regard punishment as related to certain other institutions (perhaps as necessary to them), and hence as having a role to play for that reason, we are not going to pass moral judgment on punishment without at the same time passing some sort of critical moral judgment on these other institutions. Such judgment cannot, reasonably, be passed on punishment alone and in isolation. Punishment, accordingly, should not simply be brought *directly* under some superordinate moral norm. Rather, just insofar as punishment is internally related to other political institutions, then these other institutions should also be the locus of moral judgment.

My argument here is intended to suggest, then, that the full account of any actual practice of legal punishment involves reference to other political institutions such that punishment should be neither ultimately justified nor discredited in abstraction from the network in which it is located. Thus, any ultimate moral justification of punishment will require the specification of the particular political institutions and ideals in the context of which the historically and systematically determinate practice of punishment is to be located, its functional description completed, and that justification carried through. And if these institutions are systematically related, as they may well be, then the relevant moral judgment will be of the system as a whole. In this case, then, the political or internal justification of punishment has a clear logical priority.[8]

3. JUSTIFICATION OF PUNISHMENT IN A SYSTEM OF RIGHTS

To illustrate my argument with respect to internal justification, I will draw on the schematic political system introduced earlier in this book. That is, I will talk about the role of punishment and its possible justification within a system of rights. And here I will emphasize democratically derived civil rights in particular.

3.1. *The Basic Rationale*

We can begin with a point that is fairly uncontroversial, for without it there would be no need for a discussion of punishment in a system of rights at all. I mean the point that rights can be violated.

I do not want to suggest here that no right is absolute. Instead, I want simply to say that it is logically possible for any right to be violated, whether it is a legal right or a moral right or a social–institutional one. There is nothing in the concept of rights that would rule out violations.

Every right, as I said in Chapter 5, has conditions of possession; every right has a scope (specifying what the right is to); and every right, certainly an absolute one, has or could have an ordinal weight. A way of acting is an infringement of a right only if it is contrary to norms internal to the right; thus, it would be an infringement if it is disallowed by the existing or supposed conditions of possession, scope, or weight.[9] But we do not necessarily count all infringements as violations.

Rather, a way of acting is said to violate a right when it is unjustifiably contrary to the norms internal to that right, when the questionable action infringed the right in an unacceptable way or did so for an unacceptable reason. Thus, some might say that, when the infringement of a particular legal right can be justified by reference to other incumbent *legal* values (for example, another right or a consideration such as public safety or benefit) or by reference to moral values widely accepted and accredited within the society in question, it is not a violation.[10]

Nonetheless, there are for any right some clear cases that would count as violations. They would be judged that way after all the facts were in and all considerations weighed. They would simply be actions contrary to the norms relevant to a given right which could, at the same time, be counted as unjustifiable or unacceptable infringements. And, given the way the world is, it is not unreasonable for us to expect that some, perhaps most or even all, rights will actually be violated.

Suppose now that such an infringement of a right had occurred. What responses would be appropriate? At least one level of response is indicated by a salient feature of all rights. For every right there is some significant normative direction of the conduct of others (so-called second or third parties) given or readily supposed by that right. A liberty of travel, as in the example of the path to the forest pond in Chapter 2, supposes that everybody will forbear preventing such travel in at least some ways. Now, if someone prevented travel in an unacceptable way or for an unacceptable reason, then the rightholder, or others on the rightholder's behalf, might protest. So, one response is simply to direct the offending person to do that which he or she is supposed to do, given the right in question. And such a response, where it falls within the direction that can be given for other parties, would be an entirely appropriate or characteristic response for any violation of a right. Indeed, since the capacity to give such direction or to rely on it is so intimately tied in with the right itself, there would seem to be a close—perhaps even an intrinsic or a conceptual—connection between a right, on the one hand, and this sort of response to the violation of that right, on the other.

The difficulty comes when the violator refuses to give way or returns to violate again. For any *further* response here requires rightholders to go beyond the norms already mentioned as internal to a right, that is, beyond conditions of possession, scope, and weight, and beyond the normative direction of the conduct of others afforded by these conditions in the case of a given right. Or, to put the point differently, we might want to *add* features to the right (or to the system of rights)—or explicitly to recognize features—which tell us (and others) what to do when a rights violation persists or otherwise goes too far.

We want to stop the violation in the case at hand or to prevent such violations in other cases that could arise. In fact, this is the reason one would have in the very first instance for citing the normative direction a right gave: to stop a violation in progress or to prevent future ones. Now, if this is the reason one has for citing the normative direction in the face of a violation, then it cannot be inappropriate—simply in and of itself—to stop, or try to stop, that violation or to prevent, or try to prevent, future ones. I mean it cannot be *intrinsically* wrong, from within the perspective afforded by rights, to act in this way; such conduct seems appropriate.

I would want to argue, on the assumption that mere normative direction having failed once might fail again, that the prevention of violations is no less integral to an account of rights than stopping violations on the spot. Indeed, to say that prevention is effective amounts to saying that some violations on the spot were stopped (that is, they did not occur). The two notions, then, stand or fall together. For the same rationale underlies both—that is, stopping violations on the spot and preventing future violations—namely, the rationale that rights should not be violated. (Or, if this should prove an impossible goal, the rationale would become that the violation of rights should be substantially lessened.)

This rationale, that rights should not be violated *because* rights are to be maintained, is the rationale or norm implicated with the allegiance to law in a system of rights of the typical citizen (as set forth in the previous chapter). It is also the rationale one has, in the face of an actual or likely violation, for *citing* the normative direction that a particular right enjoins upon others.

Now I have argued (in Chapter 2) that the giving of normative direction— or the capacity to give it—is intrinsic to a right. Thus, this rationale becomes intrinsic to rights to the degree that normative direction is itself intrinsic. The same rationale links the giving of normative direction and the stopping or prevention of violations. The tie between preventing violations and the having of rights, as mediated by this rationale, is thus much more intimate than might at first have been apparent. One cannot be said to take rights seriously unless the means for prevention of violations are seen to go hand in hand with rights.

So, it is appropriate to consider measures that might be employed to stop or prevent such violations. Among these would be the institution of punishment. Thus, punishment, in the form of various provisions for coercive sanctions which are then triggered after the fact by an adjudged violation of law, would appear to be appropriate to rights where punishment had the end, among others, of preventing violations of rights. We can see how such an institution might arise as a response to their violation.

But is punishment justified in this role? The argument I developed earlier suggests that it would be if no alternative to punishment will be effective or no alternative will be as effective toward that end. We can, at least, start with this suggestion.

Let us imagine that the basic *alternative* to provisions for coercive sanctions in law is some combination of the following: (1) public education, (2) reformist public policy, that is, redistribution of social roles, economic goods, welfare services, etc., and (3) public decision-making institutions, such as universal suffrage and regular elections and channels for redress. Let us assume that punishment is not included within the combination and that various combinations are possible under the headings (1), (2), and (3). Hence, there are a variety of alternatives to punishment (conceived here as a provision in law of sanctions) for before-the-fact maintenance of civil rights.

Of course, it is also possible to include punishment within these various combinations. When I speak of an option as an alternative to punishment, I mean that the practice of punishment does not constitute any part of that option. The question whether punishment is justifiable is asked, over against these feasible alternative options, with reference to its relative effectiveness in maintaining a variety of particular, determinate civil rights. Thus, if punishment constituted *some* part of the combined social response and if that response proved more effective than combinations which excluded coercive sanctions altogether, then such a scheme of sanctions would be justifiable.

In sum, the main lines of the justification proposed would go something like this. Once we grant (1) that rights might possibly be violated and (2) that violation of rights is to be prevented (because rights are to be maintained), then punishment is justified as an institution within a political system—that is, a system of rights—(3) if it would help maintain a variety of particular, determinate civil rights within such a system and (4) if it was *necessary* either in the sense that no other alternative way would do the job or in the sense that no other feasible alternative could do the job as effectively.

The basic issue is the total social response. I have in mind, then, in the account of justification here, a *total social response* that includes provisions for punitive measures and that also meets the test of relative deterrent effectiveness.

Let me emphasize again that it may be possible, up to a point, to shift the burden onto the nonpunitive elements in such a response. And it may prove desirable in a system of rights to do so (for reasons that should soon become clear). The point is, nonetheless, that if a given desirable set of nonpunitive elements is less effective in deterring lawbreaking than the same set of elements together with the practice of punishment, then punishment is justified there. And I am assuming that punishment so conceived will be justified in a typical system of rights.

3.2. *A Problem: The Rights of the Adjudged Violator*

Immediately, though, we run into the problematic status of coercive responses within a system of rights in particular. For, although provisions in law for coercive measures and even the carrying out of such measures against adjudged violators may be called for (as relatively effective), it is likely that these measures will themselves infringe (and arguably violate) the rights of violators.[11] Thus, a problem is generated. The violation of rights seems to lead to a situation in which punishment is both required (in order to protect rights) and disallowed (as seemingly a violation of rights).

The difficulty I describe here holds for *any* generalized scheme of rights (e.g., a Lockian state of nature or a society in which there are universal political or civil rights). For the problem seems inherent in the very intuitions that govern the philosophy of punishment here. (1) Rights should be maintained; they should not be violated. (2) The violation of a right should be met with an appropriate response. (3) Where mere normative direction has failed and the given violation cannot be stopped, it is nonetheless appropriate to consider the prevention of further violations. (4) Provisions in law for coercive measures may prove necessary in order to prevent violations and thereby protect rights and it may sometimes be necessary to carry out such measures, after an actual violation, upon a confined and adjudged violator. (5) Strong measures are likely to be necessary to protect stringent rights—with weaker but proportionate measures to protect weaker rights—but these measures will themselves be likely to infringe and arguably to violate the rights of violators. (6) But rights should not be violated.[12]

These intuitions do not appear mutually coherent. Thus, in a system of rights the very reason that impels people to utilize punishment, as a response to violations of rights, would forestall their employing it insofar as its use violates rights. The policy of violating the rights of violators—if that is what the infringement comes to—does not seem consistent with an original policy of not violating rights. The two policies, both apparently integral to a system of rights, cannot be worked together. Though the matter is not equally problematic for all theories of punishment (such as the utilitarian theory), this is the central dilemma for a theory of punishment within a system of rights.

I may be less successful in resolving this dilemma than I have been in posing it. But I do think it useful to note at the very beginning that the crucial issue here is not infringement of rights (for that is assumed in the very stating of the problem) but, rather, their violation by punishment. The dilemma holds only if punishment actually *violates* rights. The dilemma arises from thinking that punishment, while apparently required to protect rights, is ultimately inconsistent with them (since it operates, characteristically, by violating rights).

The way round the dilemma, then, is to show the basic compatibility of punishment with rights. Then if we can also show its role (to prevent violations) as necessary within a system of rights, we have the required justification of punishment and with it the resolution of the dilemma. For punishment in such a scheme, though it might count as an infringement of a right, is compatible with that right and would not count as its violation (because punishment is justified here) and hence would be consistent with the injunction that rights should not be violated.

3.3. *A First Step Toward Resolution of the Problem: Compatibility*

We shall approach this issue of compatibility through a series of steps. Let us first consider a typical case. Someone (a public official, say, or a banker) has large sums of money under her control and has siphoned off considerable amounts for her own personal use. For the sake of simplicity we can assume that she was not doing this to vindicate a right of any sort and that her embezzlement could be adjudged as wrong. Suppose, then, that the community decreed two responses upon apprehending and judging the culprit: one was full restitution and the other a fine, a sum of money to be drawn from the official's own account, "to deter like conduct by her or others in the future." One plausible way to view this latter sanction is to say that it served to vindicate the very same right as was being abridged by the sanction—call it A (in the case at hand, the right to security of funds).

I cannot call this right a truly stringent one, but it has in the example at hand certain interesting features which need to be brought out. First, the right A presumably had a scope; and, after note was taken of various limitations in that scope, we would be able to refer to its central core. We can assume that, whatever the banker did, it infringed A within its central core; equally, we should assume that when her funds were taken by way of sanction, that too infringed on the central core of the right A. Thus the question of scope is set aside as not germane; it has been used up in making the claim that there have been infringements of A on both sides. In the same way the issue of possession could be set aside. We assume that the banker's victims possessed the right A; they had not waived it or otherwise become dispossessed of it. This much seems implied by the claim that the banker had violated—infringed unjustifiably—their right. We also assume that the banker possessed that same right; otherwise we could not speak of its infringement in *her* case. (And without that claim the problematic issue we are trying to resolve could not even arise.) We are left, then, with only one remaining intrinsic consideration of any moment: that of weight (where the weight of a right is its standing in competition with other rights or with other sorts of normative values).

The point here can be put somewhat differently. First, unless we assumed that *all* infringements of a right's well-defined core (or all infringements of a right clearly possessed) are wrongful, then we sometimes cannot say, given simply the right's conditions of possession or scope, that an infringement of it was wrong. And, second, where we require the notions of scope and possession in order to develop a claim of infringement by sanction (and where these notions do not, as used, in themselves rule out that infringement as impermissible), then the only way in which we could determine that the infringement was in fact impermissible—without going beyond the right involved—would be to rely on comparative weight. Here, though, it would always be impermissible to infringe a right of greater weight in the interests of protecting one of lesser weight.

Let me fill in behind this argument a bit. Two points seem controversial and I will take them up in turn. First, I suggested that a certain assumption would be improper. Why? Because I argued (in Chapter 5) that rights can conflict and that some kinds of conflict are inevitable. Thus, where rights do conflict, the exercise of one right (or of one instance of a given right, e.g., A) will necessarily infringe another right (or another instance of A). It would follow then, if all infringements are violations, that at certain points one could not avoid, while exercising some rights, the violation of other rights. And rights would become incoherent at just such points, for in a system of rights it would be impossible consistently to follow the principle that rights should be maintained and not violated. At such points, then, rights could not form a system. Thus, in order to avoid the incoherence of rights, all theorists of rights need the supposition that not all infringements are violations of rights. The point here is not made specifically in reference to punishment and is in no way *ad hoc*; it is a general principle of rights theory.[13]

So some infringements are not violations of rights, specifically those infringements that are not disallowed by the relative weights of the rights involved. Conversely, those infringements that did not conform to the relevant weightings would not be allowable in a system of rights; they would be inherently or intrinsically incompatible with one of the very norms that constituted the concept of rights.

I am not saying here that there is going to be a weight ordering between each and every right in a system of rights or between any two rights in a given case. My argument (especially in Chapter 5) assumes only that there could be some such ordering and that nonarbitrary ordering of this kind is desirable (the more of it the better) in a system of rights. But individual orderings would, of course, have to be constructed (by the legislature or by the courts), and this takes time and ingenuity. Accordingly, my argument asserts simply that, where there is an ordering of inequality between two rights, it is intrinsically or inherently impermissible for the right with lesser weight (or with lesser weight in a given case) to infringe that with greater.

This brings us to the second controversial point: that I have put too much weight on weight. A critic of my account might say that things are not quite so simple. Weight may be an important factor but it is not the only relevant consideration. We could, for example, also have regard to the number of people harmed by the original violation or the number of people who would *not* be harmed in the future if such violations were significantly discouraged. We would, of course, have to set such a consideration against the number of people whose right was invaded by the employment of the punitive sanction (or whose rights were now restricted by allowing, in a provision in law, that it could be employed). The proper calculation, then, would be made by taking the relative weights and multiplying them by the relevant number of persons, with the larger aggregate preponderating. Thus, if the aggregative calculation favored it, we might permissibly jail someone for shoplifting a loaf of bread, where that penalty deterred acts of stealing bread from, say, a hundred stores; we might do so even though we also believe that the right to liberty of movement, etc. (the right invaded by the sanction) is of greater weight than the rights of property and of protection from injury on the part of the owners in the case at hand.

This is, I grant, not an implausible view to take—from a certain perspective. What it amounts to is a special case of considering general or aggregative well-being, with the enjoyment of rights (rather than other possible satisfactions or preferences) as the focal value being maximized— or, at least, appreciably increased.

But it is not the only view one could take. More crucially, it is not the characteristic view that would be taken in a system of rights. Rather, the characteristic view is that a right of greater weight should not be sacrificed to one of lesser weight on a given occasion—even if only one person is the affected rightholder on the side of the right with greater weight and many people are the affected rightholders on the other side.[14]

Why hold such a view? Suppose we said about a given right that it was weightier than another (as liberty of movement is, supposedly, weightier than a merchant's property right in loaves of bread or such an individual's right to avoid the injury of their being pilfered). It would follow that on most occasions the weightier right would outweigh the lesser right, in that the lesser right would not infringe the greater (though the greater might sometimes infringe the lesser right). If things were not so, if the infringements did not follow this pattern, then the claim that the one right was weightier would be hollow. The right in question would be merely nominal (that is, in such a case it would be, on the point of its determinate weight, like a nominal right). Thus, a fully effective right, where it is weightier, will not be infringed on many occasions by a right of lesser weight.

By the same token, it cannot be justifiably infringed even on a given occasion unless the infringing right on *that* occasion is weightier. Otherwise, we have deviated from what counts as the appropriate enjoyment of these rights, as determined by the respective rules that constitute these rights and by the authoritative decisions that do in fact set, where they are set, and fine tune the weight of these rights to one another and to other rights and to other normative considerations.

In sum, we characteristically turn to norms internal to the rights involved, within a system of rights, to decide about permissible infringements. Certainly, we do so when the weights of the rights are set or can be determined. To act otherwise with civil rights is to introduce indeterminacy and instability into the system of rights at crucial points where matters were, presumably, already settled to the benefit of each and all. Hence, we do not regard as relevant the number of people—the number of affected rightholders *per se*—where the respective weights and lines of priority have been set.

Now, admittedly, my argument has throughout emphasized *civil* rights and these are rights that every citizen has or, ideally, that everybody in a given country has. But this is not a matter of numbers of the sort we have been discussing. For civil rights count as civil, as universal, regardless of how many (or how few) actually have them—so long, that is, as everybody has them. More important, the fact that everyone has them is already impounded in the priority we accord civil rights over rights that are not universal; accordingly, the relative number of rightholders (as given in some cardinal number) is not something we take account of here *in addition* to the priority of these respective rights. So the consideration that we are peculiarly concerned with civil rights does not affect the argument I am making. And the point still stands that, where there is a relevant weight or where that weight can be determined, it is the weight (or ordinal priority) that counts in deciding permissible infringements, not weight multiplied by the number of affected rightholders.

So we can safely continue to make that point in the analysis of the case under review, the case of the banker. Here we assume that the weights are equal on each side for the simple reason, perhaps a peculiar one, that the *same* right was involved throughout. Thus, the weight of the right the banker violated was identical to the weight of the right which was infringed by the sanction—or, as we could properly say here, by the penalty. It would have to be, given that it was simply the weight of A and A was the right involved on both sides.

The fact of weight here could not be relied on, then, to overrule the penalty. Whatever the weight of the right being protected was—a matter otherwise left indeterminate—it could not rule out the penalty in question as intrinsically incompatible with the weight of A, the right being infringed by the penalty.

Indeed, such a claim could be made out only if the right so infringed had a *greater* weight (or, at least, had a greater weight on the occasion in question) than that of the right being protected; and this is impossible, by hypothesis, in the example at hand. In short, the basic compatibility we seek, between the right protected and the right infringed by penalty, is satisfied when the weight of the former right is equal to, or greater than, the weight of the latter right.

We could not assert, in the banker's case, that one right was being strengthened at the expense of another. For the right that the penalty vindicated was the same right that the penalty infringed. In any event it would be difficult to say that right A was not better maintained by these transactions. It has become a more secure right for all rightholders, the banker included, than it was before the punitive event we are here concerned with. And this strengthening persisted, if we grant preventive effect, even after a deduction had been made for the penalizing of the banker. Indeed, it is not clear that people would even perceive that penalty as reducing the effectiveness of the right or, for that matter, that even the banker herself would, in her reflective moments. Here at least one right is appreciably strengthened, and none appreciably weakened, by the penalty. So the *system* of rights is strengthened by its addition.

In the case above we have a set of arguments for saying that the penalty invoked, insofar as it is an infringement on right A, is not incompatible with A so far as any rights considerations intrinsic to A are concerned. But we cannot go from this directly to the assumption that the penalty is thereby justified and, accordingly, that the right (in the case of the banker) could justifiably be overridden by the infringing penalty.

3.4. *A Second Step toward Resolution: Relative Deterrent Effectiveness*

In suggesting a line of solution to the difficulty posed by compatibility we have introduced a new complication. For we now have the idea of a specific sanction, one that infringes a *particular* right, to deal with (for example, a fine that protects one right A but has the effect in doing so of infringing that same right, as held by the offender, or of infringing another right B, again of the offender). So we must be concerned now not just with any old rights-restricting sanction (or with sanctions generically) but with a specific one in which a particular right (for simplicity call it B) is characteristically infringed.

Thus, even after showing compatibility, we would still have to show not only that the specific sanction was effective—that the type of penalty invoked was instrumental, on the occasions when it was used, to the end of preventing (or substantially lessening) further violations of the right being vindicated—but also that there was, on balance, no significant evidence that a punitive sanction which infringed a right of lesser weight than B—or, for that matter, one which infringed no right at all—would be as effective (in preventing violations of the protected right) as the sanction we are here contemplating; and no significant evidence that another sanction which infringed a right of roughly equal weight to B would be considerably more effective or that a sanction which infringed a right of *marginally* greater weight would be *substantially* more effective. In sum, compatibility and relative deterrent effectiveness are the tests that would determine the justifiability of particular sanctions within the practice of punishment in a system of rights.[15]

But any such judgment involves, as I have already indicated, an essential background judgment about sanctions overall (or generically) in relation to a variety of complementary and alternative patterns to punishing. I mean the background judgment relied on in the basic rationale for punishment (in Section 3.1): the judgment that punitive sanctions (including those that infringed rights of adjudged violators) were themselves necessary to the end of preventing rights violations. I mean necessary in the sense that no other feasible responses could do the job of prevention at all or that no other such responses could do the job as well.

This point about overall necessity requires further elaboration in the present context, however. For the analysis has added a new wrinkle with the addition of the requirements of compatibility and relative deterrent effectiveness. What we need to do at this point, then, is compare rights-restricting sanctions (or, more properly, *kinds* of sanctions) with responses that are not punitive and that do *not* infringe rights. Such a comparison might run, for example, with mere after-the-violation giving of normative direction to the offender (telling the offender what should have been done in view of the right in question). Or, beyond that, it might include mere conventional moral criticism of the offender's wrongful conduct. Or it might include the offender's making voluntary restitution, perhaps without being blamed, and so on. In addition we would also consider such preventive, before-the-fact devices as improved public education, etc. These are, in a way, also feasible alternatives or complements to punishment. Here we would attempt to establish a *necessary* role for rights-restricting sanctions, by showing in such a comparison that they were more effective (within the total response) in preventing violations of rights than alternatives such as these that (alone or in combination) were not punitive or that did not restrict rights.

Of course, the judgments in question (as to overall necessity, as I have called it, and as to relative deterrent effectiveness) are rough-and-ready ones. Essentially they are based on commonsense beliefs about deterrent effectiveness: that undesirable conduct can be deterred by sanctions and that it doesn't make sense (and opens one to criticism) to use sanctions inefficiently. But we should not rest content with such commonsense judgments; further scrutiny is always in order. Here social scientific investigation could be called upon, as a second stage, to help establish these crucial points. In the end, then, punitive sanctions would be justified only if some such second stage of investigation showed that, besides meeting the tests mentioned above concerning certain comparative factors (for particular sanctions), the practice or institution of punishment (including sanctions that infringed rights) was *generally* necessary in preventing or reducing law violation.

Now, suppose justification on this last point—(1) the necessity of the whole practice—can be made out. Then (2) if the point about compatibility, about allowable infringement, can also be established (by reference to the competitive weight of specific rights), we could conclude that where (3) such an infringement was effective and where (4) it met the test of relative deterrent effectiveness it would be justified and would not count as a violation.[16]

If we can show these four things, then the dilemma between punishment and rights (focusing on the rights of the adjudged violator) is solved. We have in these considerations the paradigm solution to our problem. For here the right infringed by sanction is not violated.

The argument for this solution (and assuming satisfaction of the background requirement of general necessity) could now be generalized to cover any two specific rights and, hence, an entire system of rights. Thus, in considering the weight of any two rights D and E, if the right being vindicated was not outweighed by the right being infringed in the process of punishment, then nothing *internal* to the rights involved would rule out that infringement. (That is, basic compatibility is satisfied in that the weight of the former right is equal to, or greater than, the weight of the latter right. And we assume that no consideration of possession or of scope could be invoked against such a sanction either.) Then, if we could show that a particular sanction was effective in protecting a determinate right and was in fact relatively effective as a deterrent (again by reference to the weights of the rights infringed by various possible sanctions or by identifiable nonpunitive responses), then it would be irrational from the perspective of rights not to add (and sometimes use) such a measure.

The protected right, say, the right not to be physically assaulted, would be better served for all, the assailant and all others, in that future violations would be appreciably deterred. And the right to, say, freedom of movement (the right presumably infringed by penalty here) would, by reference to that same criterion, not be significantly weakened—because violation of it would not, through such infringements, thereby be increased. Here infringing one right in order to protect another is consistent with the fact that each is a right. And we have in these cases, although an infringement of the right in question, no violation of it.

By hypothesis the infringements are justifiable and hence could not be violations. There is then, in Nozick's phrase, no utilitarianism of rights— where one right is *violated* in the interests of protecting another from violation—in these cases.[17]

Nor do we have a situation where some persons (that is, adjudged violators) are treated as means only and not as ends. In a system of rights all persons are rightholders—the same civil rights are held equally by all—and no person is punished merely as a means of protecting the rights of *other* persons. Rather, the institution of punishment within a system of rights treats the rights of everyone the same and strengthens the rights of everyone, including those who are adjudged violators of the laws.

4. THE INSTITUTION OF PUNISHMENT IN A SYSTEM OF RIGHTS

Now that we have made these points, let us see how a system of rights would, characteristically, adjust to the fact of such justified infringements of rights. Once particular sanctions (that is, coercive measures in law, to be triggered by adjudged violations) are thought to be justified, on the grounds of compatibility and relative deterrent effectiveness (in relation to other, allowable sanctions), it is very likely that provisions for such sanctions would be built in—either in the rules themselves that define the rights or in the system itself, as a sort of generalized understanding of how the system worked.

For example, a provision for penalty might occur in a clause attached to the defining rule for a particular right. Thus, in the banker case, the added penalty clause might say that the bank account of "a person who embezzles" could itself be confiscated "to deter violations of the right to security of funds on deposit." Here, then, the scope of this right—to security of funds on deposit—would be defined to exclude in effect the security of funds on deposit of adjudged violators of that right. Thus, the original right of the embezzler—which we assume not to have included the clause indicated (otherwise the problem canvassed earlier simply would not have arisen)—would no longer be her right in this amended version. Or, to put the point precisely, she would continue to have the right to security of funds as a depositor but it would not be available to her as a convicted embezzler. Once she was convicted the security of her funds, up to a point at least, would no longer count as part of what the right protects. A partition has been erected. And no question of that right's being infringed or possibly outweighed would even arise in subsequent penalizations under that rule. For the sanctions specified would be included *within* the right, as defined in the amended rule.

In a maturing system of rights the direction taken would probably involve accentuating two distinct elements in this example. (1) The development of provisions for penalty and other sanctions would become part of the formulation of rights, in that penalties (for violation) would be written into the sanctions clauses attached as protections to the various rights. (2) There would be effective restriction of *other* rights in that system insofar as they figured in those penalties.

Let us consider this second point, in particular. In such a system, the right to E (the right that is to be restricted by penalty, as named in the penalty clause of right D) would be properly regarded as so restricted, by the right to D. Of course, this restricting could take quite explicit shape; the restriction could be written into the formula that defines right E, as a definite partitioning or delimitation of its scope.

Thus, once it was determined that the restriction of right E was justified in order to protect right D, the popular understanding of right D could be modified, correctly, to include the clause that violations of D would be met with a specific limitation on right E. And, correspondingly, the popular understanding of right E could now include, correctly, the statement that the right, for example, to freedom of movement, could justifiably be restricted as the penalty for violating right D. Here the penalty clause for one specific right D, a clause newly added in our example, would be directly mirrored as an explicit restriction on the scope of another specific right E, built into the very formula for defining E as a right. We would have an explicitly symmetrical (or mirror image) relation between the sanctions clause of one right (D) and the definition of scope of another (E). And here, clearly, the sanction invoked in the penalty clause of D would not, when it was carried out, infringe E as now defined—though one could still say that E (in a possible earlier definition, where its scope had not been restricted in this mirror image fashion) was allowably and justifiably *infringed* by that sanction.

Of course, our overall solution (the restriction, under well-defined conditions, of one right in the interest of another) need not take exactly a mirror image form. Scope restriction could be treated, rather, simply as a general but implicit feature of a system of rights—a feature that does not require encapsulation in the form of an explicit restriction on scope of the various specific right(s) 'infringed' by penalty. Here the partition of the scope of E (required to accommodate the justifiable restriction of E as an explicitly set penalty for violators of D) might be directly mediated, not by a clause in the definition of E, but by a free-standing institution—an agency of government—which applied the penalty clause in D, after due consideration, as a restriction on the exercise of E. There would be no formal recognition of this restriction in the statement of E, and it would be a restriction here *only* on the person who had been adjudged a violator of D. Now we have a second kind of relation between the sanctions clause of one right (D) and the definition of its scope of another (E)—not a symmetrical or mirror image kind but, instead, an implicit and systemic kind.

The advantage of this latter or institutionalizing kind is that it is more economical, conceptually, especially as the number and the internal complexity of rights increases. It leaves unchanged, on the surface at least, the scope of the rights infringed by penalty, while emphasizing the institutional mechanisms of rights restriction by which punishment proceeds.

Even so, the fundamental result of the two moves contemplated here— the move to a symmetrical or mirror image scheme or the move to a systemic and implicit one—is not substantially different. Limiting the scope of a right (E in the case at hand) by reference to the sanctions clause of another (D in the case at hand) would be equally effective in a system of rights, whether the restriction was explicitly included in the defining rule for E or not. Therefore, it is proper to view any given right within such a system as susceptible to either move. Thus, the restrictions we have described could either be built in as explicit or, alternatively, as *de jure* institutional restrictions on the scope of rights within that system.

And, equally in each case, the sanction invoked in the penalty clause of D would not, when it was properly carried out, infringe E as now defined. Thus, we are able to remove the implication, troublesome to some, that where the right to E is justifiably restricted by the sanctions clause of right D, the invoking of punitive measures under that clause infringes someone's right to E.

Now, we have assumed in the argument so far that punishment will not be confined to just one or two rights but will, in fact, be a pervasive practice, a protective measure which could attach (in principle at least) to virtually all the civil rights in a given system of rights. And I would further assume that, where this is so, much of the detail of this general practice will be spelled out as part of the background of that system, in the form of institutional devices (police, courts, jails, etc.) and the attendant institutional restrictions on the scope of rights introduced by those devices. So, we can take this approach, in which the institutional background is emphasized, as the favored case for the incorporation of punishment into a system of rights—that is, favored over explicitly including in the scope of each and every right being burdened by a sanction (say, any right E) that it was so restricted in order to protect, say, D.

This procedure for incorporating punishment is not circular or in any way question-begging. For even though the protection of rights might itself be claimed as a right, or, more properly, as a feature of rights, the institution of punishment is not thereby automatically included under such a claim. Rather, the practice of punishment, as a general background feature in a system of rights, is an allowable feature only if it is justifiable and it is justifiable only if it is compatible with determinate rights in the system and, after that, is effective in limiting the violation of civil rights.

By the same token, when punishment is established as an internally justified general background institution within a system of rights, particular safeguards can be claimed, with respect to penal codes, as rights under law by the citizens (including those who are violators). But again this involves no circularity in the justifiability of the practice of punishment. My argument assumes no antecedent right to various safeguards under a penal code, and hence no determinate rights under this code (to provide, for example, the various measures of due process), unless the general practice of punishment is justified in the first place.

Some of the safeguard measures will be added, and historically have been added, *after* the institution of punishment has been introduced. (Thus, the question of whether television cameras could be installed to monitor the cells of inmates is not one that would arise unless the practice of punishment— and, perhaps, of imprisonment—was already in place.) But some of the important measures come in, I would argue, at the same time as the title to punish. Among the most significant of these are the procedures for making a reasonable and reliable determination of guilt, as the necessary prelude to punishment. I do not mean any particular procedures here (such as trial by jury or the requirement for a unanimous jury decision in certain cases or the requirement that one be able to face hostile witnesses or one's accuser in an open court) but, rather, the very idea that there should be a reasonable procedure and, accordingly, the requirement of *some* such devices.

5. THE AUXILIARY INSTITUTION OF FAIR TRIAL

The idea of such procedures could be introduced into our account at this point on the simple ground that it is appropriate. After all, the theme of punishment was originally brought into the picture as a response to violations of law and was considered, from the very beginning, as involving adjudged violators; without some such procedures there could be no reliable way to identify (to adjudge) violators. Mention of these procedures, then, merely makes explicit what has been there, objectively, all along. Indeed, it captures the widely held belief that procedures for determining guilt are an integral feature of punishment and would be found in *any* political system in which punishment had a place.

But a claim of appropriateness, though it would fit the story we have told, would not be the only consideration. Independent reasons could be advanced. Indeed, they would have to be. For we are concerned not merely with what counts as punishment but also with whether that practice can be justified. As I argued earlier, it is not the bare definition of punishment that determines who can properly be punished in a given political system but, rather, whether that practice (when characterized as including adjudged violators) can be justified there.

We are concerned with the place of punishment in a system of rights in particular. The important reason for the inclusion of procedures for determining guilt in an account of punishment has to do here with the very features that would justify punishment in that system.

I argued in this regard that a sanction which restricted E, itself a right, could be justified if the weights of the respective rights involved were compatible and if threatening that sanction and sometimes using it had comparative deterrent effectiveness (in relation to other sanctions, or to other identifiable nonpunitive responses)—either in preventing further violations of right D (any right of roughly equal weight to E), or of F (a weightier right than E).

This judgment involved in turn, as an essential part of its background, consideration of a variety of complementary and alternative patterns to punishing (which included, we might recall, a number of things, such as public education, which were conceived of as existing and operating alongside punishment). For we are, as I argued earlier, interested in the best feasible *total social response* to the violation of law. In that regard, then, punitive sanctions would be justified only if, besides meeting the tests mentioned above concerning certain comparative factors (for particular sanctions), the *general* practice or institution of punishment was necessary in preventing or reducing law violation.

Here the *overall* practice had to be effective to that end and necessary in that no other feasible total social response was as effective as one that included the institution of punishment among its features. If punishment failed at this point—failed on the score of general or overall necessity—then it would not be justifiable in a system of rights. For to infringe rights unduly (that is, unnecessarily or for an unacceptable reason or in an unacceptable way) is to violate them and rights are not to be violated in such a system.

I want to suggest that reasonable and reliable procedures for determining guilt (e.g., in a trial of some sort) would come in as an institution complementary to punishment in that particular total social response which is justified in a system of rights. I say this because, if there were no procedures for apprehending and judging violators, or if such procedures were quite inadequate, and the practice of punishment were nonetheless persisted in, then we would be in the position of mounting a less effective response than one in which there were such procedures. And if we did, nonetheless, mount such a response, then rights (those of the persons being punished) would be infringed unnecessarily or unjustifiably. And this is wrong in a system of rights, for it counts as a violation of rights.

Imagine in this regard a social system which, through sloth or ignorance or queer belief, dealt with law violations through an elaborate scheme of 'scapegoating.' When crimes occurred someone was *always* punished. But people knew, nevertheless, that there was in such cases no relation between who had committed the crime and who got scapegoated. The authorities didn't even *try* to find the one who had actually done it. Suppose this was, more or less, the whole story—or an essential part of it. There would be, then, in that society no incentive for people not to commit crimes and, for those most likely to commit them, no good reason to refrain from doing so. Regardless of whether or not one committed a crime, scapegoating might result. Committing crimes, even habitually, did not increase a whit one's chances of being scapegoated; and scrupulously staying within the law, never violating it, did not decrease them by so much as a degree. It was all, seemingly, perfectly arbitrary. So, whatever good scapegoating accomplished (perhaps by pleasing the gods) it was quite ineffective toward the goal of preventing violations of law.[18]

Someone might claim, however, that my argument is weak at an important point. It does not consider the case where literally everyone, or almost everyone, is punished each time a crime occurs (and, presumably, such an imposition of sanctions would be effective). I don't consider such a case because the facts of the case are psychologically implausible; and, hence, it would not be at all effective. People simply would not put up with such an arbitrary arrangement. Indeed, if we are considering a polity with effective democratic institutions it is psychologically implausible that arbitrary imposition of punishment (as in the scapegoat example) on a group as large as a *majority* of the voters would be accepted as a practice or institutional arrangement there. Accordingly, scapegoating would have to be severely restricted—to an arbitrary imposition of sanctions on a relatively small subset of the whole population. It is not clear even that random imposition on *individuals* each time a crime is committed would be tolerated over the long run, but I leave this point aside in order to make a further and more important point.

A system which ties punishment to the actual commission of crime would do better at reducing crime than scapegoating (understood as the *random* imposition, each time a crime is committed, of sanctions on individuals or on arbitrarily constituted small groups). Thus, supposing we compared the two practices on this point alone, the former system would be preferred to one in which there was no connection at all (as in scapegoating) or relatively little. Hence, the same basic rationale that justifies the institution of punishment in the first place, that is, that it is necessary in that it is more effective in lessening law violations (than nonpunitive alternatives acting, alone or in combination, but without any practice of punishment), would also justify reasonable procedures for determining that someone is a violator (as a precondition for punishing that person).

The contrast here is, admittedly, stark (between having, on the one hand, procedures such as trial available as an adjunct to punishing and, on the other, simply scapegoating). But if we narrowed the gap by introducing into scapegoating procedures that were specific to crime prevention (such as better police protection), then the dialectic of the argument would always move toward the point I have suggested. For, unless reliable determination of guilt as a precondition of punishing was included, there would always be some feasible system exactly like the one we are describing except on that one crucial point (of scrupulously tying punishment to adjudged guilt) and the system that included that precondition would always be, other things equal, more effective in preventing law violations. Hence, those procedures, the satisfaction of which makes for a reliable trial in determination of guilt, would enter a system in which punishment was included as one of the features; they would come into a system of rights no less than into any other system where they helped punishment play an essentially deterrent role. Indeed, they would come in by the same door as punishment (in Hobbes's phrase), and in its train. For they would be justified in the very same way, as helping to maintain the central values of that system (as part of the best feasible *total social response* there).

We thus establish that there should be a tie between punishment and judgments of guilt. We could, given the argument just conducted, say that institutions for fairly adjudging guilt were necessary in a system of rights, and necessary for the same reason and to the same degree that the practice of punishment itself was. Correspondingly, we could say that adjudged guilt was a necessary feature of proper and justifiable punishment there.[19] But could we move from that to say that *only* the guilty should be punished?

6. PUNISHMENT OF THE INNOCENT

Perhaps, the best way to answer this question is first to develop a reasonable background hypothesis as to why, starting with the scapegoat argument, adjudged guilt turned out to play a necessary role in the total social response to lawbreaking. The plausible story that supports this conclusion would, I surmise, include two elements. One would be the claim that those adjudged guilty were, or most probably were, direct causal agents of the law violation in question. They did it; they perpetrated the violation; they were its agent; if they had not acted as they did, the violation would not have occurred. In that sense, they were responsible for the violation's having happened. They are, likely, responsible in other ways as well: they did it knowingly (and knowing that it was a violation), non-negligently, intentionally, voluntarily. Then, further, there would be the claim that it makes sense (in the construction of a total social response to lawbreaking) to invoke sanctions against identifiable persons who are, having been judicially adjudged to be, responsible causal agents of lawbreaking. For we have good reason to believe, from the scapegoating argument as it was developed, that the pertinent conduct of such persons is one of the *main* contributory causes of lawbreaking and that controlling that conduct, through sanctions and the threat of sanctions, can appreciably diminish crime.

So the incorporation, into the total social response, of punitive measures against such persons is effected. It is done on grounds of the contributory causal importance of the particular factor just cited. And this completes the plausible story I had in mind to tell.[20]

Now, suppose in the course of reaching this particular conclusion we had toyed with the idea of adding a provision that where one was an adjudged violator, members of the family could, frequently enough, be punished *instead* of the violator. On reflection, however, we came to see that the addition of such a provision would be an unlikely move to make. For, though this move is not *per se* arbitrary (since it is tied to judgments of guilt), it would be a relatively ineffective one. If the actions of family members are contributory causes of violations at all, they are far less important in that role than are those of the adjudged violators. Or, to put the point somewhat differently, evidence would tend to show that punishing family members *instead* of punishing the adjudged violator would be much less effective (in reducing crime) than simply punishing the violators themselves.

Even so, suppose we, nonetheless, next contemplated adding a somewhat different provision: that where one was an adjudged violator, members of the family could be punished *as well* as the violator. It is still not clear, however, that such a policy—of allowing punishment on these terms and of even carrying it out on occasion—would be more effective as a deterrent to law violation in a system of rights (with an otherwise viable, and presumably optimal, total social response to lawbreaking in place) than a policy of confining imposition of sanctions to those who are adjudged to be actual violators. Or, to put the point precisely, where all the other factors (the nonpunitive factors) in this total social response are held constant, it is not clear in the light of available substantive evidence that the one punitive policy would be more effective than the other as a deterrent.[21]

Behind this claim, a statistical claim, lies a causal one. Let me spell it out, by making an obvious concession and then by drawing a distinction.

I do not doubt that family members influence one another (for good or ill). And, on occasion, members of the adjudged violator's family do have some causal responsibility—through culpable negligence, through malign advice or bad example and even encouragement and planning—for that person's lawbreaking. Where the lawbreaker is a minor, such family members may have the major part of the responsibility (or, in some cases, the whole of it) for the lawbreaking incident. Such cases as these are already recognized in law and pose no special problem: indeed, they are an extension of the causal analysis already proposed (at the beginning of the present section).

But the fact remains that being a member of the functioning family of an adjudged lawbreaker is not, in and of itself, contributory. Such members are not, merely in standing in that relationship to law violators, direct causal agents of the law violations in question. Thus, we cannot generalize from the case in the previous paragraph (where family members were in fact causally contributory) to cover the case of family membership as such, of membership simply as membership. And, insofar as our understanding of the matter is *causal* and remains so, we cannot rely on notions of a blood tie or the metaphysical unity of family members with one another to bridge this particular gap—the gap between factually based causal attributions involving family members, on the one side, and family membership *per se*, on the other.

So we have a strong disposition, on grounds of relative ineffectiveness and of the causal analysis we have made, not to invoke punitive sanctions against family members in the general run of cases. And certainly not to invoke them against such members where our only reason for doing so is that they are members of the families of adjudged violators.

One important point remains to be made here. It is clear that the punishment of family members under policies of the sort we have been contemplating would invade or restrict their rights (for we are presuming that punishment often has this effect in a system of rights). Where we could not show that such an interference with rights was necessary, or could not show that we gained anything from it, in order to prevent violation of laws in such a system, then rights here are being invaded unduly.

Now, this judgment, the one we have in fact made, that rights are being invaded unnecessarily, would be reinforced and strongly supported by the analysis made earlier: that punishing the subset of members of the family of adjudged violators is considerably less effective than punishing the subset of violators *per se*, for the reason that such members (*merely* as members) are not contributory causal factors at all and are (as a group) considerably less important, statistically, as contributory causal agents of law violation than are the adjudged violators themselves. But my argument does not rest on these reinforcing considerations; they are merely supportive of the judgment that such measures are unnecessary (a judgment that can also be reached, independently, on probabilistic or statistical grounds). Rather, the fundamental consideration is that *rights* are being invaded unduly by the deployment of these ill-judged measures.

There is a strong presumption in a system of rights against infringement of or interference with rights, and it can be overcome only if certain conditions are met. They are not met here; the interference is fundamentally unnecessary, hence unjustifiable. In these cases, then, the punitive measures are violations of rights. Accordingly, the policy I have described (where others than the adjudged violator were allowed to be punished, or to be punished instead) would not be acceptable in the account I have given.

So, we conclude (1) that tying punishment to adjudged violators—as the precondition of their being punished—is effective and can be shown to meet the relevant test of belonging, as a necessary part, in the best feasible total social response within in a system of rights, but (2) that extending it to others than the adjudged violator (be they family members or fellow townspeople or co-workers) is not even allowable there. These conclusions, then, motivate the policy that in a system of rights only adjudged violators should be punished and, I would suggest, punished only for crimes they were actually judged guilty of. And, in a system of rights, the background institution of reasonable trial procedures for the determination of offenders would incorporate this policy as one of its features.

Some will balk at my account of the matter. They will point to examples, often to the example of the Nazis in the Second World War, to show that punishment of the innocent is often highly effective as a deterrent. I do not accept this. First, the record from the Nazi era is by no means conclusive on this point.[22] Second, and more important, it is not germane. The Nazis were trying to impose their rule on conquered people; they did so by in effect waging war on the civilian population of the nations subject to them, treating these people as if they were soldiers of a hostile army. Thus, they rounded up hostages (presumably innocent, most of them) in response to acts of opposition to their rule and then killed or imprisoned or tortured them. Their object here was not the maintenance of domestic codes of law, not that principally; rather, their object was the intimidation and subjugation of a hostile civilian population and the total conquest through military means of the civilian populations of the countries they had overrun. Nazi policy here should be judged, not by the standards appropriate to maintaining law through punishment, but by the standards appropriate to the theory of just and unjust war. In any event, whatever else we decide about them, the Nazis were not operating a system of rights and we cannot regard the system they were constructing as anything like a feasible total social response to lawbreaking, let alone an optimal one.

Other examples, drawn from traditional societies in which tribal solidarity or strong family bonds are very important, are actually more pertinent to our discussion. For these do, unlike the Nazi example, concern the maintenance of law-abidingness through trials and punishment. But they are, nonetheless, not telling. For, first, they probably contravene the contributory causal analysis we developed earlier and, second, they too are not concerned with punishment in a system of rights.

Though I do not want to deny flatly that rights of persons could exist in such societies, the favored cases of rights-producing societies historically have been ones in which a philosophy of individualism has taken root to some extent. And the judgment I made (as to the deterrent effectiveness of various possible punitive options) concerns what is likely to be true of societies that typically achieve successfully the status of systems of rights. My point, then, is that in a system of rights, in particular, the total social response would incorporate the policy that only adjudged offenders should be subject to punishment.

I do not, of course, want to deny that people in a system of rights would have strong feelings about the punishment of the innocent. They would regard it as arbitrary and undeserved; they would believe that it was simply wrong. But such feelings and such a belief are not enough where one inquires into the *basis* for such feelings, into a *reason* for this belief. My argument is intended to justify this policy of nonpunishment without direct regard to such feelings or such a belief, for these things themselves stand in some need of justification.

After all, what reason do we give if someone should ask why we think punishing the innocent is wrong? Surely, we would not think it sufficient to say, well, it just is wrong; that's all. And our feelings, we have reason to suspect, are not feelings appropriate simply to human nature but, rather, are feelings appropriate to a particular society or kind of society. For these feelings are not (to all appearances) shared with people in traditional societies, where a different policy may well be in place.

Thus, the argument I have been conducting, while not repudiating our feelings in the matter or denying our strong belief that punishing the innocent is wrong, could be used to justify these feelings and that belief. It would do so by showing that in a system of rights such feelings and such a belief are appropriate.

But the fact that these feelings and this belief would support the policy in question is, then, an *additional* reason for saying that in a system of rights officials (and others) would be inclined both to affirm the policy that only adjudged violators should be subject to punishment and to follow it. Thus, in such a system the incorporation of this policy and its maintenance there rests not only on the justifying grounds cited (that is, the grounds of overall necessity, within the total social response to lawbreaking, and the nonviolation of the rights infringed by punitive sanctions) but also on widespread and shared feelings and beliefs congruent with these grounds.

Once such a policy was in place, the implications for punishment in a system of rights are striking. This policy would now become a standard in the very background institution—the trial system—that served to admit people, upon the determination of their guilt, into the practice of punishment. Here the punishment of someone who was not a properly adjudged violator, under the standards now set, would always contravene these standards and thereby contravene a precondition for justifiably punishing someone in a system of rights. Thus, the punishment of those not judged guilty would always count, where that punishment infringed the right(s) of the person being punished, as an infringement done in an unacceptable way (given, that is, the relevant background institution—as we have characterized it in our account of procedures for a reliable trial). Hence, any such punishment (simply as an unacceptable infringement of that person's right) is always a violation of rights and would be disallowed.

There could, accordingly, be no such thing as justifiable "telishment" (to use Rawls's word) in a system of rights—where someone known to be innocent by the officials is represented as guilty (through an attendant clandestine perversion of the mechanisms of fair trial) in order that this individual be punished, presumably with good deterrent effect.[23] There could be no official *policy* of telishment, for reasons I've already made clear. A fair trial, under the standard we have established, is among other things one in which reasonable and reliable procedures are officially relied upon to reach a determination of guilt and have actually been employed, conscientiously, to reach such a result. Thus, there could be no authorized telishing— no carrying out of telishment—for there is no justified policy for that sort of thing, and any occasion of telishing necessarily contravenes the accredited policies relevant to punishment and is wrong.

It cannot even be done as a one-time-only or very rare exception. Suppose it is done for the reason that it will deter violations and it does, on that occasion, have that effect; it measurably decreases (in net) the violation of rights. Even so it cannot be done justifiably, and that for two reasons.

First, it must be done in an unacceptable way, for it still contravenes the standards and procedures set in the background institution for fair trial. And, second, if it is done secretly (as it must be in order to avoid popular outcry and official repudiation and in order to have the requisite deterrent effect), it contravenes principles of majority rule established in Chapter 6: the principle that administrative officials are to carry out the policies set by majority rule or that are in accordance with it (policies which, presumptively, forbid telishment) and the principle that, where administrative action is supposedly controlled by majority rule, such action must be open or at least available to inspection by lawmakers and, ultimately, the voting public. These principles are integral to the idea of a system of rights that we have been developing; it follows, then, that telishment (whether it would otherwise have had deterrent effect or not) is unacceptable in a system of rights that includes, as one of its intrinsic features, democratic institutions. Thus, since telishment is an unacceptable procedure, for the two reasons given, its deployment must violate the right(s) invaded by punishment on any given occasion.[24]

One further consideration. Many societies have treated the various trial devices as themselves rights—a complex and compendious set of rights captured under the heading of a right to a fair trial. The historic content of the constituent rights has varied considerably, but the root idea that there is a right to fair trial has not. It has long been included as a civil right in most important lists of such rights and in the actual laws (or constitutions) of states that aspire to be rights-defining and rights-maintaining. And since this right—and, in particular, the aspect we have been emphasizing (that is, the standard of subjecting only adjudged violators to punishment)—is a background institution in a system of rights, it has a systemic importance and, hence, would probably be (as in fact it has been regarded historically) a very stringent right, one that should not be outweighed, except for the strongest reasons, in competition with other normative values.

Thus, punishing those who are not judged guilty usually violates *two* rights. It violates the right invaded by the sanction and it violates the right to a fair trial at a fundamental point. And this fact of violation is always a decisive consideration in a system of rights.

I do not, however, want to assume that a right to a fair trial exists in every given system of rights. Indeed, my argument is not dependent in any way on saying that such a right exists. Rather, my argument hinges simply on the claim that a right invaded by a punitive sanction is unacceptably infringed when a person not judged guilty is subjected to punishment.

It seems clear that, once we have removed deterrent effectiveness as a motivation for occasional acts of telishment (by insisting on publicity in the actions of administrative officials), there would seem to be little point in punishing those not adjudged guilty. Indeed, it would take something like a Monty Python sketch to construct the conceivable circumstances in which such punishment might make sense and might justifiably happen.

Consider then the following. God, or perhaps a Cartesian evil demon, might point down from heaven one day and demand—everything in Technicolor, and with spoken words and curly script that could be understood by all—that some perfectly innocent person be punished by the authorities. This person is to be kept in prison and treated exactly like an ordinary felon or even put to death. (Or the demon might prove to be sly or, perhaps, whimsical and demand merely a nominal fine or a two-year jail sentence for that person.) In any event, the being who demanded this is not one to shake a stick at, for the being is very powerful and what it says is credible. This being could threaten to destroy the whole earth and everything in it unless this thing was done. People might consult and say, "If we don't do this, then everything will be destroyed, including our system of rights itself." So they do it quite openly; they punish the innocent person. And perhaps it is justifiable that they do so.[25]

For I argued in Chapter 5 that *exceptions* could be made to a given rights rule, if doing so served "to improve or, if need be, to preserve the system of equal civil rights." Now, it might appear that the punishing of the innocent person in the Monty Python sketch, though it did not make the system more secure (since the openness of the official's deed robbed punishment in this case of any deterrent effect), did serve to preserve in existence a particular system of rights. Thus such punishment (at least the lighter penalties demanded by the whimsical demon) could be construed, one might think, as a special case of the principle invoked in Chapter 5 and thus allowed to go through. But the appearance is deceiving here.

The argument in Chapter 5 was concerned with rights construction and was conducted using deliberately simplified and minimal assumptions: that all civil rights are assumed to be of equal weight and that the only normative constraint assumed was that afforded by the justifying principle of mutual perceived benefit. But the argument in the present chapter has introduced further considerations (typical of a maturing system of rights): that individual rights characteristically have definite competitive *weights* and that background institutions and rules have developed (such as democratic institutions and the institution of the trial system and the ingredient rule there that only the guilty should be punished). There is no way, then, that the punishment of an acknowledged innocent person could be made consistent with the principles of a system of rights in which such further rules and institutions had become fundamental. Punishment of the innocent here could never be done in an *internally* acceptable way, never be an *allowable* exception, given all the rules and institutions of such a system.

Thus, if we stayed strictly within the reasoning characteristic of such a system, the action would not be justifiable. For regardless of the reason for doing it, it was done in an unacceptable way. It went against the precept that only the guilty should be punished, a precept which had been embedded in the background institutions for that practice, in the very procedures for determining guilt in a fair trial that were a precondition for punishing. Thus, to punish someone in these circumstances would be to violate the rights of that person.

To justify such an action one would have to step outside the whole system. Here one would have to be understood as making an extraordinary decision. Even if the decision made was the correct one (as judged by some new and relevant standard), it would not a decision that conformed to the imperatives already built up within a typical maturing system of rights.

If the action was justifiable on utilitarian grounds (or on grounds provided by other principles of critical morality, e.g., Kantian principles), then there is a clear sense in which one could argue that the innocent person's rights, though infringed, are not violated. But to talk of justification here is now a matter of ultimate moral justification; it is not available to someone within a theoretic system of rights to provide such justification, for the principles of a system of rights are not moral principles *per se*, nor have we shown that such a system is (or could be) ultimately justified morally.

It is possible that the bizarre case I have constructed could be anticipated, at least in a general way, and, thus, could be taken account of in the background rules of a system of rights. (We could add an act of God clause to our policy.) If it were thus taken account of, the rights of the innocent would be infringed, but not violated, when they were justifiably invaded in accordance with some such rule(s). But there is no special reason to think that such a rule exists. A system of rights does not stand or fall on whether this particular feature has been incorporated into the background. Thus, in a representative account (like the present one) we need not assume that it has been. But whether it has been incorporated or not makes little difference, for in either case the determination of what was justifiable would have to be made by reference to evaluative principles, which are not themselves a feature of the system of rights (in any representative characterization).

Thus, even if one held that taking such action was necessary—that is, necessary to the very survival of a system of rights—the desirability of that survival would itself have to be determined from an appropriate evaluative or moral perspective. Whether a system of rights—taken as a whole—has ultimate value and is worth preserving for that reason can only be determined by going beyond that system and referring to those superordinate principles of critical morality which are themselves the ultimate standards of all moral judgments. But if we stayed strictly within a representative system of rights, as I have characterized it, the decision we are canvassing would not be justifiable—or, at least, there are good reasons for saying that it would not be—and the action taken (in punishing an innocent person) would, accordingly, violate that person's rights. This is the point I want to make.

In sum, I have tried in this chapter to show that punishment (in the form of provisions for coercive sanctions, to be triggered by adjudged violations of law and carried out against adjudged violators) can be justified as a political institution within a system of rights but that the punishment of people who are not adjudged violators can never be justified within such a system. It is important to note that the justification I have developed is confined to a particular political system (a system of rights) and could not be used to support the institution of punishment in other systems markedly different from that one. I suppose this is not unexpected, given the argument of the entire book. In any case, though, I have provided the general outlines of a justification of punishment, indicating the sorts of things one would do if one were to carry through such a justification in any political system.[26]

10

Modes of Punishment

THE essence of punishment, in the account I have given, is coercion. Thus, somebody (some personage at law) acquires the legal entitlement to carry out coercive measures against an adjudged violator in any number of specified ways. (For a given measure might require that the violator die, be imprisoned, pay a fine, suffer corporal punishment, lose certain rights, pay compensation to victims, undergo psychiatric confinement, be instructed as to civic responsibilities, work, etc.) The possibilities here are legion, the variety bewildering. Is there a way to reduce this complexity to more manageable form?

In this chapter I want to develop a simplifying device, by which the available sanctions can be grouped together under just a few general headings. These headings are sufficiently broad to be found in any system of punishment; thus, they can properly be described as modes of punishment. And, although I will ultimately discuss them in special reference to a system of rights, I will begin by discussing these modes in a more general way.

I. A GENERAL ACCOUNT OF THE MODES

There are, in the view I am suggesting, three main modes of punishment. They are (1) penalty, invoked against the offender, (2) compensation, to be paid to victims of crime, and (3) treatment and rehabilitation of the adjudged violator.[1]

Two factors make all of these things modes of punishment. First, all are coercive, and all can be shown to fit the formula for definition (developed at the beginning of the previous chapter) in the relevant respects. Thus, things under each of these modes could figure in a provision in law, to be applied to an adjudged violator as a specified response triggered by the violation of a given law. And, second, all these modes have deterrent effect. Each could be included under the general goal of social protection, of crime control, of preventing or significantly diminishing the violation of law. Accordingly, each could be brought under the system-located justifying aim of punishment in a system of rights, that is, the aim of maintaining rights and of preventing or reducing their violation.

This second feature, of deterrent effectiveness, is simply a generalization from my argument about justification in the previous chapter. Accordingly, we can accord it the status, in any particular scheme of punishment, of a standing but rebuttable assumption. Its inclusion in a general characteriz-ation of punishment does not, I would add, prejudge matters against a retributivist account of punishment. For holders of the retributivist theory, equally with the one I am developing, are committed to the view that we have punitive laws in the first place—or, more specifically, have laws with sanctions clauses attached——so that people will not violate these laws and thereby do that which the laws prohibit. In short, such laws do exist to discourage bad conduct. Hence, even retributivists, at the point of justifying sanctions clauses in laws, are committed to the importance of deterrence. The difference, if at all, seems to come at the point of carrying out a sanction in an individual case, for the retributivist asserts in this regard simply that the violator is to be punished because the violator did something wrong (that is, broke the law). But even here one could say, in line with the position I have developed, that a sanctioning measure is triggered by violation of law; it is carried out against an adjudged violator in accordance with the terms of a justified law, specifically, a law that has a sanctions clause attached. So there is nothing in my account so far that holders of the retributive theory need object to.[2]

I will regard that account, then, as a suitably neutral general characteriz-ation of punishment. Thus, coerciveness (and, more generally, conformity to the model definition) and the goal of social protection (or, more precisely, the prevention of violations of law) are generic traits of punishment and, hence, of its various modes. They are traits the modes have in common in virtue of being modes of *punishment*.

How, then, are the modes to be differentiated? What makes each a *distinct* mode of punishment?

Consider, first, the class of penalties (things like imprisonment or fines or the loss of some detail of one's civic status). I would suggest that all such penalties have the prevention of law violation as their exclusive or primary goal. And all such penalties operate to deter through credible examples or, as in many cases, simply through incapacitation (that is, restraint of the violator).

The notion of credible example is often discussed in terms of a distinction, of special from general deterrence; this distinction is common-place in the literature.[3] Thus, one regards deterrence by example as operating, characteristically, against people who have already committed a crime, to prevent them from committing a further one (*special* deterrence) or against people who might be inclined at some future date to commit one (*general* deterrence). But to confine general deterrence to this latter class would be a mistake. For it may well be that penalties have general deterrent effect in another way as well: they may affect not only those who are inclined to break the law but also those who are inclined to keep it. In the latter case, examples of penalization (along with the rituals of trial and publicity)—by emphatically denouncing the breaking of law, in the more serious matters at least—also express the attitude that lawbreaking in such cases is wrong and unworthy. Thus, such examples of penalization support and affirm an already settled attitude of law-abidingness. This may, indeed, be one of the most significant roles of deterrence by example.[4]

Moreover, one of the important features of punishment—at least as that institution is normally understood—takes its rise from this point. I mean the presence on the part of the violator of the feeling of having done wrong, of such feelings as shame, guilt, penitence, and so on. For one could argue that these feelings normally will occur when they have been internalized by the adjudged violator. This is, presumably, something the violator shares to some degree with fellow citizens: something he or she has acquired in much the same way as they, something stimulated by the emphatic denunciation afforded by punishment, just as in their case, and something that will continue to be shared with fellow citizens even though the people we are talking about are law violators. In a system of rights, with its emphasis on the need for reciprocity in conduct in support of civil rights, these feelings would be strongly reinforced and wholly appropriate. Hence, my account provides a solid basis for feelings traditionally associated with the judgment of guilt and with penalization.[5]

I do not want, however, to make such feelings a necessary condition of proper punishment, for there are people (outsiders, psychopaths) who may not have internalized the appropriate attitudes—not all the way down, in any case. We would want to allow, nonetheless, that they could properly be punished. For society may need protection from such individuals—sometimes *especially* from such individuals.

This latter observation leads, quite naturally, to consideration of the incapacitation of violators. Incapacitation, the other main feature of penalty, is rather more straightforward in comparison with deterrence by example. For it is deterrence by restraint. Here I refer to the fact—where it is a fact—that one consequence of someone's undergoing a penalty is the attendant inability of that person at that time to commit crimes. Thus, imprisonment is incapacitating in that prisoners are confined and carefully monitored and controlled; they are simply unable, or much less able, to commit crimes while in prison.

The suggestion I have made, in short, is that all penalties have the prevention of lawbreaking (or, more generally, the promotion of law-abidingness) as their exclusive or primary goal and that all penalties operate to achieve this goal by deterring lawbreaking through credible examples or through incapacitation. All penalties are judged, then, from a single main standpoint: their effectiveness in reducing violations of law by these means.

Compensation of victims and the treatment and rehabilitation of offenders, the other two modes of punishment, differ from penalty on these very points. Compensation is concerned principally with the well-being or good of the victim of crime. As a mode of punishment it must be *compatible* with the general aim of punishment, but it need have only an incidental or marginal effect on the reduction of crime. For it is not judged, primarily, from that standpoint. Rather, it is judged by how well it helps the victim cover the costs of crime, that is, the loss to the victim thereby incurred. In achieving this object compensation does not operate through deterrence by example or incapacitation at all; rather, it does so by offering money or in-kind aid to the victim of crime.

It should be clear that compensation to victims of crime is not always a form or species of punishment. It would not be, for example, when governments compensated victims of crime (as is done in some U.S. states today) or when the victim's own insurance company did so. For here compensation is not being paid by adjudged violators. But when a violator is *forced* to pay compensation—as a feature of the legal verdict against the violator—such compensation counts as punishment. That is, it counts as a legally specified sanction, carried out against an adjudged violator and triggered by the adjudged violation of the law in question.

Where compensation does count as punishment it achieves whatever impact it has on reduction of crime in precisely the same way that penalty does: through deterrence by example, mainly, and also through incapacitation, but only rarely. And we can assume that being forced to aid the victims of one's crime will have roughly as much deterrent effect—special or general—as being forced to pay a fine of equivalent size or to work to an equivalent degree.

Treatment/rehabilitation is the last mode of punishment to be taken up in our account. It might seem odd, initially at least, even to include it as a form or species of punishment. For one could allege that it goes against our linguistic intuitions to do so. But I am not at all sure about this. It has conventionally been asserted that reformation, or significant improvement, of the character of the offender is one of the goals or aims of punishment. If this is so, then it does not seem strange to say that measures for treatment and rehabilitation—as means to this end—can figure in punishment, can play a part in it. Hence, the idea that treatment could be a mode of the institution of punishment is not foreign to our understanding of that institution.[6]

In any event, punishment is an unsettled concept, with sometimes divergent strands. It does require, like most philosophical concepts, a bit of pressure to mold it into coherent shape.

Now, of course, treatment and rehabilitation is not always a form or species of punishment. It would not be a species, for example, when an ordinary person sought medical treatment from a doctor or visited a member of the clergy for extended counseling. But some persons are sentenced (meaning, required or coerced) to undergo psychiatric treatment as the official and specified response, carried out against an adjudged offender, for an adjudged violation of law. In such a case, then, treatment would count as punishment.

Where treatment and rehabilitation is a means of punishment, it differs from the previous two (penalty and compensation) in being concerned with the well-being of the offender as its principal initial object. As a mode of punishment it must, of course, be compatible with the general aim of punishment. However, unlike compensation, its contribution to the reduction of crime—in intention, at least—is more than merely incidental, more than simply marginal. But it achieves this object in a quite distinctive way, in a way which differentiates it from the other modes. Take, for example, penalty. Penalty (which has the reduction of crime as its primary objective) deters through credible example or through incapacitation. Reformation, though, achieves reduction of crime through measures, of treatment and rehabilitation, designed to make adjudged violators better—or at least designed to remove in their case some of the identifiable causes or motives of lawbreaking.

Thus, in the *first* instance—or at the first stage—treatment is for the violator's own good, but it is not that exclusively (for it is also, ultimately, for the good of society). There are other things that might also be for the violator's own good (and, ultimately, for the good of society also)—such as vocational training or general education, instructional films, work. When one is legally required to engage in such things, as part of the court's verdict or as an integral feature of the institutional setting in which that verdict is carried out, then it too counts as punishment.

So, in the analysis I am developing, we have before us a somewhat expanded notion of punishment (as including not only penalties but some instances of compensation and of treatment and rehabilitation as well), and I have tried to make a case for saying that these are all modes of punishment, albeit differing ones. There may be other modes as well, but I leave that issue aside.

The question remains, then, why these three categories would exist and be parts of the institution of punishment in a system of rights. Why would each be a distinct mode of punishment, and thus an option branch, in that system in particular? In attempting to answer this question, I will provide an analysis, with examples, of each mode as a mode of punishment in a system of civil rights.

2. ONE MODE: PENALTY

We can start with penalty, for it seems to be the most settled of the modes. There appears to be no special problem with the idea that some coercive responses, carried out against adjudged violators according to provisions already specified in law, exist principally to prevent violations of law and do so through measures designed to achieve deterrence by example and by incapacitation. It is not surprising, then, that penalty sanctions are commonly thought of, or thought of first, when one thinks of punishment. Indeed, the examples I used in the previous chapter (fines, confinement) were of that sort. And, given the argument of that chapter, their justification in a system of rights (insofar as we are concerned with civil rights laws) would seem a relatively straightforward and unproblematic matter.

The difficulty, though, is not with the penalty mode as such; it is, rather, that the two main contemporary forms of penalizing are thought to raise special problems in a system of rights. I refer, of course, to the death penalty and to imprisonment.

The U.S. Supreme Court has taken the position that capital punishment is not *per se* a violation of the right against "cruel and unusual punishments," as set forth in the Eighth Amendment of the Bill of Rights of the U.S. Constitution.[7] Even so, the case against the death penalty, in a system of rights, seems to me well founded. Let me suggest the main lines for this judgment.

We can assume that the right to life is very weighty; it is, in common esteem, among the weightiest (though it is not thought by many to be absolute, nor is it regarded that way officially). Thus, a penalty which invaded the right to life in order to protect a right of lesser weight (e.g., the right to security of funds on deposit, which the banker violated in our example in the previous chapter) would be intrinsically incompatible with the principles of a system of rights (as I showed in Chapter 9) and would be disallowed for that reason. But using the death penalty, against adjudged violators, to protect the right to life itself would not fail on grounds of incompatibility. We must turn, then, to relative deterrent effectiveness, the remaining consideration, to determine its justifiability in a system of rights.

In the theory of penalty the main devices for controlling unwanted conduct are the two I have stressed throughout: deterrence by example and by incapacitation. The statistical data on the success of these devices is very hard to evaluate for the case under review. But the following may well be true: although considerable evidence has been gathered, the data are uncertain; evidence is lacking, though, that the death penalty is more effective, as a deterrent against murder, than long-term imprisonment. In fact, the two seem to be equally effective.[8]

If this claim is true, then the case against the death penalty is decisive, given the argument of the previous chapter. For if a penalty infringing a right of lesser weight (as would imprisonment) is, apparently, as effective toward deterring murder as a penalty infringing a right of greater weight (as would the death penalty), then it is unnecessary to use the greater penalty. It would be unjustifiable to do so, for rights should not be invaded unnecessarily or unduly. Therefore, the death penalty constitutes a violation of rights and should not be provided for, or carried out, in a system of rights.[9]

This argument seems to me impeccable in its form; the only ground for rejecting it concerns the truth of its factual premise. But if that premise is true (or likely to be so), then there can be no ground for rejecting it at all. Now, the factual premise does rely on the claim that imprisonment is as effective as the death penalty (technically, it relies on the claim that there is no evidence that it is not as effective—or that capital punishment is more effective). And this supposes, in its turn, that imprisonment is an acceptable penalty. So we turn next to this issue.

Imprisonment means confinement: not confinement to one's own home but confinement in a penal institution, usually for a fairly long period of time, where one is required, as an additional feature of being in prison, to undergo a serious regimentation and a substantial deprivation of personal liberties. Despite this unappealing characterization, imprisonment is now pervasive—so pervasive that it has become, in popular thinking at least, almost synonymous with punishment itself.

Nonetheless, the fact that imprisonment constitutes a substantial inter-ference with the rights of the inmate, in particular, the rights of personal liberty, has led some to reject it categorically or to reject it at least as the *main* type of punishment, the punishment of choice, for even the lesser crimes against property or against the tax laws.[10] And there is growing concern that its effectiveness as a deterrent is questionable.

Granted, imprisonment does not deter crimes on its own or by itself; it operates in combination with a number of factors. Some of these come conventionally under the heading of criminal justice: police protection, the action of courts, parole and probation supervision, etc. And some are better described, in this context, as general social institutions and practices for the promotion of law-abidingness. I mean such institutions as public education or welfare and job programs, which operate before the fact of law violation, and things such as blame or pointed exhortation, which operate after the fact.

It may well be that some of these background matters are more impor-tant, in preventing crime, than imprisonment. For example, adequate police protection and the detection of criminals might be; gun control, as an inhibition on the murder rate in particular, probably is.

Nonetheless, imprisonment must be evaluated in conjunction with the set of feasible background institutions. The case for saying that imprisonment is relatively effective as a deterrent is largely made if it is believed, on reasonably reliable grounds, that crime is reduced where the total social response includes imprisonment over against a situation where various combinations of other institutions operate but without any institution of imprisonment at all.[11]

Thus, it might be alleged that prison is a deterrent to the crime of murder where, taking imprisonment as the topmost existing penalty, the whole combination of institutions, including prisons, was more effective in reducing that crime than any set of *existing* institutions which excluded imprisonment altogether. And it would be a justifiable deterrent where, on grounds of relative effectiveness, it was included with other *feasible* measures in the best total social response.

But I think we will miss an important point here if we don't stress what is peculiar about imprisonment, if we don't ask why people should be *confined*, as distinct from penalized in some other way. Presumably, they are confined either because what they have done, for example, committed murder, is very serious (that is, their crime is a violation of a very important right and can be and in fact needs to be deterred by a costly example) or because they, as convicted murderers, are dangerous (that is, they are very dangerous people, to have committed such a serious and violent crime, and need to be incapacitated).

Thus, a rough guideline for the use of this penalty emerges. The penalty of imprisonment, on one plausible account, should be limited to the crimes of murder, firearm robbery or assault ("and those involving physical injury or serious endangerment"), or the repetition of such serious crimes as simple assault or burglary.[12] To this might be added imprisonment or jail for some crimes, such as drunken driving, that run a high risk of serious bodily injury or even death to other persons.

I think a case could be made that imprisonment, as confined to serious and usually violent crimes of these sorts, would be justified in a system of rights. It would be (1) where, in contrast to institutions or responses that were not punitive, imprisonment along with other punitive sanctions was relatively more effective in deterring such crimes within the total social response, under usual or feasible circumstances, and (2) where compatibility was satisfied—when the weight of the right(s) infringed by imprisonment was less than or equal to the weight of the rights protected by that penalty—and where (3) imprisonment, in relation to the class of eligible sanctions that met this test of compatibility, was the most effective one, in combination with other relevant institutions, in deterring these particular violations of rights.

Suppose this account of the place—the necessary place—of imprisonment in a system of rights is substantially satisfied. The problem of lesser penalties would remain, the problem of how to deal with those important but lesser offenses against rights (such as, for example, the government official's or the banker's embezzlement against the right to security of money on deposit in a pension fund). I do not think the guideline here will be as clear as it was with the death penalty or with imprisonment. But something of a general sort can be said: for lesser offenses there should be lesser penalties—penalties that meet the relevant tests of compatibility and of comparative deterrent effectiveness, against a backdrop of nonpunitive institutions.

And such penalties are available. These would include fines, where the violator is required to pay out (over and beyond any amount for compensation or restitution) a sum of money, sometimes a substantial sum; and they would include such things as 'creative' sentencing, where the performance of community service might be required, and probation, where violators are required to restrict their behavior in various ways and to report back to a supervisor periodically.[13]

In sum, punitive sanctions that exist principally to deter violations of rights, and do so through example and incapacitation, have a place in a system of rights. For rights are not to be violated and such relatively effective measures, where their compatibility with rights can be made out, are indispensable to that end. Thus, penalties—even some rather serious ones such as imprisonment—have a necessary place, an internally justified one, in a system of rights. Or to put this point differently, the category of penalty will properly define one mode of punishment in such a system. Can an equally effective argument be made for compensation?

3. A SECOND MODE: COMPENSATION

It could be claimed that one of the main defects of our present system of criminal justice is that it fails to take account of the loss incurred by victims of crime. Indeed, the present system is probably insensitive to these victims in a number of ways. In a system of rights such disregard is highly problematic. After all, it was the violation of rights, that is, of the rights of someone in particular, that often lay behind the whole apparatus of detection, trial, and punishment of the law violator. So, insofar as we are dealing with a violation of rights—and have grounded punishment on that, for its justification—it seems that we should take such violations of the rights of particular persons much more seriously than we have.

Thus, it might plausibly be claimed that compensation to victims of crime is specifically required in a system of rights and that the fulfilling of this requirement should properly fall, at least in part, on the adjudged violator. Let me fill in now behind this contention with an argument, emphasizing the first of these points (for it is the more important one).

We can begin with the linchpin idea that ties penalty and compensation together in such a system. For they share a common root in the notion that rights are to be maintained.

The institutions of criminal justice—narrowly conceived as police protection and detection, trial, and penalization—rest on the rationale that rights are not to be violated, that violation of rights is to be prevented. But this rationale supposes, in its turn, that rights are to be maintained. And when rights are maintained, then ways of acting and of being treated are maintained for individual persons.

In a system of civil rights, when rights are maintained and enjoyed, certain benefits accrue to everybody: they accrue, for example, when the actions are performed that one has a liberty to perform; they accrue as one lives one's life free from certain injuries; they accrue when one receives the services provided. The having of such benefits—mutual perceived benefits, the same for each and all—is the ultimate rationale for maintaining these universal ways of acting and of being treated. This is the point, then, of socially specifying and promoting such ways of acting or of being treated, thereby making them civil rights.

When a right is violated, the way of acting or of being treated is unjustifiably infringed and, more often than not, the relevant benefit is lost, in whole or part, to someone. A particular action of that person is not allowed or an injury is inflicted or a service is denied. And this may count as loss of benefit or may itself cause such a loss for that individual.

Some response to this loss of the relevant benefit is necessary, for the whole point in a system of rights is to maintain rights. And the very reason rights are to be maintained—i.e., that there is a plausible connection, as indicated by practical inference, between (1) having certain benefits and (2) specified ways of acting or of being treated—dictates that, where a right has been violated and a benefit lost, action be taken to make up the loss or restore the benefit to the extent possible, to the person who has lost it. Otherwise rights are not being maintained for each and everyone. They are not being maintained up to the standard given in the underlying reason for acknowledging and maintaining civil rights in the first place: that some ways of acting and of being treated are to be made secure because, when secured, they afford in themselves relevant benefits or lead to them, for all.

Compensation addresses the failure to maintain rights which each violation implies. It does so by making up the loss or restoring the benefit to the individual involved. Thus, the reason for having rights is satisfied in the case at hand; and the right in question is maintained, as much as practicable, fully for all.[14]

Of course, the matter is considerably more complex than I have represented in the rather simple account so far given. Take liberty of action, for example. Making good the loss or restoring the benefit of such a liberty, in an individual case, might amount to no more than removing a hindrance, restoring the liberty *per se* (for example, removing a dangerous obstruction from a train track that had been deliberately placed there, perhaps by vandals). But it might involve some assistance to the action itself, an action which had been prevented by an earlier violation (for example, providing the services of a car or van to take older people to the grocery store, where they had previously been prevented from going by the harassment of neighborhood thugs and even muggers). Or it might involve remedial measures directed to some designated effect of the kind of action protected; hence, it might involve restoring, for example, a piece of stolen property, property that had initially and legally been obtained, or kept up, by performing an action of that sort.

What precisely is to be made good depends on a variety of contingent matters, ranging from such things as the state of society (its technology, its existing practices, its history) to things that bear rather more directly on the way of acting in question. I have in mind here such matters as whether the action is merely allowed as distinct from being encouraged, whether the damaged effect (e.g., a piece of property) is the sort of effect intended in the general maintenance of that particular liberty of action, and so on.

Much the same sort of thing can be said for avoidance of injuries and the provision of services (the other main objects of rights). Thus, making good the loss or restoring the benefit, in one of these cases, might merely involve restoring a situation of noninjury (for example, returning a stolen car to its owner in the condition it had been in at the time of the theft). Or it might involve repairing an injury already done (for example, seeing to it that a building's facade, damaged by spray-painted graffiti, is restored to mint condition by steam cleaning). Or it might involve undoing some further effect of the injury (by paying the hospital bill of an assault victim, for example). Again, in the case of a service specifically, making good (or restoration) might involve merely restoring its availability (for example, anti-abortion protesters at a university hospital, where legal abortions for poor people were being funded at public expense, after defying a court order might be effectively stopped from interfering). Or restoration might involve actually delivering the service where it was earlier denied or made unavailable (for example, the dollar amount of retirement checks, stolen from the mails and illegally cashed, might be paid into a retiree's account in a lump-sum check). Or restoration might involve repairing some effect of having failed in the first place to make the service available in the proper way (by subsequently providing remedial schooling, for instance, to pupils whose out-of-the-way school was destroyed by arson or who were altogether kept out of school, for a year, say, by the action of some religious cult or by an illegal teachers' strike).

There is no hard and fast rule that can be laid down in advance as to the focal point of restoration. But in all these cases there will be a social perception of what specific benefit is the *relevant* one in the case at hand, and hence what benefit needs restoring, what loss needs making up—as to whether, for example, it is the liberty *per se*, or the action performed under that liberty, or some expected result of performing such actions, and so on. These perceptions are constituted by popular and official understanding and, more often than not (given that we are talking about civil rights), are found in the body of law: in court decisions, in black-letter law, in administrative rules, and so on. Such perceptions form a necessary part of the setting in which restitution and compensation function as a systemic or background institution in a system of civil rights.

We should also bear in mind that restoration in full is not always practical or even possible. Cases will range, then, from full restoration (a stolen object is returned to its owner undamaged) to partial restoration (an assault victim left permanently impaired mentally and largely unable to work is partially compensated by a substantial payment of medical costs and some subsidy for subsistence). There are also costs of crime (fear in a community, increased costs of security) that are simply not compensatable (though they can be allayed, by seeing to it that the incidence of crime is diminished through punitive and police action and through other social policy measures). In the end, decisions as to compensation reflect complex judgments. What is practicable (even optimally practicable) may fall well below full restoration.

Quite simply, then, my argument is that, within practicable limits, restoration of the benefit or making up its loss to the affected individual (given the relevant social perception and the decisions just described) is something specifically required by the idea that rights are to be maintained—and by the master reason behind that idea. Hence, such restoration is a peculiar object of concern within a system of rights, when we consider the proper or mandated response to adjudged violations of rights-protecting laws in that system.

This is all that is so *required*, however. And other issues of compensation can be left aside (for now, at least) where they are irrelevant to the central case.

Consider, for example, a case of murder. Here the benefit in question— that is, a life free from certain injuries (including the injury of being murdered)—is irretrievably lost to the individual affected. And there is now no person to whom that benefit *could* be restored, or the loss made up. On the principle I have advanced, then, there is nothing practicable that could be done to compensate this affected individual; hence, there is no restitution or compensation due that particular individual, as required by the idea that rights are to be maintained. There may be, nonetheless, costs to others (the family of the victim, for example) which could be covered; but compensation here would have to be rationalized on grounds other than those I have presented. For such compensation, however desirable it might be, is not a matter I have been concerned with, one way or the other, in this argument. Accordingly, I have confined discussion to the crucial idea that compensation is required, to restore a benefit or make up its loss to the individual affected, if rights are to be maintained even in the face of violations.

But required of whom? Perhaps part of the responsibility for compensating victims should fall on the state if for no other reason than that the government is in a position to provide a social insurance program for victims of crime (as it does now for the unemployed, the disabled, and, in the case of older persons, for those who are retired or who need medical assistance). Governments could regard insuring victims of crime against loss of benefits to be a legitimate function—especially in a system of rights, where the government is the principal agency charged with maintaining rights.

Bear in mind, too, that the government has a special duty to prevent crime and many, indeed very many, crimes represent a lapse of sorts in the carrying out of this duty.[15]

But there is no reason the state—or society—should have sole responsibility in this matter. The convicted violators too could and should bear a part of the costs of compensation and restitution to victims of their respective crimes. For these violators are the agent, the party most directly responsible for their victims' loss of benefit.

We reach this conclusion by applying a well-known principle of tort law: that where one's conduct is an "adequate cause" (as Swedish law would put it) of a harm or loss of benefit to another and where one's conduct was adjudged unjustifiable, then one should bear at least a part of the cost, where practicable, of restoring that benefit or covering that loss. Thus, in a system of civil rights, someone who has violated the rights of others, causing a loss to them of the relevant benefit, should be required to help restore that benefit or make up its loss to the individuals affected.[16]

Of course, if the principle of requiring payment (or other forms of compensation) to victims of crime were widely accepted, and came to have real bite, it is likely that some sort of private insurance scheme would come into play. For this has already happened in civil matters in such areas as liability insurance for some professions and businesses, for homeowners, for operators of motor vehicles, and so on. The presence of insurance would, no doubt, complicate the picture sketched somewhat, but it would not affect the basic principle that in a system of rights adjudged violators should be required to pay compensation, personally or through their ensurers, to the victim of the crime.[17]

In this principle we can say that two distinct lines have converged. One line carries with it the idea that compensation of the injured party is necessary in a system of rights, to restore the benefit or make up the loss to that individual, so far as practicable, when a right has been violated; and the other carries with it the idea that an adjudged offender against a rights-protecting law should be forced, as part of the specified response triggered by a violation of law, to make restitution or pay compensation to the person whose right was violated and who was thereby harmed.

In this convergence compensation takes its place as a *necessary* mode of punishment in a system of rights. And from this convergence it takes its unique, distinguishing feature as such a mode: the feature that the coercion of the adjudged violator is directed principally to the well-being of the injured party, by restoring the benefit of the right or making up its loss to that individual, so far as practicable. Compensation stands, then, as a distinctive mode of punishment, alongside the mode of penalty, in a system of rights.

Some have argued that it should be the *only* mode, that there should be no mode of penalty at all in a system of rights. Thus, Randy Barnett suggests that penalties might violate rights; he then more or less assumes that they would and argues from that point, taken as settled. But compensation, he contends, is uniquely appropriate to rights and, in addition, would not have the crucial defect alleged of penalty.[18]

The reasons he offers are without merit. Punishment (including the mode of penalty) has already been shown to be appropriate in the case of violation of rights, for penalties—that is, some penalties—not only are compatible with rights but also are necessary, or so I have argued, in a system of rights. And compensation, where it is required (where it is forced on the offender), is just as much an infringement (if I may call it that) of the offender's rights, as penalization.[19] Thus, one's rights over property (including property in funds) are infringed or restricted equally by a fine (a type of penalty) or by an enforced payment of compensation; they would differ not even in degree if the dollar amounts were the same.

In neither case (forced compensation, penalization) is the offender treated as something less than an end—treated as a means only, as a mere instrument to the well-being or improvement of *other* people. For in a system of rights, all have civil rights, the offender along with others, and the modes in question (compensation, penalty) are necessary to, and strengthen, those rights—the rights of each, the offender included.

It should, however, be borne in mind that compensation by itself is sometimes only weakly deterrent. For, when accompanied by no additional measures, it may leave the offender no worse off—or not appreciably worse off—than that individual was initially, before the offense. There is no detriment to compensation in this fact, for the principal object in requiring compensation is not principally to deter future offense but to restore the benefit of a right to the injured party, or to make good its loss to that person. Nonetheless, since the deterrent effects proper to compensation are often not great, it is usually the case that compensation does not operate alone but, instead, is paired with a penalty of some sort (such as a fine or imprisonment). For if the aim of punishment in a system of rights is to reduce crime or, more generally, to help maintain rights, then some such combination of compensation and penalty is probably more effective toward that end. Thus, in the previous chapter, the punishment of the banker who had embezzled funds on deposit included both restitution and a fine. Compensation is characteristically a 'mixed mode' in a system of rights in that it often comes admixed with penalties so as to serve effectively the aims both of compensation and of deterrence.

4. RETROSPECT: THE DEFINITION OF PUNISHMENT

This point, that restitution is a mode of punishment, bears in an interesting way on the definitional account of punishment I gave at the beginning of the previous chapter. There I suggested that two important proposals for characterizing punishment have traditionally been put forward: the view held by a majority that punishment is essentially a matter of producing pain (for the violator) and the minority view that it is essentially a matter of coercing the violator. The utilitarian view (as expressed by Bentham, Mill, and Hart) can be taken as representative of the punishment-as-painful perspective.[20]

In this regard, I would want to contend that utilitarian thinkers should be inclined, on their own terms, to accept something like compensation into their account of punishment. For, if punishment is itself an evil (as penalty presumably is) and if punishment exists to counteract the evil of crime, then punishment as a response to crime merely adds evil to evil, with the result that evil (pain or bad) is increased. Of course, this is not the whole story: for it is believed that the evil of punishment deters and thus reduces future crime. It is, accordingly, this situation (where future crime is reduced through punishment) that is better on the whole than one in which crimes are unpunished and, hence, future crimes unreduced. But, by the same token, one could argue that if compensation could be made to victims (at no loss to crime reduction) then this would be even better; for more good still, or even less bad, would then be produced.

Thus, utilitarians ought to support an institution of punishment that includes both penalty and compensation over one that merely penalizes.[21] And Bentham recognized this when he allowed for the "lucrative" or pecuniary compensation of victims in his account of punishment, though it was in his view a "collateral end" rather than a main object of punishment.[22]

One could say, of course, that we have here two things, not one. There is punishment (that is, penalty) and there is compensation. All the utilitarian is required to say, given this difference, is that the response to crime is better where two distinct practices are in place—penalty and compensation— than where only one of these is. But the utilitarian is not committed to saying that compensation is itself a species of punishment. Thus, the fact that it is admitted into the picture bears in no way whatsoever on the *definition* of punishment.

We should not think, I would rejoin immediately, that compensation simply stands outside punishment. If punishment is properly characterized, in a non-question-begging way, as those measures that are to be visited upon an adjudged violator as the specified or mandated response to the violation, then required compensation counts as punishment. It follows, then, that both penalty and compensation are forms of punishment.

Those who hold the pain-producing account of punishment are committed to the view that, whatever punishment is (characterized in their preferred way), it must be understood in the non-question-begging way I have just described. For, if they were not so committed, they would be unable to distinguish the violator's punishment under law from other pains that might be visited upon that individual. And they have to be able to say when pains count as (legal) punishment. So, any *additional* characterization (including the pain-causing one) must presume this initial one. And this presumption, in turn, would bring compensation in as a species of punishment. Thus, any *additional* characterization would have to describe punishment, in general terms deemed suitable, in such a way as to capture *both* penalty and compensation.

The utilitarian proposal (which also represents the majority view) that we characterize punishment as painful or as pain-causing is relatively weak here. One principal point of having penalties, in the utilitarian account, is to produce pain (for the violator) thereby deterring further violations of law, on the part of others or on the part of the violator. Accordingly, the utilitarian is equally committed to saying that compensation belongs to punishment because *it* is painful. Otherwise, there would be no point to the general characterization of punishment as pain-producing. And the same claim could be made about nonutilitarian theories (such as Kant's) which share with the utilitarian theory that same general characterization of punishment, as measures productive of pain. Here, then, the proper characterization of punishment as painful would depend on whether mandated compensation, once we admitted it as a mode of punishment, was required to be painful, or was in fact painful.

But compensation does not exist, as a mode of punishment, in order to cause pain to the violator so that some further good can result. Rather, compensation has a role there principally because it restores a benefit or makes up a loss to the victim of crime. And, as regards violators, what is essential here is that such compensation be *required* of them. Its being so required is sufficient to give their payment of compensation a deterrent effect—at least for others. Thus, it is immaterial, in the end, whether that payment is actually painful to the violator or not. We conclude, then, that compensation as a mode of punishment is not primarily or essentially painful. It is, on the contrary, essentially something that is legally required (and enforced).

Now, we do properly describe something as *coercive* (in this case the carrying out of a sanction) when it is required regardless of whether one wants it or not. It is coercive, in particular, when it is ordinarily unwanted, when people (for the most part) do not want to do it (or undergo it) and only do so, when required, against their will. They have here no real choice; for if they try to evade this requirement, matters can only get worse—or at least that is how things have been set up to operate.[23]

Such a coercive situation is also, often correctly, describable as painful. Thus, there seems always to be some purchase for the pain-producing account of punishment whenever coercion is present in this strong form.

I do not want to deny this point of purchase. But where the idea of pain causing is simply equivalent to the correctly perceived fact of coercion, then it is not a real alternative to the idea of punishment as coercive and, in fact, rides piggyback on it. The pain-causing account can, of course, point to something other than coercion here; it can point to the fact that the violators are making payment out of their own funds or to the fact that they might have to work, expending time and energy, to pay compensation in kind. I am not really concerned to deny that this might be painful (for most people). But, of course, if the actual payment was handled by insurance, then (beyond the nuisance of the thing) no cost, no pain would attach to the transaction on the side of the adjudged violator. Even so, the point remains that the payment of compensation (as regards adjudged violators) is essentially something required of them. Thus, it is primarily a matter of their being coerced and only secondarily, if at all, a matter of their being caused pain.

My main object in all of this, then, is to force the validity of the alternative characterization of punishment as coercion onto the table. And not just for compensation but also for penalty. For, interestingly, that same characterization could comfortably be made of any penalties the violator might have to undergo: these too are (for the violator, we presume, and for most people) coerced measures.

Two considerations, then, stand out in the end: that penalties are coercive and that the measures we discussed afterwards (i.e., those in the mode of compensation) fit more readily under the heading of coercion than under that of pain causing. Accordingly, in the argument up to now we have better reason to characterize punishment as something essentially coercive than we do to describe it as something essentially painful.

Thus, a definitional account which treats punishment as primarily or essentially coercive would be endorsed by these considerations. So, we can take coercion as the favored way to characterize punishment for the two modes already analyzed. It would also provide the standpoint for the subsequent analysis of other modes, should there be any, admitted under the primary characterization (i.e., admitted under the characterization of punishment as those measures that constitute a specified or mandated response to violation of law and that are to be visited on an adjudged violator).

Now, we have already identified treatment and rehabilitation, independently of the argument just conducted, as a mode of punishment. Or, at least, I have claimed that it is plausible to consider it as such a mode. The point I want to emphasize here is that, although treatment and rehabilitation could be characterized as coercive respecting an adjudged violator—and, hence, could count as a mode of punishment for *that* reason—it could not be characterized as intrinsically painful (at least in no other respect than that it was coerced). If this is so, then we have an additional argument for preferring the general characterization of punishment as a matter of coercion over its general characterization as, always and primarily, something painful. That is, we have such an argument if treatment and rehabilitation can, in fact, be regarded as a mode of punishment.

5. A THIRD AND FINAL MODE: TREATMENT AND REHABILITATION

We come then to the third mode of punishment that I want to discuss in this chapter. In what follows I want to sketch more fully the case that can be made for saying that treatment and rehabilitation constitute an independent mode of punishment. I have in mind here (under this heading) such things as education, work and job skills training, and measures to promote health or to cure illness. Things in this mode, insofar as they are to count as punishment, must necessarily (given the argument just conducted) be coercive of the adjudged violator.

Their immediate and principal object is the betterment of the violator, with the prospect that this improvement will make the violator less likely to commit crimes. Thus, the larger object of treatment and rehabilitation, as with all modes of punishment, includes the protection of society: the reduction of crime, the encouragement of law-abidingness, the maintenance of rights in a system of rights.

It seems, accordingly, that if treatment and rehabilitation can be regarded as a mode of punishment, then the issue we have been canvassing in the previous section—the issue of the proper general characterization of punishment as painful or, alternatively, as coercive—would be concluded, as decisively as seems possible in philosophy, in favor of coercion.

I will begin with perhaps the hardest case: the treatment of the mentally ill. I have in mind specifically those who might be loosely described, at the conclusion of a trial for law violation, as criminally insane.[24]

The most obvious reason we could have for denying that such persons can possibly be punished is that they are not adjudged violators. For we can presume here the rather common verdict of "not guilty by reason of insanity." Since punishment, in the account I have been developing, can properly be carried out only against adjudged violators and never against adjudged nonviolators, then the treatment of the so-called criminally insane, in the light of such a verdict, could never possibly count as punishment.

This objection is only superficially plausible. For it overlooks the fact that the plea of insanity, on which the verdict in question is based, is a plea which, if successful, establishes a legally recognized *excuse*. Thus, insanity has a place in criminal law alongside several other such excuses, the excuse of being under age, of nonculpable ignorance of fact, of involuntariness (e.g., automatism), and so on. It is characteristic of all such excuses that their establishment, in a given case, requires the admission or the judgment (1) that there was a law which specified that the thing which had happened was the sort of thing the particular law was meant to prevent or prohibit and (2) that the person charged was the lawbreaker, the agent who had brought about the proscribed happening. Hence, the fact of violation and the fact that the accused is the perpetrator are essential material facts presupposed in any judicially established excuse of insanity (which would then issue in the verdict "not guilty by reason of insanity").[25] There is a clear sense, then, in which the person judged here to be criminally insane is, nonetheless, an *adjudged* violator.

If the person so adjudged were not a violator, it would be pointless (as the result of a criminal proceeding) to *require* that person to be confined in an institution and to undergo treatment. And yet this is often the decree of a court in such cases. It is one of the typical responses to a violation of law, characteristically visited upon the adjudged perpetrator—characteristic, that is, when a plea of insanity has been successful and the excuse (or exculpatory status) established.[26]

Still, whether the criminally insane, in being confined or treated, are being punished is a difficult question to resolve. One could argue that, after the verdict of "not guilty by reason of insanity," what they undergo is some form of involuntary *civil* commitment. The history of the treatment of the criminally insane might well bear this contention out. Or the present practice might, if we looked, for example, at American law in the last forty years or so.[27] But the fact is that, however the handling of the criminally insane is ultimately rationalized, more often than not no intermediate or independent civil proceeding intervenes or is required once the crucial verdict (of not guilty by reason of insanity) is in. And in the great majority of cases, confinement or psychiatric treatment is the standard judicial action taken in the event of such a verdict. Sometimes such a disposition is mandatory (or was), depending on the law of the state involved; and in many cases the matter was left simply to the trial judge's decision.

The fact that the criminally insane are usually judicially assigned (sentenced, if you will) to *something* at the conclusion of a criminal trial—unlike, for example, the case with very young children—seems decisive. It seems reasonable, then, to say that the thing the criminally insane are sentenced to is essentially part of a criminal proceeding; accordingly, the claim that punishment is involved here does not seem arbitrary.[28]

This brings us to a second objection, one that may prove more plausible than the first. For it could be emphasized that the perpetrator is not sentenced merely to treatment but, rather, to *confinement* and treatment. And confinement is not treatment; it is incapacitation. Primarily, then, the sentence is that the violator must be confined (incapacitated) because the violator is dangerous and this is, precisely, to bring that confinement within the orbit of penalty (at least in the account I have offered).

It is, I would add, the fact of dangerousness (the proven dangerousness to others of the offender) that distinguishes, or should distinguish, the person detained as criminally insane from most civil commitments.[29] That the mentally ill inmate is confined in a hospital or an asylum or a sanitarium, rather than in a prison, is immaterial. The required confinement is the essential point here.

Treatment as such, the objection continues, is a mere incident of confinement. For it is not uncommon for officials to treat inmates or otherwise improve their condition. Sometimes the treatment of an inmate takes on the character of protecting others in and of itself. Thus, the treatment of an inmate with a contagious disease or the requirement that an inmate be vaccinated (against smallpox or some other disease that the inmate might contract and spread to others) is of this character. Whatever good it might do the prisoner it also does good for, and is protective of, others. The treatment of the mentally ill (from the perspective here afforded in the objection we are canvassing) is on a par with such treatments.

In sum, the objection we are now considering seizes on the fact of confinement (here viewed as incapacitation, a form of penalty) and then argues that treatment of the mentally ill in such a case is not independent of confinement and, hence, is not an independent mode of punishment. It is, instead, primarily an adjunct of confinement (an adjunct of penalty) and, in being so, fits a familiar pattern of medical treatment of inmates.

But the objection fails here on two grounds. First, it overlooks the fact that the treatment in question is something *required* of the adjudged violator. Having been adjudged legally insane, that person's undergoing such treatment is part of the sentence; it is, in the case at hand, among those measures that constitute a specified or mandated response to violation of law. More precisely, we can say that it is among those that are to be visited on adjudged violators who have, as the official verdict, been declared legally insane. Not so with the medical treatment of the inmate with a contagious disease or the one who requires a vaccination. These things are not required by that person's sentence; being so treated, though it may be required on other grounds, is not something the violator was sentenced to. But the legally insane inmate has been sentenced to treatment. This distinguishes the insane inmate's treatment from that of the others.

True, the legally insane inmate is often confined, like them. And this brings us to the second point. When the inmate with the contagious disease is cured, that inmate is not released. Nor is the one who required a vaccination let go after successful immunization. They are still confined. For confinement (meaning incapacitation and, possibly, deterrence through example) is what they have been sentenced to. But the mentally ill inmate when cured is released. This suggests that the legally insane inmate was confined only because, while uncured, that individual was a danger to society. But the object of the treatment (which the inmate was sentenced to) was the cure itself, and when the inmate was cured there was no longer a need for confinement. This was the nature of that inmate's sentence.

Perhaps, 'cure' is too grand a term. The concern of the attending physician here, often with the aid of therapeutic drugs, is to bring mentally ill inmates to the point where they can begin to function in the world on their own. This does not mean release and forget; it means, rather, that upon release the former inmate continues under supervision and under treatment (indeed, these things are properly required of the inmate as a condition for release).[30]

Thus, treatment, insofar as it is a matter of sentencing, is there from the very beginning as an independent matter. It may initially run parallel to confinement but, unlike the other cases of treatment cited, it gives the term to confinement. Thus, where this is so (i.e., where confinement does not continue beyond the cure—beyond the point of reasonable release, as medically and judicially determined), the treatment of the mentally ill, those who are criminally insane, must be viewed as different from a mere incident of confinement. Such treatment is something other than a simple adjunct of penalty. And it should continue (as a requirement on the former inmate) even after the penalty phase—the confinement—has ended.

Consider next someone who was a compulsive shoplifter, who was sentenced to be treated for kleptomania but not confined. (Or, again, consider someone who was a habitual passer of bad checks, as in the *Durham* case.[31]) If the kleptomaniac (or the bad-check artist) were sentenced to treatment under a verdict of "not guilty by reason of insanity," then that person would have, so far as treatment was concerned, the same sort of sentencing requirement that the person in our earlier example had. The only difference would come on the point of confinement; the shoplifter or the bad-check passer would presumably not be thought to pose the sort of danger to society that would require confinement. The important point here, though, is that what that person *is* required to do under the sentence (that is, to be treated) is clearly independent of penalty—since there is no element of penalty involved in this case at all.[32]

Thus, if we restrict ourselves to the one factor of sentence-required treatment, the factor common to our two examples of criminal insanity, we can say for each case that the factor is independent of penalty considerations. Sentence-required treatment as such, then, can be distinguished from penalty and is independent of it (or from compensation, for that matter).

The treatment and rehabilitation of the mentally ill, under the verdict of "not guilty by reason of insanity," is required by law or by a judge; it is a feature of the sentence of a certain class of adjudged violators. It is this fact that makes such treatment a matter of punishment. But the immediate object contemplated in the treatment is the cure, if possible, of the condition described (in legal language) as insanity, and the sentencing requirement is satisfied when the treatment has been successful.[33]

Of course, it is often the case, as it was in our first example, that treatment and penalty (i.e., confinement) are both required. In those cases, then, treatment (like compensation) becomes part of a mixed mode of punishment, one that mixes both the mode of treatment and that of penalty in a single sentence.

In any event, though, we have made the case for saying that treatment and rehabilitation—insofar as criminal insanity is concerned—constitute an independent mode of punishment. Moreover, insanity is not the only example we can find within the category we are examining (that of treatment and rehabilitation as a mode of punishment). One other example merits a brief mention.

Sometimes persons who have been convicted of reckless or of drunken driving are required to undergo special driver training courses, to hear lectures and attend films about the impairments wrought on driving skills and alertness by drink or drugs, perhaps to see movies of accidents or to visit hospital emergency wards (or, in the most extreme case, to attend autopsies of victims of drunken or reckless driving). Arguably, such instruction might have in view, as its exclusive or its primary object, the improvement of the convicted driver *as driver*. Where it was required, as part of that driver's sentence, it would, I think, count as punishment.[34]

Thus, we could add to our earlier example, that concerned with the criminally insane, another clear instance of punishment in the mode of treatment and rehabilitation. That mode, then, is not a mere logical possibility; it has some significant instances. Treatment thus takes its place along with penalty and compensation as a distinctive mode of punishing.

6. THE LIABILITY OF PERSONS TO PUNISHMENT

Now that we have these three independent modes of punishment in view, we can usefully move to consider the question of the liability of persons to punishment. By 'liability' I mean not likelihood but, rather, one's eligibility to be punished.[35] The question concerns who can be subject to punishment or, better, should be. Specifically, the issue is whether anyone should be subject to punishment under the mode of penalty or under the mode of compensation or, finally, under that of treatment and rehabilitation.

Some of the main lines of an answer here have already emerged. Punishment falls on lawbreakers. For the relevant justified sanctions are provided for in laws; they are responses triggered by the violation of given laws and are carried out against adjudged violators—and, properly, only against such violators. Thus, as I argued in Chapter 9, the status of adjudged perpetrator (as determined by a reasonable procedure, such as a fair trial) is a *necessary* condition of anyone's being properly punished. Are there other, similarly general necessary conditions that could be identified for liability to punishment?

Here I would fall back on the idea of modes of punishment. The question of whether someone should be subject to undergo sanctions should be asked, not in the abstract, but with particular modes in mind.

Let me put this point more precisely now. Once we have (1) an adequate general characterization or definition of punishment as a practice and (2) a system-specific justification for that practice, as characterized, and (3) the constraint that, when a practice so characterized has been justified, only adjudged violators are properly liable to punishment, and (4) a determinate account of chief modes of punishment, then (5) the main lines of the liability of persons to punishment in a particular system is determined—within the context given—by the species-forming characteristics of the various modes of punishment that are *justified* in that system.

An important procedural principle is involved here: the principle that we first establish the justified modes of punishing, within a given system (for example, a system of rights), as the main step in determining who is properly liable to punishment there. But this principle has not always been observed.

For instance, we sometimes encounter the blanket assertion that *mens rea* (an evil or guilty mind) is a criterion of one's liability—that is, anyone's proper liability—to punishment. Thus we find Hart, perhaps the leading proponent of this view, arguing that a legally wrongful act must be done knowingly and willingly—or at least must be one that the agent could have helped doing—in order for its perpetrator to become a proper object of punishment.[36]

This contention of Hart's—insofar as it does take punishment in the abstract and in advance of any serious attempt to determine its various justified modes—represents, I would suggest, a methodological defect. But since the *mens rea* requirement is a competing alternative to the general principle for liability that I have just put forward, and since it has occupied such a prominent place within the traditional theory of punishment, we should give it some attention. More important, perhaps, the requirement must be considered here, for—in the case of many people, at least—it constitutes the main reason one might have for rejecting my claim that treatment and rehabilitation is, or could be, a mode of punishment.

There are, I suspect, two main motivating considerations that normally lie behind acceptance of the general view that persons should not be punished unless they have committed the wrongful act under scrutiny (that is, the legally wrongful act) knowingly and willingly. First, it is assumed that penalty is the paradigm, or the only significant mode, of punishing. Thus, the issue that adherents of this principle address is actually the issue of who should properly be subjected to *penalty*. Moreover, this question has been asked over against a certain background assumption. Traditional theory, in considering the assessment of penalty, has consistently and rightly held that *only* the guilty should be penalized. But, given the moralistic character of traditional theory (especially in its retributivist version), this maxim has been given a subtle, but significant, slant: it is read as if it said that only those

who are *morally* guilty should be penalized. This, then, is the second important assumption: that we are dealing with *moral* guilt, or something coinci-
dent with moral guilt.[37] And who are the morally guilty? Those who have
done wrong (that is, broken the law) knowingly and willingly. Thus the *mens
rea* requirement—that only those who have broken the law knowingly and
willingly should be subject to punishment—emerges as a general principle
of liability.

Whether the requirement would still hold across the board when we
identified the lawbreaker as not necessarily morally guilty but simply as an
adjudged violator is, of course, the exact point at issue. I think it would not.
For the locus of attention has shifted now from the very focus (on the
relevant overlap of legal and moral guilt—and, hence, on knowing and
willful misconduct) that gave the *mens rea* requirement, within the context
of traditional theory, its surface plausibility.

The wholesale importation of a moral gloss on liability is totally without
warrant in punishment theory insofar as we are concerned with punishment
under law. It is not necessarily morally bad to break a law. Law violators,
including adjudged ones, are not necessarily morally guilty of anything.
Even in a system of rights we have not made out that one ought always to
keep the civil rights laws, that is, keep them whenever they have been duly
enacted. Hence, in talking about the legal guilt of an adjudged law violator
we may not be talking about moral guilt at all, or anything much like it.
There is no standpoint, then, for bringing criteria of moral guilt in to color
the notion of one's proper liability to undergo *legal* punishment.

So, if I am right about the conceptual origins of the *mens rea* requirement,
then that requirement does not provide a sound general principle of liability. For it rests on an invalid argument: it simply does not follow from the
claim that punishment sanctions should be used only against adjudged
violators (against persons who are guilty in that sense) that we should use
such sanctions only against those who have broken the law knowingly and
willingly (or, at least, could have helped doing what they did).

One might respond, of course, that the *mens rea* requirement could have
other foundations. The one used by Hart might be cited. He argues that the
reason the *mens rea* requirement is important and worth preserving is that it
gives people a choicc, a say, in whether their conduct or their lives can be
restricted by punishment sanctions; it does so by requiring that only
knowing and willing conduct can subject one to punishment in the first
place, that only knowing and willing conduct should be allowed to bring a
person within the clutches of the law. What people cannot help doing they
cannot properly be punished for.[38]

As an argument, though, this one is defective. It begs the question. For it
is grounded on the idea that an optimal system of law is a system which
respects and even tries to maximize choices (in that legal consequences are
allowed to fall upon people only for things they could help doing). But to say

this, or to assume it, is the very thing assumed in the *mens rea* requirement. From the beginning, then, we are committed to the notion that the *only* acceptable condition on which people's conduct should be restricted (at least by punishment) is that they have knowingly and willingly done something illegal—or, at a minimum, when their illegal act was something they could have helped doing. A commitment weaker than this—one which in effect removes the *only*—will not support the *mens rea* requirement as a general or across-the-board one. But to make this particular commitment is to assume the very point that needs to be proven. Hence, it won't work in this argument.

In any event the argument is not a good argument. It seems arbitrary that the disallowed restriction should pertain to punishment alone. For the presumption seems to be, given the confinement of the argument to cases of punishment, that restrictions on conduct in *other* areas may sometimes be all right even though the crucial condition (of *mens rea*) is not satisfied.

Or, alternatively, exceptions to the *mens rea* requirement are actually allowed in the area of punishment or, sometimes, expressly countenanced (as necessary or reasonable) in other areas. Thus, it might not be wrong, for example, to limit someone's conduct through quarantine if that person has a serious communicable disease (even though that person may not have acquired the disease, nor be spreading it, knowingly and willingly or, even, in any way that the person could have helped). Again, it might not be wrong to limit someone's conduct (through civil commitment or guardianship or some similar restriction) on the ground that the person is incompetent, even though the incompetence and the behavior that stems from it may be something the person cannot help. If such restrictions as these might be all right, as the presumption of the argument leads us to think, or if these or similar explicit exceptions are expressly allowed, then we have good reason to think that like restrictions, where we are not limited simply to responding to actions that people can help, might be reasonable in punishment generally, or in some of its more specific areas of application, as well.

The point is, we cannot restrict the principle of respecting choices to the one area of criminal punishment alone. And if, in line with the presumption of the argument we have been examining (or with exceptions explicitly allowed), that principle seems not to have legitimate purchase in other areas, or in certain areas of punishment, then we have a good reason for saying that the *mens rea* requirement is not a sound general principle.[39]

Thus, Hart's theory runs into serious difficulty at the point of his preferred account of the handling of the criminally insane. Here he suggests that the *mens rea* standard should stay in place, as a necessary condition for liability to criminal conviction, "except so far as it relates to mental abnormality." He continues, "The innovation would be that an accused person would no longer be able to adduce any form of mental abnormality as a bar to conviction. The question of his mental abnormality would under this scheme be investigated only after conviction and would be primarily concerned with his present rather than his past mental state"; and, where direct evidence of present mental disorder existed, the courts would be required to "mete out ... compulsory mental treatment."[40]

The problem here is this. (1) If the criminally insane are regarded as undergoing treatment (but not as undergoing punishment) then Hart is here advocating that people who can't help what they have done should nonetheless be compelled or coerced by law. This is to make an exception to his *mens rea* requirement *outside* the area of criminal law (and, hence, to cash in the presumption I have identified). Or (2) if the criminally insane are regarded as undergoing punishment in being treated, a conclusion which Hart's argument strongly suggests, then Hart is advocating that people who can't help what they've done should nonetheless be subject to punishment. And this is to make an explicit exception to the *mens rea* requirement *within* the province of criminal law.

In either case, the *mens rea* requirement fails as an across-the-board principle for determining when a person can justifiably be compelled or coerced by law.

Nor does staying within the lines set by the *mens rea* requirement appreciably increase society-wide predictability (for individual persons within the society) as regards the sanctions that might be imposed on them. For confining punishment to adjudged violators and determining liability by reference to the accepted (and justifiable) modes of punishment, within a given political system, has in such a system an equivalent, or equally reliable, predictive value.[41]

I have shown, then, that the *mens rea* requirement is not a sound general principle for determining liability to legal punishment. Accordingly, it cannot be used as a standard against which the actual practices of punishment are to be measured. We should not be surprised to find, in addition, that important practices do not conform to the standard set by *mens rea*. This is so even in that area where the standard is most at home, the mode of penalty.

Thus, we find that the criminally negligent are made examples of, by way of sanctions, to fend people off from lawbreaking. And we find that the criminally insane (when dangerous) are in fact confined, for the protection of society. These practices stand even though the *mens rea* requirement has not been satisfied, as it arguably has not in the first case and certainly has not in the second.[42]

Despite these important exceptions, the maxim that people should not be penalized for things they cannot help doing is still given credence. I do not want to see this maxim rejected, so long as it is understood as restricted to penalties, *most* penalties, and so long as penalties, most penalties, are in fact pain-causing. But, as might be expected, the *mens rea* requirement will have considerably less vitality and much less acceptability as we move to broaden the range of punishment modes to include not merely penalty but compensation as well and even treatment and rehabilitation.

For in the case of compensation, we are principally concerned with restoring a benefit or making good a loss to victims of law violation and that concern continues to operate even when the perpetrator could not help doing that which caused the injury. Ultimately, then, it is other considerations that principally shape the liability to compensation. For, as is often the case in philosophy and in law, the value lies in the details. Thus, liability to compensation (to *pay* compensation) requires that there be someone who has been harmed, that restoring the benefit or making good the loss is practicable, that there is an adjudged violator who is responsible—at least *causally*—for this harm, and that the perpetrator is able to make restitution to some appreciable degree. Such things as these are the crucially determining factors of the liability to pay compensation as a form of punishment. But other considerations might be included as well: for example, that the victim wants compensation from the perpetrator—for it is not a foregone matter that the victim will. (If I had been mugged I might not want the person who had done it mowing my lawn or driving me to work. Or I might prefer that this person's destitute family receive the money instead of its going to me.)

And in the case of treatment and rehabilitation, where we are initially concerned with the well-being of the perpetrator, it does not seem important or even sensible to say that adjudged violators can be subjected to beneficial treatment only when those violators were brought into the hands of the law by things they could help doing. For sometimes those most in need of treatment, and who society most needs to have treated (for its own protection), are people who cannot help the things they do.

In any event, requiring that drunken drivers or persons who are incautious with medication or who suffer from certain disabilities (e.g., uncontrolled epilepsy) be educated about driving—shown movies, given counseling, etc.—does not itself require that their conduct, adjudged wrong, be willful and knowing, or something they can help. What is crucially required, though, is that they as drivers, and ultimately society, will benefit from this treatment or this training.[43]

The general thesis I have tried to advance in this discussion so far is that we should tailor the question of a person's proper liability to punishment to the species-forming characteristics of the various modes of punishment that can in fact be justified within a given system. In a system of rights, then, that means liability to penalty, compensation, and treatment, respectively.

The argument so far has shown (or, at least, suggested) that sanctions in each of these modes of punishment are necessary or conducive, in a system of rights, to the end of reducing lawbreaking and hence of preventing violations of rights or, if you will, to the end of maintaining rights. Thus, such candidate sanctions can probably be said to be justified in a system of rights. And the modes under which those sanctions have lodged could then be said to be justified there also.

7. A REMAINING DOUBT

But the person who is skeptical about including treatment and rehabilitation here could say that the argument of this chapter has *not* shown that sanctions in the mode of treatment and rehabilitation are really integral to the system we have been discussing. It is not evident, for example, that such sanctions would be required in virtue of the principle (peculiar to that system) that rights should not be violated (the ground on which penalty is required) or that rights should be maintained (the ground on which compensation is). Indeed, the skeptic continues, it is not at all clear that, unless we require treatment and rehabilitative measures of offenders (as distinct from merely incapacitating them), the protection of determinate rights of others will be appreciably weakened.

Perhaps, the skeptic's doubts here largely concern the effectiveness of psychiatric treatment of the criminally insane; perhaps they extend as well to some of the other important rehabilitative measures (such as the effectiveness of achieving basic literacy). But I do not think such concerns, even so, constitute the skeptic's main thrust.

The gravamen of the skeptic's challenge to my argument in this chapter is simply that the argument cannot really follow through on its own announced program: of showing that treatment and rehabilitation, as a mode of punishment, is specifically required by the principles of the theoretic system in question—that is, a system of rights.

How could this challenge be met? One procedure would be to show that specific sorts of treatment and rehabilitation, as required sanctions (often in conjunction with confinement or other forms of incapacitation and sometimes on their own), are effective enough to be justified, in the way already laid out, in a system of rights. I think that following this route would be successful in some cases, almost certainly in the case of drivers' rehabilitative training. But the doubts about the effectiveness of psychiatric treatment for the criminally insane (and of other important rehabilitative measures) might well remain. Such doubts will probably dog our path for the foreseeable future.

There is, nonetheless, a conclusive way to meet the skeptic's challenge here (one that would allow us, for the most part, to sidestep these very doubts). We could do so by turning to a second pattern of justification. Indeed, this pattern would be available for other cases of treatment and rehabilitation even if it did not prove successful in the case immediately at hand, that of the treatment and rehabilitation of the criminally insane.

Under this second pattern of justification we would show the necessary place of treatment and rehabilitation, as a mode of sanction within a system of rights, by arguing that adjudged violators have a right to certain kinds of treatment (or rehabilitation), have this right along with other citizens and despite the violation, and, finally, have the right in such a way as to require its exercise in the status they have as adjudged violators (that is, require its exercise as part of their sentence or as necessary to its being carried out). Let me put this last point differently. Adjudged violators—some of them at some time—will justifiably come under sanctions which in effect will be ways of being treated that the violator (along with other citizens) has a right to.

Here the idea that adjudged violators (or some of them, at least) have a proper, or system-specific, liability to undergo treatment and rehabilitation as a mode of punishment in a system of rights stands or falls, then, on whether such civil rights can be found. If they can be, the matter is resolved conclusively.

Finding any such right is a tall order. We have not succeeded in pinning one down in this chapter. Treatment of the criminally insane has been, throughout this discussion, our leading example of the application of the mode of punishment in question in a system of rights. But such treatment is singularly unsuited to fill the bill—at least given the current state of thinking in the U.S. about people's rights to care by doctors and dentists and psychiatrists. For undergoing such care is not, on the accepted view here, a right to a way of being treated (specifically, to a service) for most people.[44] Thus, it is not the sort of thing we have been seeking. There is no such civil right at all and, hence, no such right that could ground treatment or rehabilitation, as a mode of punishment, in this particular system of civil rights.[45]

Even if there was such a civil right in some other countries today (as there is, for example, in Great Britain), we would still need to show that there likely should be such a right in all countries that aspire to be systems of rights. We would have to show that such a right (or would be right) pertains to systems of rights as such, to any such country simply as a theoretic system of political institutions and concepts, or at least that it pertains to all the countries that could figure as instances in the world today.

If we are to resolve this problem and conclusively meet the skeptic's challenge, we will need to look elsewhere or to refine our argument. I will do so, in the next chapter.[46]

The Right of Inmates to Work

IN the previous chapter I argued that adjudged violators would clearly be liable to treatment and rehabilitation as a mode of punishment in a system of rights, if the peculiar status of being such a violator required the receipt of certain services or benefits that the violator (along with other citizens) had a right to. Such benefits might come through a specific sanction that was part of the violator's sentence (for example, that an offender had to undergo psychiatric treatment, which itself came under a right to medical treatment for persons in that country, as it does now in Great Britain). Or the benefits might come through the very fact that the offender was an inmate and, hence, a special ward of the state. Thus, the receipt of certain benefits or services might be required of an inmate (for example, schooling or work) in a prison setting.

In the present chapter I want to follow this idea out in some detail. For focus—and because of the signal importance attached to imprisonment (as the punishment of choice) in contemporary jurisprudence—I will concentrate the discussion on prison inmates. The issue, then, becomes whether there are any civil rights of the inmate that could ground treatment and rehabilitation as a mode of punishment in a system of rights. Or ground that mode, at least, in all countries that aspire to be systems of rights in the world as we know it today (and for the foreseeable future).

I. FORFEIT

Some might be inclined to answer summarily here. They think the prisoner has no rights; they think that at the point of imprisonment an inmate's legal status is no different from a slave's. There may have been some basis for such a belief, in popular or judicial sentiment, at an earlier date in our history.[1] The important thing we want to consider here, though, is not the belief itself but, rather, the animating reasons behind it.

In our society the old natural rights philosophy still exercises considerable sway. And many have been led to argue that it is true of morally justified rights (particularly of natural or human rights and, hence, of many important civil rights) that when one violates the rights of another, one forfeits one's own rights—or at least some of those own rights, including especially that very right which has been violated. Thus, a violator becomes dispossessed of one or a few or even all morally justified rights. And by being an adjudged violator one becomes dispossessed of legal rights—one right or a few or all of them—insofar as these are morally based.

The claim here is not that the scope of certain rights is redrawn so as to allow for the punishment of violators; rather, the claim is that the adjudged violator does not have important civil rights any longer; the violator has simply lost some or many or all morally based civil rights. Indeed, the argument continues, if adjudged violators had not surrendered these important civil rights, whether temporarily or permanently, it is not clear that we could punish them at all (without violating those very rights).[2]

In my view such an argument has things turned around completely. We do not say that a sanction can be justifiably attached (and employed) *because* the adjudged offender has forfeited a particular right; rather, we say that the offender's rights can be abridged (in the defining rules or in the background institutions of a system of rights) because sanctions which invade that right are justifiable.

In any event, I have already addressed the issue of justifying punishment without the supposition of forfeit (in Chapter 9). So I will not retrace those steps; instead I will concentrate on the independent claim that adjudged violators, simply in virtue of being in that status, have forfeited important civil rights, insofar as these are morally based. This claim, if sound, would effectively undercut the analysis I am advancing: for it is likely there would be no significant measures of treatment and rehabilitation that inmates could have as a matter of right, where they had forfeited all or many of their important civil rights simply by entering the status of adjudged violators.

I do not regard the idea of a general or total forfeit of rights as sound. It certainly is not sound in the context in which it is usually advanced (that is, natural rights theory). For one important supposition of that theory or of human rights theory is that individuals have rights as a feature of their being human individuals or human selves. Now, if individuals have rights in this way they will continue to have them even after they have committed violations (for they are still selves, still human beings, though perhaps less worthy ones than they were). Thus, since such persons haven't lost the status in virtue of which they are said to have these important, morally based civil rights, it really isn't open to theorists of natural or of human rights to say that the original offenders have forfeited or become dispossessed of their basic constitutional rights—certainly not in any wholesale or general way.[3]

One might reply, even so, that in some cases (when an important or morally based civil right has been violated) an adjudged violator, simply in virtue of being in that status, completely forfeits, not all important civil rights, but only one or two of them—in particular, the one that had been offended against. Here we move from a theory of general forfeit to one of particular forfeit. Thus, Kant says, "If you vilify him, you vilify yourself; if you steal from him, you steal from yourself; if you kill him, you kill yourself."[4]

But the doctrine of particular forfeit—here the doctrine that one automatically and completely forfeits the very right violated—has unwelcome implications, when taken as a principle across the board. For example, one would not say, presumably, that persons guilty of rape or of torture should themselves be raped or tortured as the penalty for their crime.[5] By the same token, one would not want to say that such persons had forfeited their rights not to be raped or not to be tortured—for this would allow the disreputable penalty in question and the very point here is that it should not be allowed.

I am not saying here that moral reasons *alone* can give us (or deny us) rights. My point, rather, is that when a right exists (for example, the right not to be tortured), for which supporting moral reasons can be advanced, then that right is not forfeited—by reference to those supporting reasons—if we *still* have them even after it is established that a particular rightholder has in fact violated that very right.

Even if we reached the judgment (that such things are not allowable) by reference to independent moral considerations, without regard to whether the offender had or did not have a right in these cases, that judgment would, nonetheless, support the assertion—in any theory of morally based civil rights—that the offender did have the right in question, or that the offender should have it. Some of these rights, accordingly, have not been forfeited.

It follows in such a theory, then, that the selfsame civil right is not forfeited in every case simply in virtue of the fact that adjudged offenders have violated something that is a morally based civil right. Hence, we no longer have the crucial basis—the ground of generality—for saying that one always automatically forfeits the very right one has violated.

Nonetheless, it is still open for a defender of the view I am criticizing to say that *sometimes* there is a complete forfeit of an important civil right by an adjudged violator simply in virtue of the violator's being in that particular status. The most common example here, which Kant and Locke and others cite, is the convicted murderer's forfeit of the civil right to life.

Let me add that Locke's idea of forfeit is by no means straightforward at this point, for he qualifies it by speaking, in the context of forfeiting one's right to life, of an "act that deserves death" and this clearly shifts the issue. More important, by speaking of desert, Locke has left behind any idea of automatic forfeit at all, even in the case of murderers. For the appropriate penalty is now grounded on what is deserved (and, in the case at hand, what murderers deserve, Locke thinks, is to be put to death). And some such principle of desert will hold, presumably, in every case of determining the kinds of penalties for other serious offenses.

Thus, no right is ever automatically forfeited in these cases; rather, the judgment whether it should be forfeited or otherwise abridged is made on independent grounds (for example, on grounds of desert or, more properly, of what is justifiable). And this removes the basis for saying that one ever forfeits, simply in virtue of being in the status of adjudged violator, the very right one has violated.[6]

But is it correctly believed in a system of rights that the murderer deserves to lose his or her life and has thereby completely forfeited it? For if murderers had, there would be nothing wrong with simply killing them upon conviction. But were there nothing wrong, we might wonder why police officers (or citizens) should try to prevent the lynching of a convicted murderer, or guards break up a knife fight in prison (even one on death row), or doctors revive from suicide attempts a convict under sentence of capital penalty (as Utah officials ordered done in the case of Gary Gilmore). Or why we feel a sense of revulsion when it is suggested that doctors should be able to "harvest" vital organs from such prisoners.

One could say, of course, that the things identified as suspect here (such as the suicide of a condemned murderer, etc.) are illegal, are contrary to the relevant institutional rules. Convicted murderers can be killed but only in the right way—as specified by the rules. But, I think, one might also suppose that such things are not merely illegal but also morally doubtful. Some of them, at least, are presumably unjustifiable morally. Now, if the governing moral theory in such cases is one appropriate to human rights or to natural rights (which is our supposition here), then the judgment that these things would be *morally* wrong suggests that we do not, when occupying the perspective of such a theory, subscribe to what the forfeit doctrine might imply. We could conclude, in short, that the convicted murderer has not simply and deservedly forfeited the human right to life (as this notion is understood in the theories in question).

The defenders of the forfeit doctrine, sensitive to this line of criticism, might want to moderate their claim. Now they would want to say, not that the convicted murderer has completely forfeited the human right to life and liberty or, more narrowly, the right not to be killed, but instead say that such a person has forfeited it in a certain respect or at a particular point. I cannot fault this move.

Indeed, it presupposes things I have already said. For it would not be possible to develop a theory of restricted forfeit without doing the sort of abridgment of rights analysis that I employed in Chapter 9 (in Section 4 especially). Thus, the idea of restricted forfeit poses no fundamental challenge to my general account of the justification of punishment. However, the character of this general account is not at issue here; for we are concerned at this point, not with punishment in general, but with the death penalty in particular.

As I argued in Chapter 10, there is good reason for saying (in a system of rights) that a capital penalty is not justifiable even for murderers. Thus, there is no ground here at all for alleging that the murderer properly and justifiably forfeits (even in a restricted way) the very right that the murderer has violated.

Some may still be inclined to say that the murderer has forfeited *some* right, for an offender always does, they believe. But such a claim seems perfectly arbitrary. We have no reason to say that the murderer has forfeited any right at all, or forfeited all or many of the important civil rights, if we mean that the murderer has done so as a kind of given.

Such a claim of prior forfeit, let me say again, has things turned around completely. We do not say that a sanction can be justifiably attached (and employed) *because* the adjudged offender has forfeited a particular right; rather, we say that the offender's rights under law can be abridged (in the defining rules or in the background institutions of a system of rights) because sanctions which invade that right are justifiable.

This abridgment may sometimes take the form of allowing for dispossession of a right at specific points; or it may take the form of delineating a restriction of scope for that right, again at specific points. But in each case this is another matter from what we have been discussing, for forfeit (to stay with that as our central case) is here never automatic, never simply assumed, never a given; it is, therefore, not presupposed in any fundamental determination of what is justifiable. Arguing from forfeit, then, cannot provide a general strategy for admitting punishment into a system of rights (a point presupposed in my argument in Chapter 9) or for denying that inmates, even though they are adjudged violators, may have rights to significant benefits and the provision of important services.

2. RIGHTS OF PRISONERS

I think the best way to state the matter, accordingly, is to say that prisoners retain their rights *in general*; these rights have not, as a matter of course, been forfeited or lost. But in a given case, a particular right may be given up entirely, if only temporarily (e.g., the right to vote), or seriously interfered with (e.g., as the right to certain liberties is by imprisonment), or even so drastically abridged—whether by dispossession or by restriction of scope— as to be said to be annulled at a specific point (e.g., as is the right to life by capital punishment, where the convict's right not to be killed is dramatically altered so as to allow for the convict's death at the hands of the state). But there is nothing automatic even in this last case. Convicted murderers do not lose the full right to life *because* they took the life of another; rather, they lose it or have its scope restricted (if that is so) because they were convicted of a crime under a statute which includes, among its provisions for penalty, capital punishment. If the statute included no such provision, and I have argued that it should not, then a murderer could not legally be put to death.

The leading idea in all these cases is that interference with rights or restriction of rights, insofar as we are concerned with the convicted person, is something that is itself determined by law. It is a provision in a statute that determines which rights will be restricted, on the part of the convict, and to what degree. Even a right abridged is often still preserved—though its scope or conditions of possession may be significantly altered. And rights not abridged are retained in full.

My thesis, then, is that convicted persons lose or have restricted those rights that are specifically provided for in the sanctions clause of the statute under which they have been convicted. But not those *only*. The convict may also lose or have restricted those rights which it is reasonably determined must be lost or restricted consistent with the carrying out of the specified sanction. So we have two kinds of abridgement: statutory or specific-sanction abridgements and secondary or administrative ones. Both kinds may be justifiable (a point I am not here concerned with).[7]

Imprisonment, the penalty we are chiefly concerned with, is not merely confinement (say, to one's house). Rather, it involves removing the convicted person to a prison setting, often for a substantial period of time. And being a prisoner may, no doubt will, involve the inmate in a wide network of administrative infringements. Prison life is regimented life, seriously regimented life, and it opens up a person to much more than mere deprivation of liberty to come and go as one pleases, to live at a place of one's choosing, and so on. Hence, the status of inmate will involve a substantial interference, both statutory and administrative, with the liberty rights of those who are inmates. But inmates also retain rights; in particular, they retain those rights that are not statutorily deprived or restricted and those that are not administratively constricted.

In a system of rights, inmates are persons who had, before conviction, the full range of rights of any citizen or person in the society and who retain, even while in prison, many rights. Some of their rights may be, arguably, more like the full rights of citizens than like the reduced and restricted rights of convicts. Inmates are not outlaws, not outside the system of rights. Their rights too must be taken seriously.

This brings us, then, to the crucial question I want to address. What rights do inmates retain? The inmate retains the right to be free of the injury of torture. This no one contests. Presumably, the inmate should also retain First Amendment rights (such as freedom of speech and conscience, free exercise of religion) but we note that these are usually severely restricted, especially the right of freedom of speech and personal communication.[8] I do not here question this restriction, or justify it, but merely note it.

It is difficult to generalize about what rights the prisoner effectively retains.[9] One might be on firmer ground to ask specific questions about specific rights.

Education and work are sometimes cited as measures of treatment and rehabilitation that should, appropriately, be made available to inmates as a matter of right. So one issue we want to determine is whether a civil right to either of these things would include prisoners. But that is only a part of the issue we are canvassing. For we must also determine whether these things can be *required* of them, in their status as inmates, and hence count as a part of their punishment. Only by successfully taking this second step can we establish that such schooling or work is a feature of the distinctive mode of punishment (that is, treatment and rehabilitation) we are here concerned with.

On this very point, though, there is doubt they can fill the bill. In the normal case neither is *required*. True, education is required of all citizens (up to a certain age). But if it were required of inmates, for example, it would be because they were within the specified age group and not because of their status as adjudged violators. Of course, some people don't learn or aren't well taught; still, there seems to be no legal requirement that such persons undergo remedial schooling and no special requirement that adjudged violators undergo it either.[10] So we can say that schooling—in the form either of basic school attendance or of remedial schooling—is not something provided for in law as a specified response, to be visited upon an adjudged violator, for the breaking of a particular law. Such a thing is not part of the violator's sentence, not part of that person's punishment.

Much the same could be said for work. Work is not required in Western countries of citizens in general (though in some of the former socialist-bloc countries it is, or was, regarded as a social duty).[11] Nor is it, in most cases, at least, required of adjudged violators.

Of course, both educational and work opportunities have found a pervasive place in the modern prison setting. But my point is that unless the schooling or the work is *required* of inmates—as a matter of administrative necessity in that setting, for example, or as a feature of their having the status of prisoners, or as specified in a law as a response to breaking that law—then it will not count as punishment. These things, insofar as they are opportunities as distinct from requirements, are really more like adjuncts to confinement (to penalty).

Now it is conceivable that sometimes schooling or even work might actually be required of a young offender (or a poorly educated one or a poorly motivated one) in lieu of confinement or alongside it. Let us assume, moreover, that a primary and significant object of such a sentence was the improvement of the offender (the hallmark object of treatment and rehabilitation) rather than deterrence of that person or others, through example, from the commission of further crimes.

Thus, we might be able to find some cases of required treatment and rehabilitation functioning as punishment. Even so, such instances are probably much too rare to support a general case for saying that the education of offenders (or work, understood as rehabilitative) counts as punishment. And we have, in allowing even for this concessionary instance, departed from our initial concern with prison inmates *qua* inmates.

The matter is complex, however; so we had best not dismiss such things as education or work from consideration too readily. Indeed, I think a case could be made for work in prisons as a measure of rehabilitation that inmates should be encouraged to undertake, that could even be required of them in a prison setting, and that arguably they could be said to have a right to. I will, accordingly, turn my hand to making that case in the remainder of the present chapter.

3. WORK IN A PRISON SETTING

Sometimes persons are actually sentenced to hard labor. This is a common and age-old practice. Prisoners in classical Greek times worked the mines; prisoners in recent memory did hard labor in work camps in the Soviet Union and elsewhere: the chain gang, the work force in the field, the convicts breaking rock in the quarry or in the coal mine, are all part of the folklore of American prison experience. I do not think such things are what we have in mind when we ask about the right of inmates to work.

If hard or unpleasant work or pointless work is something one is sentenced to, if work is deemed administratively necessary to prison life (as, for example, inmate farm work might help feed the prison population), if work is not compensated or is barely compensated, then it is more like a penalty the inmate undergoes than it is like a right the prisoner retains while undergoing penalty.

Much work in prisons is in that gray zone somewhere between out-and-out penalty and a full-fledged right to work. We could imagine some pure cases where work was simply a penalty and in no way an inmate's right. And we could imagine other pure cases where it was a right wholly removed from penalty (as, ideally, to cite another example, the right to free exercise of religion would be). But, for the most part, the work of inmates today is so bound up with issues of discipline and efficiency—with administrative maintenance of the prison itself and the provision of goods and services to the prison or to the state, with the need to help pay for the inmate's own keep, or with the earning of pin money which the prisoner then spends at the prison store—that we cannot see the inmate's work either as a pure case of penalty (as a mere adjunct to confinement, for example) or as a pure case of a right to work.[12]

Accordingly, I think it especially useful to inquire into the right to work and, more particularly, to ask why one might think the inmate had such a right and to inquire into the nature of that right in a prison setting. As a result, we might better be able to distinguish the inmate's work from standard cases of the right to work, on the one hand, and penalty, on the other, and possibly to identify the specific character of the inmate's right to work, with equitable compensation, in prison.

3.1. *The Right to Work: A Preliminary Account*

The doctrine of human rights, unlike the old natural rights tradition, has not been particularly reticent in claiming that there is a right of persons to work. The human rights movement has, from the beginning, been concerned to identify certain important rights or rights norms that apply equally to all persons and to formulate them in an authoritative declaration, the UN's Universal Declaration of Human Rights (of 1948). In the Universal Declaration, among several listed social and economic rights, it is affirmed that

1. Everyone has the right to work, to free choice of employment, to just and favorable conditions of work and to protection against unemployment. 2. Everyone, without any discrimination, has the right to equal pay for equal work. 3. Everyone who works has the right to just and favourable remuneration ensuring for himself and his family an existence worthy of human dignity. ... (article 23)

So, there is no failure of express acknowledgment, as there was in the natural rights tradition, of a human right to work with fair compensation. The problem comes at another point. For it is not clear that what is to be distributed, either jobs or the opportunity to work, can be distributed literally to everyone. This might be judged a serious *practical* problem. But the problem runs even more deeply. What the UN Declaration contemplates is socially useful work—useful jobs or the opportunity for such employment—and it is unlikely that a society can *guarantee* for each and every person in it the availability of socially useful work. Failing that sort of guarantee, it is doubtful we can talk of a human right to work as a right in the strictest sense. Indeed, the Declaration tacitly recognizes this when it asserts that there is also a right to "protection against unemployment" (article 23, see also articles 22 and 25). The right to useful work, then, has a restricted scope; for it includes an implicit exceptive clause: "Everyone has a right to useful work except where that proves impractical; then a related right takes over, the right to adequate unemployment compensation." Thus, the right to work, so understood, does not guarantee or set a goal of socially useful work, or the opportunity for such work, as available to each and every person.[13]

3.2. *Full Employment Standards*

The matter is further complicated by the theory of full employment current in advanced industrial nations. A goal or target of full employment has been set by law in both Great Britain and the United States. It is also one of the guarantees of the 1977 Soviet Constitution (article 40). Again, the employment contemplated is socially useful work. There is no desire to set people to 'make work' tasks, to digging holes and then filling them up at the end of the day. The rub comes, though, in the fact that full employment is defined in such a way that it is said to exist when most but not literally all of the available work force are gainfully employed. There is always, in short, a margin of unemployed persons allowed for under the aegis of so-called full employment. The percentage figure has been set differently at different times, but in all cases the policy has never been intended to attain a maximum goal of socially useful employment for literally every person available for and willing to work.[14]

These two factors, that we are contemplating only socially useful work and that there is no policy goal of providing such work, or opportunity to work, for literally everyone who could work and wants to work, seem to me to militate against the idea that there is an appropriately recognized and maintained right of every person to work with fair compensation. Or, at least, they go against the idea that there is such a right in the strict sense, that of something which can be guaranteed equally to each and all. For this is what the human right to work, if it were a strict right, would require in its operational setting as a civil right in this country, and that one, and so on. Thus, the human right to work must be seen as more a "manifesto" right, a desirable or praiseworthy goal, than as a right in the strictest sense.[15]

The goal of full employment is a goal (legislatively set in the U.S. and in Great Britain, constitutionally set in the USSR) which depends, for its *ethical* justification, on the prior idea that it would be a good and desirable goal to guarantee, if we could, useful work (or the opportunity for useful work) to each and every available and willing hand. Thus, the policy of full employment is governed and set by the idea that there is a human right to work to this degree: that it would be morally desirable to distribute useful work, or the opportunity for it, on a guaranteed basis to each and every individual.[16]

Under ideal circumstances such a right would actually be recognized and maintained; under less than ideal circumstances we can at least specify that there is, or would be, such a right and set out to come tolerably close to what it requires. But we realize at the same time that the maximum aim can never be achieved but, at best, only approximated. This is why we set the goal of full employment at less than 100 percent employment and why provision is made for unemployment compensation.

3.3. *A Rights-Tending Policy*

I would say, then, that the policy of full employment is a rights-tending policy. This description is meant to capture the ambivalence we have noted. The policy of full employment has its rights feature in the idea that the policy is animated and justified by the goal of guaranteeing useful work or its opportunity to each and every person; however, since this policy can never, practically speaking, be fully attained (though it can be approximated), we call it a policy rather than, simply, a right.

Accordingly, full employment is not technically a civil right; and a socially useful job, or the opportunity to work at one, is not guaranteed as a matter of right to each and every person. If there is a right involved in this matter at all, it is best contained in this notion of a rights-tending policy.

Now, the civil right to work—if it were, strictly speaking, a right—would be a human or morally based right.[17] Accordingly, it would be an important right. But, though there is no such right, there is a rights-tending policy of full employment—at least in most advanced industrial societies.

We can presume, then, that such a policy has importance (given its moral pedigree and rights-related status). And we can presume that each citizen can claim to come under that policy equally.[18]

We could expect, then, if everyone were actually under such a policy, that useful work would be widely distributed, in the normal course of things, over the entire population. There would still be unemployment; there could even be pockets of unemployment, as representing a failure to adjust to the market through, for example, the decline of a given industry in a given area. But noticeable pockets of unemployment—if they involved discriminatory impact, in that a constitutionally "suspect class" was through state action being disproportionately disadvantaged, for example, blacks or persons of Latin American origin—might well be subject to exacting legislative or judicial remedy.

3.4. *An Application*

Let us apply this analysis, by way of a loose—but not wholly fanciful—analogy, to prison inmates. We can start from the premise that inmates retain the rights they possess as citizens or persons, except for rights that are removed or restricted either statutorily, as part of the sentence, or administratively. I would suggest, then, that the right to work would be among those retained. Inmates have the same right to work as any other citizen, the same right to work they had before they became inmates, subject only to the limitation that the work is to be work in a prison setting and that it can be restricted by administrative considerations that do not apply to non-inmates. In short, the inmates' right to work is a general or society-wide right of all persons and not a special right peculiar to their status as prisoners (as, for example, the right to a limitation on the number of occupants to a cell would be, that is, if it were in fact a right).[19]

That it is not a right removed or abridged by the punitive sanction itself (or the legislative provision for the sanction) is a matter of fact. Sanctions do not, usually, explicitly include the loss or restriction of the particular opportunity or benefit identified in the right to work. Prisoners are not literally sentenced to idleness, at least this is not usually contemplated in the statute under which sanction is passed. And idleness is not administratively necessary (or even desirable) in a prison setting. These are all considerations in favor of the contention that a right to work, insofar as it is a right of all persons in our society, is retained by inmates. Or to be precise on this point: inmates along with other citizens come under the full-employment policy.

But if inmates have the same right to work as any other person, subject only to some justifiable administrative restriction, we would not expect to find such a wide disparity between their situation of economically useful employment and that of the larger population. For we are confronted, in most cases, with abnormally high unemployment (as defined by prevailing employment standards): the level of unemployment—and under-employment—in prisons is far higher than it is in the public at large.

There are, of course, mitigating factors here—such as the purpose of prisons (to deter crime through incapacitation and example and to protect society) and the additional costs of employment programs—which would need to be taken into account. But even when these additional considerations are factored in, a significant disparity remains.

Many more persons who want to work and are able to work lack socially useful jobs, or the opportunity for useful jobs, in prison than out of prison. These pockets of idleness and unemployment might, then, be matters of special concern for legislatures and for courts. There appears to be a discriminatory impact here and, though no "suspect classification" is involved, inmates are arguably a "discrete and insular minority," that is, an identifiable group of people who are vulnerable (at least in the sense that they have historically been discriminated against) for having a trait they cannot help and who are politically powerless or relatively weak. They have *intentionally* been denied opportunity to work by state officials. Since no compelling, or even substantial, state interest could be cited in justification of this inequality, it probably should count as constitutionally impermissible.[20]

Some degree of useful work is consistent with prison life, for it already exists there—and is more prevalent in some countries (e.g., Japan) than in our own. A sentence to prison is not automatically, as though by logical necessity, a sentence to idleness and forced unemployment. Nor should it be if inmates retain, as I have suggested they do, a right to work.

There is good reason for societies to arrange things, as much as practicable, for individuals to have useful jobs—or, at least, the opportunity for them. The reason is given in our earlier discussion of full employment as a rights-tending policy. What crucially counts here is the maintenance, at an appropriate level, of a policy of full employment. It is not enough, then, merely to provide unemployment compensation (or meals and a bed, the prison equivalent of that). And I have tried to show that such a policy, of full employment, has not been well served in the prison setting.[21]

4. THE REQUIREMENT OF WORK

The considerations raised—or similar ones—have been so convincing to some people that they have advocated that prisoners should be *required* to work.[22] Accordingly, some attention should be paid to the implications of treating inmate work as something that should be strongly encouraged on the part of all prisoners, or even required. The important implications for a theory of punishment in a system of rights can be brought out most strikingly where work is required of all or almost all inmates. I will, accordingly, simplify the discussion by assuming for now some such requirement.

I have been arguing in this chapter that what is at issue is a policy—a policy of full employment under equal protection standards—and have contended, further, that this policy is a rights-tending one. That is, what supports and justifies the policy, from an ethical perspective, is an ideal of making useful work available to every person, an ideal which would be a true rights norm if it were fully realizable.

Now, the thing which might seem odd in the light of this analysis is that if we *required* everyone to work—or everyone within a certain subset of the population—we would in effect be saying that the right to work, supposing such a rights norm to have been recognized in law and duly maintained, amounts to a requirement to work, for those people. And it might seem a bit strange to say that someone has a right which that person is *required* to exercise. One might even urge that these two notions, of having a right and of being required to exercise it, are incompatible.

I do not think, however, that there is any real logical difficulty in this matter. For we are in fact familiar with rights whose exercise is required. The right to an (elementary) education is one example. In many modern societies schooling—education in that sense—is thought to be a right of children and its exercise is required. Indeed, the UN's Universal Declaration of Human Rights couples these two ideas closely when it says, "Everyone has the right to education. ... Elementary education shall be compulsory" (article 26). It might be contended in response that it is the parents, not the child, who are being compelled here. But this rejoinder seems rather hollow when we consider that the school-leaving age in many societies is as high as 16. The requirement would seem to be on the child or teenager as well as on the parents. In any event, there are other examples. The right to vote is one whose exercise is required, in some contemporary societies (e.g., Australia, Belgium, Costa Rica), without losing the name of right. In some countries the requirement is even enforced, with a fine for those who do not vote.[23]

It is difficult, of course, to regard a right to a liberty of action as a right that one is required to exercise. Here there may be a genuine incompatibility.[24] But not all rights are of this nature. The right to vote involves, admittedly, something that the rightholder does or can do but, where it is required (as it is in some countries), it is a right, though clearly not a right to a *liberty* of conduct. We might, then, prefer to call such a right a power or a competence, as I suggested in Chapter 2, rather than a liberty. For powers can be commanded. Some rights, of course, are not rights to a way of acting at all; they are rights to a way of being treated (at the hands of others).

Such rights concern the avoidance of injury at the hands of others (e.g., torture) or concern the receipt of beneficial services (e.g., an education, medical care, or social service benefits). And among rights of these two kinds (avoidances of injury, receipt of services) we may find some that are compulsory with respect to the rightholder. Education, I have suggested, is one such. This is one reason why education could be thought—and has quite persistently been thought—to figure as a part of one's punishment: for, although it is a measure of treatment and rehabilitation that one has a right to, it can nonetheless count as something *required*. The right not to be tortured has a similar feature, for it too significantly restricts the liberty of the rightholder. It is not a right which one can waive nor is the avoidance in question an optional one.

Thus, to regard work as both a right and a requirement is to think of it not as a liberty of conduct but, more likely, as the requirement of an avoidance of injury or as the required receipt of a service of some sort. There may be peculiar reasons why it is required of prisoners while only being allowed for or encouraged of others outside the walls, but the fact that it is required of prisoners, where it is required, does not derogate from its status as a right— or, for our purposes, from its coming under the ideal embedded in a rights-tending policy of full employment.

A further significant feature of requiring work of inmates is that it might seem to break down the distinction between work as a penalty and work as a right from which the main argument in this chapter started. I did note, of course, in making this distinction originally that work in prison marked a sort of gray zone in which the distinction tended to blur. And it may well be that if we required work of inmates it would make retention of that particular distinction extremely difficult. I do not think, however, that this follows.

In the end, the decision as to which it is—penalty or nonpenalty— probably comes down to deciding whether the requirement is, in the main, administratively necessary to running a prison in an acceptable way (as providing for the health of prisoners and preventing disease might be) or whether it is intended primarily for the benefit of the individual prisoner, and ultimately for the attendant good of society (as making sure everyone is able to read might be). The argument of this chapter has suggested that talk of the prisoner's right to work—that is, of an inmate's coming under a policy of full employment—concerns something that is mainly to his or her individual benefit, specifically, as the avoidance of an injury or the receipt of a service. Thus, I would want to say that required work as a right and required work as a penal sanction (or as something administratively necessary in a prison setting) can be distinguished, conceptually at least.

But the important thing here is that almost anything required of prisoners, in their status as prisoners, will be part of their punishment. I do not mean to include those things undergone on a one-time-only or irregular basis (like being required to pile sandbags along a levy to help prevent flooding) but, rather, only those things which are pervasive features of prison life, for all prisoners—things which have become part of the institutional backdrop and which, for that reason, could be anticipated in advance. The same would go for things that prisoners are properly and routinely encouraged to do or undergo in a prison setting. Hence, if we mean by punishment, as regards inmates, those things that are standardly undergone by the inmates in virtue of their being inmates, then the *requirement* that such persons work, as distinct from having a mere option to work, would be a part of their punishment.

5. PRISON WORK IN THE MODE OF TREATMENT AND REHABILITATION

Where inmates come under a rights-tending policy of general full employment and where work is so arranged, in consequence, that it is for the benefit of the inmates, then providing such work in prisons would count as one of the things public officials do, in a system of rights, specifically to maintain rights—or, as in the case at hand, specifically to carry out rights-tending policies. And where such work is required of inmates, or is something they are encouraged to do and that they routinely do, then it would likely count as part of a distinctive mode of punishment, that of treatment and rehabilitation.

Work in prisons might, of course, serve other goals in addition and, hence, slot into other modes as well. When it did, work in prisons would itself be a mixed mode of punishment. Even when mixed, though, work in prisons, if it is to stay within the pattern just described, should retain its character as *primarily* rehabilitative. We can determine most readily whether this crucial point has been met by looking at the other modes of punishment—compensation and penalty—that might play a part in such a mix.

It is unlikely that compensation to victims would ever be the main rationale for requiring inmates to work; for it is unlikely that the compensation to victims afforded by inmate labor could ever be more than nominal. Indeed, if the level of compensation ever did turn out to be substantial, we could rightly suspect here a *public* subsidy of victims of crime disguised as payment by adjudged violators. And this would prove to be, if the main point was compensation, an extraordinarily inefficient way to effect such transfers. For I assume that any program of work—let alone of providing income from work—would always cost more than it could earn or contribute and, hence, would always have to be subsidized, perhaps heavily subsidized; and it clearly would be better, then, if compensation to victims is the object, to make these payments directly from the public coffers. Accordingly, even if all the money earned by inmates went to compensate victims, we would still justifiably conclude that the payment of such money was not the *main* point of requiring prisoners to work.

One might say that, of course, inmates should work. They should because it is good for *them* to contribute to restitution to their victims and to know that they are doing so. Quite so. And this shows that a rehabilitative idea is at work here, not primarily the idea of compensating victims.

Thus, we could plausibly conclude (in view of the argument to date) that the point of encouraging or requiring work by inmates is mainly a matter of the work itself—that is, a matter of rehabilitation, of something that will improve their capacities and prospects—and only secondarily a way of providing income to them or others. Thus, even if there are some prisoners who could not provide the sort of compensation to victims outlined in Chapter 10 (as, for example, convicted murderers could not), it would still make sense to encourage or require them to work on rehabilitative grounds (and as a way of avoiding the idleness and attendant apathy which are the common lot of all prisoners). More important, a program of work and job skills training on these grounds would make sense in prisons—and might well be strongly encouraged or required there—even if it generated no personal income for the inmate (or others) at all. And here, clearly, the payment of compensation to victims of crime could not be the primary purpose of requiring work in prisons.

Now we turn to penalty. It is consistent with the argument just made, where we rank work *per se* as more important than the income earned by work, to say that the point of such work is *mainly* prison maintenance or some other administratively necessary feature of inmate life in that setting. Again, I do not want to deny that prison maintenance, and so on, might constitute some part of the reason for requiring work of inmates. But it could not be the main reason: the requirement to work, in the case we are contemplating, could never be primarily a matter of prison efficiency or administrative necessity—so long, that is, as the work in question is being conceived of as a matter of right. For, in a system of rights, civil rights have priority in the normal course of things over policies that serve some interests (those of prison and other state officials or of a cost-conscious public) in preference to other interests (those of inmates) and, accordingly, have priority over the efficient administration of such policies. And I assume it is plausible to say (though I will not argue the point) that a rights-tending policy, where the right involved is or approximates to a civil right, would also have priority over matters of efficiency or administrative necessity that attach to policies of differential advantage. Hence, work in prisons, insofar as it serves matters of administrative necessity (such as prison maintenance), must always be compatible in such cases with its having a beneficial character for the inmate. Indeed, such work could be encouraged or required in a system of rights when it was not administratively necessary—or even when such work was at some cost to efficiency or to administrative convenience—as long as the overriding benefit was one the inmate had a right to (or, as in the case at hand, so long as it came under a rights-tending policy). In such cases, then, any requirement of work—for whatever reason that requirement is made—must meet the conditions laid down, in a system of rights, by the priority of civil rights over mere efficiency or over policies of differential advantage. Accordingly, the work required of inmates (where that work comes under the rights-tending policy of full employment) must always be primarily rehabilitative.

The only ground on which this primacy might fail is where work that was hard and unpleasant (or pointless), work that was more nearly penal than rehabilitative, was specifically and justifiably a part of the sanction that the convict was sentenced to. But in most systems of rights today such sanctions do not exist. Or, to put the point more precisely, most of the penalties invoked in such systems do not include a component of nonrehabilitative work as a specific feature of the sentence. Thus, this particular reason for denying that work by inmates is primarily rehabilitative is not usually present.

Hence, we are able to conclude that the work of inmates in prison today, insofar as it is a matter of rights, is and should be primarily for the inmates' benefit. And we can say, where such beneficial work is required (or routinely encouraged), that it belongs to one mode of punishment in particular, that of treatment and rehabilitation. And this mode is and should be the dominant one in cases of so-called mixed modes.

One important consequence of admitting work as a sanction under the mode of treatment and rehabilitation is that it would change our conception of the sanction of imprisonment. Under the present system, confinement often includes as one of its features extensive idleness. This idleness is not a part of the inmates' penalty, but it does reflect public neglect and in that way does result from public policy. It is an unwanted side effect of imprisonment. If, however, we were—for reasons given in this chapter—to require or routinely encourage work of prisoners, then its being *required* (or strongly encouraged) would be a part of the sanction standardly visited on inmates. And imprisonment would then include, as one of its characteristic features, work by the inmates. The character of the sanction of imprisonment would have been changed thereby, for the better.

Of course, if we merely made work available to all those who wanted it and were able to do it, that also would change the character of life in prison, again for the better. It would not, however, change the character of the sanction of imprisonment—by *mixing* the mode of penalty with that of treatment and rehabilitation—as would the *requirement* of beneficial work or the strong encouragement of inmates to do such work.

Now, the issue of fair compensation for inmate work becomes especially pressing precisely at this point, of requiring or strongly encouraging such work in a prison setting. Unless the compensation is perceived as suitable then the inmate can be regarded, perhaps justifiably, as exploited and inmate's work as itself an injury, whatever good reasons might have been advanced in the first place for such work.[25]

Societies are very complex. I hesitate in the face of this complexity to suggest a straightforward answer to the question of fair compensation. I am especially reluctant to do so when the cost factors and the necessary measures for implementation have not been worked out.[26] Also, I am inclined to leave aside discussion of fair compensation in order to retain focus on the crucial issue of requiring (or encouraging) beneficial work by prisoners.

Accordingly, I will simply leave undetermined the matter of fair compensation; it is not our principal concern. The main point of relevance has been the *need* to provide beneficial work for inmates, primarily that, and then, only secondarily, to provide equitable and appropriate compensation for that work.

Though I think this chief need has been established by the present argument, there are some important loose ends which must be gathered together in order to make the overall argument conclusive. Let me attend to them briefly. I will begin with what I take to be the least problematic consideration.

6. SOME PROBLEMATIC FEATURES OF THE ANALYSIS

The main device I have used to capture the right to work was the idea of a full-employment policy. The argument, then, was that under a standard like "equal protection of the laws" such a policy would cover inmates (as well as other citizens). But, it could be contended, the standard in question is peculiar to American law, belonging to the jurisprudence of the Fourteenth Amendment to the U.S. Constitution. It is by no means clear, the objection continues, that such a standard would exist in all systems of right I do not accept this contention.

The standard of equality for persons under rights-tending policies (however that standard is worded) would probably be found, and should be found in some form, in any system in which the rights themselves were civil rights (or approximated civil rights) and, hence, were equal rights. I have argued in the present book that civil rights are equal rights (see Chapter 5).[27] My claim here is that where civil rights are equal ones, then insofar as *all* persons in a given society come under rights-tending policies, they should come under them *equally*. This claim would hold good in any system of rights.

We move now to a second contention, somewhat like the first one, that could be lodged against my argument. I have in mind here the claim that full-employment policy, in particular, is a feature of *some* systems of rights but not necessarily of all, nor of systems of rights *per se*. This contention has some merit. There are probably specific historical conditions under which the right to work (or the rights-tending policy of full employment) is appropriately recognized and maintained. Thus,

the issue of the right to work typically arises when the supply of labor exceeds the demand, when large numbers of people have no choice but to work for others, and when the social fabric characteristic of tribes and extended families who share whatever is available breaks down. Historically, the right to work becomes an issue with industrialization, because only a few own the means of production and the typical person earns his living by working for a wage.[28]

I would say, nonetheless, that these *are* the conditions of the present day and of the foreseeable future. Such conditions will continue to hold, we can expect them to. And they will be determinative so long as citizens define themselves and their self-worth largely by their work—or, at least, so long as full and effective membership in the body politic is difficult, almost impossible, to achieve in the normal case without useful employment.[29]

Work is important in the world as it is and as it will be; accordingly, the present need for a policy of full employment will persist. All societies today, if they aspire to be systems of rights, are thus motivated to establish a civil right to work in the form of a policy of full employment. And, simply because this is so, that particular policy seemed a good one to use as the illustration in my argument.

The United States has, as I pointed out earlier, recognized such a right and pursued such a policy. It is not a fundamental right there; but it is, as I have made clear, an important right of all persons in the country (given its moral pedigree) and that right has been enfolded in American law in the policy of full employment (a policy in effect since 1946).

Now, the critic of my account would be fully justified in calling attention to one of the points just made: that this right is not a fundamental right in American law. Hence, the critic could stress that this right would not be accorded the highest level of protection (the level of so-called strict scrutiny) in Fourteenth Amendment jurisprudence. More important, the critic continues, American courts have been reluctant to extend the equal protection standard to prisoners at all and certainly have proven unwilling to afford inmates this highest level of protection when they do. Thus, so far as persons in prison are concerned, the official recognition of the equal protection standard and its degree of maintenance are relatively weak, too weak to carry the burden of the argument I have conducted. If we apply the same criteria to rights-tending policies that we do to rights strictly conceived, the critic concludes, then there is no policy of full employment applicable to prisoners in American law at all and, hence, my argument about a right to that kind of service (the provision of a job) simply fails to work in a prison setting.

The critic's main claim is merely the fact of the matter: that American law has not actually effected the extension of full-employment policy (under Fourteenth Amendment standards or any others) to cover inmates in prisons. The critic's point is that, even if the extension were justified, it is illegitimate to say that this particular rights-tending policy has actually been extended in American law to inmates. There simply is no such right of inmates in this country today.

This is the third criticism of my overall argument. It is a criticism that makes a significant point. It says something true about American law. But it does not touch the essentials of my argument.

My argument was meant to have an application beyond American law. I have tried to develop the idea that in a model system of rights—a typical system of rights under modern conditions—there is a space for certain characteristic civil rights or rights-tending policies that provide benefits or services; among them is a policy of full employment. This space has been filled, at one point or another, to one degree or another, in actual systems by such rights, including the policy of full employment (the one under discussion). In this sense, that particular policy is a characteristic one.

And I have used a standard argument, drawing (1) on the retention of certain rights by inmates, including the right to work (as wholly incorporated into a rights-tending policy of full employment) and (2) on equal protection norms actually present in all or most systems of rights today, to say that inmates should come under such a policy. But I did allow, though, for some relaxation of the standard of full employment in their case, to take account of the actual level of unemployment in a given society and of the special goals and costs of imprisonment.

When the particular space in question has been filled, as it should be, by official recognition and maintenance of a policy of full employment even for inmates, then we can speak of inmates having a right to a job. And where the receipt of that service is required or strongly encouraged of inmates, for reasons appropriate to their status as prisoners, then it counts as part of their punishment.

Work in prisons would then be one feature of treatment and rehabilitation functioning as a mode of punishment in a typical system of rights. And this mode would be, under the specifications in the paragraph above, characteristic of such a system—indeed intrinsic to it.

But why should work be *required* or routinely encouraged in prisons? Why should it, in a system of rights, be required of inmates in their status as prisoners? Or be something they are strongly encouraged to do.

These questions constitute the fourth and most important concern raised by my account. Let me sketch an answer here.

If it is true that enforced idleness and attendant apathy in prisons threaten the very *ground* for there being a right to work in the first place—that useful work is essential to the status of membership in a typical system of rights under modern conditions—then it seems that work must be encouraged or even required in prisons in such a system. Otherwise, we fail to maintain the right in question (the right to work), in a prison setting, to an appropriately general degree; and many prisoners are effectively cut off from the benefit which exercise of that right provides. It is an important benefit; idleness in prisons deprives one of that benefit by encouraging its opposite, the sense of worthlessness (just as prolonged and involuntary unemployment beyond the walls does). And the more prison life in general undermines the status of inmates as effective members of a system of rights—as it surely does—the more incentive we have to encourage and often to require the participation of prisoners in receiving those benefits and services (including those grounded in rights) that help counteract such a tendency. Thus, the reason for requiring work in prisons is, in effect, the same as the reason one would have for instituting a civil right to work (or a rights-tending policy of full employment) to begin with. And this, to my mind, gives the strongest reason one would have in a system of rights for requiring inmates to work.

In sum, I have suggested that, in a model system of rights under modern conditions, adjudged violators have a right to certain kinds of treatment or rehabilitation (with the provision of or opportunity for work included among them), that they have this right along with other citizens and despite the violation, and, finally, that they may hold this right (with the right to work as a case in point) in such a way as to require its exercise in the status they have as adjudged violators, specifically as prison inmates. (That is, require its exercise as part of their sentence or as a characteristic feature of its being properly carried out.)

Now, it may well be that today American law falls outside my account of this particular aspect of prison life, of this particular detail of treatment and rehabilitation that prisoners in fact have or should have a right to. Nonetheless, I have indicated the path that might be followed in American law to reach a right to work for inmates and to incorporate that right as one aspect of a distinctive and intrinsic mode of treatment and rehabilitation of prisoners in the American system of rights. And this mode could even become at points, where there are well-established reasons to require or routinely encourage inmates (in virtue of their status as inmates) to receive the benefit in question, a distinctive and intrinsic mode of punishment in that system.

My argument has been, in short, a standard or general argument that applies to American law though it is not peculiar or limited to it. Perhaps the argument, though, so far as U.S. law specifically is concerned, belongs more to the future than to the present.

7. A SUMMARY OF MAIN CONCLUSIONS ABOUT PUNISHMENT IN A SYSTEM OF RIGHTS

We have come, at this point, to the end of our rather lengthy discussion of punishment in a system of rights. The main conclusion we have been able to draw overall is that coercion, especially and specifically in the form of punishment for crimes (in which rights are violated), could be justified in a system of rights. This is so even when rights of an adjudged violator are themselves infringed by punitive sanctions. And I have shown, in addition, that three distinctive modes of punishment are justifiably employed and, indeed, are characteristic modes in a typical system of rights.

Penalties (the object of which is incapacitation and the deterrence of crime through example) provide an indispensable means of preventing the violation of rights and, in a system of rights, even such severe penalties as imprisonment would probably prove justified. Compensation to victims, required of some adjudged violators, is necessary in a system of rights in order that rights be maintained and, thus, constitutes the second characteristic mode of punishment there. Finally, specific forms of treatment and rehabilitation are necessary for adjudged violators in a system of rights, if there is a civil right to some such form there (or if it comes under a rights-tending policy). And where that measure of treatment or rehabilitation is required (or even routinely encouraged) of adjudged violators in their status as, say, inmates, then we have identified a third characteristic mode of punishment in a typical system of rights, the mode of treatment and rehabilitation.

The effect of viewing punishment in the way indicated, as justified in a system of rights by reference to the principle that rights should be maintained and as breaking down into three main modes, could be considerable. For one thing, significant practical changes would ensue (the death penalty would probably be abolished, compensation to victims of crime would be paid by both the government and the adjudged violator, work in prisons would be made available, probably encouraged and possibly even required there). And some of these changes, especially the latter two (compensation and prison work), would likely turn out to be very expensive.

For another, the conception of liability to punishment would undergo some change. Here liability would be determined by reference to which modes of punishment were characteristically justified in a given political system (in the case at hand, a system of rights). Thus, people (if adjudged violators) would be liable to penalty, the requirement to pay compensation to victims of crime, and probably some forms of treatment and rehabilitation in a typical system of rights. And it might prove to be the case, and very likely would if this third category of liability was realized, that persons would be liable to punishment (in particular, to required treatment or rehabilitation) even if they did not satisfy the *mens rea* requirement, even if their lawbreaking was something they couldn't help.

And, for a third thing, we would have witnessed a significant rectification of names. Not only have we seen grounds for extending the concept of punishment beyond penalty, where it is largely lodged today, but we have also learned to view punishment as something essentially coercive rather than as something essentially painful.

These are three of the sorts of reforming changes, some of them practical changes, we could expect to encounter, then, if the scheme of punishment I have outlined, within a system of rights, ever came to be.

Punishment is an old institution and exists in many political systems, not just in a system of rights. And many of our ideas about punishment antedate the development of rights systems in particular and are in no way intrinsically tied to them. For example, many of the rights of persons who are charged with crimes or who are to be punished are of this sort. They were developed, not in a full system of rights, but in a fledgling one, one in which the government itself (in line with the times) was autocratic, undemocratic, and not primarily attuned to identifying and maintaining rights for all its citizens. It is necessary, then, to reexamine these rights in order to establish their fitness within an overall system of determinate rights and to decide which of them are fundamental rights and which are not. And like all rights—even fundamental rights—those that survive this scrutiny will be subject to definitional balancing in scope and content, to the establishment of criteria of possession and dispossession, to being weighed against other rights and other normative considerations.

In short, there is an ever pressing and constantly renewed need to rethink punishment, and the rights of persons on trial and under sentence, within the context of a system of rights, within a system of determinate rights and with a view to the principles of the relevant theoretic system of political institutions and conceptions. This is one of the main reasons I have devoted these three chapters to the theory of punishment. Not the only reason, though. Without this extended treatment, we could have given little sense, or less than it deserved, to the claim that punishment is justified in a system of rights in order that rights be maintained.

There are, of course, other issues than punishment that could have been addressed in a book about systems of rights. My strong emphasis on allegiance (including the duty to obey rights laws) and on punishment (conceived as certain justified coercive responses to lawbreaking) was necessary, however, given the topic from which we started, that is, the topic of political authority (as developed in Chapter 1). This topic has been the sustained focus of the entire book.[30]

A System of Rights

WE have now completed our survey of the institutions and conceptions of a system of rights, or at least those that touch on the main elements of political authority in particular.[1] I mean here such elements as (1) the presence of governmental agencies entitled to make law, (2) a reasonable expectation of compliance by citizens with laws duly made, and (3) the government's rightful monopoly in the use of coercive force—or, if not that, at least the propriety of the government's use of coercion to secure compliance with law (paired, at the same time, with a well-founded ability to forbid the use of force to its subjects).

It is time now to summarize the results of this study with respect to that system. I do so in order to determine the bearing of these findings on political authority within a system of rights and, hence, to help determine the possibility of political authority in general. This project is taken up in the present chapter, where I hope to join the main lines together and directly to address again the focal topic of political authority.

I. INTERNAL JUSTIFICATION OF POLITICAL AUTHORITY

Let me begin here by recalling some of the main features in the topography of the present book. Its first part concerned rights. Here the various practices and institutions involved in rights (especially in the most important kinds of rights) were spelled out in Chapters 2–5. It was shown in Chapter 5, in particular, that active civil rights—the principal kind of right in a system of rights and the core of the most important rights, human rights and constitutional rights—require an agency (or a coordinated set of agencies) to formulate and maintain and harmonize them. And it was shown next, in Chapters 6 and 7, that democratic institutions—universal franchise, contested voting, majority rule, the checking devices—can, acting as a coordinated set (on a majority electoral base), perform this job nicely. For, characteristically, these institutions, operating as essential parts of a carefully designed constitution, have a decided tendency to produce, protect, harmonize, and promote precisely such rights.

A definite line of connection ran, then, between the having of determinate active civil rights by individual persons, on the one hand, and the formulation and maintenance and harmonization of these rights by a well-defined set of democratic institutions, on the other. In Chapter 7, in particular, it was shown that this connection was not a matter of happenstance. It was a systemic one; for the two poles here, civil rights and democratic institutions, each supplied what the other needed and were thus mutually supporting.

Such a system was possible, we saw there, because two independent elements could be systematically connected to one another, by argument. And this particular connection was underwritten, in its depths, one might say, by the intrinsic affinity each element exhibited (under analysis) for the other, based on their shared justification by the standard of mutual perceived benefit.

The upshot of the argument (in Chapters 5–7) is that in order for people to have civil rights a set of rule-issuing agencies is required; and democratic institutions have a peculiar title, given that argument, to serve as the agencies that do this issuing. Hence, in a system of rights *one* of the authority elements is necessarily present: for there is and must be an agency, or set of agencies (and of a fairly definite sort), entitled there to pass and harmonize and promote civil rights laws.

The systematic connection of civil rights with democratic institutions (as set forth in these chapters) constitutes the main axis in the system of rights. From this particular nexus certain additional lines of connection were traced in subsequent chapters: first to allegiance and then to punishment.

It was noted in Chapter 8 that the character of allegiance in any particular kind of state will be defined in part by the peculiar standing the representative citizen has toward the laws typically generated in such a state. The discussion then turned to the case of a rights-producing state (a state of the sort we are interested in, a system of rights). It was argued, specifically, that citizens there would have (among other things) an institutional duty to comply with civil rights laws, as well as with certain other laws that had been duly issued on a democratic foundation.

The relevant duty here took shape through a series of moves, a sequence of considerations. As was shown in Chapter 2, rights always involve normative directions for the conduct of second parties—and thus rights lay the hand of duty, or something like it, on such persons. Given the argument of Chapters 3–5, the rights in question, the rights of principal interest, were *civil rights* (and could only be civil rights). It followed then, in view of the argument of Chapters 6–7 (summarized above), that the relevant duty of second parties is defined by democratically derived civil rights laws. The duty here is to do what these laws prescribe. In the case of any given civil right, it is a duty incumbent on and thereby a normative constraint on the conduct of second parties (who are, if we may call them that, the primary dutyholders under any such right). In a harmonized or coherent scheme of civil rights laws (as set forth in Chapter 5), there are a number of such duties that fall, variously, on each and every citizen. These duties, then, are part of the allegiance of the typical citizen, part of the standing of persons before the laws within a system of rights (given its scheme of democratically derived civil rights laws). The duties in question are, all of them, institutional duties (all of them system-specific duties) and were described, for purposes of summarization in Chapter 8, under the heading of the institutional duty to comply with civil rights laws. And the carrying out of this duty through conformity to law, in manifold ways, helps maintain a variety of active civil rights and thus fulfills the primary object of the scheme of democratically derived civil rights laws (that is, the object of seeing to it that the benefits provided by active rights, justifiable by the standard of mutual perceived benefit, are enjoyed by each and all, so far as possible, at an appropriate level).

Again, then, a relationship of mutual support—of reciprocal support— holds good here. It holds, as we have just seen, between (1) the institutions on the main axis—active civil rights of individual persons, democratic institutions—and (2) the institutional duty of typical citizens to conform to democratically derived civil rights laws.

This duty, once it had been carefully specified, was not one that typical citizens would find it unreasonable to perform (even when that duty required conduct from them that was contrary to conduct which would maximize the dutyholder's individual utility in a given case). For the rights maintained by the carrying out of this duty were themselves active rights that the dutyholders themselves also benefited from.

Thus, the *second* of the authority elements is necessarily present in a system of rights: for here there is and must be a reasonable presumption of general law-abidingness with respect to the most important laws. The rationally expected thing (given the substantive connection of civil rights and democratic institutions, on the one hand, and of democratically derived civil rights laws with the institutional duty of citizens, on the other) is that each citizen would comply with these laws. Or, more specifically, it is that they would comply at least with laws that establish civil rights or that bear certain identifiable and well-established relationships to such laws.

Now, it was also noted in Chapters 7 and 8 that the tendency of democratic institutions to issue laws of the appropriate kinds was (though decided) an imperfect one; accordingly, a highly constrained form of citizen disobedience had to be provided for. Even so, making such a provision did not detract from the reasonable expectation of compliance already established but was, rather, fully compatible with it. For civil disobedience, when so constrained, is within the ambit of the allegiance of the typical citizen.

At that point (once the point about the reasonable expectation had been established and the great value of law-abidingness had been affirmatively settled) the appropriateness of considering coercive enforcement of the laws was introduced into the discussion. And I then proceeded to provide, in the next few chapters (9–11), a summary sketch of how such enforcement might be justified and what shapes it might take in a rights-producing state.

Since punishment has been discussed in the chapters immediately previous to this one, I do not think it necessary to provide a detailed summary of conclusions there. I suggest instead that we go directly to the issue of how punishment is tied in to the other institutions in a system of rights.

Punishment was characterized from the very outset as a political or legal practice within a context. In the case at hand, it was a practice that operated within the setting provided by civil rights laws and by the democratic institutions that formulated, promoted, harmonized, and gave priority to such laws, and by the allegiance owed such laws by typical citizens in a democratic system of rights.

The practice of punishment made sense and was justified in that context on the ground that it was not only compatible with these other things (with active civil rights, democratic institutions, allegiance to laws) but was also required, in the strong sense of *necessarily* required, for the deterrence of violations and for the maintenance of democratically derived civil rights laws. Thus eligible, punishment (and the attendant institution of fair trial) helped ensure that civil rights (justifiable by the standard of mutual perceived benefit) remain active and that the relevant benefits and their enjoyment are at hand for all so far as possible.

Thus, there is here again a note of mutual support, of reciprocity, this time between (1) the elements on the main axis—active civil rights of individual persons, democratic institutions—and (2) the institution or practice of punishment and the modes that make it up (penalty, compensation, treatment and rehabilitation) in a system of rights. For, on the one hand, the elements in the axis provide a justification for punishment—an appropriate legal or political justification—through the idea that civil rights laws are to be maintained and not violated (as the argument in Chapter 9 showed). On the other, punishment (in the form of sanctions clauses attached to law) exists to deter substantially violations of such laws. Punitive measures (as spelled out in the clauses) are invoked in cases where conformity to law has failed, through the violation of civil rights and other relevant laws, and this invoking has deterrent effect as well. The point of punishment, so conceived, is to see to it as far as possible that such violations are minimized and, thus, that rights are maintained for each and all up to a certain standard, even in the face of violations.

There is, I would note before we conclude this particular discussion, an additional relationship of mutual support worth considering here. For, on the one side, the practice of punishment presupposed, as I said, the norm that individual civil rights are to be maintained (a norm that was implicated in the allegiance to the laws of the typical citizen) and, equally important, presupposed the norm that the typical citizen should abide by civil rights laws. In return, the practice of punishment (in the form of sanctions clauses in laws and of the invoking of those sanctions on appropriate occasions) effectively supported the called-for conformity to civil rights laws by citizens and encouraged an attitude favoring law-abidingness, an attitude proper to the typical citizen. More significantly, perhaps, civilly disobedient persons (insofar as they acted acceptably and in accordance with the allegiance they owed to law in a system of rights) were normatively directed to accept measures of punishment, if these were properly invoked. Thus, the institution of punishment (as justified in a system of rights) actually helped define the allegiance of the representative citizen there.

In the further development of the overall line of argument respecting punishment, in Chapters 10 and 11, it was shown (as conclusively as can be shown in philosophy) that the measures centrally involved in the practice of punishment are essentially coercive (rather than pain-causing) in character. Accordingly, the *third* and last of the authority elements is necessarily present in a system of rights: for there is and must be—if civil rights are to be maintained and their violation prevented or, at least, substantially lessened—an eligible and justified use by government of coercion against adjudged lawbreakers to help secure compliance with civil rights laws (paired, at the same time, with that government's well-founded ability to forbid the use of rights-violating force to its subjects).

Whether we could take the matter one step further, to include the government's prohibition of the use of force in principle—that is, *all* use of force—is not clear. It does seem, rather, merely that a use of force which violated determinate rights could be prohibited, with justification, by building sanctions clauses into laws and by invoking the allowed-for coercive measures against adjudged violators. Even so, we have here a criterion for deciding the issue; and it is a powerful one in principle, since it would be possible to prohibit all—or almost all—use of force by ordinary citizens on the basis it provides. Here, then, at least the *possibility* of a government's rightful monopoly in the use of coercive force has been established.

I would prefer, though, something more than a mere possibility. Accordingly, I suggest that we stay with what has actually been established in this matter: that it is proper for a government in a system of rights to use coercion against adjudged violators of civil rights laws, so long as the terms of justified use have been met. And pair that with something else already established: that the government in a system of rights has a well-founded ability to forbid the use of rights-violating force to its subjects. This seems to state the matter (of a monopoly of coercive force) in a sufficiently clear but restricted way, and we can leave it at that.

In sum, then, the basic constitution of the system of rights sketched in this book consists of a number of institutional essentials: (1) active civil rights laws, (2) the democratic institutions, (3) allegiance to law of the typical citizen, with the duty of each to conform to civil rights laws, but with allowed-for civil disobedience, (4) the institution of fair trial and the practice of punishment, the latter in a variety of appropriate modes. And there are, as we have seen and can now put schematically, important mutually supporting or reciprocal relationships between these institutions: (*a*) most especially between (1) and (2) but also (*b*) between (1)–(2) and (3) and (*c*) between (1)–(2) and (4) and, finally, (*d*) between (3) and (4).

As I have sketched out in the present chapter, the overall arrangement of these relationships of mutual support among the institutional essentials of a system of rights is such that the main elements in the idea of political authority—that is, the title to issue rules, a reasonable presumption of compliance, the propriety of a government's both using force and refusing that use to its subjects—are all necessarily present in such a system.

Accordingly, the authority elements are proper to that system and can be regarded as ingredient within it. They are not only necessary in a system of rights but, more important, are systemically connected with one another there. They arise, connected to one another, as we have seen, on the foundation provided by the reciprocal relationships of the institutional essentials in a system of rights. Thus, the authority elements are necessary as part of the completion—of the achievement of systemic closure—of that particular theoretic system of political institutions and conceptions. And they would be necessary, practically necessary, for that particular system to exist—for a system of rights to be exemplified, even if only imperfectly—in the world of human affairs.[2]

The necessity here, as I argued in Chapter 1, is not a matter of logical entailments among the authority elements themselves. (For I do not think any such entailment exists.) Rather, the necessity is generated on an altogether different basis: that is, through the reciprocal connection of the institutional essentials themselves in a system of rights. Thus, it is the coherence of that system (of the background theory, as it was called in Chapter 1)—the coherence of a reciprocally related institutional setup in which each of the elements of authority can be shown to be present—that justifies political authority for such a system.

The justification so achieved is *internal*. It is a justification accomplished by analyzing the institutional essentials of a given political system and determining that the system, shown to be a coherent one in virtue of the systematic interrelationship of its constituent institutions, has other important features as well—among them, the necessary presence of the authority elements. That these other features are—or at least that the authority elements are—in a sense supervenient on the underlying institutional setup does not diminish the claim that an internal justification has been achieved.

Such a justification is *political*, for it operates on political institutions and stays, more or less, at the level of these institutions. Or, to be strictly accurate, it does not ascend beyond that level to the level of a critical justification, to the justification of these institutions by the standards of a critical morality, such as, for example, philosophical utilitarianism. Political justification, so conceived, presupposes the possibility of a critical moral justification but does not exhibit or rely on it. For this reason, then, I have felt rather comfortable in calling by the name *political* the kind of justification I have been describing.

In the case at hand, then, the relevant institutions included civil rights, democratic institutions, an institutional duty (to comply with civil rights laws), and the political and legal institutions of punishment and fair trial. A political justification of political authority, as I have been conceiving it in the argument of the present book, is an internal justification. It is complete when the institutional essentials have been shown to constitute a coherent arrangement, a systematic setup, and when the authority elements have been shown to arise, to be present on that basis, in such a setup.

Of course, it would follow from what I have been saying that an internal political justification is a quite limited affair. It is limited to one kind of justification in particular (an important kind, no doubt, and usually indispensable) but it leaves other forms or levels of justification untouched—or at least relatively open. And, even when accomplished, an internal political justification is not a justification of political authority as such but, instead, only a justification of such authority within a particular theoretic political system (in the case at hand, only a justification of political authority within a system of rights, of the sort set out in this book).

Nonetheless, we can say that political authority—and, withal, the presence of the authority elements—is internally justified in this theoretic political system of rights. And this is the conclusion I have drawn in the present chapter, in the present book, about such authority in a system of rights.

2. THE PRIORITY OF BASIC CONSTITUTIONAL RIGHTS

The notion of a system of rights has been characterized in this book in three distinct but related ways. First, as a harmonious or coherent scheme of civil rights laws (in Chapter 5). Then, as a particular system of political institutions. Here it was characterized (in Chapters 6–11) as an arrangement in which civil rights are substantively and reciprocally related to other institutions—to democratic institutions, to the institutional duty of citizens to conform to civil rights laws, to the institution of fair trial and to the institution of punishment, in each of its modes (penalty, compensation, treatment and rehabilitation)—and these other institutions are similarly related to one another. Finally, a system of rights was characterized (especially in Chapter 7 and also in Chapter 8 and to a degree in 11) as one in which civil rights are compatible with these other institutional essentials while having a standing priority, individually and as a set, over other normative values: over corporate or aggregative nonrights (like national security or the growth of

GNP or mere majority interests) and over rights that are not universal (not civil in that sense).

Clearly, the most controversial claim and, in the end, the most deeply entrenched idea in this rather complex characterization has been the priority of civil rights (as just described). I want to consider now an important challenge to my account.

Many people—American judges in particular—seem to distinguish basic rights from other rights and to identify constitutional rights with basic rights in particular. One could say, then, that my analysis has been defective on this very point. The tie-in of rights with constitutionality, with the status of being among the institutional essentials, should run only to *basic* civil rights. And priority—which continues, by the way, to attach to basic civil rights—becomes now a secondary and derivative criterion for that status, the first being basicness.

Of course, there is and always has been considerable diversity of opinion as to how basicness is to be determined. One plausible candidate (and one consistent with the argument of this book) is that basicness is grounded on a shared estimate of importance, by fellow citizens in the past and by fellow citizens today, as mediated in the history of their common nation. Thus, on this view, the most secure standard for regarding some rights as basic is the conventional judgment—both popular and expert—that they are basic.

At this point, though, a further note is often introduced. For some want to say that it is not basicness or importance as conventionally perceived that counts decisively—not even when that convention constitutes a widely shared and long-run social consensus—but, rather, the written constitution itself is what counts. In short, the best ground, on this amended version, for regarding some rights as basic is that they are enumerated in the written constitution, the supreme law of the land. This is still a conventionalist account of sorts, for it does focus on the convention embodied in and expressed in the constitution so conceived, but it limits attention to that one convention, as written down, and to it alone.

Thus, Robert Bork (who exemplifies this view) says, respecting the American constitutional system, that both majority rule and judicial review are profoundly limited by those rights, but only by those rights, that are specified in the *text* of the U.S. Constitution or that *derive* "from the governmental processes established by the Constitution." These are the only basic rights Americans have. Save for these rights, majority rule can do anything it wants. And judges (paying attention to the text and to the intentions of the Framers) can hold up only these rights, and no others, as grounds for annulling an otherwise legitimate statute.[3]

In my judgment, this account has things backwards. We do not say that the rights of the U.S. Bill of Rights (to cite one example) are basic *because* they are incorporated in the written constitution; instead, we say that they should be, or have been, so incorporated because of the inherent importance they have. They cannot have *this* importance, the requisite importance, simply by being incorporated into the written constitution. To put the same point differently, one might believe as an act of piety toward the constitution that the rights of the Bill of Rights have an overriding importance simply in virtue of their being *in* the constitution; but one could not explain or justify their being there in the first place, for that reason.

Thus, to assign special importance or basicness to the rights of the Bill of Rights solely on the ground of their being incorporated into the written constitution, or solely on the basis of appeal to the history of successful written constitutions (as Rawls in effect does) is to beg the crucial question.[4] For the crucial question is what could *explain* that incorporation in the first place.

Why should the rights found in the body of the U.S. Constitution, such as habeas corpus, that is, the right not to be held in involuntary confinement unless charged or sentenced (found in article 1, section 9), and the rights in the Bill of Rights (in Amendments 1–8), and the right to vote (as originally secured in article 1 and then modified by subsequent amendments: 15, 17, 19, 24, 26) be incorporated into the written constitution? An appropriate explanatory answer would, I think, include two kinds of considerations: (1) those bearing on such a constitution itself and (2) those bearing on civil rights as constitutional rights.

Regarding (1), that is, regarding the written constitution itself, an appropriate answer would include the claim that these rights should be incorporated because the written constitution (if it is to be at all useful or successful toward its intended end) identifies the institutional essentials and directs the behavior of legislators and administrators and judges. The citizens want the governmental agents to specify and promote certain rights—certain ways of acting and of being treated—for everybody. They do not want, presumably no one wants, these ways to be superseded by other concerns. Accordingly, the constitution attempts, so far as practical, to put the legislative and judicial and other political agents on notice and to prevent action hurtful to these matters. So the especially important rights—the rights of the Bill of Rights and so on—are incorporated into the written constitution (for example, of the U.S.), or the citizens (and the political agents) include them in some other way among the institutional essentials.

Such rights are identifiable on grounds independent of incorporation, or so it has been argued. The written constitution's job is simply to list the basic or fundamental rights. Ideally, then, the constitution of a particular state should list *all* the basic rights, as appropriately (and independently) recognized by the people and the authoritative lawmaking agencies there. And that list should be added to, deleted from, modified as time goes on.

The point is, once a given right is appropriately thought to be basic, there is good reason to incorporate that right into the written constitution—that is, where a state has such a constitution. For the written constitution is a public, authoritative, agreed-on charter (usually on a supermajoritarian basis) having the status of supreme law of the land and designed to lay out the institutional essentials of the body politic in a given case.

We have here, then, a reason for listing basic rights in the written constitution (given the character such a document has) that is properly thought to be a paramount consideration. And this reason holds even though listing such rights there does not *establish* their status as basic but merely registers it.

We must ask, though, what *would* establish a basic or fundamental status for civil rights? For this, clearly, is the fundamental question. What would count as an appropriate and decisive explanatory rationale for saying that certain civil rights had, or should have, that status?

Here we turn to (2). For regarding (2), that is, regarding civil rights as constitutional rights, another line of argument comes into play. What *explains* the constitutional status of some civil rights is that they are widely regarded as ways of acting, or ways of being treated, that should be recognized and maintained for everyone—*because* they are perceived to be in the interest of each and all (presumably reasonably perceived, for example, as long-established civil rights which continue to enjoy a highly concurrent favorable social opinion). Thus, here it is the widespread and long-run perception of mutual benefit for all (the judgment, upon reflection, that these things really are for the perceived good of each, or a means to it) that makes these particular ways of acting, or of being treated, peculiarly important.

If this is so, then it is also reasonable, in a scheme of democratic institutions, to accord priority to such long-term rights. And when people are willing to pay the costs, as we expect they would be, of giving these ways priority over nonrights values and over rights that are not similarly universal, then the civil rights in question have the status—and ought to have the status—of constitutional rights.

The correct (explanatory) account of civil rights as constitutional rights, then, is wholly consistent with—indeed, it is a further working out of—the argument given earlier in the present book, in Chapter 7.[5] For the explanatory account assumes, among other things, that a high social consensus exists; it exists here, indeed, on the basis provided by the self-correcting character of democratic institutions, and that consensus has been recognized and reinforced as well (and quite explicitly) in the checking devices or institutions. (Thus, it has been recognized, for example, in a written constitutional bill of rights or in some oft-repeated and authoritative interpretation of constitutional law found, over a long period of time, in judicial review or in parliamentary debates and enactments.)

An important point is thereby established: that any such determinate way of acting or of being treated is, with these credentials and when formulated as a civil right, justifiable by the standard of mutual perceived benefit. Civil rights other than the long-standing ones may, of course, also be justifiable by that standard; the point is, the long-standing ones are the definitive example of such rights in a *democratic* system of rights (for the self-correcting character of the democratic institutions has been allowed to operate in their case and the rights have been explicitly incorporated into—or recognized by—the checking devices as well). Hence, they are the paradigm case of the kind of civil right that should have priority in that *particular* theoretic system of rights, in the one I have identified as democratic.

In this explanatory account, the 'correct' account I have called it, the gloss provided by constitutional piety (of the Borkian text-based sort) is abandoned as explanatorily (and justificationally) empty. And the conventional judgment of basicness (referred to at the very beginning of the present discussion) is not taken at face value, as a mere assertion or a sociological judgment; rather, it takes a rather complex institutional form, one that is regimented by familiar concerns. It is, in fact, structured by considerations recognizable from themes developed in previous chapters of this book.

Specifically, this explanatory account is structured (1) by the *universal character* of a particular designated way of acting (or of being treated) within the body politic (as set out in Chapters 2–5); and (2) by the satisfaction, by that particular way, of the justifying criterion of mutual perceived benefit (and, hence, by the *importance* of that way of acting or of being treated, a point emphasized in Chapter 5). It is structured (3) by what I have called the paradigmatic status of at least the long-standing civil rights already included under (2), that is, by the peculiar *support provided by the self-correcting character of democratic institutions and by appropriate and explicit recognition in the checking institutions.* Accordingly, it is structured (4) by the expressed *willingness* (upon due reflection) of the political agencies and of the citizens generally *to pay the costs of affording priority* to that paradigmatic way of acting, or of being treated, and by their commitment to bring that way within the set of rights that, having priority over other kinds of normative considerations, must itself be continuously harmonized.

Such a commitment involves, as we have seen, the identification of the central contents of these various rights and subsequent scope adjustments and competitive weightings—these transactions all having the goal of adjusting paradigmatic civil rights to nonrights (like national security) and of harmonizing such rights with one another (so as to avoid conflicts and thereby achieve coherence). Thus, any such commitment points to a messy and time-consuming and often frustrating business. So the account is structured, finally, (5) by the citizens' willingness and the political agencies' *willingness to tolerate* and live with *such a messy and controversial business* as this.[6]

These five points, as summarized in the italicized words in the two paragraphs above, constitute the points of conceptual structure, of rigor, that my analysis of civil rights as constitutional rights introduces into the conventional account of basicness with which we began. These points, in effect, identify hurdles that ways of acting or of being treated must surmount in order to become constitutional rights. (In particular, points [3]-[5] do, for they mark the key distinction between civil rights *per se* and those that are constitutional rights.) Or, at least, we can say that a successful negotiation of all these points would *explain* such status in a given case.

What I have tried to suggest, in this discussion, is that a non-question-begging account (one that actually explains why some civil rights are constitutional rights) should focus on what plausibly explains the constitutional status of such civil rights. For we can assume that not every civil right will make all the jumps indicated. The civil right to cosmetic dental care and hair transplants (mentioned in Chapter 5), were there such a right, probably would not, and the right to work (discussed in Chapter 11) has not in fact; but the civil right to an education through age 16 (also mentioned there) probably would. At least it is making progress in that direction. And the rights in the text of the current U.S. Constitution (if I may again use that example)—the rights of habeas corpus and universal franchise and *some* of the rights in the Bill of Rights—seemingly have.[7]

In sum, then, my argument to this point has been that some civil rights, as established in law, can be shown to have the support of a highly concurrent social opinion. These, then, are clearly justifiable on the regulative standard of mutual perceived benefit. As so justified these civil rights are precisely the sort of thing that is to be given constitutional priority in a system of rights. And I have taken those long-standing ones that enjoy not only popular support but also the support of the checking devices to be the paradigmatic basic or constitutional rights in a *democratic* system of rights.

It follows, of course, that some civil rights by law, even some that can reasonably be acknowledged to be justified on the basis of mutual perceived benefit, will not have priority in this particular sort of theoretic system. For, though they are civil rights, they cannot count as *constitutional* rights, as full-fledged institutional essentials, unless the right kind of effort and commitment (as spelled out in points [3]-[5], above) has been put behind them.

Let me put my argument now in a somewhat different way. I have been arguing that, in a democratic system of rights, there are *two* fundamental considerations that determine the status of a basic right and hence the status of the constitutional priority of basic civil rights. First, such a right must actually have the support of a highly concurrent social opinion and, hence, be properly regarded as justifiable on the standard of mutual perceived benefit. I suggested, then, that long-standing rights were a paradigm case of rights that enjoyed such support. But, in addition, these rights enjoyed additional support, support that was peculiar to a democratic system of rights in particular. And this brings us to the second fundamental consideration: that a basic or fundamental right should also have the support of the self-correcting character of democratic institutions and, among rights that had this support, be recognized as well (and quite explicitly) in the constitutional checking devices.

Thus, the account I have given in this chapter of the character of politically basic or constitutional rights qualifies (but does not revoke) what I said earlier in the book. Specifically, it qualifies the argument in Chapter 7 by suggesting that not all civil rights, or even all civil rights justifiable by the standard of mutual perceived benefit, but only some civil rights are to be counted among the institutional essentials in the constitution of a democratic system of rights.

Thus, the idea (developed in Chapter 7) that civil rights, as a proper subset of things that are for the good of each and all, have a certain priority over other normative considerations is qualified in the present chapter. Here being a civil right of the sort just characterized is a necessary condition of that right's being a constitutional right; but it is not sufficient.

This qualified account is, I think, a more plausible one. For it does not suggest that civil rights are constitutionally basic, or have priority, *simply* in virtue of being civil rights in law (or simply in virtue of being civil rights justifiable as in the interest of each and all)—a suggestion that would in effect give strong priority literally to every justified civil right.

And it is a better account in another respect too; it does not ignore the fact that civil rights are themselves political constructions, and that constitutional rights are not merely civil rights (rights by law and justifiable by mutual perceived benefit) to which sound theory has added the correct spin. Rather, it emphasizes that constitutional rights themselves are political constructions, involving certain express undertakings.

Quite properly, then, the modified account politicizes the notion of constitutional rights. It recognizes that decisions must be taken here, and lived with, that such rights must be formulated and maintained and harmonized, like all rights, in political give and take.

But its greater measure in these respects cannot be *the* decisive consideration. Instead, we must have good reason to believe that the revised account is fully acceptable in the light of what has gone before.

The decisive consideration here, then, is whether the two lines of argument—the one in Chapter 7 and the one in the present chapter—can be regarded as consistent. The first line of argument (as developed in the beginning half of Chapter 7) was designed to show that civil rights required agencies of formulation (and so on) and that democratic institutions, where they stayed in character by reference to that which justified them, could be presumed to be apt to produce precisely such rights and not to invade them tyrannically, by allowing other considerations to supersede civil rights. This line still stands.

More importantly, what I have said in the present chapter draws, it should be noted, on what was said in Chapter 7 *after* that first line of argument had been concluded. For, in order to support that first line and its conclusions, further considerations were drawn into play there. The most important of these, for our present purposes, are the need to have constitutional checking devices (like judicial review or a written bill of rights) and the importance of the self-correcting character of democratic decision making over time. The identification of certain long-standing civil rights as paradigmatic basic constitutional rights (an identification made initially near the end of Chapter 7 itself) was clearly done on the basis of these new materials, introduced in the second half of that chapter. And priority was attached to such rights especially.

Thus, if we take all that was said in Chapter 7, as material intended to give full content to the account of a *democratic* system of civil rights in particular, then we are able to conclude, as we have in the present chapter, that the idea of the priority of civil rights is fully satisfied by according priority to those long-standing civil rights that have met the two fundamental considerations summarized above. In that particular theoretic system we call a *democratic* system of rights, these rights are the privileged ones. They are the politically basic or fundamental civil rights in the constitution of that system. As such they have priority over nonrights considerations and over rights that are not universal within the body politic—and, we might now add, over civil rights that were not themselves politically basic or constitutional.

Now that this point has been made, let me go on to add (what I said in Chapters 5 and 9) that I can see no objection to developing an account of the weighting of basic rights *within* the class of constitutional rights. Indeed, some such move will probably be necessary if the task of harmonization (of rights with one another and of rights with other considerations) is to be carried out successfully.

It should be noted, for the point is not obvious, that a difference in competitive weight *between* two constitutional rights, between two politically basic or fundamental rights, can be allowed for in the account I have been giving. It would not disrupt the earlier analysis of the priority of civil rights.

For that priority, as we understood it in our last summary of that idea, was simply the priority of basic civil rights over nonrights considerations and over rights that are not universal within the body politic—and, we have just added, over universal rights that were not themselves constitutional. Hence, the status of these civil rights as constitutional (or politically fundamental) would not be jeopardized, where the priority just named persisted, even though the exercise of one constitutional right might yield to another and weightier one, generally or on a given occasion.

Thus, to cite a possible example (from American constitutional law), the First Amendment right to the nonestablishment of religion (as the superordinate right in a given case) might outweigh certain features of one's right to an education (as subordinate there). Or (from an example in Chapter 5) the policy of not burdening the marketplace with racial discrimination (and the rights this policy gave rise to) might have greater weight *in a given case* than the right to free personal association. Or, from that same chapter, one of two exercises of the self-same right (say, free exercise of religion) might have greater weight over the other on a given occasion, for merely technical reasons. And so on.

I will not, however, press this idea of differential competitive weights between constitutional rights. It has in effect already been discussed (and the last two examples developed more fully) in Chapter 5. More important, it takes us away from what has been our chief concern in this discussion, away from our concern with what makes something a fundamental *constitutional* right in the first place.

One final point. The present account, as a modification of the earlier one (in Chapter 7), allows us to distinguish clearly between two closely related but not identical notions. It allows distinction between, on the one hand, the priority of civil rights (as that notion has now been reformulated, so as to include the priority of basic or constitutional civil rights over those civil rights that are not constitutional) and, on the other, the competitive weight of individual rights. The former and more specialized idea is, perhaps, the deepest and most distinctive feature in my account of a system of rights; the latter and more general idea is a rather ordinary and workaday idea, but one that has proven to be useful, perhaps essential, in the harmonization of rights (Chapters 5, 7) and in the theory of punishment (Chapters 9–11) within a system of rights.

3. THE DEMOCRATIC SYSTEM OF RIGHTS

The idea of a system of rights (as it has gradually unfolded in this book) is a quite distinctive one. As developed, it has (as we have seen) four identifiable but related constituent elements: civil rights, democratic institutions, the institutional duty to conform to civil rights laws, and the conjoint institutions of punishment and fair trial. And special emphasis has been given here to the democratic element and its implications, thereby creating a particular and distinctive theoretic political system the *democratic* system of rights— in which the priority is given to certain basic or fundamental constitutional rights (that is, to long-standing civil rights that meet the two fundamental considerations developed earlier).

The idea of a system of rights (and, within it, that of a democratic system of rights) is distinctive in part, of course, simply because there are theoretic models of states—and many actual states—that could not possibly be systems of rights. Thus (as was argued in Chapter 5), a sharply class-divided state, on the model of Plato's republic, cannot have civil rights, that is, identical across-the-board political rights for all its citizens. Nor can a rigid caste society.

The whole point of such societies is to deny recognition and maintenance to any particular way of acting or of being treated that holds alike for each and every person there. Members of a given class may perhaps have some rights (rights peculiar to their class or caste status), but there are no rights which are common to all the persons in the whole society.

Some such societies include a class or caste of chattel slaves. Here the denial of universal rights is coupled with a further denial, the denial of rights altogether to one class, the slaves. Indeed, I think it characteristic of any society in which the institution of chattel slavery exists to deny rights to the slave (as was the case in antebellum America, before the Thirteenth Amendment [1865] that abolished slavery). Thus, for these societies too universal political rights, that is, rights of each and all within the body politic, are ruled out.

Some states, however, fail to be systems of rights at another point, at the point of affording *priority* to civil rights. Thus, a state that modelled itself on an Islamic theocracy (like Iran) or on classical Marxist socialism (like the USSR during almost all its history) could not, while staying in character and given the models they are following, accord fundamental political priority to civil rights (or to any subset of civil rights). Unless it be a 'right' that merely reproduces the doctrinal grounds of that system—to serve the revealed and authoritatively interpreted will of Allah and not be an enemy of God, in the one case, or objectively to help build communism, to the best of one's abilities, and not be an enemy of the Revolution or the Party, in the other. Goals different from civil rights have the priority in such states. And civil rights, even if they existed there, can be superseded (or denied or suppressed) on the basis of these goals. Where this is so, then the state that exemplifies such goals would necessarily fail to be a system of rights (as was argued in Chapter 8).

Last of all, some states are not close to having democratic institutions (of the sort described in Chapters 6 and 7). Some states, indeed, may actively oppose efforts to establish or strengthen these institutions (for expressed contempt for parliamentary institutions and for actual parliamentary democracies is a deep and pervasive theme in nineteenth- and twentieth-century political thought and action). Such states, then, could not be modeled on the kind of system of rights described in this book (in particular, in the present chapter), that is, on a *democratic* system of rights.

As I have tried to emphasize, then, the interesting thing about all these examples—of states that cannot have civil rights, of states that cannot accord priority to civil rights (or at least to some civil rights), of states that cannot or are not likely to develop democratic institutions—is that none of them can (while staying true to form) possibly be exemplifications of that particular theoretic system, the democratic system of rights, which has been the focus of attention in the present book. I do not mean to suggest, in saying this, however, that any presently existing state actually is a proper exemplification. Indeed, I think no state today is a system of rights state.

The reason for this seems clear enough. Almost all the states that might be described as *aspiring* to be systems of rights have constitutions that were developed over several centuries. These constitutions were, in their beginnings, nondemocratic and they contain many institutional essentials (even to this day) that are not fully compatible with democratic institutions. And others (like present-day Germany or Japan) have relatively new constitutions that were imposed on them, in unpromising circumstances, at the end of the Second World War (or shortly after). Thus, the newly written Japanese Constitution was erected on the foundations, not wholly expunged, of an autocratic imperial state and the German on the ruins of a popularly supported totalitarian dictatorship. The German situation has been even further complicated by the recent incorporation into its constitutional fabric of East Germany (which, for the last forty years, had been an independent Marxist socialist state). And many of the states remaining (insofar as they even count as democratic or as rights-producing states, as perhaps India does and possibly Israel) had their constitutions, like their borders, imposed on them as part of an often makeshift post-colonial settlement.

Clearly, then, in the case of all these 'aspiring' constitutions, the point of delineating a theoretic system of rights is not to help unearth their origins or to structure the ideologies that prevailed in their beginnings, but, rather, to mark one plausible direction for further institutional development. The delineation serves principally to identify what such constitutions would become if they became systems of rights. It indicates, as a sort of goal, what institutional essentials would need to be present and how they should relate to one another in the constitution of a democratic system of rights.

If one wanted to assess progress toward this goal, what primarily should be looked for? In terms of the argument of this book, three things seem of paramount importance.

First, there would be movement in the direction of establishing the democratic institutions (identified in Chapters 6 and 7): universal franchise on the principle of one person, one vote; contested voting, on a regular basis and with free discussion, at both the electoral and legislative levels; majority rule in lawmaking (*on a majority electoral base*); and the checking devices (such as judicial review, a written bill of rights, separation of powers with attendant checks and balances, congenial traditions of parliamentary interpretation and activity, what have you). Of these, I think the one furthest from achievement in any present-day parliamentary democracy (and probably the most difficult to achieve and retain) is that feature of majority rule I have italicized here.

Then, next, there would be movement in the direction of establishing active civil rights: ways of acting or of being treated that are formulated in law and maintained for all citizens or all persons individually (or almost all) and that are reasonably thought to be justifiable by the standard of mutual perceived benefit. Finally, and perhaps most important, there would have to be movement in the direction of according political priority to some civil rights (in particular, to those that are basic or fundamental constitutional rights and that have this status in virtue of their being long-standing rights for which there is the support of a high level of social consensus and explicit recognition by and incorporation into the checking devices).

What counts crucially here, then, is not the founding documents of states or the myths of their civic religions (to which I, for one, would attach great importance) or their self-understanding and representation to others, but, rather, the evolutionary development, the actual tendencies of states in the directions indicated. In sum, the theoretic system I have sketched in this book explicates *one* important feature of the tendencies of *some* existing political societies.

But no state today or in the past can claim to exhibit more than that: for none of them has passed beyond the status of aspirant, the status of being guided fitfully and only in part by the system of rights idea; none of them has become anything like a wholesale exemplification of that idea. Thus, though the idea of a system of rights might be in fact a goal of some existing states (and one that the politicians and judges and citizens gradually have become more and more conscious of), that idea is, right now, best understood as only a partial goal of any one of them.[8]

Even if a given state ever came to the point of realizing these tendencies sufficiently to count as an exemplification, as a more or less proper instance, of a system of rights, it would be an imperfect exemplification, an approximation at best. For we can suppose that there would always be some civil rights in law there that were not justifiable on the standard of mutual perceived benefit or some justifiable civil rights that *should* be accorded priority, though they were not, or some that should *not* be accorded priority, though they were, and so on.

With this final point made about the 'reading' of actual states in the light of this (or any other) determinate ideal, let us turn to the most engaging problem that faces the particular theoretic system of rights I have sketched in the present book. At a number of points, I have acknowledged that justifications are possible other than the internal kind I have been developing. Indeed, this was granted from the very beginning (in Chapter 1).

4. JUSTIFICATION OF THE DEMOCRATIC SYSTEM

What I have argued for in the book (mainly in Chapter 1 but at other points as well) is that, if these other justifications are to be justifications of *political* institutions or of political arrangements, one needs to bear in mind that these political things do not typically come one by one but, instead, are often, if not usually, systemically related to one another. And one would need, or so I have argued, to take account of these systemic relationships.

There are, of course, exceptions to this rule of thumb. For some states actually are ramshackle, jerry-built affairs. And some state models, some theoretical ideals of states, are equally hodge-podge. But these exceptions do not concern us here.

Let me put my crucial point in a somewhat different way: the intellectual interest, and the challenge, of attempting to justify political practices and institutions typically arises in view of the fact that these things, characterized as they are, have a 'logic' of their own, a systemic interplay which must be captured and taken into account. I would suspect that many long-established political institutions, and functioning states with such institutions, have precisely this character. They do exhibit the systemic, interactive affinities I have described (though these affinities differ, of course, from one basic arrangement or theoretic system of institutions to another); and the institutional setup to which each is attached needs to be brought into view and its essential coherence established (or, at least, assayed) in any serious normative evaluation.

Even more strongly, I would suspect that *theories* of states and of politics (whether we have in mind Plato's theory or the theory of Augustine or that of Locke or Rousseau or Marx) would exhibit a fairly high degree of internal coherence. Again, such theories will differ from one another in a variety of important ways. But each will be coherent (or can be made coherent, using resources taken from the theory itself); this at least is my operating assumption. Hence, one of the tasks of political philosophy is to try to establish this coherence, to see it first hand (as best one can) and to assay the result.

Sometimes the theory in question is associated with a particular named individual (as in the previous paragraph). But sometimes (as in my account of a theoretic system of rights) it is associated with no one person's name but, rather, is 'in the air' and can be traced, at one point or another, to a variety of theorists who have contributed to its development. Such a theoretic system often owes as much to direct reflections on politics and institutional development and recent history as it does to the counsels of an explicit political philosophy.

More often than not, any theory we are seriously interested in is a sort of amalgam of all these things (of political philosophy in the grand manner, of theory appropriate to a given system, of reflection). The theory that results may be somewhat amorphous, to be sure, but it is no less palpable for that. The theoretic system of rights we have reviewed in this book is, I believe, an example of theories in this particular genre. Such theories too must be made coherent, if that is possible.

The attempt to achieve internal coherence, to achieve internal justification of political authority, in a given theoretic system (in particular, in one that is being advocated or is being held up as a model) is the marching order, the first task, of a political philosopher. And if the claims made in the previous several paragraphs here are sound, then the *other* justifications (by reference, for example, to conventional moral norms or to religious beliefs) are probably better conceived as complementary to internal political justification. Such ancillary or supervenient justifications show that a soundly conceived political regime, itself coherent, can also be endorsed by conscientious practitioners of a given religion or moral code.

In sum, any further attempt at justification has to be conceived as presupposing and building upon that internal political justification. Thus, if these other kinds of justification are really to satisfy us here as justifications of political institutions or practices, then they must take as their starting point the achievement of precisely the sort of internal political justification that this book has been at pains to set out and, as regards a system of rights, to accomplish.

In the argument of the book I have emphasized, even though internal justification has remained the principal focus throughout, that another sort of justification would be called for—were the first sort (the internal justification of authority in a theoretic system of rights) to be achieved. A critical justification of that system will be called for then, a further justification that uses critical standards—the standards of an accredited moral theory like utilitarianism, say, or the standards of rational choice theory—to assay its essential features (insofar as these have gone together to make up one whole). Here the move to bring such critical standards to bear, as a further level or sort of justification, is to perform the second main task of political philosophy.

From the perspective of the present book we have now reached the point of requiring a second-level or critical justification of a theoretic system of rights. We need, then, to take a preliminary survey of that task, to begin to chart our route up the face of that next climb, and to gather some notion of the tools we have on hand to use. It is time now to turn to that task.

13

Critical Justification

THE present chapter is the concluding one in the book. In the short space of this one chapter I will be able to provide only a brief first sketch of some of the features and problems of a critical justification of the democratic system of rights. In order to simplify matters appropriately, I will be concerned in what follows only with attempts at a critical *moral* justification. I should add that I will develop no theory of what counts as such a justification here; I will, rather, assume merely that it would widely be thought to be a *critical* moral justification if one were to achieve that justification by using the resources of an accredited comprehensive and general moral theory (a theory like that of philosophical utilitarianism, for example).[1]

In order to simplify matters even further, at least in this very preliminary discussion, I will assume that what we are looking for here is simply a critical moral justification for according civil rights to individual persons and for giving priority to at least some such rights over policies that serve corporate or other aggregative considerations and over other important moral values, deep values like the perfection of some important trait such as holiness or wisdom or Nietzschean self-transcendence.

Let me elaborate a bit on this particular simplifying claim. Throughout the book, I have stressed the idea of a *system* of rights and the need to justify not so much particular rights as the whole system of civil rights. Or, to put the point differently: though it is important to be able to justify named rights, it is even more important that one be able to justify that there should be determinate civil rights which, individually and as a set, have priority. The priority intended is a familiar one (priority over corporate goods and mere majority interests, over rights that are not universal, and over civil rights that are not basic and constitutional), but here we go beyond this. The intended priority also includes, as a second feature, the claim that the critical moral justification of a scheme of basic constitutional rights will give those rights, individually and as a set, priority over at least some deep moral values.

I should add that I will not emphasize here (except to mention by way of backdrop) that the rights in question are systemically connected with other institutions and practices (with democratic institutions, with the practices of punishment and fair trial, etc.) and, hence, that a full and proper critical justification of a system of rights would have to take this systemic connection into account and incorporate it as well, as something that could itself be critically justified. So, the problem we are addressing in this preliminary sketch is but a truncated version of a fuller and deeper problem.

One appropriate way to deal with the problem at hand, it seems to me, even in the rather constrained format we are here contemplating, is to consider *first* those substantive theories of critical justification that have grown up in proximity to serious talk about human and constitutional rights. For we could presume these to be particularly sensitive, then, to the issues such rights pose.

Three important *contemporary* theories fit this description: utilitarianism (in particular, the theory developed by J. S. Mill and advocated recently under the name of "indirect" utilitarianism), the theory of John Rawls, and rational choice ethical theory (especially that of David Gauthier). I will not take time to discuss all three, certainly not in any detail (for the larger part of another book would be required to do so).

But I will say something about the apparent prospects of Millian utilitarianism for providing a critical justification of the leading idea in a democratic system of rights, that is the idea of the priority of certain basic constitutional rights. And after that I will say a few words, in the same vein, about one of the main alternatives to it, the Rawlsian theory. This very brief discussion should prove sufficient to give us at least a feel for some of the main issues in and problems of the project of critical justification that we are previewing here.

I. MILL'S UTILITARIANISM

In Mill's view the "general happiness principle" supported a number of important rights (chief among them rights to liberty, as described in his celebrated essay *On Liberty*, 1859, and rights to personal security, as set out in chapter 5 of his equally famous essay on *Utilitarianism*, 1863). Mill believed that the rights in question were human rights—that is, basic constitutional rights which were morally justifiable by the happiness standard.

Many people have thought, however, that utilitarianism (including Mill's version) was somehow incompatible in principle with basic constitutional rights, or at least with their priority. The intuition that lies behind their view—I have adapted it somewhat to conform to the issue presently under discussion—goes something like this.

They do not deny that the general happiness principle could support certain rights. For rights are plausibly regarded as ways of acting or of being treated available to every person and justifiable by reference to the benefit of each and all. And, no doubt, some such policies for action (some such rights) would be justified as conducing to the general happiness. Rather, the problem they see is that no one can think that following any such policy or acting in accordance with any given right (especially if the social rules that formulate such things are kept fairly simple) will always and on every occasion yield up a result that is compatible with the general happiness principle. Sometimes deviating from the policy will have the greater welfare value. And, given the general happiness principle itself, the principle that the greater benefit should be preferred to the lesser and that normative requirements on action can always be set to achieve the greater benefit, that deviation *should* be taken.

It follows, then, that rights cannot have an overriding priority over corporate good or aggregate welfare considerations, insofar as these are supported (in the way just described) by the general happiness principle. Sometimes a right ought to yield to such considerations: it should do so where they hold the prospect of greater well-being. To deny this—once one accepts that sometimes deviations can, all things considered, conduce to more net benefit than would keeping with rights—is to repudiate the foundational idea itself, the idea that a greater welfare is always to be preferred to a lesser and that action is always to be normatively regimented to that end. Hence, the general welfare or general happiness principle is incompatible with the idea that constitutional rights can be politically basic or fundamental (in having a sort of standing priority over corporate good and other aggregate considerations) within a body politic.

The theory of indirect utilitarianism (found in Mill, advanced for a time by David Lyons and more recently by Wayne Sumner, and systematized by John Gray) is an attempt to deal with this problem. Roughly, these theorists assert that direct appeals to general welfare are self-defeating, all things considered, and that putting standing constraints on the principle—such as by installing a system of moral rules or a coherent set of civil rights justifiable by the standard of general happiness—is in fact productive of the greater well-being.[2]

The indirect utilitarian does not, however, assert that moral rules should never be overridden nor individual rights ever broached. Rather, on this view, where rules conflict or rights do (for they inevitably will, as I argued in Chapter 5), some sort of appeal to the general happiness is in order. And here is where the notion of an *indirect* utilitarianism comes crucially into play.

Building on what has already been said in favor of a constrained utilitarianism, they argue that the principle of general happiness should *not* directly determine what is to be done here; one does not say, for example, that action *A*, which comes under one rule, is to be done because on this occasion doing so produces the greater well-being. Rather, the principle operates only indirectly in such cases. It bears down, not on individual actions *per se* (some of which might, as already noted, be described as deviating from the established rule), but on the rules themselves. It is used to determine which rule is weightier, all things considered and over the long run, or to help determine a policy (a rule of conduct), all things considered, for conduct when these particular moral rules (or these particular rights) conflict.[3]

Thus, on their account it is possible to have policies for action (to have both moral rules and rights) that are justifiable by the standard of general happiness and, at the same time, to shield these policies from direct confrontation with (and possible overthrow by) the happiness principle on individual occasions. And it is possible to do so while still allowing these policies to remain sensitive to what produces the greater aggregate benefit on given, individual occasions—a sensitivity that is registered in the differential weights assigned the various rights and policies, an assignment that occurs gradually (over time and with experience) and cumulatively.

The rationale for this particular approach is, as I said earlier, that direct appeal to the happiness principle does not tend to produce greater welfare where social rules are involved—perhaps necessarily involved—and where these rules are themselves justifiable by general happiness. Thus, indirect utilitarianism (if all its arguments and presumptions are allowed) seemingly establishes that utilitarianism is compatible with basic constitutional rights and their priority—at least in the case of those rights that are themselves justifiable in accordance with the general happiness principle.

One point I would raise, in challenging this view, is that appeals to the general happiness on a given occasion should not be limited simply to cases of conflict between moral rules or between rights. For example, sheer deviations from or exceptions to the rules could also be allowed on indirect utilitarian grounds. There are three crucial points in favor of my claim here.

First, the indirect utilitarian accepts that appeals (on given occasions) to the idea of promoting general welfare can have a cumulative determinative effect upon moral rules or upon rights practices, to some significant degree or other. Once this has been granted, we have removed perhaps the most important ground for saying that a constitutional right should not be overridden if, all things considered, a contrary corporate good or a certain aggregate interest better serves the general well-being on a given occasion.

The indirect utilitarian could reply that rights are in fact allowed to be overridden in the account they have given—rights can be overridden by other (and weightier) rights. But this is not a helpful reply. For, on utilitarian grounds, this response (with its built-in limitation to weightier rights) is quite arbitrary.

Here we come to my second point. Utilitarianism is, it was acknowledged at the very beginning, a comprehensive and general critical moral theory. It is, perhaps, peculiar among such theories, in that it rests conclusive weight on a single and relatively simple master principle—that the greater aggregate benefit or welfare is to be preferred to the lesser—in all determinations, normatively, about human good and, ultimately, about human conduct. But the point is that utilitarianism, like any other comprehensive and general theory, casts a wide net. Its determinations range over the consequences of moral rules for conduct and also over the consequences of civil rights (conceived as politically universal ways of acting or being treated) and over the consequences of states of character, of motives for acting, of other social institutions, of nonrights political and social policies, of individual pieces of conduct (on given occasions), and so on. There is no reason *within* utilitarianism, as a comprehensive and general critical moral theory based on a single foundational principle, to restrict its scope to *moral* rules and to *rights* (even constitutional rights) or to give these any sort of privileged status. Only one thing has privileged status in this theory: the master principle of general happiness itself (and, of course, whatever follows from that principle).

Again, the indirect utilitarian might concede all this, but reply in turn that it has proven to be very important to shield moral rules and constitutional rights from having exception taken to them and from being overturned on individual occasions by the actions of individuals who were, although perhaps conscientious utilitarians, also simply fallible, self-interested, and limited human beings (like all the rest of us).[4] And the indirect utilitarian might add, if the case is as serious as the one here contemplated, where a moral rule might be overturned by a rule-less action or a constitutional right by a one time-only exception, that these individuals are, no doubt, also rattled and under considerable internal turmoil and pressure as well.

Surely, what the indirect utilitarian says here is true. But it is largely irrelevant. This brings me to my third point.

What we are contemplating at this juncture, often enough, is not the isolated acts of given individuals in exceptional circumstances. Rather, many and perhaps most times, we are considering political or social *policies* (themselves more like rules for acting than they are like individual pieces of conduct), policies that are arguably in the interest of some corporate or other aggregate good and supportable by the standard of general happiness. When such policies conduce, all things considered, to greater welfare than would conforming to the norms of a competing right, then it is difficult on utilitarian grounds (if not impossible) to resist overturning the right.

Let us put this last point into a framework that the indirect utilitarian finds particularly congenial. Here an assessment in accordance with the principle of general well-being probably would indicate that one rule (the policy) is cumulatively weightier than the other (the right), all things considered, or that a policy—a rule—for conduct (when these particular rules conflict) cumulatively favors the nonrights interest, all things considered. If these things proved so in a given case (and I have suggested they probably would), then even the indirect utilitarian could not resist the overturning of a constitutional right by the consideration of corporate good or aggregate welfare in question.[5]

In sum, we began with the claim, characteristic of indirect utilitarianism, that moral rules and constitutional rights are shielded from direct overthrow by the principle of general happiness. My argument has shown, given the three points made, that this claim is *not* to be taken as a theoretical or conceptual truth about utilitarianism. Thus, if the indirect utilitarian's claim is true at all, it must be true in some other way. It must be true as a claim about utilitarianism in the light of certain expectable facts, certain independent but relevant facts of experience and of the world.

Here some room is still left for the indirect utilitarian to maneuver. Let me foreclose that remaining space with a simple counterclaim. Considerations of corporate good and of aggregate welfare (including those that serve mere majority interests or that mark but a marginal increase in general welfare or that amount to nothing more than the increased well-being of some individuals at the expense of others) *can* in fact override constitutional rights, on given occasions. And, in this regard, we will, of course, consider only those corporate or aggregate considerations that are supportable by the principle of general happiness.

If such considerations *could not* in fact take precedence (on this foundation) over constitutional rights, then there would have been little point in my raising (in Chapters 6 and 7) the issue of such overriding in the first place and no point at all in my claim that civil rights (or at least some of them) should be given a standing priority in such cases and that checking devices should be installed in the interest of that priority. More important, if we allowed that considerations of corporate or aggregate welfare *could not* in fact override constitutional rights, then the very jumping-off point of indirect utilitarianism would disappear along with the problem it was designed to solve. And the basic strategy of indirect utilitarianism would be rendered meaningless; I mean the strategy of shielding moral rules and constitutional rights from being overridden by corporate or aggregate political policies even when such policies were arguably supported as preferable by *direct* reference to the standard of general happiness.

Thus, when it is clearly seen that the *could not* here does not represent a conceptual claim about utilitarianism, then the indirect utilitarian is forced (on pain of self-contradiction, given the basic strategy just outlined) to make the fatal admission that social policies *could* in fact override constitutional rights. Once this is granted, all the indirect utilitarian can do is argue that in fact no corporate or aggregative social policy will ever, cumulatively and with all things considered, outweigh a constitutional right with respect to overall happiness. But this is not an argument that can be conducted a priori. We turn instead to facts of the world and of experience and it is likely, for the reasons just given (in the paragraph above) that such facts would tell against the indirect utilitarian.

I conclude, then that, if this is so, the general happiness principle could not support the assignment of basic rights—constitutionally guaranteed benefits—to individual persons even where it was acknowledged that important benefits might accrue to those individuals as a result. That is, such rights would not be assigned to each and every person in advance, so to speak, and across the board—if, in effect, such rights tied the utilitarian politician's hands (as it does in indirect utilitarianism) against allowing corporate or aggregate interests to override or supersede constitutional rights on those occasions when, cumulatively and all things considered, those interests could be seen to conduce to greater benefit.

I do not say here that utilitarians cannot support constitutional rights at all. Nor do I deny that utilitarians might prefer such rights to other purportedly deep values (like holiness, as religiously conceived, or Nietzschean elitism). I say here only that they cannot allow for politically fundamental constitutional rights that have priority over corporate or aggregate considerations even when those considerations are supported, as preferable, by the general happiness standard.

In that sense, then, philosophical utilitarianism is incompatible with the notion of basic rights developed in the present book. For it cannot plausibly provide a critical justification of the democratic system of rights in which constitutional civil rights have a standing priority over policies favoring corporate goods or aggregate welfare.[6]

This conclusion is not, I would surmise, a terribly surprising one.[7] In any event, certainly given contemporary discussion, Rawls's theory would appear a much likelier prospect for close consideration. So we turn to it.

2. RAWLS'S THEORY OF JUSTICE

On first inspection, that theory does seem to fulfil its promise—at least it does in its later (or post-1980) versions. For the later theory does, in my judgment, provide an initially plausible justification for saying that some civil rights—some "liberties," as Rawls calls them—should be regarded as basic constitutional rights. Let us begin, then, by reviewing that particular line of argument.

Rawls claims (in his Dewey Lectures [1980] and in the Tanner Lectures [1982a]) that there are two fundamental moral capacities or powers and, correspondingly, two "highest-order interests" of every individual citizen. Thus, each person has, over that person's entire life, (1) an interest in being able to have, formulate, revise, promulgate, live according to, and advance one's particular determinate conception of the good and (2) an interest in exercising one's "sense of justice." That is, each person has, over that person's entire life, (2) an interest in living cooperatively with fellow citizens, on terms of mutual respect and for mutual benefit, under a unified and stable scheme of basic political and economic institutions that has been organized by a shared set of principles of justice which each citizen can rationally affirm both publicly and in the heart.

Rawls then identifies which liberties—which ways of acting or of not being injured—should be among the basic constitutional rights, or among the most weighty such rights, by considering what he calls "two fundamental cases." Thus, those liberties that are part of or a means of achieving the *first* interest or power constitute the first of these cases and those that are a part of or a means of achieving the *second* constitute the second of the "two fundamental cases." There are, apparently, some liberties that fall under both cases and, finally (though this point is not as clear as it should be), some that fall under neither case directly but are, nonetheless, necessary for the proper exercise of those that do so fall.[8]

For Rawls, then, all the liberties just specified should be counted among the basic constitutional rights (though even among them there are, as I said, evidently some variations of weight). These are the basic rights to liberty and noninjury, the "equal basic liberties," as Rawls often calls them. For the most part, these rights are rather standard civil rights, of the sort that would be found, for example, in the UN's Covenant on Civil and Political Rights (1966) or on a list of important rights in current American constitutional law.

It is difficult to be entirely confident of the account I have just given. Problems loom. For example, Rawls claims that the "Reasonable" (roughly, interest [2]) enframes and subordinates the "Rational" (roughly, interest [1]);[9] this claim suggests that the two fundamental interests or powers are not really equal (contrary to what the language of two "highest-order interests" would indicate). Thus, we almost immediately have an impediment to clear interpretation of Rawls's justificatory idea of the two highest-order interests or powers of the person.

More important, Rawls never succeeds in making an adequate case for the priority of the first principle of justice over the second—of the basic liberty rights over elements in the second principle, of those basic rights over policies designed to achieve fair equality of opportunity or to achieve maximization of the level of goods and services available to the least well-off income group (say, the bottom 20 percent).[10] Indeed, for that matter, we cannot say even that Rawls makes a satisfactory case for putting basic constitutional rights (here: the basic rights to liberty and noninjury) over policies advancing corporate goods or other aggregate considerations. This, then, is the crucial failure of Rawls's theory insofar as it attempts to provide a justification of the standing priority of basic constitutional rights over such considerations.[11]

I would not claim that Rawls's theory altogether lacks the resources to deal with the priority problems just identified.[12] But, rather than pursue this particular matter to conclusion, I think we would be well advised to concern ourselves here with a more fundamental consideration—whether Rawls's theory, taken on its own terms, can really count as an acceptable theory of *critical* justification at all.

The complicated procedure whereby Rawls attempted (in his *Theory of*

Justice, 1971) to justify his two principles of justice—a procedure centering on the notion of an "original position" for deciding about candidate principles of justice—has, I think, two important defects.[13] First, it assumed some of the very things (the values of liberty and equality, for example) that a sound *critical* justification would need to vindicate, not assume. And, second, in making these very assumptions, Rawls's theory seemed to rule out from serious consideration certain rival candidates to his own two principles (especially those candidates, such as Platonic perfectionism or Nietzschean elitism, that did not take equality or liberty of individuals as fundamental).

Such ruling out is not, in itself, a defect. But, given the role of framework for an objective assessment of various historically available candidate principles of justice that Rawls had assigned the original position, it is a defect.[14] I will return to this particular problem in Rawls's theory after I have made my first point of criticism a bit clearer.

I am not claiming, in that first criticism, that Rawls's justificatory theory surreptitiously includes a substantive principle of equality among its background ideas. If it did, that would count as a clear and decisive reason for rejecting it, at least on its own terms, as a foundation for a critical moral theory. What I want to claim is rather like that, however.

My claim here is simply that the "parties" in the deliberations of the original position are said to have an equal status. That is, all are capable of contributing significantly, in accordance with their individual lights and over their complete lifetimes and as appropriate (given the institutions and accredited practices of a given well-ordered society), to the well-being of themselves and of fellow citizens in that society. Hence, each is capable of being a full member of a given well-ordered society, one that is to be lived in by all. Rawls treats full membership, in the sense just described, as entitling the citizen to *equal* membership.[15]

Accordingly, then, each citizen as a party to the fundamental determination (or, alternatively, each representative of the citizens) is to have an equal weight in the deliberations within the original position about the substantive principles of justice for their common society. And, given the Rawlsian requirement of unanimity in these deliberations, each has an equal veto over any candidate principle considered there. Thus, the only principles of justice that can survive scrutiny by the parties—by the body of fellow citizens (or their representatives), each one of them having equal status and an equal voice and full veto power—are principles that treat people as substantive equals. Here both the Rawlsian first principle of justice (the principle of equal basic liberties) and the second principle appeal to this fundamental idea of equal status in the arguments that crucially support them.[16]

My point in this first criticism, then, is simply that Rawls's two principles of justice presuppose and draw upon a substantive idea of equal status, an idea that is required if these principles are to be established as justified. Rawls in effect merely assumes this idea, or rests content with characterizing it as a "Kantian conception of equality."[17] In this respect, Rawls's initial theory assumes something that amounts to a substantive moral norm; in so doing, the theory takes as given what needs to be proven. This, then, is a crucial defect in Rawls's theory of the moral justification of the two principles of justice.

And given the standards the theory has imposed on itself, the theory (with its resultant preference for the two Rawlsian principles of justice) must be accounted a failure as an acceptable theory of *critical* justification simply insofar as it excludes anti-egalitarian options, as it necessarily must (with this assumption as its starting point), from any serious consideration. Let me make this particular objection a bit sharper now.

As I said earlier, the original position "model" (as it subsequently comes to be called), in effect, outlines a procedure or a set of objective considerations for *assessing* rival substantive principles of justice. Accordingly, if any such principle or set of principles survived the scrutiny of the original position model and emerged as preferred, among the rival candidates, then that principle or that set would constitute *the* critically justified substantive principle(s) of justice. And the normative theory that elaborated this particular principle or set of principles, with the support afforded by the original position model as backdrop, and that applied the principle(s) to the project of organizing the basic institutions of given society would be an accredited theory of critical moral justification. My point, then, is simply that Rawls's theory of the two principles, given the defects I have outlined in the assessment procedure, is not, on its own terms, such an acceptable or accredited theory of critical moral justification.

Again, it might be possible to repair Rawls's theory at the points where it fails. I doubt it; but I cannot say for sure without extended additional reflection that would take us well beyond Rawls's theory in the form that it had in *A Theory of Justice*, in 1971, and had for about a decade afterward. In any case, such repair was not the direction Rawls himself chose to take.

For Rawls seems, beginning with his Dewey Lectures in 1980, to be reconfiguring his entire justificatory account. A number of important changes have occurred as he has moved further from positions he occupied in *A Theory of Justice*. For example, he now claims that his theory is specifically a *political* theory of justice, which is itself not a comprehensive critical moral theory, nor part of one. In this newer account, such comprehensive moral theories (like Kant's or like Mill's utilitarianism) merely "overlap" with or converge on the independently justified "political conception of justice." And the values that Rawls uses to construct this independent political justification of the so-called two principles of justice are themselves said to be latent in the culture of a contemporary democratic society.[18]

More specifically, political justification, in Rawls's later writings, sets out from four "model conceptions": the idea of the person, the idea of social cooperation for mutual benefit, the idea of the well-ordered society, and the idea of a linking or mediating conception which lays out the standards for decision making that fellow citizens could be expected to follow in reaching a rational decision respecting the governing principles of political justice (that is, the principles of justice for the basic structure of *their* well-ordered society). Not surprisingly, this mediating conception captures many of the features familiar from Rawls's earlier discussion of the original position (including, of course, many of the restrictions imposed by what he calls the "veil of ignorance").[19]

In sum, then, fellow citizens—acting in accordance with the principles of decision making specified in the mediating model, with each of them interested in formulating, revising, and advancing their own particular determinate conception of the good but also interested in living their entire lives cooperatively with fellow citizens, as free and equal citizens and on terms of mutual benefit—rationally affirm (both publicly and in the heart) a shared set of principles of justice that they would prefer to see used to organize a unified and stable scheme of basic political and economic institutions under which they can all live together. The principles so selected are not principles for the whole of life; they are not comprehensive and general moral principles; rather, they are merely the appropriate principles for governing the life of fellow citizens *in the public domain*.

Establishing some such set of principles is the main object of Rawls's new *political* conception of justice. In this account, the principles that emerge as preferred are, presumably, the principles that are best supported from within the nexus formed by the model conceptions (and Rawls thinks that those best-supported principles will be his own two principles of justice, understood now as *political* principles).

Starting points other than the four model conceptions would, no doubt, yield different principles of political justice. The relevant principles of Rawlsian justice are thus politicized—not in any unattractive sense, but merely in the sense of focusing on and emphasizing the basic political and economic and social institutions of a particular body politic or *kind* of body politic. The relevant principles of Rawlsian political justice are thus localized, for any given body politic or kind of body politic, to a specific systemic and historical setting. In this respect, Rawls's theory of political justice is quite like the notion of internal political justification that I have been developing in the present book.

Rawls is aware, of course, that the account of political justice he is now offering is profoundly different from his earlier theory, the one in *A Theory of Justice*. He in effect acknowledges that people quite reasonably could (based on what he had said in that book) persist in thinking that "justice as fairness" (one of the names he habitually uses to describe his own theory) is and always has been essentially a *crit*ical theory of moral justification (analogous, say, to historic utilitarianism). But he goes out of his way to indicate that he is not now offering such a theory.[20]

Questions, though, continue to press forward. What exactly is the relationship between theories of critical moral justification and Rawls's new political theory of justice? Can Rawls's political theory be critically morally justified? These are very like the questions I raised respecting my own account of a system of rights, in particular, once that system was seen to be a coherent one and thus able to have an internally justified political authority.

For Rawls, the stakes here, in answering these questions, are quite high. He thinks that, unless his political theory can be critically morally justified, it will strike people as a mere *modus vivendi*. I would point out that it is already more than that: it is a carefully crafted vindication of political institutions as *just* by reference to standards actively embedded within a living political culture, standards that would be reflectively acknowledged as sound by members of that culture. (It is even possible that such standards would be reflectively acknowledged as sound, or at least reasonable, by persons from other cultures or different times as well, but this is not his main concern.) Rawls thinks this vindication, solid as it is on its own terms, lacks deep moral credentials (of the sort afforded by a comprehensive critical theory). Thus, one point (in Rawls's view) of critical moral justification would be to *moralize* the *modus vivendi*, to give the political justification the moral grounding it otherwise lacks.[21]

Rawls characteristically describes the critical moral justification in question as being one of "overlapping consensus." This reflects his view that no single comprehensive critical moral theory could support the politically justified system in every detail. More important, it reflects his view that that system could be partially supported by several different critical moral theories, each of them controversial, no one of them accepted by everybody (or almost everybody), and all of them subject to endless and apparently unresolvable disputation.

The point of multiple support here is not to moralize the system even further (by taking in every detail, covering every base, from one angle or another). Rather, the point of multiple support by a variety of accredited (or at least widely acknowledged) critical moral theories is to lend greater stability, over time and for the long run, to the political system itself. That, and to ensure that the system will have and continue to enjoy widespread support from its citizens, regardless of their individual religious or ethical commitments and regardless of whether they have internalized the political justification in its own terms (for here other terms of justification—those provided by the various competing moral and religious theories—are readily available to *these* citizens).[22]

Rawls thinks, if we descend now to specifics, that several such supports can be afforded his politically justified system. Among them (as I already mentioned) are two well-known and presumably accredited theories of critical moral justification: Kantian ethical theory and Mill's utilitarianism.[23]

Rawls's language for expressing this support is sometimes quite misleading. He speaks, for example, of the critical theories themselves as "premises" with respect to which the leading propositions of his political conception can be regarded as "theorems."[24] Such a characterization is not at all likely to be helpful. If critical moral theories are true, itself a controversial and even doubtful claim, they are not true in the same way that, say, arithmetical axioms are true; that is, they are not *analytic* truths.[25] In any event, the relationship between the critical theories, on the one hand, and the political conception, on the other, is *not* typically one of *logical* entailment. Clearly, then, any suggestion of "moral geometry" would be singularly out of place here.[26]

What he had in mind, however, can probably be put much more simply. It is that *each* of the accredited theories of moral justification he refers to can afford reasons, on balance, for accepting the two principles and the other elements of the Rawlsian political conception—for accepting them as governing principles for the public domain of a given well-ordered society that has the sort of background and formation we find in contemporary democratic societies.

But even this notion of support will not do for one of the suggested theories of critical moral justification, Millian utilitarianism, that Rawls had in mind. For, if my earlier argument respecting so-called indirect utilitarianism is sound, the utilitarianism of Mill cannot support the priority of the first principle (the principle of equal basic liberties) over the elements of the second principle, or support the priority of basic constitutional rights (at least the rights identified with the equal basic liberties) over corporate good or other aggregative welfare policies insofar as these can be adjudged to be preferable or even supportable on utilitarian grounds. Since the factor of priority, as just described, is as important to Rawls's political conception as a somewhat similar notion of priority has proven to be to my own account of a system of rights, this defect (if I may call it that) of Millian utilitarianism is decisive. Rawls is wrong, then, to think that that particular accredited theory of critical moral justification supports his political conception of justice and can thus be a part of the "overlapping consensus" that underwrites it morally.

Of course, Millian utilitarianism could probably support a political conception *like* Rawls's own (that is, could support one that was like Rawls's in every respect except that the supported conception lacked the crucial feature of priority). And I do not doubt that indirect utilitarianism could support a political system *like* the democratic system of rights (except that the supported system, again, would necessarily lack the crucial feature of priority). Such support is beside the point. For the fact remains that Millian utilitarianism cannot support the specific political conception of justice that Rawls advocates and with which his name is justly and indelibly identified.[27]

It could, of course, still be true that Kantian moral philosophy might provide support, the support of an accredited critical moral theory, for Rawls's political conception. But I cannot confidently say that it would, for largely Rawls merely asserts that (like Millian utilitarianism) it would; but he nowhere exhibits this support in anything like a rigorous fashion.[28] In any event, even if such support was there (and could convincingly be shown to be so), more than mere Kantian support would be required if we were to have an "overlapping consensus" and were to avoid thereby the partisanship and controversy of endless speculative disquisitions between and among the critical moral theories.[29]

We reach in the end, then, a rather unsatisfactory result for Rawls's theory of justice. In the form his theory had initially, in 1971, it is not an acceptable or creditable theory of critical moral justification. And in the form it has had more recently, after 1980 and especially since 1985, it does not represent itself as a critical moral theory at all. It is not clear, moreover, that Rawls's theory would be supported by any of the accredited theories of critical moral justification that he names, and, contrary to his express expectation, very unlikely that it would be in one such case—that of Millian utilitarianism.

The upshot of this brief survey of likely candidates for critical justification of a system of rights is somewhat disquieting. For the results have been more negative than positive. But I must emphasize again that my intention here was not to provide such a justification—or even the sketch of one—but, rather, to survey in brief compass some of the issues and problems that would attend such a task.

I have not, as should be clear, tried to push either a utilitarian or a deontological line in this initial survey. Nor am I inclined to say, for example, that utilitarianism must fail as a critical moral theory because it cannot justify a system of rights or because it is seemingly incompatible with the central idea of such a system, the idea of the priority of basic constitutional rights. Indeed, I would expect that there will be difficulties in achieving fit between a theoretic system of rights, which is, after all, the formulation of a complex scheme of political institutions and practices, and a high-level general and comprehensive critical moral theory like philosophical utilitarianism. The point is simply that whatever merits contemporary consequentialist or deontological theories might have, they may not be able, at least as judged by the representative samples of each kind of theory we examined, to offer a satisfactory critical moral justification of the democratic system of rights.[30]

Perhaps the most helpful thing to say, then, is that achieving such a justification may not be so easy or simple a matter as it may have seemed at first. Clearly, though, the issue of justification has not been foreclosed by these preliminary failures. For one thing, we have not even considered the third of the plausible contemporary candidates, Gauthierian rational choice theory, nor have we taken at all seriously Rawls's implicit claim that Kantian moral theory, perhaps more than any other modern theory, could be expected to take on a justificatory role for the system of rights idea.

3. TWO TASKS OF POLITICAL PHILOSOPHY

I would not want, either, to lose sight of the fact that one of the important tasks of political philosophy has now been accomplished for the democratic system of rights—the task of internal justification. And that a powerful unifying theme has emerged in that justification (in particular, in Chapter 7), in the idea of mutual perceived benefit. Thus, there is a sense in which the idea of a system of rights already has a significant justification, even before we turn our hands to the task of critical moral justification. And this justification would survive failure to achieve justification at that new level.

But it could not comfortably survive repeated failures of that sort. For it is still a part of our normative outlook that some things require critical moral justification, among them theoretic systems of political institutions and concepts. These latter are things which, if they cannot be adjudged morally good or right in accordance with appropriate (and prevailing) standards, are thought to be defective not just ethically but as theoretic systems of politics. It appears that justification must go more deeply than we have yet been able to go.

The outlook or attitude just expressed may not be an appropriate one. I cannot say with certainty that it is. In the face of repeated failures at the task of critical justification, the attitude here might in fact be relaxed or even discarded. That would be one way things could go. Or, alternatively, the prevailing attitude might be affirmed and deep doubt roused about the moral credentials of even the most attractive of state models. And that would be another.[31]

These speculations about which way to turn at the end of the road are decidedly premature. In any event, at this early point (and despite the two failures we have registered, albeit rather cursorily, in the present chapter) I am not inclined to give in to skepticism about the prospects of a critical moral justification of the democratic system of rights.

There are a number of traditional philosophical theories that might afford eligible critical principles which could, perhaps, play a foundational role here. (For example, Platonic forms or Aristotelian wholes and their ends or Thomistic human nature or Lockian natural law or Kantian respect for persons, the candidate Rawls suggested, or even utilitarian general happiness, suitably reworked, of course.) And there are contemporary theories, in ethics and more generally in philosophy, which might do so as well.

It would be a grave mistake, in my view, however, to think that we could mechanically match up rights theory with the principles of one of these critical theories in a more or less comfortable fit and consider the job of critical justification well done. Straightforward justification, moving directly from superordinate justifying principle to subordinate theoretic system (as Rawls's notion of moral geometry suggested we should), is probably not a workable scheme.

Having it in mind, as a model, may in fact have been part of the problem we encountered in our initial failure to provide a critical moral justification for the democratic system of rights. Something more complicated may be called for by civil philosophy in performing this, its second important task. Something more like Mill's famous inverse deductive method[32] than like Rawlsian deduction from moral "axioms" may be needed here.

It seems likely (to me, at least) that a subject matter fairly distinctive historically—like civil rights and their priority, individually and as a set—will involve some fairly distinctive justificatory ideas, ideas not easily captured, certainly not directly captured deductively, by traditional philo-sophical ethics. This business of hooking thumbs (in Melden's phrase), as we traipse from one partner to another, from one form of justification (internal) to another (critical), may not be the way to go.

My thinking, rather, is that we should try to generate requisite principles out of the ongoing system itself (as we did in the internal justification of a system of rights), principles which could then be seen on suitable reflection to be both reasonable and in some plausible sense foundational. In the end, I think the best model for justification will probably be one that not only handles this point (difficult as it is) but also successfully shows the location of a settled way of life and its emergent norms within some broader process of development over historical time.[33]

This two-pronged attack on the problem of justification might be described (for purposes of ready recall) as the tracking and bringing to equilibrium of two distinctive lines of reasoning—that of dialectical and that of historical reason. Here the critical justification of a theoretic scheme of rights is not simply or primarily a matter of bringing the institutional theory of the practice of rights (if I may call it that) under some austere, lucid, unchanging, abstract, transhistorical formula—be it a simple one in the manner of the utilitarian's general happiness principle or a more complex one in the manner of Rawls's two principles—under a formula which has, for its own reasons, gained widespread currency.

More is surely involved, and I have tried to suggest what that 'more' is in my brief discussion (of the two-pronged attack) in the preceding two paragraphs. I realize that what I have said is very sketchy and ill-formed. It may not prove fruitful. It is a prospective suggestion.

If we wanted to stay simply with solid results, on the retrospective side of the ledger, we could say two things in sum. One of the several tasks of political philosophy has been successfully accomplished in this book: an internal justification for political authority in a theoretic system of rights (specifically, the democratic system) has been achieved. Another of those tasks, the critical justification of that system (whatever that amounts to), awaits doing.

4. RETROSPECT AND PROSPECT

The idea of a democratic system of civil rights, and of the priority there of constitutional civil rights, is a distinctive one. It marks off a definite political 'style' and it sets a goal (never too clearly articulated) that has been the object of aspiration of many people, and many societies, for several centuries now. It is an idea that has, even to this day, an almost worldwide appeal.

It has been the task of this book, by no means a modest task, to set this idea out, not shunning some of its harder edges, and to begin to consider some of the implications it has for the further conduct of political philosophy. The idea of a system of rights is one of the great ideas of political philosophy and, unlike many of those great ideas, it is still a living one. It is, or can be, one of the ideas for our time.

Notes

NOTES TO CHAPTER 1

1. Gerald MacCallum stresses that a political community (or what I am calling a politically organized society) must occupy a more or less settled territory (see MacCallum 1987: 3, 7, 10). Accordingly, he thinks nomadic and hunter-gatherer societies do not constitute political communities (1987: 7–9). By the same token, states (which are a species of political communities) must themselves occupy definite territories (1987: 39).

   MacCallum's views here are quite different from my own inclinations in this matter; for I would definitely allow that nomadic and hunting-gathering peoples can constitute politically organized societies. And, as will become clear as we proceed, I tend to identify states principally by reference to whether a given politically organized society has a government (that is, whether it typically *uses* coercion itself in a more or less coordinated fashion to enforce its laws, its definitive interpretations of principles and other norms, its decrees, and so on) and do so without any special consideration being given to whether or not a definite territory is also occupied in that case. In any event, what MacCallum calls a state (*simpliciter*) I would call a *territorial* state.

   MacCallum's general approach here contravenes what I regard as one of the deep insights of traditional political theory, that the laws of a politically organized society can be laws over a people (or over peoples) as well as "laws of the land" (see McIlwain 1932, ch. 5, pp. 168–80, esp. 170, 179–80). For further discussion of the state as territorial, see Fain (1972).
2. Raphael (1970: 78; see also 68–9, 72–4).
3. Wolff (1970: 9; see also 4–5, 40).
4. McPherson (1967: 59; see also 60–2 and 64–5). A similar view is expressed in Raz (1985: 3–6, esp. 5).
5. Wolff (1970: 11). For additional discussion of this point, see Simmons (1979: 39–43).
6. I have interpreted the point of agreement between anarchist and statist as "if a government has rule-issuing authority then [by logical entailment] its subjects have an obligation to obey its rules" ($R \rightarrow O$). It is quite likely there would also be agreement to ($O \rightarrow R$). We could then describe both camps as holding a thesis of mutual entailment ($R \leftrightarrow O$). I have chosen to evaluate in what follows only the first entailment ($R \rightarrow O$). It is a weaker thesis than ($R \leftrightarrow O$) and, of course, if it fails ($R \leftrightarrow O$) fails also.
7. For those interested in the details of Socrates' arguments in the *Crito*, I would suggest a reading of that part which deals with Socrates' dialogue with the personified Laws of Athens. (See Plato, *Crito*, tr. F. S. Church, 2nd edn. [New York: Library of Liberal Arts, 1956], 60–5.) I have argued (in "Socrates on Disobedience to Law," *Review of Metaphysics* 24 [1970], 21–38) that Socrates should here be taken as saying that, where a person cannot dissuade the author of the law from putting it into effect, then that person *must* obey the law. (For

criticisms see Wade 1971 and Farrell 1978.)

Lucas (1988), also drawing on the *Crito*, argues formalistically that the considerations vetted there do establish a general duty to obey the law. His position differs from mine in that, although we agree Socrates believed that he or anyone else must obey the law, Lucas thinks Socrates' judgment here is well grounded.

Many writers, of course, have rejected the view that Socrates advocates an absolute obligation to obey the law. They do so largely by drawing on statements made by Socrates in Plato's *Apology*. The best essays in defense of this position are Wade (1971), Woozley (1971), and Vlastos (1974). (For criticisms of the papers by Woozley and Vlastos, see Euben 1978: 150–6.) In addition interesting studies focused on the rhetorical character of the *Crito* have been published, most notably by Allen (1972, 1980), Pateman (1985: 98–102), and Young (1974). (For criticisms of Young, see Euben 1978: 156–9 and McLaughlin 1976.)

The discussion of Socrates' position has begun, of late, to grow into a literature of some proportion. The essays by Farrell (1978), McLaughlin (1976), and especially G. G. James (1973) might prove helpful in providing some overview.

The book by Woozley (1979) does not attempt any such overview of the literature of the preceding dozen years or so. It is, rather, an extended and closely written commentary on the *Crito*, followed by Woozley's own translation. (For discussion of the commentary, see Kraut 1981.) In general I am much more sympathetic to the treatment Woozley provides in the book than in the earlier article (1971). Woozley is not intent here on reconciling any presumed inconsistency between the *Apology* and the *Crito*; he concerns himself instead principally with the argument of the *Crito*. He does not, as he did in the project of reconciliation in the earlier article, turn Socrates into a kind of utilitarian. And, in another contrast with the article, he here says Socrates' idea that one can (indeed should) attempt to get bad laws changed is, indeed, an alternative to simply obeying them; but he is now decently inconclusive as to whether such attempts at dissuasion actually count as disobeying them. The important point for him is that the arguments of the *Crito*, in the end, seem to weigh against disobedience to law; hence, one does on this view have an obligation of sorts to obey laws *qua* laws and the possibility of doing injustice through such obedience is not simply dismissed from consideration.

8. "Obey the authority which has power over you (in everything which is not opposed to morality) is a categorical imperative" (*Kant's Philosophy of Law*, ed. and tr. W. Hastie [Edinburgh: Clark, 1887], 256). That Kant took his dictum quite seriously is attested to by his own conduct. In 1794, Kant was rebuked by the monarch for his *Religion within the Bounds of Reason Alone* and was enjoined to discontinue publication on this subject. Kant assured the king of the honesty of his motives and of his conscience but, nonetheless, complied: "As Your Majesty's most loyal subject, I will abstain in lectures or in writing. ..." He had earlier said in a letter, "If new laws order me to do what is not against my principles, I will precisely obey them." He said, also, "But to be silent in a case like the present is the duty of a subject." (All three quotes come from Lindsay 1934: 12.) The reader might want to consult on this point the interesting essay by Lasky (1969).

9. The subject's "right" here is neither moral nor political but a "right of nature,"

the right of self-preservation. (See T. Hobbes, *Leviathan*, ed. M. Oakeshott [Oxford: Blackwell, 1957], ch. 21, esp. pp. 141–3.) Indeed, the scope of this right, even in civil society, is rather wide; for it encompasses such cases of resistance as immediately involve, in Hobbes's words, "death, wounds, and imprisonment" (ch. 14, p. 91). Thus, anyone might resist being executed, might flee the scene of battle though commanded to stay, or might refuse to give testimony which could be self-incriminatory and hence punishable. (See ch. 14, pp. 86–7, 91–2, and ch. 21, p. 142, for these examples.)

10. Locke asserts a strict obligationist position: "And thus every Man, by consenting with others to make one Body Politick under one Government, puts himself under an Obligation to everyone of that Society, to submit to the determination of the *majority*, and to be concluded by it. ..." (J. Locke, *Two Treatises of Government*, ed. P. Laslett, 2nd edn. [Cambridge: Cambridge University Press, 1970], sect. 97 of the *Second Treatise*, p. 350; see chs. 7 and 8 of the *Second Treatise*, esp. pp. 347–51.)

    However, Locke limited the political obligation of the subject to the case of a constitutionally legitimate government which was acting justly or lawfully towards the "property" of its subjects (see ch. 11 of the *Second Treatise*, sects. 134–5, and ch. 13). But since the Lockian "right of revolution," as we call it today, can arise only at the point where these conditions are not fulfilled, the proper exercise of this right effectively annuls any political obligation of any of the subjects to the government. (See here the entire argument of ch. 19 of the *Second Treatise*, esp. pp. 426 [sect. 212], 430 [sect. 222], 434 [sect. 227], and 437 [sect. 232].) It should be noted that the essence of this right of "rebellion" (as Locke himself called it) is the removal and canceling of all obligation on the part of the citizens and not the taking up of arms by them. Indeed, the rebellion can exist (the return to the "state of war") even though there is no fighting. It also appears, although this is not entirely clear, that Locke lodged the exercise of the right of rebellion in the hands of the whole body of "the people," presumably the majority, and not in the hands of the individual citizens severally, as Hobbes had done (see ch. 19, sects. 240–3 of the *Second Treatise*, but note Locke's use of the notion of an "appeal to Heaven"). For further discussion, see Pateman (1985, ch. 4, last sect., esp. pp. 76–8).

11. For the main points (body politic, constitutional consensus, avoidance of state of nature), see Locke, *Second Treatise*, chs. 7 and 8, esp. sect. 97; and also sects. 89, 95–6, 98–9. Locke's account of the powers of government (specifically, the legislative, executive, and federative powers) is found in *Second Treatise*, chs. 11 and 12. Locke's discussion of *express* consent, that is, the permanent or standing consent of citizen-members, occurs in *Second Treatise*, ch. 8, sects. 116–18; and his further account of it and contrast with *tacit* consent, that is, the temporary consent of visitors etc., is found in *Second Treatise*, ch. 8, sects. 119–22. The idea of implied consent has been developed by Simmons (1979: 88–91), and my discussion has drawn on his, with modifications.

    It should be noted that the duty to obey which comes in under tacit consent is, for Locke, quite strict. What is different between express and tacit consent, then, is not the strictness of the duty but, rather, the ground of the duty in each case. In the case of travellers and temporary visitors and even resident aliens, it is their enjoyment of certain benefits (security, roads, etc.) that grounds the duty (and possibly explicit promises to conform to law as well). In the case of citizens, however, the ground is as described in the text to which this note is appended.

I owe some of the points made in the second paragraph (above) to Ed Abegg.

12. The argument for this interpretation is developed in my paper "Hobbes and the Doctrine of Natural Rights: The Place of Consent in his Political Philosophy," *Western Political Quarterly* 33 (1980), 380–92. The vital interests are those identified in note 8 above (i.e., the avoidance of "death, wounds, and imprisonment"). For another discussion that, in general, supports the reading I have given, see Pateman (1985, ch. 3).

13. See J. J. Rousseau, *The Social Contract*, tr. and ed. C. M. Sherover (New York: Meridian Books [New American Library], 1974), IV. ii. 181. For additional discussion of Rousseau's doctrine of contract, see Pateman (1985: 142–62, esp. 151; also 186).

14. See David Hume, "Of the Original Contract," in Ernest Barker (ed.), *Social Contract* (New York: Oxford University Press, 1947), 145–66: 150, 160; see also 151, 161. For discussion of Hume's contentions, see Lewis (1989: 794–5).

I should add that the texts of Hobbes and Locke were known to him. Rousseau's work, of course, comes after Hume's essay.

15. For the obligationist, the establishment of a strict obligation to obey the law is *necessary* for there to be rule-issuing authority (otherwise the entailment $R \rightarrow O$ fails). Some of the important obligationists in the history of political philosophy may well have regarded it as *sufficient* as well (as in $O \rightarrow R$). But whether obligation is being conceived as merely necessary or as both necessary and sufficient to rule-issuing authority, the point is that the justification of strict political obligation must be, given the program outlined here, an external one.

16. See Reiman (1972, esp. 44–5, 53–5).

17. See Reiman (1972, pp. xxv, xxvii, 21; also 29, 31, 42). In this brief discussion I have drawn on my review of Reiman's book in the *American Political Science Review* 71 (1977), 1650–1.

18. Bernard Gert lists "Obey the law" as one of ten justified moral rules, among which he also numbers such rules as "Don't deceive" and "Keep your promise." (See Gert 1973: 125; also 114–8, 120–1, 224–5).

19. It is, of course, possible that a critical theory of moral justification is sufficiently complex as to individually and directly gather in and validate, one by one, each of the elements of authority. That is, these elements (rule issuing, compliance, coercion) are not authorized as parts of an integral whole. Instead each is validated on its own by being brought under and supported by a different feature of this complex moral theory. I do not deny this possibility (though I think it unlikely, given the actual history and present prospects of philosophical ethics).

My point is, rather, that the elements so validated are still not being treated as parts of a political whole; they are not being authorized in *that* format. For we have no sound idea, absent a prior internal justification, whether the political conceptions and institutions of a given theoretic system are in fact coherent. In this case, then, we still are unable to say that the political system is coherent as a *political* system and, hence, unable to say whether the elements of authority could arise in it on *that* foundation. We still lack, then, a moral justification of political authority (that is, of authority *qua political* within a given theoretic system).

20. I am grateful to Ed Abegg for his helpful comments on this and the next three chapters. The (anonymous) reader for Oxford University Press also provided many helpful criticisms and comments on an earlier draft of this and subsequent chapters of the present book—comments and criticism which I much appreciate. I have taken account of them in my final redraft, as reflected in the book in hand.

NOTES TO CHAPTER 2

1. See Ronald Dworkin (1978, esp. 90–1). For discussion see R. Martin and J. W. Nickel, "Recent Work on the Concept of Rights," *American Philosophical Quarterly* 17 (1980), 165–80: 171–2.

2. The notion of customary here requires some care. In law we speak of custom as having the force of law. But this simple claim can express two distinct views.

   What often is meant here is that customary practice, in being accepted into law, becomes so-called customary law. Thus, on this view, a customary right would be, say, a customary way of acting that has become, *when accepted into law*, a customary right—or, as is often the case, the modification of an existing common law right. In some jurisdictions this is probably the way customary law, and with it a customary right, is best viewed. (For discussion, see Leivestad 1938, part 1, pp. 98–102, and much of part 2; see also Law Review Note 1955: 1203–4 and, for another interesting example, pp. 1194–5; also 1208–9).

   But an alternative view is possible. Here some customs—some customary practices—are viewed as themselves having (on their own) the force of law. They have this character, then, even before they are accepted into law (by statutory law or constitutional law or common law). On this second view, customary law is law simply as customary (subject, of course, to the proviso that even as customary it is *regarded* as having normative force). A customary right could be a right on this same understanding. Any such right accepted into statutory or other law would be accepted *as* a right, that is, as *already* a right. Custom—that is, customary law, customary rights—apparently had this character in Norway, and was a recognizable type of law in that country as recently as fifty years ago. (See Leivestad 1938, part 1, pp. 95–7, 102 ff., esp. 106–7. An example rather like my path example is discussed in Leivestad 1938, part 2, p. 283.)

   This second view of customary law largely gives the sense of customary right that I want to capture in the account I am giving. Here, then, a customary right would amount to this: a customary practice (say, a customary way of acting) has or is assumed to have the various features I have been introducing into the discussion (in the present chapter) and is or is assumed to be, simply as customary, already equivalent (or identical) in normative force to whatever normative force a legal right (say, a statutory legal right) would have.

Let us take now one final step. Most historic and prehistoric human societies, so far as we know, have several distinct sources (or kinds) of normative practice going on at once. Accordingly, we could imagine a society in which custom provided one of these sources, but there was no sharp differentiation made there between customary and legal. This, then, would give us more or less precisely the sense of customary right I am here using. Thus, a customary practice has certain familiar rights-making features; in addition it has, simply as customary, considerable normative force (in that one can permit or even require or prohibit a given act on the basis it provides): that customary practice, then, would be a customary right in the sense I intend.

3. For a discussion of action as intelligible or plausible or reasonable and, more generally, of soundness in an explanation of action, see my book *Historical Explanation: Re-enactment and Practical Inference* (Ithaca, NY: Cornell University Press, 1977), esp. chs. 5 and 8. For the relevant markers in the theory of practical inference, see ch. 4 (esp. pp. 77–8) and also pp. 158–9.

   For a short, accessible account (one that emphasizes the issue of plausibility or reasonableness, in particular), see my paper on "Intelligibility," *Monist* 74 (1991), 129–48, sect. 1. For further discussion of intelligibility and of what might be called the necessary and sufficient conditions to *account* for actions said to be done for a reason, see my "G. H. von Wright on Explanation and Understanding: An Appraisal," *History and Theory* 29 (1990), 205–33.

4. I will return to this important point in Chs. 3 and 4 of the present book.

5. This thesis has deep roots in the philosophical literature on rights and has been advocated, without commitment to the parallel thesis that duties logically entail rights, by Macdonald (1946–7), Hart (1955), Mayo (1965), Feinberg (1970b, 1973), Sumner (1987: 8, 12, 15–17, 35, 36), and Rawls (1971). For a discussion of Rawls, in particular, on this point see my book *Rawls and Rights* (Lawrence, Kan.: University of Kansas Press, 1985), ch. 2, sect. 2. For some of the main criticisms of the rights-entail-duties thesis, see Martin and Nickel, "Recent Work on the Concept of Rights," esp. 165–7.

6. Hohfeld (1964: 36, 39). The four italicized elements were thought by Hohfeld to give legal "advantage" (1964: 71) and their correlates legal "disadvantage." Thus Hohfeld conceived rights as devices for the parceling out of legal advantage and disadvantage to individuals in four distinct patterns.

7. The two passages quoted are from David Lyons (1970: 50–1). In this interpretation of the constitutional right of free speech Lyons is actually following Hart closely (see Hart 1961: 242, note to p. 64).

8. Braybrooke (1972: 361).

9. For citations and for a more detailed account of Hobbes's views, one which would provide background to the discussion I have sketched in this section, see my paper "Hobbes and the Doctrine of Natural Rights: The Place of Consent in his Political Philosophy," *Western Political Quarterly* 33 (1980), 380–92.

10. Morton White emphasizes the point that, for Locke, rights *logically* imply duties (see White 1978: 71–2, esp. 72; also 187, 219n., 254). For further discussion on this important point see my paper "Politics and Political Ideas in Seventeenth-Century Europe," in J. W. Woelfel and Sarah Trulove (eds.), *Patterns in Western Civilization* (Needham Heights, Mass.: Ginn, 1991), 243–59.

11. 'Privilege' is his preferred term; see Hohfeld (1964: 36; also 38–50, esp. 42).

For the wonderful salad example, see pp. 41–2. Hohfeld took the example, but added all the interesting refinements himself, from John C. Gray's classic *The Nature and Sources of the Law* (New York: Columbia University Press, 1909), sect. 48.

I should add that some of the curious features of Hohfeld's analysis can be traced back to questions of ownership. However, if we specify that no one of the people at the table owns the salad or the bowls or the table, and add that the actual owner has left only a very loose set of rules for behavior at meals and each agrees that each has a liberty right (as Hohfeld understood that term) to eat a bowl of salad, then something very chaotic (rather like a Hobbesian state of nature—but without the mayhem) could result within the confines (such as they are) that are provided by a Hohfeldian liberty and given his emphases.

The term 'no-claim' I have taken from Carl Wellman. For a helpful discussion of the Hohfeld elements, in short compass, see Sumner (1987, ch. 2, sect. 1). I will return to the question of Hohfeldian liberties again, briefly, in the next chapter.

12. *A* and *B* here are not particular actions. Rather, they are placeholders, for particular kinds of action, within a very general schema. When I say that some such action is specified I mean that it is the sort of action specified by the conditions of the "if . . ." part of the formula. But it should be noted that a *particular* action would be specified when certain particular facts fulfill or instantiate these conditions. And such a particularizing would tell us what, materially, the practical thinking of an agent would be if that agent acted in accordance with those conditions. For elaboration, see my book *Historical Explanation*, 189–98 (esp. 193, 195) and 211–13.

13. By 'internal' here I mean roughly what Hart meant: that the endorsement represents a "general standard to be followed by the group as a whole" and that members here have a "critical reflective attitude" towards patterns of behavior on the basis of such a common standard (see Hart 1961: 55–6, 86–8, and 244, note to p. 86). I have suggested that customs can fit this model, not of course when they are wholly unthinkingly engaged in, but, rather, when people become aware of how they are in fact behaving and then take this, if only implicitly, as their standard for how things are done.

Thus, when I say customary rights could be based on common acceptance, which is the mode of social ratification appropriate to them, I mean custom that has been raised to this level of reflectiveness. At this level customary conduct, if it meets the criteria for rights that I have worked out in this chapter, in being determinate, individuated, etc., is recognized or accepted *as* a right.

14. My notion of a generic sense of 'should' draws on White (1981: 82 and esp. 83).

15. The schema in question might, as I said, be represented by the "if . . . then . . ." formula introduced in the text or, better, by the one in my book *Historical Explanation*, 158–9. For the main argument here against entailment see *Historical Explanation*, chs. 9 and 10.

16. My analysis of rights is deeply indebted to discussions I had with G. H. von Wright in Helsinki. My account of practical inference, in particular, has been heavily influenced by his own. Thus, his view that the direction of others' conduct amounts to an expectation that has arisen as a matter of "practical

necessity" has duly filtered into my account, in the form that it has in the current presentation.

The governing intuition in both our cases is that where something is an end, then under certain specifiable conditions one does that which is necessary (or sufficient) to that end. The fragment of reasoning displayed in the "if . . . then . . ." formula in the text is a special case of this; here, when an end is established, one does not take action that is inconsistent with this end or that would tend to make its realization impossible. (Or, to be precise, such conduct would be ruled out insofar as that end is to be allowed, encouraged, or required.)

17. A liberty, as analyzed by MacCallum (1967) always has three elements: a liberty holder, a freedom *to* . . ., and a freedom *from*. . . . I should add that my account is a rather loose adaptation and I have omitted mention of an important stipulation made by MacCallum.

18. The objection recounted here has been made separately by Janet Sisson, G. H. von Wright, and Carl Wellman.

19. As I have said a couple of times above, it is true of the classical rights found in the American documents, as well as in the roughly contemporaneous French Declaration, that they are rights of two main types: rights *to* certain ways of acting and rights *to* certain ways of being treated. The interesting thing, though, is that rights in the seventeenth and eighteenth centuries were by and large discussed— in the abstract, so to speak—as if they were simply ways of acting on the part of the rightholder. (For example, Morton White asserts that the U.S. Declaration rights were conceived as rights to do or act; see White 1978: 288; also 195, 205 8, esp. 208; 211.)

This tendency to conceptualize rights as rights simply to ways of acting is deeply rooted in the tradition of rights discourse. It is hard to say when 'a right' was first spoken of in a way continuous with current usage (a usage that had become clear sometime in the seventeenth century). Many careful expositors— e.g., Villey (1969, ch. 10), Wellman (1990), Golding (1991)—locate that first full blown use with William of Ockham (1300–49), when he talked of a right (*ius* or *jus*) as a power or capacity (*potestas*) to act in accordance with "right reason" or, in the special case of a legal right (*ius fori*), with an agreement. (See Ockham, *Opera Politica*, ii [Manchester: Manchester University Press, 1965], 579; cited in Golding 1991: n. 3; see also pp. 54, 56–7. For important qualifying discussion here, see Tuck 1979, ch. 1.) Thus, as we can see, the tendency was there at the very beginning.

And it was well established by the seventeenth century. Hobbes, as we have seen, typically conceived rights as liberties of action, and Locke largely does the same (see Wellman 1990, esp. 22). It is understandable, then, why this way of capsulizing the idea of rights has become so widespread, even to the present time.

Today it constitutes, nonetheless, a drastic oversimplification—if the rights referred to are, as they usually are, the classic rights of the eighteenth-century documents; for these rights include important rights to ways of being treated and such rights are *not* things the rightholder does or can do. Even so, the oversimplification continues to prevail in philosophical literature; for example, Rawls's "equal basic liberties" (enshrined in his first principle of justice) include both liberties of action *and* ways of being treated, typically ways of not being injured by the actions of others. (For discussion see my book *Rawls and Rights*, 47–8.)

This oversimplification has often led to deep confusion, as in the muddled distinctions of "positive" and "negative" liberty or of freedom "from" and freedom "to." And the oversimplification (emphasizing the centrality of liberty, as it does) has tended to discourage some philosophers and politicians from accepting, or being comfortable with accepting, rights to the services of others as proper rights. The oversimplification is philosophically pernicious and should be eschewed.

One final point. My use of the term 'ways of' (as in "ways of acting," "ways of being treated") is meant to capture part of what was intended in talk of rights as capacities (or powers in that sense) and to thereby establish continuity with the original sense of 'rights' and the deep tradition that developed around it.

20. The point to which I am replying in this paragraph I owe to Richard DeGeorge.
21. The point to which I am replying in this paragraph was suggested by Jack Bricke.
22. Here I draw on the distinction (taken from Shue 1978, esp. 131–6) between terroristic torture and other main kinds of torture (e.g., interrogational torture). The rule against interrogational torture might be able to countenance a rare exception (but only if that exception were morally approvable; see Shue 1978: 140–3). The rule against terroristic torture would, however, countenance no exceptions (since none could be morally approved).

   The Timerman case does not fall exactly under either heading, but it is more like interrogational torture. It does not, of course, aim to elicit verbal information; but it does convey information to the torturers and to others, nonetheless. We might call this special subcase, then, clinical torture. Interestingly, in the UN Covenants on Human Rights (1966), the one important gloss added to the right not to be tortured was a prohibition on one's being subject to medical research without one's consent.

   In the clinical case, then, the subject's consent could make a difference (as to whether the medical research in question was admissible). But such consent would not always determine permissibility or justifiability—as the discussion of informed consent in the case of medical research on prisoners should make clear. There are other cases (e.g., the ordeal undergone, in so-called judicial torture, by persons to show whether or not they were guilty of some crime as charged, such as witchcraft) where consent does not count at all; for, under contemporary standards, the activity counts as torture regardless of consent and is unjustifiable. My suggestion, then, is that the Timerman case falls under a subclass of interrogational torture (under the subclass called clinical or judicial torture) and is, under those same contemporary standards as well as under Shue's, unjustifiable.

   I am indebted to Ed Abegg and Karen Bell (not to mention the Salem witch trials) for helping me sharpen the analysis of torture, in the paragraph in the text and in the present note.
23. G. H. von Wright would say that having a right means "it's up to you." Joel Feinberg claims that "one cannot have a right which is not also a liberty, for rights can be understood to contain liberties as components" (1973: 58). Morton White treats rights generically as deontic "permissions" (1981: 58). And

Carl Wellman sees a certain function as common to all rights: the function of creating an area of autonomy for the rightholder. Thus, for example, a "legal right is the allocation of a sphere of freedom and control to the possessor of the right in order that it may be up to him which decisions are effective within that defined sphere" (1975: 52). This same analysis is extended to moral and to human rights (see Wellman 1978b: 56). Indeed, for Wellman, autonomy is so central to rights (definitionally) that only beings capable of the exercise of autonomy can have rights; thus, infants—and, presumably, the terminally unconscious and the radically senile—are said by him to have no rights (1979, sect. 3; 1984: 441).

Perhaps the fountainhead of all these views of rights and certainly the most influential of them is Hart's account of rights. Hart argued (1973: 196–7) that what was common to many, but not all, legal rights is that they confer on the rightholder the ability to choose what shall occur within some limited domain. Thus, such rights involve, on Hart's view, a legally respected individual choice. (See also Hart 1954, esp. 49 and n.; 1955.) For further discussion of the choice theory of rights, see Sumner 1987, ch. 2, sect. 2; also pp. 96–101, 109–10; for further discussion of Hart, in particular, on this point, see MacCormick (1977).

My argument here goes against the grain of Hart's contentions and of all the others cited—contentions deeply rooted in the traditional understanding of rights—and would force a different root characterization of rights, along the lines of the more pluralistic account developed in this chapter. But the position I argue against (the so-called rejoinder to my own) is a construct. So far as I know it has been advanced in exactly this form by no one else, though it does have especial affinity with libertarian theories of rights such as Nozick's (see his 1974, ch. 9, in particular).

24. For these notions (action-universal, generic description) see my book *Historical Explanation*, 103–4, 221–2, 228, and 242.

25. The notion of the "central content" (or core or range) of a right is adapted from Rawls (see 1982a: 9, 11, 12, 26, 56–7, 63, 71, 74).

26. Both Carl Wellman and Wayne Sumner have recently attempted to construct a comprehensive theory of rights using the Hohfeld elements and the notion of the function or uses of rights. (See here Wellman 1985, esp. chs. 1–3, and Sumner 1987, ch. 2; also the entries listed under Wellman in the Bibliography.) In each case, though, they have merely installed the elements and put them to work without doing the sort of background analysis that the present chapter has been concerned with, up to this point. Accordingly, they tend to ascribe more significance to the Hohfeld elements and to give them more centrality than I think is warranted.

27. Wellman "follows Alf Ross (1958) in holding that every right is a complex ... structure which typically involves *several* [Hohfeld] elements. In order to keep these complex entities within manageable bounds Wellman distinguishes between the *defining core* of a right—which consists in that Hohfeld element (or pair of elements) which is fundamental to the existence of the right—and the *associated elements* (i.e., other of the Hohfeld elements) which contribute to the satisfaction of the core" (Martin and Nickel, "Recent Work on the Concept of Rights," 170). See here Wellman 1978b: 52–3, 56; also 1978a: 218–20, and 1975: 59. (For a view similar to Wellman's see Sumner 1987: 45.) Of course, in order

for Wellman's analysis to be applied to moral rights, *ethical* analogues of Hohfeldian legal liberties, claims, powers, and immunities have to be developed; this, then, becomes another important feature in Wellman's subtle and interesting account of rights (see, e.g., Wellman 1978b: 55).

I am indebted to Gerry MacCallum—and indirectly to Ralf Dreier—for the idea that a Hohfeldian power, as described, is an important feature of the right to vote. (See MacCallum 1987: 158.) A somewhat similar point could be made about the right to own property: that it is complex and that some of its important features are not captured, in any apparent way, in the characterization of it as a liberty of conduct. I address this point—ultimately a point of complaint against my account—in the paragraphs that follow in the text, in particular the next three.

28. In sum, I have suggested that some rights, as their primary characterization, designate things the rightholder does or can do. An action by the agent is what the right is a right *to*; an action of some definite sort (or, better, a determinate way of acting) constitutes the central core or content of such rights. We can call these agency rights.

Agency rights are of two main sorts: liberties of action and competencies (or capacities, in that particular sense) for action. The main difference between these two main sorts is that liberties cannot be compelled (and remain liberties) but competencies can be compelled, required, or mandated (without losing their character either as competencies or as ways of acting). Thus, in the example, voting officials, even though they might be said to have the right (i.e., the official competence) to decide about and tabulate and announce the votes, can be compelled (by an individual voter or the voter's agent or even by another public official) to do any one of these things.

In what follows I will generally refer to both species of agency rights as liberties of action. I do this simply because liberty rights are, by far, a more interesting species of agency rights than competencies. It should also be clear that competencies are, for the most part, ultimately quite incidental to my main project, the project of capturing main features of what might be called basic rights—human rights, fundamental constitutional rights of individuals, etc.

Normally, nothing of substance is lost by the simplification I propose (of emphasizing just the one species—that is, liberty rights). Where a distinction is helpful I will, of course, revert to distinguishing liberties from competencies (as the two species of agency rights).

29. The crucial fragment of reasoning would go something like this. We first suppose that a certain condition or state of affairs of person 1—call that condition C— is accredited in a community. And person 2 is an eligible second-party agent, picked out by some sort of independent argument, with respect to that condition. Now,

IF   (*a*) the relevant end in view here is that C is to be accomplished or brought about, and

          (*b*) doing D can be judged by an agent (person 2) to be a means to or part of accomplishing C, and

          (*c*) the agent has no adequate countervailing reason to prefer a relevant alternative course of action—call it E—to doing D, where E is to be

distinguished from *D* (as in effect its contradictory) in the very respect
mentioned in (*b*), and

    (*d*) the agent is personally and situationally able to do *D*,

THEN   the action specified and expected, where the agent acts in accordance
with those conditions, is that the agent does *D*.

My claim is simply that, given *C* (a state of affairs, of noninjury or of beneficial service, to be achieved for person 1) and the chain of practical reasoning
displayed here, the mandated or expected conduct for person 2 is *D* (where *D*,
then, is either an action of avoidance of the injury or an action of providing the
service). Here *D* is the conduct picked out as proper; such conduct is normatively directed. But I do not regard the conclusion—"then ... the agent does
D"—as an entailment. It would not be an entailment even if the fragment was
developed further, so that the "if ..." part had more elements and the "then ...
the agent (as second party) does *D*" part became fully expectable. (For the main
argument here, again see *Historical Explanation*, chs. 9 and 10.)

30. I have been urged, by both Jay Atlas and Arthur Skidmore, to end this chapter
by specifying explicitly the necessary and sufficient conditions for something to
be a right. Thus, we might take *A*, a way of acting or a way of being treated, and
ask what the necessary and sufficient considerations are which must be satisfied
for it to count as a right. Accordingly, we might ask whether (1)–(6) are necessary and jointly sufficent for *A* to be a right (taking points [1]–[4] from an earlier
part of the text in the present section and using as point [5] the set of items
[*a*]–[*d*] in the schema developed in the previous note and using as point [6] the
idea that the second party is normatively directed with respect to *A*).

I am, I must confess, reluctant to undertake this suggested project at this
point. For not nearly enough has been said up to now. In subsequent chapters
(especially in Chs. 3–5) I hope to say more. And in Ch. 8, for example, I hope to
elaborate the notion of normative direction further.

In the end, I trust that enough will have been said to supply an answer to a
series of relevant questions: What are the necessary and sufficient conditions for
something, an *A*, to be a right; for it to be a proper human right; for it to be a
proper civil or constitutional right; for it to be a fully justified civil or constitutional right? Of course, we are *close* to having an answer to this first question (as
regards a right to a way of being treated) in the material summarized in the first
paragraph of this note. Still, I beg the indulgence of my two friendly critics to be
allowed to proceed in a more roundabout and piecemeal and—I think, ultimately—more orderly fashion.

NOTES TO CHAPTER 3

1. I particularly have in mind those theorists, like Hobbes or Locke, who emphasize the concept of a state of nature in their theories. Nozick's position,
which he explicitly associates with that of Locke, is developed in his book (1974).
Others, e.g., Gauthier (1986, ch. 7; also pp. 277–80), have attached a somewhat
similar "Lockean proviso" to their theories.

2. "Justice as fairness rests on the assumption of a natural right of all men and women to equality of concern and respect, a right they possess not by virtue of birth or characteristic or merit or excellence but simply as human beings with the capacity to make plans and give justice" (Dworkin 1978: 182). In this chapter of his book (ch. 6, "Justice and Rights," originally published in 1973, and also chs. 1, 5, 7), Dworkin argued that the "deep theory" implicit in Rawls's contractarian notion of the original position is the view that each individual has a right to equal concern and respect. This right, then, becomes the basis of Dworkin's own theory.

However, in subsequent writings (e.g., in 1978, ch. 4, originally published in 1975) Dworkin moves away from the Rawlsian contract apparatus, as a justificatory mechanism, and adopts instead a method familiar from jurisprudence: the "constructive" model for developing background principles, in which the judge or legal scholar examines the relevant body of law and precedent in order to construct "a scheme of abstract and concrete principles that provides a coherent justification for all common law precedents and, so far as these are to be justified on principle, constitutional and statutory provisions as well" (1978: 116–17). Dworkin's strong emphasis on the judicial notion of constructive interpretation would call his earlier natural rights reading into question.

In his most recent book (1986) Dworkin develops the notion of constructive interpretation in a systematic way. He continues to see the principle of equality of concern and respect as fundamental; the question is how best to embed it for juristic use, in natural rights theory or in constructive interpretation. Perhaps the best overview statement of his current position on this issue can be found in the concluding chapter of that book.

3. "When we call anything a person's right, we mean that he has a valid claim on society to protect him in the possession of it, either by force of law or by that of education and opinion" (J. S. Mill, *Utilitarianism* [1863], ch. 5, para. 24; in S. Gorovitz [ed.], *"Utilitarianism" [by] J. S. Mill, with Critical Essays*, Text and Critical Essays [Indianapolis: Bobbs-Merrill, 1971], 50). Important studies of Mill's theory of rights, which I follow here, are provided by David Lyons (see Bibliography). Lyons's interpretation of Mill is discussed in my book *Rawls and Rights*, ch. 1, sect. 1, and more briefly in the concluding chapter of the present book.

It has not been much noted, however, that Mill sometimes talks of rights, not as valid claims, but as "legitimate and authorized expectations" (*Utilitarianism*, ch. 2, para. 19). In doing so Mill may be signaling, perhaps inadvertently, adherence to a somewhat different view of rights. Though the two ideas can be forced together, important differences may nonetheless surface in accounts that stress the one (valid claims) or the other (legitimate expectations). For discussion see *Rawls and Rights*, ch. 2, sects. 1 and 2.

4. See *The Works of Jeremy Bentham*, ed. John Bowring, ii (Edinburgh: Tait; London: Simpkin, Marshall, 1843), 501. The more important point here, though, is that for Bentham (1) rights attach to the qualified recipients of benefit-conferring obligations and (2) such obligations, in turn, are viewed as created by legal or other social sanctions attached to coercive rules. It follows from this that (3) there are no rights other than those given such social sanction.

For (1) and (2) see Bentham, *Works*, iii. 159, 181, 217–18; for (3) see also *Works*, iii. 221.

5. "The right to the possession of them, if properly so called, would not be a mere power, but a power recognised by a society as one which should exist. The recognition of a power, in some way or another, as that which should be, is always necessary to render it a right" (T. H. Green, *Lectures on the Principles of Political Obligation and Other Writings*, ed. Paul Harris and John Morrow [Cambridge: Cambridge University Press, 1986], sect. 23, p. 45).

This emphasis on the role of social recognition lies behind Green's notorious remark that "rights are made by recognition. There is no right 'but thinking makes it so' ..." (sect. 136, p. 106; see also sect. 41, p. 38). Note also sects. 23–6 (pp. 24–7), 31 (p. 29), 99 (pp. 79–80), 103 (pp. 82–3), 113 (pp. 89–90), 116 (pp. 91–2), 121 (p. 96), 139 (p. 108), 142 (p. 111), 144–5 (pp. 113–15), 148 (pp. 116–17), and 208 (pp. 150–61).

Since Green (1836–82) has been an important influence on the development of the account I am advancing in the present book, a brief word about his principal writings is in order here. The *Works of T. H. Green* was edited by R. L. Nettleship, in 3 volumes (London: Longmans, Green, 1885–8; subsequently reprinted). These volumes contain everything of note except Green's *Prolegomena to Ethics*, virtually completed before his death in 1882 and published separately in 1883. Green's *Lectures on the Principles of Political Obligation* first appeared in print in *Works*, ii (1886) and was reprinted as a separate book (1895), with a preface and a brief appendix by Bernard Bosanquet; an introduction by A. D. Lindsay was added in 1941. This book was, until recently, still in print (London: Longmans, Green, 1963; Ann Arbor, Mich.: University of Michigan Press, 1967).

The version edited by Harris and Morrow is now the definitive one. This edition takes account of Green's unpublished papers (on deposit in the library of his college, Balliol, Oxford) and indicates variants etc. between the subsequent edited versions and the original unpublished lectures. All my page references in the present book are to the Harris and Morrow edition.

6. After noting the "interesting phenomenon of Communism retaining, in its first phase, 'the narrow horizon of bourgeois rights,'" Lenin added, "Bourgeois rights, with respect to distribution of articles of *consumption*, inevitably presupposes, of course, the existence of the *bourgeois state*, for rights are nothing without an apparatus capable of *enforcing* the observance of the rights" (V. I. Lenin, *State and Revolution*, ch. 5, sect. 4, [New York: International Publishers, 1932, repr. 1969], 81–2; first publ. in 1918).

7. See, in particular, Raz (1986, ch. 7); here he says, "'X has a right' if and only if X can have rights, and, other things being equal, an aspect of X's well-being (his interest) is a sufficient reason for holding some other person(s) to be under a duty" (1986: 166). For other examples, see Dworkin (1978: 335–6), MacCormick (1983: 164–5), and Held (1984: 15, 116, 170–1, 222).

8. See Raz (1986: 181; also 1984a: 5; 1984b: 213). Raz lays special stress on the duties others can be held to in such cases.

9. Feinberg's texts are listed in the bibliography and will be discussed in this chapter. Another important statement of the view that rights are essentially claims is found in Mayo (1965); see also Barnhart (1969) and Bandman (1973).

Roughly the same conception of rights is implicated in the thesis that rights are entitlements; see here especially the papers by McCloskey (cited in the Bibliography). The essential connection between these two characterizations, that rights are claims and that rights are entitlements, is brought out in Martin and Nickel, "Recent Work on the Concept of Rights," 169–70.

Again, let me emphasize that my main reason for examining the valid claims theory is not merely that it is one of the main ways in which rights have been characterized. Rather, it is examined here as the best articulation of the fundamental alternative to my own account.

10. See Feinberg (1966; 1970b, esp. 249–52), and Lyons (1979: 8, 11–12). Feinberg's account is also criticized in Alan White (1983, esp. 144–6, 152).

11. See Feinberg (1970b: 255; 1973: 67). Note, in particular, his gloss on *validity* here as "justification of a peculiar and narrow kind, namely justification within a system of rules." For the passage quoted in the previous paragraph, see Feinberg (1974: 43–4).

12. See Feinberg (1970b: 256). Although Feinberg does not himself do this, I will (following the style of the Martin and Nickel paper "Recent Work on the Concept of Rights") hyphenate these phrases for purposes of clarity.

13. See Feinberg (1970b: 253–5; also 1973: 66–7). The language of "a threshold of satisfaction" I owe to Jim Nickel. Gerry MacCallum helped me sharpen points made in this paragraph.

14. See Feinberg (1966, esp. 137–8).

15. This particular feature of his analysis is called the "directional element" by Feinberg (see 1970b: 250); it gives a logical priority to claims-to over claims-against. In Feinberg's account, it's not simply that an obligation is owed someone that makes something due that person; rather, the crucial fact is that something can be due an individual (on the basis of the claim-to element) regardless of whether anyone owes it to that person in particular. And what is owed is determined, in some instances at least, by what is due.

At this point we reach the common ground between Feinberg's account of rights and Raz's. For Raz's account is but another version of the valid claims theory of rights, when that theory is understood in the way I have described it in the text. Thus, we could describe Raz's position to be that a right of person $A =_{df}$ a ground ("an aspect of [A's] well-being") sufficient for justifiably holding person B to be under a relevant duty (see Raz 1984a: 1, 5; 1986: 166; also 1984a: 12, 14, 17, 20).

16. For Feinberg's analysis of the concept of rights see esp. Feinberg (1970b: 253–7; 1973: 64–7). Unfortunately the important discussion (1970b: 256–7) of rights (i.e., valid claims) as having "two dimensions," as merging "*entitlements to* do, have, omit, or be something with *claims against* others to act or refrain from acting in certain ways" is omitted from Feinberg's book (1973).

17. See Feinberg (1973: 84–5).

18. For the notion of a "manifesto sense" of rights see Feinberg (1966: 143; 1970b: 255–6; 1973: 63–4, 66–7, 95).

19. Immediately after he states that (1) "a man has a legal right when the official recognition of his claim (as valid) is called for by the governing rules" we find Feinberg saying that (2) "a man has a moral right when he has a claim, the recognition of which [as valid] is called for—not (necessarily) by legal rules—

but by moral principles, or the principles of an enlightened conscience" (see Feinberg, 1973: 67; the same passage is found in 1970b: 255).

20. Feinberg (1970b: 257; see also 1974: 43–4; and 1978: 96). The generic characterization is not found, however, in Feinberg (1973).

21. "Legal claim-rights are necessarily the grounds of other people's duties toward the right-holder. A legal right is a claim to performance, either action or forbearance as the case may be, usually against other private persons. It is also a claim against the state to recognition and enforcement" (Feinberg 1973: 58).

22. See Feinberg (1973, ch. 5); also DeCew (1988).

23. See also Feinberg (1978: 98–103, esp. 101–3).

24. For a discussion of the notion of a prima facie right and, more generally, the issue of the defeasibility of rights, see Martin and Nickel, "Recent Work on the Concept of Rights," 172–4.

25. See Feinberg (1973: 75).

26. For Feinberg's discussion see (1973: 73–5, esp. 74).

27. See Feinberg (1973: 79–82, also 76–9), for his discussion of an absolute constitutional right. I take it also that Feinberg's point about an "established right" as not being merely "presumptive" (see 1973: 75) has weight principally in that, for an established right, practices of promotion and maintenance can be said to prevail, for the most part, in its competition with other rights or with interests, such as the general welfare or national security, which are not themselves rights.

28. One of the more interesting footnotes to the recent history of the philosophical discussion of rights concerns Gregory Vlastos. In his important paper "Justice and Equality" (1962), Vlastos devotes a long note (n. 23, on p. 38) to developing the view that a right is a justified claim. In a reprinting of the first two parts of that essay (Melden 1970: 76–95) Vlastos's long note (again n. 23) this time is devoted to developing the view that a right is best understood as an "associated class of actions" to which is attached an "associated class of demands" (Melden 1970: 82). The material in the Melden volume is represented (see p. 76n.) as a reissue, "with slight change," of the first two parts of the original essay together with an added new note (n. 45, on p. 95) at the end. There is nothing to indicate that a new note concerning what Vlastos conceives a right to be has replaced the one from the earlier version; and, of course, no reason for Vlastos's change of mind is given.

My analysis in the present chapter, which treats rights as involved in practices or, in Vlastos's words, in "classes of actions," can be taken as providing some of the main reasons one might have for switching from the view that rights are justified claims to the view that they are practices of some sort. In addition my analysis attempts to specify which practices in particular are crucial to rights, or at least to legal rights.

29. The relevant section of the Articles of Confederation (1781) is article 4. See Chafee (1968, ch. 3, esp. pp. 188–213) for the constitutional standing of the liberty to travel.

30. Hart speaks (1973: 180) of a "right to scratch my head."

31. The term 'perimeter' is cited from Hart (1973: 180–1). The discussion of liberty rights as involving both (1) the absence of a duty to do *X* and (2) the absence of a duty not to do it is also drawn from Hart (who calls this, on pp. 175–6, a "bilateral" liberty). Hohfeld, it will be recalled from Ch. 2, meant by a liberty only part (2), as Hart notes.

I have been much helped, in constructing the argument of this and the previous paragraph, by comments, etc. made by Carl Wellman and by Jim Nickel. And, of course, one's debt to Hart in this as in other matters is enormous.

32. The term 'competition rights' is taken from Rawls (1971: 239n.). The rules relevant to the baseball example are rule 2.00 and rule 7.06. The example of competition over an unclaimed bank note is from Hart (1955: 179; see also 1968: 126–7, for a related example).

I am indebted to Gerry MacCallum for forcefully bringing the notion of competition rights to my attention, in an unpublished paper on competition, and for suggesting that such rights pose a challenge to my account. It is, perhaps, worth mentioning in this regard that if one regards competition rights as liberties and if one means by liberty roughly what MacCallum meant by freedom (in his essay [1967] on that topic) then such rights will necessarily direct the conduct of others at some point, at the point where it is specified what the freedom is a freedom *from*.

33. Feinberg delivered a paper to the American Section of the International Association for Philosophy of Law and Social Philosophy (familiarly called AMINTAPHIL) in February 1970; this paper serves as the basis for the 1970b article (see 1970b: 243), which in turn is the basis of the text of ch. 4 ("Legal Rights") of Feinberg's book *Social Philosophy* (see 1973, p. x). The AMINTAPHIL paper, which bears the same title as the 1970b paper, has never been published; the pages I am referring to, pp. 33–9, have not been included in any of Feinberg's subsequent publications.

The quotations later in the textual paragraph, to which this note is attached, both come from p. 34 of Feinberg's AMINTAPHIL paper. For additional discussion, as to how this paper underlies Feinberg's *generic* characterization of rights as *valid claims*, see my article on "The Development of Feinberg's Conception of Rights," *Journal of Value Inquiry* 16 (1982). 29–45. sect. 3, esp. pp. 40–2.

34. *Brown* v. *Board of Education* (of Topeka, Kansas), 347 U.S. 483 (1954). It is a considerable oversimplification of the existing constitutional situation in 1954 to interpret it as representing the mere absence of explicit authoritative recognition/denial. Nonetheless this interpretation is substantially accurate.

For a competent and interesting account of what might be called framer's intent, with respect to segregated schooling in light of the Fourteenth Amendment (1868) to the U.S. Constitution, see Bickel (1955). For a concise and revealing history of the relevant constitutional law leading from the case in point, *Plessy* v. *Ferguson*, 163 U.S. 537 (1896), to the *Brown* decision, see Jack Greenberg (1974, esp. 323–34, and app. 1 on 355–6). Note too Greenberg's summary remark, "By the time of *Brown* v. *Board of Education*, the precedents necessarily implied, but did not state, that segregation [in public schools] was unconstitutional, but the Court reserved the right to disavow the clear implications of its decisions" (1974: 330).

35. I owe the objections, to which this paragraph has responded, to Carl Wellman.

36. The position I am criticizing, at what I have called the third level, is that of Dworkin. (See, in particular, Dworkin 1978, ch. 2, and ch. 3, pp. 46–64). Dworkin never really faces up to a serious problem that confronts his ideal judge, Hercules. Dworkin does admit (1986: 412) that two equally Herculean judges

might reach different legal conclusions about the rights involved in a given case, and this is a problem of sorts. But he never confronts the problem that would occur if Hercules were in the minority on a given rights decision; for here the right constructed by reference to the standards of law as integrity, that is, according to the best coherent theory of American law, would *not* prevail. Could it, then, in such a circumstance, really be considered a right in American law? Dworkin masks this problem (from himself) by characteristically representing Hercules as the sole judge, but once Hercules is elevated to the U.S. Supreme Court (as in Dworkin, 1986: 379), one has to face the problem of Hercules in the minority; one cannot assume as Dworkin does that Hercules will always be with the majority (or write all their opinions, for that matter).

Actually, the gulf between my account and Dworkin's is not so great as might first appear. The main difference is that he does not distinguish, or distinguish sharply, between principles (as justifying reasons for rights, often moral reasons) and rights *per se*. But if that distinction were made, at least in law, as my argument suggests it should be, then the two positions would be much more similar at this third level. Indeed, Dworkin's strong emphasis that the moral or political principles which belong to a particular theory of law must have institutional support—in order to underwrite (that is, explain or justify) concrete rights—would go a long way toward assuring the virtual coincidence of the two positions there. (See Dworkin 1978, esp. ch. 4, and also pp. 40, 66–7, 79; also 1986, ch. 11.) And the arguments I have developed in this chapter, in particular, in considering the three levels, should complete the job so far as legal rights are concerned.

37. See Greenberg (1974: 348–9).
38. See Raz (1984a).
39. My account becomes somewhat hypothetical at this point, for Raz appears to agree with and accept points such as these (see Raz 1984a: 10–21, esp. 14). Thus, he does not *identify* rights merely with interests—or important interests—that can ground duties, for he does not see legal rights simply as such interests. The problem is that his *general* account of rights (as in Raz 1986, ch. 7) suggests otherwise. There may also be an important difference between our accounts at the point of human rights, a matter I will turn to in the next chapter.
40. I also want to acknowledge the very helpful remarks by Chuck Yablon on ideas contained in this chapter and in the next two. The present section was written, largely, in response to criticisms he had made. (See his review of my book *Rawls and Rights*, in the *Michigan Law Review* 85 (1987), 871–94, esp. sect. 2.)
41. Feinberg talks of a definition (see 1970b: 253, 255; 1973: 65–6, 67); so does Raz (1986: 166). The quoted phrase is from Feinberg (1973: 64).

NOTES TO CHAPTER 4

1. See Brownlie (1981) for the texts of these documents. Recent philosophical studies of human rights include Donnelly (1985), Macfarlane (1985), Milne

(1986b), Nickel (1987), and Nino (1991). The older concept of the "rights of man" (or natural rights) and the nineteenth-century critique of such rights (by Burke, Bentham, and Marx) are ably set out in Waldron (1987a; see also my review of Waldron's book, in *Canadian Philosophical Reviews*, 8 [1988], 332–4).

2. See Feinberg (1973: 84) for the first quoted passage and (1970a: 85 n. 27) for the second.

   Feinberg *defines* 'human rights' as "generically moral rights of a fundamentally important kind held equally by all human beings, unconditionally and unalterably" (1973: 85). The particular use of 'moral' which we are here discussing is what Feinberg meant by 'generically moral'; on this point see also Feinberg (1973: 84–5; 1970a: 39–40).

3. See Cranston (1973: 5–6).

4. Some philosophers, e.g., Hart (1955) and Rawls (1971, esp. 505–6 n. 30) continue to talk of *natural* rights, but probably do so in the restricted sense indicated.

5. See Feinberg (1973: 85).

6. See Young (1978: 66); Haskell (1987: 984–5, 995, 1007–9; also the "puzzle about rights," 988, 994, 996). I discuss the issue of critical moral principles, again, in Ch. 13 of the present book.

7. For the quoted phrase see Feinberg (1970b: 255; 1973: 67 and also 84–5; 1974: 43–4). For his discussion of human rights as morally valid claims, see Feinberg (1973, ch. 6, esp. pp. 84–5; 1978: 96–7); and also the argument in his paper (1974).

8. In Feinberg's view some of the rights listed in the UN's Universal Declaration are full-fledged moral rights; others—the ones he calls "manifesto" rights—lay claims to things which are not fully practicable at present. Chief among these truncated or "manifesto" rights are most of those listed among the "social and economic rights" (in articles 22–7) of the UN Declaration (see 1970b: 255; 1973: 67, 94–5). Such claims function, principally, as "ideal directives" to bring about that requisite practicable state of affairs on which their full validity depends (see Feinberg 1973: 71–2, 86; and also 1970b: 255).

   But Feinberg's account does show that such claims belong within the theory of human rights. His theory indicates that these claims have now some standing, some credit amassed in a scheme for justifying claims, and that, if certain steps were taken, they would actually become rights (in the full or technical sense). Thus, these "manifesto" rights fit into a pattern of valid claims; they are emerging or proto-rights.

9. The formulation of the problem in this paragraph I owe to Jim Nickel.

10. This and the previous three paragraphs have been taken, largely, from two of my papers: "Green on Natural Rights in Hobbes, Spinoza and Locke," in A. W. Vincent (ed.), *The Philosophy of T. H. Green*, Avebury Series in Philosophy (Aldershot: Gower, 1986), 104–26, and "Absolute Rights and the Right Not To Be Tortured," paper presented at a meeting of AMINTAPHIL at the Westminster Institute, London, Ontario, Apr. 1981.

11. I owe the formulation of this sentence to Diana Meyers.

12. For discussion of the Aztec practice and the beliefs behind it, see León-Portilla (1963, ch. 2, esp. pp. 45, 56, 60–1, also ch. 3 and p. 177; and 1964, esp. 41–5). Perhaps a similar conclusion could be drawn about the Greek and Roman

practice of exposing (that is, leaving to die) healthy newborn babies. Or about the Ancient Egyptian (and the Scythian and the Sumerian and the Chinese) practice of burying a great lord with his servants, concubines, animals, etc.— who were killed for that purpose as part of the funeral rites, or left to die in the tomb (see Harris 1977: 115). Or about the practice in nineteenth-century Bali of cremating dead kings, in an elaborate and expensive ceremony, along with several young wives—living women—from their retinue (see Geertz 1980, esp. 98–102, also 104, 116–20, 214–15, 231–5).

Note also Waldron's contention (1987a: 16–17) that awareness of deep cultural or transhistorical moral differences, which he claims began with "Enlightenment anthropology," significantly eroded the acceptability of the idea of natural rights (the precursor of today's idea of human rights).

13. I think it generally agreed that Kantians hold such a view. It is not so clear, however, that utilitarians do or would. That Mill, at least, held some such view should be evident from combining what he says in *Utilitarianism* about the importance of the intention or end in view of a dutiful action (in ch. 2, n. 3, a note which appeared, interestingly, only in the 2nd edn. [1864] of *Utilitarianism*) with what he said about the relation of virtue and habit at the end of ch. 4 (in para. 11).

14. This filling in behind my line of argument, which has taken the last several paragraphs to do, responds to certain questions and criticisms Carl Wellman had raised about that line.

15. See the Universal Declaration of Human Rights, article 13. The details of the right to travel are spelled out at substantially greater length in article 12 of the UN's International Covenant on Civil and Political Rights. See also the interesting but rather eccentric attempt to justify this right, morally, in Roger Nett (1971, esp. 218–19, 225–6).

16. Carl Wellman asks an important question here: "Does recognition consist in mere intellectual assent unconnected with practice or does it require that those who recognize the right refrain from infringing it and even protect it?" (Wellman 1970: 257).

17. For one example see Cranston (1967b, esp. 48).

18. "Rights, whenever operative in society, that is, whenever existing as rights, are themselves a social reality. Having the right to meet freely with other people, whenever effective, that is, normatively penetrated in social behaviour, does not 'cover' any other reality but that I can freely meet other people without risking to be sent to prison. ... In a society, whenever rights are only formally proclaimed but not socially implemented, there are no rights at all" (La Torre 1988: 375).

19. "[A]s a matter of fact men speak of their moral rights mainly when advocating their incorporation into a legal system" (Hart 1955: 177). Human rights are explicitly represented, in the preamble to the UN Declaration, as rights to be secured "among the peoples of Member States"; they are enjoined on governments, in particular, as rights that "should be protected by the rule of law." In the two United Nations Covenants (1966, entered into force 1976), one on "economic and social rights" and the other on "civil and political rights," it is the "States Parties," as they are called, that expressly undertake to do these things, as specified in the earlier Universal Declaration (1948).

20. Cranston (1973: 69; see also 6–7, 21, 67); roughly the same view is advanced in Cranston (1967a).

21. See Raphael (1967a: 66, and, for the passage quoted, 65). See also Raphael (1967b, esp. 108–10, 112–13). A view similar to that of Raphael and Cranston is also found in Wasserstrom (1964: 632).

22. See Cranston (1967b: 43; 1973: 65).

23. In the Declaration on Protection from Torture (1975), a resolution of the UN General Assembly, the language focuses entirely on the relevant obligations of governments (as the parties primarily addressed). For the text see Brownlie (1981) and note esp. his introductory paragraph (1981: 35).

24. On the right to an education see also article 13 of the UN's International Covenant on Economic, Social and Cultural Rights.

25. See Roshwald (1958–9, esp. 370–1, 379).

26. Feinberg sees human rights as falling largely into two kinds: ideal rights and conscientious rights (see 1973: 84–5; and 1970a: 85[–86] n.). Both ideal rights and conscientious rights draw their validity from what might be called, in the narrower sense of 'moral,' moral principles; they differ mainly in this: ideal rights are addressed to governments, and laws are the kind of thing that satisfies them; whereas conscientious rights are addressed to "private individuals for a certain kind of treatment" (1973: 85). Feinberg notes, significantly, "Human rights are sometimes understood to be ideal rights, sometimes conscientious rights, and sometimes both" (1973: 85). Those that are both Feinberg describes elsewhere (1978: 96) as "double-barreled" in that they are addressed both to government (see 1978: 96, 103–4) and to "all other private individuals or groups" (see also 1973: 3, 84–5). Most conspicuous among the "double-barreled" human rights is the right to life.

27. "Declarations of the Rights of Man did not include his right to be told the truth, to have promises kept which had been made to him, to receive gratitude from those he had benefited, etc. The common thread among the variety of natural rights is their *political* character" (Macdonald 1946–7, 240).

28. The citations here are to Mayo (1965; for the two points made, see 227, 231, 234–5, and 233, 235, respectively). This paper is reprinted in shortened form in Raphael 1967b (see there esp. 73, 75, 77–8; also 78–80).

29. For the notion of the unconditionality of human rights see Martin and Nickel, "Recent Work on the Concept of Rights," pp. 176–7; for the somewhat more problematic notion of universality, see pp. 175–6.

30. This is how I treat Rawls's contention that the human rights he is especially concerned with—that is, valid claims to the so-called basic liberties—are natural rights. (See Rawls 1971: 505–6 n. 30; and, for discussion, see my book *Rawls and Rights*, ch. 2, sect. 2.) The other main likeness to natural rights of such claims is, Rawls's note suggests, that such claims are not easily overridden. I will address this issue, specifically, in Chs. 5 and 7 of the present book.

31. The distinction between special and general rights is drawn from Hart (1955: 187–8). My discussion here is also indebted to William Nelson's analysis (1974, esp. 411).

32. A. I. Melden extends the point about special rights to cover all moral rights (see esp. 1977, ch. 5); the only exception in his view is the basic right "to conduct [one's] own affairs in the pursuit of [one's] interests" (1977: 166), which is

presupposed by all special (moral) rights. (The point is argued in Melden 1977, ch. 6.) It is not clear to me whether Melden regards this basic right as the only human right; in any event, most of the rights conventionally called human rights are considered by him to be special rights.

33. I am following T. H. Green in using the term 'civil rights' to designate those political or legal rights which attach to all persons within a society. See, e.g., his *Lectures on the Principles of Political Obligation and Other Writings*, ed. Paul Harris and John Morrow (Cambridge: Cambridge University Press, 1986), sects. 23–5 (pp. 24–6).

In the next chapter I will differentiate the terms 'constitutional' (or 'basic') and 'civil.' But for now we can treat them as roughly synonymous.

34. As might be expected, there is in my book a division of labor on this point. Thus, the present chapter is concerned with human rights *claims* and the proper response to them (that is, in civil rights laws); Ch. 8 is concerned with civil rights *laws* and the assignment of duties and other normative direction to second parties. In this and the previous paragraph I have attempted to respond to a criticism made by Carl Wellman.

35. It should also be noted that where international mechanisms exist, as they do under the European Convention on Human Rights (where effective enforcement procedures are available) and arguably under the United Nations Covenants of 1966, some intergovernmentally created institutional rights may be called human rights as a matter of course. It is unlikely that all of these will prove to have adequate moral title. Thus it may become necessary to distinguish between those human rights that have clear and independent moral standing and those that are principally merely institutional. The point I am making (to which this note cue is attached) concerns human rights only in the first of these two cases.

36. Here I respond to criticisms of any account that have been made by Jim Nickel, Diana Meyers, and H. J. McCloskey.

37. The remarks in this paragraph were stimulated by an observation Gerry MacCallum made to me.

38. In my account of morally valid claims, such claims must, in order to attain the status of human rights, be reflectively connectible not only with a society's conventional morality but also with critical moral principles. Both points of connection are required. But only the former bears on the criticism I am now addressing; so I have left aside, in this brief résumé of my account, the issue whether the second connection holds as well.

39. Thus we find Feinberg saying that "an ideal right is not necessarily an actual right of any kind" (1973: 84); it is, rather, "what *ought* to be a positive (institutional or conventional) right and would be so in a better or ideal legal system" (1973: 84; see also 1970a: 85n). But human rights, as I have tried to show, cannot be reduced to such "ideal" moral rights. This indicates, then, a basic conceptual limitation of Feinberg's theory of rights as valid claims.

In addition, I want to acknowledge the helpful comments of Carl Wellman and of David Duquette on the ideas contained in this particular chapter.

NOTES TO CHAPTER 5

1. See Walzer (1983: 70, 73–4 and also ch. 8).
2. "A people is an assemblage of reasonable beings bound together by a common agreement as to the objects of their love; then, in order to discover the character of any people, we have only to observe what they love. Yet whatever it loves, if only it is an assemblage of reasonable beings and not of beasts, and is bound together by an agreement as to the objects of love, it is reasonably called a people; and it will be a superior people in proportion as it is bound together by higher interests, inferior in proportion as it is bound together by lower" (Augustine, *City of God*, book 19, ch. 24, p. 706).

   See also book 2, ch. 21, p. 63, book 15, ch. 8, p. 489, book 1, ch. 15, p. 21. The page numbers cited and the English text quoted are from the version translated by Marcus Dods and others (New York: Modern Library, 1950). For further discussion, see my paper "The Two Cities in Augustine's Political Philosophy," *Journal of the History of Ideas* 33 (1972), 195–216: 209–16 (esp. 209–10).
3. For Rawls's idea of the basic structure of a society, see his two papers (1977, 1978); for discussion, see my book *Rawls and Rights*, ch. 1, sect. 2, and p. 240 (for further citations).
4. The present paragraph is taken from my article "On the Justification of Political Authority," in R. Baine Harris (ed.), *Authority: A Philosophical Analysis* (University, Ala.: University of Alabama Press, 1976), 54–75: 68.
5. For the relationship of freedom of speech to the rational participation of free and equal citizens in political life, see Rawls (1982a: 24, 47–51, also sects. 10–12); for discussion, see *Rawls and Rights*, ch. 3, sect. 1, esp. pp. 50–1. For the relationship of freedom of thought and speech to good character, see Robert H. Hall, "J. S. Mill's *On Liberty* and Freedom of Thought," Ph.D. dissertation, University of Kansas, Lawrence, Kan., 1986, ch. 5 (esp. sect. *c*).
6. The idea that citizens can have an interest in identical ways of acting (or of being treated), even though they differ as to whether these ways are a means to some good or are themselves intrinsically good, is similar to, and partially overlaps, the Rawlsian idea of an "overlapping consensus" (see Rawls 1971: 220–1; 1985: 225, 229–30, 246–8, 250–1; and 1987).

   In his discussion (in 1987), Rawls emphasizes the notion of "everyone's advantage," or what I call "identical interests" of each and all, at three points: in 1987, n. 16; in sect. 3, esp. at p. 12; and in sect. 6, esp. at pp. 19–20. My account differs from his, principally, in that I leave it wholly open as to whether (or not) such interests can be endorsed by higher-order considerations of critical morality. Rawls argues (in 1987, sect. 3), that they *can be* but also asserts (in 1987, sects. 5 and 6) that they *need not be*. Thus, his idea of the "political conception of justice" and mine, of a system of civil rights justified by mutual perceived benefit, are together on all fours.
7. For a brief discussion of the value of the exercise of a right, see *Rawls and Rights*, 55–6.
8. The idea of multitrack (or "many-track") and single-track descriptive categories is taken from Gilbert Ryle. (See Ryle 1949: 43–4 and 118 in particular. Hempel's notion of "broadly dispositional" [see Hempel 1962, esp. 13–15]

would also be serviceable here to describe a multiple-track category.) For the account of action descriptions that lies behind my brief remarks here, see my book *Historical Explanation: Re-enactment and Practical Inference* (Ithaca, NY: Cornell University Press, 1977), 109–14. And for a fuller treatment, exploring yet further dimensions of the problem, see *Historical Explanation*, chs. 10 and 11 (esp. pp. 222–40), and my article "Collingwood's Doctrine of Absolute Presuppositions and the Possibility of Historical Knowledge," in L. Pompa and W. H. Dray (eds.), *Substance and Form in History: A Collection of Essays in Philosophy of History* (Edinburgh: Edinburgh University Press, 1981), 89–106, sect. 4 (esp. pp. 101–105).

The interested reader should bear in mind the important difference between an *explanation* of the deeds and thoughts of persons in one period or culture by persons in another (through the use of transhistorical or cross-cultural general principles) and the *justification* of civil rights within a single given society. My account in the present chapter concerns only the latter.

9. For the constitutional right of abortion (under the right of privacy), see *Roe* v. *Wade*, 410 U.S. 113 (1973). For the development of the right of privacy itself, see *Griswold* v. *Connecticut*, 381 U.S. 479 (1965).

10. For a general account of Plato's theory, see my paper "The Ideal State in Plato's *Republic*," *History of Political Thought* 2 (1981), 1–30, esp. sect. 1. For the point about kindergarten education *for all*, see Plato, *Republic*, II. 337a, III. 401b–402a, VII. 536e–537a, 540c, 541a.

So far as I am aware no theorist claims that Plato advocates a theory of civil (or human) rights in the *Republic*. Gregory Vlastos, who has devoted more attention to this issue than any other theorist, sometimes suggests something like the view I am here criticizing (see, e.g., Vlastos 1978: 178); but in the end he is quite explicit that Plato's *Republic* neither develops nor affords a theory of universal political rights (see Vlastos 1977, esp. 35; 1978; 173, 182, 188, 191, in particular).

11. The main argument is elaborated in *Rawls and Rights*, ch. 3, sect. 2, esp. pp. 58–61. Though the argument there concerns Rawls, it should be clear from the present chapter that the argument would cover the case of mutual perceived benefit as a justifying norm as well.

12. For general discussion of these notions see Martin and Nickel, "Recent Work on the Concept of Rights," sect. 2; also Schauer (1981, sect. 3), and Sumner (1987: 11–13).

13. For general discussion of the crucial notion of inalienability (and for references to the literature) see Martin and Nickel, "Recent Work on the Concept of Rights," sect. 3.

14. It does not follow, of course, that courts would allow, without further ado, any and all attempts at censorship of obscene speech (for example, in the form of so-called prior restraint, that is, refusal to publish by a newspaper). Courts might still want to determine that the speech was, in the legal sense, obscene or libelous. My point is simply that, where such a determination has been made and judicially supported, obscene or libelous speech is not protected speech (under the First Amendment).

15. Robert's compendium of rules, originally published in 1876, codifies and adapts the rules of the U.S. House of Representatives for general use.

16. The key ideas developed here can be found in Rawls (1982a), as follows: (1) the

distinction between regulating and restricting, pp. 9f., 71; (2) the notion of the
central core or range of a right, pp. 9, 11, 12, 26, 56- 7, 63, 71, 74; and (3) the idea
that a right is "self-limiting" at its central core, pp. 56, 71–2. For (2) see also
Rawls (1974: 640).

17. See Rawls (1982a: 69), for the two passages quoted and for discussion.

18. The relevant reasoning, as set out in this and the paragraph above (in the text), is
adapted from *Rawls and Rights*, 61. To that should be added the supporting
material in the next three paragraphs of the text.

19. The main Supreme Court sources of the "clear and present danger" test are
Justice Holmes's decisions, for a unanimous court, in *Schenk* v. *United States*,
249 U.S. 47 (1919), and *Debs* v. *United States*, 249 U.S. 211 (1919). The first uses
of the test to attempt to *protect* freedom of political speech are found in the
dissenting opinions of Justices Holmes and Brandeis, in *Abrams* v. *United States*,
250 U.S. 616 (1919). For discussion see Rawls (1982a, sect. 11).

 The constitutional right of habeas corpus is interesting in this regard. The
U.S. Constitution expressly asserts (I.9.ii) that persons can be held only when
charged and allows writs to that end "unless when in Cases of Rebellion or
Invasion the public safety may require [suspension of the privilege of such
writs]." The test here invoked, a weighting test, is rather more like the one we
might usefully have in mind in talk of a "constitutional crisis of the requisite
kind."

20. Rawls (1982a, sect. 7 and pp. 10–13) has been my main source for the discussion
of the right to liberty of political speech and the press in this chapter. All the
distinctions drawn (in the various partitionings, etc.) are his, except the exclusion of obscene speech; this is drawn directly from American constitutional law.
I am also indebted to the very helpful article by Alan Fuchs (1981, esp. 113,
and—for the idea that the scope and, within that, the zones of overlap could be
represented graphically—120–1). I should add that I have also drawn on an
earlier version of Fuchs's paper, presented at the Conference on the Moral
Foundations of Public Policy: Rights, meeting at Virginia Polytechnic Institute,
in Blacksburg, Va., in May 1980.

21. The famine example is from Benn and Peters (1965: 110–11). Similar examples
are used by Thomson and by Feinberg. The highway example is from Feinberg
(1973: 71). A similar example (concerning rights of motorists and pedestrians) is
used by Hart. Additional examples can be found in Sumner (1987: 1–4); Waldron (1989: 506–7; also 509, 512, for discussion); Nino (1991, sect. 6.1, esp.
pp. 187, 194).

22. The idea that rights "of the *same* kind" can conflict is drawn from Feinberg
(1973: 95). He emphasizes, in particular, that rights to liberties are not *internally* "nonconflictable" (see pp. 95–6 and, for further general discussion of
possible conflicts of rights, ch. 5 of Feinberg's book). Waldron (1989) calls such
conflicts "intraright" conflicts, as distinct from 'interright" ones.

 Unfortunately, most examples of internal conflict, including Feinberg's, are
not good ones; therefore I have had to supply one of my own. For additional
discussion of conflict within a right, with examples, see Sher (1984, esp. sects. 1
and 6); Fishkin (1979, esp. 63; for additional discussion see also Fishkin 1984a:
191, 193); Waldron (1989: 514).

23. I want to acknowledge here the helpful critical remarks that have been directed

at this particular example by Michael Bayles, Bernard Gert, Robert Hall, and Carl Wellman.

Admittedly, my example has a peculiar feature or two. It arises in a domestic context and raises issues of paternalism and of the proper influence and control of family members toward one another. And it draws on facts about religion, not so much the specific creeds as the very character of religious attachment, in determining the right to free exercise of religion and the place of that right within liberty of conscience.

But conflicts of rights always arise in a context. Sometimes the context is scarcity (temporary or sudden) of necessary resources, or ignorance of the true causes of things, or an inadequacy in the technology called upon to meet a pressing problem. Thus, conflicts could arise for a right to a liberty (as in the free exercise of religion example) or, on the grounds given, for a right to a noninjury or to a service.

24. My argument in the present section, as regards internal conflict within a given right, would pose a serious problem for Dworkin's well-known "rights thesis." See Dworkin (1978, ch. 4 in particular); the thesis is also elaborated, under the notion of "law as integrity," in Dworkin (1986).

25. One final point of amplification is perhaps in order before we move on. For it may be useful to distinguish between the primary and secondary guidance provided by a civil right. The primary guidance provided by the right to a fair trial, for example, pertains to the procedures that are to be used in determining a person's guilt or innocence in a criminal case. But if this primary guidance is justifiably or unjustifiably not complied with in a particular case, the right may yet provide secondary guidance by requiring that any infringement be done in a certain way or that the rightholder be compensated in a certain way. Thus a right might yield to stronger considerations, or to a competing exercise, in a given case and yet still operate in that case by providing secondary guidance. If this suggested approach is taken, then an individual civil right might become an exceedingly complex normative structure. In addition to its primary content it must also provide guidance about what to do when the right is going to be or has been violated or infringed. The inclusion of such a wide range of guidance in the formulation of the right is, of course, possible. (And Wellman 1975: 49–53 clearly envisions such complexity as part of what is to be included.)

One should hasten to add, however, that the fact that a right may be this complex does not imply that every right actually will be this complex. For it would seem equally reasonable to treat some general principles of compensation and other matters of secondary guidance as a background and frequently invoked feature of a whole set of rights rather than view them as ingredients, as a part of the content, of most individual rights taken singly.

I turn to this matter again in Ch. 9. There I will discuss further complications, concerning either the formulation of a given right or background features to the whole set of such rights, introduced into civil rights by the need to respond to violations of rights by individual persons.

For additional discussion of the issue raised in this amplification, see Martin and Nickel, "Recent Work on the Concept of Rights," sect. 2 (esp. the last paragraph). Much of the text of the present note is from that article and from my article "On the Theory of Legal Rights as Valid Claims," *Midwest Studies in Philosophy* 7 (1982). 175–95: 185.

26. The term 'incumbent' is taken from Feinberg (see 1973: 80ff.). I mean by it roughly what he meant: a right is incumbent when it has been previously (and expertly) partitioned, its scope adjusted in relation to other rights, and its competitive weight assigned by the relevant bodies.

27. The idea of a "family" of rights is from Rawls (see 1982a: 72, 74). I take such a family to be equivalent to what I here call a coherent or harmonious set of civil rights.

28. The term 'compossible' is taken from Steiner (1977). In a similar vein R. G. Collingwood (1940: 66–7) spoke of theoretical first principles, in a loose set, or of constituent elements in such principles (1940: 331) as being "consupponible."

29. This formula for justified civil rights—the main points of which are italicized— has been adapted from my book *Rawls and Rights*, see pp. 69, 82–3, 119–20, 125–6, 152–3.

30. Two of the leading ideas in this chapter—that civil rights are justified by the fact of mutual perceived benefit and that such benefit refers to identical interests each citizen has in certain ways of acting or of being treated—are taken from T. H. Green. See his *Lectures on the Principles of Political Obligation* (ed. Paul Harris and John Morrow [Cambridge: Cambridge University Press, 1986]) for these two points: sects. 29 (p. 28) and 217 (p. 168); also sects. 25–7 (pp. 25–7), 30 (pp. 28–9), 38–9 (pp. 36–7), 41 (p. 38), 99 (pp. 79–80), 114 (pp. 90- 1), 121 (pp. 95–6), 143–4 (pp. 111–14), 151 (pp. 117–18), 206 (pp. 158–9), 208 (pp. 159–61), and 216 (pp. 167–8).

What I call here mutual perceived benefit (often called "common good" by Green) has much likeness, I suspect, with the idea of "humanistic social ethics," as presented in Milne (1986a). See also Gerald N. Matross, "T. H. Green and the Concept of Rights," Ph.D. dissertation, University of Kansas, Lawrence, Kan., 1972, chs. 4–6; my paper "Green on Natural Rights in Hobbes, Spinoza and Locke," pp. 104–5, 116–19; and my review of the book by Geoffrey Thomas, *The Moral Philosophy of T. H. Green*, in *International Studies in Philosophy* 24 (1992), 143–5.

For a criticism of my account of Green, see Simhony (1989: 495n.). That I think this criticism can be readily turned aside should be clear from the argument of the present chapter.

NOTES TO CHAPTER 6

1. For the idea of an essentially contested concept, and for discussion, see Gallie (1968: 157–91, esp. 161 and 168). For democracy, in particular, as such a concept and for an interesting typology of contemporary competing versions, see Macpherson (1966, chs. 1–3). A different typology of competing models, this one ordered historically, is developed in Macpherson (1977).

2. See J. S. Mill, *Considerations on Representative Government* (1861), ch. 8.

3. The U.S. Supreme Court, for example, has used the principle of one person, one vote to determine that electoral districts should be roughly equal in size of population throughout a given state. (The principal cases here are *Baker* v. *Carr*, 369 U.S. 186 [1962], on justiciability, and *Wesberry* v. *Sanders*, 376 U.S. 1 [1964] and esp. *Reynolds* v. *Sims*, 377 U.S. 533 [1964], on point.)

In the latter case, one person, one vote is not so much a qualification on universal franchise as it is an attempt at equalization, across electoral districts, of individual votes (expressed as a fraction of the total number of eligible votes in respective districts of residence). Thus, if $1/a$ expresses that fraction in district A and $1/b$ in district B, then the numerical value of these two fractions should be roughly identical in a given state S. Where this standard is met, then farmers, for example, who predominate in district A (which is larger in land area than district B, though roughly the same in population) do not have a greater proportionate vote, in the state assembly or in the Congress, through their elected representative than do the urban dwellers of district B through theirs.

Now, there clearly is a problem with unequal electoral districts; such inequalities (where the districts are concerned with the election of representatives to the same lawmaking body) can lead to significant distortions in the electoral basis of law or policy making. The Supreme Court's view here is correct. Accordingly, this and other acceptable qualifications will be assumed throughout when I talk of the principle of one person, one vote. Nonetheless, the central understanding of that principle—which will be emphasized throughout—is to see it in the way it is represented in the text proper, as a qualification on universal franchise when voters are compared one by one.

4. Rawls, in the context of contested or competitive voting, has argued that individual citizens should be guaranteed "fair value" there, a rough equality of access to political participation (see Rawls 1982a, sect. 7, also pp. 75–8). "[T]his guarantee means," he says, "that the worth of the political liberties to all citizens, whatever their social or economic position, must be approximately equal, or at least sufficiently equal, in the sense that everyone has a fair opportunity to hold public office or to influence the outcome of political decisions" (1982a, 42). And this equalizing of the opportunity to count politically is to be achieved through such measures as (1) limits on campaign spending or (2) government funding of campaigns or (3) public subsidy (or a mandate for ready and inexpensive availability of air time) to candidates and political parties and other relevant points of view.

Again, as I said in the previous note (about the Supreme Court), Rawls's notion here of "fair value" or "equal worth" has considerable merit. His point is, there must be allowance not only for real contestation, real opposition between options, but also for the real input of individual persons in the political process if the standard of competitive voting (with universal franchise and one person, one vote) is to be a meaningful one. Accordingly, this and other acceptable qualifications will be assumed throughout—or at least left open for further deliberation—when I talk of contested voting. Nonetheless, the central understanding of that institution, as a real contest between genuine alternatives, as presented in the text proper, is the one I will continue to emphasize throughout.

5. We should also stipulate that in all these votes (in both electoral voting as in [1]

and in votes in the lawmaking body as in [2]) the requirement of interchangeability—or anonymity—is met (see May 1952: 681; Dahl 1956: 65–6). By interchangeability is meant, roughly, the replaceability at random of any one of the individuals that help constitute the losing portion (in a vote) by an arbitrarily chosen different voter who also holds (by hypothesis) the same view on the desired outcome of the vote as the individual replaced. Or, to make the same point, we can imagine a switch of places between any two voters, one originally in the majority and the other in the minority (or vice versa); after the switch the hypothesis in the previous sentence is said to operate, as if a magical change of mind had occurred in the crossover. The intuition in either of these formulations is that if voting really is decided by majority rule, the substitution will make no difference to the original outcome.

In the discussion that follows in this chapter, I will presume that both the stipulations—the one introduced into (2) in the text and the one in the first paragraph of the present note—hold and are satisfied. However, it is sometimes difficult or awkward to build the stipulations in explicitly; so I say this now to cover those cases.

6. This typology of party forms is drawn from Macpherson (1977: 66).

7. My account of democratic institutions in this chapter draws on the work of Karl Popper (1950, ch. 7, sects. 2 and 3; ch. 17, sect. 7; and ch. 19, sects. 2 and 5), Joseph Schumpeter (1950, part 4), and Robert Dahl (1956, ch. 3). All three writers have emphasized the notion of institutionalized contested voting, in particular (see, e.g., Schumpeter 1950, ch. 22).

There are, however, important differences between these accounts and my own. For instance, Schumpeter restricts his account to representative government, while I have allowed for the two conventional models—direct and indirect. Nor does Schumpeter's, unlike my account, have any commitment to the notion of universal franchise (see 1950, ch. 20, sect. 4). None of the three authors, again unlike my account, has emphasized the institution of majority rule; indeed Dahl (1956, ch. 2) criticizes the main forms that the institution has taken historically and clearly opts (1956, ch. 3) for a plurality model at the electoral stage. And, as befits a professor of political science, Dahl (1956: 71, 84) puts especially strong emphasis on what he calls the "interelection stage" (as equivalent, roughly, to "the proviso" mentioned in the previous paragraph of the text in my account).

In none of these cases, however, including my own account, is any serious attempt made to explain how democratic institutions have arisen. And the focus in none of these cases is put on how these institutions are best to be maintained or coordinated with other institutions.

8. For advocacy of the feasibility of electronic direct democracy, see Wolff (1970: 34–7).

9. "Democratic laws generally tend to promote the welfare of the greatest possible number; for they emanate from the majority of the citizens, who are subject to error, but who cannot have an interest opposed to their own advantage" (Alexis de Tocqueville, *Democracy in America* [1835], ch. 14).

10. The pioneer works in the theory of social choice are by Duncan Black (1968) and Kenneth Arrow (1963). For discussion and elaboration, especially as regards voting, and for a helpful bibliography, see Michael Dummett (1984).

The argument I have developed (in two parallel formulations) is adapted from Brian Barry (esp. 1967 and 1965: 292–3). See also Rawls (1971, sects. 36, 37, 54, esp. p. 358). The point about stability is taken from Dummett (1984, ch. 4).

Ultimately, the argument in Barry's case and my own is based on a probabilistic analysis developed by Black (1968: 159–80, esp. 163–72). Black in turn was here explicating the theory of Condorcet (a mathematician and social reformer, member of the French Academy and of the Academy of Sciences, and permanent secretary of the latter organization). Condorcet's main treatise here is his *Essai sur l'application de l'analyse à la probabilité des decisions rendues à la pluralité des voix* (1785). This essay has never been translated, in its entirety, into English. A useful translation of a good chunk of the nonmathematical part of the essay, however, is found in *Condorcet: Selected Writings*, ed. Keith M. Baker, Library of Liberal Arts (Indianapolis: Bobbs-Merrill, 1976), 33–70.

11. Aristotle's argument is found in his *Politics*, book 3, esp. ch. 11 and also chs. 12–13. For discussion see Keyt (1985, esp. sects. 5–6).

Marsilius of Padua is probably the most distinguished proponent of the theory of democracy in the ancient or medieval world. Unfortunately, his main argument here, which follows lines laid down by Aristotle, is clumsy (in that it ultimately depends on the inappropriate claim that the whole body of voters is analogous to a *geometrical* whole and thus that any such whole is obviously "greater than" any of its parts—in wisdom, for example); the argument is probably unsound to boot (because, from it, one could derive both p and not-p) Marsilius's arguments are found in his *Defender of Peace* (1324). See Discourse (*Dictio*) I, esp. ch. 12, parts 3, 5–7; also chs. 8, part 3, and 13, part 3. The objectionable discussion of geometric wholes is found in Discourse I, ch. 13, part 4.

The essence of Jean-Jacques Rousseau's argument is his contrast of the "will of all" with the "general will." See *The Social Contract* (1762), esp. book 2, chs. 3–4, and book 4, ch. 1. See also (for further elaboration of the general will and its properties) book 1, chs. 6–7; book 2, chs. 1–2; book 4, ch. 2.

All these arguments are epistemic, in that they judge the reliability of claims to correctness and opt for one claim over others. In the end they all support the claim that the citizens deciding as a whole (in accordance with institutions recognizably democratic) are more likely to reach a sound decision in public matters than any individual citizen or small group acting alone or on its own.

There is, it should be noted, no logical connection between the epistemic rationale itself and the probabilistic analysis that supports it in my text. Thus, the epistemic rationale *per se* does not *require* the probabilistic analysis. And none of the authors mentioned in this note appear, at least at first glance, to use that analysis in their arguments. Some have suggested, however, that Rousseau can be explicated on the model provided by the probabilistic analysis (see here Grofman and Feld 1988, esp. 568, 571).

One final point. As Aristotle's argument, in particular, makes clear, expert opinion is not to be despised. But who is the expert? In some matters the individuals affected are the experts; in others (in mores, in matters of right and wrong so conceived) virtually any normal "freeborn" citizen is an expert. His point, though, is that specialized expert opinion (the opinion of "the wise," for example), when voiced in the context of democratic institutions, is likely to help yield a *majority* decision having a greater probability of correctness than that of the expert on his or her own (see *Politics*, book 3, ch. 11, at 1218^a 15).

12. As Robert Bork, for example, says. Thus, "Every clash between a minority claiming freedom and a majority claiming power to regulate involves a choice between the gratifications of the two groups." Bork continues, "Courts must accept any value choice the legislature makes unless it clearly runs contrary to a choice made in the framing of the Constitution" (1971: 9–11). For "political truth is what the majority decides it wants today" (1971: 30–1).

   According to Waldron a roughly similar idea (as to political 'truth') lies behind what might be called the Benthamite conception of democracy (see Waldron 1990). Here, presumptively, the democratic or majoritarian result reflects the preponderant weight in the overall balance or aggregation of individual desires.

13. See John Locke, *Second Treatise of Government* (1690, sects. 95–7; the passage in question is found in sect. 96).

14. Barry (1967: 122). The cardinal formulas indirectly referred to in my text, and relied on by Barry in the illustration there, can be found in Black (1968: 164–5). These formulas are expansions from Bernoulli's theorem. The crucial formula used by Barry is one of several cited by Black; it is found in Barry (1965: 293), and reads:

   More precisely, if each member of the group is right in proportion v of the cases dealt with, and wrong in proportion e, where $v + e = 1$, then if in a given instance h members of the group give one answer and k members the other answer ($h > k$), the probability that the h members are right is:

$$\frac{v^{h-k}}{v^{h-k} + e^{h-k}}.$$

15. Black is careful to distinguish the ordinal form of the argument (1968: 170–2) from the cardinal form (1968: 164–5) and to indicate that Condorcet's argument (despite initial appearances, as in the formula in n. 14, from which the argument starts) is of the *ordinal* form. Black's point here is that Condorcet did not rely on the formula in any simplistic or straightforward way, applying it mechanically to all cases; rather, he relied on the complex ordinal claim—and here we use the notation introduced in the text—that $p(s) > p(c)$ and thus (1) in a contest between two options the decision should go to the majority and (2) in a contest among three or more options, that option which was supported by a majority over all the others (if there was any such option) should be selected. (See Black 1968: 163–4, 170–2; also 57.)

   One advantage of the ordinal form, in addition to the one already mentioned in my text, is that the cardinal form—unlike the complex ordinal form introduced in the previous paragraph—will give an unwanted result where, among three options, one of the pairwise majority votes is exceptionally large relative to the other two. (See Black 1968: 168–70.)

   Of course, one of the most interesting issues in the Condorcet–Black theory is to apply the ordinal analysis to the case where different majorities within the same voting population can be established for three different options in the following cyclical pattern: $A > B, B > C$, and $C > A$. (See Black 1968: 171–3.) I will return to this particular matter in the next chapter.

16. By majority decision I mean (here and at further points) a decision in accordance with the complex ordinal form specified in n. 15: $p(s) > p(c)$ and thus (1) in a contest between two options the decision should go to the majority and (2) in a contest among three or more options, that option which was supported by a majority over all the others (if there was any such option) should be selected.

17. The ambiguity identified here is frequently, indeed, almost universally, overlooked. One exception is Gaus (1990: 51–2); see also (1989: 93); another is Gewirth (1982: 174).

18. For the language of compatible/incompatible interests I am indebted to Robert Hall (who calls them "consistent/inconsistent"). See Robert H. Hall, "J. S. Mill's *On Liberty* and Freedom of Thought," Ph.D. dissertation, University of Kansas, Lawrence, Kan., 1986, 6–7 and *passim*.

19. The notion of interchangeability, discussed in n. 5, requires, roughly, that *who* is doing the voting makes no difference to the outcome; all that counts is the number of first-place votes, with the decision going to the majority of these.

   Children are excluded from the vote, not because they have no interests, but because they lack the relevant capacity for judgment. For it is true, presumably, of children—below the age, say, of 18—that in their case (and for the most part) $p(c) < 1/2$.

20. My account of the role of uncertainty in the abstract model has many points in common with the discussion of "constitutional choice," as it is called there, in Buchanan and Tulloch (1965: 77–80). My account differs from theirs, however, at other points. They stress that constitutional choice requires unanimity (Buchanan and Tulloch 1965: 110–11, 188, 251–2, 256); mine requires, as we shall see, only a more or less universal subjective consensus. They give no special role to majority rule in everyday legislative or "operational" choice; indeed, they make a number of dismissive comments about such rule (see, e.g., Buchanan and Tulloch 1965: 81–2, 89–90 [esp. 89], 92, 95–6, 186, 188, 194, 201, 302, 311, 339); mine, of course, gives majority rule an essential place. I should add, however, that materials are present in their argument for giving majority rule a more central role in operational choice than they do (see, e.g., Buchanan and Tulloch 1965, ch. 6, pp. 70ff. [esp. 83] and pp. 126–8, 166–7).

21. Rawls's own summary of his "original position" model is given in Rawls (1971: 146–7; see also 126–7, 137). The metaphorical phrase "veil of ignorance" is, of course, his; see Rawls (1971: 12, 19, 169, and esp. sect. 24, pp. 136–42). For further discussion, see my book *Rawls and Rights*, ch. 1, sect. 2, and Ch. 13 of the present book.

22. For further discussion see Rawls (1971, chs. 1–3). By "social primary goods" Rawls had in mind (1982b: 162, to cite but one of many such accounts spread throughout his writings from 1971 on):

   (a) First, the basic liberties as given by a list, for example: freedom of thought and liberty of conscience ... ;
   (b) Second, freedom of movement and choice of occupation against a background of diverse opportunities;

(c) Third, powers and prerogatives of office and positions of responsibility, particularly those in the main political and economic institutions;

(d) Fourth, income and wealth;

(e) Finally, the social bases of self-respect.

One obvious additional difference between Rawls's account and mine here is that I generate the abstract model (analogous to Rawls's original position) out of a generalized account of democratic institutions; whereas Rawls does the very opposite. He generates the various political practices which collectively add up, roughly, to those included under the heading of democratic institutions out of features of the original position (see Rawls 1971, sects. 36, 37, 54, all cited earlier).

In his most recent writings (1985, 1987, 1988, 1989a), Rawls stresses that his primary concern now is to develop, not a moral theory, but a "political conception" of justice. Among the features of this political conception is the crucial claim that all the background elements (the original position, and so on) that ground the justification of the substantive principles of justice are themselves latent or implicit in the practices and attitudes of a contemporary democratic society. (For this last point see, e.g., Rawls 1985: 231 n. 14; 1987: 6, 8; 1988: 252; 1989a: 240. For general discussion see the last chapter of the present book.)

It follows, then, in this new political conception of justice, that the original position model can no longer be used to generate the so-called democratic institutions or to justify them; for the original position model necessarily presupposes these very institutions in the work of constructing the political conception of justice in the first place. This same problem does not, however, arise for my account. For there democratic institutions continue to be justified on independent grounds (as afforded by the resources of the Black–Condorcet theory); they are brought in to justify a particular interpretation of the rationale for democracy only after that rationale has been independently established—a point made clear earlier, I hope.

23. See _Rawls and Rights_, 16, 20.

24. Accessible discussions of the theory of decision making under uncertainty can be found in many of the standard introductions to or surveys of rational choice theory; see, e.g., Resnik (1987, ch. 1). Prakash Shenoy has suggested to me, as particularly useful here, the essays by North (1990) and by Shafer (1990) and, for more advanced and technical discussion of this branch of decision theory and for further bibliography, Shafer and Pearl (1990).

25. I concur in the _spirit_ of Duncan Black's observation that "the individual values; the group does not; it reaches decisions through some procedure in voting" (1968: 167); see also Dummett (1984: 15), and Buchanan and Tulloch (1965: 32, 35–6, 332, and app. 2 n. 13 [p. 359]).

26. I want to acknowledge here the help and advice of Krister Segerberg, Prakash Shenoy, and many of my colleagues in philosophy at Kansas, all of whom read and commented on an earlier draft of this chapter.

NOTES TO CHAPTER 7

1. The things in (3) all come under the heading of what economists call public goods. Public goods have, in order to be provided at all, to be provided publicly or at large. Such goods (like the light cast by a lighthouse) are indivisible; hence, they must be provided for everyone—whether the good is needed or can be used by every single individual—and they must be provided for everyone without regard to any one person's willingness or ability to pay. They are paid for, then, by the public: either by government or on the basis of some cooperative, non-voluntary arrangement. For this reason public goods are said by economists to represent market failures. (For further discussion of public goods, see my book *Rawls and Rights*, 224 nn. 10 and 12.)

   I leave it open whether every public good in this sense is best regarded as a corporate or collective aggregative good. The ones I have named in (3) probably are. But it may be that others, for example, clean air and water or measures for public health (say, the freedom from certain contagious diseases, which may require, among other things, vaccinations or other shots), are not; these may be rather more distributive than aggregative in character (in that everyone needs or wants them and, hence, that they are goods for each person). At this point in the present chapter, suffice it to say, my discussion is restricted to public goods that are aggregative in character.

2. My discussion in these two paragraphs rather loosely follows the argument of Gauthier (1986, chs. 3 and 6; also pp. 116–19). The Prisoner's Dilemma is described there (and analyzed in the way I have indicated). It should be noted that in conducting this particular discussion to this point I have not relied on arguments previously made about uncertainty and about risk taking.

3. In terms of my analysis, the famed principle of utility (the "general happiness" principle, as Mill sometimes called it) is something of a hybrid: sometimes it ranges over corporate aggregative interests (identified as [2] in the paragraph to which this note is attached) and sometimes over partial aggregative interests (identified as [3]). I leave the matter open whether it can range over civil rights (identified as [1]), but I am disinclined to say that it can.

   For one thing, civil rights, though they may be justified on consequentialist grounds (as they are in my account), are inherently distributive in character; whereas utilitarianism, as it has been conceived historically and is usually understood today, is, though consequential, *not* distributive (but, rather aggregative) in character. For another, even if the utilitarian principle were allowed to range over the interests in (1), it is not clear that its argument structure would allow civil rights to be given the strong priority over (2) and (3) that one finds in my account. In short, utilitarianism may be unable in principle to accommodate or justify what might be called basic rights (that is, basic within a given political system, a system otherwise justifiable on utilitarian grounds). I will return to this point in the last chapter of the present book.

4. There is a structural similarity between my account of the justification of democratic institutions and that of Nelson (1980, 1988). There are differences, though, as well. The main difference is that Nelson makes *contractarian morality* part of the justifying standard for democratic institutions and I make *civil rights*

a main part of that standard. Or, to be precise, it is civil rights, individually and as set, justifiable by reference to the interest of each and all, that plays the italicized role in my account. In Nelson's case, the leading idea is that democratic constitutional standards are justifiable when they can be unobjectionably justified to each member by reference to the "contractualist conception of morality that underlies the strongest argument for representative government itself" (Nelson 1988: 81; also 77–9. 85, 87, 89n.). This ideal of justification is somewhat different from the one he had earlier proposed (in Nelson 1980, ch. 6, sects. 2 and 3, esp. pp. 102–7). In any event, Nelson is dubious that one can lay down, "in advance, a system of rights that represents the requirements of morality . . ." (Nelson 1988: 77).

Another difference is that, in my analysis, justifiable civil rights are a part of the standard, when seen from the perspective of democratic institutions themselves (in particular, the institution of majority rule). This part of the justifying standard is not something *external* to democracy. In contrast, Nelson regards his approach as "instrumental" (Nelson 1988: 77) in the sense that the justifying standard is extrinsic to democratic processes *per se*. But he qualifies this with the observation that *if* "the underlying [contractualist] account of morality is itself recognizably democratic, this position [of his] may not differ . . . much from that of theorists who regard democracy as intrinsically desirable" (Nelson 1988: 77).

5. The clarification provided in this and the previous three paragraphs is in response to a question raised by Dennis Lowden.

6. For Rawls's idea of the basic structure of a society, see his papers (1977, 1978); for discussion, see my book *Rawls and Rights*, ch. 1, sect. 2, and p. 240 (for further citations). The phrase "institutional design" is also his (see Rawls 1988: 272).

7. *The Federalist Papers* are a collection of letters published in New York newspapers in 1787–8, under the pseudonym "Publius," advocating New York's ratification of the new U.S. Constitution. The authors were John Jay (5 letters), Alexander Hamilton (51 letters), and James Madison (26 letters plus 3 jointly with Hamilton).

For Madison's celebrated discussion of "faction," see *The Federalist*, no. 10; also no. 51. The premier philosophical study of the papers is by Morton White (1987). For White's discussion of *Federalist* no. 10, see esp. (1987, ch. 5).

8. In the interests of historical accuracy, however, I think a few points should be noted respecting the addition of the Bill of Rights, in particular. *Federalist* no. 84 (by Hamilton) points out that a number of rights are secured in the body of the original Constitution of 1787 (e.g., habeas corpus, no *ex post facto* law—both in article 1, sect. 9) and that no separate and additional bill of rights was needed. Madison apparently concurred in this judgment at the time of his co-authorship of the *Federalist* papers—and thus was subject to criticism by his friend Jefferson—but he did later advocate such an addition to the U.S. Constitution, and became one of its prime movers in the First Congress (meeting in 1789–91).

The device whereby Madison reconciled his earlier judgment (as to the dispensability of a bill of rights) with his subsequent support for such a bill is afforded by amendment 9 (which states that "the enumeration in the Constitution, of certain rights, shall not be construed to deny or disparage others retained by the people"). This amendment removed the objection that a bill of rights might allow the (incorrect) conjecture that the rights enumerated were the *only* rights the citizens actually had. Such a conjecture would, of course, be intolerable to persons (like Madison) who accepted rights under common law, rights under state constitutions and state laws, and even rights under natural law. In addition, Hamilton and Madison (and others who held the dispensability thesis) wanted to avoid the further incorrect conjecture that, absent a federal bill of rights, Congress did in fact have a constitutional power to control the press, to establish religion, and so on.

9. Thus, a distinguished historian of the U.S., Henry Steele Commager, captures the conventional rationale well, when he speaks in his Richards Lectures, of the "fundamentally contradictory" relationship between majority rule and civil rights; the judicial protection of such rights is said to *deny* "the principle of majority rule," and the checking devices themselves are called "impediments" to majority rule government (Commager 1943: 4–8). A similar note is regularly struck in the literature of American legal theory, especially regarding the institution of judicial review. John Hart Ely, for example, argues that judicial review, where it acts in support of substantive values (such as by specifying—or specifying further—and then protecting the right of privacy under the Fourteenth Amendment), is antimajoritarian (see Ely 1980, ch. 1, esp. pp. 4–7, and ch. 3, esp. pp. 67–9). Ely allows only for a *procedural* type of judicial review, one that helps make the democratic institutions more effectively democratic, say, by extending universal franchise or one person, one vote even further. For further discussion and additional citations, see Griffin (1987: 772–5; and 1989, esp. sect. 2).

And some of the most prestigious contemporary philosophers of politics and law subscribe to the idea of a fundamental conflict, a conflict in principle, between majority rule and universal political or civil rights.

See, for one example, Rawls 1971, sects. 36, 37, 53, 54. For another, Ronald Dworkin speaks famously of "rights as trumps over the majority will" (1985: 59) and develops a theory of judicial protection of rights, where rights are understood as held, in principle, *against* the majority. See Dworkin (1978, ch. 5; 1985, ch. 2, but also pp. 23–8; 1986, ch. 10, esp. pp. 375–7).

10. And here my account echoes a prescient observation of Tocqueville's. "If, on the other hand, a legislative power could be so constituted as to represent the majority without necessarily being the slave of its passions, an executive so as to retain a proper share of authority, and a judiciary so as to remain independent of the other two powers, a government would be formed which would still be democratic, without incurring hardly any risk of tyranny" (*Democracy in America*, ch. 15).

11. I have, it should be noted, indicated no priority relationship between civil rights and individuated public goods (goods such as clean air and water). In terms of the justifying rationale appropriate to both, there is no assignable priority. However, priority does get built in in other ways.

Suppose, first, that there is no public policy respecting such public goods at all; then they are not competing with civil rights within the same space (the so-called public domain). Here they are either simply unrecognized or treated as exclusively economic in nature (and left to the market). In either event, it is unlikely any such good could ever outweigh a civil right.

Suppose, second, the likelier case that such public goods are recognized and maintained by public policy. Here they would enter the picture either as rights themselves or, at a minimum, as normative considerations that would be considered in rights construction. Here scope adjustment and competitive weighting would ensue (between these goods and [other] civil rights) along the lines set out in Ch. 5. Thus, their emergence as policy matters, their having a place in the public domain, should work no significant change in the picture already drawn in Chs. 5, 6, and 7. And the main priority, as described in (2) would remain intact, as stated there.

More will be said about the relation of civil rights to individuated public goods in the next chapter.

12. This paradox is set out briefly in Popper (1950, ch. 7 n. 4).

13. This important point is emphasized by Buchanan and Tulloch (1965: 121, 285, 328).

14. This particular rationale has been much insisted upon, and given its most extensive development (on Peircean grounds), in Thorson (1962, esp. ch. 8; also pp. 120–4). I am grateful to Richard Cole for pointing out that this rationale is both sensible and popular.

15. It would be naïve, of course, to believe that the abolition of slavery (in the Thirteenth Amendment) came about solely or even mainly from the operation of democratic institutions. For it took the American Civil War (1861–5) to bring about the event. Even so, many responsible antislavery leaders (such as Lincoln) believed that the abolition of slavery would have occurred, in time, through the operation of these institutions.

   The example I have used is not crucial; others are at hand. I have in mind, for instance, the extension of the franchise to women (in the Nineteenth Amendment [1920]), which changed the character of the civil right to vote—or, to speak precisely, transformed that right (as initially embodied in article 1 of the U.S. Constitution, where it was vested *de facto* in men only) into a universal political (or civil) right. Or, for a second instance, one could cite the repudiation (in the *Brown* decision, 1954) of the notion that the right to an education allowed for "separate but equal" schools, that is, allowed for public schools legally segregated by race (a notion that had held sway for roughly sixty years before *Brown*).

16. The notion of cyclical majorities was independently discovered in 1785 by Condorcet and in 1876 by the Oxford mathematician and logician Charles L. Dodgson (better known by his pen name of Lewis Carroll). It is Dodgson who coined the term 'cyclical majorities'; Condorcet called them "inconsistent" or "contradictory" sets. For helpful discussion of the problem of cyclical majorities, see Black (1968, ch. 7 and pp. 166–8, 173–8, 225) and Dummett (1984, ch. 6 and pp. 11, 54, 85, 298).

   Some have suggested that there may be majoritarian ways to determine which option should be chosen in cases of cyclical majorities (through considering the comparative size of each pairwise majority vote and the revealed preferences of the voters). Thus, Black (following Condorcet) attempted to sketch such a procedure; see Black (1968: 171–2). In the end, though, he expresses doubts (Black 1968: 172–3) as to the commonsense appeal of this procedure. (See also Dummett 1984, ch. 10 and pp. 115–28.)

In the final analysis there probably is no way to avoid appeal to such things as common sense and a sense of fairness, and probably no merit in sticking with any single decision procedure as suitable for literally all occasions of voting. Perhaps the best view to hold, then, respecting the merits, taken in the abstract, of the two main decision procedures—that of weighted preference scores (associated with the name of Borda, Condorcet's colleague in the Academy of Sciences) and that of majority decision (associated with the name of Condorcet)—is that neither can do entirely without the other, certainly not in cases of ties (see Dummett 1984: 134, 165, 176, 178–9, 182). More generally, I must agree with Dummett's wise remark: "Anyone seeking a criterion that will select a unique fairest outcome in almost every case must have recourse both to the criterion of majority preference and to the preference score criterion: the question at issue is to which to give the priority" (1984: 141–2; see also 143 n., 179, 227, 241, 295).

17. See Ch. 6, nn. 15 and 16, where this particular notion of majority decision is introduced.
18. One of May's requirements on group choice is that "each set of individual preferences leads to a defined and unique group ... decision (even if this decision is to be indifferent)" (May 1952: 681). Thus, this requirement is satisfied here.
19. Others think otherwise. For discussion, see Gordon Tulloch's appendix in Buchanan and Tulloch (1965: 323–40, esp. 326–30).
20. See Buchanan and Tulloch (1965, ch. 8) for another pattern, this one depending on a systematic concealment of preferences by voters. For yet another such pattern, see Plott and Levine (1978); they rely on the notion of a fixed agenda, set at the beginning and unchanged (1978: 147–8), and on certain restrictions on allowable exchanges of information (see 1978: 151–2, 158). For a general discussion of strategic voting, see Dummett (1984, chs. 1, 11–13, and p. 56), and Farquharson's brief monograph (1969). I am indebted to Ann Cudd for calling two of these references—Plott and Levine, Farquharson—to my attention.

It is important to note that strategic voting (unlike cyclical majorities *per se*) does affect—but, presumably, not to any great degree—the tendency of majority rule *strictly conceived* to produce justifiable civil rights. This point should be kept in mind in the ensuing discussion in the present chapter.
21. Krister Segerberg asks, Can one be *wrong* about perceived interests? A full answer to this question bears, in important ways, on whether the line of argument I have set out in Chapters 5 through 7—and, in particular, the point to which this note attaches—is ultimately acceptable or not. However, one can follow that argument, perfectly well, through all of Chapter 7 (and even beyond) without having such an answer in hand. And the answer itself is wholly self-contained. Accordingly, I have relegated it to an appendix at the end of the book. Interested readers can consult it at their leisure.
22. The term 'model conception' (used above in the paragraph to which this note is appended) is taken from Rawls. See, e.g., Rawls (1980: 520).
23. See, e.g., Rousseau, *The Social Contract*, book 2, ch. 3, and book 4, ch. 1.
24. See, e.g., Rawls (1971: 357–8).
25. *Condorcet: Selected Writings*, ed. Keith M. Baker, Library of Liberal Arts (Indianapolis, Ind.: Bobbs-Merrill, 1976), 47.

26. See also Waldron (1990: 63–4).

NOTES TO CHAPTER 8

1. I have taken the term from Goldsmith (1977). Allegiance is a relation of citizens to the laws; it is a status and may include, as one factor, a principled compliance with what the laws require (in virtue of their being authoritatively issued in a certain setting).

2. See Green, *Lectures on the Principles of Political Obligation and Other Writings*, ed. Paul Harris and John Morrow (Cambridge: Cambridge University Press, 1986), sect. 1 (p. 13). More precisely, Green's interest is in determining our moral duty to perform our political obligations (see sect. 10, p. 17). Simmons approaches the problem in much the same way (see Simmons 1979: 23, 29; also 4). I would contend that we could make little sense of the issue, posed in this way, unless we had first determined what the citizen's political obligations actually were.

3. For the *distinction* of duties from obligations, see Rawls (1971, sects. 18–19, 51–2, esp. pp. 114–15); Hart (1955, esp. 179n.). See also Simmons (1979: 11–16).

4. See Rawls (1971: 350, 354; also see sect. 19 and pp. 109–10 and sect. 51, esp. pp. 334–7). The view I have just described, in the text, is found in Rawls's book (1971). In his more recent writings (as found in his published works in the 1980s) he would probably set the matter up somewhat differently—a point I cannot make with certainty since he does not address the duty in question in these articles.

5. Jim Nickel has suggested that my account of allegiance is like that of the well-known fair play view of obligations (see Simmons 1979, ch. 5). I have, in the paragraph in the text, indicated crucial points at which my account is *unlike* that of fair play. There is, however, an even more important difference: the fair play idea introduces a deep *duty* (to be fair) which underwrites the *obligation* of fair play in a variety of circumstances. But my account draws on no such notion (of fairness or a duty of fairness).

   There are, of course, similarities as well between my account and that of fair play. In each an institutional context is presupposed and, within that, a practice of some sort. And in each some benefit—potential or actual—of every individual is identified as the ground of the institutional obligation (or duty) at issue.

   Fair play here, however, requires the *actual* receipt—or, better, the positive acceptance of some such actual receipt—of the benefit, or a fair share of the benefit, by an *actual* individual (where that benefit is brought about through the actions of others); whereas my account stresses potential or unrealized benefits (as well as actual ones) of the *typical* citizen. Moreover, on my account, innkeepers would have the duty imposed by the Civil Rights Act (of 1964) whether or not they themselves ever stayed in inns owned or managed by other innkeepers. But this is not so in the fair play account.

6. The present section (and, subsequently, part of Sect. 6) draw on discussions I

had with Jack Bricke about conventions (in particular, Hume's account of them) and the way in which strictly conforming conduct might become a reasonable expectation, despite the porosity that actual conventions exhibit. Some of the ideas are, of course, his—and even some of the language, for example, the term 'ruleworthy.' I will return to this question of appropriate discretionary unspecified exceptions in Scct. 5 of the present chapter.

7. For a discussion of the duties of understanding and argument, see my paper "The Ideal State in Plato's *Republic*," *History of Political Thought* 2 (1981), 1–30, esp. sect. 4; for a discussion of the duty to fight, see Walzer (1970, essays 5 [pp. 99–119] and 6 [pp. 120–45]; also essay 4 [pp. 77–98]). It should be clear that I am not advocating the inclusion of these duties within the citizen's allegiance but merely nominating them for consideration.

The standard of (good) citizenship varies, of course, from society to society and, over time and class status, within a given society. For a helpful suggestion as to how the ideals of citizenship have varied, between high Victorian times and our own, see Vincent and Plant (1984, ch. 9).

What I am talking about, under the heading of allegiance, is in effect a sort of ideal type of citizenship: citizenship conceived as typical or characteristic or representative from within the confines of some complex institutional scheme. My idea of a typical citizen in a system of rights is structurally like Rawls's "ideal of a good citizen of a democratic state" (see Rawls 1988: 263).

8. As noted, Congress did pass (in April 1987) a law allowing higher speed limits (65 m.p.h.) on certain multilane, divided rural highways (with limited access) and on sections of the interstate highway system outside city limits. And state legislatures did, subsequently, enact such limits within many of the states. Nonetheless, these higher limits still conform to the argument I have been conducting and the duty in question would apply to them as well. My argument is by no means tied specifically to the 55 m.p.h. limit and to it alone.

9. Thomas Aquinas says that "something may be derived from the natural law in two ways: first, as a conclusion from premises, secondly, by way of determination of certain generalities" (*Summa Theologica*, 1a 2ae, quest. 95, art. 2). The point I am making about highway speed limit laws here is like Aquinas's second way; whereas a law against murder (that is, against people being killed by other people) would be like his first way.

10. It should be noted, first, that not all public goods are things one could be said to have a civil right to (see my book *Rawls and Rights*, 114–20, 125–6, for the development of this point). But, second, those primary goods that could be justified in the way just described (in the text) *could* constitute civil rights, if they were otherwise eligible and had been established as rights by governmental action. My point, though, is that the duty to obey would be supported by the mutual perceived benefit argument even if a civil right had not been specified in that particular case.

11. See Hart (1961, ch. 3, sect. 1). The idea of such laws plays a crucial role in Hart's general concept of law (see, e.g., 1961, ch. 4, sect. 3, and esp. chs. 5 and 6; also pp. 8–9, 238–40).

12. Simmons discusses a number of such grounds in his book (1979): fidelity or consent (chs. 3 and 4), fair play (ch. 5), Rawls's natural duty of justice (ch. 6), and gratitude or repayment (ch. 7); see also pp. 15–16, 54–5.

13. For Simmons's discussion of the particularity requirement and the problems it poses, see (1979: esp. 31–5, and also 37, 43, 54, 64, 155–6). It is, I think, a merit of Simmons to have identified this requirement (and its problems—in particular, the problem that standard theories of political obligation can't meet the requirement). I should add that he does not set the requirement in two stages (as I do in the present paragraph and the paragraph next but one in the text). Ultimately, though, Simmons admits that he himself cannot solve the problems posed by the requirement (see Simmons 1979, ch. 8, esp. pp. 192, 198); the main reason he cannot is that he continues to retain the perspective of a classical externalist.

14. I continue to find persuasive much of what Simmons says in his criticism of consent or contract theory (see Simmons 1979, chs. 3 and 4). For additional critical discussion, see Waldron (1987b: 136–8). I admit, of course, that there are sophisticated defenses of traditional consent theories; among these I particularly recommend Lewis (1989).

15. For helping me clarify the contention in this paragraph I am indebted to Mauro Nobre.

16. Walzer provides an interesting discussion of a citizen's characteristic duty, in a socialist country (Cuba), not to commit suicide; see (1970, essay 8, pp. 169–89, esp. 172–3, 180–4).

17. The notion of a basic right has not, up to this point, been defined. What I have in mind are, paradigmatically, those civil rights (such as the right of habeas corpus), mentioned at the end of Ch. 7, that enjoy a very high level of social consensus support and that have survived the self-correcting processes of the democratic institutions and now enjoy explicit endorsement by various of the checking devices. I will turn to the issue of such basic or constitutional rights in Ch. 12 of the present book.

18. A similar view is also set forth by MacCallum (see 1987: 156–7). It is important to see that allegiance, as here conceived, is a kind of receptacle. It is filled by various justified duties, apt feelings, and so on that typical citizens have or could reasonably be expected to have. But allegiance does not itself justify these feelings or duties in any way; rather, what justifies them is the particular features of an overall political system of some determinate sort (in the case at hand, a system of rights).

19. In this paragraph I reply to points raised by Richard Bellamy. Gibbard (1990, ch. 13) provides a helpful discussion of how such shared focus might in fact develop and come to have weight. The phrase "apt feeling" is, of course, taken from his book. For additional discussion, emphasizing the "transformation" of "affective ties" and the high degree of social cohesion and stability afforded by reciprocity, see McClennen (1989, esp. 8).

Rawls (from 1982 on) puts great emphasis on the pluralistic character of modern societies—that is, of Western societies after the wars of religion ended. (See Rawls 1982a: 17–18; 1982b: 160.)

20. I associate my account here with Tocqueville's idea of "another species of attachment," when he says (in *Democracy in America* [1835] ch. 14): "But there is another species of attachment to country, which is more rational than the one we have been describing [concerning the quasi-religious attachment of the French patriot under the absolute monarchy]. It is, perhaps, less generous and ardent, but it is more fruitful and more lasting: it springs from knowledge; it is

nurtured by the laws; it grows by the exercise of civil rights; and, in the end, it is confounded with the personal interests of the citizen. A man comprehends the influence which the well-being of his country has upon his own; he is aware that the laws permit him to contribute to that prosperity, and he labors to promote it, at first because it benefits him, and secondly because it is in part his own work."

21. This important point is also found in Rawls. He emphasizes that *any* institutional constitutional setup will be only an imperfect device for realizing values that can be described, but not instantiated, independently of such a setup. Thus, in his own account the constitutional system, even the best one, is a necessary but imperfect device for embedding the principles of justice in the basic structure of a well-ordered society. This is a general point he makes. It is not a point about voting and majority rule procedures *per se*; but it does, of course, apply to them. (See Rawls 1971, sects. 31, 36, 53, 54, and pp. 296–7, 315.) The rubric under which Rawls developed his overall analysis is that of imperfect procedural justice (see 1971, esp. 84–88). Hence, the name of the present section: "Democratic Process as an Imperfect Procedure."

22. On the Rawlsian duty to obey unjust laws, see (1971, sect. 53, esp. pp. 351, 354–5). Rawls says elsewhere that (natural) duties hold "unconditionally" (1971: 115). This might strengthen the impression that Rawls thinks citizens are supposed to obey unjust laws. But he means by 'unconditional' here simply that the duty is not conditional upon such things as some prior transaction or the fact that such a transaction was engaged in knowingly and voluntarily—not conditional, that is, on those things that would make it an obligation (as distinct from a duty) in Rawls's technical sense. In any event, Rawls makes it clear that disobedience to law is allowed for in a "state of near justice" —under two distinct headings, "civil disobedience" and "conscientious refusal" (see Rawls 1971, ch. 6, esp. sects. 55–9 and, for the phrase quoted, p. 389).

23. I take the term "positional duties" from Simmons; for discussion, see (1979: 4, 12–13, 16–24, 26, 150).

24. The Supreme Court decision I refer to is *Roe* v. *Wade*, 410 U.S. 113 (1973).

25. Childress (1971: 11).

26. See Rawls (1971: 367 and 363, respectively) for these passages.

27. See Wolff (1969: 610–11, esp. 611). The definition I offered in my paper "Civil Disobedience," *Ethics* 80 (1970), 123–39, was of this latter, authority-recognizing sort (see pp. 123–7 and also 129).

It should be noted that the account in the present chapter allows disobedience to a law not itself thought to be defective, if that is an effective way of protesting some law or policy that *is* thought to be radically unsound. Trespass laws are often violated in this way, and I would want to allow that such cases could count as civil disobedience. For I do not think there is any significant difference in principle between direct civil disobedience (where the law disobeyed, or its application, is itself thought to be an evil) and indirect civil disobedience (cases like trespass, mentioned at the beginning of this paragraph). It may, nonetheless, be true that indirect civil disobedience is in most cases more difficult to justify than direct, especially where major disruption and unrest occur or where the law violated is only symbolically or only tangentially related to the evil being protested.

28. For discussion see my paper on "Civil Disobedience," esp. 137 nn. 1 and 2.

29. See Henry D. Thoreau, "On the Duty of Civil Disobedience" (1849), reprinted

in *Walden and On the Duty of Civil Disobedience* (New York: New American Library, 1964), 222–40: 223. For discussion, see my paper "Civil Disobedience," 138–9 n. 8.

30. See Zinn (1968: 30 and 120–1, respectively) for these quotations.

31. For the political sense of "civil disobedience," see also my paper "Civil Disobedience," 123, 133, 135.

32. See *Republic*, book 10 (the Myth of Er); for discussion, see my paper "The Ideal State in Plato's *Republic*," sect. 4 and also pp. 8–9, 13–14.

33. "[T]here can be no right to disobey the law of the state except in the interest of the state; i.e., for the purpose of making the state in respect of its actual laws more completely correspond to what it is in tendency or idea, viz. the reconciler and sustainer of the rights that arise out of the social relations of men" (T. H. Green, *Lectures on the Principles of Political Obligation*, ed. Harris and Morrow, sect. 142, p. 111). For discussion of Green's interesting views on this point, see Harris (1986) and my paper on "Civil Disobedience," 128 and n. 6 (pp. 137–8).

34. For elaboration of the argument here, esp. on point (1), see my paper "Civil Disobedience," 131–3 and also 129–31. Of course, there is room, under the heading of civil disobedience, for what might be called the revolutionary form of civil disobedience, where radical change in the form or character of government was intended (see pp. 134–5 of that same paper). The point here though is that revolutionary civil disobedience which aimed at overthrowing a system of rights and replacing it with something else (a communist utopia or a rule of the saints) could not be countenanced as justifiable within the theoretic system—a system of rights—that we are concerned with in the present chapter.

35. For elaboration on this point, see my paper "Civil Disobedience," 135–6.

36. For elaboration on this conclusion, see my papers "Civil Disobedience," 136–7, and "Wolff's Defence of Philosophical Anarchism," *Philosophical Quarterly* 24 (1974), 140–9: 147–9.

Rawls develops the notion of strict compliance or ideal theory (see 1971: 8–9, 145, 241–2, 245–6, 351, and 391). By these terms he refers to the situation where a well-ordered society conforms without defect, in the appropriate way and at the appropriate level, to the principles of justice. And one of his principal claims is that civil disobedience could arise and have a role only in a "state of near justice," one that failed of strict compliance and, hence, is "nonideal" or in "partial compliance" (see 1971: 8–9, 351, 353–5, 363, 391).

But I cannot follow him on this point: if constitutional devices can give us only an imperfect procedural justice, then we must build in and accommodate this fact in any state—and not merely in any well-ordered or "near just" state (or in any nondefective system of rights). Moreover, there will always be contested judgments about civil rights; hence there will always be a space for civil disobedience even in an "ideal" system of rights. The Rawlsian (natural) duty to obey the laws in a just or "near just" society goes hand in hand with politically justified civil disobedience; they are *doppelgängers*, ultimately two facets of the same basic understanding of political life. Accordingly, I have suggested that we collapse these notions into the single idea of allegiance (in a system of rights, the case at hand); and this conclusion, then, represents precisely such a view.

37. Some have advocated that a degree of legal toleration be extended to civilly disobedient conduct. For example, Dworkin (1978, ch. 8) argues in favor of

lenient prosecutorial discretion in some such cases, and Hall (1971: 145–51) argues that "conscientious disobedience" should be an allowable legal defense, with the jury left free to mitigate punishment or (in the likely successful outcome) to absolve from guilt in such cases.

One thing seems clear: if punishment for lawbreaking is justifiable in a system of rights, then the burden of proof (in favor of special leniency) will fall on the civilly disobedient and their legal counsel; and prosecutorial discretion will be somewhat restricted. In the end, then, such proposals as those of Dworkin and Hall are best addressed, not in the context of conscientious disobedience, but in that of justifiable punishment within a system of rights. And I will simply leave the matter at that.

38. For Hume's account of the "sensible knave," see his *Enquiry Concerning the Principles of Morals* (1751). The passage in question can be conveniently found in Hume, *Enquiries*, ed. L. A. Selby-Bigge, with text revised by P. H. Nidditch, 3rd edn. (Oxford: Oxford University Press, 1975), 282–3. I owe this citation and the point about akrasia to my discussions with Jack Bricke.

NOTES TO CHAPTER 9

1. "The right to punish contained in the penal law is the right that the magistrate has to inflict pain on a subject in consequence of his having committed a crime" (I. Kant, *The Metaphysical Elements of Justice*: part 1 of the *Metaphysics of Morals* [1797], in *Werke*, ed. E. Cassirer [Berlin, 1916], vii. 138, and in Kant, *The Metaphysical Elements of Justice*, tr. John Ladd, Library of Liberal Arts [Indianapolis: Bobbs-Merrill, 1965], 99). "But all punishment is mischief: all punishment in itself is evil"; it is clear from the context that by evil Bentham meant painful. (See J. Bentham, *An Introduction to the Principles of Morals and Legislation* [1789, reprinted 1823], ch. 13, sect. 1, para. 2, for the passage quoted; also ch. 14, para. 26, and ch. 3. And see J. Bentham, *Of Laws in General*, ed. H. L. A. Hart [London: University of London, The Athlone Press, 1970], ch. 6, sect. 4, p. 54.)

2. For example, take S. I. Benn's encyclopedia article. He says, "Characteristically, punishment is unpleasant. It is inflicted on an offender because of an offense he has committed; it is deliberately imposed, ...and the unpleasantness is essential to it, not an accidental accompaniment to some other treatment (like the pain of the dentist's drill)" (Benn 1967: 29; see also 34).

3. For example, see Plato, *Protagoras* 324–5, *Laws* IX, and esp. *Gorgias* 479–80, 525–6, *Laws* V. 735–6; Aristotle, esp. *Nicomachean Ethics* II. 1104^b 15–19; also *NE* X. 1180^a 1–13, and *Politics* VII. xiii. 6–7 (1332^a).

4. See G. W. F. Hegel, *Philosophy of Right* (1821), sects. 90–103, esp. 94, 97, 99.

5. See J. S. Mill, *Utilitarianism* (1863), ch. 4, esp. para. 10; also ch. 4, para. 2, and ch. 2, para. 2. Mill suggests an analogy between visibility and desirability and then says, "[T]he sole evidence it is possible to produce that anything is desirable is that people do actually desire it" (*Utilitarianism*, ch. 4, para. 3). I

assume he would say, in parallel fashion, that something is properly said to be undesirable (that is, positively not desirable) if, when faced with it, people desire not to have it. My account in the text assumes this particular connection.

6. The definition here is different from the one I provided in "On the Logic of Justifying Legal Punishment," *American Philosophical Quarterly* 7 (1970), 253–9: 253. The idea of dividing the institution into two stages—(1) having a provision for coercive sanctions and (2) carrying out that provision—is adapted from an important idea developed by several thinkers; see Mabbott (1969: 48, 51); Quinton (1969: 62–3); Rawls (1955: 3, 16, 18, 30–2). When I speak of carrying out the provision I do not mean carrying it out on any *one* occasion (unless so specified) but, rather, on *all* those occasions on which it is carried out.

7. See Hart, "Prolegomenon to the Principles of Punishment," in Hart (1968: 3–4, 8–11).

8. We should, of course, recognize the fact that some societies make no significant distinction between their political–legal systems and their religious institutions or between their political–legal institutions and their conventional morality and its institutions. My account does not require any such distinction; what it does require is the existence of agencies of the following sort: a rule-making agency (or authoritative interpreter of principles, customs, the divine will, or what have you) that itself enforces these rules with punitive measures (or is in close coordination with some such coercive agency). Whether the society in question would call such agencies political (or legal) or whether that society even has the concept of law or of the state and politics is not material.

Furthermore, most societies (perhaps all) exhibit a considerable overlap between the content of the commands and prohibitions of law and the content of the commands and prohibitions of their conventional morality. Thus, it is always possible to refer the system-located practice of punishment to conventional morality for justification of a sort. That is, it is possible so long as the two are not literally identical. Since such identity is rare (I mean identity not only in content but also between the theoretic systems, so that no distinction is made at all), we can set this caveat aside and allow for conventional–moral justifications of punishment.

Nonetheless, the main points I made still stand. (1) The practice of punishment must be considered in the light of surrounding political institutions— including the existence of law (and whatever the purpose of law is there)—if it is to be understood as a functional political practice. Thus, justification by reference to conventional morality does not supersede my claim that punishment, insofar as it is a political–legal practice, must be evaluated in relation to other political institutions. And where these institutions are systematically related, then the conventional moral evaluation would have to be of the whole system. And (2) such a practice or such a network of practices and institutions, even if justified by conventional morality, would still be subject to scrutiny by the standards of ultimate or critical morality.

Accordingly, though we could count conventional moral justification as a third kind of justification, that would not change the main lines of the theory of justification I have already sketched. I am greatly indebted to Neale Mucklow for helping me think through the doctrine of internal justification in this chapter.

9. The notions of possession, scope, and weight were worked out in Martin and

Nickel, "Recent Work on the Concept of Rights," esp. sect. 2 and also 3. The notion of normative direction, introduced in the text three paragraphs below, is also discussed in that paper (in sect. 1, esp. pp. 165–7). For further discussion of these two points see Chs. 5 and 11 (possession etc.) and Chs. 2 and 8 (normative direction) in the present book.

One further point. In Ch. 5, I suggested that all civil rights, simply as civil rights and as justified by the standard of mutual perceived benefit, could be assumed to have equal weight. Nonetheless, it was asserted there that weighting differences could and should be introduced to deal with cases of conflict, and the argument there allowed for weighting differences between rights. The argument in the present chapter assumes that such weighting differences have been installed; the assumption here is that a reasonably well-articulated scheme of ordinal weights (for when rights conflict and between some rights) is in place. No particular *theory* of weighting (e.g., a theory of basicness) is implied, however. We will assume merely that the ordinal weights are established in common and popular estimation (as reflected in a particular society's traditions and arguments) and that the weights themselves are exhibited in law and in judicial decisions.

10. The distinction of infringement from violation is frequently made (see Martin and Nickel, "Recent Work on the Concept of Rights," 173). For discussion see Feinberg (1978: 101–2), Thomson (1977a: 10–11; 1977b: 47–8; 1980, esp. sects. 1–2, 7–8; 1986b: 253–5), Fletcher (1980: 146–7, 150), and Gewirth (1981: 2). The distinction is challenged in Montague (1984).

11. It should be clear in any account where punishment is *defined* as a deprivation of rights, on the part of the person punished, that punishment is actually being conceived as an infringement of rights. (See Bedau 1982b: 341, and Rawls 1955: 10, for examples of such definitions.) But even where punishment is not so defined, we know for a fact that the *effect* of punishment, in the form of coercive sanctions triggered by adjudged violations of law, might be a deliberate infringement of the rights of those punished. Thus in a system of rights, where all have rights and some rights are the same for all, a problem is posed for all such coercive responses.

12. I have assumed throughout the argument in this chapter that adjudged violators do not automatically forfeit or become dispossessed of their rights—nor do they automatically forfeit the one they have offended against. Thus, forfeit is not available as a general strategy for dealing with rights violation; accordingly, the dilemma I have identified must be faced by any theory of rights. For further discussion of forfeiture, see Ch. 11 of the present book.

13. For development of the idea that rights can, indeed must, conflict see Feinberg (1973, ch. 5 and pp. 95–6); Martin and Nickel, "Recent Work on the Concept of Rights," sect. 2; Martin, *Rawls and Rights*, ch. 7; and Ch. 5 of the present book.

I should add that the factors I am pointing to in this argument—the features of possession, scope, and weight (all introduced initially in Ch. 5)—are not the only intrinsic features of rights. A number of other such features—normative direction, and so on—were adduced in Ch. 2 as well. My reason for emphasizing the former set of features in the present argument (while by and large neglecting the latter set) is simply that I think the features of scope etc.

are more likely to figure, in a material way, in any discussion of the
permissibility of allowing one right to infringe on another.

I am indebted to Mike Young for urging both the clarification in the previous
paragraph of this note and the clarification in the text to which this note is
attached.

14. The argument in the text is a response to a point raised by Don Marquis. I have
adapted the bread loaf example from the one he offered. The point I made in the
text, in the sentence immediately preceding the note cue, is also made by Alan
Goldman and by Thomas Hurka; see Goldman (1979: 52–3), and Hurka (1984:
142–3 and 143n.).

15. One interesting criticism of my account, which I owe to Donna Martin, is that
the account provides no decision procedure as between penalties within the
range of roughly the same deterrent effectiveness that operate by infringing
rights of roughly equal weight. A ready response here would be that, in such a
case, the matter is indifferent from the perspective of rights. Choice could,
nonetheless, be made on other grounds; for instance, a penalty that was
aesthetically unattractive or that violated some rule of propriety (by being
exceedingly impolite, for example) might be disallowed on that basis. However,
some of the penalty options might actually be morally repugnant (disfigure-
ment, for example, such as by lopping off fingers or a hand) and it seems odd to
say that these are equally justified, along with other eligible penalties, from the
perspective of rights. A reply might be that the situation envisioned here is
unlikely to occur. Hence, such a problem simply would not come up in the
normal course of things. Nonetheless, it could come up, one notes with disquiet;
its doing so is not inconceivable. It seems to me, then, that if it did, the best
response would be to say, in such a case, that the infringement of a right by that
penalty was objectionable on grounds of conventional or accepted morality
(unlike alternatives to it), was thus prima facie morally unjustifiable, and, as
such, arguably constituted a *violation* of rights: it would therefore be ineligible,
for further consideration or for use, from among the alternative penalties that
had been admitted simply on grounds of weight and relative deterrent
effectiveness.

16. Some will object, quite plausibly I think, that where these conditions are met, it
is not proper to speak of the right in question (a right held by the adjudged
violator) as *infringed* by the sanction. I accept this criticism and will attempt to
show, in the next section of this chapter (Sect. 4), how it can be accommodated.

One further point. I have not addressed the question of responses (to
lawbreaking) that are nonpunitive but that do infringe rights. I am not sure there
are such responses. But, assuming that there are certain identifiable ones, we
could, for completeness' sake, include these within the tests for compatibility
and relative deterrent effectiveness. The latter test would, of course, become
somewhat more complicated to state and to perform; but the complexity would
be kept manageable by the requirement that the responses, like the sanctions
they were being compared with, were specific and identifiable.

17. See Nozick (1974: 28).

18. This argument is adapted from one developed by Hart; see Hart, "Legal
Responsibility and Excuses" in Hart (1968: 44–50); "Prolegomenon to the
Principles of Punishment" in Hart (1968: 22–3); "Punishment and the

Elimination of Responsibility" in Hart (1968: 181–3). A similar argument is developed by Lemos (1986: 71–2).

19. I assume the same sort of argument as the one just used (as to scapegoating) would show—if we are concerned with a specific law, and not with laws in general—that being punished under a law that one was adjudged guilty of violating was also a necessary feature of proper and justifiable punishment. For any such law is more effectively maintained where this feature is included (along with the other conditions of justifiable punishment) than it would be in a scattershot approach where, once it is determined that one had violated *some* law, one could be punished under the sanctions clauses of *any* eligible law. I will not, however, pursue this particular point further in the present book.

20. For a discussion of contributory causation in the special case of intentional actions (the case we are here contemplating), see my paper "Collingwood on Reasons, Causes, and the Explanation of Action," *International Studies in Philosophy* 23 (1991), 47–62, esp. n. 20; also my paper 'G. H. von Wright on Explanation and Understanding: An Appraisal," *History and Theory* 29 (1990), 205–33, esp. sects. 4 and 5.

21. Examples of collective punishment, of the punishment of persons who are not—by our standards—adjudged violators, are well known to cultural anthropologists. For an example of such punishment, of a member of the violator's family (among the Tlingits of Alaska) and for discussion, see Wall (1970–1: 492–5).

The general principle by which he evaluates such a practice is similar to the one I propose—but unlike mine will work only if one is committed to utilitarianism (see Wall 1970–1: 498). For a more formal statement of the general principle I have employed in this section, see my book *Historical Explanation: Re-enactment and Practical Inference* (Ithaca, NY: Cornell University Press, 1977), 125–32.

22. The main problem, as will become clear, is whether the things the Nazis did can really count as punishment. We can certainly call them victimizations and allow, if only for argument's sake, that they are enough like punishment (loosely conceived) for us to count them as cases of punishing the innocent. Even so, the record is not clear that these punishment-like victimizations of the innocent served the object intended: that is, the object of providing motivation to subject people not to oppose the Nazi regime in any way. For there are cases, e.g., punishing other prisoners in a P.O.W. camp when one of the prisoners had escaped or had tried to, in which the Nazi practice actually stiffened the resolve of its victims while not impeding the proscribed actions. See here Walzer (1970: 159, esp. n. 22, continued on p. 160). I would add that wholesale repression and victimization of the sort the Nazis practiced has not proven, historically, to be a viable long-term policy—as the breakup first of Stalinism and then of the Soviet system, in the Soviet bloc and in the USSR itself, bear witness.

23. For Rawls's discussion of telishment, a term he made up, see Rawls (1955: 11–13).

24. Rawls's point is that (1) utilitarians would not select the practice involving telishment over the more standard practice, where only the adjudged violator—the conscientiously adjudged violator—is liable to punishment. Thus, (2)

where the practice *as justified* serves to *define* the relevant concept (i.e., punishment) then it follows that only the guilty could be punished. H. J. McCloskey argues, successfully in my view, that Rawls's point (1) is not so clear: for utilitarians *might* actually opt for a practice incorporating telishment (if it was assured, additionally, that the cases of telishment would be very rare in fact, and could be successfully kept dark). Hence, this would resolve the definitional issue in favor of telishment. More important, McCloskey argues that even if a standard practice of punishment was preferred, as justifiable, there is always the possibility that utilitarian reasoning would allow, on some given occasion and all things considered, a utilitarian-justified *exception* to that standard practice. (See McCloskey 1971a: 207; 1971b: 361–6.)

I think, in sum, that these problems will prove intractable for any utilitarian-justified deterrence theory of punishment. My proposal, in effect, then, is quite simply to detach deterrence from its historic connection with utilitarianism and to couple it instead with a rights theory, as its justification. My contention here is that the practice as defined—including the controversial delimitation to adjudged offenders—would be justified in a rights theory and the policy would be endorsed there that only the guilty should be punished. And this solves—in a way that the reiterated turns to utilitarianism could not, or have not done decisively and convincingly—the problem facing the deterrent theory of punishment.

25. Of course, we could vary the scenario a bit. For it might be a nuclear terrorist, holding a whole city hostage, who makes such a demand. Now, admittedly, terrorists are known to be less imaginative and less credible and less patient than Cartesian evil demons. Nonetheless, a similar chain of reasoning might ensue, leading to the punishment of the innocent (or, more likely, to the victimization of some designated individual).

26. I want to thank, for helpful comments and suggestions on this chapter at various stages in its development, Neale Mucklow especially and also Don Marquis, Diana Meyers, Warner Morse, Mohammad Muqim, Bill Roberts, Ingmar Pörn, Carl Wellman, Susan Daniel (who helped me develop, in its initial stages, the argument about punishment of the innocent), and, in particular, Michael Young (who pointed out that, even in a system of rights, there is still need to solve the problem of allowing for the punishment of the guilty only).

NOTES TO CHAPTER 10

1. A similar account of modes of punishment—called there "categories of methods"—can be found in Thompson (1975: 7–8). As in my account Thompson includes compensation to victims and therapy among the modes.

2. For further discussion of the retributionist's commitment (in this case Kant's) to deterrence, see Scheid (1983, 1986). The compatibility of my theory with traditional retributive theory extends even beyond the points in the text. For it includes, as developed in Ch. 9, the idea that only adjudged violators can properly be punished and the idea that the severity of sanctions should be

proportionate, in some way, to the gravity of the law violated. Indeed, the only point at which my account deviates from retributivism is on the claim that *all* the guilty should actually be punished. This tenet has been held by only a few such thinkers (Kant comes to mind as a significant example; see Goldinger 1965: 462–4), and thus the tenet may not be an essential feature of traditional retributivist theory at all. Mundle, for instance, explicitly repudiates this tenet in an important postscript, after earlier holding it in his article (1954).

The points to which this paragraph responds were first made to me by Ingmar Pörn. I am also grateful to Arthur Skidmore for urging this clarification.

3. See, e.g., Wertheimer (1982: 374–5), Lyons (1984: 157–8), Hart, "Intention and Punishment," in Hart (1968: 128–9), and Murphy and Coleman (1990: 118).

4. The view that punishment represents an "emphatic denunciation" of crime has been put forward by a number of thinkers: Bishop Butler in the eighteenth century, James Fitzjames Stephen in the last, and in this century Lord Denning (the author of the phrase quoted), E. F. Carritt, A. C. Ewing, M. R. Cohen, and John Plamenatz. Among the important recent defenses of this theory are Feinberg (1963, 1965), Nozick (1981: 369–80, 393), Walzer (1983, esp. 268–70), and Duff (1986, ch. 2 and pp. 150, 166, 184–5, 234–9).

It should be noted, in the account I have offered, that denunciation does not figure as a part of the definition of punishment. Nor is it a feature of the justification—except indirectly, insofar as it bears on deterrence (in the way that I have indicated).

5. The point about finding a basis for the appropriate feelings, to which this paragraph was a response, was made to me separately by Georg Henrik von Wright and Michael Young.

6. Early on, American prisons took the names of penitentiary and reformatory. But few philosophers have been willing to make reformation the *exclusive* object of punishment. (Collingwood is one of the exceptions; see his book *Religion and Philosophy* [London: Macmillan, 1916], part 3, ch. 2, esp. pp. 178–9, 187. Duff is another; see 1986, ch. 9, esp. sects. 4 and 5, also chs. 2, 8 [sect. 4], 10, and pp. 150, 185.) Many, though, have been willing to let it figure as one end, or possible end, of punishment. (Even Hart; see 1968: 240–1 note to p. 26.)

The objection that this paragraph (in the text) addresses was raised by Georg Henrik von Wright.

7. The governing decision here is *Gregg v. Georgia*, 428 U.S. 153 (1976). That is, imposition of the death penalty for (1) serious crimes which involve the taking of a life is not unconstitutional provided that three procedural criteria are met. (2a) The penalty is not mandatory. (2b) The judge or jury is guided by specific, express standards which take into account the mitigating or aggravating circumstances of the offense and the offender. And (2c) there is provision for appellate review of the sentence. The Court also expressed a preference for, but does not require, (3) a bifurcated trial in which the sentence is determined in a separate proceeding. This allows the jury to review the appropriateness of the death penalty apart from the evidence by which they determined the criminal defendant's guilt.

For (1) see *Coker v. Georgia*, 433 U.S. 584 (1977); for (2a) see *Woodson v. North Carolina*, 428 U.S. 280 (1976); for (2b) see *Furman v. Georgia*, 408 U.S. 238

(1972) and *Gregg* and *Woodson*; for (2c) and (3) see *Gregg*. The above paragraph and these citations were provided by Heather Bussing.

8. Support for the main contention can be found in Hart, "Murder and the Principles of Punishment: England and the United States," in Hart (1968, ch. 3, esp. pp. 83, 85; see also the notes on pp. 246–7, 251–2), and in Bedau (1986, sects, 21, 24). And Bedau (1982a, ch. 4), collects together a number of supporting studies. Justice Marshall, in his dissent in *Gregg* (1976), argued that the available statistical evidence did not show the deterrent superiority of the death penalty and, thus, concurred with this main contention. Curiously, Justice Stewart, who wrote the opinion for the Court, agreed with this finding.

   The problem of recidivism, in the case of murderers specifically, is statistically slight and, hence, is a negligible issue in the overall account. (See Hart 1968: 64, and the note on p. 250; Bedau, 1986: 197.)

   Finally, though there is probably little controversy in this matter, Bedau (1986, sect. 16) does spell out some of the considerations for saying that the death penalty invades a weightier right than does imprisonment (even imprisonment for a long term).

9. Thomas Hurka uses this same line of argument; See Hurka (1982: 652–4, 656–7, and esp. 659). Brennan, in his dissent in *Gregg* (1976), relied on it also.

10. See, e.g., Goldman (1979: 49). I am indebted to Roni Bwalya, who, through his reaction of amazement, first alerted me to the essential severity and to the often disproportionate character of imprisonment.

   The phrase "punishment of choice," as applied to imprisonment, is from Sherman and Hawkins (1981: 88 and 109; see also 83, 86, 94).

11. In this argument I have combined, for simplicity, two considerations that were put forward in the previous chapter as distinct features of justification: overall necessity and relative deterrent effectiveness. The kind of reasoning involved in my account of imprisonment here is very like that used by historians to establish the comparative weight of various factors—for example, Robert W. Fogel's study of the practical contribution of railroads to the U.S. GNP in 1890 (in comparison with other feasible factors: canals, rivers, roads, etc.). For helpful discussion see McCullagh (1984, ch. 8, sect. 1, esp. p. 198).

12. The main contention here is advanced by Sherman and Hawkins (1981, see 100–1, 109–11, 114ff., 120; and 109 for the phrase quoted in the parentheses). For imprisonment they advocate a usual five-year maximum term (see 1981: 110, and also 103, 118–19).

   Others think that for murder a longer period of confinement, say, fifteen years, should be the rule. Kansas (my state of residence, which, incidentally, does not allow the death penalty) recently introduced the rule of 'hard 40': forty years' imprisonment, without possibility of parole, for some cases of murder.

13. Similar penalties that might be considered are frequent-furlough jailing and house arrest (supplemented, perhaps, by computer-controlled electronic surveillance of the sort now in use in Oklahoma and other states).

14. We must, of course, acknowledge that there are cases other than the ones examined in this chapter where rights are infringed (sometimes justifiably infringed) and where compensation might be owed. Such cases are often the province of civil, as distinct from criminal, law. They are civil matters when the harm done is simply harm to a private individual but not to the public at

large—though this suggestion is easier to make than it is to spell out (see Murphy and Coleman 1990: 110–17, 143–6, 161–5, and 211–13 for discussion). My account is not concerned with such cases; my exclusive focus is on losses due to specifically criminal violations of civil rights.

15. The point about the state's duty is made by Del Vecchio (1969: 203). Del Vecchio does not, however, tie the matter here specifically into a system of rights.

16. Epstein (1980) argues for what he calls a "strict liability" formulation of tort law; here a prima facie case of liability to pay damages "rests on causal notions alone, subject to a series of defenses, replies, and the like, which are designed to reduce the gap between notions of causation and those of responsibility" (1980: 133). In this account, liability on causal grounds holds, or should hold, "regardless of whether [the defendant] intended to harm the plaintiff or had conducted his activities with reasonable care" (1980: 74; see also 75). Much of the force of Epstein's argument rests on the fact that his reformulation and the law of negligence (the main apparent exception to his view) have in common a cause-based theory of tortious responsibility (see 1980: 133–5).

We can take this cause-based theory, then, as our starting point. Thus, Thomson (1984) claims that "under traditional tort law, the plaintiff had to show three things in order to win his case: (*a*) that he suffered a harm or loss, (*b*) that an act or omission of the defendant caused that harm or loss, and (*c*) that the defendant was at fault in so acting or refraining from acting" (p. 101). Her point is that causal agency (item [*b*]), in the presence of (*a*) and (*c*), is *sufficient* to ground the liability of an individual to pay damages (see Thomson 1984: 111–12, 116–17). She also wants to argue, more controversially, that causality should be a *necessary* condition of all such liability (see Thomson 1984: 104, 132–3; 1986a: 60, 63; and for discussion see Fischer and Ennis 1986, esp. 38, and Kagan 1986, esp. sects. 3 and 5).

I am not concerned here with the necessary condition claim. The position I advocate is simply the modest thesis (common to both Epstein and Thomson and to "traditional tort law") that, under conditions of the sort described in the text, causal agency is sufficient to ground liability to pay damages. For an account very like the one I have developed see MacCormick (1977–8), where there are at least two important points of similarity: (1) basing the requirement that compensation is owed on facts about rights and (2) treating causality, in the context of things like (*a*) and (*c*) above, as a sufficient condition for the liability to make such payment.

I realize that my account in the present chapter occurs in the context of *criminal* law. Not all illegal acts under the criminal code concern harms to identifiable individuals; those that do, however, should involve a requirement of compensation. Or, at least, this is what I am contending. And there is no point of principle, especially in view of what I said about causation in Sect. 6 of the previous chapter, that would prevent the application, as I have done in the present note, of relevant standards of tort law to cases of this sort.

17. Some would argue that such insurance payments should not be allowed in restitution; see, e.g., Abel and Marsh (1984: 189).

18. See Barnett (1977: 283–4; 1980: 120–2, 125, and esp. 132). Barnett says *punishment* here but he has penalty, specifically, in mind. Forcing violators to pay

compensation to victims is not, in my view, an alternative to punishment but a mere mode of punishment. (The same view is taken in Abel and Marsh 1984, ch. 2, also ch. 3; they too regard forced restitution as a form of punishment.)

19. I owe this point to Heather Bussing. I should add, too, that compensation as a mode of punishment must conform to the standards established for that practice. Thus, provisions for such sanctions are justifiable where there was compatibility in the weight of the rights involved, between that of the right restored by compensation and that of the right infringed by the requirement that compensation be paid, and where the provision (and its carrying out) had some deterrent effect—or, at least, did not reduce the preventive effect of other measures already in place there.

20. For John Stuart Mill's account of punishment, see *Utilitarianism* (1863), ch. 5, where he associates punishment with "hurt" (paras. 19, 20) and with "evil for evil" (paras. 34, 36). For Hart's definitional association of punishment with *pain*, see his "Prolegomenon to the Principles of Punishment," in Hart (1968, esp. 4 and also 26), and "Murder and the Principles of Punishment: England and the United States," in Hart (1968: 77). Hart's somewhat elusive utilitarian commitment is avowed explicitly (at least so far as punishment is concerned) in "Murder and the Principles of Punishment," in Hart (1968: 80–1), and in "Postscript: Responsibility and Retribution," in Hart (1968: 210).

21. I want to acknowledge the help of Dana Young in formulating this point; it was he who first brought this idea to my attention and who gave it its initial development.

22. See J. Bentham, *An Introduction to the Principles of Morals and Legislation* (1789, republished 1823), ch. 13, sect. 1.

    Locke also, I would add, regards "reparation" (restitution) as an important feature of punishment, at least in the state of nature and presumably in civil society; see here Locke, *Second Treatise* (1690), esp. sect. 8 and also sects. 10, 11, 20. Note too his discussion of a parallel case (conquest in a just war) in sects. 183, 196. I want to thank Ralph Lindgren for suggesting that, in the interests of rounding out the historical record, I mention not merely Bentham's but also Locke's inclusion of compensation within the conception and practice of punishment.

23. In my account punishment sets up a coercive situation having two main features: the general threat of a sanction and the carrying out of that threat on occasion. At this point in the text I am concerned with the second of these features. But we could also develop an account of the first of these features; this account would draw on—and, in fact, derive from—the essentially coercive character of the use of sanctions (as described in the text). Such an account would be roughly compatible with the one developed by Nozick (1972), Bayles (1972), and Airaksinen (1984). In the situation envisioned by Airaksinen (1984, esp. 105–9) person B is coerced when B is put in a situation where it is better to follow A's instructions toward x than to have A's threat carried out (though either of these options counts as a loss of some sort to B). A, on the other hand, prefers the carrying out of these instructions over the carrying out of the threat, for in the former case A realizes a positive gain (or, at least, a relatively positive one).

    The main modification I would suggest here is to say that B's following A's instructions (toward *x*) may count as a loss to *B* but, again, it may not. For people might actually want to do that which the law says they ought to do. Nonetheless, even they are in a coercive situation insofar as the law's instructions are attached to general coercive threats (addressed to everyone), threats that are backed up in turn by sanctions which are sometimes invoked. For here, as elsewhere, it is the "ordinarily unwanted" character of the sanctions themselves (the phrase is Neale Mucklow's) that grounds the threat and gives it the coercive character described in the paragraph above.

Accordingly, I would further modify Bayles's account, as summarized in (1972: 24–5), by dropping his stipulation that person *B* is being coerced only if *B* actually follows *A*'s instructions toward *x*. For *A*'s carrying out the threat against *B*, which *A* would do only if *B* failed to carry out the instruction, is a part of the coercive situation as initially envisioned (by *both* parties). Indeed, were it not for the relatively unwanted character of the sanction, the initial threat would have been empty and uncoercive. And when that sanction *is* employed against *B*, because *B* had *not* followed the instruction respecting *x*, *B* is being coerced in the fundamental way already identified (that is, required to do or undergo something ordinarily unwanted).

I would dissent, however, from von Wright's suggestion (in discussion) that coercion always involves *physical* compulsion or its threat. In my view (and, I am sure, that of many people), if I park my car at some distance from my office in order to avoid a ticket, then the situation is coercive. And when I pay a parking ticket (by mail, let us say), it is also coercive. In neither case, though, is physical compulsion present, or its immediate threat. Thus, a situation can be coercive in the absence of these things. The point is, coercion here doesn't begin merely with the advent of physical compulsion or its immediate threat; it begins, rather, in somebody's being required to do something (whether they want to or not) in the sort of situation characteristic of punitive law and legal punishment (i.e., the two-pronged coercive situation mentioned at the beginning of this note). It is important, though, to bear in mind that the schedule of coercive sanctions is often so arranged in law that physical compulsion (or its immediate threat) will most likely emerge at some point. Here, then, von Wright's emphasis is sound.

24. Insanity is a legal, not a medical, notion. It has been subject to a variety of legal definitions (also called 'rules' or, more often, 'tests'). The one I have tended to follow, or at least had in the back of my mind, is the one proposed in the Model Penal Code of the American Law Institute (1962, sect. 4.01; this section is slightly different from the text originally proposed in 1955):

> A person is not responsible for criminal conduct if at the time of such conduct as a result of mental disease or defect he lacks substantial capacity either to appreciate the criminality [wrongfulness] of his conduct or to conform his conduct to the requirements of the law.

"This test, or some variant of it, has been adopted within the last twenty years by all of the federal courts of appeals and by a substantial number of states" (Moore 1984: 220).

Other tests have played an important role and I list them, briefly. The most important is the M'Naghten test. This test focuses on cognitional matters, such as whether the accused, when the illegal act was performed, knew "the nature and quality of the act he was doing." If this failure of knowledge could be traced to a "disease of the mind," as its cause, then a verdict of insanity would be proper. (See *R.* v. *M'Naghten*, 10 Cl. and Fin. 200 [1843], 8 Eng. Rep. 718 [H.L., 1843]. The M'Naghten rules actually originated in the judges' answers, defending the *M'Naghten* decision, to questions put to them by the House of Lords. [See 8 Eng. Rep. 718 (1843), esp. 722–3, and for background, see Hansard, 3rd series, vol. lxvii (1843), 714–43.] For discussion, see Walker 1968, esp. ch. 5 and also ch. 6.)

Many jurisdictions have used another test, emphasizing volitional aspects (sometimes called irresistible impulses) to replace or, more often, to supplement the M'Naghten test. The ALI test, in effect, does so, supplementing the M'Naghten test with this one. Such a supplementary test has had a well-established standing in U.S. law since *Davis* v. *U.S.*, 165 U.S. 373 (1897). (For discussion see Goldstein 1967: 271 n. 1, and American Psychiatric Association 1983: 682; for discussion of the rather more complicated situation in the U.K., see Walker 1968, ch. 6, and Hart, "Changing Conceptions of Responsibility," in Hart 1968, ch. 8.)

Another test, called variously the Durham or the New Hampshire test, defines insanity simply as an unlawful act which is "a product of mental disease or of mental defect." Though this test was in use in the District of Columbia from 1954 to 1972 (at which point—1972—the D.C. Court of Appeals, U.S. Second District, abandoned the Durham test and adopted the ALI test), it is not today in use in the U.S. (except in the state of New Hampshire) or in the U.K. It, or a test substantially like it, is still used, however, in many other countries. (See *Durham* v. *U.S.*, 214 F. 2d 862 [D.C. Circuit 1954], and *State* v. *Pike*, 49 N.H. 399 [1870]. A footnote occurs in the latter case: "This case was decided June term, 1869, and should have appeared in 48 N.H. It was examined and reaffirmed in *State v. Jones*, Rockingham June term, 1871 [i.e., 50 N.H. 369 (1871)].")

Finally, the American Psychiatric Association has recently supported the so-called Bonnie rule, which in the main applies the M'Naghten test. The rationale here appears to be that psychosis "is usually defined in terms of the 'cognitive' failure of reality testing" (Radden 1985: 160). (See American Psychiatric Association 1983; Bonnie 1983, 1984: 15–18; and, for discussion, Radden 1985: 159–61.)

For useful discussion of these (and various other) tests, see Fingarette (1982), Hart, "Changing Conceptions of Responsibility," in Hart (1968, ch. 8), Moore (1984, ch. 6), and Radden (1985, chs. 9 and 11).

25. For an account of legal excuses, see Hart, "Prolegomenon to the Principles of Punishment," in Hart (1968, esp. 13–14, 17–24), and "Legal Responsibility and Excuses," in Hart (1968, ch. 2); also Moore (1984: 84–7, 221–4). Excuses so understood are to be distinguished from legal justifications (and from subsequent extenuations, at the point of imposing sanctions).

26. Some writers have advocated that insanity be regarded as an excusing status analogous to that of childhood. (See Moore 1984: 65–6, 222–3, 226; Radden 1985: 3, 24–5, 70, 121, 145, 151–2; and, for the more general argument, Radden 1985, chs. 9–11.) The important sense in which both statuses are exculpatory is

that we cannot *blame* people for their illegal conduct in either status, for they cannot help what they have done. But, even though this claim might be granted, the point remains that the under age (at least very young children) and the criminally insane are treated differently *after* the excusing status has been established. For very young children are let go, but not the criminally insane. And neither Moore nor Radden advocates that the matter be any different at this point. The criminally insane are treated differently because the status they occupy, unlike that of children, is thought to be especially and inherently dangerous (or at least threatening) to the rights of others. So the analogy breaks down here.

27. See Goldstein (1967, ch. 10, also p. 20 and ch. 12); American Law Institute (1962, sect. 4.08, and explanatory note, pp. 71–2).

28. The American Psychiatric Association refers to "the quasi-criminal nature of the insanity defense and of the status of insanity acquitees" (1983: 686).

29. Some have argued that confinement (in its routines and in its removal from distraction) is itself a form of treatment; see Brooks (1974: 854). The point I am making, though, is that those who are adjudged criminally insane (for having committed a violent act) should be confined, if dangerous; and this is so whether or not such confinement is itself therapeutic. On the point about the dangerousness of such detainees, and the reason for drawing a distinction (in law and fact) between them, and the great bulk of those who have been civilly committed (whether involuntarily or not), see American Psychiatric Association (1983: 686–7).

30. See American Psychiatric Association (1983: 686–687), and Bonnie (1983: 194).

31. *Durham* v. *United States*, 214 F. 2d 862 (D.C. Circuit 1954), esp. 864. Monte Durham, in this case, was technically accused of housebreaking. But he had a long history of motor theft, parole violation, and bad-check writing—which had led to his confinement in St. Elizabeth's Hospital on earlier occasions. Of course, the person in this case *was* in fact confined; so my example in the text is, to that degree, hypothetical. I am indebted to Les Mazor for helping me sharpen the analysis here.

32. The issue of detention, especially for an indeterminate period, of the criminally insane is one of the most vexing concerns. In the argument I have developed, the criminally insane can be incapacitated by confinement only if the crime they committed would have led to imprisonment when committed by a person who was *not* adjudged insane. But if that standard is met, the criminally insane can be confined. Thus, if a psychopath has committed a crime normally requiring confinement and that person has been judged insane (in a fair trial) then he or she can be confined, but a mere shoplifting kleptomaniac cannot.

33. The insanity plea, in cases of murder, has virtually been replaced in British courts (since 1957) by that of diminished responsibility (see Hart, "Changing Conceptions of Responsibility," in Hart 1968: 191–2, esp. 192). A defense of insanity sufficient to constitute an independent ground for the traditional verdict of "not guilty by reason of insanity" (or, sometimes, "guilty, but insane") is still found in most American courts—with some exceptions, however (e.g., Idaho and Montana). In the latter case it was removed by statute in 1979 (see *State* v. *Korell*, 690 P. 2d 992 [Montana 1984], esp. 996–997). The verdict allowed in Montana is enough like the traditional verdict to constitute no special

problem for my analysis; the sentencing aspects indicate, however, that confinement of the inmate for a statutory term is the primary consideration (see p. 997). I am indebted to John Robinson for calling the Montana case to my attention and for the citation.

34. And if that sentence were combined with a significantly long suspension of that person's driver's license (a case of incapacitation), we would have yet another example of a mixed mode of punishment.

35. I take the term 'liability' from Hart; see "Prolegomenon to the Principles of Punishment," in Hart (1968: 11), "Murder and the Principles of Punishment," (1968: 80), and "Intention and Punishment" (1968: 113).

36. See Hart (1968: 14, 28, 31, 35–40, 90–1, 114–15, 139–40, 173–6, 186–7, 206 n. 31, 218–19, 233; 1961: 173–4). The main idea Hart wants to advance here is that people should not be punished (penalized) for things they cannot help doing. In this regard, see also the discussion of Moore and Radden in n. 26 of the present chapter.

37. Hart's position seems to be that legal guilt (of the sort that subjects one to punishment) approximates moral guilt, or overlaps it in certain respects. See Hart, "Punishment and the Elimination of Responsibility," in Hart (1968, esp. 174–5), "Postscript: Responsibility and Retribution," in (1968, esp. 225–6), and Hart (1961: 173–4).

38. For the main argument, see Hart (1968: 44–50, 181–3, and 206–9). For the idea (developed in the next paragraph of the text) that the object of law is to maximize choices, see Hart (1968: 46, 48, 181). Hart develops a second main line of argument, which I will merely mention here: that it is unfair or unjust to punish (that is, penalize) those who cannot help what they have done—see Hart (1968: 22–3, 38–9, 77–9, 181, 201).

39. Hart sometimes makes the presumption I have identified. (For example, most of his examples and citations in effect limit the *mens rea* requirement to the area of criminal law alone.) But it should be noted that Hart also explicitly argues that the principle of giving weight to the mental condition of the agent has purchase outside the area of criminal law; for he argues, specifically, that the same conditions which constitute legal excuses (in the case of criminal conduct) also constitute grounds for invalidating such civil transactions as "wills, gifts, contracts, marriages, and the like." (See Hart 1968: 34–5, 44–6; the matter quoted appears on p. 45.) The problem, however, comes with express exceptions that Hart is willing to allow—as I show, next, in the text.

40. All quotations are from Hart (1968: 205; for his account see pp. 205–6).

41. Hart puts considerable emphasis on predictability (from the perspective of the agent); see Hart (1968: 23, 47, 181–2).

42. For Hart's discussion of negligence, see Hart (1968: 132, 136, 240 n., 245 n.). His view seems to be that penalizing people for negligent conduct does not violate the *mens rea* requirement. For they were able to act differently (that is, to act non-negligently); it was in their power to do so. In that sense, they could help what they were doing.

43. This constitutes a partial reply to Hart's point (raised in n. 38 above) that it is unfair or unjust to compel people to undergo something for conduct they couldn't help in the first place, for it does not seem wrong (under certain conditions) to compel such people to undergo treatment or rehabilitation.

44. The insane, in a criminal trial, do not have a constitutional right to the availability of the insanity defense (see American Psychiatric Association 1983: 682). And along with the rest of us in the U.S. today, the criminally insane do not have a right to treatment *per se*. Instead they have only a right to undergo psychiatric treatment *when they are confined* (just as they have a right to other medical or dental care, similarly, *when they are confined*). Thus, it is always possible to count such treatment, once we have modified the existing tenor of sentences, as a mere adjunct of penalty (of confinement) and no more. For it is probably true that we cannot require treatment of them in all cases (even in those where it is, apparently, needed).

    The relevant legal background appears to be as follows. Some state statutes on the commitment of mentally ill criminal offenders specify a right to treatment; others are simply silent. Two of the leading cases are *Rouse* v. *Cameron*, 373 F. 2d 451 (D.C. Circuit 1966), and *Wyatt* v. *Stickney*, 325 F. Supp. 781 (M.D. Ala. 1971) and 344 F. Supp. 373 (M.D. Ala. 1972). The latter case concerns civil commitment but the holding was sufficiently broad to include the medical and psychiatric treatment of criminal inmates as well.

    I owe the content and the citations in the previous paragraph of this note to Philip Kissam. For further discussion see Brooks (1974, ch. 14 and also pp. 397–9) and Krantz (1983: 190–208).

45. A right to get medical care, for most people, is simply a right to a way of acting, to a liberty of conduct. I am not sure whether such a right is a civil right. It may be what I called earlier (in Chs. 3, 5) a weak right; if it is, then it cannot possibly be a civil right (for reasons given there). Even if it is not a weak right, such a right could never be coerced or required (and remain a right to a *liberty* of conduct). Thus, in either case, it is not, as it stands in the U.S. today, a civil rights matter that could be required of adjudged violators and, hence, could never be or figure as a part of their punishment.

46. I have acknowledged help from a number of people in various notes in this chapter; I would like to add as well, with my appreciation for their useful comments, the names of Warner Morse, Paul Roth, Wayne Mastin, and Tony Genova.

    In particular, I want to thank Margaret Holmgren for written comments on material found in the present chapter. (I have attempted, at various points in this and in the previous chapter, to reply to some of the criticisms she raised: see esp. Ch. 9, Sects. 1 and 2, and Sects. 1, 4, 6 of the present chapter.) I also want to thank Deborah Johnson for helpful written comments on this chapter and on the next one. I have taken account of her comments at a number of points.

NOTES TO CHAPTER 11

1. See, e.g., *Ruffin* v. *Commonwealth*, 62 Va. 790, 796 (1871), where it is said that a prisoner is a slave of the state and has no rights. Kant held a similar view (see n. 4 of the present chapter). Many people read the Thirteenth Amendment to the U.S. Constitution as if it said that "involuntary servitude" (and slavery) were ruled out *except* in the case of convicts.

2. This argument is made, for example, in Goldman (1979: 43, also 45, 48); and in Pilon (1985: 828–30, also 822–4).

Richard DeGeorge suggested to me that the forfeiture doctrine needed to be discussed, that it could not be shunted aside in any full account of the justifiability of punishment. The argument that follows does, I think, address his point.

3. See Thomson (1977a: 14–15) and Martin, *Rawls and Rights*, 131. See also Brennan's dissent in *Gregg* v. *Georgia*, 428 U.S. 153 (1976).

4. Kant, *The Metaphysical Elements of Justice*, tr. John Ladd, Library of Liberal Arts (Indianapolis: Bobbs-Merrill, 1965), 101. Kant prefaces his discussion of punishment with the observation that a person who violates the criminal law is thereby made "unfit to be a citizen" (p. 99). His argument about the penalty for theft is especially revealing:

> Inasmuch as someone steals, he makes the ownership of everyone else insecure, and hence he robs himself (in accordance with the Law of retribution) of the security of any possible ownership. He has nothing and he can also acquire nothing, but he still wants to live, and this is not possible unless others provide him with nourishment. But, because the state will not support him gratis, he must let the state have his labor at any kind of work it may wish to use him for (convict labor), and so he becomes a slave, either for a certain period of time or indefinitely, as the case may be. (p. 102)

One possible interpretation of Kant's doctrine here is that the individual forfeits—temporarily or permanently—the very right the individual has violated (in the example just cited, the right to property). The point of *lex talionis*, then, is not so much to set penalties as it is to prepare the ground for an appropriate penalty in the idea of forfeit. The eye for an eye element is not given by the "characteristicalness" (in Bentham's term) between crime and penalty but, instead, by the right forfeited. Thus, the penalty in the example cited (being a convict laborer or "slave") is not identical to the crime (robbing someone of a particular possession, a VCR, say), but there is an identity, nonetheless, between the right violated and the right forfeited. For they are the same right.

5. Kant, of course, admits this point. See his discussion of the problem posed by rape, pederasty, and bestiality in "Supplementary Explanation of the Metaphysical Elements of Justice" (in *Metaphysical Elements of Justice*, tr. John Ladd, 132–3).

6. For Locke's doctrine of forfeit (and for the item quoted—an "act that deserves death"), see *Second Treatise*, sect. 23. For criticisms of forfeit see Bedau (1968: 567–70 [in an essay largely devoted to forfeit doctrine in William Blackstone's *Commentaries of the Laws of England* (1795)]), and Bedau (1982b: 323–8, esp. 326–8; 1986: 177–81), and Fletcher (1980: 135 and esp. 142–5), and Thomson (1977a, sect. 2).

It is interesting to note that Locke, in his long discussion of punishment in the state of nature (*Second Treatise*, sects. 7–13), does not rely on any doctrine of forfeit. But in sects. 85 and 172 and in ch. 16 ("Of Conquest") he reverts again to forfeiture. However, this entire later discussion—a discussion that concerns not the state of nature *per se* but, rather, the state of war, especially as that occurs in the setting of civil society—depends on what Locke had said earlier about an "act that deserves death." Thus, the idea of such desert is the linchpin of his whole account of forfeiture (though not, as should be clear, of his whole theory of punishment).

A similar discussion of forfeit (this time of parental prerogatives) can be found in Locke, *First Treatise*, sect. 100. (I am indebted to Peter Cvek for this reference and the one to *Second Treatise*, sect. 85.) For additional discussion of Locke's doctrines of punishment and forfeit, see von Leyden (1981: 109–19) and Simmons (1991, esp. sect. 4).

Kant, of course, also says that murderers "must forfeit" their right to life (see Kant, *Metaphysical Elements of Justice*, tr. John Ladd, 106). But, again, the interpretation and criticism I make of Locke here (i.e., that the issue is not automatic forfeit but instead what is deserved or, better, what is justifiable in the way of sanctions) also seems to me to be the proper interpretation (and basis for criticism) of Kant's theory of punishment.

A discussion of the relation of forfeit to desert, likeminded with my own, can be found in Lemos (1986: 80).

7. A principle somewhat like the one I have spelled out here has been enunciated by the courts; see, e.g. *Coffin* v. *Reichard*, 143 F. 2d 443 (6th Circuit, 1944). The court in this case emphasized that the rights of prisoners can be restricted not only by express sanctions (as set forth in their sentences) but also by considerations of administrative necessity or efficiency (see also *Price* v. *Johnston*, 334 U.S. 266 [1948]). Bedau as well draws attention to the importance of considerations based on "necessary conditions of institutional security" (1982b: 343, also 342). The issue, though, is the appropriate level of administrative and judicial restriction on the rights of prisoners—in particular, on grounds of administrative necessity or efficiency—and this is one issue I want to address in the present chapter.

8. See *Pell* v. *Procunier*, 417 U.S. 817 (1974), 822.

9. For a survey of these rights see Krantz (1983, ch. 5; also pp. xix–xx, 4, 91–102, 109–16, 238–40, 243–4, 259–66). See also, for a close analysis of the prisoner's right to write letters, Bedau (1981).

10. Gerald Baliles, the Governor at that time, proposed that all Virginia prisoners—about 38 percent of whom were functionally illiterate—be required to read at a sixth-grade level or better before parole could be granted. Inmates who attend the prison school, to attain this level, would be paid at the prevailing rate for work in that prison. This, of course, was merely a proposal. If adopted, it would have come close to a requirement for remedial schooling. Nonetheless, it would fall short in that (1) it is technically a requirement for parole and not a requirement of prison status as such and (2) it effectively applies only to inmates who cannot meet the relevant literacy standard. (The information cited here comes from a column by Mary McGrory—copyright 1986 by Universal Press Syndicate—printed in Kansas City by the *Star* on 1 June 1986.)

11. See, e.g., the Constitution of the USSR (1977), article 60.

12. For an excellent historical survey of work in prisons, up through the end of the nineteenth century, see Melossi and Pavarini (1981). This work, written from a Marxist perspective, studies England, Italy, Holland, and the U.S. in part 1 and the U.S. situation in the Jacksonian era in part 2. The interview, conducted by Beaumont and Tocqueville, with the Warden of Sing Sing in that

period (Mr. Elam Lynds), quoted on pp. 177–81, makes quite instructive reading.

13. For helpful discussions, see Nickel (1978–9), Becker (1980), DeGeorge (1984). I am also indebted to Carl Wellman's "The Right to a Job" (section of an unpublished MS).

14. The classic text of the theory of full employment is Beveridge (1944). My reference to just digging holes is taken from that book (1944: 20).

15. The idea of a "manifesto" right is taken from Joel Feinberg. See, e.g., Feinberg (1973: 63–4, 66–7, 95).

16. I distinguish the *ethical* justification for full employment, as given here, from its *economic* justification. In the latter, full employment, as one instance of the utilization of existing resources, is regarded as a necessary feature or precondition of market efficiency.

The relevant U.S. law (the Full Employment and Balanced Growth Act of 1978) begins by referring to "the right of all Americans who are able, willing, and seeking to work to full opportunity for useful paid employment at fair rates of compensation." Interestingly, the earlier law (the Employment Act of 1946) made no reference to any such right whatsoever.

17. It is appropriate here to recall to mind that in my account human rights are civil rights (see Ch. 4 of the present book). That is, they are practicable ways of acting or of being treated that are recognized in law and maintained by government for every citizen or every person in a given society. They constitute a special class of civil rights in being morally based (whether on conventional moral judgments or critical ones is immaterial); and they are said—from the moral perspective identified—to cover all persons in a given society simply in virtue of those persons' being human individuals who can relevantly count as within that society or under its domestic law.

18. The relevant constitutional writ here for Americans is the Fourteenth Amendment, which applies to the states. In constitutional adjudication the equal-protection feature of the Fourteenth Amendment has been applied to the federal government, as distinct from state governments, through incorporation into the due process clause of the Fifth Amendment.

19. For the case I am citing, rather indirectly here, see *Rhodes* v. *Chapman*, 452 U.S. 337 (1981).

20. The phrase "discrete and insular minorities" and the idea behind it are taken from the famous footnote 4, by Justice Harlan F. Stone, in *U.S.* v. *Carolene Products Co.*, 304 U.S. 144 (1938), 152. This idea has become one of the principal strands in the present-day theory of adjudication under the Fourteenth Amendment.

"Suspect classification" identifies a legislative or administrative classification of persons that will bring a close, hard look from the court because the group in question has, among discrete and insular minorities, been especially abused, or subject to abuse, over a long period. The list of suspect classifications, though not permanently fixed, is surprisingly short and includes invidious racial classifications (largely directed against blacks or orientals), classifications by national origin, and alienage (having to do with noncitizens).

Classifications that single out or mention prisoners are not, as such, constitutionally suspicious in the eyes of judges (see, e.g., *Morales* v. *Schmidt*, 340 F.

Supp. 544 [Western District of Wisconsin, 1972]). Nor are classifications by gender suspect (at least not in the eyes of an official *majority* of the Court) or classifications that single out those people who are impoverished. My point here, then, is that the rationale for determining a protected "discrete and insular minority" could well apply to prisoners (even though they, like long-term aliens, are to some extent responsible for their status).

The Supreme Court in its adjudication under the Equal Protection clause of the Fourteenth Amendment has evolved the idea of two tiers or levels of judicial scrutiny. (1) The most severe or "strict scrutiny" is reserved for cases that involve a violation of fundamental rights (in particular, many of those identified in the Bill of Rights—but not, I would add, the right to work) or that involve a suspect classification. Here the courts are not at all deferential toward legislative or administrative judgment and require a compelling state interest in order to tolerate laws or decrees that make for unequal treatment. And judicial remedy is very exacting and assiduous where the unequal treatment has been disallowed. (2) A much less severe scrutiny is mandated, however, in cases that do not involve a fundamental right or a suspect classification. Here the courts are quite deferential to legislative or administrative judgment and require only a very loose "rational basis," in the statute or the decree, in order to rule that unequal treatment is justifiable in a given case.

Recently, the idea of an intermediate tier of scrutiny, somewhere between the "compelling state interest" and the "traditional" or "rational basis" tests, has been accepted. (See, e.g., the dissenting opinion of Justice Thurgood Marshall in *San Antonio Independent School District* v. *Rodriguez*, 411 U.S. 1 [1973] where such an intermediate level was argued for.) It is in this intermediate tier, where a reasonably important or "substantial" state interest is required for unequal treatment to be justifiable, that cases of discrimination by sex are currently being adjudicated. My analysis, then, is meant to suggest that the unequal treatment of prisoners, as regards the policy of full employment, could well be judged under this intermediate test as well.

21. Additional reasons, beyond the principle of full employment itself, which I have emphasized, could be offered that favor a course of action designed to end the policy of idleness in prisons. They come under the following headings: (1) making possible compensation or restitution to victims of crime, (2) contributing to the costs of imprisonment, (3) support of families on the outside, (4) personal savings as a stake for the future, (5) the morale of inmates. These reasons are sketched in more fully in my paper "The Human Right of Inmates to Work with Just Compensation," *Journal of Social Welfare* 9 (1983), 41–60: 50–2.

22. "All prisoners under sentence shall be required to work, subject to their physical and mental fitness as determined by the medical officer" (First UN Congress on the Prevention of Crime and the Treatment of Offenders, 1955, reaffirmed and reissued in the UN's "Standard Minimum Rules for the Treatment of Prisoners," 1957; see part 2a, sect. 71.2).

23. On a problem posed by the legal requirement to vote, see Singer (1973: 55–6). On the requirement to vote in Australia in particular, see Singer (1973: 56) and Pateman (1985: 86 and 200 n. 20).

24. Sumner (1987: 34) accepts the idea of a *required* liberty of action as coherent; so

does Hohfeld. The reason for this is that they have in mind only a "half liberty" (Sumner's phrase): here one has no duty not to do *A*; thus, one *may* do it. But nothing is said at all about whether one might have (or not have) a duty to do it. The governing intuition, on their view, then, is that it is not inconsistent to have a duty to do what one is permitted to do. The law, for example, might allow me to make right turns at a red light, after stopping, and sometimes require me to do so. I do not share this intuition as to liberties, however; for I do not see how a person can, at one and the same time, be permitted to *not* do something and be required to do it.

In any event, where one has, in Sumner's phrase, a "full liberty" or, in Hart's phrase, a "bilateral liberty" (that is, where one has no duty to do *A* and no duty to not do *it) one cannot, logically* cannot, be required either to do or not do the relevant action *A*. Since a "full" or "bilateral" liberty is what I mean by a liberty (as the argument in Ch. 3 suggested) it follows on this account that one cannot both have such a liberty, respecting *A*, and be legally required either to do that thing or not do it.

25. "In the early 1970's ...[t]he average inmate wage in both federal and state industry programs was $.13 per hour; some inmates earned no wages" (Grissom and Lewis 1981: 43). For a helpful chart summarizing prison wages in this period, see Callison (1983: 136). The situation is not significantly different today. Inmates, typically, earn well below the standard set by the federal minimum wage (currently $4.25 per hour). And in Canada "at present inmates earn a base pay ranging from $1.15 up to $2.20 per day, with a $3.00 per day bonus for those employed in industrial areas" (David 1981: 74).

26. The matter of fair compensation is discussed briefly in my paper "The Human Right of Inmates to Work with Just Compensation," 56–7.

27. For a similar argument, by Rawls, see Martin, *Rawls and Rights*, ch. 3, sect. 2; also pp. 82–3, 119–20, 125–26, 144.

28. DeGeorge (1984: 19; see also 20).

29. See Walzer (1983: 105–7, 278), and Harrington (1985, ch. 6, esp. pp. 146–50).

30. I am indebted to Herbert Callison and David Gottlieb for their written comments on an earlier draft of this chapter. And especially indebted to Robert McKay, who was visiting Rice Professor in the School of Law, University of Kansas, for helping me improve my knowledge and understanding of constitutional law and for bibliographic help.

The initial version of this chapter was presented as a paper, delivered to an audience of inmates and others, at the Kansas State Penitentiary, in Lansing, in May 1982.

NOTES TO CHAPTER 12

1. I have taken the term 'system of rights' from Green. See T. H. Green, *Lectures on the Principles of Political Obligation and Other Writings*, ed. Paul Harris and John Morrow (Cambridge: Cambridge University Press, 1986), sects. 1 (p. 13), 9 (p. 16), 16 (p. 20), and 22 (p. 23).

Certain "main elements" in the notion of authority are referred to here, in the sentence to which this note is attached. These elements are, of course, the ones identified and discussed in Chapter 1 of the present book.

2. It is important to avoid misunderstanding and confusion here. At an earlier point I said (in Ch. 7) that democratic institutions were not *necessary* to a system of rights. I claimed there, rather, merely that historical experience indicated that the two tended to go together—that the two seemed to develop more fully, each in the presence of the other. On this basis, and on the basis that political agencies of *some* sort were required, I specified that democratic institutions should be among the institutional essentials of the system of rights under construction in the present study.

In short, other systems of rights are conceivable (or, at least, possible) than the one I have sketched here. But, for the reasons indicated, the one I have had in view is a *particular* theoretic system of rights, one that has among its institutional essentials not only civil rights but also democratic institutions (and, of course, the institutional duty to obey civil rights laws, and the institutions and practices of fair trial and of punishment).

The earlier claim that democratic institutions, though sufficient to produce rights, are not strictly necessary in any conceivable system of rights is fully compatible with the claim I am now making, the claim that the *authority elements* are necessarily present in the system of rights which I have sketched in this book. For these two claims concern quite different matters: the earlier one concerned the necessity of democratic institutions in order for there to be civil rights at all; the present one, assuming the democratic institutions to be among the institutional essentials in a *particular* theoretic system of rights (as constructed), concerns the necessary presence within such a system of the authority elements—that is, of agencies with a title to issue rules, etc.

3. See Bork (1971). Some of the key points made here and the passage quoted can be found on p. 17 of that essay.

A brief aside. It is often unclear, when one talks about constitutions, whether one refers to a document called *the* Constitution (that is, to the written constitution of a particular country) or whether one means to refer to the set of institutional essentials that make up the constitutional system of that same state (for the U.S., for example, it would be institutions or practices like separation of powers, federalism, and so on). I have tried, at various points in the text, to make my meaning clear.

In any event, since almost every contemporary state does have a written constitution, it is important to take some account of such documents and of their role. There are, of course, contemporary states that do not have such constitutions (for example, Great Britain and Israel). Every state, though, does have some privileged or canonical pattern of institutional essentials that marks out its political groundform. In the end, I will come back to this very important consideration, as the decisive one. In the meantime, my remarks will concern only those states (such as the U.S.) that have written constitutions.

4. See Rawls (1982a, sect. 9, esp. pp. 51–3). For discussion, see *Rawls and Rights*, ch. 6, sect. 1, esp. pp. 111–14.

5. Specifically, it is a further working out of the argument in Ch. 7, Sect. 7, as

found at roughly that point in the text where note cue 21 occurs. This argument is further amplified in the Appendix.

6. Points (4) and (5) here follow lines set out in Chs. 5 and 7, principally. Point (5), the importance of which is often neglected, is mentioned in Haskell (1987:1005).

7. For further discussion, of the *current* U.S. Constitution, see my paper "Civil Rights and the U.S. Constitution," in Gary Bryner (ed.), *The Bill of Rights: A Bicentennial Assessment* (Provo, Utah: Brigham Young University [distributed at Albany, NY, by SUNY Press], forthcoming), sect. 5.

8. Gary Shapiro and Allan Hanson have suggested that I needed a hermeneutical dimension in my account of a system of rights, some way of identifying and gauging what is involved in saying that an actual state tends (or does not tend) to exemplify a theoretic system of rights. I have tried to supply this dimension in the last several paragraphs. As regards the historic development of the U.S., in particular, along the second parameter, that of having a harmonious scheme of active civil rights, see ibid., esp. sect. 5.

NOTES TO CHAPTER 13

1. The term 'comprehensive and general' is from Rawls. Critical theories are general, Rawls says, when they apply to "a wide range of subjects of appraisal (in the limit of all subjects universally)" and comprehensive when they include and integrate "conceptions of what is of value in human life, ideals of personal virtue and character and the like, that are to inform much of our conduct (in the limit our life as a whole)." He adds, "Many religious and philosophical doctrines tend to be general and fully comprehensive" (Rawls 1987: 3 n. 4). For further discussion and examples, see Rawls (1987: 6 and 14 n. 23; 1988: 252–3 and 253–4 n. 2; 1989a: 240). I should add that, in the end, he regards most actual critical moral theories, though comprehensive and general in intent, as only *partially* comprehensive and general (see Rawls 1987: 19; 1988: 274–5). Thus, we should properly speak of such theories as *relatively* comprehensive and general.

As I said in the text, I will provide no general account of what is to count as an acceptable critical moral theory. A comment or two on the notion of a critical theory would be helpful, nonetheless. Part of the force of calling such theories critical is that they can be sustained, more or less effectively, in the face of careful philosophical criticism (and have done so over time); and they are compatible with the findings of natural and social science and of historical investigation, as these have developed over time. This at least is an ideal any such theory aspires to, though it is an ideal at best only imperfectly or partially met by actual given theories. Rawls captures this ideal of rational sustainability in his discussion of "free public reason" (see Rawls 1987: 8 and 20, for the phrase; for his further discussion, see 1980: 539–40, also 541–2, where he applies the idea of rational sustainability to the principles of political justice in particular, and 1989a: 244). One further point, to which I would give strong emphasis (though Rawls does not), is that principles found reasonable in a given society (say, for instance, our own) would also, when understood, be thought reasonable (or at least intelligible and plausible) by representative reflective persons in other cultures or in different times.

Thus, critical moral principles are (1) general and comprehensive, even if only relatively so, (2) ideally rationally defensible or sustainable, and (3) judgeable as reasonable across cultures or historical epochs. Rawls addresses this last point (3) in (1989a 245 and 251–2 n. 46). Some of the important points at issue (in [3]) are discussed in my book *Historical Explanation: Re-enactment and Practical Inference* (Ithaca, NY: Cornell University Press, 1977), in the last two chapters, and in two recent papers: "The Problem of Other Cultures and Other Periods in Action Explanations," *Philosophy of the Social Sciences* 21 (1991), 345–66, esp. sects. 2 and 3, and "Intelligibility," *Monist* 74 (1991), 129–48.

2. This way of interpreting Mill stems from an important essay by J. O. Urmson (1953). For the essays by David Lyons that favor this line of interpretation of Mill and that support indirect utilitarianism, see Lyons (1976, 1977, 1978, 1979a,*b*, 1982a). For John Gray, see (1981, esp. 87, 91, 106, 109, 111; 1983, esp. chs. 1 and 2 and pp. 59, 63, 66, 111, 116, 121; and his very judicious paper, 1984: 75, 78–80, 83–4, 85 ff.). See also Fred Berger (1984, esp. ch. 3) and David Brink (1992, esp. 92–103). For the point about the self-defeating character of direct utilitarianism, see Gray (1984: 75, 80–4).

Gray, in particular, provides a useful summary of what he calls the "new wave of Mill scholarship" (1983: 10). For his citation of recent literature see (1981: 113–15 nn. 11 and 14; 1983: 131–2 n. 17 to ch. 1, and 133–4 nn. 14 and 29 to ch. 2; 1984, footnotes *passim*).

Others have recently supported indirect utalitarianism without special or essential reference to Mill. For example, R. B. Brandt (who, incidentally, has little to say about rights *per se* in Brandt 1979, but more to say in Brandt 1983 and 1984a,*b*) and Peter Railton (1984, esp. sects. 6 and 7). And several such theorists are concerned with rights, in particular: see here Wayne Sumner (1987, ch. 6); R. M. Hare (1981, esp. ch. 9, also chs. 1–3, 5–6, and 12 [sects. 6–9]); Allan Gibbard (1984). For discussion of Hare (1981), see Brandt 1984*b*, sect. 3, and Frey (1984), in particular the essays by Frey, Mackie, and Hare on pp. 61–120 and, for background, Hare (1976). For discussion of Gibbard (1984), see Fishkin (1984b) and Gibbard (1990: 221–2, esp. 222).

The idea of constraining the principle of general happiness so as to maximize (or at least increase) general happiness is found at a number of points, for example, in Gray (1983, esp. 65, 68, 94–5, 124). I should add one brief qualification to something said in the text, however. Unlike the others, Lyons says not so much that it is self-defeating as that it is *conceptually improper* to refer moral rules and morally approved basic rights directly to the general happiness principle. He grounds the latter claim by generating the idea of a special realm of morality in which such rules and rights are to be located (see here Lyons 1976: 105; 1978: 7; 1979a: 7).

I am indebted, for discussion and bibliographical suggestions, to Conrad Johnson. I would like to call attention, also, to his book (1991, esp. chs. 5, 9).

3. For Mill's account of the conflict of moral rules, see *Utilitarianism*, ch. 2, last para.; also ch. 5, paras. 32–3, 37. For Gray, see (1983: 42; 1984: 84, 88–90). For Lyons the point of appealing to the general happiness in the event of a conflict of

rules is merely to contribute to an ongoing cumulative ranking of "the opposing obligations" so as to achieve a refined and resultant clear ranking of those obligations, for use on particular occasions of conflict (see Lyons 1976: 115).

4. See Sumner (1987: 187–8 ff., 196–7), and Gray (1984: 85–6, 89).

5. One final consideration is, perhaps, relevant here; we can list it, then, as a *fourth* point in favor of the claim I am making. It is a consideration that many, possibly most, utilitarians would accept (and it was accepted by the great nineteenth-century founders of the doctrine, Bentham, Mill, Sidgwick). It is this: though the general happiness principle (which Bentham called the principle of "the greatest happiness of the greatest number") is related to conventional moral beliefs and practices, it is, nonetheless, a principle that can be stated and accepted (as sound or reasonable) independently of them. It is not necessary, then, to accept the principle (as sound or reasonable) on the basis that it was actually generated as a sort of extrapolation from existing rules (or from existing rights) or as a kind of Baconian generalization from a vast number of occasions (or instances) of good things and of acting well. The principle of general happiness is a self-sufficient one and reasonable in its own terms; thus freed from conceptual or causal dependence on moral rules and constitutional rights, it is able to sit in judgment on them.

6. I have tried to set out and to criticize the utilitarian attempt at a critical justification of basic constitutional rights in several things I have written. See esp. *Rawls and Rights*, ch. 1, sect. 1 (in particular, pp. 4–5 on indirect utilitarianism). See also my review of Sumner (1987)—in *Ethics* 100 (1990), 408–11—and the discussion of Lyons in my article "On the Justification of Rights," in G. Fløistad (ed.), *Contemporary Philosophy: A New Survey* iii: *The Philosophy of Action* (The Hague: M. Nijhoff, 1982), 153–86: 159–66.

I should add that David Lyons has had second thoughts about indirect utilitarianism and has mounted cogent arguments *against* that theory in two of his more recent essays (1980) and (1982b). Here Lyons now disputes the presumed conceptual connection or mutual entailment (referred to in n. 2 above) between moral rules and rights, on the one hand, and a special realm of morality, distinct from but subordinate to the general happiness principle, on the other. For discussion of Lyons (1982b) in particular, see Gewirth (1982, sect. 1), Hare (1982), and Brandt (1984b, sect. 2).

7. Indeed, in Ch. 7 n. 3 it was suggested that this conclusion would be drawn.

8. See Rawls (1982a: 23–9, 47–51, also 74). Rawls offers liberty of conscience or freedom of personal association as examples of liberties justified under the *first* power or interest and freedom of political speech or of assembly as examples under the *second* power. Presumably, all of these liberties could be justified under *both* powers or interests. And some liberties (or protections from injury), for example, the due process rights to such things as fair trial, are justified as necessary to the full flourishing of the liberties justified in the "two fundamental cases." For further discussion, see my book *Rawls and Rights*, ch. 3.

9. For the claim see Rawls (1971: esp. 530–532 and also 533–4). See also Rawls (1982a: 55, 83; 1985: 237 n. 20).

10. Rawls's most recent version of the two principles of justice (from 1982a: 5) reads as follows:

1. Each person has an equal right to a fully adequate scheme of equal basic liberties which is compatible with a similar scheme of liberties for all.
2. Social and economic inequalities are to satisfy two conditions. First, (a) they must be attached to offices and positions open to all under conditions of fair equality of opportunity; and second, (b) they must be to the greatest benefit of the least advantaged members of society.

This formulation is repeated in (1985: 227) and (1989a: 251 n. 43). The relevant priorities here are the usual ones with Rawls, as follows: 1 > 2a, 1 or 2a > 2b.

11. For discussion, see *Rawls and Rights*, ch. 6, sect. 1.
12. In fact, I think it does possess the necessary internal resources to do so; see *Rawls and Rights*, ch. 6, sects. 2–4, esp. 2. But here pursuit of that particular issue is set aside, in deference to consideration of the more fundamental matter raised next in the text of the paragraph to which this note is attached.
13. See Rawls (1971, ch. 3) for his most complete account of the so-called original position. Perhaps, the leading idea in this account, as I suggested in Ch. 6 n. 21 of the present book, is the notion that the "parties" decide about candidate principles of justice behind a "veil of ignorance" (see 1971, ch. 3, sect 24). The veil here is metaphorical. It stands for the idea that certain identifiable, particular facts about the parties (for example, their strength, intelligence, religion, determinate conception of the good) are bracketed off from the discussion, as being prejudicial or irrelevant matters. Here, then, the parties are not allowed to rely on these facts, or to appeal to them in effect, in their arguments or in the decision they make about which candidate principle is to be preferred. In this respect, the veil functions like the instructions a judge makes to a jury to overlook or disregard certain points in their deliberations.
14. Three points are crucial here. First, Rawls consistently identifies the candidates for selection as principles of justice as being those principles afforded by a short list of historically available theories of justice. (For citations here see my book *Rawls and Rights*, 206 n. 27.) Second, the choice problem is typically characterized as an attempt to *rank* these candidate principles (see Rawls 1971: 18; 1978: 61). Finally, Rawls regards the original position as an *objective* forum for making such a ranking among those principles provided by the short list of historical theories. (See Rawls 1971, sect. 78, esp. p. 516, and sect. 87, esp. p. 581; for a similar discussion, of objectivity in Kant's moral philosophy, see Rawls 1989b: 91, also 100–1; in addition, see his discussion of a *fair* decision procedure: 1971: 136, as spelled out in pp. 84–8.) My claim in the text (as to the role Rawls assigned the original position idea in *A Theory of Justice*) follows from these three points.
15. See Rawls (1971, sect. 77; also 1980: 546–51, also 529, 532; 1982a: 15–17, 52, 86; 1985: 233–4, 244–5; 1988: 255 together with 270).
16. For the relevant argument for the first principle, see *Rawls and Rights*, ch. 3, sect. 2; and for the second (for part 2b, the part called the difference principle), see ch. 5, sect. 3, and pp. 104–5.
17. See Rawls (1975; also 1971, sect. 40; 1980, Lecture 2).
18. The main works to consult here are Rawls (1980) and some of his writings thereafter. All the claims cited in this paragraph can be found in each of his later papers (specifically, in Rawls 1985, 1987, 1988, 1989a).

19. In these later writings, as I said, Rawls treats the original position as one of four "model conceptions" (the others are, as noted in the text, the model of the person and the model of the well-ordered society). The original position model is explicitly described as the "mediating" conception among these more fundamental conceptions (see Rawls 1980: 520, 522–3, 533, 566–7; 1982a: 18–19) or as a "device of representation," a device for representing certain considerations as regards moral persons or their cooperation for mutual benefit (see Rawls 1985, sect. 4). And in his *most* recent writings, the original position idea is mentioned only perfunctorily and relegated to the footnotes (see Rawls 1987: 7 n. 13; 1988: 274 n. 32; 1989a: 247 n. 32 and 252 n. 46).

Actually, Rawls introduces (e.g., in 1989a: 240) a fifth model conception: that the idea of the basic structure of a society identifies a unified set of main institutions (unified in the sense that they work *together* to satisfy the two principles of justice) and that the basic structure, so understood, is the principal subject of justice (i.e., the principal object of construction in accordance with the two principles). In any event, since the basic structure and these other models have now assumed more importance in Rawls's account, the original position model recedes considerably, and with it the veil of ignorance. Nonetheless, that model continues to play a modest but necessary role in Rawls's theory, as I have indicated in the text.

20. See, e.g. Rawls (1985: 223–5, esp. n. 2; 1988: 253–4 n. 2).

21. For this point (about moralizing the grounds of the political conception), see Rawls (1985: 247; 1987: 2, 11; 1988, p. 274). See also, in this regard, Rawls's interesting comment on his use of the term 'moral' (in Rawls 1987: 3 n. 2).

22. Two considerations are raised in this paragraph of the text: (1) the role of overlapping consensus in affording stability, (2) the attendant provision of support by the citizens on grounds other than the political conception itself. For (1) see Rawls (1985: 250–1, and 251 n.; 1987: 10–11, 22–4; 1988: 275); for (2) see Rawls (1988: 269).

23. See Rawls (1985: 245–6, esp. n. 28, and 250; 1987: 6, esp. n. 11, and 9). Rawls often refers to these theories as the "liberalisms of Kant and Mill" (e.g., in 1985: 6).

24. See Rawls (1987: 9).

25. Rawls begins his Dewey Lectures with, among other things, the observation that "the search for reasonable grounds for reaching agreement rooted in our conception of ourselves and in our relation to society replaces the search for moral truth interpreted as fixed by a prior and independent order of objects . . . (1980: 519). And in (1980, Lecture 3), he contrasts his own theory (which he calls "constructivism") with rational intuitionism. The rational intuitionist holds to an ideal of moral truth based on the claim that first principles (of morality) are self-evident, reflecting a moral order that has been fixed by "the nature of things" (1980: 557 ff; 1989b: 95–6, 98, 100). The constructivist, to the contrary, sets aside the idea of a fixed and independent moral order and holds that the relevant principles are at best merely " 'reasonable' . . . instead of 'true' " (1980: 569; also 560–1, 564, 566, 570; 1985: 230).

But in (1987: 13 n. 21, 15, and 20 n. 30) Rawls takes a somewhat different tack. He alleges simply that the notion of truth (or moral truth) is not *needed* in the project of constructing the *political* conception of justice (and is not available in any event, for historical and sociological reasons).

The interesting thing, though, is that he now wants to repudiate "scepticism" about certain religious, philosophical, and moral "truths" (1987: 13, 24). He goes so far as to say that his theory, with respect to the idea of "a prior and independent moral order," does *not* "presuppose the controversial metaphysical claim that there is no such order" (1987: 13 n. 21).

In the end, then, I find Rawls's position on moral truth puzzling. It may well be that his political conception *presupposes* neither skepticism nor the *denial* of an independent moral order. But the fact remains that in (1980, Lecture 3) he did seem to deny the usefulness of thinking both that there was such an order (fixed "in the nature of things") and that there could be "truths" about it (knowable by rational intuition). One bit of sorting out that the later writings of Rawls require is to decide whether or not he still adheres to the rigorous and austere constructivism of the Third Dewey Lecture.

In any event, Rawls's more modest claim that talk of moral truth is not required in "justice as fairness" (conceived as political, not metaphysical) would disallow his idea that moral theories (like Kant's) could be "premises" to which the principles of the Rawlsian political conception are "theorems" (cited in the previous note). And it would disallow any idea of "moral geometry" or deductivity (as discussed in the next note).

26. Rawls initially endorsed deductivity as the ideal for the derivation of the two principles from the original position model and the other background elements: "The argument [of *A Theory of Justice*] aims eventually to be strictly deductive .... We should strive for a kind of moral geometry with all the rigor which this name connotes" (Rawls 1971: 121; see also 119, 185). At the very end of the Dewey Lectures, though (and not unexpectedly), he repudiates this ideal quite explicitly when he says "the original position is not an axiomatic (or deductive) basis from which principles are derived" (Rawls 1980: 572).

It may be, though, that Rawls has again had second thoughts and is of a mixed mind. For we find him saying (Rawls 1985: 239 n. 21) that, in *A Theory of Justice*, the "acceptance of ... particular principles of justice is not conjectured as a psychological law or probability but rather follows from the full description of the original position." He then says, in the very next sentence, "Although the aim cannot be perfectly achieved, we want the argument to be deductive, 'a kind of moral geometry.'" (See also Rawls 1985: 237-9, esp 237 n. 20.)

I do not know how to take this particular sentence. It could be taken, first, as a further account of what he had said in *A Theory of Justice*, in which case there is no problem. Or, second, he could be expressing an ideal that he now adheres to (that is, in Rawls 1985, and presumably in subsequent writings), in which case he would have gone back on what he had said at the very end of the Dewey Lectures. Since he seems to be distancing himself from the Third Dewey Lecture this (second) possibility should not be dismissed out of hand. But my inclination is to go with the first reading here.

In the end, though, the substance of the conclusion I want to draw is straightforward and quite simple. A Rawlsian deployment of "moral geometry," in the derivation of the two principles from the original position and other background models, is ruled out by two main considerations. First, such a deployment, even as an ideal, is not consistent with a point that he emphasizes, repeatedly, in his later writings, the point that the choice of the principles of political justice is to be made on the "overall balance of reasons." (This phrase is used in Rawls 1985: 238, to cite just one example.) Second, the balance of reasons idea comports well with Rawls's notion that the ultimate object here is to *rank* competing conceptions of justice; however, if deductivity were the preferred procedure in such a case, then the other conceptions would not be simply downgraded in the ranking but, rather, eliminated altogether, as underivable. (For further discussion see my book *Rawls and Rights*, 16–20 and esp. ch. 1 n. 40, on p. 207.)

If we shifted the focus of Rawlsian "moral geometry" from its initial home (the derivation of the two principles from a description of the original position) to a new one (the derivation of the two principles as "theorems" from "axioms" provided by the comprehensive moral conceptions), we would encounter equally discouraging results. For consider: if the principles of comprehensive moral conceptions were *axioms*, as in the role just described, then moral truths would be *required* in Rawls's theory (in order that the theorems be deductively derivable from the axioms) and this would contradict Rawls's claim (discussed in the previous note) that moral truths are not required in his theory. Not only this. If we sought an *overlapping* consensus here, then the principles of all (or, at least, several) of the competing moral conceptions would have to be true (indeed, would be *required* to be true by Rawls's own theory). This is an implausible result in its own right. Also, it too contradicts Rawls's initial claim that his theory does not require moral truth (let alone truths). And, finally, it goes against Rawls's emphasis on the persistence of reasonable pluralism, where a variety of comprehensive moral and religious conceptions are to be accepted as reasonable but no one of them thought to be true, except from *within* that conception. (On the last of these points, see Rawls 1989*a*, esp. sect. 9.)

27. It is clear that when Rawls cited Mill's theory, as possibly part of the overlapping consensus, he particularly had in mind ch. 3 of Mill's *On Liberty* (1859) as the *locus classicus* of Mill's "liberalism" (the term Rawls normally used to refer to Mill's theory and to group it with Kant's). He does say at one point that Mill's liberalism is not a form of utilitarianism (see Rawls 1982b: 160n.). But the more important point here is that Rawls does not exclude the possibility that Mill's utilitarianism, suitably interpreted, could (unlike Benthamite utilitarianism) be part of the overlapping consensus that supports the Rawlsian political conception of justice. (See here Rawls 1987: 12, esp. nn. 18 and 20; 1989a: 249, esp. n. 39).

I, of course, have tried in my argument (in the previous section of the present chapter) specifically to exclude this very possibility. The main barrier to utilitarian acceptance arises with the element of priority, in Rawls's account as in my own. Specifically, what would bar utilitarians from concurring in the Rawlsian political conception is its inclusion of the claim that the two principles (or, at least, the equal basic liberties) have priority over the common or public good and over "the net balance of advantages." (See Rawls 1980: 562 [for the quoted phrase]; 1982a: 8; 1982b: 183; 1985: 249–50; 1987: 17–18; 1988: 275–6.)

28. For his most recent discussion of Kantian moral philosophy, see Rawls (1989b).

29. For discussion of the point about endless speculation and all but unresolvable dispute, see Rawls (1985: 225–6, 230–1, 249; 1987: 5–6, 12–15; 1989a: 236–8, 249).

I have, in the rough sketch of Rawls's theory of justification offered here, tried to take account of points raised in the review of my book *Rawls and Rights*, in *Ethics* 99 (1988), 155–9, esp. 158. I am indebted to Bart Schultz for those helpful comments.

30. Ted Vaggalis suggested that I make clear that I am not here trying to *refute* indirect utilitarianism, or the Rawlsian theory of justice, or to offer a special ground for rejecting either of them (as accredited critical moral theories) in their apparent failure to do the job of justification for the democratic system of rights. Instead, my point has simply been to assess each of them, preliminarily, as to whether they can accomplish such a justification for that system, given that each could be (and has been) offered as a plausible candidate for the performance of precisely this task.

I am also indebted to Vaggalis for suggesting some of the points made in the paragraph in the text.

31. Again we enter the orbit of issues emphasized by philosophical anarchism, a theory discussed in the very first chapter of the present book. Let me say, then, briefly the bearing I see in the present discussion for that theory.

Philosophical anarchism, historically conceived, is a *moral* critique of the idea of political authority. Its essential claim, put simply, is that such authority, even if politically justified, is morally undesirable. To this extent, then, philosophical anarchism is parasitic on there being at least some creditable theories of critical moral justification. (For discussion see my paper "Anarchism and Skepticism," in J. R. Pennock and John W. Chapman [eds.], *Anarchism*, Nomos, xix [New York: New York University Press, 1978], 115–29, esp. sect. 3.)

The upshot here is this. The failure so far recorded (of utilitarianism and of Rawls's theory of justice to accord a critical moral justification to the democratic system of rights idea) would not support an anarchist conclusion. A total failure to achieve such justification would, however, but only under one condition: that at least one such accredited critical moral theory would support the crucial anarchist claim that no plausible instantiation of the democratic system of rights is morally preferable to the morally best comparable instance of a working social system that lacked government altogether.

In sum, the anarchist scheme itself is one of the competing options that is under judgment by any given theory of critical moral justification. Thus, the favored case for philosophical anarchism is one where a theory of critical moral justification, one that was reasonably thought to be supportive of the democratic system of rights, turned out, on close scrutiny, not to provide that support while, at the same time, affording an endorsement of the overall or systemic features of an anarchist alternative.

In the end, though, I remain doubtful that a case can be made for saying that some relevant variant of an anarchist society—presumably politically organized but without a government—would be morally preferable to *any* workable instantiation of one or another politically justified governmental system. The case that has to be made here is, I am sure it will be recognized, a generalized analogue to what I called earlier in this note the "crucial anarchist claim." (The difference here is that the generalized version is not restricted merely to the subset of instances afforded by the democratic system of rights model.) It is this broader claim, respecting the moral undesirability of *all* state models and all governmental systems, that must be made out if philosophical anarchism is to establish its base contention that a morally justified political authority is, in some deep sense, impossible.

Obviously, then, more needs to be said in this dispute between the partisans of politically justified authority and philosophical anarchism. It is probably best to leave things at that for now.

32. As described in book 6 of Mill's *Logic* (1872 [final edn.]), ch. 10.

33. These remarks are terribly vague. Some suggestions as to the direction of my thinking here might be afforded by the discussion of some issues raised by Wittgenstein, in my book *Historical Explanation*, ch. 10, pp. 203–12, and of some rather obscure sayings of Collingwood, in my paper "Collingwood's Claim that Metaphysics Is a Historical Discipline," *Monist* 72 (1989), 489–525. To this should be added the items cited in the first note of the present chapter.

If my sketchy remarks, at some later point, prove to have merit, then what results will go some way toward repairing the breach that currently exists between philosophy of history and political philosophy. It is often said that analytic philosophy, taken more generally, is a victim of this breach—that analytic political philosophy has no real 'sense of history.' If this is so, and if it is a serious defect, then a successful filling in behind my concluding comments would address this signal defect and try to set things right.

APPENDIX

Addendum to Chapter 7

KRISTER SEGERBERG asks (as I said in Chapter 7 note 21) an important question: Can one be *wrong* about perceived interests? One aspect under which this question could be asked regards the relation of laws and public policies to perceived interests; this aspect was dealt with in Chapter 6. There I suggested that voters might be correct better than half the time as to whether policies did serve their perceived interests— thus, to use the symbolization introduced in that chapter, $p(c) > \frac{1}{2}$. Once we assumed $p(c) > \frac{1}{2}$ for every voter, the desirable thing about majority rule, then, was said to be the epistemological superiority of the social decision—$p(s)$—as regards policies and their relation to perceived interests, when the perceived interests of each of the voters was fed into the mix; for here the probability of correctness was even greater (as to which policies were in the perceived interests of an indeterminately large number—presumably a majority—of these voters). Thus, $p(s) > p(c)$. It was never claimed, of course, that the social decision was infallible, that is, that $p(s) = 1$.

The interest of Segerberg's query, then, must be that it concerns *another* aspect under which the question could be asked. Thus, it could be asked about ways of acting or of being treated, identically the same ways for everyone, whether these ways belonged to or reliably led to perceived benefits. It is to this question, or aspect of the question, that I here reply.

Let us grant that citizens are at least as reflective on this second matter as they were on the first (the Chapter 6 case treated above) and that they are at least as assiduous in gaining relevant knowledge and information in the second case as in the first. Starting thus, we can assume that the probability of judging correctly, as to whether determinate ways of acting or of being treated are parts of, or a means to, perceived beneficial states, is fairly high for any ordinary given individual—say, $p(W_c) > \frac{1}{2}$ but, probably, $p(W_c) < \frac{9}{10}$.

It should not be necessary to assume that the probability of correct judgment is likely going to be lower for such an individual in this second case than the relevant individual judgment was in the first case (the Chapter 6 case). In any event, though, and on parity with the reasoning developed in Chapter 6, we could assume, further, that a *concurrent* social opinion, where a registering of judgment by all people showed that way *A*, say, was relevantly favored by almost all of them, would have a probability of correctness—$p(W_s)$—of very close to 1. Indeed, the probability of correctness of such a highly concurrent social judgment would approximate 1 (i.e., $p(W_s) = 1^*$).

In sum, then, individuals can be wrong, in a given case, as to whether a determinate way of acting or of being treated is part of, or a means to, a state they perceive as beneficial. That does not, however, adversely affect the extremely high probability of correctness of the *social* opinion that could be generated out of these individual judgments, if the resultant social opinion is highly concurrent.

For any civil right to be reasonably thought to be justified, the supporting social opinion must be highly concurrent. The argument I conducted (in particular in

Chapter 7) requires, then, only that *some* social opinions be highly concurrent, specifically those that concern civil rights, or at least many such rights.

And many of those concerning civil rights are highly concurrent, especially if time and experience are factored in. For here the individual's judgment would be one that would be persisted in upon reflection; it would be one that held up under self-examination, under scrutiny by others, under the addition of information from history, from other cultures, and from the facts of science, natural and social.

I do not, of course, say that the probability of correctness of a concurrent social opinion, in the case of any civil right, is 1. It could not be (and need not be). In any event, such opinions, like the judgments of individuals, must be left open to revision and change of mind.

There is one other aspect under which Segerberg's question could be viewed. Here we grant, for purposes of argument, the correctness of the judgment that a given way of acting or of being treated is either a part of or a means to a state perceived as beneficial. We ask, then, whether, when an individual perceives a state as beneficial, it *really* is beneficial. I do not know how to deal with this question. If we were in Plato's heaven, perhaps I would know (if I were one of the gold people rather than a silver or bronze one). But I do not—we do not—occupy that epistemological perspective.

I can identify, then, only one relevant way to address this aspect of Segerberg's question. We would need to move the whole issue back into the arena of *perceived* benefit. Thus, we might then ask about the probability of correctness that a state unfailingly perceived as beneficial up to now would still be perceived as beneficial under some ideal condition (under, say, conditions of sustained reflection on a full life lived in an optimal setting).

I would not know how to answer this question, either. But if we relaxed the conditions to allow for merely adequate reflection and to allow the life to be the sort of life that people, most of them ordinary normal adult citizens, have actually lived and to allow the setting to be, say, an actual parliamentary democracy, then I think we can hazard an answer. For we have, in effect, returned to something like the conditions of our *second* case.

In this second case, individual people do make judgments about whether determinate ways of acting or of being treated are parts of, or do lead to, states they perceive as beneficial. Some of these judgments are incorrect. And people can change their minds, about these judgments and about other things. Thus, they might decide, for example, that they no longer regarded a certain end state, hitherto perceived as beneficial, as beneficial. And this could, in turn, affect their judgment that, for example, a determinate way of acting was a means to a beneficial state.

But it need not affect that particular judgment. For such a change of mind (as to what states are beneficial) is neither a necessary nor a sufficient condition for change of mind about determinate ways of acting or of being treated (as to whether *they* are parts of, or do lead to, states that the individual perceives as beneficial).

In the end such changes by individuals can be interesting to us only if they remove a way of acting or of being treated from the category of mutual perceived benefit, when that way had previously been in it, or only if they add a way to that category, when it had hitherto been absent from that category. Even so, what counts in the evaluation of civil rights is not the correctness of judgment of this individual or that but, rather, the probability of correctness of the relevant social opinion. It is that which must approximate 1 (i.e., $p(W_s) = 1^*$), as it does in cases of concurrent social opinion. And, as I said (in discussing the second case earlier), it is only these social opinions that we are crucially interested in.

It is important that Segerberg's question be answered. But the answer I have given—that individual people can be wrong about many things, even about their own perception of certain states as beneficial—is not threatening to the general drift of my argument. For, if we are seeking evidence for the soundness of the judgment that a given policy can—upon reflection, over time, given experience—reasonably be seen to be for the benefit of each and all, we have that evidence in the claim (rendered true by a highly concurrent social opinion) that $p(W_s) = 1^*$. Such a well-supported judgment is enough to warrant saying that the regulative standard of mutual perceived benefit—the standard of the interest of each and all—has been satisfied by a given policy or a given civil right.

Select Bibliography

Most of the items I have written (or co-authored) that are relevant to this study are listed in Part 2 of this bibliography. A few additional items have been cited in individual notes. These items are not repeated here. Nor are books originally published before 1919 (the end of the First World War) listed again in this bibliography, for all are adequately cited in individual notes. Nor are the doctoral dissertations, court cases, or laws mentioned in the text (or notes) listed again, for the same reason. With these exceptions, everything cited in the present book is listed in Part 1 of the bibliography below, as are a few other pertinent items as well.

A (b) at the end of an entry indicates that the item in question contains a particularly useful bibliography.

PART 1

ABEL, Charles F., and Frank H. MARSH (1984), *Punishment and Restitution: A Restitutionary Approach to Crime and the Criminal* (Westport, Conn.: Greenwood Press).

ACTON, H. B. (ed.) (1969), *The Philosophy of Punishment: A Collection of Papers* (London: Macmillan; New York: St. Martins Press). (b)

AIRAKSINEN, Timo (1984), "Coercion, Deterrence, and Authority," *Theory and Decision* 17: 105–17.

ALLEN, R. E. (1972), "Law and Justice in Plato's *Crito*," *Journal of Philosophy* 69: 557–67.

——(1980), *Socrates and Legal Obligation* (Minneapolis, Minn.: University of Minnesota Press). (Includes new translations of the *Apology*, pp. 37–62, and the *Crito*, pp. 115–28.)

American Law Institute (1962), *Model Penal Code: Official Draft and Explanatory Notes*, adopted May 24, 1962 (Philadelphia: American Law Institute, 1985).

American Psychiatric Association (1983), "Statement on the Insanity Defense," *American Journal of Psychiatry* 140. G: 681–8. (This statement was adopted in December 1982.)

ARROW, Kenneth J. (1963), *Social Choice and Individual Values*, Cowles Foundation Research in Economics at Yale University, monograph no. 12, 2nd edn. (New Haven, Conn.: Yale University Press). (First pub. New York: John Wiley, 1951.)

BANDMAN, Bertram (1973), "Rights and Claims," *Journal of Value Inquiry* 7: 204–13.

BARNETT, Randy E. (1977), "Restitution: A New Paradigm of Criminal Justice," *Ethics* 87: 279–301.

——(1980), "The Justice of Restitution," *American Journal of Jurisprudence* 25: 117–32.

BARNHART, J. E. (1969), "Human Rights as Absolute Claims and Reasonable Expectations," *American Philosophical Quarterly* 6: 335–39.

BARRY, Brian. (1965), *Political Argument* (London: Routledge and Kegan Paul).

——(1967), "The Public Interest," in Anthony Quinton (ed.), *Political Philosophy*

418   Select Bibliography

(Oxford: Oxford University Press), 112–26. (Reprinted from *Proceedings of the Aristotelian Society*, suppl. vol. 38 [1964], 1–18.)

BAYLES, Michael D. (1972), "A Concept of Coercion," in J. Roland Pennock and John W. Chapman (eds.), *Coercion*, Nomos, xiv (Chicago: Aldine-Atherton), 16–29.

BECKER, Lawrence C. (1980), "The Obligation to Work," *Ethics* 91: 35–49.

BEDAU, Hugo A. (1968), "The Right to Life," *Monist* 52: 550–72.

——(1981), "How to Argue about Prisoners' Rights: Some Simple Ways," *Rutgers Law Review* 33: 687–705. (The original version of this paper is found in Bedau 1982b: 335–44.)

——(ed.) (1982a), *The Death Penalty in America*, 3rd edn. (New York: Oxford University Press).

——(1982b), "Prisoners' Rights," in Elliston and Bowie (1982: 321–46). (Also pub. in *Criminal Justice Ethics* 1 [1982], 26–41.)

——(1986), "Capital Punishment," in Tom Regan (ed.), *Matters of Life and Death: New Introductory Essays in Moral Philosophy*, 2nd edn. (New York: Random House), 175–212. (First pub. 1980.)

BENN, S. I. (1967), "Punishment," in Paul Edwards (ed.), *Encyclopedia of Philosophy*, vii (New York: Macmillan and Free Press), 29–36.

——and R. S. PETERS (1965), *The Principles of Political Thought* (New York: Free Press). (First pub. as *Social Principles and the Democratic State* [London: Allen and Unwin, 1959].)

BERGER, Fred R. (1984), *Happiness, Justice, and Freedom: The Moral Philosophy of John Stuart Mill* (Berkeley, Calif.: University of California Press).

BEVERIDGE, William (1944), *Full Employment in a Free Society: A Report* (London: George Allen and Unwin).

BICKEL, Alexander M. (1955), "The Original Understanding and the Segregation Decision," *Harvard Law Review* 69: 1–65.

BLACK, Duncan. (1968), *The Theory of Committees and Elections* (Cambridge: Cambridge University Press). (First pub. 1958.)

BONNIE, Richard J. (1983), "The Moral Basis of the Insanity Defense," *American Bar Association Journal* 69: 194–7.

——(1984), "Morality, Equality, and Expertise: Renegotiating the Relationship between Psychiatry and the Criminal Law," *Bulletin of the American Academy of Psychiatry and the Law* 12. 1: 5–20.

BORK, Robert H. (1971), "Neutral Principles and Some First Amendment Problems," *Indiana Law Journal* 47: 1–35.

BRANDT, Richard B. (1979), *A Theory of the Good and the Right* (Oxford: Oxford University Press).

——(1983), "The Concept of a Moral Right and its Function." *Journal of Philosophy* 80: 29–45.

——(1984a), "Comments on Professor Card's Critique," *Canadian Journal of Philosophy* 14: 31–7.

——(1984b), "Utilitarianism and Moral Rights," *Canadian Journal of Philosophy* 14: 1–19.

BRAYBROOKE, David (1972), "The Firm but Untidy Correlativity of Rights and Obligations," *Canadian Journal of Philosophy* 1: 351–63.

BRINK, David O. (1992), "Mill's Deliberative Utilitarianism," *Philosophy and Public Affairs* 21: 67–103.

BROOKS, Alexander D. (1974), *Law, Psychiatry, and the Mental Health System* (Boston: Little, Brown).

BROWNLIE, Ian (ed.) (1981), *Basic Documents on Human Rights*, 2nd edn. (Oxford: Oxford University Press).

BUCHANAN, James M., and Gordon TULLOCH (1965), *The Calculus of Consent: Logical Foundations of Constitutional Democracy* (Ann Arbor, Mich.: University of Michigan Press). (First pub. 1962.)

CALLISON, Herbert G. (1983), *Introduction to Community-Based Corrections*, Series in Criminology and Criminal Justice (New York: McGraw-Hill).

CHAFEE, Zecharia, Jr. (1968), *Three Human Rights in the Constitution of 1787* (Lawrence, Kan.: University Press of Kansas).

CHILDRESS, James (1971), *Civil Disobedience and Political Obligation* (New Haven, Conn.: Yale University Press).

COLLINGWOOD, R. G. (1940), *An Essay on Metaphysics* (Oxford: Oxford University Press).

COMMAGER, Henry Steele (1943), *Majority Rule and Minority Rights*, the James W. Richards Lectures in History at the University of Virginia (New York: Oxford University Press).

CRANSTON, Maurice. (1967a), "Human Rights: A Reply to Professor Raphael," in Raphael (1967b: 95–100).

——(1967b), "Human Rights, Real and Supposed," in Raphael (1967b: 43–53).

——(1973), *What Are Human Rights?* 2nd edn. (London: Bodley Head).

DAHL, Robert A. (1956), *A Preface to Democratic Theory* (Chicago, Ill.: University of Chicago Press).

DAVID, Marjorie M. (1981), "Canadian Correctional Industries: The Total Perspective," *Corrections Today* (Nov.–Dec. 1981), 73–6.

DECEW, Judith Wagner (1988), "Moral Rights: Conflicts and Valid Claims," *Philosophical Studies* 54: 63–86.

DEGEORGE, Richard T. (1984), "The Right to Work: Law and Ideology," *Valparaiso University Law Review* 19: 15–35.

——(1985), *The Nature and Limits of Authority* (Lawrence, Kan.: University Press of Kansas). (b: "Bibliographic Essay," 293–9)

DEL VECCHIO, Giorgio (1969), "The Struggle against Crime," tr. from the Italian by A. H. Campbell, in Acton (1969: 197–203). (First pub. in Italian, 1965.)

DONNELLY, Jack (1985), *The Concept of Human Rights* (New York: St. Martin's Press).

DUFF, R. A. (1986), *Trials and Punishment*, Cambridge Studies in Philosophy (Cambridge: Cambridge University Press).

DUMMETT, Michael (1984), *Voting Procedures* (Oxford: Oxford University Press).

DWORKIN, Ronald (1978), *Taking Rights Seriously* (Cambridge, Mass.: Harvard University Press). (First pub. 1977; repub. with appendix added, pp. 291–368.)

——(1985), *A Matter of Principle* (Cambridge, Mass.: Harvard University Press).

——(1986), *Law's Empire* (Cambridge, Mass.: Harvard University Press).

ELLISTON, Frederick, and Norman BOWIE (eds.) (1982), *Ethics, Public Policy, and Criminal Justice* (Cambridge, Mass.: Oelgeschlager, Gunn, and Hain). (b)

ELY, John Hart (1980), *Democracy and Distrust: A Theory of Judicial Review* (Cambridge, Mass.: Harvard University Press).

EPSTEIN, Richard A. (1980), *A Theory of Strict Liability: Toward a Reformulation of Tort Law*, Cato Paper no. 8 (San Francisco, Calif.: Cato Institute). (Part 1 is a reprint of "A Theory of Strict Liability," *Journal of Legal Studies* 2 [1973], 151–204; part 2 is a reprint of "Defenses and Subsequent Pleas in a Theory of Strict Liability," *Journal of Legal Studies* 3 [1974], 165–215.)

EUBEN, J. Peter (1978), "Philosophy and Politics in Plato's *Crito*," *Political Theory* 6: 149–72.

FAIN, Haskell (1972), "The Idea of the State," *Nous* 6: 15–26.

FARQUHARSON, Robin (1969), *Theory of Voting* (New Haven, Conn.: Yale University Press).

FARRELL, Daniel M. (1978), "Illegal Actions, Universal Maxims, and the Duty to Obey the Law: The Case for Civil Authority in the *Crito*," *Political Theory* 6: 173–89.

FEINBERG, Joel (1963), "Justice and Personal Desert," in Carl J. Friedrich and John W. Chapman (eds.), *Justice*, Nomos, vi (New York: Atherton Press), 69–97. (Reprinted, with slight change, in Feinberg 1970a: 55–87.)

——(1964), "Wasserstrom on Human Rights," *Journal of Philosophy* 61: 641–5.

——(1965), "The Expressive Function of Punishment," *Monist* 49: 397–423. (Reprinted, with virtually no change, in Feinberg 1970a: 95–118.)

——(1966), "Duties, Rights and Claims," *American Philosophical Quarterly* 3: 137–44.

——(1970a), *Doing and Deserving: Essays in the Theory of Responsibility* (Princeton, NJ: Princeton University Press).

——(1970b), "The Nature and Value of Rights," *Journal of Value Inquiry* 4: 243–57. (This paper is a revised version of the paper Feinberg delivered to the American Section of the International Association for Philosophy of Law and Social Philosophy [AMINTAPHIL] in 1970.)

——(1973), *Social Philosophy*, Foundations of Philosophy (Englewood Cliffs, NJ: Prentice-Hall). (Ch. 4 follows Feinberg 1970b closely.)

——(1974), "The Rights of Animals and Unborn Generations," in William T. Blackstone (ed.), *Philosophy and Environmental Crisis* (Athens, Ga.: University of Georgia Press), 43–68.

——(1978), "Voluntary Euthanasia and the Inalienable Right to Life," *Philosophy and Public Affairs* 7: 99–123.

——(1980), *Rights, Justice, and the Bounds of Liberty* (Princeton, NJ: Princeton University Press). (A collection of Feinberg's writings; includes 1966, 1970b, 1974, and 1978.)

FINGARETTE, Herbert (1982), "What is Criminal Insanity?", in Elliston and Bowie (1982: 228–44).

FISCHER, John Martin, and Robert H. ENNIS (1986), "Causation and Liability," *Philosophy and Public Affairs* 15: 33–40.

FISHKIN, James (1979), "Moral Principles and Public Policy," *Daedalus* 108: 55–67.

——(1984a), *Beyond Subjective Morality: Ethical Reasoning and Political Philosophy* (New Haven, Conn.: Yale University Press).

——(1984b), "Comment on Gibbard: Utilitarianism versus Human Rights," *Social Philosophy and Policy* 1: 103–7. (Reprinted in Paul et al. 1984.)

FLETCHER, George P. (1980), "The Right to Life," *Monist* 63: 135–55.

FREY, R. G. (ed.) (1984), *Utility and Rights* (Minneapolis: University of Minnesota Press).

FUCHS, Alan (1981), "Taking Absolute Rights Seriously," *Filosofia del Derecho y Filosofia Politica* 2: 107–21. Memoria del X Congresso Mundial Ordinario de Filosofia del Derecho y Filosofia Politica, Mexico City (Mexico, DF: Universidad Nacional Autonomia de Mexico).

GALLIE, W. B. (1968), *Philosophy and the Historical Understanding*, 2nd edn. (New York: Schocken Books).

GAUS, Gerald F. (1989), "A Contractual Justification of Redistributive Capitalism," in John W. Chapman and J. Roland Pennock (eds.), *Markets and Justice*, Nomos, xxxi (New York: New York University Press), 89–121.

——(1990), "The Commitment to the Common Good," in Paul Harris (ed.), *On Political Obligation* (London: Routledge), 26–64.

GAUTHIER, David (1986), *Morals by Agreement* (Oxford: Oxford University Press).

GEERTZ, Clifford (1980), *Negara: The Theatre State in Nineteenth-Century Bali* (Princeton, NJ: Princeton University Press).

GERT, Bernard (1973), *The Moral Rules: A New Rational Foundation for Morality* (New York: Harper Torchbook). (First pub. 1966.)

GEWIRTH, Alan (1981), "Are There Any Absolute Rights?" *Philosophical Quarterly* 31: 1–16.

——(1982), "Can Utilitarianism Justify Any Moral Rights?" in J. R. Pennock and J. W. Chapman (eds.), *Ethics, Economics, and the Law*, Nomos, xxiv (New York: New York University Press), 158–93.

GIBBARD, Allan (1984), "Utilitarianism and Human Rights," *Social Philosophy and Policy* 1: 93–102. (Reprinted in Paul *et al.* 1984.)

——(1990) *Wise Choices, Apt Feelings: A Theory of Normative Judgment* (Cambridge, Mass.: Harvard University Press).

GOEHLERT, Robert (1976), "Anarchism: A Bibliography of Articles, 1900–1975," *Political Theory* 4: 113–27. (b)

GOLDING, Martin (1991), "The Significance of Rights Language," *Philosophical Topics* 18: 53–64.

GOLDINGER, Milton (1965), "Punishment, Justice, and the Separation of Issues," *Monist* 49: 458–74.

GOLDMAN, Alan H. (1979), "The Paradox of Punishment," *Philosophy and Public Affairs* 9: 43–58.

GOLDSMITH, M. M. (1977), "Allegiance," in Preston T. King (ed.), *The Study of Politics: A Collection of Inaugural Lectures* (London: Frank Cass), 245–63. (Goldsmith's lecture was given on the occasion of his induction into the chair of Politics at the University of Exeter, 12 Nov. 1970.)

GOLDSTEIN, Abraham (1967), *The Insanity Defense* (New Haven, Conn.: Yale University Press).

GOROVITZ, Samuel (ed.) (1971), *"Utilitarianism" [by] J. S. Mill, with Critical Essays*, Text and Critical Essays (Indianapolis: Bobbs-Merrill).

GRAY, John (1981), "John Stuart Mill on Liberty, Utility, and Rights," in J. R. Pennock and John W. Chapman (eds.), *Human Rights*, Nomos, xxiii (New York: New York University Press), 80–116.

——(1983), *Mill on Liberty: A Defence* (London: Routledge and Kegan Paul).

——(1984), "Indirect Utility and Fundamental Rights," *Social Philosophy and Policy* 1. 2: 73–91. (Reprinted in Paul *et al.* 1984: 73–91.)

GREENBERG, Jack (1974), "Litigation for Social Change: Methods, Limits, and Role in Democracy," *The Record of the Association of the Bar of the City of New York* 29: 320–75. (Greenberg's paper, the thirtieth annual Benjamin Cardozo Lecture, for 1973, has been reprinted, under the same title, as a separate hardback volume: New York: Association of the Bar of the City of New York, 1974.)

GRIFFIN, Stephen M. (1987), "Reconstructing Rawls's Theory of Justice: Developing a Public Values Philosophy of the Constitution," *New York University Law Review* 62: 715–85.

—— (1989), "What Is Constitutional Theory? The Newer Theory and the Decline of the Learned Tradition," *Southern California Law Review* 62: 493–538.

GRISSOM, G. R., and C. N. LEWIS (1981), "The Evolution of Prison Industries," *Corrections Today* (Nov.–Dec.), 42–3, 46–8, 50.

GROFMAN, Bernard, and Scott L. FELD (1988), "Rousseau's General Will: A Condorcetian Perspective," *American Political Science Review* 82: 567–76.

HALL, Robert T. (1971), *The Morality of Civil Disobedience* (New York: Harper and Row).

HARE, R. M. (1976), "Ethical Theory and Utilitarianism," in H. D. Lewis (ed.), *Contemporary British Philosophy: Personal Statements*, 4th series (London: George Allen and Unwin), 113–31.

—— (1981), *Moral Thinking: Its Levels, Method and Point* (Oxford: Oxford University Press).

—— (1982), "Utility and Rights: Comment on David Lyons's Essay," in J. R. Pennock and J. W. Chapman (eds.), *Ethics, Economics, and the Law*, Nomos, xxiv (New York: New York University Press), 148–57.

HARRINGTON, Michael (1985), *The New American Poverty* (New York: Penguin Books). (First pub. New York: Holt, 1984.)

HARRIS, Marvin (1977), *Cannibals and Kings: The Origins of Cultures* (New York: Random House).

HARRIS, Paul (1986), "Green's Theory of Political Obligation and Disobedience," in Andrew Vincent (ed.), *The Philosophy of T. H. Green* (Aldershot: Gower), 127–42.

—— (ed.) (1989), *Civil Disobedience* (Lanham, Md.: University Press of America). (b)

HART, Herbert L. A. (1954), "Definition and Theory in Jurisprudence," *Law Quarterly Review* 70: 37–60. (This article is Hart's inaugural lecture as Professor of Jurisprudence at Oxford, which was published under the same title in a lecture pamphlet, by Oxford University Press, 1953; the article and the inaugural lecture are identical except that the article omits the very first para. of the lecture.)

—— (1955), "Are There Any Natural Rights?" *Philosophical Review* 64: 175–91.

—— (1961), *The Concept of Law* (Oxford: Oxford University Press).

—— (1968), *Punishment and Responsibility: Essays in the Philosophy of Law* (New York: Oxford University Press).

—— (1973), "Bentham on Legal Rights," in A. W. Simpson (ed.), *Oxford Essays in Jurisprudence*, 2nd series (Oxford: Oxford University Press). 171–201. (Reprinted, unchanged, as ch. 7, pp. 162–93 in H. L. A. Hart, *Essays on Bentham: Studies in Jurisprudence and Political Theory* [Oxford: Oxford University Press, 1982].)

HASKELL, Thomas (1987), "The Curious Persistence of Rights Talk in the 'Age of Interpretation,'" *Journal of American History* 74: 984–1012.

HELD, Virginia (1984), *Rights and Goods: Justifying Social Action* (New York: Free Press).

HEMPEL, Carl G. (1962), "Rational Action," *Proceedings and Addresses of the American Philosophical Association* 35: 5–23.

HOHFELD, Wesley N. (1964), *Fundamental Legal Conceptions* (New Haven, Conn.: Yale University Press). (The two papers printed under the above title first appeared as articles in the *Yale Law Journal*, one in vol. 23 [1913], 16–59, and the other in vol. 26 [1917], 710–70. Subsequent to Hohfeld's untimely death in 1918 the articles were reprinted, with manuscript changes by the author, in a single book by Yale University Press, 1919, edited and with an introduction by Walter W. Cook. This book has been reprinted twice: once in 1923 and again in 1964, in the latter case with an additional foreword [by Arthur L. Corbin].)

HURKA, Thomas (1982), "Rights and Capital Punishment," *Dialogue* 21: 647–60.

——(1984), "Rights and Punishment: A Reply to McKerlie," *Dialogue* 23: 141–48.

JAMES, G. G. (1973), "Socrates on Civil Disobedience and Rebellion," *Southern Journal of Philosophy* 11: 119–27.

JOHNSON, Conrad D. (1991), *Moral Legislation: A Legal–Political Model for Indirect Consequentialist Reasoning* (Cambridge: Cambridge University Press).

KAGAN, Shelly (1986), "Causation, Liability, and Internalism," *Philosophy and Public Affairs* 15: 41–59.

KAMENKA, E., and A. E. S. TAY (eds.) (1978), *Human Rights* (London: Edward Arnold; New York: St. Martin's Press).

KEYT, David (1985), "Distributive Justice in Aristotle's *Ethics* and *Politics*," *Topoi* 4: 23–45.

KRANTZ, Sheldon (1983), *The Law of Corrections and Prisoners' Rights*, Nutshell, 2nd edn. (St. Paul: West). (First pub. 1976.)

KRAUT, Richard (1981), "Plato's *Apology* and *Crito*: Two Recent Studies," *Ethics* 91: 651–64.

LASKY, Melvin J. (1969), "The Sweet Dream: Kant and the Revolutionary Hope for Utopia," *Encounter* 33 (4 Oct.), 14–27.

LA TORRE, Massimo (1988), "Reason in Rights: Reflections on Rationality and Law," in *Reason in Law*, Proceedings of the Conference held in Bologna, 12–15 December 1984, iii (Milan: A. Giuffrè), 359–79.

Law Review Note (1955), "Custom and Trade Usage: Its Application to Commercial Dealings and Common Law," *Columbia Law Review* 55: 1192–1209.

LEMOS, Ramon M. (1986), *Rights, Goods, and Democracy* (Newark, Del.: University of Delaware Press).

LEÓN-PORTILLA, Miguel (1963), *Aztec Thought and Culture: A Study of the Ancient Nahuatl Mind* (Norman, Okla.: University of Oklahoma Press). (*La Filosofía Náhuatl* was first pub. in 1956; a 2nd edn. was issued in 1959 by the National University of Mexico. "The present English edition is not a direct translation of the second edition in Spanish, but rather an adaptation and rewriting of the text" [p. viii]. Translated from the Spanish by Jack Emory Davis.)

——(1964), "Philosophy in the Cultures of Ancient Mexico," in F. S. C. Northrop and Helen H. Livingston (eds.), *Cross-Cultural Understanding: Epistemology in Anthropology* (New York: Harper and Row), 35–54.

LEIVESTAD, T. (1938), "Custom as a Type of Law," *Law Quarterly Review*, part 1: 213: 95–115; part 2: 214: 266–86.

LEWIS, Thomas J. (1989), "On Using the Concept of Hypothetical Consent," *Canadian Journal of Political Science* 22: 793–807.

LINDSAY, A. D. (1934), *Kant* (London: Benn).

LUCAS, Billy Joe (1988), "Plato's *Crito* as a Contribution to Philosophy of Law," in S. Panou, G. Bozonis, D. Georgas, and P. Trappe (eds.), *Philosophy of Law in the History of Human Thought*, part 1 (Stuttgart: F. Steiner), 27–31.

LYONS, David (1969), "Rights, Claimants, and Beneficiaries," *American Philosophical Quarterly* 6: 173–85.

——(1970), "The Correlativity of Rights and Duties," *Nous* 4: 45–55.

——(1976), "Mill's Theory of Morality," *Nous* 10: 101–20.

——(1977), "Human Rights and the General Welfare," *Philosophy and Public Affairs* 6: 113–29.

——(1978), "Mill's Theory of Justice," in Alvin I. Goldman and J. Kim (eds.), *Values and Morals* (Dordrecht: Reidel), 1–20.

——(1979a), Introduction, in D. Lyons (ed.), *Rights* (Belmont, Calif.: Wadsworth), 1–13.

——(1979b), "Mill on Liberty and Harm to Others," in W. E. Cooper, Kai Nielsen, and S. C. Patten (eds.), *New Essays on John Stuart Mill and Utilitarianism*, *Canadian Journal of Philosophy*, suppl. vol. 5: 1–19.

——(1980), "Utility as a Possible Ground for Rights," *Nous* 14: 17–28.

——(1982a), "Benevolence and Justice in Mill," in H. B. Miller and W. H. Williams (eds.), *The Limits of Utilitarianism* (Minneapolis: University of Minnesota Press), 42–70.

——(1982b), "Utility and Rights," in J. R. Pennock and J. W. Chapman (eds.), *Ethics, Economics, and the Law*, Nomos, xxiv (New York: New York University Press), 107–38.

——(1984), *Ethics and the Rule of Law* (Cambridge: Cambridge University Press).

MABBOTT, J. D. (1969), "Punishment," in Acton (1969: 39–54). (First pub. in *Mind* 48 [1939]: 152–67.)

MACCALLUM, G. C. (1967), "Negative and Positive Freedom," *Philosophical Review* 76: 312–34.

——(1987), *Political Philosophy*, Foundations of Philosophy (Englewood Cliffs, NJ: Prentice-Hall).

MCCLENNEN, Edward F. (1989), "Justice and the Problem of Stabillity," *Philosophy and Public Affairs* 18: 3–30.

MCCLOSKEY, H.J. (1965), "Rights," *Philosophical Quarterly* 15:115–27.

——(1971a), "An Examination of Restricted Utilitarianism," in Gorovitz (1971: 204–16). (First pub. in *Philosophical Review* 66 [1957]: 466–85.)

——(1971b), "Utilitarian and Retributive Punishment," in Gorovitz (1971: 361–75). (First pub. in *Journal of Philosophy* 64 [1967]: 91–110.)

——(1975), "The Right to Life," *Mind* 84: 403–23.

——(1976), "Rights: Some Conceptual Issues," *Australasian Journal of Philosophy* 54: 99–115.

MACCORMICK, D. N. (1977), "Rights in Legislation," in P. M. S. Hacker and J. Raz (eds.), *Law, Morality and Society: Essays in Honour of H. L. A. Hart* (Oxford: Oxford University Press), ch. 11, pp. 189–209.

——(1977–8), "The Obligation of Reparation," *Proceedings of the Aristotelian Society*, n.s. 78: 175–93.

——(1983), "Rights, Claims, and Remedies," in M. A. Stewart (ed.), *Law,*

Morality, and Rights, Royal Institute of Philosophy Conference, University of Lancaster, 1979 (Dordrecht: D. Reidel), 161–81.

McCULLAGH, C. Behan (1984), *Justifying Historical Descriptions* (Cambridge: Cambridge University Press).

MACDONALD, Margaret (1946–7), "Natural Rights," *Proceedings of the Aristotelian Society* 47: 225–50. (Reprinted in Melden 1970: 40–60.)

MACFARLANE, L. J. (1985), *The Theory and Practice of Human Rights* (London: Maurice Temple Smith).

McILWAIN, Charles H. (1932), *The Growth of Political Thought in the West: From the Greeks to the End of the Middle Ages* (New York: Macmillan).

McLAUGHLIN, Robert J. (1976), "Socrates on Political Disobedience," *Phronesis* 21: 185–97.

MACPHERSON, C. B. (1966), *The Real World of Democracy*, The Massey Lectures, Canadian Broadcasting System, 1965 (Oxford: Oxford University Press).

——(1977), *The Life and Times of Liberal Democracy* (Oxford: Oxford University Press).

McPHERSON, Thomas (1967), *Political Obligation* (London: Routledge and Kegan Paul).

MAY, K. O. (1952), "A Set of Independent Necessary and Sufficient Conditions for Simple Majority Decision," *Econometrica* 20: 680–4.

MAYO, Bernard (1965), Symposium on Human Rights, II, *Proceedings of the Aristotelian Society*, suppl. vol. 39: 219–36. (Reprinted in shortened form as "What Are Human Rights?" in Raphael 1967b: 68–80.)

MELDEN, A. I. (ed.) (1970), *Human Rights* (Belmont, Calif.: Wadsworth).

——(1972), "The Play of Rights," *Monist* 56: 479–502.

——(1977), *Rights and Persons* (Oxford: Blackwell; Berkeley, Calif.: University of California Press). (Ch. 1 incorporates, with revisions, Melden 1972.)

MELOSSI, Dario, and Massimo PAVARINI (1981), *The Prison and the Factory: Origins of the Penitentiary System*, tr. G. Cousin, Critical Criminology (London: Macmillan). (First pub. as *Carcere e fabbrice* [Bologna: Società editrice il Mulino, 1977; 2nd edn. 1979]. The English-language text is based on the 1979 edn.)

MILNE, A. J. M (1986a), "The Common Good and Rights in T. H. Green's Ethical and Political Theory," in Andrew Vincent (ed.), *The Philosophy of T. H. Green* (Aldershot: Gower), 62–75.

——(1986b), *Human Rights and Human Diversity: An Essay in the Philosophy of Human Rights* (Albany, NY: State University of New York Press).

MONTAGUE, Phillip (1984), "Rights and Duties of Compensation," *Philosophy and Public Affairs* 13: 79–88.

MOORE, Michael S. (1984), *Law and Psychiatry: Rethinking the Relationship* (Cambridge: Cambridge University Press).

MUNDLE, C. W. K. (1954), "Punishment and Desert," *Philosophical Quarterly* 4: 216–28. (The Postscript [1968] is found in Acton 1969: 81–2.)

MURPHY, J. G., and Jules COLEMAN (1990), *Philosophy of Law: An Introduction to Jurisprudence*, rev. edn. (Boulder, Colo.: Westview Press).

NELSON, William N. (1974), "Special Rights, General Rights, and Social Justice," *Philosophy and Public Affairs* 3: 410–30.

——(1980), *Justifying Democracy*, International Library of Philosophy (London: Routledge and Kegan Paul).

NELSON, William N. (1988), "Constitutional Limits on Majoritarian Democracy," in Diana T. Meyers and Kenneth Kipnis (eds.), *Philosophical Dimensions of the Constitution*, an Amintaphil volume (Boulder, Colo.: Westview Press), 75–90.

NETT, Roger (1971), "The Civil Right We Are Not Ready For: The Right of Free Movement of People on the Face of the Earth," *Ethics* 81: 212–27.

NICKEL, James W. (1978–9), "Is there a Human Right to Employment?" *Philosophical Forum* 10: 149–70.

——(1987), *Making Sense of Human Rights: Philosophical Reflections on the Universal Declaration of Human Rights* (Berkeley, Calif.: University of California Press).

NINO, Carlos Santiago (1991), *The Ethics of Human Rights* (Oxford: Oxford University Press). (This book is based on Nino's book, in Spanish, *Ética y derechos humanos* [Buenos Aires: Paidós, 1984; 2nd edn. Buenos Aires: Astrea; Barcelona: Ariel, 1989].)

NORTH, D. Warner (1990), "A Tutorial Introduction to Decision Theory," in Shafer and Pearl (1990: 68–78). (First pub. under the same title in *IEEE Transactions on Systems Science and Cybernetics* SSC-4. 3 [Sept. 1968].)

NOZICK, Robert (1972), "Coercion," in P. Laslett, W. G. Runciman, and Q. Skinner (eds.), *Philosophy, Politics, and Society*, 4 series (Oxford: Blackwell, 1972), 101–35. (First pub. in slightly different form in S. Morgenbesser, Patrick Suppes, and Morton White [eds.], *Philosophy, Science, and Method: Essays in Honor of Ernest Nagel* [New York: St. Martin's Press, 1969], 440–72.)

——(1974), *Anarchy, State, and Utopia* (New York: Basic Books).

——(1981), *Philosophical Explanations* (Cambridge, Mass.: Harvard University Press).

PATEMAN, Carole (1985), *The Problem of Political Obligation: A Critique of Liberal Theory* (Cambridge: Polity Press, in association with Blackwell, Oxford). (First pub. New York: John Wiley, 1979.)

PAUL, E. F., Fred D. MILLER, Jr., and Jeffrey PAUL (eds.) (1984), *Human Rights* (Oxford: Blackwell).

PENNOCK, J. R., and John W. CHAPMAN (eds.) (1978), *Anarchism*, Nomos, xix (New York: New York University Press). (b: pp. 341–65)

PILON, Roger (1985), "Legislative Activism, Judicial Activism, and the Decline of Private Sovereignty," *Cato Journal* 4: 813–33.

PLOTT, Charles R., and Michael E. LEVINE (1978), "A Model of Agenda Influence on Committee Decisions," *American Economic Review* 68: 146–60.

POPPER, Karl R. (1950), *The Open Society and its Enemies*, rev. edn. (Princeton, NJ: Princeton University Press). (First pub. in 2 vols., London: Routledge and Kegan Paul, 1945.)

QUINTON, Anthony (1954), "On Punishment," in Acton (1969: 55–64). (First pub. in *Analysis* 14 [1954]: 133–42.)

RADDEN, Jennifer (1985), *Madness and Reason* (London: George Allen and Unwin).

RAILTON, Peter (1984), "Alienation, Consequentialism, and the Demands of Morality," *Philosophy and Public Affairs* 13: 134–71.

RAPHAEL, David Daiches (1967a), "Human Rights, Old and New," in Raphael (1967b: 54–67). (Reprinted from the Symposium on Human Rights, *Aristotelian Society* suppl. vol. 39 [1965], 205–18.)

——(ed.) (1967b), *Political Theory and the Rights of Man* (Bloomington, Ind.: Indiana University Press).

—— (1967c), "The Rights of Man and the Rights of the Citizen," in Raphael (1967b: 101–18).

—— (1970), *Problems of Political Philosophy* (London: Pall Mall Press).

RAWLS, John (1955), "Two Concepts of Rules," *Philosophical Review* 64: 3–32.

—— (1971), *A Theory of Justice* (Cambridge, Mass.: Harvard University Press).

—— (1974), "Reply to Alexander and Musgrave," *Quarterly Journal of Economics* 88: 633–55.

—— (1975), "A Kantian Conception of Equality," *Cambridge Review* (Feb.), 94–9. (The essay, slightly revised, has been reprinted twice, most recently in Virginia Held (ed.), *Property, Profits, and Economic Justice* [Belmont, Calif.: Wadsworth, 1980], 198–208.)

—— (1977), "The Basic Structure as Subject," *American Philosophical Quarterly* 14: 159–65.

—— (1978), "The Basic Structure as Subject," in Alvin I. Goldman and J. Kim (eds.), *Values and Morals* (Dordrecht: Reidel), 47–71. (This essay is a considerable revision of the previous entry; sects. 2 and 3 are new.)

—— (1980), "Kantian Constructivism in Moral Theory," *Journal of Philosophy* 77: 515–72. (A published version of three lectures given as the John Dewey Lectures, at Columbia University, 14–16 Apr. 1980).

—— (1982a), "The Basic Liberties and their Priority," in S. M. McMurrin (ed.), *The Tanner Lectures on Human Values*, iii (Salt Lake City: University of Utah Press), 3–87.

—— (1982b), "Social Unity and Primary Goods," in A. Sen and B. Williams (eds.), *Utilitarianism and Beyond* (Cambridge: Cambridge University Press), 159–85.

—— (1985), "Justice as Fairness: Political not Metaphysical," *Philosophy and Public Affairs* 14: 223–51.

—— (1987), "The Idea of an Overlapping Consensus," *Oxford Journal of Legal Studies* 7: 1–25. (This paper is the text of the 1986 Hart Lecture in Oxford University.)

—— (1988), "The Priority of Right and Ideas of the Good," *Philosophy and Public Affairs* 17: 251–76.

—— (1989a), "The Domain of the Political and Overlapping Consensus," *New York University Law Review* 64: 233–55.

—— (1989b), "Themes in Kant's Moral Philosophy," in Eckart Förster (ed.), *Kant's Transcendental Deductions: The Three "Critiques" and the "Opus postumum"* (Stanford, Calif.: Stanford University Press), 81–113.

RAZ, Joseph (1984a), "Legal Rights," *Oxford Journal of Legal Studies* 4: 1–21.

—— (1984b), "On the Nature of Rights," *Mind* 93: 194–214.

—— (1985), "Authority and Justification," *Philosophy and Public Affairs* 14: 3–29.

—— (1986), *The Morality of Freedom* (Oxford: Oxford University Press).

REIMAN, Jeffrey H. (1972), *In Defense of Political Philosophy: A Reply to Robert Paul Wolff's "In Defense of Anarchism"* (New York: Harper Torchbooks).

RESNIK, Michael D. (1987), *Choices: An Introduction to Decision Theory* (Minneapolis, Minn.: University of Minnesota Press).

ROSHWALD, Mordecai (1958–9), "The Concept of Human Rights," *Philosophy and Phenomenological Research* 19: 354–79.

ROSS, Alf (1958), *On Law and Justice* (London: Stevens; Berkeley, Calif.: University of California Press, 1959).

RYLE, Gilbert (1949), *The Concept of Mind* (New York: Barnes and Noble).

SCHAUER, Fred (1981), "Can Rights Be Abused?" *Philosophical Quarterly* 31: 225–30.

SCHEID, Don (1983), "Kant's Retributivism," *Ethics* 93: 262–82.

——(1986), "Kant's Retributivism Again," *Archiv für Rechts- und Sozialphilosophie* (hereafter: *ARSP*), 72: 224–30.

SCHUMPETER, Joseph A. (1950), *Capitalism, Socialism, and Democracy*, 3rd edn. (New York: Harper).

SHAFER, Glenn (1990), "Decision Making," in Shafer and Pearl (1990: 61–7). (Introductory essay [with bibliography] to ch. 3.).

——and Judea PEARL (eds.) (1990), *Readings in Uncertain Reasoning* (San Mateo, Calif.: Morgan Kaufmann). (Relevant bibliographies are included at the end of the introductory essay for each of chs. 2–9.)

SHER, George (1984), "Right Violations and Injustices: Can we always Avoid Trade-Offs?" *Ethics* 94: 212–24.

SHERMAN, Michael, and Gordon HAWKINS (1981), *Imprisonment in America* (Chicago: University of Chicago Press).

SHUE, Henry (1978), "Torture," *Philosophy and Public Affairs* 7: 124–83.

SIMHONY, Avital (1989), "T. H. Green's Theory of the Morally Justified Society," *History of Political Thought* 10: 481–98.

SIMMONS, A. John (1979), *Moral Principles and Political Obligations* (Princeton, NJ: Princeton University Press).

——(1991), "Locke and the Right to Punish," *Philosophy and Public Affairs* 20: 311–49.

SINGER, Peter (1973), *Democracy and Disobedience* (London: Oxford University Press).

STEINER, Hillel (1977), "The Structure of a Compossible Set of Rights," *Journal of Philosophy* 74: 767–75.

SUMNER, L. Wayne (1987), *The Moral Foundation of Rights* (Oxford: Oxford University Press).

THOMSON, Judith J. (1977a), *Self-Defense and Rights*, Lindley Lecture, 1976 (Lawrence, Kan.: University of Kansas, Department of Philosophy). (Reprinted, unchanged, in Thomson 1986b: 33–48.)

——(1977b), "Some Ruminations on Rights," *Arizona Law Review* 19: 45–60. (Reprinted, unchanged, in Thomson 1986b: 49–65.)

——(1980), "Rights and Compensation," *Nous* 14: 3–15. (Reprinted, with the correction of an important typographical error, in Thomson 1986b: 66–77.)

——(1984), "Remarks on Causation and Liability," *Philosophy and Public Affairs* 13: 101–33. (Reprinted, unchanged, in Thomson 1986b: 192–224.)

——(1986a), "A Note on Internalism," *Philosophy and Public Affairs* 15: 60–6.

——(1986b), *Rights, Restitution, and Risk: Essays in Moral Theory*, ed. William Parent (Cambridge, Mass.: Harvard University Press). (A collection of Thomson's writings: includes 1977a,b, 1980, 1984.)

THOMPSON, D. F. (1975), "The Means of Dealing with Criminals: Social Science and Social Philosophy," *Philosophy of the Social Sciences* 5: 1–16.

THORSON, Thomas L. (1962), *The Logic of Democracy* (New York: Holt, Rinehart and Winston).

TUCK, Richard (1979), *Natural Rights Theories: Their Origins and Development* (Cambridge: Cambridge University Press).

URMSON, J. O. (1953), "The Interpretation of the Moral Philosophy of J. S. Mill," *Philosophical Quarterly* 3: 33–9. (Reprinted in Gorovitz 1971: 168–74.)

VILLEY, Michel (1969), *Seize essais de philosophie du droit* (Sixteen Essays in the Philosophy of Law) (Paris: Dalloz).

VINCENT Andrew, and Raymond PLANT (1984), *Philosophy, Politics and Citizenship: The Life and Thought of the British Idealists* (Oxford: Blackwell).

VLASTOS, Gregory (1962), "Justice and Equality," in R. B. Brandt (ed.), *Social Justice* (Englewood Cliffs, NJ: Prentice-Hall), 31–72. (Reprinted, sects. 1 and 2 only, with changes, in Melden 1970: 76–95.)

——(1974), "Socrates on Political Obedience and Disobedience," *Yale Review* (Summer 1974), 517–34.

——(1977), "The Theory of Social Justice in the *Polis* in Plato's *Republic*," in Helen F. North (ed.), *Interpretations of Plato: A Swarthmore Symposium. Mnemosyne*, suppl. series (Leiden: E. J. Brill), 1–40.

——(1978), "The Rights of Persons in Plato's Conception of the Foundations of Justice," in H. Tristram Engelhardt, Jr. and Daniel Callahan (eds.), *Morals, Science, und Socialty,* The Foundations of Ethics and its Relationship to Science, iii (Hastings, NY: The Hastings Center), 172–201.

VON LEYDEN, Wolfgang (1981), *Hobbes and Locke: The Politics of Freedom and Obligation* (London: Macmillan). ("The State of Nature and Locke's 'Strange' Doctrine of Punishment," pp. 109–19 in this book, originally appeared in a shorter and somewhat different version, as "Locke's Strange Doctrine of Punishment," in Reinhard Brandt [ed.], *John Locke: Symposium Wolfenbuettel 1979* [Berlin: Walter de Gruyter, 1981], 113–27.)

WADE, F. C. (1971), "In Defense of Socrates," *Review of Metaphysics* 25: 311–25.

WALDRON, Jeremy (ed.) (1987a), *Nonsense Upon Stilts: Bentham, Burke and Marx on the Rights of Man* (New York: Methuen). (This book consists mainly of excerpts from the three theorists named plus introductions to each by Waldron and a lengthy general introduction and concluding essay by him.) (b)

——(1987b), "Theoretical Foundations of Liberalism," *Philosophical Quarterly* 37: 127–50.

——(1989), "Rights in Conflict," *Ethics* 99: 503–19.

——(1990): "Rights and Majorities: Rousseau Revisited," in J. W. Chapman and A. Wertheimer (eds.), *Majorities and Minorities*, Nomos, xxxii (New York: New York University Press), 44–75.

WALKER, Nigel (1968), *Crime and Insanity in England*, i: *The Historical Perspective* (Edinburgh: Edinburgh University Press).

WALL, George B. (1970–1), "Cultural Perspectives on the Punishment of the Innocent," *Philosophical Forum* 2: 489–99.

WALZER, Michael (1970), *Obligations: Essays on Disobedience, War, and Citizenship* (Cambridge, Mass.: Harvard University Press).

——(1983), *Spheres of Justice: A Defense of Pluralism and Equality* (New York: Basic Books).

WASSERSTROM, Richard (1964), "Rights, Human Rights, and Racial Discrimination," *Journal of Philosophy* 61: 628–41.

WELLMAN, Carl (1970), Commentary, *Journal of Value Inquiry* 4: 257–58. (On Feinberg 1970b.)

——(1975), "Upholding Legal Rights," *Ethics* 86: 49–60.

WELLMAN, Carl (1978a), "Legal Rights," in *Uppsalaskolan: och efterât* (Stockholm: Almqvist and Wiksel), 213–21.

——(1978b), "A New Conception of Human Rights," in Kamenka and Tay (1978: 48–58).

——(1979): "Consent to Medical Research on Children," 85–105 in Lyman T. Sargent (ed.), *Consent: Concept, Capacity, Conditions, and Constraints. ARSP* Beiheft n.s. 12 (Wiesbaden: Steiner).

——(1984), "The Growth of Children's Rights," (*ARSP*) 70: 441–53.

——(1985), *The Theory of Rights: Persons under Laws, Institutions, and Morals* (Totowa, NJ: Rowman and Allanheld).

——(1990), "Locke's Right to Revolution Reexamined," in W. Maihofer and G. Sprenger (eds.), *Revolution and Human Rights. ARSP* Beiheft n.s. 41 (Stuttgart: Steiner), 21–6.

WERTHEIMER, Alan (1982), "Criminal Justice and Public Policy: Statistical Lives and Prisoners' Dilemmas," in Elliston and Bowie (1982: 370–89).

WHITE, Alan (1983), "Rights and Claims," in M. A. Stewart (ed.), *Law, Morality, and Rights*, Royal Institute of Philosophy Conference, University of Lancaster, 1979 (Dordrecht: Reidel), 139–60.

WHITE, Morton G. (1978), *The Philosophy of the American Revolution* (New York: Oxford University Press).

——(1981), *What Is and What Ought to be Done: An Essay on Ethics and Epistemology* (New York: Oxford University Press).

——(1987), *Philosophy, "The Federalist," and the Constitution* (New York: Oxford University Press).

WOLFF, Robert Paul (1969), "On Violence," *Journal of Philosophy* 66: 601–16.

——(1970) *In Defense of Anarchism* (New York: Harper and Row Torchbooks). (Reprinted in 1976 with "A Reply to Reiman" added as appendix, pp. 83–113.)

WOOZLEY, A. D. (1971), "Socrates on Disobeying the Law," in Gregory Vlastos (ed.), *The Philosophy of Socrates: A Collection of Critical Essays* (Garden City, NY: Doubleday Anchor), 299–318.

——(1979), *Law and Obedience: The Arguments of Plato's "Crito"* (Chapel Hill, NC: University of North Carolina Press). (Includes a new translation of the *Crito*, pp. 141–56.)

YOUNG, Gary (1974), "Socrates and Obedience," *Phronesis* 19: 1–29.

YOUNG, Robert (1978), "Dispensing with Moral Rights," *Political Theory* 6: 63–74.

ZINN, Howard (1968), *Disobedience and Democracy* (New York: Random House [Vintage]).

PART 2

I have used some of my own writings, substantially rewritten, as sources of various chapters of the present book, as indicated (in each case) by the chapter numbers in parentheses after the entries below. A co-authored item is listed at the very end.

"Authority and Sovereignty," in Peter Caws (ed.), *The Causes of Quarrel: Essays on Peace, War, and Thomas Hobbes* (Boston: Beacon Press, 1989), 36–49. Copyright 1989 of Peter Caws; used by permission of Beacon Press (Chs. 1, 2).

"The Character of Political Allegiance in a System of Rights," in Paul Harris (ed.), *On Political Obligation* (London: Routledge, 1990), 184–217 (Chs. 1, 8).

"Civil Rights and the U.S. Constitution," in Gary Bryner (ed.), *The Bill of Rights: A Bicentennial Assessment* (Provo, Utah: Brigham Young University [distributed at Albany, NY, by SUNY Press], forthcoming) (Chs. 5, 7, 12).

"Democracy and Rights: Two Perspectives," in Werner Maihofer and Gerhard Sprenger (eds.), *Law and the State in Modern Times*, Selected Proceedings of the 14th IVR World Congress on Philosophy of Law and Social Philosophy, Edinburgh, 1989, *Archiv für Rechts- und Sozialphilosophie* (hereafter: *ARSP*) Beiheft 42 (Stuttgart: F. Steiner, 1990), 9–18 (Chs. 6, 7).

"The Development of Feinberg's Conception of Rights," *Journal of Value Inquiry* 16 (1982), 29–45. Copyright 1982 of Martinus Nijhoff Publishers, The Hague; used by permission of Kluwer Academic Publishers (Ch. 3).

"Explanation in History and the Theory of Rights," in S. Panou, G. Bozonis, D. Georgas, and P. Trappe (eds.), *Human Being and the Cultural Values*, *ARSP* Supplementa, vol. iv, a volume of plenary and other selected papers from the 12th IVR World Congress on Philosophy of Law and Social Philosophy, Athens, 1985. (Stuttgart: F. Steiner, 1988), 76–92 (Ch. 2).

"Green on Natural Rights in Hobbes, Spinoza and Locke," in A. W. Vincent (ed.), *The Philosophy of T. H. Green*, Avebury Series in Philosophy (Aldershot: Gower, 1986), 104–26 (Chs. 2, 4, 5).

"The Human Right of Inmates to Work with Just Compensation," *Journal of Social Welfare* 9.1 (Winter 1983), 41–60 (Ch. 11).

"Human Rights and Civil Rights," *Philosophical Studies* 37 (May 1980), 391–403. Copyright 1980 of D. Reidel Publishing Co., Dordrecht; used by permission of Kluwer Academic Publishers (Ch. 4).

"Justifying Punishment and the Problem of the Innocent," *Journal of Social Philosophy* 20 (1989), 49–67 (Ch. 9).

"Modes of Punishment," *Public Affairs Quarterly* 1 (1987), 73–85 (Ch. 10).

"The Nature of Human Rights," in *Contemporary Conceptions of Law*, Proceedings of the 9th IVR World Congress on Philosophy of Law and Social Philosophy, Basle, 1979, *ARSP* Supplementa, vol. i, part 1 (Wiesbaden: F. Steiner, 1982), 379–93 (Ch. 4).

"On the Justification of Political Authority," in R. Baine Harris (ed.), *Authority: A Philosophical Analysis* (University, Ala.: University of Alabama Press, 1976), 54–75 (Chs. 1, 8).

"On the Logic of Justifying Legal Punishment," *American Philosophical Quarterly* 7 (1970), 253–9 (Ch. 9).

"On the Theory of Legal Rights as Valid Claims," *Midwest Studies in Philosophy* 7 (1982), 175–95 (Chs. 2, 3).

"Punishment and Rights," in Jan Broekman, K. Opatek, D. Kerimov (eds.), *Social Justice and Individual Responsibility in the Welfare State*, Selected Proceedings from the 11th IVR World Congress on Philosophy of Law and Social Philosophy, Helsinki, 1983, (*ARSP*) Beiheft 24 (Stuttgart: F. Steiner, 1985), 274–81 (Ch. 9).

Rawls and Rights (Lawrence, Kan.: University Press of Kansas, 1985) (Chs. 4–7, 13).

"Treatment and Rehabilitation as a Mode of Punishment," *Philosophical Topics* 18 (1990), 101–22 (Ch. 11).

"Two Ways of Justifying Civil Disobedience," in Peter Caws (ed.), *Two Centuries of*

Philosophy in America, American Philosophical Quarterly Library of Philosophy (Oxford: Blackwell; Totowa, NJ: Rowman and Littlefield, 1980), 291–7 (Ch. 8).

"Two Models for Justifying Political Authority," *Ethics* 86 (1975), 70–5. Copyright 1975 of the University of Chicago; used by permission of the University of Chicago, publisher (Ch. 1).

"Wolff's Defence of Philosophical Anarchism," *Philosophical Quarterly* 24 (1974), 140–9 (Ch. 1).

MARTIN, Rex, and James W. NICKEL, "Recent Work on the Concept of Rights," *American Philosophical Quarterly* 17 (1980), 165–80 (Chs. 2–4).

Index

Abel, Charles 391
abstract model 146–7, 167
  knowledge in 147–9, 156–8, 163, 371
  relation to justification of
    democracy 147–50, 372
  subjective consensus 150–1, 158
Airaksinen, Timo 392
allegiance 185–7, 354, 378–9, 380
  argument for (in a system of
    rights) 188–91, 197–9, 205–7, 212–13,
    304–5; convention (and uniform
    conformity) 191–3, 213, 215–17, 379;
    problems, secondary 194–9
  particularity, problem of 199–202, 380;
    solution 203–5
  relation to other authority
    elements 214–17, 306–7, 308
  see also civil disobedience
Allen, R. E. 341
anarchism (philosophical) 9–10, 15, 16–17,
  23, 91, 221, 411–12
Anscombe G.E.M. (example) 105
Aquinas, Thomas 6, 379
Aristotle 95, 132, 142, 167, 183, 220, 369,
  383
Arrow, Kenneth 368
Augustine 321, 362
authority:
  elements 2, 7–9, 21, 303, 307–8
  justification (externalism, simple and
    direct) 12, 14–18, 21, 199–201, 249–50,
    343–4
  justification (internal) 3, 4, 18–19, 21,
    302, 304–9, 320–2, 337, 339
  see also critical justification
Aztec priest (example) 78

Baliles, Gerald (example) 399
Bandman, Bertram 353
banker (example) 229–30, 233, 237, 264
Barnett, Randy 263, 391
Barnhart, J. E. 353
Barry, Brian 142, 143, 369, 370
baseball (example) 62–3
basic rights, see priority of civil rights: in
  relation to basic rights
Bayles, Michael 392, 393
Beaumont, Gustave de 399
Becker, Lawrence 400
Bedau, Hugo 385, 390, 398, 399
benchmark goal (of democracy) 141, 182
Benn, S. I. 364, 383

Bentham, Jeremy 51, 220, 265, 352, 353,
  358, 383, 392, 398, 406
Berger, Fred 405
Bernoulli's Theorem 370
Beveridge, William 400
Bickel, Alexander M. 356
Bill of Rights (US, 1791) 30–1, 41, 61, 93,
  170, 172, 173, 177, 256, 310, 311, 314,
  316–17, 374–5
Black, Duncan 183, 368, 369, 370, 371,
  372, 376
Blackstone, William 398
Bonnie, Richard 394, 395
Borda (Comte de) 377
Bork, Robert 310, 370, 403
Bosanquet, Bernard 353
Brandeis, Louis 364
Brandt, R. B. 405, 406
Braybrooke, David 345
Brennan, William 390, 391
Brink, David 405
Brooks, Alexander 395, 397
Brown v. Board of Education (US, 1954) 67,
  84, 95, 356, 376
Brownlie, Ian 357, 360
Bryner, Gary 404
Buchanan, James M. 371, 372, 376, 377
Burke, Edmund 358
Butler, Joseph 389

Callison, Herbert 402
Calvin, John 29
capital punishment 256–7, 282–3, 301,
  389–90
Carritt, E. F. 389
Carter, Jimmy 196
Chafee, Zacharia, Jr. 355
Chapman, John 411
checking devices, constitutional 172–5,
  182, 312–13, 314, 316, 319, 320, 380
Childress, James 381
civil disobedience:
  definition 208–9, 210, 212, 381–2
  justification: mixed 213; moral 209–10;
    political 210–11, 212
  relation to allegiance: argument for
    211–14, 305, 382
  in relation to punishment 214–17, 306–7,
    308, 382–3
civil law, distinction from criminal
  law 390–1

civil rights:
   character, general 92, 100, 102, 110–15,
      126, 127, 187, 233, 361, 373
   and constitutional rights 101–2, 172,
      312–14
   and human rights 92–7, 98, 100, 400
   and majority rule democracy 2, 127,
      140, 166–7, 169–71, 181–2, 303–4, 319,
      375, 403
   and nonuniversal rights 98–9, 105–7,
      317–18
   as rights that can lack strong moral
      backing 100–1
   see also mutual perceived benefit; rights:
      conflict
Civil Rights Act (US, 1964) 66, 84, 176,
   189–90, 194
Civil War Amendments (US,
   1865–1870) 173, 176, 177, 297, 298–9,
   318, 376, 397, 400
coercion 221–2, 251–2, 266–8, 302, 307,
   392–3
   see also punishment
Cohen, M. R. 389
Coleman, Jules 389, 391
Collingwood, R. G. 366, 389, 412
Commager, Henry Steele 375
compensation (civil) 254, 262, 265
   compensation (as punitive), see modes of
      punishment: compensation
Condorcet (Marquis de) 183, 184, 369,
   372, 376, 377
conformity to law (uniform), see allegiance:
   argument for, convention
consensus, see abstract model: subjective
   consensus; majority rule: social
   consensus
constitution:
   constitutional system 403
   written 310–11, 403
constitutional crisis, see system of rights:
   harmonization
contested voting 130–1, 147, 167, 319, 367
contract 10–12, 13, 200, 380
convention, see allegiance: argument for
Cranston, Maurice 74, 87, 88, 358, 359,
   360
critical justification 22–3, 309, 322, 323–4,
   336, 337–9, 404–5, 412
   in Rawls 329–36
   in utilitarianism 324–9, 373
   see also authority: justification (internal)
custom 344–5, 346
cyclical majorities, see majority rule: other
   problems

Dahl, Robert A. 368
David, Marjorie 402

Declaration of Independence (US,
   1776) 95, 125
DeGeorge, Richard 400, 402
Del Vecchio, Giorgio 391
DeLorean, John (example) 109
democracy, justification of 137–8, 143–4,
   165–6, 167–8, 303, 374
   ambiguity in, dispelling the 144–6,
      149–50, 163–6, 371
   epistemic character 142, 167, 183, 369
   motivational assumptions 150, 154–5,
      156–8, 163
   probabilistic character 138–40, 142–3,
      176, 181, 182, 369
   see also abstract model; benchmark goal;
      civil rights; democratic institutions;
      publicity
democratic institutions:
   characterization, general 127, 190, 303,
      304, 318–20
   model: direct 137, 140, 146;
      representative 131–2, 133–4, 137,
      140–1, 146
   relation to other authority
      elements 303–4, 306, 308
   see also checking devices; contested
      voting; majority rule; universal
      franchise
Denning (Lord) 389
deterrence, see modes of punishment;
   punishment
direction, see normative direction
Dodgson, Charles L. 376
Donnelly, Jack 357
Dray, W. H. 363
drunken driving (example) 258, 272, 277
Duff, R. A. 389
Dummett, Michael 368, 369, 372, 376, 377
Durham, Monte (example) 395
Dworkin, Ronald 26, 51, 52, 116, 173,
   344, 352, 353, 356, 357, 364, 375, 382,
   383

Ely, John Hart 375
Ennis, Robert 391
entitlements, rights as 354
Epstein, Richard 391
equality 107–8
   equal protection 290–1, 297–9, 400–1
   temporary inequality 108–9
Euben, J. Peter 341
Ewing, A. C. 389

Fain, Haskell 340
Farquharson, Robin 377
Farrell, Daniel 341
Federalist Papers (US, 1788) 172, 374
Feinberg, Joel:
   conflict of rights 59, 364, 385

Feinberg, Joel (*contd.*):
  human rights 56, 74, 358, 360, 361
  liberty element (in rights) 348
  manifesto rights 56, 358, 400
  punishment 389
  rights imply duties 345
  rights as incumbent 366
  rights as valid claims 54–6, 58, 64–6, 71,
    353–7
Feld, Scott 369
Fifteenth Amendment (US, 1870), *see* Civil
  War Amendments
Fingarette, Herbert 394
Fischer, John M. 391
Fishkin, James 364, 405
Fletcher, George 385, 398
Fløistad, G. 406
Fogel, Robert 390
forfeiture (of rights) 280–4, 385, 398–9
Fourteenth Amendment (US, 1868), *see*
  Civil War Amendments
Frey, R. G. 405
Fuchs, Alan 364
full employment policy 288–9, 298–9, 400,
  401
  relation to prisoners 290–1, 293–7, 298
  relation to rights 288, 289–90, 292,
    298–9, 314

Gallie, W. B. 366
game-theoretic reasoning, *see* democracy,
  justification of: motivational
  assumptions; sensible knave (Hume)
Gandhi, M. K. 209
Gaus, Gerald 371
Gauthier, David 324, 351, 373
Geertz, Clifford 359
Gert, Bernard 343
Gewirth, Alan 371, 385, 406
Gibbard, Allen 380, 405
Gilmore, Gary (example) 283
Golding, Martin 347
Goldinger, Milton 389
Goldman, Alan 386, 390, 398
Goldsmith, M. M. 378
Goldstein, Abraham 394, 395
Gorbachev, Mikhail 201
Gray, John (on Mill) 325, 405, 406
Gray, John Chipman 346
Green, T. H. 51, 185, 353, 361, 366, 378,
  382, 402
Greenberg, Jack 356, 357
Griffin, Stephen 375
Grissom, G. R. 402
Grofman, Bernard 369

habeas corpus (example) 159, 311, 314,
  364, 380
Hall, Robert H. 362, 371

Hall, Robert T. 382
Hamilton, Alexander 374, 375
Hare, R. M. 405, 406
Harrington, Michael 402
Harris, Marvin 359
Harris, Paul 382
Harris, R. Baine 362
Hart, H. L. A.:
  capital punishment 390
  choice theory of rights 349
  competition rights 356
  conflict of rights 364
  duty and obligation 185, 378
  Hohfeld elements 345, 355, 402
  internal point of view 346
  laws that create capacities 379
  liability to punishment (*mens rea*) 273–6,
    396; criticism 274–6
  natural rights 358, 359
  punishment (other issues) 265, 384, 386,
    387, 389, 392, 394, 395, 396
  special/general rights 360
Haskell, Thomas 358, 404
Hawkins, Gordon 390
Hegel, G. W. F. 221, 383
Held, Virginia 353
Hempel, Carl 362
Hobbes, Thomas 1, 10, 11, 32, 33, 34,
  35, 89, 214, 242, 342, 343, 345, 347,
  351
Hohfeld, Wesley 29, 30, 31, 32, 33, 34, 35,
  46, 47, 61, 64, 345, 346, 349, 355, 402
Holmes, Oliver Wendell 111, 364
human rights 73–4
  as institutionalized 75, 87–94, 98, 124–6,
    361
  and legal rights 71–2, 84–5, 92–4, 96–7
  and moral rights 74–5, 85–6, 89, 90, 94–6
  and valid claims 75–7, 81, 85, 92, 95–6,
    97; criticism 77–86
Hume, David 11, 216, 343, 379, 383
Hurka, Thomas 386, 390

imperfect procedure, democracy as, *see*
  majority rule: imperfect procedure
imprisonment:
  character, general 257, 258, 285, 293–4,
    296
  justification of 257–8
incapacitation, *see* modes of punishment:
  penalty
infringement of a right 225–6, 230, 231,
  238, 250, 301, 385, 386
insanity 268–71, 278–9, 393–6, 397
institutional design, *see* checking devices

James, G. G. 341
Jay, John 374

Jefferson, Thomas 95, 374
Johnson, Conrad 405
Jong, Erica (example) 105
justification (as treated under several
    topical headings), *see* abstract model;
    authority; civil disobedience; critical
    justification; democracy, justification
    of; mutual perceived benefit;
    punishment

Kagan, Shelly 391
Kant, Immanuel 10, 220, 266, 281, 282,
    332, 341, 383, 388, 389, 397, 398, 399,
    407, 408, 409
Keyt, David 369
King, Martin Luther, Jr. 208, 209
kleptomania (example) 271
Krantz, Sheldon 397, 399
Kraut, Richard 341

Lasky, Melvin J. 341
Laslett, Peter 342
LaTorre, Massimo 359
Leivestad, T. 344
Lemos, Ramon 387, 399
Lenin, V. I. 51, 353
Léon-Portilla, Miguel 358
Levine, Michael 377
Lewis, C. N. 402
Lewis, Thomas J. 343, 380
liability:
    to punishment 272–8, 301, 396
    in tort law 391
liberties:
    competition rights 61–4, 356
    Hohfeldian liberty 30, 32, 35, 355, 401–2
    liberty rights 32–5, 61, 292–3, 350
    mere liberties 36, 62, 63
    waiving a right 42–4
Lincoln, Abraham 170, 376
Lindsay, A. D. 341, 353
Locke, John:
    contract and consent 10, 11, 200
    forfeiture (of a right) 282, 398, 399
    majority rule 142, 370
    obedience to law 214, 342, 343
    political society 6, 321
    punishment and compensation 392
    rights, concept of 1, 34, 345, 347
    state of nature 351
Lucas, Billy Joe 341
Lynds, Elym 400
Lyons, David 54, 325, 345, 352, 405, 406

Mabbott, J. D. 384
MacCallum, Gerald 40, 340, 347, 350, 356,
    380
McClennen, Edward 380
McCloskey, H. J. 354, 361, 388

MacCormick, D. N. 349, 353, 391
McCullagh, C. Behan 390
Macdonald, Margaret 345, 360
MacFarlane, L. J. 357
McGrory, Mary 399
McIwain, Charles H. 340
Mackie, J. L. 405
McLaughlin, Robert J. 341
Macpherson, C. B. 366, 368
McPherson, Thomas 9, 340
Madison, James 374, 375
majority rule 132–4, 171–5, 319, 368
    definition 136–7, 178, 371
    imperfect procedure 175–7, 182, 184,
        205–7, 305, 381
    Locke on 142, 370
    other problems 134, 148–9, 175, 177–81,
        182–4, 369–70, 376–7
    plurality rule 135–6, 179–80, 181
    Rawls on 183, 369, 372, 375
    self-correcting character 176–7, 181,
        312–13, 314, 316, 376, 380
    social consensus 182, 205, 312–13, 314,
        320, 380
    see also civil rights; democracy,
        justification of; mutual
        perceived benefit: justification of
        majority rule democracy
Marsh, Frank 391
Marshall, Thurgood 67, 68, 390, 401
Marsilius (of Padua) 142, 183
Marx, Karl 6, 321, 358
Matross, Gerald N. 366
maximizers, rational, *see* democracy,
    justification of: motivational
    assumptions; sensible knave (Hume)
May, K. O. 368, 377
Mayo, Bernard 89, 345, 353, 360
Melden, A. I. 338, 355, 360, 361
Melossi, Dario 399
mens rea, see Hart: liability to punishment
Mill, John Stuart:
    critical justification 75, 324, 325
    democracy and participation 129, 132,
        366
    dutiful action 359
    indirect deductive method 338, 412
    liberty (example) 83
    punishment and pain 221, 265, 383,
        392
    Rawls on 332, 408, 410
    rights 51, 352
    utility 373, 405, 406; cannot support the
        priority of rights 335
Milne, A. J. M. 357
modes of punishment 251, 272–3, 277–8,
    301
    compensation 253–4, 259–64, 277, 294–5,
        301, 391, 392

penalty 252–3, 255–9, 273, 276–7, 295–6, 301, 396
  treatment and rehabilitation 254–5, 268–72, 277–80, 286–7, 294–7, 299–300, 301–2, 389, 395, 396
Montague, Phillip 385
Monty Python (example) 248–9
Moore, Michael 393, 394, 395, 396
Mundle, C. W. K. 389
Murphy, J. G. 389, 391
mutual perceived benefit:
  identical ways of acting or being treated 104–5, 107, 366
  justification of civil rights 102–4, 113, 121, 188, 197, 202, 249, 304, 312–13, 314, 319, 366
  justification of majority rule democracy 168–9, 304
  Segerberg's problem (can one be wrong about one's own perceived interests?) 377, 413–15

natural rights:
  criticism 124–6
  and human rights 74, 89–90, 280–2
  and moral rights 89
Nazis, punishment under 245, 387
Nelson, William 360, 373, 374
Nett, Roger 359
Nickel, James W. 344, 345, 349, 354, 355, 360, 363, 365, 385, 400
Nino, Carlos Santiago 358, 364
Noriega, Manuel (example) 109
normative direction 26, 29, 38, 83–4, 104, 123, 365, 385
  duties, moral 79–81, 82
  practical inference, relation to 36–9, 49–50, 260, 350–1
  rights involve (imply) duties 30–1, 32–6, 77–9, 188, 190–1, 226–7, 304
North, D. Warner 372
Nozick, Robert 1, 51, 116, 236, 349, 351, 386, 389, 392

obligation:
  contrast with allegiance 185–6
  contrast with duty 185–6, 378, 381
  neighborly obligation (example) 13
  obligationists, strict 10–12, 213–14, 340, 343
  political obligation 13–14, 18, 186, 378
  see also allegiance
Ockham, William of 89, 347
one person, one vote, *see* universal franchise

particularity, *see* allegiance
Pateman, Carole 341, 342, 343, 401
Paul (St.) 15, 16

Pavarini, Massimo 399
Pearl, Judea 372
penalty, *see* capital punishment; imprisonment; modes of punishment: penalty
Pennock, J. R. 411
Peter (St.) 15
Peters, R. S. 364
Pilon, Roger 398
Plamenatz, John 389
Plant, Raymond 379
Plato 6, 10, 105, 106, 107, 185, 211, 220, 317, 321, 340, 363, 379, 382, 383, 414
Plott, Charles R. 377
Pompa, Leon 363
pond, going to (example) 25–8, 226
Popper, Karl 368, 376
possession, scope, and weight of rights 42–4, 110–14, 118, 123, 225, 231–2, 236–8, 249, 281, 283–4, 316–17, 355, 366, 384–5
  see also forfeiture; infringement of a right; liberties: waiving a right; system of rights: harmonization
practical inference 36–9, 49–50, 260, 345, 346–7, 350–1
priority of civil rights 159–61, 163–5, 172, 174–5, 203, 309–10, 312, 316, 318, 323, 328, 338
  argument for 152–8, 161–3, 164, 315–16
  in relation to basic rights 116, 310–13, 314, 316, 380
  in relation to constitutional rights 312–16, 339
  in relation to nonrights 161, 164, 375–6, 379
  in relation to Rawls 330, 335–6, 410, 411
  in relation to utilitarianism 328–9, 335–6, 373, 411
prisoners:
  requiring them to work 291–3, 298, 299–300
  right to work of 286–7, 290–1, 294–300
  rights of 284–6, 300, 399
  wages of 296–7, 402
  work in prisons 287, 293–6, 301, 399
  see also full employment policy
privacy, right to (example) 106, 107–8, 363
publicity (as a requirement on democratic government) 133–4, 148
  relative to punishment theory 247–8
punishment:
  characterization, general 218–22, 251–2, 253, 264–8, 273, 274, 293–4, 302, 306, 384, 385, 388–9
  of the innocent 219, 241–50, 272–3, 387–8
  justification (standard) 222–3, 249–50, 255, 273–4, 384; (in a system of rights) 225–36, 238–9, 244–50, 273, 277, 281, 301, 306

punishment (*contd.*):
　method of argument on 219–20, 222,
　　273, 390; internal justification (of
　　punishment) 223–5, 227–8, 233–6,
　　239–40, 243–4, 250
　relation to fair trial 239–42, 247–8, 249,
　　272, 308
　relation to other authority
　　elements 214–17, 229–34, 302, 306–7,
　　308
　see also coercion; liability; modes of
　　punishment

Quinton, Anthony 384

Radden, Jennifer 394, 395, 396
Railton, Peter 405
Raphael, D. D. 9, 88, 340, 360
Rawls, John:
　basic structure 102, 362, 374
　bill of rights (in a written
　　constitution) 403
　citizenship 379
　civil disobedience 381; criticism 382
　"competition rights" (phrase) 356
　constitution as an imperfect
　　procedure 381
　constitutional crisis 364
　critical justification 324, 329–39, 404–5,
　　411
　duty and obligation, distinction of 378
　equal basic liberties 362, 364, 406
　"fair value" and competitive voting 367
　"family of rights" (phrase) 366
　"free public reason" 404
　"institutional design" (phrase) 374
　majority rule and democracy 375;
　　on Black-Condorcet model 183, 369
　model conception(s) 408
　moral truth 408, 409–10;
　　deductivism 409–10
　mutual advantage 363
　natural duty of justice 206, 378, 379, 381;
　　criticism 187
　natural rights 360
　original position 352, 371, 407–8; and
　　democracy 372
　overlapping consensus 408, 410
　pluralism 380
　political conception of justice 407, 408
　principles of justice 38, 406
　priority 407, 410
　punishment 384, 385, 402;
　　telishment 387–8
　rights 345
　social primary goods 371
Raz, Joseph 53, 66, 71, 340, 353, 354, 357

rehabilitation 254, 269–71
　see also modes of punishment: treatment
　　and rehabilitation
Reiman, Jeffrey 16, 343
Resnik, Michael 372
rights:
　character, general 1, 2, 4, 24, 29, 60–1,
　　83–4, 292–3, 345, 347–8, 351
　conflict 28, 58–9, 109–10, 115, 122–3,
　　126, 230–1, 364, 385; internal 118–22,
　　364–5
　main types 40–2, 45–8, 292–3, 347–8
　see also civil rights: and constitutional
　　rights; Feinberg: manifesto rights;
　　human rights; normative direction:
　　rights involve (imply) duties; system of
　　rights; valid claims
Robert's Rules of Order (example) 111
Roshwald, Mordecai 360
Ross, Alf 349
Rousseau, Jean-Jacques 11, 25, 142, 167,
　　182, 183, 321, 343, 369, 377
Ryle, Gilbert 362

salad (Hohfeld's example) 35, 346
sanctions, *see* modes of punishment;
　　punishment
Schauer, Fred 363
Scheid, Don 388
Schultz, Bart 411
Schumpeter, Joseph 368
scope (of a right), *see* possession, scope,
　　and weight of rights
Segerberg, Krister 377, 413–15
sensible knave (Hume) 215–16, 383
Shafer, Glen 372
Sher, George 364
Sherman, Michael 390
Shue, Henry 348
Sidgwick, Henry 406
Simhony, Avital 366
Simmons, A. John 340, 342, 378, 379, 380,
　　381, 399
Singer, Peter 401
Socrates 10, 12, 214, 340, 341
state 5–7, 340
Steiner, Hillel 366
Stephen, James Fitzjames 389
Stewart, Potter 390
Stone, Harlan F. 400
strategic voting, *see* majority rule: other
　　problems
Sumner, L. Wayne 325, 345, 349, 363, 364,
　　401, 402, 405, 406
system of rights 3, 19–22, 169, 307–8,
　　309–10, 314–16, 317–20, 323, 339, 402,
　　403
　harmonization 115–18, 121–4, 126,
　　158–61, 166, 317

Taylor, Harriet 83
telishment, *see* punishment: of the
    innocent; Rawls
tendencies of democratic law, *see* majority
    rule: imperfect procedure
Thirteenth Amendment (US, 1865), *see*
    Civil War Amendments
Thomas, Geoffrey 366
Thompson, D. F. 388
Thomson, Judith J. 364, 385, 391, 398
Thoreau, Henry David 6, 381
Thorson, Thomas 376
Timerman, Jacopo (example) 44, 348
Tocqueville, Alexis 170, 368, 375, 380, 399
travel (example) 61, 82–3
treatment and rehabilitation, *see* modes of
    punishment: treatment and
    rehabilitation; rehabilitation
Trulove, Sarah 345
Tuck, Richard 347
Tulloch, Gordon 371, 372, 376, 377

Universal Declaration of Human Rights
    (UN, 1948) 24, 73, 88, 170, 288, 292,
    359, 360
  Covenants (1966) 73, 88–9, 330, 359, 361
universal franchise 128–9, 147, 319, 367,
    371
Urmson, J. O. 405
utilitarianism 405–6
  see also critical justification

valid claims:
  analysis, importance of 51–2, 73–4
  character, general 52–3, 54–6
  as rights 56–7, 85; criticism 57–8, 64–71,
    77–86

Villey, Michel 347
Vincent, A. W. 358, 379
Vlastos, Gregory 341, 355, 363
Von Leyden, Wolfgang 399
Von Wright, G. H. 346–7, 393

Wade, F. C. 341
Waldron, Jeremy 358, 359, 364, 370, 380
Walker, Nigel 394
Wall, George 387
Walzer, Michael 362, 379, 380, 387, 389,
    402
Wasserstrom, Richard 360
weak rights 62, 99–100, 397
weakness of will (*akrasia*), *see* allegiance:
    argument for, convention
weight (of a right), *see* possession, scope,
    and weight of rights
Wellman, Carl 346, 347, 349, 350, 359,
    365, 400
Wertheimer, Alan 389
White, Alan 354
White, Morton 345, 346, 347, 348, 374
Wittgenstein, Ludwig 412
Woelfel, J. W. 345
Wolff, Robert Paul 9, 208, 340, 381
Woozley, A. D. 341

Yablon, Chuck 357
Young, Gary 341
Young, Robert 358

Zinn, Howard 210, 382